AI-driven Cyber Risk Management

RIVER PUBLISHERS SERIES IN DIGITAL SECURITY AND FORENSICS

The "River Publishers Series in Security and Digital Forensics" is a series of comprehensive academic and professional books which focus on the theory and applications of Cyber Security, including Data Security, Mobile and Network Security, Cryptography and Digital Forensics. Topics in Prevention and Threat Management are also included in the scope of the book series, as are general business Standards in this domain.

Books published in the series include research monographs, edited volumes, handbooks and textbooks. The books provide professionals, researchers, educators, and advanced students in the field with an invaluable insight into the latest research and developments.

Topics covered in the series include:-

- Blockchain for secure transactions
- Cryptography
- Cyber Security
- Data and App Security
- Digital Forensics
- Hardware Security
- IoT Security
- Mobile Security
- Network Security
- Privacy
- Software Security
- Standardization
- Threat Management

For a list of other books in this series, visit www.riverpublishers.com

AI-driven Cyber Risk Management

Editors

Hooman Razavi
Tecnologico de Monterrey,
Monterrey, Mexico

Muriel Figueredo Franco
Federal University of Rio Grande do Sul (UFRGS),
Porto Alegre, Brazil

Mariya Ouaissa
Cadi Ayyad University,
Marrakech, Morocco

Mariyam Ouaissa
Chouaib Doukkali University,
El Jadida, Morocco

Gautam Srivastava
Brandon University,
Brandon, Canada

River Publishers

Routledge
Taylor & Francis Group
NEW YORK AND LONDON

Published 2025 by River Publishers
River Publishers
Broagervej 10, 9260 Gistrup, Denmark
www.riverpublishers.com

Distributed exclusively by Routledge
605 Third Avenue, New York, NY 10017, USA
4 Park Square, Milton Park, Abingdon, Oxon OX14 4RN

AI-driven Cyber Risk Management / Hooman Razavi, Muriel Figueredo Franco, Mariya Ouaissa, Mariyam Ouaissa and Gautam Srivastava.

Routledge is an imprint of the Taylor & Francis Group, an informa business

ISBN 978-87-4380-806-0 (hardback)
ISBN 978-87-4380-811-4 (paperback)
ISBN 978-87-4380-808-4 (online)
ISBN 978-8-743-80807-7 (ebook master)

DOI: 10.1201/9788743808077

Contents

Preface

In today's hyper-connected digital landscape, organizations increasingly rely on complex cyber systems, spanning cloud computing infrastructures, enterprise applications, financial platforms, and critical operational technologies, to sustain their business operations. While these advancements drive efficiency and innovation, they also expose organizations to an expanding spectrum of risks far beyond traditional security threats. System downtime, data breaches, ransomware attacks, and financial fraud can trigger severe operational, reputational, and financial consequences. In such an environment, conventional risk management practices are no longer sufficient. To effectively navigate these evolving challenges, enterprises must embrace intelligent, adaptive, and proactive strategies, powered by Artificial Intelligence.

This book is designed as a comprehensive guide to how AI is transforming cyber risk management, equipping organizations with the knowledge and tools needed to anticipate, assess, and mitigate threats with unprecedented accuracy. By integrating AI with big data analytics and emerging technologies, businesses can move from reactive defense to predictive, real-time risk mitigation. Through this lens, the book explores the cutting-edge methodologies and frameworks that define the future of cybersecurity resilience.

The content is organized to provide readers with both conceptual understanding and practical insights. It begins by laying the foundational principles of cyber risk management before examining the evolution of AI in cybersecurity, the role of big data in risk analytics, and the application of AI in threat intelligence, fraud detection, and automated incident response. Further chapters introduce AI-driven risk quantification models, intelligent mitigation strategies, and their integration into broader security ecosystems, including business continuity planning and disaster recovery frameworks. To bridge theory with practice, the book features industry-specific case studies demonstrating the tangible impact of AI across various sectors. In addition, forward-looking discussions address emerging technologies, such as the Internet of Things, blockchain, large language models, explainable AI, and advanced machine learning techniques, highlighting their transformative role in shaping the future of cyber risk management.

This book is written for a diverse audience, including cybersecurity professionals, risk managers, technology leaders, researchers, and students, who seek to understand and apply AI-driven innovations to real-world cyber risk challenges. Combining technical depth with practical clarity, it offers readers a holistic perspective on both the opportunities and challenges of AI adoption in cybersecurity.

List of Contributors

Abu Al-Haija, Qasem, *Department of Cybersecurity, Jordan University of Science and Technology, Jordan*

Adnan, Muhammad, *Abasyn University Peshawar KPK, Pakistan*

Agrawal, Shyam Sunder, *Lovely Professional University, India*

Al-Faouri, Mohammad I., *Department of Cybersecurity, Jordan University of Science and Technology, Jordan*

Al-Khasawneh, M. A., *Hourani Center for Applied Scientific Research, Al-Ahliyya Amman University, Jordan; School of Computing, Skyline University College, UAE*

Al Mamoon, Ishtiak, *CSE Department IUBAT, International University of Business Agriculture and Technology, Bangladesh*

Alhyan, Mohamed, *LTI, Chouaib Doukkali University, Morocco*

Alasoully, Abdallah O., *Department of Cybersecurity, Jordan University of Science and Technology, Jordan*

Al-Alawneh, Ahmad I., *Department of Cybersecurity, Jordan University of Science and Technology, Jordan*

Al-Omari, Qusai R., *Department of Cybersecurity, Jordan University of Science and Technology, Jordan*

Atieh, Omar A., *Department of Cybersecurity, Jordan University of Science and Technology, Jordan*

Benaich, Rihab, *Engineering Sciences Laboratory, National School of Applied Sciences, Ibn Tofail University, Morocco*

Bilal, Hazrat, *College of Mechatronics and Control Engineering, Shenzhen University, China*

Chaudhry, Vipin Kumar, *School of Computer Science and Engineering, Lovely Professional University, India*

El Mendili, Saida, *Engineering Sciences Laboratory, National School of Applied Sciences, Ibn Tofail University, Morocco*

Fayaz, Muhammad, *Department of Computer Science and Engineering, Sejong University, South Korea*

Ga, Youssef, *Engineering Sciences Laboratory, National School of Applied Sciences, Ibn Tofail University, Morocco*

Haider, Zeeshan Ali, *Department of Computer Science, Qurtuba University of Science and Information Technology, Pakistan*

H Khan, Tabassum, *Artificial Intelligence Department, G H Raisoni College of Engineering and Management, India*

Islam Sourav, Md Tanvir, *Department of Computer Science and Engineering, Varendra University, Bangladesh*

Khan, Amreen, *Computer Science & Engineering Department, MIT School of Computing, MIT ADT University, India*

Khan, Fida Muhammad, *Department of Computer Science, Qurtuba University of Science & Information Technology, Pakistan*

Khan, Rahim, *College of Information and Communication Engineering, Harbin Engineering University, China*

Khan, Zahid Ullah, *College of Information and Communication Engineering, Harbin Engineering University, China*

Kartit, Ali, *LTI, Chouaib Doukkali University, Morocco*

Lippert, Kari, *University of South Alabama, USA*

Lippert, Karri, *University of South Alabama, USA*

Mahajan, Divya, *University Business School, Guru Nanak Dev University, India*

Masud, Nasrullah, *Department of Electrical and Electronic Engineering, Varendra University, Bangladesh*

Munawar, Madiha, *Stanley College of Engineering and Technology for Women, India*

Nadifi, Zineb, *LTI, Chouaib Doukkali University, Morocco*

Ouaissa, Mariyam, *LTI, Chouaib Doukkali University, Morocco*

Ouaissa, Mariya, *LISI, Cadi Ayyad University, Morocco*

Powar, Swati, *Computer Science & Engineering Department, MIT School of Computing, MIT ADT University, India*

Puttanapura, Jagadeshwari, *Stanley College of Engineering and Technology for Women, India*

Qasaymeh, Mohammad R., *Department of Cybersecurity, Jordan University of Science and Technology, Jordan*

Rahman, Taj, *Department of Computer Science, Qurtuba University of Science & Information Technology, Pakistan*

Reddy C, Kishor Kumar, *Stanley College of Engineering and Technology for Women, India*

Sharadgah, Shahed M., *Department of Cybersecurity, Jordan University of Science and Technology, Jordan*

Sharma, Anshu, *School of Computer Science and Engineering, Lovely Professional University, India*

Sharma, Nidhi, *University Business School, Guru Nanak Dev University, India*

Sher, Taj, *Daqing Normal University, China*

Singh T, Monika, *Stanley College of Engineering and Technology for Women, India*

Sowmya, Pasham, *Stanley College of Engineering and Technology for Women, India*

Syan, Amanjot Singh, *Canadore Stanford International College, Canada*

Sobhan, Abdus, *Department of Computer Science and Engineering, Varendra University, Bangladesh*

Ullah, Inam, *Department of Computer Engineering, Gachon University, Republic of Korea*

Ullah, Tahseen, *Abasyn University Peshawar KPK, Pakistan*

Zeb, Asim, *Department of Computer Science, Abbottabad University of Science & Technology, Pakistan*

Zeeshan, Mohammad, *Department of Computer Science, Abbottabad University of Science & Technology, Pakistan*

List of Figures

List of Tables

List of Abbreviations

AML	Anti-money laundering
APT	Advanced persistent threat
APTs	Advanced persistent threats
ARIMA	Auto regressive integrated moving average
AST	Application security testing
CBLS	Cloud-based location services
CDO	Collateralized debt obligation
CICOIN	Contract intelligence
CNNs	Convolutional neural networks
CASP	Critical appraisal skills program
CRM	Cyber risk management
CPS	Cyber-physical systems
DDoS	Distributed denial of service
DID	Decentralized identifiers
DIDs	Decentralized identities
EBMs	Explainable boosting machines
ETL	Extract, transform, and load
ERM	Enterprise risk management
FAIR	Factor analysis of information risk
FATF	Financial action task force
GDPR	General data protection regulation
GTD	Global terrorism database
IAM	Identity and access management
ICS	Industrial control systems
IEC	International committee for electrical engineering
IDS	Intrusion detection systems
ISMS	Information security management system
ISO	International organization for standardization
KYC	Know your customer
MFA	Multi-factor authentication
MSSPs	Managed security service providers
NIST	National institute of standards and technology

NLP	Natural language processing
NVD	National vulnerability database
OCR	Optical character recognition
OT	Operational technology
PII	Personally identifiable information
PoS	Proof-of-stake
QSA	Qualified third party
RBAC	Role-based access control
SIEM	Security information and event management
SLR	Systematic literature review
SMEs	Small and medium enterprises
SOAR	Security orchestration, automation and response
SSI	Self-sovereign identity
TTPs	Tactics, techniques, and procedures
UEBA	User and entity behavior analytics
XAI	Explainable ai

1

Foundations of Cyber Risk Management

Zineb Nadifi[1], Mohamed Alhyan[1], Mariyam Ouaissa[1], Mariya Ouaissa[2], and Ali Kartit[1]

[1]LTI, Chouaib Doukkali University, Morocco
[2]LISI, Cadi Ayyad University, Morocco

Email: zinebnadifi5@gmail.com; mohammedalhyan@gmail.com; ouaissa.mariyam@ucd.ac.ma; alikartit@gmail.com; m.ouaissa@uca.ac.ma

Abstract

The evolution and increase in organizations' need for digital transactions has automatically led the world to the need to digitize services; this has helped organizations and users to offer and benefit from services easily, but it has also increased the threats that can confront an IT system, which requires the deployment of an approach supporting organizations throughout their service, hence the importance of risk management.

Risk management is a well-organized process designed to help organizations better manage cyberattacks by effectively identifying threats and assessing their severity to put in place the right countermeasures. Once corrective measures have been put in place to deal with these threats, it is important to note that this correction does not always mean elimination of the risk, because risks cannot always be circumvented, but risk management guarantees good dealing with them, either through avoidance, mitigation, transfer, or acceptance.

Certain norms and standards have been put in place to meet this need and to standardize a number of guidelines for effective risk management, on the other hand, regulations are in place which ensure that organizations comply with the measures to be taken to manage risks in order to protect user data, and improve user experience, and which impose sanctions where appropriate in the form of fines, penalties, legal proceedings, and many others.

DOI: 10.1201/9788743808077-1

A good risk management application guarantees an acceptable level of data protection and helps to ensure that sensitive data is not put at risk, as it accompanies companies throughout their entire lifecycle.

1.1 Introduction

For years before, and especially after the COVID-19 pandemic, the world has definitively decided and expressed that digitalization is not an improvement in the quality of communications and the user experience; but a necessity and an obligation, which has caused a growing and increased need in organizations for service providers who manage operations via the internet, especially those who operate with critical and sensitive data [1].

The increase in online operations has systematically increased the number of threats and attacks that present major security risks to critical and sensitive data, such as alteration of information, unauthorized access to resources, theft, disclosure or loss of sensitive data, and service interruptions. This increases the number of organizations offering cybersecurity services to deal with cyberattacks in cyberspace, by identifying threats in advance, detecting and mitigating them, and monitoring and continuously improving them as they occur, hence the importance of risk management [2].

Risk management then becomes a major challenge in helping to anticipate threats and unforeseen events that could have a negative impact on the production and continuity of services, and security in general, thereby reducing these impacts limiting the negative consequences of incidents, systematically guaranteeing positive and effective decision-making, and strengthening resilience in the face of crises, bouncing back and restoring quickly and effectively after incidents have occurred [3].

Risk management is not a time-limited process, but practices that follow the deployment of projects throughout their lifecycle, given that risks cannot be managed and controlled only at the outset, but are generated and created as a function of change and modification of the working environment, which requires the risk management process to be re-launched [4].

1.2 Risk Management Life Cycle

Before initiating risk management, and to better clarify and explain risk management, we must first of all, know what risk is, and what risk is a group of terms that define them, and which react together in an equation to generate risks, including [5]:

Figure 1.1 Risk management steps.

Vulnerability

A flaw or weakness in an IT system that reduces and minimizes the security of an asset and makes it vulnerable to attack, such as a PC left without a password, a PC without antivirus software, incorrectly configured equipment, etc.

Threat

Potential that can exploit a vulnerability in an IT system, which can lead to the likelihood of the asset falling victim to an attack, e.g., a cybercriminal, malicious software, human error, etc.

Risk

Presents the probability of the association and exploitation of a vulnerability by a threat which can cause a negative impact on the asset, and damage on different levels, i.e., financial, production stoppages, fall in the image of targets.

Cyber-risk is therefore very often formulated in terms of the equation:

$$\textbf{Risk} = \text{Vulnerability} \times \text{Threat} \times \text{Impact}$$

Risk management is a structured, sequenced, and systematic process that aims to protect IT systems and assets against cyberattacks in order to guarantee their availability, integrity, and confidentiality, and to ensure continuity of production and business activities. It also complies with the regulations and standards in force, by following a series of successive steps: identifying risks, risk assessment, risk treatment, continuous monitoring, and risk improvement (Figure 1.1).

1.2.1 Identifying risks

Risks are identified by:

- Detecting and mapping assets in order to quantify the attack surface.
- Identifying the vulnerabilities and threats associated with the assets.

1.2.2 Risk assessment

Risk assessment consists of determining:

- An estimate of the likelihood of a threat occurring.
- Examine the potential impact if the threats occur on several aspects: financial, operational, functional, reputational, etc.
- Define the criticality of the risks in order to classify them and prioritize the most critical.

1.2.3 Risk management

The idea is to eliminate all risks to the target in order to guarantee a safe and healthy environment. However, this is not always easy given the conditions, threats, and factors that do not always depend on security experts, which gives rise to four main strategies for dealing with risks on a case-by-case basis.

Risk avoidance
This strategy aims to eliminate a risk outright by removing the underlying cause, in cases where the risks are unacceptable, and/or it is not possible to avoid, mitigate, or circumvent them in any other way, the elimination of the risk in this case can be done by completely abandoning the use of the service or functionality that is causing the risk, for example:

- Disabling USB ports on machines to ensure that external storage sources are not connected to company workstations, as USB sticks are one of the most common methods of infecting machines with external malware, especially as the use of USBs is not always related to business activities.
- Disabling unsecured and unused services, such as telnet, FTP, NBT-NS, LLMNR, etc.

Risk mitigation
Aims to minimize the probability of the presence and occurrence of very high risks so that they can be ignored, or so that risk mitigation does not impact the performance of the business and the company's production, by applying security measures:

- Technical – such as the deployment of security and monitoring tools including SIEM solutions, firewalls, DLP, IPS/IDS, NDR/EDR/XDR, data encryption to guarantee confidentiality, MFA.
- Organizational – through awareness campaigns aimed at company employees to mitigate the human errors that can lead to attacks such as phishing, and implementation of security policies (access management and regular audits).

Risk transfer
Consists of transferring and shifting the handling of, and responsibility for, risks to a third party, or third party, this is applicable when risk management is hyper-costly and complicated for the company, or when the third-party entity will be able to better handle and manage the risks in view of its expertise via:

- Cyber insurance: This is similar to personal life insurance or car insurance, except that in this case only financial losses in the event of incidents can be covered by insurance.
- Outsourcing: Making a service provider responsible for an operation such as migrating from one infrastructure to another, or upgrading links, or for the complete management of part of the business, as in the case where a cloud provider is responsible for storing customers' data in their database.

Risk acceptance
This consists of accepting and tolerating a risk if it has a low impact and does not significantly affect the company's production, or if the cost of mitigating the risk far exceeds the financial losses that may result if it occurs. For example, not ensuring a high level of data protection because the data is already public and exploded on the internet.

1.2.4 Continuous monitoring and risk improvement

This final stage consists of implementing regular audits of log files, as well as intrusion tests aimed at challenging the company in question, in order to reassess the security measures already in place, and also to reassess the risks previously dealt with in order to adjust the strategies for managing them as new updates become available.

1.3 The Difference Between Cyber Risk and IT Risk

Cyber risk and IT risk are two terms that intersect, but each has a meaning that differs from the other [6].

Cyber risk refers to threats related to cyberattacks, and to harmful and malicious activities that impact the operation of IT systems, networks, and data in motion and/or stored. These activities can be the result of internal attacks by negligent, ignorant, professional, or malicious employees, as well as external attacks by cybercriminals who can deliver ransomware, send phishing emails, apply DoS/DDoS attacks, etc., all of which can cause damage such as data leakage and exfiltration, disruption, malfunction, and loss of data. This can cause damage, such as the leakage and exfiltration of data, interruption, malfunction, or stoppage of production, for example:

- A hacker exploits a vulnerability to steal customer data.
- A ransomware attack blocks access to a company's files.

IT risk is a broader term than cyber risk, since it covers not only the aspect of cyber risk, but also the other risks associated with computer systems and information technologies, whether intentional or unintentional, such as IT failures, i.e., software bugs, hardware problems in servers, saturation of the bandwidth of a computer network, or the consumption of machine resources (CPU, RAM, etc.). It also affects human errors such as configuration errors, the entry of personal data on untrusted sites through negligence or ignorance, the accidental deletion or modification of files or data, in addition to problems of non-compliance with norms and standards, such as ISO 27001, RGPD. Examples of IT risk include:

- A server that is saturated and has no more storage space.
- A misconfiguration that blocks access to a business application or a tender site.

1.4 Risk Analysis Methodologies

1.4.1 Qualitative analysis

Qualitative analysis is an analysis which, in order to identify and assess threats, is based on approximate scales, very often on two axes: the first is the probability and frequency of occurrence, which ranges from rare, unlikely, moderate, likely and almost certain, and the second is the impact, which varies from insignificant, minor significant, major, and severe.

The designation of degrees of appearance and impact of threats is subjective, which requires a considerable level of expertise to better judge the appropriate levels of the scales, this analysis is used in the early stages of projects, where there is no measurable basis of figures to work with and calculate, also to give a ranking and sequencing of threats in order to prioritize the treatment of threats with greater criticality [7].

There are a number of methods that can be adopted to ensure a qualitative analysis, including:

- Risk matrices (probability vs. impact).
- SWOT analysis (strengths, weaknesses, opportunities, threats).
- Rating scales.
- Brainstorming and interviews.

Although this approach is quick and easy to carry out, it remains subjective, lacking in figures and statistics, and limited in precision.

1.4.2 Quantitative analysis

Quantitative analysis is distinct from qualitative analysis in that it is measurable and quantified rather than approximate, and relies on mathematical and statistical models, as well as numerical data and figures to arrive at estimates of the financial or temporal impact of risks. This method is objective, and ideally used in the decision-making phases, particularly in terms of the budget, timetable and resources required for risk management.

Some methods are based on quantitative analysis, such as:

- Probabilistic analysis (distribution law, Monte-Carlo simulation).
- Value-at-risk (VaR) analysis.
- Statistical modelling

The quantitative analysis approach is suitable where precise, measurable results of risk exposure are required, as well as for strategic and budgetary decision-making, and for comparing risks on a numerical scale.

It is not possible to judge that one analysis is better or more effective than the other, as the two complement each other and each is better suited to certain conditions and more responsive in certain cases, which can clarify and provide a clear overview of risk management [8].

1.5 Cyber Risk Management Frameworks and Standards

1.5.1 ISO/IEC 27005

ISO/IEC 27005 is an international standard that presents the main and essential guidelines for ensuring risk management. It is a framework that guides organizations in making the right decisions to effectively and efficiently mitigate cybersecurity risks and build their defense against potential threats via a risk identification, assessment, and mitigation approach aimed at managing cyber risks in a systematic way.

Compliance with the steps offered by ISO/IEC 27005 plays a vital role in maintaining a robust IT system posture.

ISO/IEC 27005 has come to complete a suite of international ISO standards designed to build a secure, managed, and supervised information system, more specifically ISO 27001, which is dedicated to establishing an Information Security Management System (ISMS). The major difference between the two ISOs is that ISO 27001 presents a framework to help set up an ISMS, whereas ISO 27005 offers guidelines for better managing the risks of systems in organizations.

ISO 27005 can be seen as a global standard, as it covers the establishment of a risk management context, through the assessment of identified risks, the implementation of a plan to deal with and correct these risks, and continuous monitoring and review of the risks as they arise [9].

1.5.2 NIST cybersecurity framework (CSF)

The CSF is a framework developed by the National Institute of Standards and Technology (NIST) in the United States. It publishes a set of guidelines outlining best practices for organizations to follow in order to better manage cyber risks and reduce attack surfaces.

What makes the CSF framework unique is its flexibility and adaptability to different sectors, domains, and organizations to cover new threats and its continuous improvement.

To ensure effective risk management, the NIST Cybersecurity Framework (CSF) is based on five main functions:

1. Identify: Consists of determining resources, assets, and risks by understanding how the environment works.
2. Protect: Putting in place and deploying security prerequisites and defense tools and techniques as a proactive action to limit the impact of events that may occur.

3. Detect: Identifying malicious cybersecurity events using the detection tools deployed in the previous phase.
4. Respond: Responding to cybersecurity incidents with prompt responsiveness.
5. Recover: Rapidly and securely restore impacted resources and services after incidents have occurred.

The NIST Cybersecurity Framework (CSF) consists of three essential elements: the core, implementation tiers, and profiles.

1.5.2 Core

The core acts on the five functions presented above (identify, protect, detect, respond, recover) and breaks them down into categories and sub-categories that will be referenced to other standards such as ISO 27001, COBIT, NIST SP 800-53.

For example, the second function (protect) can be broken down into different categories, such as access control, awareness and training, data security, etc and others, each category can in turn be broken down into other sub-categories. For example, from the 'access control' category, we can derive a sub-category. 'Only legitimate users who have only the right access to only the right data for only the right reason,' can be referenced to another external standard such as COBIT.

1.5.2.2 Implementation tiers

Implementation tiers present four levels for assessing the maturity and compliance of organizations in terms of applying the Framework. Levels x, known as tiers x, are listed respectively from 1 to 4, from the least to the most compatible with the NIST CSF framework, in order to make it easier to identify the organization's weak points and areas for improvement:

- Tier 1: Ad hoc approach, unstructured, and therefore biased.
- Tier 2: Some cybersecurity processes exist, but are not always formalized, known as Risk Informed
- Tier 3: Well-defined processes, regularly applied and improved, known as Repeatable
- Tier 4: The organization adapts dynamically to threats. Highly mature and adaptive processes.

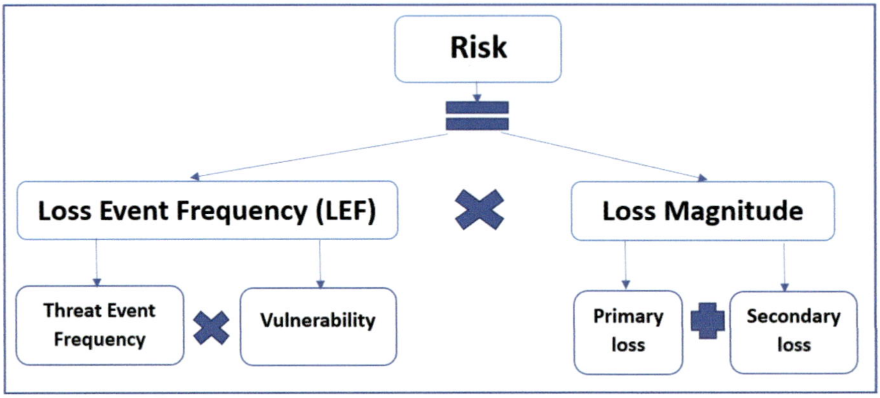

Figure 1.2 Risk equation following FAIR model.

1.5.2.3 Profiles

The profiles are presented in two parts: one presenting the current state of the system, and the other describing the desired and targeted state. For example, in the "Access control" category, we might have a Tier 2 profile, and we aim to complete the Tier 3 profile.

1.5.3 FAIR model (factor analysis of information risk)

The factor analysis of information risk (FAIR) model is a methodology that aims to assess, identify, understand, and deal with cyber-risks quantitatively, i.e., based on numerical values, and not on estimates as in the case of qualitative approaches, which enables predictions to be made about the criticality of risks, and help IT managers to deal with threats more effectively, by prioritizing the most critical and impactful ones, and encourage them to make decisions on a solid basis that can be justified by figures and calculations [10]. This approach also justifies budget investment in protection and security solutions (Figure 1.2).

The factor analysis of information risk (FAIR) model deals with the risk equation by breaking down, structuring, and detailing the two elements in question:

Risk = Loss Event Frequency (LEF) × Loss Magnitude

Loss event frequency (LEF): is defined as the frequency with which a loss event can occur, and is broken down into two factors: Threat event frequency (TEF) × Vulnerability.

Threat event frequency (TEF): This is the number of times a threat interacts with assets.

Vulnerability: The probability that threat attempts will result in a loss, and will succeed in exploiting it.

Loss magnitude: Estimate of loss in the event of a successful incident or malicious event, defined according to the equation: Primary Loss + Secondary Loss

Primary loss: These are the direct damages and immediate losses that can affect, for example, the financial and operational levels, such as theft of money, interruption and malfunctioning of the system, etc.

Secondary Loss: These are indirect losses with medium or long-term consequences such as litigation, fines, damage to the organization's image and reputation, etc.

1.6 Compliance and Regulations

Regulations are laws with measures to be applied in order to ensure an acceptable level of security and prevent organizations from falling victim to threats that can be averted and removed by complying with the guidelines [11].

To ensure that organizations have a level of security that protects them against common threats, regulations require them to align and apply a set of security measures, such as data encryption, strong authentication, logging to ensure traceability, etc. There are numerous regulations, including:

1.6.1 General data protection regulation (GDPR)

General Data Protection Regulation (GDPR) is a European regulation designed to protect and secure the personal data of the population of the European Union against disclosure, alteration, and leakage, by putting in place technical and organizational measures and by making organizations that store and process individuals' data liable for non-compliance with the GDPR through the application of very heavy fines against organizations violating the measures granted by the GDPR of up to 20 million euros and 4% of annual worldwide turnover [12].

1.6.2 Network and Information Security Directive 2 (NIS2)

Is a regulation that aims to improve the level of cybersecurity at the European Union level, and align and harmonize the requirements and prerequisites of all EU countries by inviting them to provide cybersecurity training to all staff and managers in particular to avoid human errors that can lead to cyber-risks, and by implementing operational and organizational security measures such as access control, NIS2 also relies on regular audits to verify the level of compliance of organizations with the regulations, and makes them accountable where necessary by imposing financial penalties of up to €10 million or 2% of worldwide turnover.

1.6.3 Health Insurance Portability and Accountability Act (HIPAA)

For a regulation originating in the United States, the main aim of it is to protect information and data relating to the health of American citizens, whether stored, transmitted, used, or shared. It is intended for any organization that processes data relating to patients and health, such as health insurers, hospitals, clinics, and healthcare providers, to guarantee the confidentiality and security of protected health information (PHI). PHI identifies any kind of information linked to an individual and which ensures a certain uniqueness in relation to others, such as surname, first name, address, date of birth, medical records, medical history, healthcare billing, test results, etc.

HIPAA aims to ensure the confidentiality and privacy of patient data, during its collection and use, against any kind of disclosure or leakage to other unauthorized entities, and that the patient's authorization is compulsory and necessary before any sharing, except in the most urgent and extreme cases, HIPAA also aims to put in place security measures at different physical, operational, organizational, and administrative levels, so it obliges organizations that in the case of incidents in this sense to send notifications to the parties concerned, such as the patients themselves, to the government, and the public if the incident impacts a large number of people.

And like the other regulations, HIPAA imposes penalties on organizations that fail to comply with the recommended security measures, in the form of fines of up to $1.5 million per year (per type of violation), as well as criminal prosecution.

1.6.4 Payment Card Industry – Data Security Standard (PCI-DSS)

Is an international standard created by the major card companies such as Visa, MasterCard, American Express, Discover, and JCB, which aims to protect bank card data, i.e., card number, name, expiry date, CVV code, etc. It applies to all organizations that deal with banking data, whether they store it, process it, or transmit it, such as banks, online payment service providers, e-commerce sites, etc.

The PCI-DSS standard is based on twelve requirements grouped into six major security control objectives:

1. Building, installing, and maintaining a secure network and systems:
    a. Harden and ensure correct configuration and reinforcement of firewalls.
    b. Ensure that passwords are strong and unique and that systems and accounts do not have the same password while changing the default settings provided by the supplier.
2. Protect cardholder data:
    a. Protect stored card user data.
    b. Hide cardholder banking data on open public networks by encrypting the information transmitted.
3. Maintain a vulnerability management program:
    a. Protect computer systems against malware by installing an antivirus, and keeping it up to date in order to keep its virus signature database up to date and guarantee that it can know the signatures of all viruses, including new ones.
    b. Keeping systems up to date, by periodically checking available updates and applying them to stay up-to-date, and developing and maintaining secure systems and applications.
4. Implement strict access control measures:
    a. Restrict and limit access to cardholder data and systems according to justified business needs.
    b. Allocate unique and strong identifiers to each cardholder, ensuring identification and authentication prior to any access to a system.
    c. Restrict physical access to cardholder data.
5. Monitor and test networks regularly:
    a. Ensure logging by tracing and monitoring every access to the network and to cardholder data components.
    b. Regularly test security systems and networks.

6. Maintain a security policy:
   a. Maintain an information security policy and organizational programs for all staff, through periodic awareness campaigns and the drafting of documented procedures.

PCI-DSS defines four levels of compliance depending on the annual volume of card transactions:

- Level 1: Dedicated to transmissions that exceed 6 million transactions per year, requiring an annual audit plus a quarterly scan, and the audit must be carried out by a qualified third party (QSA).
- Level 2: Dedicated to transmissions with an annual volume of transactions of between 1 and 6 million, requiring a self-assessment (SAQ) with a scan sometimes required.
- Level 3: Dedicated to transmissions with an annual volume of transactions of between 20,000 and 1 million, and requiring self-assessment (SAQ) with scanning sometimes required.
- Level 4: Is dedicated to transmissions with an annual volume of transactions of less than 20,000 and requires a self-assessment (SAQ) with a scan sometimes required.

In the event of non-compliance, organizations risk fines imposed by the card networks (Visa, MasterCard, etc.), and a loss of the right to process payments, as well as a fall in their public image and reputation. It is also important to remain compliant in order to gain and maintain the trust of customers and business partners, as well as to limit and reduce fraud, data leaks, and penalties linked to security breaches [13].

1.7 Conclusion

With the rapid growth in cyber threats and cyberattacks, and given the increasing number of cyberattacks and constant evolution of threats, it is essential to adopt a proactive, structured, and continuous approach. Risk management is no longer an optional extra; it is becoming now increasingly mandatory and essential, and a key strategic challenge for all organizations, also it is not a time-bound process, but a continuous technique that accompanies organizations from the start of their projects, and during their deployment and operation, which consists of identifying threats, assessing them, correcting them, and tracking and monitoring them.

Various standards have been put in place to provide a better framework for the measures to be taken, the steps to be applied, and the prerequisites to be met, so that organizations can ensure compliance with known regulations and standards. Any negligence or complacency on the part of organizations risks sanctions and fines, as well as consequences that have a negative impact on their reputation, operations, organization, and much more. Each standard corresponds to specific cases and sectors and is applied under given conditions.

In the end, it should be noted that the aim of cyber risk management is not to eliminate all risks, but to control, prioritize, and reduce them to an acceptable level in line with the organization's objectives and resources, this can only be ensured with an effective approach and strategic risk management.

References

[1] A. Shostack, Threat Modeling: Designing for Security, Wiley, 2014.

[2] P. Mell and T. Grance, "The NIST definition of cloud computing," National Institute of Standards and Technology, vol. 800, no. 145, 2011.

[3] ISO/IEC 27005:2018, Information technology – Security techniques – Information security risk management, International Organization for Standardization, 2018.

[4] Z. Nadifi, M. Ouaissa, M. Ouaissa, M. Alhyan, and A. Kartit, "Security, privacy, and trust in IoT networks," In Artificial Intelligence for Blockchain and Cybersecurity Powered IoT Applications, pp. 19–29, CRC Press, 2024.

[5] D. Hubbard and R. Seiersen, How to Measure Anything in Cybersecurity Risk, Wiley, 2016.

[6] A. A. O. Zanella, N. Bessis, and S. Sotiriadis, "Risk management in cyber-physical systems: A review," Future Generation Computer Systems, vol. 91, pp. 555–565, 2019.

[7] L. Deleris and E. Madnick, "Risk management and decision analysis with Bayesian networks," Communications of the ACM, vol. 49, no. 3, pp. 56–61, 2006.

[8] B. Schneier, "Attack trees," Dr. Dobb's Journal of Software Tools, vol. 24, no. 12, pp. 21–29, 1999.

[9] M. Ouaissa and M. Ouaissa, M. (2020, September). "Cyber security issues for iot based smart grid infrastructure," In IOP Conference Series: Materials Science and Engineering (Vol. 937, No. 1, p. 012001). IOP Publishing.

[10] M. S. Islam, M. M. Hassan, and A. Almogren, "A blockchain-based privacy-preserving data sharing for cyber-physical systems," IEEE Access, vol. 7, pp. 11980–11990, 2019.
[11] A. Radanliev et al., "Cyber risk management for critical infrastructure: A review," Computers & Security, vol. 95, 2020, p. 101827.
[12] N. Z. Alwan, K. M. Elleithy, and N. Ahmed, "Cybersecurity risk assessment framework for smart grid," Procedia Computer Science, vol. 155, pp. 715–720, 2019.
[13] M Ouaissa and M. Ouaissa, "Analyzing and Mitigating Attacks in IoT Smart Home Using a Threat Modeling Approach-Based STRIDE," International Journal of Interactive Mobile Technologies (iJIM), vol. 19, no. 2, pp. 126–142, 2025.

2

The Rise of AI and Risk Management

Muhammad Adnan[1], Tahseen Ullah[1], Sher Taj[2], Rahim Khan[3], Zahid Ullah Khan[3], M. A. Al-Khasawneh[4,5], and Inam Ullah[6*]

[1]Abasyn University Peshawar KPK, Pakistan
[2]Daqing Normal University, China
[3]College of Information and Communication Engineering, Harbin Engineering University, China
[4]School of Computing, Skyline University College, UAE
[5]Applied Science Research Center, Applied Science Private University, Jordan
[6]Department of Computer Engineering, Gachon University, Republic of Korea

Email: adnanthana@gmail.com, tahseenjan007@gmail.com; shertajkhan002@gmail.com; rahimkhan9001@yahoo.com, dr.khan8003@yahoo.com; malkhasawneh@outlook.com; inam.fragrance@gmail.com

Abstract

In today's business landscape, embedding artificial intelligence (AI) into risk management is being done as a strategic measure for companies to improve their operational performance and resilience. This chapter will go into the applications, advantages, and challenges of AI risk management. Miglior risk mitigation through more accurate and proactive AI of supply chain optimization, cybersecurity, natural language processing (NLP), and predictive analytics. However, there is some large trouble getting data quality, getting out of the model, ethical considerations, and regulatory compliance to work effectively with AI in risk management. This chapter, in addition, covers different AI risk management frameworks, e.g., the NIST AI Risk Management Framework (AI RMF) and the EU AI Act, that generate a structured way for

DOI: 10.1201/9788743808077-2

keeping hold of risks, once they talk about the full AI lifecycle. Using real-life case studies and grounded practical advice, this chapter intends to deliver to the reader a full grasp of how AI is transforming risk management and what needs to be done in order to reap the benefits. As AI progresses, its role in risk management will surely extend, giving new chances for development and further enhancing valuable business quality in an ever more complex and versatile business environment.

2.1 Introduction

Artificial intelligence (AI) has arrived to start a new age of technological development, therefore changing many industries, including risk management. A vital task for companies and institutions, risk management is the process of spotting, evaluating, and reducing possible hazards to guarantee operational stability, financial health, and strategic success. Risk management has historically molded proven methods that include human knowledge, historical data analysis, brainstorming, checklists, SWOT research, and risk formation. These methods succeed in handling various situations, but they might fail to address contemporary risk elements that demonstrate complexity and flux. Modern AI development provides new possibilities for finding better data control options and alternative change methods to reduce risks in traditional risk management approaches [1].

Businesses improve risk reduction through decisions and reduce the probability of vulnerabilities when they analyze extensive datasets with AI processing skills to identify patterns and make risk predictions. AI generates essential changes in multiple domains, which include predictive analytics, natural language processing (NLP), cybersecurity, and supply chain optimization. The implementation of these technologies enables businesses to complete precise risk assessments while raising production speeds and pre-empting risks, which leads to overall cost-efficiency [2]. AI tools that integrate into risk management operations cause numerous integration challenges. AI applications in risk management operate efficiently and responsibly by appropriately addressing issues of data quality, complex models, ethical matters, and other issues.

This chapter considers the increasing use of AI in risk management. We explore how AI can transform traditional risk management strategies by providing more valuable and proactive opportunities to find and reduce risk. It also highlights the need to use powerful AI risk management systems, such as the NEST framework (AI RMF) of the NIST AI-Risk Recalculation (AI RMF) and the EU-AAI Act, to manage the complexities and ethical issues associated with artificial intelligence. Through thorough case studies and practical ideas, this chapter hopes to convey complete knowledge of how AI can change risk management and which measures maximize. AI is constantly changing, and AI certainly plays a more significant role in risk management in the development of opportunities for inventions, improving organizational resilience in the context of more complex and dynamic enterprises.

AI is revolutionizing chance administration by presenting phenomenal levels of effectiveness, precision, and prescience. Conventional hazard administration methods, frequently dependent on manual data analysis and human judgment, are being replaced by AI's ability to handle massive amounts of data at extraordinary speeds. This empowers organizations to distinguish and survey dangers more precisely and proactively. Prescient analytics, fueled by machine learning calculations, can presently identify potential dangers based on historical and real-time data, permitting convenient interventions. NLP permits AI frameworks to analyze unstructured information, such as news articles and social media, to identify rising dangers and estimation patterns [3]. In cybersecurity, AI-driven frameworks can screen and analyze activity for irregularities, recognizing and reacting to potential breaches in real time.

2.2 Application of AI Risk Management

2.2.1 Predictive analytics

Prescient analytics utilizes advanced AI and machine learning algorithms to analyze historical data and predict future outcomes. This innovation plays a basic part in risk management, engaging organizations to anticipate potential risks and implement proactive measures to mitigate them. Its applications span different businesses, illustrating its flexibility and esteem. Within the monetary administrations division, prescient analytics models are utilized to survey credit hazard by assessing verifiable information on advance reimbursements, wage levels, and investing designs [4]. Banks can use these models for their appearance to predict the likelihood of credit cases, set appropriate attractive tariffs, and minimize budget accidents. Presidential analysis is used within the conservation industry and assesses the likelihood of a claim by analyzing authentic information, climate rules, and statistical data. This allows you to set a more accurate premium and identify false exercises that guarantee an adapted hazard portfolio.

2.2.2 Natural language processing (NLP)

NLP could be a transformative innovation that includes the KI framework for understanding, interpreting, and creating human dialects. In the cessation of random dosing, NLPs demonstrate invaluable value in the analysis of unstructured information such as content documents, emails, and social media contributions that can ignore traditional strategies. Turning dialects into amazing recordings of knowledge makes a difference for organizations that preempt potential dangers and make better-trained decisions. One of the foremost compelling applications of NLP is assumption investigation. By filtering social media platforms, news articles, and online discussions, NLP can gauge public sentiment toward a company or industry. This gives organizations early notice of developing dangers, such as reputational dangers or moving advertising recognition [5]. For example, a sudden surge in negative estimation on social media may flag an approaching emergency, permitting businesses to reply quickly and deliberately.

NLP also exceeds expectations in record classification, a basic task in hazard evaluation. By analyzing the substance of legitimate reports, contracts, or compliance reports, NLP calculations can consequently categorize and prioritize data. Typically, especially valuable in legitimate and compliance risk management, where recognizing pertinent documents rapidly can make the difference between mitigating a risk and facing expensive consequences. Envision a compliance group filtering through thousands of pages of legitimate content. NLP can streamline this preparation and basic problems, and save profitable time.

Additionally, NLP creates chatbots and virtual employees, key devices in random management. These great frameworks combine clients and representatives to ensure that something else remains unknown. In the case of chatbots, the chatbot can identify concerns that customers express intelligently in the middle of the day and take over random management groups in real time. Virtual employees can also make a difference in providing quick warnings of potential risks and ensuring that representatives investigate complex situations.

2.2.3 Cybersecurity

AI is a cybersecurity sentinel that, in real time, filters huge amounts of information to identify inconspicuous designs that escape human witnesses. These frameworks learn from a wide dataset, distinguish between special features that characterize potential violations, and act as frameworks for attention to attacks. In the arrangement, check the AI calculations of all information bundles and customer activity. This will display indescribable exercises such as sudden climbing areas of information or registration from new areas [6].

These irregularities that cannot be detected regularly on regular devices cause fast precautions and allow for quick mediation. Suddenly, strange exchanges and deviations from everyday investment trends raise the red flag and predict potential financial accidents. Computer-aided landscapes are used to improve locations. AI Control Framework Mining Program Code and Screen Behavior Learn to recognize malware signs. These frameworks adapt to unused risks and are aware of them recently and neutralize them. It can cause damage recently. AI-controlled frameworks analyze real-time data from MasterCard exchange information to identify messy designs and can cause false actions. This reduced the fear tor episodes by 40%, indicating AI control in securing gel frames.

2.2.4 Supply chain risk management

In all relationships, impotence is hidden within today's supply chain. From unexpected shop window shifts to eccentric crashed grunts, obstacles can paralyze operations and destroy productivity. However, false knowledge provides effective healing that changes the receptive response to positive techniques. By using machine learning explanatory skills, Ki-Frameworks is a huge data record that reveals hidden designs and predicts potential obstacles that have recently been realized [7]. This careful ability allows companies to create flexible supply chains that can optimize stocks, streamline adjustments, and ultimately study weaknesses in the globalized world. AI can act as a progressive sentinel, providing early messages, allowing businesses to mitigate risks and ensure a smooth flow of products and management in increasingly unstable scenes.

Demand forecasting: AI models analyze external components, such as authentic offer information, advertising patterns, regularity, and financial changes to plan future demands with incredible accuracy. This allows companies to optimize stock levels, reduce the risk of confirmation, and adapt plans to generate expected customer requirements. By participating in real information and progressive calculations such as LSTM and ARIMA, companies can spur powerful changes in numbers to accommodate changes in presentation terms.

Risk assessment: AI models analyze external components, such as authentic offer information, advertising patterns, regularity, and financial changes to plan future demands with incredible accuracy. This allows companies to optimize stock levels, reduce the risk of confirmation, and adapt plans to generate expected customer requirements. By participating in real information and progressive calculations such as LSTM and ARIMA, companies can spur powerful changes in numbers to accommodate changes in presentation terms.

Logistics optimization: The AI-controlled framework streamlines the morphology of transport and dispersion by analyzing activity design, climatic conditions, and transportation planning. AI-driven course optimization, energy planning, and Armada management reduce transportation costs, create transportation times, and improve maintenance. Together, these AI-driven skills create an integrated supply chain environment. This is not so competent and inexpensive, and also spy and flexible within disability denominations.

2.2.5 Other applications

Manufactured insights revolutionized risk management in various sectors. In healthcare systems, AI analyzes vast amounts of information and predicts complications such as illnesses and infectious diseases. By recognizing high-risk patients and prescriptions for preventive measures, AI enables personalized care, provides an understanding of outcomes, and reduces costs. This aggressive approach improves supply quality and minimizes the burden on health frameworks. In managing natural opportunities, AI analyzes information such as climate design, seismic behavior, and climate patterns to predict normal fiasco and examine the impact of climate. These knowledge reports allow organizations to implement disaster and maintenance functions planning. This reduces risks and ensures communities and biological systems. In the compliance field, AI makes a difference when organizations consider complex management scenarios by adapting their corporate approach to management conditions [8]. By mechanizing compliance, observation, and row-to-line distinctions, AI reduces the risk of legal punishment and reputational damage and maintains operational effectiveness.

In human resources (HR), random administration of AI is varied by analysis of representative information regarding sales rate expectations, perceptions of potential conflicts, and evaluation of staff patterns. By providing representative performance and commitment experience, AI allows organizations to expose themselves to maintenance techniques and arbitration programs. This is not the same as workers' guarantees, but it also reduces sales, promoting a more profitable and more comfortable work environment. In general, AI-controlled risk management improves decision-making, drives outcomes, and ensures outstanding versatility across different segments.

2.3 Benefits of AI in Risk Management

AI poses imaginative measures to successfully address, research, and mitigate dangers. By using progressive innovations such as machine learning,

Table 2.1 Benefits of AI in risk management.

Benefit	Description	Examples
Enhanced accuracy and efficiency	AI processes large datasets in real time, identifying patterns and correlations.	Fraud detection in banking, healthcare diagnostics
Proactive risk mitigation	AI predicts and addresses potential risks before they escalate.	Detecting fraud, preventing equipment failures, and averting cybersecurity threats
Cost reduction	AI identifies and addresses risks early, preventing costly issues.	Predictive maintenance, fraud detection, and automation of routine tasks
Improved decision-making	AI provides data-driven insights and comprehensive risk assessments.	Forecasting market volatility, supply chain disruptions, and cybersecurity threats

general dialect preparation, and predictive analysis, AI improves traditional hazard management practices, allowing businesses to work more productively and proactively. See Table 2.1 for a detailed comparison of traditional and AI-enhanced hazard management practices.

2.3.1 Enhanced accuracy and efficiency

The ability of AI to process and analyze large data records in real time is one of the most notable advantages of random administration. The KI framework is B. It can be information from a variety of sources, including adjustments, customer behavior, presentation patterns, and actual outside variables, such as climate design and geopolitical opportunities. This comprehensive information survey allows AI to distinguish between inconspicuous relationships and increases the risk that human auditors can ignore. To illustrate, KI can look at the world market around the clock within the budget sector and recognize early signs of financial fluctuations and current instability.

AI makes significant advances in the Fright Tor Center when managing your accounts and health checks. When managing accounts, AI improves the location of fear by analyzing millions of transactions in real time using designs that show false measurements and machine learning calculations that recognize irregularities. It may be approved by displaying the registration operation, such as an IP address or device [9]. With this constant learning from unused information, the AI framework becomes more persuasive over time, reducing false positives and increasing progress accuracy.

During health checkups, AI-equipped devices analyze recovered images, such as X-rays, MRIS, CT scans, and other fields, lending high accuracy and effectiveness. These devices use progressive machine learning methods, particularly deep learning, to identify abnormalities and analyze cancers, such as cancer and cardiovascular disease, with accuracy that exceeds traditional strategies.

2.3.2 Proactive risk mitigation

Active coincidence moderation using AI's dedicated organizations predicts and counters potential risks these days. Recently, they have become more and more fundamental issues. By analyzing verifiable information, recognizing patterns, and determining weaknesses, AI frameworks companies can take precautions such as threats, disappointment, or deflecting cybersecurity risks. This careful ability, combined with real-time observation and mechanized responses, ensures that risks are monitored quickly and visually, minimizing the impact on operations and accounts.

AI demands decisions by conveying amazing knowledge and repeating various dangerous scenarios [10]. This allows businesses to prioritize risk, distribute assets productively, and create strong possibilities. As a company is gradually being used by the AI-controlled random empire, they are building facilities for practical development in a versatile but quirky world.

2.3.3 Cost reduction

The risk transfer systems controlled by AI technology help organizations save money while providing distinct hazard identification abilities to analyze potential risks. Organizations can request precautionary measures through AI systems that analyze verifiable information and real-time data about disappointment, supply chain failures, and cybersecurity risks. The deployment of AI-controlled pensions decreases production stoppages in addition to reducing maintenance expenses and the implementation of AI-based tor frame systems decreases financial problems [11]. Organization leaders should use these positive measures only as tools to improve operational efficiency without granting them independence for free action.

AI-controlled risk transfers minimize costs while separating various potential risks through the process of distinguishing potential hazards. AI frameworks that analyze verifiable information and real-time data help organizations take precautions through their processing of disappointment, supply chain failures, and cybersecurity risks. The AI-powered pension system decreases the need for voluntary system downtime and repair expenses, while the AI-controlled ship frame system minimizes budgetary accidents [11]. These beneficial measures function as tools for operational enhancement instead of providing independence to achieve productive operations and distribution of assets.

2.3.4 Improved decision making

AI upgrades decision-making in risk management by giving organizations data-driven insights and comprehensive risk assessments. By analyzing endless amounts of information from numerous sources, AI distinguishes designs, patterns, and potential dangers that would not be clear through conventional strategies. For illustration, AI can assess budgetary information, advertising conditions, and operational measurements to estimate dangers, such as market instability, supply chain disruptions, or cybersecurity threats [12]. This empowers pioneers to make educated choices, prioritize dangers, and execute techniques that effectively relieve potential impacts.

AI bolsters situation examination and prescient modeling, permitting organizations to mimic the results of distinctive hazard administration procedures. By testing different scenarios, pioneers can evaluate the potential results of their choices and select the foremost ideal course of activity. This proactive approach is not as it diminishes vulnerability but also makes strides the in general strength of the organization. With AI's capacity to handle complex information and convey noteworthy bits of knowledge, decision-makers can explore dangers with more noteworthy certainty and accuracy.

2.4 Challenges of Implementing AI in Risk Management

2.4.1 Data quality and access

AI frameworks depend on high-quality, exact, and comprehensive information to provide dependable bits of knowledge. Be that as it may, numerous organizations battle with fragmented, obsolete, or conflicting information, which can lead to imperfect forecasts and ineffective risk management. Furthermore, information silos inside organizations can anticipate AI frameworks from getting to the total run of data required for an all-encompassing viewof dangers [13]. Guaranteeing information quality and availability requires critical speculation in information foundation, administration, and integration, which can be an obstruction for numerous organizations.

Additionally, getting to outside information sources, such as advertising patterns or worldwide event information, can be challenging due to lack of access, accessibility, or administrative limitations. Without a vigorous information foundation, AI frameworks may struggle to supply significant bits of information, constraining their effectiveness in risk management. Organizations must prioritize information administration tools and contribute to tools that upgrade information collection, cleaning, and integration.

2.4.2 Complexity and transparency

AI frameworks, especially those utilizing progressed machine learning models, can be exceedingly complex and troublesome to decipher. This "dark box" nature of AI poses a challenge for hazard administration, as partners may struggle to understand how the framework arrives at a specific expectation or proposal. The need for straightforwardness can lead to doubt and delay in embracing AI-driven arrangements, particularly in businesses where responsibility and explainability are basic, such as finance or healthcare [14].

To address this, organizations are progressively centering on Reasonable AI (XAI), which aims to create AI decision-making forms that are more straightforward and justifiable. In any case, achieving this adaptation between complexity and no complexity remains a challenge, as the model can reduce accuracy and careful control. Organizations need to contribute to instruments, prepare to fill this gap, and ensure that they can successfully interpret the KI framework.

2.4.3 Ethical and legal considerations

AI implementation in risk management creates significant moral issues, specifically about fair treatment and avoiding mix-ups. AI models that receive authentic and unilateral data input might generate various imbalances that organizations must prevent by making sure their frameworks follow ethical principles.

From a legitimate perspective, AI-controlled random choices can lead to risk issues if they cause budgetary injuries or management injuries. Responsibility decisions are challenged as they are engineers, information suppliers, or end users when AI frameworks make incomplete forecasts. Without a clear, legitimate system for monitoring AI in risk management, organizations face compliance and potential legal instability.

2.4.4 Regulatory compliance

Financial institutions and other businesses must guarantee that AI applications comply with existing laws and industry benchmarks. However, AI models frequently advance powerfully, making it troublesome to adjust them to inactive administrative necessities. Controllers are still catching up with AI advancements, leading to ambiguity in compliance desires and potential clashes with chance administration hones.

Moreover, distinctive words have shifting controls on information security (e.g., GDPR), algorithmic reasonableness, and AI straightforwardness [15]. Multinational organizations must explore these complex legitimate scenes, which can increase the complexity and AI usage. Disobeying directions can result in fines, sanctions, or limitations on AI utilization, restricting its viability in risk management.

2.5 Challenges of Implementing AI In Risk Management

2.5.1 The NIST AI risk management framework (AI RMF)

The NIST AI Hazard Administration System (AI RMF) may be a comprehensive, direct system created by the National Institute of Standards and Technology (NIST) to assist organizations in overseeing risks related to AI frameworks (Figure 2.1). It is planned to be adaptable and versatile to different sorts of AI frameworks and organizational settings [16].

Govern: To successfully oversee AI dangers, organizations ought to receive an organized approach, including governance, mapping, estimation, and management. To begin with, administration structures such as AI Administration Committees ought to be built up to supervise hazard administration, ensuring responsibility and alignment with organizational objectives. Authorities must develop a risk-aware culture, emphasizing moral AI utilization and proactive risk management.

Map: Organizations must implement AI risks by contextualizing them in production environments. This includes examining the potential impact on professional, social, and moral measures to understand how AI risks are related to a wider variety of trading formats. In partnerships that create employees, customers, and supervisory authorities in risk assessments, they are guaranteed.

Measure: Estimates are the basis of well-discovered decisions. Organizations should perform both quantitative and subjective random assessments and use measurements to assess the risk that the analysis will exceed the average. Creating important measurements will make a difference over time and enhance the data-controlled changes.

Manage: Hazards need to be effectively monitored by prioritizing those with the most prominent potential effects. Performing professional and procedural

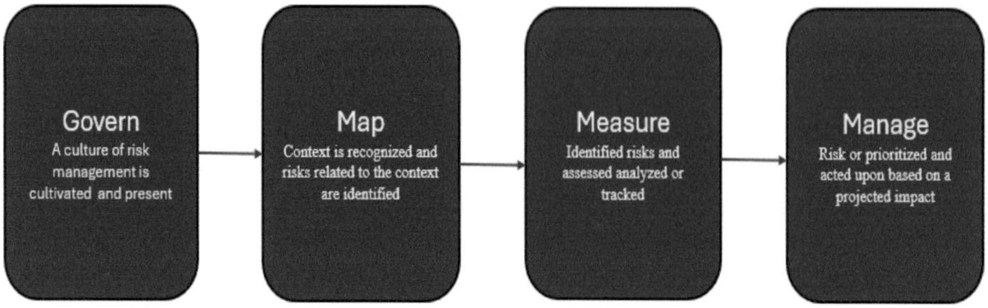

Figure 2.1 The NIST AI risk management framework (AI RMF).

controls, such as finding trends and calculations for discovery by moral research committees, can serve to mitigate risk. Sustainable improvements from normal research ensure that risk management progresses near AI head paths and rising danger.

2.5.2 The EU-AI Act

EU-AI Act could be the management system pointed out to ensure the security and critical rights of EU citizens when connecting to the AI framework conditions. We classify the KI framework into four levels of risk: insufficient, large, limited, and negligible risk [17]. The law does not allow for the use of a particular AI suited to low-risk and sets strict prerequisites for high-risk AI frameworks, including risk management frameworks, information management, human supervision, and uncomplicated (Figure 2.2).

Risk assessment: To investigate and monitor AI threats, organizations must classify AI frameworks at risk levels, as outlined in the Systems and EU-AI Act. This classification distinguishes asset prioritization and moderation techniques based on potential injuries. Once classified, a careful risk assessment must be conducted for each AI frame, where special, moral, and legitimate proposals are evaluated to provide a comprehensive understanding of potential weaknesses.

Compliance: Compliance can be a fundamental part of reliable AI placement, especially for high-risk frames. Organizations must follow their administrative needs. B. Implement strong random frames for management frameworks, ensure legitimate information management, maintain human supervision, and maintain simple benchmarks. Compliance efforts, random review counting, moderation techniques, and documenting review paths are about responsibility and administrative verification.

Figure 2.2 The EU AI Act.

Monitoring: Advanced reviews ensure that the KI framework remains compliant and persuasive over time. The constant implementation of framework conditions, the discovery of temperament, and moral influences recognize the development of danger. Furthermore, organizations must remain trained to improve industry control and best honor and adapt arrangements and methods as needed. By participating in organized random ratings, rigorous conformance measurements, and aggressive reviews, companies can send AI to minimize meeting risks and legitimate obligations.

2.5.3 ISO/IEC Standards

The International Organization for Standardization (ISO) and the International Committee for Electrical Engineering (IEC) have developed standards that affect various aspects of AI risk management [18]. These standards highlight transparency, accountability, and ethical considerations and provide implementable guidelines for managing AI risks throughout the AI lifecycle. Key standards include ISO/IEC 23894:2023 (Figure 2.3).

Adopt standard: To ensure robust AI management, organizations need to incorporate internationally recognized standards such as ISO/IEC into their processes. The first step is to determine whether a standard such as ISO/IEC 23894 (AI Risk Management) or ISO/IEC 42001 (AI Management System) is most relevant to the AI system and risk profile. As soon as these standards are identified, these standards should be systematically integrated into the organization's risk management framework to ensure consistency, reliability, and compliance.

Integrate into processes: During the design and development of AI systems, compliance with these standards contributes to risk mitigation by entering best practices in areas such as data quality, detection, and algorithm transparency. Similarly, compliance with standards established during the operational

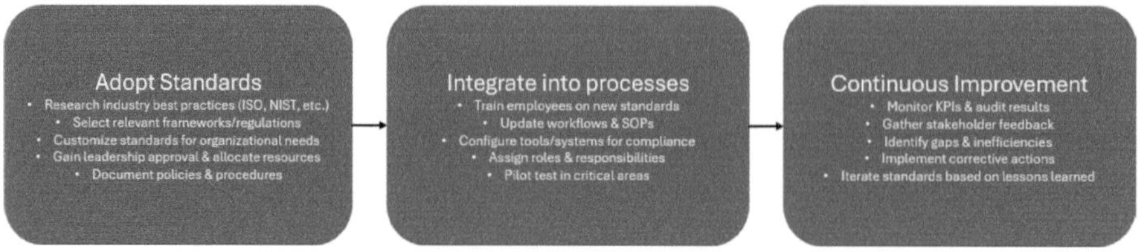

Figure 2.3 ISO/IEC Standards.

and development phases ensures that AI systems function as intended, providing appropriate safety measures for security, accountability, and ethical use.

Continuous improvement: To maintain long-term effectiveness, businesses need to carry out a continuous improvement process. This includes regular reviews of risk management practices to adapt to development standards and regulatory requirements. Additionally, a structured feedback loop with insights from audits, stakeholder inputs, and real performance data can help improve your risk strategy over time. By embedding standards based on every stage of the AI lifecycle and continuous improvement, businesses can promote trust, reduce risk, and ensure sustainable adoption of AI.

2.5.4 Additional framework

The morally adapted IEEE Plan (EAD) contains comprehensive rules for prioritizing moral reflection in excellent independent framework conditions. To implement EAD, organizations need to begin determining moral standards and specific proposals at a high level. This must guarantee agreement with the values of truth, liability, human rights, etc. Closing with various partners, including ethics, engineers, and political decisions, is important to participate in AI progress and agreements. Also, tending to social settings is fundamental, as moral dangers may shift over locales; this includes surveying potential inclinations, societal impacts, and long-term results in several scenarios [19]. In the interim, MITRE's Sensible Administrative System for AI Security emphasizes improving AI framework security and versatility through collaboration among industry, government, and the scholarly community, alongside persistent risk evaluation. In differentiation, McKinsey's system takes a business-centric approach, centering on proactive hazard administration by cultivating collaboration between trade, legal, and specialized groups to relieve AI-related dangers effectively.

2.6 Case Study With Real-World Example

2.6.1 Financial institution using AI for fraud detection

As advanced exchanges became increasingly common, JP Morgan Chase, one of the world's biggest financial institutions, was faced with increasing challenges of financial fraud. Ordinary extortion location frameworks that are based on rule-based calculations and manual checking are reactive, leading to a high number of false positives [20]. It was clear that a few sorts of advanced proactive solutions were required.

Implementation: A long time ago, JP Morgan Chase created a sophisticated AI framework to spot fraud. Utilizing machine learning, the show checks gigantic numbers of exchanges in real time. It continually screens exchanges, examining client investing propensities to identify its normal behavior [21]. On the off chance that an exchange looks abnormal compared to past designs, the framework flags it for a human to review. Since the AI was connected to the bank's frameworks, alarms may well be taken care of promptly.

Results: JP Morgan Chase altogether improved its extortion location capabilities after implementing an AI solution. The AI framework distinguishes and banners false exchanges with greater accuracy and speed than conventional rule-based strategies. According to JP Morgan Chase's information, modern AI has moved forward in extortion location rates by 25% and decreased false positives by 50%. This progression has fortified client beliefs, as fewer wrong cautions result in fewer disturbances, and clients feel more secure knowing that the progress of innovation shields their accounts. Moreover, AI sending has conveyed considerable financial benefits to banks.

2.6.2 Retail company using AI for supply chain optimization

These dazzle spots made expensive, wasteful aspects overloaded distribution centers, missed conveyances, and disappointed clients [22]. Without clearer perceivability, indeed, little disturbances get snowballed into greater issues, harming both operations and client belief.

Implementation: The company executed AI arrangements to optimize its supply chain. These arrangements included real-time information collection and examination, predictive analytics, stock administration, course optimization, and distribution center robotization. AI calculations were utilized to decide the most proficient and cost-effective transportation routes, considering components like activity conditions, fuel utilization, and plans.

AI-powered robots were sent to computerize assignments like picking, pressing, and sorting in stockrooms.

Results: The usage of AI arrangements led to effective changes within the company's supply chain. Real-time information collection and investigation have given superior visibility and transparency into stock levels and shipment areas. Prescient analytics made a difference in distinguishing potential disruptions or supply chain vulnerabilities, permitting the company to take pre-emptive measures. Stock administration was optimized, lessening costs related to overloading or understocking. Course optimization comes about in more proficient transportation, decreasing fuel utilization, and transportation costs. Distribution center mechanization made strides in speed, exactness, and effectiveness in stockrooms. In general, the company experienced upgraded supportability, increased client involvement, and expanded benefits.

2.6.3 Healthcare provider using AI for risk management

A healthcare supplier battled to successfully oversee dangers in persistent care, finances, and compliance [23]. Obsolete hazard administration approaches could not keep up with real-time requests or adjust to changing controls and operational challenges. As a result, wasteful aspects added up costs, workflows got strained, and quiet fulfillment endured. Without convenient experiences, the organization is confronted by mounting pressures on both care quality and financial stability.

Implementation: The healthcare supplier has made AI arrangements to improve its risk management capabilities. These arrangements included real-time information collection and investigation, predictive analytics, and situation arranging. AI calculations were utilized to analyze information from different sources, including understanding records, monetary exchanges, and administrative necessities. Prescient analytics distinguished potential dangers and vulnerabilities, permitting the supplier to take pre-emptive measures [24]. Situation arranging empowered the supplier to recreate different circumstances and create possible plans.

Results: The execution of AI arrangements led to critical enhancements within the healthcare provider's hazard management capabilities. Real-time information collection and examinations give superior visibility and transparency into understanding care and financial operations. Prescient analytics made a difference in identifying potential dangers and vulnerabilities, permitting the supplier to take pre-emptive measures. Situation arranging empowered the supplier to create compelling possibility plans, guaranteeing commercial coherence. By and large, the healthcare supplier experienced improved quality of care, made strides in financial performance, and expanded administrative compliance.

2.7 Future Trends and Directions

As counterfeit insights proceed to advance at a quick pace, the future of AI risk management will be shaped by both technological advancements and the expanding scope of societal concerns [25]. Here are a few rising patterns and headings that are anticipated to characterize another chapter of AI administration, with more humanized points of interest:

2.7.1 AI regulation becomes mainstream

Governments around the world are progressively recognizing the ought to direct AI to guarantee it is created and utilized capably. The European Union's AI Act may be a prime case, setting a worldwide benchmark for transparency, accountability, and decency in AI frameworks. Comparative systems are being investigated and embraced by other districts, signaling a move towards worldwide administrative arrangement [24]. This implies that organizations will have to be more watchful of compliance, as non-compliance may lead to critical punishments and reputational harm.

2.7.2 Widespread adoption of ethical AI toolkits

Organizations are becoming more mindful of the moral implications of AI and are receiving AI morals toolkits and automated management platforms [26]. These toolkits can offer assistance to distinguish inclination, guarantee interpretability, and produce compliance reports, making it less demanding for engineers to coordinate moral contemplations into the AI improvement lifecycle. For instance, cloud framework suppliers are advertising built-in AI morals toolkits that bolster inclination discovery and fairness testing, making a difference companies to adjust their AI frameworks to their values.

2.7.3 Explainable and Interpretable AI (XAI)

The request for AI models that can be effectively adopted and applied is developing, particularly in segments like healthcare, law, and finance, where decisions can have significant consequences. XAI will end up more predominant, permitting partners to trust AI systems and guaranteeing compliance with legal requirements. For example, in healthcare, specialists and patients have to understand how an AI framework arrives at a specific determination to believe its proposals.

2.7.4 Privacy-preserving AI

Advances such as combined learning, differential protection, and homomorphic encryption will become more standard. These advances empower AI frameworks to learn from information without compromising client protection, making it conceivable to utilize AI capably in delicate applications. For example, unified learning permits numerous organizations to collaboratively prepare AI models without sharing their information, in this way protecting security while improving the model's precision.

2.8 Conclusion

The fast rise of AI has been introduced in a modern period of both boundless opportunities and phenomenal challenges. As we stand on the brink of a future where AI is profoundly woven into the texture of our everyday lives, the significance of viable AI hazard management cannot be exaggerated. This chapter has dug into the complicated and multifaceted nature of AI decision-making, shedding light on the moral, operational, legal, and societal challenges that must be explored to guarantee that AI is delivered consistently and fairly.

Within the domain of morals, we confront the overwhelming task of ensuring that AI frameworks do not sustain or compound existing biases. For example, AI-enlisting devices that incidentally favor certain socioeconomics over others can have far-reaching results for reasonableness and correspondence. Operational challenges emerge from the complexity of AI frameworks, which regularly work as "black boxes," making it troublesome to understand how choices are made. Legitimately, the scene is quickly advancing, with controls such as the EU's AI Act setting a point of reference for straightforwardness, responsibility, and reasonableness in AI frameworks. Societal concerns range from uprooting work to the potential for AI to be utilized in ways that conflict with human values.

As AI frameworks end up more complex and independent, the requirement for comprehensive systems that advance straightforwardness, decency, responsibility, and security gets to be progressively pressing. The rise of AI chance administration is not a fair response to potential dangers; it speaks of a fundamental move towards implementing obligation at every arrangement of AI improvement. This move is basic, not as if it were to relieve dangers, but moreover to construct beliefs and guarantee that AI frameworks are adjusted with societal values.

Looking ahead, the end of the AI chance administration will be formed by a few key patterns. The worldwide collaboration will play a pivotal part, as seen in activities like the Worldwide Association on Manufactured Insights (GPAI), which brings together governments, the scholarly world, and industry to share best hones and harmonize approaches. Mechanical advancement will proceed to drive the improvement of devices and procedures for overseeing AI dangers, such as explainable AI (XAI) and privacy-preserving innovations. Open calls for moral benchmarks will increase, and the future will demand a unified effort from governments, researchers, industry leaders, and society at large. By working together, ready-to-make AI frameworks that not as it were perform viably but do so with judgment and care for humankind. Grasping this duty nowadays will guarantee that AI becomes a driver for great, enabling social order while minimizing harm.

References

[1] S. Campos, H. Papadatos, F. Roger, C. Touzet, O. Quarks, and M. Murray, "A Frontier AI Risk Management Framework: Bridging the Gap Between Current AI Practices and Established Risk Management," pp. 1–20, 2025, [Online]. Available: http://arxiv.org/abs/2502.06656

[2] M. Awadalkarim, A. Ali, Y. A. Elmubarak, and H. Abdalla, "The Role of Artificial Intelligence in Risk Management and Underwriting Optimization in the Insurance Industry," vol. 22, pp. 17626–17642, 2024.

[3] I. Ullah, S. Qian, Z. Deng, and J. H. Lee, "Extended Kalman Filter-based localization algorithm by edge computing in Wireless Sensor Networks," *Digit. Commun. Networks*, vol. 7, no. 2, pp. 187–195, 2021, doi: 10.1016/j.dcan.2020.08.002.

[4] A. Wasil, J. Clymer, D. Krueger, E. Dardaman, S. Campos, and E. Murphy, "Affirmative Safety: An Approach to Risk Management for Advanced Ai," *SSRN Electron. J.*, 2024, doi: 10.2139/ssrn.4806274.

[5] K. Šekrst, J. McHugh, and J. R. Cefalu, "AI Ethics by Design: Implementing Customizable Guardrails for Responsible AI Development," 2024, [Online]. Available: http://arxiv.org/abs/2411.14442

[6] R. Powell, "The US Executive Order on AI : National Security Implications," no. November, pp. 1–11, 2024.

[7] A. Jedličková, "Ethical considerations in Risk management of autonomous and intelligent systems," *Ethics Bioeth. (in Cent. Eur.*, vol. 14, no. 1–2, pp. 80–95, 2024, doi: 10.2478/ebce-2024-0007.

[8] I. Ullah, D. Adhikari, X. Su, F. Palmieri, C. Wu, and C. Choi, "Integration of data science with the intelligent IoT (IIoT): current challenges and future perspectives," *Digit. Commun. Networks*, 2024, doi: 10.1016/j.dcan.2024.02.007.

[9] "Generative AI in Action : Opportunities & Risk Management in Financial Services," no. January, 2025.

[10] M. A. Khan, S. Javaid, S. A. H. Mohsan, M. Tanveer, and I. Ullah, "Future-Proofing Security for UAVs With Post-Quantum Cryptography: A Review," *IEEE Open J. Commun. Soc.*, vol. 5, no. November, pp. 6849–6871, 2024, doi: 10.1109/OJCOMS.2024.3486649.

[11] S. Barnaby, N. Pope, L. Derczynski, and C. Parisien, "Frontier ai risk assessment," no. August, 2025.

[12] "Optimizing-Risk-Management-Using-AI-ECI-Working-Group-Paper".

[13] I. Ullah, X. Su, X. Zhang, and D. Choi, "Simultaneous Localization and Mapping Based on Kalman Filter and Extended Kalman Filter," *Wirel. Commun. Mob. Comput.*, vol. 2020, 2020, doi: 10.1155/2020/2138643.

[14] D. M. Douglas, J. Lacey, and D. Howard, "Ethical risk for AI," *AI Ethics*, 2024, doi: 10.1007/s43681-024-00549-9.

[15] S. Taj *et al.*, "Machine Learning Applications in Unmanned Aerial Vehicle Swarms," in *Unmanned Aerial Vehicles Swarm for Protecting Smart Cities: Future Trends and Challenges*, O. Arshi, I. U. Khan, K. Kaushik, N. Iqbal, I. Ullah, and K. Slimani, Eds., Berkeley, CA: Apress, 2025, pp. 45–89. doi: 10.1007/979-8-8688-1047-3_2.

[16] M. Yazdi, E. Zarei, S. Adumene, and A. Beheshti, "Navigating the Power of Artificial Intelligence in Risk Management: A Comparative Analysis," *Safety*, vol. 10, no. 2, pp. 1–48, 2024, doi: 10.3390/safety10020042.

[17] S. Taj *et al.*, "Introduction to Unmanned Aerial Vehicles Swarm and Smart Cities," in *Unmanned Aerial Vehicles Swarm for Protecting Smart Cities : Future Trends and Challenges*, O. Arshi, I. U. Khan, K. Kaushik, N. Iqbal, I. Ullah, and K. Slimani, Eds., Berkeley, CA: Apress, 2025, pp. 1–43. doi: 10.1007/979-8-8688-1047-3_1.

[18] G. Ai, "Effective Mitigations for Systemic Risks from," pp. 1–78, 2024.

[19] S. U. Amin *et al.*, "EADN: An Efficient Deep Learning Model for Anomaly Detection in Videos," *Mathematics*, vol. 10, no. 9, pp. 1–15, 2022, doi: 10.3390/math10091555.

[20] M. Weismann, *University of Miami Business Law Review The Ethical Governance of Artificial Intelligence Using the AI Integrative Risk-Based (AIRB) Model to Achieve Compliance Risk Management The Ethical Governance of Artificial Intelligence : Using the AI Integrati*, vol. 33, no. 2.

[21] S. Ul Amin, B. Kim, Y. Jung, S. Seo, and S. Park, "Video Anomaly Detection Utilizing Efficient Spatiotemporal Feature Fusion with 3D Convolutions and Long Short-Term Memory Modules," *Adv. Intell. Syst.*, vol. 6, no. 7, 2024, doi: 10.1002/aisy.202300706.

[22] R. O. Ajirotutu, B. Matthew, P. Garba, and S. O. Johnson, "AI-driven risk mitigation: Transforming project management in construction and infrastructure development," 2024.

[23] T. Ullah *et al.*, "Machine Learning-Based Cardiovascular Disease Detection Using Optimal Feature Selection," *IEEE Access*, vol. 12, no. January, pp. 16431–16446, 2024, doi: 10.1109/ACCESS.2024.3359910.

[24] M. Yasir, I. Ullah, and C. Choi, "Depthwise channel attention network (DWCAN): An efficient and lightweight model for single image super-resolution and metaverse gaming," *Expert Syst.*, vol. 41, no. 4, pp. 1–13, 2024, doi: 10.1111/exsy.13516.

[25] S. U. Amin, Y. Kim, I. Sami, S. Park, and S. Seo, "An Efficient Attention-Based Strategy for Anomaly Detection in Surveillance Video," *Comput. Syst. Sci. Eng.*, vol. 46, no. 3, pp. 3939–3958, 2023, doi: 10.32604/csse.2023.034805.

[26] A. Shah, B. Ali, M. Habib, J. Frnda, I. Ullah, and M. Shahid Anwar, "An ensemble face recognition mechanism based on three-way decisions," *J. King Saud Univ. - Comput. Inf. Sci.*, vol. 35, no. 4, pp. 196–208, 2023, doi: 10.1016/j.jksuci.2023.03.016.

3

The Future of Cyber Risk Management in an AI-driven World

Fida Muhammad Khan[1], Asim Zeb[2], Taj Rahman[1], Inam Ullah[3*], M. A. Al-Khasawneh[4,5], Ishtiak Al Mamoon[6], and Hazrat Bilal[7]

[1]Department of Computer Science, Qurtuba University of Science & Information Technology, Pakistan
[2]Department of Computer Science, Abbottabad University of Science & Technology, Pakistan
[3]Department of Computer Engineering, Gachon University, Republic of Korea
[4]School of Computing, Skyline University College, UAE
[5]Applied Science Research Center. Applied Science Private University, Jordan
[6]CSE Department IUBAT, International University of Business Agriculture and Technology, Bangladesh
[7]College of Mechatronics and Control Engineering, Shenzhen University, China

Email: fida5073@gmail.com; asimzeb1@gmail.com; tajuom@gmail.com; inam.fragrance@gmail.com, mahmoudalkhasawneh@outlook.com; ishtiak.cse@iubat.edu; hbilal@mail.ustc.edu.cn

Abstract

Cyber threats are growing smarter and harder to predict as our lives become more connected and dependent on digital systems. Traditional cybersecurity methods are no longer sufficient to address these dynamic risks. As a result, artificial intelligence (AI) is emerging as a game-changing force, poised to revolutionize how organizations manage and mitigate cyber risks. This study explores the transformative role of AI in cyber risk management, examining its impact on threat detection, prevention, and response. AI technologies,

DOI: 10.1201/9788743808077-3

including machine learning and deep learning, offer advanced capabilities for identifying emerging threats, automating risk assessments, and responding to incidents in real time. The study highlights the challenges associated with AI implementation, such as data quality, ethical concerns regarding privacy and bias, and resource constraints, particularly for small- and medium-sized enterprises. Furthermore, the study discusses the integration of AI with emerging technologies like quantum computing, blockchain, and the Internet of Things (IoT), which presents both opportunities and risks in securing critical infrastructure and interconnected systems. The study concludes by emphasizing the need for organizations to invest in AI, improve data practices, ensure transparency and ethics, and collaborate to create robust and scalable cybersecurity systems. By addressing these challenges, AI can become a critical tool in building a proactive, secure, and resilient digital landscape.

3.1 Introduction

Cyber risk management is the essential process that organizations use to determine, evaluate, and mitigate the threat. With the speed of digitization progressing, the risks of cyber threats have scaled beyond imagination. Past cyber risk management was to protect info as well as systems using basic protective actions such as firewalls, antivirus, and upgrades of the security [1]. But as more advanced attacks like ransomware, malware, and increasingly sophisticated phishing campaigns start to grow rapidly beyond these legacy approaches, we have exposed significant vulnerabilities in traditional methods. While these integrated systems are continuing to grow and continue to offer tremendous business benefits, they have also massively expanded the cybercriminals' attack surface [2]. Cyber risk management aims to minimize the risk of attack by implementing controls to either reduce or eliminate the chance of a successful attack. Risk management frameworks typically only consider vulnerability assessments and apply some mitigation countermeasures to prevent breaches. Yet, given today's rapid and rapidly changing threat environment, the complexity and scale of cyberattacks have necessitated changes in dynamic, proactive, and predictive risk management practices. Such a shift is necessary since organizations now operate in an environment where they are threatened by complex, targeted systems that have become much more persistent [3]. For example, ransomware attacks have become increasingly sophisticated campaigns of either simple extortion or data theft and public shaming of victims. For state-backed advanced persistent threats (APTs), the actors may stay hidden for an extended period as they infiltrate an organization undetected.

Moreover, modern businesses are increasingly dependent on digital infrastructures, and a successful cyberattack may have dire consequences, such as financial losses, a damaged brand, and even loss of customer trust. Constantly exposed to data breaches and privacy invasions, regulators around the world have implemented stricter safeguards to protect customer data. Additionally, local laws in many regions, including the General Data Protection Regulation (GDPR) and the California Consumer Privacy Act (CCPA), and at times international agreements, make it difficult for organizations to neglect effective practices in the management of cyber risk [4]. Thus, the remit of cybersecurity has grown beyond simply fixing technical weaknesses to negotiating compliance with new privacy regulations, protecting trade secrets, and keeping customer data secure.

3.1.1 The rise of AI in cybersecurity

The digital landscape has rapidly evolved, and conventional security systems that depend on signature-based detection have struggled to catch up with the sheer volume and complexity of cyber threats. Artificial intelligence has heralded unprecedented solutions in cybersecurity, significantly more efficient than the already existing systems. Leveraging advances in machine learning (ML) and deep learning (DL), AI systems can analyze massive quantities of data at virtually no delay, events, behaviors, interconnectedness, and pobable and anomalous patterns by employing algorithms far quicker and more accurately than any human analyst can. Blind spot finding AI uses machine learning to cover new attack vectors emerging like a new poison, thus acting as a strong protector for future threat detection [5]. AI's capacity to identify both known and new threats in real time is another significant advantage. Traditional cybersecurity models are based on knowledge of known types of malware or attack patterns. This works well with known threats but is helpless against zero-day attacks and new variants of known malware. AI avoids this limitation by constantly learning from new data and identifying patterns that signal malicious activity, even if the attack has not been previously encountered [6]. In an era where cybercriminals are adapting their tactics to beat traditional security systems, this capability becomes a necessity.

Moreover, AI has vital functions in predictive cyber risk management as well. AI trained on data through advanced algorithms to recognize trends of historical attacks and determine the patterns of a potential future threat. This enables organizations to proactively fortify their defenses instead of waiting to react to incidents as they occur [7]. For instance, AI helps to detect early warning signals of a coordinated campaign against the

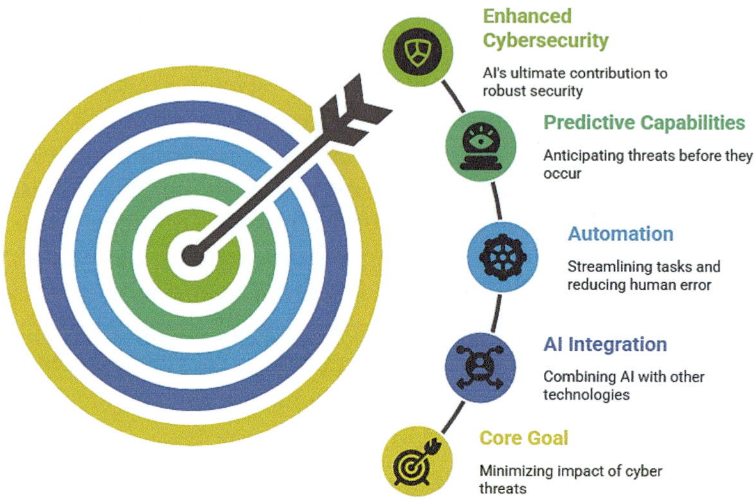

Figure 3.1 AI-driven cybersecurity key contributions and core goals.

organization, or a change in an attacker's tactics, by surfacing information that allows security teams to take preventive action before a compromise occurs. Additionally, with the incorporation of AI in cybersecurity modules, there is a potential for a greater degree of automation. AI-based automated systems handle repetitive, real-time tasks, such as malware scanning, network monitoring, and incident response. This not only saves time but also eliminates the pressure on human analysts, who can then concentrate on more difficult issues in terms of security. They provide faster response times, which is essential to mitigating a cyberattack, by automating tasks such as detecting anomalous behavior, isolating infected devices, or blocking malicious network traffic [8]. This also reduces human error, which is one of the top reasons for falling short in security for many businesses. Another major advantage of AI is its flexibility. Gone are the days when cybersecurity simply applied a passive posture. Organizations now require solutions that continuously adapt to the wide-ranging and evolving tactics cyber adversaries deploy. Such dynamic protection is made possible with the use of AI, as cyber security systems learn from new data, allowing them to continuously strengthen their defenses to respond effectively as attack strategies evolve [9]. The key contributions of AI-driven cybersecurity are illustrated in Figure 3.1, emphasizing security improvement, threat prediction, process automation, and integration with other technologies. The fundamental objective is to reduce the impact of cyber threats with smart and proactive defensive mechanisms.

AI plays a very important role in cyber risk management. As technology continues to evolve, from the proliferation of solutions on the edge with the IoT, to the rise of quantum computing, the sophistication of cyber threats continues to grow, creating an even stronger demand for innovative and AI-driven solutions. As new technologies emerge, they introduce new vulnerabilities and attack vectors that legacy security systems cannot accommodate, and AI plays an essential role in controlling the risks associated with them [10]. Moreover, the fusion of AI with other cutting-edge technologies, like blockchain and 5G, is anticipated to enhance cybersecurity even more, fostering stronger and safer digital landscapes as these cyber threats evolve in sophistication and scale, AI certainly becomes a very much a part of the future of cyber risk management. This heralds a new paradigm in which organizations can adopt Generative-AI principles, yielding a more proactive, adaptive, and scalable neural network defense against a growing wave of cyber threats. This book chapter further delves into the vast potential of AI in transforming enterprise threat detection and response, and how organizations can utilize such technologies to improve their overall security [11].

3.2 The Evolution of Cyber Threats and Risk Management

3.2.1 Increasing sophistication of cyber threats

In the last couple of decades, cyber threats have changed dramatically; they are now more complex, targeted, and sustained. Early cyber threats from simple viruses, worms, and drive-by attacks were generally used to cause disruption or steal personal data. However, modern-day cybercriminals are incredibly well organized and are using advanced methods to target deficiencies in digital systems. Advanced malware, ransomware, APTs, and insider threats have risen steeply, causing organizations to reevaluate their cybersecurity strategies. For organizations to formulate appropriate risk management plans, it is imperative to grasp these evolutions and complexities of the threats. The evolution of this cyber challenge and the associated risk management issues is presented in Figure 3.2.

3.2.1.1 Malware and ransomware

Malware is still one of the most common and destructive types of cyber threats. Malware types and behaviors have evolved from simple viruses, or "worms," to polymorphic malware and more sophisticated types today that adapt for evasion of the basic security tools. Some examples of these threats are viruses, trojan horses, spyware, and worms that exploit vulnerabilities

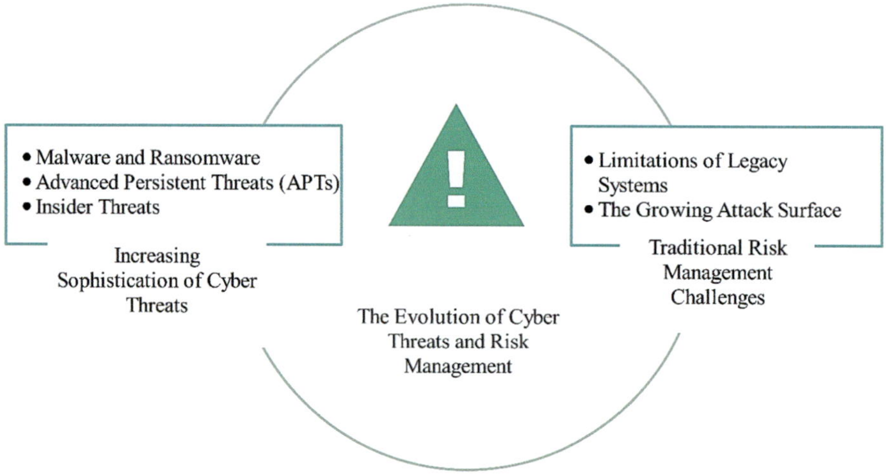

Figure 3.2 The evolution of cyber threats and risk management.

in the software, hardware, or network of a system. Once inside, malware can extract sensitive data, corrupt files, or cause an entire system to become defective. Malware that has become increasingly prevalent over recent years is ransomware, a form of malware that is particularly harmful [12]. In these types of attacks, the attacker encrypts the victim's files and requests a ransom, which is usually paid in cryptocurrency, in exchange for the decryption key. Recent ransomware attacks like those from WannaCry, NotPetya, and more recently, Ryuk, show us just how large in scale and financially damaging these attacks can be. Ransomware is usually used with data exfiltration techniques to maximize impact. Ransomware groups are becoming ever more organized, and their toolkits are increasingly sophisticated; traditional cybersecurity approaches are becoming less effective at preventing these attacks.

3.2.1.2 Advanced persistent threats (APTs)

APTs are targeted, long-term cyberattacks, often involving well-resourced attackers that include nation-state actors or organized criminal enterprises. Unlike regular cyberattacks, they are focused on breaking into a network and keeping themselves embedded within for prolonged periods without detection. APTs typically aim at valuable data or critical infrastructure and, in such cases, the attackers operate on a long-term basis and stealthily in the network to exfiltrate sensitive information or stop operations without raising alarm [13]. Instead, APTs are far too complex and persistent, requiring a more sophisticated risk management approach than your average cyberattack.

Attackers apply a variety of techniques to gain and maintain access, including spear-phishing, malware delivery, and privilege escalation. Inside, they commonly leverage tools that obfuscate their activities, allowing them to go unnoticed by standard security systems [14]. As organizations become more reliant on interconnected systems, the threat of APTs becomes more dangerous, specifically within financial, healthcare, and government sectors.

3.2.1.3 Insider threats

External cybercriminals are still a major factor to consider; however, insider threats have become a dangerous and underappreciated threat. Insider threats are malicious or negligent acts whenever employees, contractors, or others who have trusted access to an organization's internal systems are involved [15]. These threats can be intentional, like employees stealing intellectual property, or accidental, like an employee accidentally publishing sensitive information via poor data protection. Detecting insider threats can be difficult because insiders know the organization's systems, business processes, and common practices, allowing them to evade traditional security measures. Also, a lot of insider threats develop over long timelines, so they are challenging to detect without advanced detection systems. AI and machine learning also help mitigate the risk of insider threats by helping to monitor end users, flagging suspicious behavior, and detecting anomalous activity or unusual patterns that may indicate a potential threat [16]. However, organizations also need to consider the human aspects of data security by creating a cybersecurity culture along with proper training of employees to securely handle sensitive information in the workplace.

3.2.2 Traditional risk management challenges

The growing regularity and sophistication of cyberattacks have rendered traditional cybersecurity approaches inadequate. The increasing reliance on legacy systems and static defense mechanisms, characterized by signature-based detection and manual monitoring, has made it more and more challenging to keep pace with the evolving threat landscape. We discuss the potential challenges posed by conventional defense mechanisms given the expanding threat landscape and traditional risk management systems.

3.2.2.1 Limitations of legacy systems

Legacy cybersecurity systems like signature-based detection tools have formed the core of traditional risk management strategies for decades. These systems operate on the principles of matching the incoming data with known attack signatures or known genome techniques that are used. Signature-based detection relies on memorized patterns to detect threats, which works well for previously discovered threats but cannot detect a new implementation of the same attack [17]. Even the best algorithms can struggle when it comes to threats like ransomware or APTs, since those techniques are new and have never been seen before, let alone have a tensor model trained on them. Furthermore, legacy systems depend too much on manual monitoring and responses, which can slow down processes and create opportunities for human error. Cyber threats become more complex and widespread, so organizations need more agile, automated, and scalable solutions [18]. As networks and devices generate increasingly high volumes of data, legacy systems struggle to handle this data and detect real-time anomalies or potential threats in a sea of data.

3.2.2.2 The growing attack surface

Digital technologies and interconnected systems have expanded at an exponential rate, broadening the attack surface within organizations. The growth of cloud computing, IoT, and increasing dependence on mobile and remote workforces has widened the opportunities for cybercriminals to exploit. The joint influence of these diverse identity types has been the driving force behind the implementation of additional layers of security in systems as organizations continue to undergo digital transformation, exposing more of their infrastructure to potential threats, and making it increasingly difficult to maintain visibility and control over their entire environment [19]. Due to a limited understanding of security, costs, and hardware constraints, IoT devices tend to have a poor implementation of security. Likewise, cloud environments can be highly dynamic and may require third-party vendors, adding new complexities for organizations to manage when trying to protect their data. Due to certain vulnerabilities or the use of some weak authentication methods in these systems, attackers can take advantage of them and gain access to sensitive information [20]. Such remote access has become commonplace amid the COVID-19 pandemic, also elevating the level of risk as employees frequently connect to corporate networks via personal devices with less protective security setups. This expanding attack surface demonstrates that traditional risk management approaches, which utilize perimeter-based protections considering the dangers from external actors, are no longer applicable [21]. Organizations need to take a more integrated approach that leverages AI, machine learning, and continuous monitoring to protect and respond to threats in a much broader and more diffuse landscape.

3.3 AI in Cyber Risk Detection and Prevention

AI is widely used for cybersecurity and automates risk detection, prevention, and response in an organization. As cyber threats continue to evolve in complexity and sophistication, AI systems offer increasingly proactive, scalable, and efficient solutions to protect against potential intrusions. In this section, we will determine how to utilize AI for the detection and prevention of cyber risk, including the contributions from ML and DL for pattern recognition, real-time anomaly detection, predictive risk management, and autonomous incident response systems.

3.3.1 AI-driven threat detection

Machine learning approaches an AI-based threat detection system that analyzes large amounts of data much more quickly and accurately than humans [22]. These systems cannot only detect known threats but also discover new ones by analyzing complex patterns and behaviors in real time.

3.3.1.1 Machine learning and deep learning for pattern recognition

Modern AI threat detection platforms are built on ML and DL. These two techniques rely on trained models and historical datasets to make predictions on the detection of suspicious activities. AI- and ML-enabled cybersecurity applications, such as AI-based threat detection, predictive risk management, and autonomous response systems, are illustrated in Figure 3.3. These components add up to improved detection and prevention of cyber risks so that security can be proactive.

Machine learning: Traditional cybersecurity models relied upon static identification methods based on signatures or signatures created by rules. On the other hand, machine learning techniques allow the system to adapt and learn from new data, making it more effective at recognizing new types of attacks. All are used to analyze network traffic, system logs, and historical attack data, including supervised learning, unsupervised learning, and reinforcement learning. Supervised learning uses labeled data, which tells whether a specific event is benign or malicious, as the input to train the model [23]. After training, the model effectively recognizes known threats by detecting similar patterns in other, never-before-encountered data. In contrast, unsupervised learning allows AI to discover anomalies without the need for pre-labeled data. This AI simply establishes a baseline of normal behavior and flags anything that deviates from this baseline, thereby

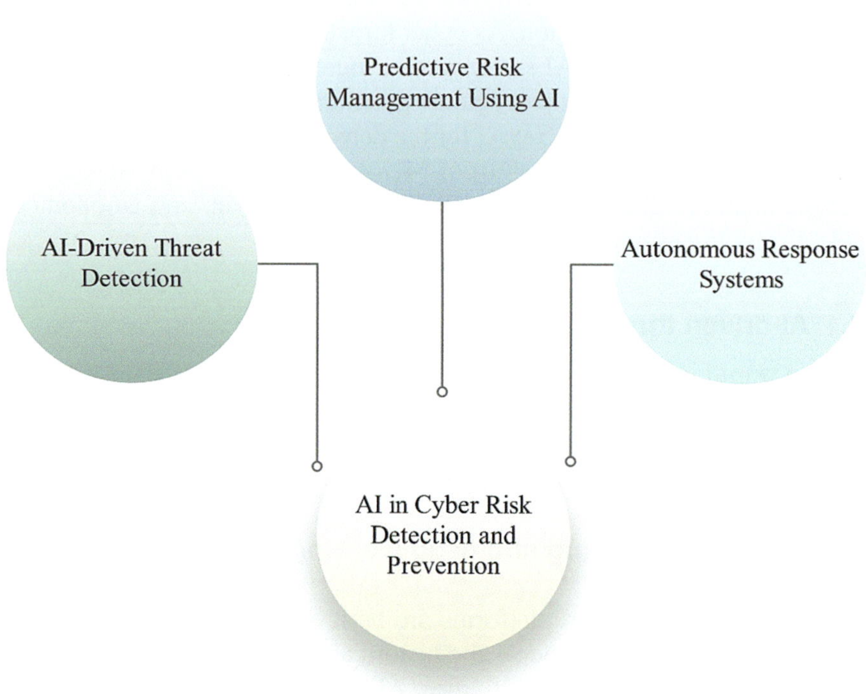

Figure 3.3 AI in cyber risk detection and prevention.

helping it to identify novel attack methods that have not been encountered before

Deep learning: Deep learning, which is a specific type of machine learning that machines use to replicate the way the human brain's neural network works, which utilized when you are dealing with unstructured data such as network traffic, system logs, and even multimedia data such as images or videos. This is where techniques such as convolutional neural networks (CNNs) and recurrent neural networks (RNNs) come into play, as they are used to parse and analyze these data sources, resulting in the system's ability to detect threats with improved accuracy and efficiency. Deep learning is also capable of recognizing complex, multi-dimensional things that traditional rule-based systems overlook, which is one of the main reasons it is useful for identifying sophisticated threats like APTs or zero-day vulnerabilities [24].

3.3.1.2 Real-time anomaly detection and behavioral analytics

The curiosity AI also opens doors for this kind of system to be used in anomaly detection, which is instrumental in the identification of new and dynamic threats. Unlike signature-based traditional systems that detect known attacks using signatures, anomaly detection employs artificial intelligence to find those deviations from normal system behavior and is thus able to find not only known but also unknown threats, in real time.

Anomaly detection: Machine learning models such as random forests and support vector machines learn incrementally from data to profile a "normal" baseline of behavior for a network, system, or user. If the limitation deviates from this baseline, the AI system marks it as anomalous and needs more investigation. The most basic example is if any accounts belonging to the employee start logging in from an unfamiliar location or start accessing sensitive information that the employee has not previously used [25]. Likewise, if it notices abnormal traffic patterns, either too much network traffic or attempts to access certain applications that should not be accessible, it will raise an alarm. This is crucial for detecting novel attack methods that do not conform to known threat signatures.

- **Behavioral analytics**: Behavioral analytics add a layer of analysis over anomaly detection and monitor user identity behavior and alerts on any deviations from historical behavior. This allows organizations to detect insider threats and advanced threats that may be slowly evolving over time [26]. For example, if an employee or an insider attacker starts to take actions that are not consistent with their normal behavior, like downloading skyrocketing amounts of data or trying to penetrate systems that are out of their job description, the system can give out alerts, potentially stopping data breaches before they happen.

3.3.2 Predictive risk management using AI

AI's capacity to process not only historic but also current data can be integrated into predictive risk management to anticipate potential cyber threats and vulnerabilities. AI analyzes data to identify trends and patterns, enabling organizations to take a proactive approach to emerging risks and prevent attacks before they happen.

3.3.2.1 Leveraging historical and real-time data for risk prediction

The predictive nature of AI makes it easier for cybersecurity teams to pinpoint potential risks from past behaviors and attack trends. AI models analyze huge amounts of historical threat data, enabling them to detect patterns that are indicative of a successful cyberattack [27]. These patterns can be certain patterns of network activity, specific types of malwares, or certain user behaviors that are seen before the attack occurs.

Risk prediction: Machine learning analyzes years of historical cybersecurity data and identifies the circumstances in which past attacks occurred. They then train predictive models on this data, which can predict the probability of certain types of attacks occurring. For instance, if an attacker typically obtains entrance to a system through a specific vulnerability at certain times of the year, an AI can determine when this vulnerability is most likely to occur. AI systems are useful in predicting the outcome of security threats by analyzing data streams in real time, with the ability to send actionable advice to security teams [28]. This enables organizations to remediate proactively rather than reactively.

Threat intelligence: AI also ingests external threat intelligence feeds that include up-to-the-minute information on known vulnerabilities, attack signatures, and emerging trends in cybercrime. Utilizing information by cross-referencing it with our internal data, AI systems ensure that any significant threat can potentially target the organization, and when [29]. For example, if a new strain of malware is detected in the wild then AI can look at historical trends and take the most likely candidate targets of that malware and analyze them to see which organization is most at risk to help IT teams proactively prevent the threat by taking steps like patching their vulnerability stack or blocking routes patterns which gives the malware a vector for propagation vs ensuring their networks and systems are closed against this new vector.

3.3.3 Autonomous response systems

In addition to detection and prediction, AI has a major role to play in incident response and mitigation. AI-enabled systems for autonomous response identify, examine, and react to cyber events, sometimes even without human input. This automation is important for organizations that need to act swiftly to contain the damage of a cyberattack.

3.3.3.1 AI's role in incident response and mitigation

In the classical security model, incident response is usually a manual and resource-heavy process, as human analysts analyze threats, contain breaches, and minimize damage. After we detect a threat, the AI autonomous response system reduces the time to address it significantly by automating many such tasks.

- **Automated threat containment**: The moment a potential threat is detected, AI systems immediately activate to contain the threat and prevent it from spreading. In this case, if malware is found on one endpoint, the system automatically quarantines the affected device from the network to stop the malware from spreading to other systems. When it comes to Distributed Denial of Service (DDoS) attacks, for instance, AI systems are used to recognize abnormal traffic patterns and reroute or filter out malicious traffic, ensuring critical services remain accessible. This decreases the response time and lessens the effect of the attack [30].
- **Real-time decision making**: AI-based systems offer the advantage of making decisions in real time, powered by a large amount of contextual data like threat intel, historical patterns of attacks, and active network activity. In an APT context, for example, AI systems detect a possible breach and take appropriate action, such as blocking unauthorized access, alerting the security team, or even shutting down the compromised systems to limit the attack [31]. They act autonomously and proactively the moment a threat is detected, which decreases the opportunity window for the attacker and helps to limit damage from a breach.
- **Continuous learning and adaptation**: The most notable way that AI helps incident response is through its capacity for continual learning against new threats. The system ends up improving its response strategies as it is exposed to novel attack vectors or types of methods [32]. This means that if, for instance, an AI system comes across a new variant of ransomware, it can analyze the behavior of the attack and learn from the incident, updating its detection and mitigation protocols for future incidents. This iterative learning process improves AI response systems over time and also equips them better to tackle the ever-evolving landscape of cyber threats.

3.4 AI and Automation in Cyber Risk Management

Detection and response have become significantly difficult, as cyber threats have drawn inordinate attention, and organizations no longer rely solely on traditional, manual methods to secure their data. Because cyber risk management now requires a more dynamic and responsive approach, AI and automation are emerging as very important parts of modern security strategy [33]. From risk assessment and continuing monitoring to scaling efforts to the

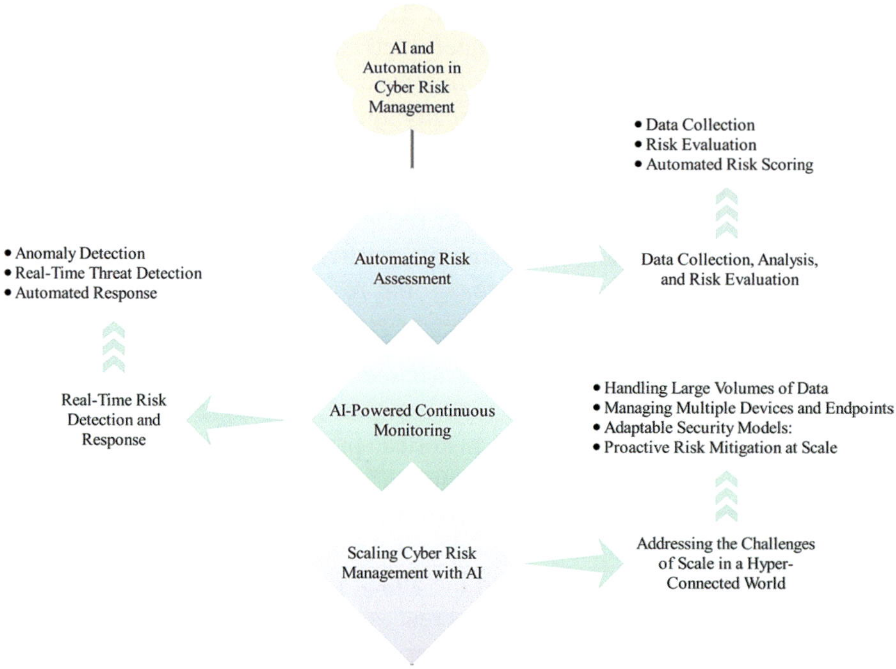

Figure 3.4 AI-driven cyber risk management framework.

demands of an increasingly interdependent world, AI allows organizations to automate all aspects of cyber risk management [34]. This section covers how AI is helping to automate risk assessment, improve continuous monitoring, and overcome the difficulties related to scaling cyber risk management to the hyper-connected world we live in today.

An AI-based cyber risk management framework is shown in Figure 3.4, which illustrates the key processes, including automated risk assessment, continuous monitoring, and scalable risk avoidance. It leans towards real-time detection of threats, evaluation of the risk of any data, and honeypots for security while on the run from cyber threats.

3.4.1 Automating risk assessment

Risk assessment was traditionally a manual process where cybersecurity professionals analyze vulnerabilities, evaluate threats, and prioritize risks based on the type of factors, but it can be time-consuming, error-prone, and reactive [35]. ML is revolutionizing the process of risk evaluation with the use of detailed data collection in real-time, which is used to carry out comprehensive analysis, automated assessments of cyber risks, and so on.

3.4.1.2 Data collection, analysis, and risk evaluation

AI systems are capable of gathering and processing vast amounts of information from multiple sources, such as hard network traffic, system logs, threat intelligence feeds, and even external databases. AI ensures risk assessments are based on the most updated and detailed information available by automating the data gathering process.

Data collection: AI systems pull the data automatically from various sources, i.e., internal security logs, user activity reports, network traffic patterns, and external threat [36] feeds, to perform risk assessments autonomously. Being able to gather large volumes of data from various sources enables the private entity to achieve a better understanding of its security state, which constitutes a basis for adequate risk assessment.

Risk evaluation: After collecting data, AI analyzes the data efficiently to discover vulnerabilities and threats that may result in a security breach. For instance, AI models learn through machine learning algorithms to recognize patterns of malicious activity, enabling the system to flag risk based on behavioral or known attack signatures. For instance, AI analyzes system vulnerabilities, matching known weaknesses (e.g., out-of-date software or unpatched security vulnerabilities) against upcoming threats such as newly discovered types of malware or phishing methods [37]. This assessment allows companies to allocate resources effectively and focus on the most significant risks.

Automated risk scoring: Risk scores can also be generated with AI based on how likely it is that a given risk could occur, as well as how much damage it would do to the organization. In turn, these scores suggest risk exposure dynamically in real time to new data that surfaces, thus providing an enterprise exposure score of the organization [38]. Automated risk assessment leading to decision-making allows the organization to make better-informed decisions about risk treatment strategies so that the most significant risks are addressed promptly.

3.4.2 AI-powered continuous monitoring

Cyber threats are ever-evolving, with attackers leveraging new and ingenious ways to circumvent established security. This means that organizations must monitor their systems in real time for any indications of a breach or suspicious activity as soon as it happens [39]. AI-driven continuous monitoring systems provide automated, round-the-clock vigilance, enabling organizations to stay ahead of new and evolving threats.

3.4.2.1 Real-time risk detection and response

The ability of AI to analyze massive datasets in real time means ongoing monitoring systems can spot anomalies and risks when they happen. This real-time response is vital in reducing the harm done during cyber assaults. AI can watch everything from user behavior to system processes, network traffic, and application activity to identify anything out of the baseline of normal behavior.

Anomaly detection: AI systems identify slight deviations from routine system operation that may signal a looming attack. If a user suddenly starts accessing files they do not usually use, or if there is an abnormal spike of outbound data traffic, AI systems flag this behavior for follow-up [40]. AI also learns what baseline and normal activity looks like by employing machine learning models and detects any abnormalities as anomalies even before they impact performance or are even visible to the naked eye.

Real-time threat detection: AI systems monitor data feeds in real time to identify known threats and newly emerging modes of attack. Deep learning models leverage patterns to identify malicious domains, malware, or phishing attempts from email contents, web-tracking, or other data sources [41]. These systems enable real-time threat alert of security teams, helping to respond on the spot to prevent or minimize any potential damage.

Automated response: AI systems are also vital in responding in real time to identified threats. However, once the threat is discovered, AI is capable of automatically activating those process recovery procedures, for example, isolating the infected system, blocking suspicious network traffic, or raising the alert to security teams on the problem [42]. Automating these responses allows organizations to rapidly contain incidents and decrease the time to remediation, thus reducing the impact of an attack considerably.

3.4.3 Scaling cyber risk management with AI

Cyber risk management has necessarily matured into a more powerful practice as organizations have adopted digital transformation and more heavily relied on interconnected systems, and the scale of preventing and mitigating risk in cyberspace has grown exponentially. Traditional security models are typically not geared to manage the large volume of data, devices, and endpoints requiring monitoring and protection [43] but AI provides a solution that can scale, making it possible for organizations to expand their cybersecurity posture to suit the needs of a hyper-connected world.

3.4.3.1 Addressing the challenges of scale in a hyper-connected world

The transition to cloud computing, the proliferation of IoT devices, and the increasing dependence on mobile workforces have significantly broadened the attack surface for businesses. With the proliferation of devices and systems built for on-demand services, cybersecurity teams can no longer manage the widening task of addressing endpoints, networks, and applications ad hoc. This complexity makes scaling traditional security systems slow and expensive [44]. AI, on the other hand, can do this in a much more effective and scalable manner.

Handling large volumes of data: Notably, the vastness of data that modern networks and devices generate constitutes one of the biggest barriers to implementing scalable cybersecurity solutions. AI-based systems shine in processing and analyzing this information at scale, allowing organizations to monitor massive amounts of activity without getting flooded [45]. Machine learning models can process vast amounts of data coming from tens of thousands or even millions of devices and are therefore indispensable in large organizations with huge digital infrastructures.

Managing multiple devices and endpoints: Additionally, the rapid growth in IoT devices has greatly increased the total count of endpoints that must be monitored and secured. So, they take all the pictures of a lot of devices together and continuously monitor them. INEQE security is training AI systems on this data that can see the logs from numerous sources, such as mobile devices, industrial control systems, and personal computers, giving holistic protection across the whole of an organization's network [46]. The AI also ensures faster patch management and configures the devices, automating updates and security fixes across billions of devices.

Adaptable security models: New-age AI-driven cybersecurity solutions are susceptible to new technologies and network architecture changes while allowing organizations to scale security operations based on the phase of their digital transformation. For instance, as a business continues to adopt cloud computing or incorporate new IoT devices, AI security systems automatically adapt to accommodate these changes, evolving with the business to combat new challenges [47]. This flexibility allows organizations to have a robust security posture as their digital footprint expands.

- **Proactive risk mitigation at scale**: AI empowers organizations to take a proactive approach towards risk management. Through continuous monitoring and data analysis across numerous channels and segments, AI systems can detect trends and new risks before they are exploited [48]. By identifying and mitigating these risks before attackers exploit them, organizations prevent cyberattacks from being successful.

Organizations need to be secure as the world connects more, and cybersecurity efforts need to expand to meet the need for improvement. AI provides the automation, efficiency, and scalability required to cater to these demands, enabling an organization to protect its digital assets, data, and systems without being weighed down by the complexities of an increasingly hyper-connected world.

3.5 Ethical and privacy considerations

The integration of AI into cyber risk management offers tremendous advantages such as enhanced efficiency, predictive capabilities, and real-time threat detection, but it also poses substantial ethical and privacy challenges. Organizations are leaning more towards AI-based systems for monitoring, analyzing, and mitigating cyber threats, It is important to address the implications for data privacy, compliance, and ethical AI use. In this section, we delve into the challenges and considerations of data privacy and protection, as well as the ethical aspects surrounding the deployment of AI systems in cybersecurity.

3.5.1 Data privacy and protection

AI is commonly employed to help with cyber risk management, which involves the collection, analysis, and processing of potentially significant quantities of data, much of which includes sensitive personal and organizational information. Because AI systems that provide the human-in-the-loop monitoring of networks, devices, and user behaviors all tap into massive datasets, it is conceivable that this data may contain private, confidential, or personally identifiable information (PII). It also raises data privacy concerns, considering AI accounts for sensitive information that could be exposed or misused if disclosed inadvertently [49]. Figure 3.5 highlights the key ethical and privacy considerations in AI, including compliance, data privacy,

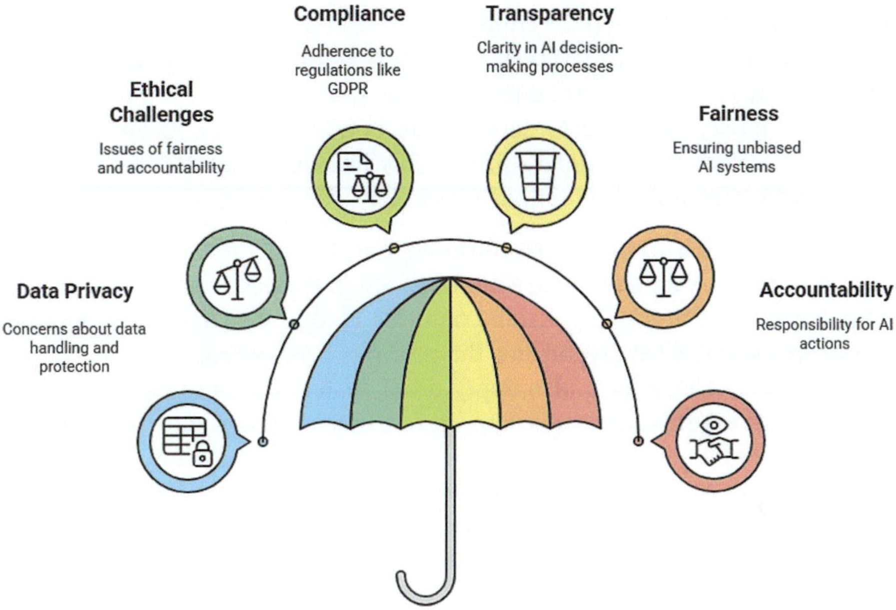

Figure 3.5 Ethical and privacy considerations in AI governance.

transparency, fairness, and accountability. It emphasizes the need for responsible AI governance to ensure fairness, security, and regulatory adherence.

3.5.1.1 Handling sensitive data and compliance (e.g., GDPR)

Today, organizations need to ensure their AI systems meet strict data privacy and protection standards to maintain trust, live up to regulations, and protect against risks from data breaches or unauthorized access. For AI systems to function respectfully and ethically, they need to be developed and implemented with privacy in mind.

Data minimization and purpose limitation: AI systems avoid gathering and processing more data than is vital to accomplish the desired objectives, to reduce privacy risks. This is especially true of sensitive information such as health data, financial records, or personal identifiers [50]. Such guidelines are intended to prevent the use of data for other purposes, be it profiling or surveillance, unless users have specifically consented to it, known as the principle of purpose limitation.

Consent and transparency: Informed consent is one of the foundational pillars of data privacy governing regulations such as the General Data Protection Regulation (GDPR) in the European Union, ensuring that individuals are fully aware of how their data will be collected, processed, and how it will be used is a requisite of AI systems. Users have the opportunity to consent to their data being processed, and to revoke that consent at any point [51]. Furthermore, organizations are also able to demonstrate how AI systems make decisions that could impact an individual's privacy, for instance, flagging user behavior or triggering alerts when a user engages in unusual activity.

Compliance with privacy regulations: Laws applicable to data protection and privacy vary across jurisdictions; while Europe follows GDPR, the USA has CCPA, and many Asian countries abide by PDPA. They require certain responsibilities regarding the storing, processing, and sharing of personal data. These laws also apply to AI systems used in cybersecurity, ensuring that organizations take appropriate measures to secure individuals' data and rights. For instance, practices like data anonymization, encryption, and establishing transparent retention policies are obligatory for organizations under GDPR [52]. Furthermore, AI systems need to allow individuals to access their data as well as the ability to request changes or deletions of their information.

Data security and encryption: Data security is another component that AI systems must implement; sensitive information needs to be protected from unauthorized access, manipulation, or theft. This is creating a reality where an organization using a database or cloud environment must implement various measures to prevent such attacks, one must use encryption, whether that be both in transit and at rest [53]. Moreover, AI models that handle sensitive data should be equipped with privacy-preserving mechanisms like differential privacy, which enables guaranteed Sybil resistance where individual data points cannot be reconstructed from the model's output.

3.5.2 Ethical challenges

The systems of AI are becoming more involved in the management of cyber risk, and ethical issues surrounding their usage are increasingly coming to the fore. There is growing concern about the transparency, fairness, accountability, and bias of AI in cybersecurity, which needs to be addressed so that individuals, organizations, and society are not harmed by the AI systems used in cybersecurity.

3.5.2.1 Transparency, fairness, and accountability in AI systems

ML-based AI systems are often referred to as "black boxes" because of the difficulty in interpreting their internal workings and understanding how decisions are made. This lack of transparency does bring significant challenges, as the use of AI systems in cybersecurity must remain responsible.

Transparency: Transparency becomes all the more important as we take AI systems towards the path of impact and innovation. In cybersecurity, for example, AI-driven systems are left alone to make decisions that will affect users, whether it is flagging an employee as a potential insider threat or blocking network traffic based on anomalous behavior. When these decisions are made in this opaque way, it becomes difficult to hold that system accountable when things go wrong or biases arise [54]. Hence, interpretability and explainability are paramount for AI models. To help address these biases, new techniques such as Explainable AI (XAI) explain this root cause, allowing users to better understand how complex machine learning models work, uncover decision systems within vulnerabilities or biases, and help cybersecurity professionals test or even improve their machine learning models.

Fairness: One of the major ethical concerns with AI is the potential for bias. AI systems learn from historical data and if that data has underlying biases, whether gender-related, bias toward a race, or socioeconomic status, these can percolate into the AI system's predictions and actions. Another example is a cybersecurity system trained on biased data, which results in discriminatory practices by disproportionately flagging certain demographic groups as suspicious [55]. To the present, organizations must know that AI systems trained on diverse, representative datasets are the same, and their decision-making processes must be regularly audited, identifying and correcting any biases.

Accountability: Accountability in AI systems is necessary for their trustworthiness and for ensuring responsible use at all levels. When an AI system makes a decision that deeply impacts people's lives, like blocking legitimate traffic, incorrectly identifying an employee as a threat, or letting a data breach happen, it is critical to know who is responsible for that decision. They also need to know who is responsible for training the AI model, specifying how the system makes decisions, and if the system is never allowed to monitor when it makes errors [56]. Furthermore, cybersecurity experts need to intervene whenever there is incorrect decision-making by AI systems, ensuring human intervention is guaranteed whenever vital decision-making is taking place.

Ethical use of surveillance: Many AI systems implemented in cybersecurity require the surveillance of user behavior and network activity. Although this is essential for recognizing possible hazards, it raises apprehensions regarding personal privacy and independence. However, where employees or users feel constantly monitored, it could be seen as invasive or an infringement of their rights. Organizations must be transparent about what they monitor and ensure that AI systems are only used for legitimate cybersecurity reasons [57]. These organizations also put in place well-defined policies outlining their plans on how to handle, store, and utilize the data they expect to collect, so that the implementation may not violate employee or user rights.

3.6 Challenges in Implementing AI for Cyber Risk Management

There is great potential in leveraging AI-driven systems for cyber risk management, but also some serious challenges associated with implementation. The first involves the AI technology itself, its inherent complexity, appropriate data sets for such tools to work efficiently, operational bottlenecks, and the financial provisions required for organizations to embed AI tools in their security frameworks. This section outlines the main challenges that organizations face when implementing AI for cyber risk management data quality and availability, handling false positives and false negatives, and resource constraints and cost hurdles.

3.6.1 Data quality and availability

High-quality data availability and diversity are some of the most critical challenges to implement. AI for cyber risk management requires the availability of high-quality, clean, and diverse data. Data is one of the fundamental building blocks of AI models, without which it is impossible to identify patterns, make decisions, or automate predictions, but the accuracy of such models depends on the reliability and relevance of the data used for training and testing purposes.

3.6.1.1 The need for clean, diverse, and representative data

AI systems for cybersecurity are trained on data from a variety of sources, which include network traffic, system logs, and historical attack data. The accuracy of an AI system's prediction is adversely affected if the data on which the models were trained is missing, inconsistent, or biased [58]. However, the challenge for any AI-driven cyber risk management solution is to have clean data that reflects real-life events and is not skewed or lacks critical events needed for prediction.

Data quality: High-quality data is crucial for building AI models, as they process vast amounts of data to detect complex patterns and anomalies. Data with poor quality, like missing values, incorrect labels, or noise, can result in incorrect model predictions and lower the effectiveness of the whole system [59]. For example, if data used to train a threat detection model includes erroneous logs or is outdated, the AI may overlook current threats or label legitimate behavior as suspicious.

Data diversity: As threats become more sophisticated, organizations ensure that AI models are trained on diverse datasets that encompass a range of possible attack scenarios. Models that are too biased towards certain types of threats end up missing new or innovative attack forms, due to data that is insufficiently diverse [60]. A model trained predominantly on financial institution data, for instance, might have a hard time during detection relevant to the healthcare sector due to differences in data and risk landscape.

Data representation: The efficacy of using AI in cybersecurity also relies on the availability of data that accurately reflects the population of users, devices, and environments that an organization will encounter. If the information used to teach the systems is not representative of different user behaviors, device forms, and system configurations, these AI models might act with biases, resulting in unfair or inaccurate assessments [61]. If a model, for instance, was built mostly based on data from big enterprise networks, it may not be well prepared to tackle the distinctive challenges that smaller or remote working environments present. We highlight some of the challenges faced in adopting AI into cyber risk management practice in Table 3.1. For instance, challenges of data quality, false positives/negatives, and resource constraints matter. It details the restrictions associated with each challenge, including unreliable predictions or disruption of operations, and proposes potential remedies, such as enhancing data quality, honing the AI models, and deploying scalable and cost-effective AI systems.

3.6.2 Addressing false positives and false negatives

Integrating AI into cybersecurity threat detection systems trade-off between sensitivity and specificity. Threat detection in AI-based cybersecurity systems, balancing these considerations, is nontrivial and one of the major challenges of using AI systems for cyber risk management.

3.6.2.1 Balancing sensitivity and specificity

False positives: A false positive is when a legitimate event or activity is incorrectly identified as a threat. In cybersecurity, false positives can cause unnecessary notifications and actions like blocking access to essential systems or

Table 3.1 Challenges in implementing AI for cyber risk management.

S.No	Challenges	Description	Limitations	Solutions
1	**Data quality and availability**	Ensuring the availability of high-quality, clean, and diverse data for training AI models.	Poor data quality, such as missing values or incorrect labels, leads to inaccurate predictions, reducing AI model effectiveness.	Ensure data is clean, diverse, and representative of real-world scenarios. Apply advanced techniques for data cleaning and preprocessing.
2	**Data diversity**	Cybersecurity threats are constantly evolving. AI models need diverse datasets to represent various attack vectors.	Lack of diversity in data may lead to models missing emerging threats or being over-tuned to specific risks, reducing effectiveness in diverse environments.	Ensure AI models are trained on diverse datasets that represent a wide range of attack scenarios.
3	**Data representation**	AI models must represent the range of users, devices, and environments accurately.	Misrepresentation of data could cause biases and inaccuracies in AI predictions.	Balance the data representation to ensure it accurately reflects user behaviors, device types, and network configurations.
4	**False positives and false negatives**	The balance between detecting real threats (sensitivity) and avoiding unnecessary alerts (specificity) is critical.	False positives create unnecessary disruptions, while false negatives allow cybercriminals to operate undetected.	Fine-tune the AI models to reduce both false positives and false negatives. Integrate continuous learning and model refinement.
5	**Resource constraints and cost barriers**	Deployment of AI systems requires significant resources and financial investment, especially for SMEs.	AI implementation is resource-intensive, and smaller organizations may not have the budget, infrastructure, or skilled personnel required.	Consider cloud-based or third-party AI solutions to reduce resource demands, particularly for SMEs.
6	**Financial costs**	Developing, training, and implementing AI systems can be costly, especially for SMEs.	High initial costs for AI implementation and continuous expenses for model maintenance, data updates, and compliance.	Prioritize investment in scalable AI systems or opt for cloud-based AI solutions to reduce initial costs.
7	**Expertise and talent**	AI cybersecurity systems require specialized skills, which may be difficult to find in smaller organizations.	Small organizations may not be able to compete for AI talent with larger firms, leading to challenges in developing and maintaining effective systems.	Upskill existing employees, collaborate with AI specialists or outsource AI system management to third-party providers.

disrupting business processes. Too many false positives can drown security teams in unwanted alerts, creating alert fatigue and causing important things to be missed. False positives can therefore create a large cost, not only financial but also in operational terms, especially when it is needed to deal with them regularly [62]. Blocking legitimate traffic because of a false positive on a DDoS attack detection system may lead to revenue loss and business degradation.

False negatives: A false negative represents a scenario in which a real threat is completely skipped over, so an actual breach/attack will not be detected. False negatives are especially disruptive since cybercriminals can act without being detected, leading to significant data loss, financial loss, or even a system takeover [63]. For instance, if an AI application encounters a new form of malware that it has not seen before and was not accounted for in the data used to build the model, your organization may experience a devastating attack.

The trick for organizations is to adjust their AI models so that both false positives and false negatives are fine-tuned. Canada allows local and provincial reporting only, so this is a very sensitive issue without the ability to report on any national level. Finally, human oversight is critical to verifying that AI-generated alerts are accurate and contextualizing the decisions made outside of these parameters. Frequent assessment of AI performance, including changes to thresholds of suspicious activity, is key to minimize these mistakes.

3.6.3 Overcoming resource constraints and cost barriers

AI offers evident advantages in managing cyber risk, but the implementation of AI-driven cybersecurity solutions is resource and cost-intensive and thus remains a challenge for small and medium-sized enterprises (SMEs). The deployment of AI systems requires a sizable investment of people, infrastructure, and maintenance assets that not all organizations have at their disposal.

3.6.3.1 AI deployment challenges for small- and medium-sized enterprises

Financial costs: Building, training, and deploying AI systems can be expensive. Despite their potential, the cost of obtaining high-quality data, developing AI models, and deploying the infrastructure of hardware and software is prohibitively expensive for smaller organizations. The costs associated with the maintenance of AI models and the continuous updating of data to ensure compliance with the growing privacy regulations can also put a dent in resources aside from the initial setup costs [64]. For many small and medium enterprises (SMEs), these costs are a major hurdle to embracing AI for cybersecurity.

Expertise and talent: The development, deployment, and maintenance of AI-driven cybersecurity systems require specialized expertise. Organizations need to recruit or train data scientists, machine learning engineers, and cybersecurity experts who possess a dual understanding of both the technology and the needs of cyber risk management. Yet, it is difficult to find and keep high-quality AI specialists, especially for smaller companies that cannot compete with larger corporations or technology companies that pay higher wages [65]. Smaller organizations, such as enterprises and non-profits, may find it difficult to implement and maintain AI-based systems without the necessary expertise.

- **Scalability and infrastructure**: The underlying architecture of AI systems lends itself to the use of large computing systems that can process huge data sets in real time. This will often require investment in high-performance computing systems, cloud services, and advanced security monitoring tools. For SMEs, the financial and logistical challenges associated with obtaining and deploying this infrastructure can be formidable [66]. Moreover, ensuring AI systems work in tandem with current cybersecurity measures is also a complicated task that necessitates thorough technical reconfiguration. This is often a challenge for smaller organizations that struggle to maintain pace with the ever-evolving nature of threats and the capability needed to provide effective AI-enabled solutions.
- **Third-party solutions**: To address such resource limitations, a majority of the SMEs rely on AI-powered third-party cybersecurity solutions and have been sourcing them as an alternative for flexibility and cost-effectiveness. Managed security service providers (MSSPs) and AI-powered cybersecurity platforms can provide smaller organizations with access to AI-driven risk management tools without requiring a heavy up-front investment. The aforementioned services provide organizations the ability to outsource AI complexity, which allows them to devote resources to their core operations and simultaneously leverage advanced cybersecurity capabilities [67]. But picking a trustworthy provider and making sure the third-party solution fulfills the requirements of the enterprise can be a difficult task.

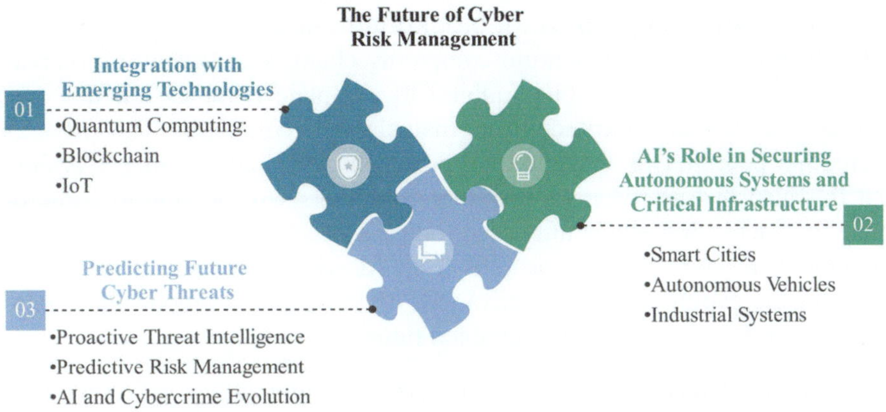

Figure 3.6 Future trends in cyber risk management.

3.7 The Future of Cyber Risk Management

The world of cyber risk management is ever-changing, with new industries emerging with the evolution of technology and the growth of cyber threat sophistication. The challenges of modern cyber risk require innovative, progressive solutions. The evolution of cybersecurity is greatly driven by the impact of artificial intelligence (AI), which presents a dynamic and scalable approach to detect and mitigate any cyber threat. So, moving ahead, find out how emerging technologies, quantum computing, blockchain, and the Internet of Things (IoT) will change cyber risk management, what role AI will play in securing autonomous systems and critical infrastructure, and how AI itself will take on new shapes as it prepares for cyber threats yet to come. Figure 3.6 presents key aspects of cyber risk management, focusing on the integration of emerging technologies, AI's role in securing autonomous systems, and predictive threat intelligence. It highlights advancements such as quantum computing, blockchain, and AI-driven risk mitigation.

3.7.1 Integration with emerging technologies

With rapid advancements in technology, emerging technologies such as cloud computing, blockchain, and IoT are now woven into the digital ecosystems that are fundamentally propelling world economies. These technologies come with cybersecurity challenges that are distinctive but also provide an opportunity to adapt cybersecurity risk management strategies.

3.7.1.1 Quantum computing, blockchain, and IoT

Quantum computing: Quantum computing changes the game of computing by utilizing quantum bits (qubits) to complete complex calculations, which are orders of magnitude faster than classical computers. This presents incredible potential in areas like cryptography, AI, and machine learning, but this also has its risks. As quantum computers will be able to compromise the encryption algorithms used today, it becomes essential to develop quantum-safe encryption algorithms [68]. AI will prove crucial to solving risks for the evolution of these advanced cryptography methods and secure data transmission in a quantum-enabled future.

Blockchain: Blockchain, a decentralized and immutable technology, is increasingly being used in cybersecurity to provide enhanced transparency, secure data integrity, and strengthen trust in digital transactions. Blockchain can be used to create secure, distributed networks for storing and sharing critical data, making it more resistant to tampering and attacks; blockchain can be used to create secure distributed communications networks, open-source protocols, and marketplaces that enable seamless data sharing; and blockchain can be used to certify data provenance, authentication, and verification over time [69]. This decentralization, along with the analytical prowess of AI to recognize anomalies or to prevent fraud (and thus to secure the integrity of transactions), has been an investment worth making.

IoT (Internet of Things): The IoT has facilitated the growth of connected devices across sectors, from smart homes and healthcare devices to industrial machinery and transport networks. Although IoT carries huge benefits, it also expands the attack surface, opening untold new avenues for cybercriminals. AI technology is not just limited to malware or malware-like lockdown methods in IoT security; it also combines various solutions like log analysis, event correlation, etc. AI analyzes the connected IoT devices for anomalous activity work or determines areas of vulnerability and takes automated action, such as isolating affected devices from operating on a network to reduce the spread of malware [70]. As the number of IoT devices is increasing exponentially, AI will be critical to understanding how to scale to manage these systems and ensure they are protected from new threats.

3.7.2 AI's role in securing autonomous systems and critical infrastructure

Two of the most vulnerable, high-stakes areas of cyber risk management are autonomous systems and critical infrastructure. With the convergence of autonomous vehicles, smart cities, and industrial systems into everyday life, securing the devices is paramount. AI would also be critical for safeguarding such systems against a variety of cybersecurity threats.

3.7.2.1 AI for smart cities, autonomous vehicles, and industrial systems

Smart cities: Smart cities utilize a network of technologies to improve aspects of urban life, such as transportation, energy, infrastructure, and healthcare systems. But as cities become "smarter" and more connected, they are also becoming prime targets for cyberattacks. AI can also be used to detect and prevent traffic management systems, energy grids, and public services. AI can play a vital role in preventing or mitigating the damage caused by cyberattacks that can severely compromise the operation of a smart city [71] through real-time anomaly detection, predictive risk analysis, and automated response systems. For instance, AI can also analyze the power grid for suspicious activity that may suggest a cyberattack, like a DDoS attack on a substation or the compromise of a control system.

Autonomous vehicles: Autonomous vehicles such as self-driving cars and drones use a combination of sensors, communications systems, and machine learning algorithms to navigate and make decisions in real time. These systems pose an enormous security risk because a malfunction in one element (e.g., GPS, sensors, vehicle-to-vehicle communication) can have catastrophic consequences. Real-time monitoring and intrusion detection, identification of potential vulnerabilities, and autonomous combat of security threats are how AI can secure these vehicles [72]. AI systems spot abnormalities in the vehicle's communication channel or unauthorized access attempts to the vehicle's software, as this serves as a failsafe that ensures any breach is delightful before a compromise occurs.

Industrial systems: Industrial control systems (ICS) and operational technology (OT) used in manufacturing, energy, utilities, and sectors are becoming easier targets for cyberattacks as they connect more to the internet and enterprise systems. AI-enabled data analytics can enhance the security of these systems by evaluating and exposing anomalous behavior from a massive volume of data issued, which is generated by different control devices and sensors to predict failures of equipment and capture the accessibility of potential attacks [73]. Moreover, automation in AI equips worthwhile capabilities to maintain the resilience essential for such systems against cyberattacks, allowing for instant responses.

3.7.3 Predicting future cyber threats

The future of cyber threat intelligence will focus on the ability to anticipate and mitigate emerging risks, enabling organizations to maintain secure digital ecosystems. AI will play a critical role in predicting attack vectors, as well as addressing potential risks before they happen.

3.7.3.1 How AI will evolve to anticipate and mitigate emerging risks

Proactive threat intelligence: Conventional cybersecurity is mostly reactive to known threats. Unlike humans, AI systems also proactively identify emerging risks, as they can continuously analyze historical and real-time data to detect patterns and correlations that could signal a new method of attack. By using machine learning algorithms, the AI will constantly adapt and increase its capacity in predicting future cyber threats, considering evolving behaviors, new vectors, and evolving threat landscape [74]. For instance, artificial intelligence can recognize trends in phishing attacks, detect new social engineering techniques, and anticipate future patterns, giving companies time to amend their defenses before the next attack.

Predictive risk management: AI will help organizations move from reactive risk management to predictive risk management because organizations will be able to anticipate threats before they become fully realized. By parsing through vast amounts of cybersecurity data and integrating it with threat intelligence feeds, AI can reveal vulnerabilities, anticipate exploitations, and suggest mitigation measures. The combination of the two mentioned above and their scopes helps organizations to secure their networks, systems, and data against future threats, minimizing or eliminating as many damaging incidents as possible and increasing adaptation and resistance [75]. AI systems, for instance, anticipate which vulnerabilities are more likely to be exploited based on historical attack information, allowing businesses to prioritize patching activities or deploy targeted defenses.

- **AI and cybercrime evolution**: As cybercriminals embrace ever more sophisticated techniques, AI will be central to understanding and fighting these dynamic threats. As such, machine learning models will work for detecting patterns in cybercrime activities, particularly the AI-based and automated attacks and the levels of operations attempted by attackers. Organizational AI will continue to learn from new data; these technologies will adapt their detection and response capabilities with the evolution of risk indicators [76]. AI even helps teams anticipate what cybercriminals will use next, allowing security to plan to patch what AI has predicted will be their targets.

3.8 Conclusion

Artificial intelligence (AI) has significantly turned the landscape of cyber risk management with faster and much more precise detection, prevention, and response. AI is powerful because it can process huge amounts of data, uncover activities and patterns, and project what will occur next, enabling organizations to respond successfully to the risk at hand and ensure the security of the digital space. Despite all the above-mentioned challenges, AI has already been widely employed, albeit with certain limitations, which include the lack of high-quality and diversified data, addressing the ethical issues regarding privacy, bias, and accountability, and there is still a shortage of resources for small and medium enterprises. Furthermore, as AI emerges as a new technology assisted by quantum computing, blockchain, and IoT, new challenges arise while trying to safeguard critical infrastructure and integrated systems. To make the most of how the art business can be transformed by AI, companies prioritize changing the way they approach data, ensuring that there is transparency in the way they implement AI in making their decisions, ensuring ethical standards, and investing in the talent and technologies required. Addressing these challenges and embracing the future promise of AI, organizations can create more proactive, scalable, and, importantly, secure approaches to addressing cyber risk in a world where the challenges are becoming more complex and interrelated.

References

[1] Bharadiya, J. P. (2023). AI-driven security: how machine learning will shape the future of cybersecurity and web 3.0. American Journal of Neural Networks and Applications, 9(1), 1–7.

[2] Sarker, I. H. (2024). AI-driven cybersecurity and threat intelligence: cyber automation, intelligent decision-making and explainability. Springer Nature.

[3] Yaseen, A. (2023). AI-driven threat detection and response: A paradigm shift in cybersecurity. International Journal of Information and Cybersecurity, 7(12), 25-43.

[4] Prince, N. U., Faheem, M. A., Khan, O. U., Hossain, K., Alkhayyat, A., Hamdache, A., & Elmouki, I. (2024). AI-powered data-driven cybersecurity techniques: Boosting threat identification and reaction. Nanotechnology Perceptions, 20, 332–353.

[5] Ijiga, O. M., Idoko, I. P., Ebiega, G. I., Olajide, F. I., Olatunde, T. I., & Ukaegbu, C. (2024). Harnessing adversarial machine learning for advanced threat detection: AI-driven strategies in cybersecurity risk assessment and fraud prevention. J. Sci. Technol, 11, 001–024.
[6] Chinta, P. C. R., Jha, K. M., Velaga, V., Moore, C., Routhu, K., & Sadaram, G. (2024). Harnessing Big Data and AI-Driven ERP Systems to Enhance Cybersecurity Resilience in Real-Time Threat Environments. Available at SSRN 5151788.
[7] Pulyala, S. R. (2024). From detection to prediction: AI-powered SIEM for proactive threat hunting and risk mitigation. Turkish Journal of Computer and Mathematics Education, 15(1), 34–43.
[8] Shahana, A., Hasan, R., Farabi, S. F., Akter, J., Mahmud, M. A. A., Johora, F. T., & Suzer, G. (2024). AI-driven cybersecurity: Balancing advancements and safeguards. Journal of Computer Science and Technology Studies, 6(2), 76–85.
[9] Camacho, N. G. (2024). The role of AI in cybersecurity: Addressing threats in the digital age. Journal of Artificial Intelligence General science (JAIGS) ISSN: 3006-4023, 3(1), 143–154.
[10] Rehan, H. (2024). AI-driven cloud security: The future of safeguarding sensitive data in the digital age. Journal of Artificial Intelligence General science (JAIGS) ISSN: 3006-4023, 1(1), 132–151.
[11] Lakhani, A. (2023). AI revolutionizing cyber security unlocking the future of digital protection. doi: https://osf. io/cvqx3.
[12] Habbal, A., Ali, M. K., & Abuzaraida, M. A. (2024). Artificial Intelligence Trust, risk and security management (AI trism): Frameworks, applications, challenges and future research directions. Expert Systems with Applications, 240, 122442.
[13] Salem, A. H., Azzam, S. M., Emam, O. E., & Abohany, A. A. (2024). Advancing cybersecurity: a comprehensive review of AI-driven detection techniques. Journal of Big Data, 11(1), 105.
[14] Rangaraju, S. (2023). Secure by intelligence: enhancing products with AI-driven security measures. EPH-International Journal of Science And Engineering, 9(3), 36–41.
[15] Aziz, L. A. R., & Andriansyah, Y. (2023). The role artificial intelligence in modern banking: an exploration of AI-driven approaches for enhanced fraud prevention, risk management, and regulatory compliance. Reviews of Contemporary Business Analytics, 6(1), 110–132.
[16] Javaid, H. A. (2024). Ai-driven predictive analytics in finance: Transforming risk assessment and decision-making. Advances in Computer Sciences, 7(1).

[17] Saxena, D., Gupta, I., Gupta, R., Singh, A. K., & Wen, X. (2023). An AI-driven VM threat prediction model for multi-risks analysis-based cloud cybersecurity. IEEE Transactions on Systems, Man, and Cybernetics: Systems, 53(11), 6815–6827.

[18] Manoharan, A., & Sarker, M. (2023). Revolutionizing Cybersecurity: Unleashing the Power of Artificial Intelligence and Machine Learning for Next-Generation Threat Detection. DOI: https://www. doi. org/10.56726/IRJMETS32644, 1.

[19] Galla, E. P., Rajaram, S. K., Patra, G. K., Madhavram, C., & Rao, J. (2022). AI-Driven Threat Detection: Leveraging Big Data For Advanced Cybersecurity Compliance. Available at SSRN 4980649.

[20] Ganesh, A. D., & Kalpana, P. (2022). Future of artificial intelligence and its influence on supply chain risk management–A systematic review. Computers & Industrial Engineering, 169, 108206.

[21] Madhavram, C., Galla, E. P., Sunkara, J. R., Rajaram, S. K., & Patra, G. K. (2022). AI-Driven Threat Detection: Leveraging Big Data For Advanced Cybersecurity Compliance. Available at SSRN 5029406.

[22] Nair, M. M., Deshmukh, A., & Tyagi, A. K. (2024). Artificial intelligence for cyber security: Current trends and future challenges. Automated Secure Computing for Next-Generation Systems, 83–114.

[23] Ekundayo, F. (2024). Leveraging AI-Driven Decision Intelligence for Complex Systems Engineering. Int J Res Publ Rev, 5(11), 1–10.

[24] Xu, J., Wang, H., Zhong, Y., Qin, L., & Cheng, Q. (2024). Predict and optimize financial services risk using AI-driven technology. Academic Journal of Science and Technology, 10(1), 299–304.

[25] Olutimehin, A. T. (2025). Advancing cloud security in digital finance: AI-driven threat detection, cryptographic solutions, and privacy challenges. Cryptographic Solutions, and Privacy Challenges (February 13, 2025).

[26] Sindiramutty, S. R. (2023). Autonomous threat hunting: A future paradigm for AI-driven threat intelligence. arXiv preprint arXiv:2401.00286.

[27] Yaseen, A. (2022). Accelerating the SOC: Achieve greater efficiency with AI-driven automation. International Journal of Responsible Artificial Intelligence, 12(1), 1–19.

[28] Khan, M. I., Arif, A., & Khan, A. R. A. (2024). The Most Recent Advances and Uses of AI in Cybersecurity. BULLET: Jurnal Multidisiplin Ilmu, 3(4), 566–578.

[29] Ajala, O. A., Okoye, C. C., Ofodile, O. C., Arinze, C. A., & Daraojimba, O. D. (2024). Review of AI and machine learning applications to predict and Thwart cyber-attacks in real-time. Magna Scientia Advanced Research and Reviews, 10(1), 312–320.

[30] Arif, H., Kumar, A., Fahad, M., & Hussain, H. K. (2024). Future horizons: AI-enhanced threat detection in cloud environments: Unveiling opportunities for research. International Journal of Multidisciplinary Sciences and Arts, 3(1), 242–251.

[31] Khan, M. I., Arif, A., & Khan, A. R. A. (2024). AI's Revolutionary Role in Cyber Defense and Social Engineering. International Journal of Multidisciplinary Sciences and Arts, 3(4), 57–66.

[32] Arefin, S., & Simcox, M. (2024). AI-Driven Solutions for Safeguarding Healthcare Data: Innovations in Cybersecurity. International Business Research, 17(6), 1–74.

[33] Sugureddy, A. R. (2024). Proactive Data Governance: Using Ai and Ml to Anticipate and Mitigate Risks. International Journal of Artificial Intelligence & Machine Learning (IJAIML), 3(02), 173–185.

[34] Olutimehin, A. T., Ajayi, A. J., Metibemu, O. C., Balogun, A. Y., Oladoyinbo, T. O., & Olaniyi, O. O. (2025). Adversarial threats to AI-driven systems: Exploring the attack surface of machine learning models and countermeasures. Available at SSRN 5137026.

[35] Olabanji, S. O., Marquis, Y., Adigwe, C. S., Ajayi, S. A., Oladoyinbo, T. O., & Olaniyi, O. O. (2024). AI-Driven cloud security: Examining the impact of user behavior analysis on threat detection. Asian Journal of Research in Computer Science, 17(3), 57–74.

[36] Khan, F. M., Akhter, M. S., Khan, I. U., Haider, Z. A., & Khan, N. H. Clinical Prediction of Female Infertility Through Advanced Machine Learning Techniques.

[37] Ramachandran, K. K. (2024). The role of artificial intelligence in enhancing financial data security. International Journal of Artificial Intelligence & Applications (IJAIAP), 3(1), 1–13.

[38] Nadella, G. S., Gonaygunta, H., Kumar, D., & Pawar, P. P. (2024). Exploring the impact of AI-driven solutions on cybersecurity adoption in small and medium enterprises. World Journal of Advanced Research and Reviews, 22(1), 1190–1197.

[39] Nwaimo, C. S., Adewumi, A., & Ajiga, D. (2022). Advanced data analytics and business intelligence: Building resilience in risk management. International Journal of Scientific Research and Applications, 6(2), 121.

[40] Adewusi, A. O., Chiekezie, N. R., & Eyo-Udo, N. L. (2022). The role of AI in enhancing cybersecurity for smart farms. World Journal of Advanced Research and Reviews, 15(3), 501–512.

[41] Obioha Val, Onyinye, et al. "Investigating the feasibility and risks of leveraging artificial intelligence and open source intelligence to manage predictive cyber threat models." Temitope and Olaniyi, Oluwaseun Oladeji and Gbadebo, Michael Olayinka and Olisa, Anthony Obulor,

Investigating the Feasibility and Risks of Leveraging Artificial Intelligence and Open Source Intelligence to Manage Predictive Cyber Threat Models (January 23, 2025) (2025).
[42] Moolchandani, S. (2025). AI-driven risk platform automating data aggregation and risk insight generation. International Journal of Science Engineering and Technology, 13(1), 12.
[43] Ramachandran, K. K., Vinjamuri, L. P., Al-Taee, M., & Alazzam, M. B. (2023, May). Using AI for risk management and improved business resilience. In 2023 3rd International Conference on Advance Computing and Innovative Technologies in Engineering (ICACITE) (pp. 978–982). IEEE.
[44] Haider, A., & Bano, S. Recurrent Neural Network and Multi-Factor Feature Filtering for Ransomware Detection in Android Apps.
[45] Aziza, O. R., Uzougbo, N. S., & Ugwu, M. C. (2023). AI and the future of contract management in the oil and gas sector. World Journal of Advanced Research and Reviews, 19(3), 1571–1581.
[46] Rahmani, F. M., & Zohuri, B. (2023). The transformative impact of AI on financial institutions, with a focus on banking. Journal of Engineering and Applied Sciences Technology. SRC/JEAST-279. DOI: doi. org/10.47363/JEAST/2023 (5), 192, 2–6.
[47] Chukwunweike, J. N., Yussuf, M., Okusi, O., & Oluwatobi, T. (2024). The role of deep learning in ensuring privacy integrity and security: Applications in AI-driven cybersecurity solutions. World Journal of Advanced Research and Reviews, 23(2), 2550.
[48] Umoga, U. J., Sodiya, E. O., Ugwuanyi, E. D., Jacks, B. S., Lottu, O. A., Daraojimba, O. D., & Obaigbena, A. (2024). Exploring the potential of AI-driven optimization in enhancing network performance and efficiency. Magna Scientia Advanced Research and Reviews, 10(1), 368–378.
[49] Bonagiri, K., VS, N. M., Gopalsamy, M., & SJ, S. (2024, August). AI-Driven Healthcare Cyber-Security: Protecting Patient Data and Medical Devices. In 2024 Second International Conference on Intelligent Cyber Physical Systems and Internet of Things (ICoICI) (pp. 107-112). IEEE.
[50] Nnaomah, U. I., Odejide, O. A., Aderemi, S., Olutimehin, D. O., Abaku, E. A., & Orieno, O. H. (2024). AI in risk management: An analytical comparison between the US and Nigerian banking sectors. International Journal of Science and Technology Research Archive, 6(1), 127–146.
[51] Ramesh, P. N. (2025). Advancements in AI-Driven Communication Systems: Enhancing Efficiency and Security in Next-Generation Networks.

[52] Usman, F. O., Eyo-Udo, N. L., Etukudoh, E. A., Odonkor, B., Ibeh, C. V., & Adegbola, A. (2024). A critical review of ai-driven strategies for entrepreneurial success. International Journal of Management & Entrepreneurship Research, 6(1), 200–215.

[53] Mollashaik, A. S. (2025). Advancing data security through AI-driven classification: A framework for intelligent threat detection and privacy preservation. International Journal of Computer Engineering and Technology (IJCET), 15(6), 467–481.

[54] Khan, F. M., Rahman, T., Zeb, A., Haider, Z. A., Khan, I. U., Bilal, H., ... & Ullah, I. (2024). Vehicular Network Security Through Optimized Deep Learning Model with Feature Selection Techniques. IECE Transactions on Sensing, Communication, and Control, 1(2), 136–153.

[55] Badmus, O., Rajput, S. A., Arogundade, J. B., & Williams, M. (2024). AI-driven business analytics and decision making. World Journal of Advanced Research and Reviews, 24(1), 616–633.

[56] Quinn, T., & Thompson, O. (2024). Applying large language model (llm) for developing cybersecurity policies to counteract spear phishing attacks on senior corporate managers.

[57] Folorunso, A., Adewumi, T., Adewa, A., Okonkwo, R., & Olawumi, T. N. (2024). Impact of AI on cybersecurity and security compliance. Global Journal of Engineering and Technology Advances, 21(01), 167–184.

[58] Khan, I., Tian, Y. B., Vllah, H., Rahman, S. U., & Kamal, M. M. (2018, May). Design annular ring microstrip antenna based on artificial neural network. In 2018 2nd IEEE Advanced Information Management, Communicates, Electronic and Automation Control Conference (IMCEC) (pp. 2033–2037). IEEE.

[59] Ajayi-Nifise, A. O., Odeyemi, O., Mhlongo, N. Z., Ibeh, C. V., Elufioye, O. A., & Awonuga, K. F. (2024). The future of accounting: Predictions on automation and AI integration. World journal of advanced research and reviews, 21(2), 399–407.

[60] AL-Dosari, K., Fetais, N., & Kucukvar, M. (2024). Artificial intelligence and cyber defense system for banking industry: A qualitative study of AI applications and challenges. Cybernetics and systems, 55(2), 302–330.

[61] Arinze, C. A., Izionworu, V. O., Isong, D., Daudu, C. D., & Adefemi, A. (2024). Predictive maintenance in oil and gas facilities, leveraging ai for asset integrity management. International Journal of Frontiers in Engineering and Technology Research, 6(1), 16–26.

[62] Oereshi, M. S., Khan, I. U., Qureshi, S. M. B., Khan, F. M., & Aleshaiker, S. (2023). Empowering the Blind: AI-Assisted Solutions for Visually Impaired People.

[63] Ohalete, N. C., Aderibigbe, A. O., Ani, E. C., Ohenhen, P. E., Daraojimba, D. O., & Odulaja, B. A. (2023). AI-driven solutions in renewable energy: A review of data science applications in solar and wind energy optimization. World Journal of Advanced Research and Reviews, 20(3), 401–417.

[64] Joshi, S. (2025). Review of Gen AI models for financial risk management. International Journal of Scientific Research in Computer Science, Engineering and Information Technology, 11(1), 709–723.

[65] Gupta, S., Modgil, S., Lee, C. K., & Sivarajah, U. (2023). The future is yesterday: Use of AI-driven facial recognition to enhance value in the travel and tourism industry. Information Systems Frontiers, 25(3), 1179–1195.

[66] Ajayi, A. J., Joseph, S., Metibemu, O. C., Olutimehin, A. T., Balogun, A. Y., & Olaniyi, O. O. (2025). The impact of artificial intelligence on cyber security in digital currency transactions. Available at SSRN 5137847.

[67] Radanliev, P. (2024). Cyber diplomacy: defining the opportunities for cybersecurity and risks from Artificial Intelligence, IoT, Blockchains, and Quantum Computing. Journal of Cyber Security Technology, 1–51.

[68] Dhoni, P., & Kumar, R. (2023). Synergizing generative ai and cybersecurity: Roles of generative ai entities, companies, agencies, and government in enhancing cybersecurity. Authorea Preprints.

[69] Khan, I., Tian, Y. B., Ullah, I., Kamal, M. M., Ullah, H., & Khan, A. (2018). Designing of E-shaped microstrip antenna using artificial neural network. Int. J. Comput. Commun. Instrum. Eng, 5(1), 23–26.

[70] Khan, F. M., Rahman, T., Zeb, A., Ullah, I., Khan, I., & Akhter, M. S. (2025). The Essential Role of Cybersecurity in UAV Swarm Operations. In Unmanned Aerial Vehicles Swarm for Protecting Smart Cities: Future Trends and Challenges (pp. 403–441). Berkeley, CA: Apress.

[71] Khan, F. A., Li, G., Khan, A. N., Khan, Q. W., Hadjouni, M., & Elmannai, H. (2023). AI-driven counter-terrorism: Enhancing global security through advanced predictive analytics. IEEE Access, 11, 135864–135879.

[72] Bello, O. A., Ogundipe, A., Mohammed, D., Adebola, F., & Alonge, O. A. (2023). AI-Driven Approaches for real-time fraud detection in US financial transactions: challenges and opportunities. European Journal of Computer Science and Information Technology, 11(6), 84–102.

[73] Sodiya, E. O., Umoga, U. J., Amoo, O. O., & Atadoga, A. (2024). AI-driven warehouse automation: A comprehensive review of systems. GSC Advanced Research and Reviews, 18(2), 272–282.

[74] Faheem, M. A., Anwer, S., Rayhan, Z., Ullah, M. A., Paudel, R., Ahmed, M. F., & Khan, H. (2024). AI-Driven Innovation In HRM And Its Impact On Business Management: An In-Depth Study Of Technology Advancement And Strategic Implementation. Nanotechnology Perceptions, 20, 1174–1204.

[75] Ullah, I., Adhikari, D., Su, X., Palmieri, F., Wu, C., & Choi, C. (2024). Integration of data science with the intelligent IoT (IIoT): Current challenges and future perspectives. Digital Communications and Networks.

[76] Shishehgarkhaneh, M. B., Moehler, R. C., Fang, Y., Aboutorab, H., & Hijazi, A. A. (2024). Construction supply chain risk management. Automation in Construction, 162, 105396.

4

Artificial Intelligence in Cyber Risk Management: Revolutionizing Threat Detection and Resilience

Soufiane Ouariach[1], Fatima Zahra Ouariach[2], Veerpratap Meena[3], Mariya Ouaissa[4], and Mariyam Ouaissa[5]

[1]Computer Science and University Pedagogical Engineering (S2IPU), Higher Normal School of Tetouan, Abdelmalek Essaadi University, Morocco
[2]Educational science, language didactics, human and social sciences, Higher Normal School of Tetouan, Abdelmalek Essaadi University, Morocco
[3]Department of Electrical Engineering, National Institute of Technology, India
[4]Computer Systems Engineering Laboratory, Cadi Ayyad University, Morocco
[5]Laboratory of Information Technologies, Chouaib Doukkali University, Morocco

Email: soufian.ouariach@etu.uae.ac.ma; fatimazahra.ouariach@etu.uae.ac.ma; vmeena1@ee.iitr.ac.in; m.ouaissa@uca.ac.ma; ouaissa.mariyam@ucd.ac.ma

Abstract

As the cyber threat environment evolves more sophisticatedly and at a greater scale, traditional measures remain inadequate. Thus, this chapter explores how artificial intelligence can transform cyber risk management (CRM) by delivering dynamic, scalable, and proactive approaches to detect, prevent, and respond to cyber threats. It therefore also considers the integration of AI technologies, including machine learning, natural language processing, and predictive abilities, for better detection of threats, response to incidents, and risk assessment. Furthermore, this chapter discusses how AI can provide a

DOI: 10.1201/9788743808077-4

faster incident response capability through more precise threat detection and scalability to address issues, including evolving ethical considerations, data privacy, and resource constraints. Future leaps, such as AI joining hands with quantum computing and federated learning, will transform CRM by enabling firms to take an active role in managing risks and building cyber resilience. This chapter highlights the need for teamwork across fields, new rules, and the use of ethical AI to ensure that strong and smart practices for managing cyber risks are in place.

4.1 Introduction

Traditional cybersecurity measures, such as detection systems based on signatures, cannot identify and mitigate sophisticated threats as the threat landscape evolves. Due to cybercriminals' ability to create increasingly complex malware, adapt quickly, and exploit vulnerabilities, static, rule-based defenses have become inadequate. This is where artificial intelligence (AI) comes into play, offering dynamic, adaptive solutions that address the rising complexity of cyber threats [1], [2].

The role of AI in cyber risk management is due to the shortcomings of traditional methods in spotting, reacting, and responding to an attack. In the past, approaches to cybersecurity were passive; they dealt with damage control after an attack had taken place. The development of interconnected systems and the vast growth in data volume have made it mandatory to change systems into proactive, preemptive ones. Organizations have started using AI-based solutions to improve their enterprise risk management (ERM) frameworks because they now understand that cyber risks are not standalone but linked with operational, financial, regulatory, and reputational layers of business [2], [3].

AI technologies, namely machine learning, natural language processing, and predictive analytics, are the driving forces behind the elevation of cyber risk management capabilities. Anomaly detection and adaptive response to threats are made possible for ML models by large dataset analysis for pattern recognition and anomaly identification. Another contribution of NLP is the extraction and analysis of critical threat intelligence from unstructured data reports, social media, and forums for actionable insights. The organization is further enhanced by predictive analytics, which forecasts potential risks based on historical data and current trends [4], [5].

Using AI in cyber risk management also helps deal with the greater problems of cyber threats coming from more IoT devices, external links, and supply chain ties. Every connected device shows a potential entry point, and

AI solutions are needed to monitor, assess, and mitigate these dangers immediately [6], [7]. AI's ability to handle large data at high speed boosts firms' power to foresee and counter sophisticated attacks that might exploit these vulnerabilities.

Besides its technical use, AI is also very important in building organizational cyber resilience. Resilience here does not only mean preventing breaches but also ensuring that organizations can continue to function during and after a cyber incident. In response to this need, AI-driven incident response systems, staff training, and automated disaster recovery processes become integral parts of the strategy [8], [9]. Cooperation from different domains – economics, law, cognitive sciences, and so on – contributes significantly towards evolving holistic CRM strategies based on AI. These strategies should equally address vulnerabilities from both technical and human perspectives [10].

Even though AI could greatly help, there are many challenges in using it for CRM. These include ethical issues and data privacy, as well as cost factors associated with AI systems. Strong regulatory bodies, ethical actions towards AI, and teamwork from different fields are needed to overcome these obstacles so that all responsible use and effectiveness of these technologies can be achieved [11], 12]. To sum up this chapter, discusses how AI can close the gap between old practices in cybersecurity and having new, modern, proactive ways to manage cyber risks. The chapter also brings out the transformational impacts that artificial intelligence technologies have had on cyber threat detection, prevention, and mitigation, as well as bringing out some of the accompanying challenges and numerous opportunities during implementation. Artificial intelligence would therefore bring about an organizational change from reactive measures to proactive strategies in ensuring resilience amidst cyber complexity.

4.2 The Need for AI in the Evolving Cybersecurity Landscape

The evolution of cyber risk management (CRM) experienced a total transition from traditional manual defense mechanisms to smart technological systems that combat escalating cyber threat sophistication. The development of cyber risk management passes through distinct phases that show different methods for handling cyber operation-related risks. The development of cyber risk management through technology, organizational behavior, and regulatory frameworks has achieved its peak in today's society, which requires proactive management of sustainable cyber risks.

The initial stage of CRM depended on traditional security methods that used perimeter controls, including firewalls and antivirus programs as main defenses. The dominant perception at this time demanded that organizations establish security measures following the occurrence of events rather than proactively. The approach proved unproductive when faced with growing, sophisticated, and widespread cyber threats that required organizations to adopt a comprehensive enterprise risk management (ERM) framework for cybersecurity. Organizations started implementing cybersecurity strategies into their complete risk management practices after realizing cyber risks form connections across their organizational framework. Organizations must integrate cybersecurity approaches because it enables them to treat security as an essential organizational element that affects operational security alongside reputation and finance, and regulatory compliance [2], [3].

The rising level of cyber threats demanded that organizations become ever more thoughtful and intelligent in identifying and managing risks on a proactive basis. An approach scrubbed through the lens of AI and ML into CRM underlines this migration. The role of AI technologies is aimed at escalating the capacity of cybersecurity systems both in the sphere of detection and response to security issues as well as facilitation of better threat intelligence to predict, find, and react to possible breaches in real time [4], [5]. The growing amount of data, as well as the actors of threats, means that traditional solutions do not adequately keep up with either the speed or assortment of threats in the cybersecurity landscape; therefore, efficacious AI technologies are not just beneficial but required within contemporary CRM.

Advanced analytics and threat intelligence platforms have also upgraded CRM activities by a long shot. Companies, through frameworks that use AI and real-time monitoring to adjust risk management strategies dynamically in light of the evolving threat landscape, can change risks imperatively. The pivot to data-driven and automated cyber risk management is important as it will allow actions that proactively seek to close down vulnerabilities before they can be leveraged by adversaries [6]. Such innovation finds its best relevance in a sector characterized by high interconnectedness and information sensitivity that makes the system highly vulnerable, hence the need for intelligence synchronization across a myriad of levels in an organization [4].

The dynamic expansion in the IoT drives the ever-complex landscape of cyber risks. Every single connected device becomes a potential entry point for hackers to attack, so the attack surface is growing exponentially. In turn, that demands a full-fledged CRM inside the perimeter and up to the perimeter of all interactions with devices outside the company and third-party vendors [7]. In combination with supply chain risk management, organizations further enhance their resilience against attacks exploiting vulnerabilities in interconnected systems and services [8].

Regarding modern CRM, cyber resilience has come to be the core where organizations are to adequately and effectively withstand cyber incidents and recover from them. This requires pivoting from the traditional model of attack prevention, focusing on ensuring uninterrupted breach-impacted essential functions [9], [10]. Maintaining strong incident response plans, staff training and periodic drills, and execution of backup and disaster recovery procedures make cyber resilience strategies an integral part of the operational health of organizations [9].

Cross-disciplinary collaboration also plays a very important role in the advancement of CRM. As the complexity of cyber threats has grown, it has become necessary to involve several disciplines, like economics, law, and cognitive sciences. Such an interdisciplinary approach betters the understanding of cyber risks and leads to the existence of more truly comprehensive and therefore more effective strategies for cyber risk management [11]. In evolving CRM, enterprises gradually give importance to ensuring that an environment of safety consciousness is inculcated among the employees, accepting that the human element's weaknesses are the most used ways of attack.

Insurance coverage from cyber adversaries now plays a significant role in the grounding of the CRM, shielding an organization against possible breaches and inducing the firms to implement more robust risk management practices though this concept is proven by insurance products that help them avoid any financial losses to incidents while in turn inducing better cybersecurity measures to avoid a risk exposure [12]. However, the liability emerging from cyber threats means quantifying cyber risk in the insurance market is fraught with liability and indeed prompts a need for improved modeling and risk assessment methodology that captures the complexity of these emerging dynamics correctly [12].

A major challenge facing firms as they advance their CRM practices is the adaptation of regulatory frameworks to rapidly changing technology alongside an evolving landscape of cyber threats. Policy-making authorities have to decide on how best to channel governance and incentives for cyber investments into improved cybersecurity while simultaneously ensuring that companies are made accountable for cyber risk management as a part of their operational activities [13], [14]. In such a background of regulation, the way organizations work is defined, which in turn defines the resilience of society to a multitude of cyber threats.

In summary, the evolution of cyber risk management describes the ever-changing environment where technology strategies and products become one throughout the enterprise. Advancing the transition from manual processes to intelligent-system defenses can indicate if and how an organization is responding to the changing nature of cyber threats. As an organization continues to improve its CRM approach, it goes without saying that several other factors are very important – for instance, proactive strategies, collaboration across disciplines, and all built around resilience. Technology such as AI and advanced analytics will enable organizations to take an active approach in securing their assets against the threats in the cyber risk landscape.

4.3 Role of Artificial Intelligence in Cyber Risk Management

The role of AI in CRM is bridging the age-old strategies of managing cyber risks with modern approaches to bring on board sophisticated methods of threat detection, response, and mitigation. The capacities of AI, particularly those of ML, NLP, and predictive analytics, uplift the effectiveness of cybersecurity actions to proactively and smartly mitigate ever-transforming risks from within and without. In the sections that follow, we will explore how these technologies revolutionize cybersecurity practices, enabling organizations to stay ahead of ever-evolving cyber threats.

Machine learning for threat detection and pattern recognition: One of the major applications of ML, therefore, is the ability to spot patterns and anomalies in extensive datasets characteristic of cyber threats. Once trained on historical data, ML models can spot malicious activities within an IT architecture and adapt swiftly when new information becomes available. This feature allows the organization to achieve real-time discovery of anomalies that could be early indicators of breaches or attacks. For example, recent studies suggest the use of machine learning models in the analysis of security intelligence feeds and security-centric big data for real-time discovery of threats and vulnerabilities in the organization [15]. Other research also indicates that ML-based techniques are more amenable to easing the identification burden of cybersecurity analysts to find out about threats that previously required manual detection [16], [17]. By the use of techniques like anomaly detection or intrusion detection, organizations can enhance their threat response capabilities to an enormous extent [18].

Natural language processing (NLP) for analyzing cyber threat intelligence: NLP functions as an AI subdiscipline that enables human language data processing and understanding, and its cybersecurity applications have gained significant importance. The analysis of threat intelligence from various sources, such as social media, reports, and technical documentation, becomes more effective through NLP techniques. NLP technology allows quick threat identification through automatic extraction of important data from unstructured text, which leads to faster understanding of active cyber threats [19]. AI systems that use NLP technology detect cyber threat patterns to create practical intelligence that supports security teams in their critical operational decision-making [20]. Through its applications, NLP facilitates the consolidation and contextualization of threat data extracted from different languages, which extends the reach of threat intelligence both during collection and response activities [21].

Predictive analytics for identifying potential risks before they occur: Predictive analytics runs through learning machines; it works toward helping an organization forecast future cyber risks based on patterns and trends imbibed by historical data. Assessment results of previous incidents of breach or vulnerability of the system to cyber threats may be projected by ML models along with the circumstances under which cyberattacks happened [22]. This, therefore, would become a very effective proactive method to prepare defenses well before and not after any breach has occurred. For example, advanced predictive models are being developed to enhance ransomware and malware detection, which will therefore help security teams to identify and mitigate any threats long before breaches occur [23]. Furthermore, the integration of such predictive functionalities within larger CRM approaches allows firms to appropriately prioritize cybersecurity endeavors toward those areas most at risk [24].

One area where automation is increasingly leveraged in CRM is in the area of risk assessment and monitoring of risks that are associated with cyber operations. It is usually done through AI, mainly by using machine learning, NLP, and predictive analytics in the corporate system. The integration helps in expediting the process of identifying, assessing, and mitigating cyber risks, thereby increasing organizational resilience against potential threats.

The technology to automate risk assessment and monitoring with AI is solely based on the characteristic of artificial intelligence to handle large amounts of data at a speed that is above the normal range, enabling companies to detect the weaknesses and the elements that are anomalous that could lead to a security breach rather quickly. Machine learning models, particularly those using algorithms such as artificial neural networks (ANN), have shown efficiency in predicting cyber risks with exceptional accuracy [25]. Furthermore, these models rely on ongoing data acquisition to enhance their threat detection capabilities and, in addition to that, minimize false negatives in risk assessment, such as the case where the identified vulnerabilities might have been missed.

Natural language processing would thus come in to extract and analyze the critical threat intelligence from different sources – be it social media, technical reports, etc. Thereby providing a support factor that enhances the aspect of pattern and trend analysis to enable organizations to be more proactive in addressing the mid-emerging threats [26]. NLP can automate the classification of threat-related information to thus quickening the process by which security analysts make decisions, thereby enabling them to act faster and in the right direction in their risk management strategy. NLP techniques should be applied to the analysis of unstructured data extracted from multiple sources like threat intelligence reports, social media, and other forums to develop actionable insights into potential vulnerabilities. Through context and semantic comprehension of the substance of information, AI systems would be able to produce synthesized critical information that, in turn, would support organizations in making informed decisions in the context of the establishment of strategies on risk management [27]. In the context, for example, summarizing security alerts for organizations and translating them into formats that are much more understandable and easier to analyze for quick actions would be possible through the use of NLP [28].

Predictive analytics are literally made possible by the respective historical data and real-time metrics vested in predicting vulnerabilities to cyber threats as well as risks. Through machine learning applications that help spot patterns of risks and predict future breaches, even more preventative measures can be taken long before any incident occurs, and respond post facto [29]. Investments can thus be channeled more effectively by identifying the risks beforehand, with a demand for the allocation of resources to close key vulnerabilities.

Furthermore, organizations can predict upcoming risks through AI-powered predictive analytics before threats become actual security threats. AI platforms examine patterns to estimate threat probabilities while helping security staff allocate resources towards active threats first. The predictive analysis models leverage three types of variables, such as historical security incidents and system parameters, and external threat analysis to predict future vulnerabilities [30]. Organizations need this proactive strategy to protect against escalating complex cyber threats because it helps them prevent expensive breaches before they occur [31].

4.3.1 Benefits of AI in cyber risk management

Cyber risk management advantages emerge from using artificial intelligence (AI) because it demonstrates several benefits that enable organizations to better combat cyberattacks. AI implementation enables faster incident response as well as increased security threat detection precision and expanded security operation scalability. A stronger cybersecurity position results from the combination of these security benefits.

AI-operated systems demonstrate superior performance by analyzing vast data sources and detecting possible security dangers during their processing time. The current security systems that depend on human analysts create detection delays and response delays because of limited human speed. AI automation detects threats directly through immediate anomaly detection, which allows security personnel to rapidly respond to potentially harmful activities. Darktrace leverages unsupervised machine learning to deploy automatic threat responses during detection events, thus minimizing the average time needed for response. The immediate response capability stands as a key factor to reduce the damage caused by cyberattacks [32].

Using AI technologies to secure systems results in stronger threat detection accuracy. Traditional systems generate numerous false alarms that cause security personnel to experience exhaustion from receiving non-threatening alerts at high rates. The learning process of AI models makes continuous improvements to threat identification precision by analyzing historical data. AI anomaly detection software distinguishes legitimate user actions from malicious activity, which lowers the number of false security alerts [33], [34]. The predictive capabilities of deep learning neural networks and other machine learning algorithms improve through their ability to detect faint threat indicators [35]. Organizations achieve better security operations through threat prioritization made possible by genuine threat identification.

AI solutions are inherently scalable, capable of managing extensive datasets without a proportional increase in human resources. As organizations grow, their cybersecurity needs become more complex, and AI systems adapt to handle increased workloads efficiently. By leveraging AI, companies can monitor more endpoints, analyze larger volumes of network traffic, and incorporate new data sources without substantial investments in additional personnel or infrastructure. This scalability is particularly advantageous for small and medium-sized enterprises (SMEs), which may lack the resources to expand their cybersecurity teams. Moreover, AI technologies can be integrated across different platforms, allowing for a cohesive approach to risk management.

Scalability is an inherent quality of AI technology that enables the effective handling of big datasets without requiring additional human staff. An AI system enhances its cybersecurity capabilities when organizations expand their operations through efficient workload adaptability. AI technologies allow businesses to maintain surveillance of a larger domain of endpoints and analyze extensive network traffic volumes through a system requiring minimal new personnel and infrastructure costs. The scalability benefits of AI systems prove highly beneficial for small- and medium-sized enterprises (SMEs) due to their limited capabilities to increase their cybersecurity teams [36]. Multiple platforms can unify their risk management approaches through AI technology integration.

Organizations use AI to analyze both historical data and real-time metrics for implementing predictive analytics solutions that protect their cybersecurity. Organizational success in detecting potential dangers enables preemptive action for strengthening defense systems. Models for predictive analysis use present vulnerabilities to generate attack scenarios that help organizations determine which defenses to protect first [37], [38]. The preventive security strategy contributes to better defense capabilities and builds organizational resistance to future security threats.

The implementation of artificial intelligence across cyber risk management produces numerous significant advantages, which include swift response times alongside better accuracy, scalability features, and prediction enhancement. Organizations that aim to lead against modern sophisticated cyber threats need these advantages to thrive. Organizations obtain a resilient cybersecurity framework through automated threat detection and response processes and advanced analytical techniques that safeguard their assets through an evolving digital landscape.

4.4 Key Applications of AI in Cyber Risk Management

4.4.1 Threat detection and prevention with AI

Artificial intelligence has become indispensable for improving cyber risk management because it allows organizations to establish better threat detection and prevention systems. The main concern in phishing detection requires AI mechanisms that implement machine learning algorithms for recognizing different cyber threats, including phishing schemes and malware, and ransomware attacks.

The combination of multi-layer adaptive systems with optical character recognition (OCR) functionality and high-tech machine learning elements serves as an effective phishing attempt detection solution. OCR functions as part of the detection system [39] to extract text from phishing website images before random forest and LSTM networks process this data for detailed assessment, thus elevating phishing detection performance above standard textual approaches. The joint application of evidence theory and machine learning processing solutions for linguistic features achieved improved accuracy when detecting phishing scenarios, according to Gutiérrez et al. [40].

Machine learning algorithms achieve superior results both in detecting phishing activities and showing exceptional performance against various security threats. The research by Govea et al. proved that machine learning solutions achieve 98% detection success while cutting incident response times by 70% [41]. The high level of operational efficiency represents a fundamental advancement for organizations that need to handle their cyber risks. Research from Sarker et al. demonstrates that AI-based systems depend on large datasets to forecast security threats, and they acquire new data patterns continually, which enhances detection and intrusion prevention systems [42].

Intelligent phishing detection methods have progressed by combining ensemble machine learning classifiers into their development process. The detection accuracy of phishing websites increases through the implementation of support vector machines (SVM) and extreme learning machines (ELM) [43], [44]. Research by ANDRIU demonstrates AI solutions that adapt to protect email security by detecting phishing email attacks with great precision [45].

Modern phishing tactics demand that organizations sustain their defensive technologies in constant development. The integration of AI systems into threat detection measures provides an efficient way to look at historical data patterns, which leads to enhanced overall threat recognition [46]. PhishHaven uses real-time detection of phishing URLs by exploiting machine learning adaptability to combat new IoT security threats [47]. The changes in cybersecurity call for proactive adoption of AI-based solutions by organizations in their security strategies. AI applications oriented toward cybersecurity protect organizations by not only improving operational speed and detection efficiency but also establishing continuous learning systems to handle complex digital threats.

4.4.2 Enhancing incident response with artificial intelligence

Artificial intelligence operates as an essential tool that helps incident response teams in cyber risk management efforts. AI technologies provide organizations with multiple functional abilities that speed up their response mechanisms to cyberattacks. The analysis of enormous data quantities by machine learning programs in AI solutions allows for better identification of security threats while dramatically speeding up response operations. Organizations using AI-based security systems achieved a remarkable 98% better threat detection capability, combined with under 70% shorter response times to cyberattacks, according to recent research findings [48]. Through AI-enabled monitoring systems, organizations can create a proactive incident response because these platforms detect upcoming cyber threats before they develop. AI-based threat prediction depends on its ability to study historical data for pattern recognition, which leads to better threat forecasting and safeguards organizations from various upcoming attacks [49], [50]. Through the utilization of machine learning models that operate with data based on previous attacks, organizations maintain a proactive position against cyber adversaries by allowing constant adaptation [51], [52].

AI systems use automation to enhance security incident response, which minimizes errors and boosts operational performance during a situation of rapidly developing cyber threats. AI-integrated incident response enables faster breach discovery along with automatic corrective measures to control cyber incidents [53]. Security systems collect and analyze user engagement conditions alongside network traffic patterns from security-oriented events to detect abnormal operations, which enables immediate alerts and responses [54]. Organizations gain dynamic threat response capabilities through implementing AI-based cybersecurity systems. Security infrastructure resilience improves through the continuous evolution of detection capabilities enabled by deep learning frameworks with natural language processing, which enables performance enhancement based on processed data [55], [56]. Traditional security measures fail to protect complex systems like the Internet of Things (IoT) environments, yet this issue becomes crucial since the failure point [57]. AI is now recognized for its capability to enhance incident response frameworks so these become more resistant against known and unknown security threats [58].

4.4.3 AI-powered fraud detection: Revolutionizing security

Artificial intelligence (AI) use in fraud detection technology brings revolutionary changes for real-time fraudulent activity identification and prevention. Business rules and static detection approaches from previous methods lack the ability to respond speedily to newly emerging or adjusted fraud schemes. AI through machine learning algorithms uses new data to perpetually improve its ability to identify fraudulent patterns that it had not detected before [59]. The dynamic nature of AI systems provides essential benefits because they stay current with constantly changing fraudulent patterns in the environment [60].

Deep learning-based AI models demonstrate outstanding abilities to process large transactional datasets with great effect. Anomalies signaling fraudulent behavior become detectable through analysis of historic patterns as well as undisclosed variables that human analysts might miss [60], [61], [62]. Deep learning models achieve superior performance in detecting sophisticated fraudulent transactions through their ability to reveal complex data interrelations, according to research reports [61]. Science-based research shows that AI-based detection systems achieve better identification results with fewer incorrect alarms than typical analytical methods [63], [64].

Time-sensitive fraud identification through AI works as an essential tool across sectors, including financial services and healthcare. The price of missing fraudulent transactions becomes massive in these specific industrial sectors. AI systems use transaction analysis to spot unusual transactions and speed up the process of stopping fraudulent events and ensuring trust for customers [59], [64]. By implementing AI in banking fraud detection systems, the operational effectiveness of organizations has improved so much that they now react instantly to security threats [65].

AI detectors are used across multiple sectors to find irregularities in credit card payments as well as to validate insurance applications and perform banking security checks. The combination of institutions using federated learning technology, which permits model training across various organizations with secure protection of sensitive data, provides promising solutions for fraud detection [66]. The method showcases how AI advances both operational speed and strict privacy requirements in a single application.

AI teams up with natural language processing (NLP) and predictive analytics to identify fraud patterns successfully. Start-time detection systems utilize both structured and unstructured data to find valuable insights that help prevent fraud [67]. The combination of multiple data sources generates a better understanding of incoming threats which helps organizations build much stronger security frameworks for fighting fraud.

4.5 Challenges in Implementing AI for Cyber Risk Management

The implementation of artificial intelligence (AI) for cyber risk management presents multiple difficulties that organizations must handle in their processes. This chapter discusses the moral issues of AI decision systems as well as data protection threats and the expense of maintaining systems while depending on extensive source materials and expert staff. It presents solutions to minimize these barriers.

The main obstacle when deploying AI systems is the set of moral concerns associated with biased algorithms. The occurrence of bias in artificial intelligence systems produces major effects, including unfair treatment outcomes, and these problems have been observed in healthcare applications that utilize patient data [68]. A flawed dataset used for training algorithms allows such systems to both sustain and increase biases that already exist within the data. AI tools that faced discrimination complaints demonstrated clear bias issues during their development, as shown in multiple company incidents, particularly through the exposed Amazon hiring problem that discriminated against female applicants [69]. Ethical review processes and algorithm development evaluation programs should exist as mandatory components to confirm data representation validity while conducting routine tests for unintended bias [70].

The protection of sensitive data and system security has become a major obstacle of its own kind. Large-scale personal data requirements by AI systems become a cause for data security concerns since the information must be adequately protected from breaches and unauthorized access [71]. The exposure of user-sensitive data by generative AI and machine learning applications demands robust protective measures because these systems accidentally leak personal data [72]. The AI technique of federated learning enables decentralized training of models by allowing analysts to perform operations on disbursed data without consolidating sensitive information [73]. This method enhances security and privacy protection. The evaluation process of privacy policies according to AI-related changes will help users feel comfortable while complying with relevant legal mandates [74].

AI adoption imposes heavy financial challenges on organizations, especially those with reduced financial resources. Significant sums of money must be allocated to software and hardware acquisition as well as employee training before companies can adopt AI technologies. This high initial cost proves challenging for numerous potential implementers. Intelligent system implementations for improved cybersecurity become inaccessible to small companies due to high implementation costs, which restrict market diversity [75]. Organizations that wish to spread the benefits of technological improvement should adopt long-term deployment strategies with trial implementations and partnership agreements that distribute financial burdens and educational resources throughout the network of users [76].

Large datasets needed for AI training represent fundamental constraints because of their dependency [70]. Successful algorithms require datasets that cover multiple dimensions because they lead to reliable results. Obtaining such datasets along with their correct labels can become costly and time-consuming due to their extensive demands on resources. AI systems face difficulties with unfamiliar circumstances that their training data lacks because of insufficient recent data and inadequate context, which leads to system breakdowns in real-world implementations [69]. Organizations solve this challenge by implementing active learning methods to keep training sets updated, together with synthetic data generation serving as a temporary solution [73].

Comprehensive AI systems require expert personnel who possess knowledge of data science alongside machine learning and cybersecurity expertise. The implementation of AI solutions becomes inefficient when there is an inadequate number of skilled professionals in these specialist fields [72]. Organizations must spend on employee education programs, together with incentives and academic institution partnerships to create future talent capabilities in essential fields [78]. A combination of interdisciplinary teams that unite professionals from cybersecurity and AI allows organizations to implement a comprehensive approach that properly handles all risks related to cyber operations and system implementations.

The implementation of AI in cyber risk management brings enormous advantages for better performance, along with numerous obstacles that need unified work to solve them. Companies must tackle essential barriers, which include ethical concerns alongside privacy threats and cost expenditures, as well as big datasets demands and staff expertise shortages. Organizations can overcome the complexities in AI implementation through strong ethical frameworks combined with innovative privacy protection methods, cost-sharing networks, dynamic data management practices, and purpose-directed training sessions to achieve successful AI integration in cybersecurity.

4.6 Future Outlook: AI and the Evolution of Cybersecurity

AI-powered autonomous systems have grown in popularity to the extent that they now provide automated cybersecurity functions. These systems serve as essential tools for organizations to monitor actively in real time, detect anomalies, and take preemptive action [79]. Autonomous features have proven effective in decreasing the time to react against threats, making it possible for organizations to respond swiftly to potential breaches before they turn into major damages [80]. Future predictions expect improved cyber defense capabilities from machine learning algorithm integration within autonomous systems despite their developing state [81]. Federated learning represents an advancement that enables distributed AI model training across multiple devices while maintaining privacy standards [81].

The combination of AI and quantum computing creates an additional enhancement for cyber risk management systems. The computational strength of quantum systems allows them to handle sophisticated algorithms together with substantial datasets more rapidly than conventional computers, thereby improving security threat identification and reaction times [82]. The application of quantum algorithms strengthens encryption methods so unauthorized data access becomes considerably harder [81]. Scientific studies show that quantum cryptography enables secure communication channels that resist any form of undetected monitoring to secure sensitive messages [80]. Organizations can defend themselves from evolving security threats thanks to the new security pathways created by quantum technology integrated with artificial intelligence systems.

The effectiveness of cyber risk management heavily relies on upgraded deep learning along with natural language processing capabilities within AI algorithms and tools [83]. Assisting algorithms have the ability to examine large datasets, which helps them discover anomalies that signify security breaches [84]. AI technologies currently under advancement will add explainable AI models that will enable organizations to develop trust in automated systems [85]. Modern opinion supports transparency in AI operations since it establishes an understanding between stakeholders about AI cybersecurity functions [86]. Due to improved algorithms, organizations will benefit from reduced false positive incidents, which will streamline their incident response and management procedures [81].

The integration of AI throughout cybersecurity generates heightened requirements for regulations that guide the field. Governments around the world will begin implementing regulations that determine how businesses use AI technologies to control cyber risks [87]. Organizations must implement AI responsibly according to societal values by using benchmarks that regulations provide for data privacy and ethical AI use, and accountability purposes [81]. Organizations that create standardization initiatives for AI-based cybersecurity solutions will build best practice guidelines that can facilitate wider market acceptance, thus enabling improved cyber risk management across various industries [88].

Many experts analyze the potential of AI to modify how the cyber risk management industry operates. Organizations will shift their cybersecurity practices from reactive to proactive through increasingly proficient AI tools by detecting threats ahead of time, according to [89]. AI-powered threat intelligence platforms let organizations instantly share threat data, which enhances their collective cybersecurity initiative implementation [90]. Industry leaders will incorporate AI technologies into all digital security aspects to achieve holistic cyber resilience in domains where AI becomes prevalent [90]. The current industry transformation permits AI to become a fundamental organizational partner, which forms an integral part of protective cyber defense strategies.

4.7 Conclusion

The role of artificial intelligence in cyber risk management encompasses the evolution of detection, response, and mitigation strategies toward cyber threats. Outdated approaches that rely heavily on static defenses can no longer cope with the sophisticated strategies of cyber attackers. Information and proactive machine learning-based NLP augmented predictive analytics empower organizations to adopt scalable approaches in making threat discovery, incident response, and risk evaluation more proactive. All these possibilities serve real-time anomaly recognition, exact threat discovery, and predictive models for forecasting vulnerabilities so that an organization can organize its defense. Although AI solutions promise several strategic advantages for CRM implementation, there lie numerous challenges as well – ethical considerations, data privacy risks, high costs, and expertise. Addressing these barriers through strong ethical frameworks, new ways to protect privacy, and teamwork is essential to ensuring AI works well. In the future, when AI joins quantum computing and federated learning, it will have life-changing power for CRM, allowing quicker calculations, better encryption, and more distributed intelligence. By combining technological progress with moral and regulatory changes, companies can develop a robust, intelligent, and flexible way to manage cyber risks for what lies ahead.

References

[1] Naayini, Prudhvi and Myakala, Praveen Kumar and Bura, Chiranjeevi, How AI is Reshaping the Cybersecurity Landscape (February 14, 2025). Available at SSRN: https://ssrn.com/abstract=5138207

[2] Marotta and M. McShane, "Integrating a proactive technique into a holistic cyber risk management approach", Risk Management and Insurance Review, vol. 21, no. 3, p. 435–452, 2018. https://doi.org/10.1111/rmir.12109

[3] L. Holder, "Cyber risk management with the help of artificial intelligence in smes: analysis of barriers and needs", 19th International Scientific Conference on Industrial Systems, p. 454–461, 2023. https://doi.org/10.24867/is-2023-vp1.1-1_00941

[4] P. Trim and Y. Lee, "Combining sociocultural intelligence with artificial intelligence to increase organizational cyber security provision through

enhanced resilience", Big Data and Cognitive Computing, vol. 6, no. 4, p. 110, 2022. https://doi.org/10.3390/bdcc6040110

[5] N. Vemuri, N. Thaneeru, & V. Tatikonda, "Securing trust: ethical considerations in ai for cybersecurity", Journal of Knowledge Learning and Science Technology ISSN: 2959-6386 (Online), vol. 2, no. 2, p. 167–175, 2023. https://doi.org/10.60087/jklst.vol2.n2.p175

[6] M. Alwaheidi, "A Data-Driven Threat Modelling Language for Ensuring Cyber Security Assurance," Doctoral dissertation, University of East London, 2024.

[7] P. Radanliev, D. Roure, P. Burnap, & O. Santos, "Epistemological equation for analysing uncontrollable states in complex systems: quantifying cyber risks from the internet of things", The Review of Socionetwork Strategies, vol. 15, no. 2, p. 381–411, 2021. https://doi.org/10.1007/s12626-021-00086-5

[8] V. Mavroeidis and A. Jøsang, "Data-driven threat hunting using sysmon", Proceedings of the 2nd International Conference on Cryptography, Security and Privacy, p. 82–88, 2018. https://doi.org/10.1145/3199478.3199490

[9] Kanthimathinathan, S. Saravanan, & P. Anbalagan, "A novel cyber resilience framework – strategies and best practices for today's organizations", International Journal on Recent and Innovation Trends in Computing and Communication, vol. 11, no. 8s, p. 86–96, 2023. https://doi.org/10.17762/ijritcc.v11i8s.7178

[10] F. Mızrak, "Integrating cybersecurity risk management into strategic management: a comprehensive literature review", Pressacademia, 2023. https://doi.org/10.17261/pressacademia.2023.1807

[11] Marotta and M. McShane, "Integrating a proactive technique into a holistic cyber risk management approach", Risk Management and Insurance Review, vol. 21, no. 3, p. 435–452, 2018. https://doi.org/10.1111/rmir.12109

[12] E. Kopp, L. Kaffenberger, & C. Wilson, "Cyber risk, market failures, and financial stability", IMF Working Papers, vol. 17, no. 185, 2017. https://doi.org/10.5089/9781484313787.001

[13] Z. Riaz Pitafi and T. Mumtaz Awan, 'Perspective Chapter: Cybersecurity and Risk Management – New Frontiers in Corporate Governance', Business, Management and Economics. IntechOpen, May 13, 2024. doi: 10.5772/intechopen.1005153.

[14] V. Mavroeidis and S. Bromander, "Cyber Threat Intelligence Model: An Evaluation of Taxonomies, Sharing Standards, and Ontologies within Cyber Threat Intelligence," 2017 European Intelligence and Security

Informatics Conference (EISIC), Athens, Greece, 2017, pp. 91–98, doi: 10.1109/EISIC.2017.20.
[15] H. Naeem, "Analysis of network security in iot-based cloud computing using machine learning", International Journal for Electronic Crime Investigation, vol. 7, no. 2, 2023. https://doi.org/10.54692/ijeci.2023.0702153
[16] Shaukat, K., Luo, S., Varadharajan, V., Hameed, I. A., & Xu, M. (2020). A survey on machine learning techniques for cyber security in the last decade. IEEE Access, 8, 222310–222354. https://doi.org/10.1109/access.2020.3041951
[17] Atadoga, E. Sodiya, U. Umoga, & O. Amoo, "A comprehensive review of machine learning's role in enhancing network security and threat detection", World Journal of Advanced Research and Reviews, vol. 21, no. 2, p. 877–886, 2024. https://doi.org/10.30574/wjarr.2024.21.2.0501
[18] M. Ling, W. Qi, D. Chang, X. Zhang, & C. Zhang, "Machine-learning-based network sparsification modeling for iots security analysis", 5th International Conference on Information Science, Electrical, and Automation Engineering (ISEAE 2023), p. 188, 2023. https://doi.org/10.1117/12.2690061
[19] N. Camacho, "The role of ai in cybersecurity: addressing threats in the digital age", Journal of Artificial Intelligence General Science (JAIGS) ISSN:3006-4023, vol. 3, no. 1, p. 143-154, 2024. https://doi.org/10.60087/jaigs.v3i1.75
[20] H. Alturkistani and S. Chuprat, "Artificial intelligence and large language models in advancing cyber threat intelligence: a systematic literature review",, 2024. https://doi.org/10.21203/rs.3.rs-5423193/v1
[21] P. Ranade, S. Mittal, A. Joshi, & K. Joshi, "Using deep neural networks to translate multi-lingual threat intelligence", 2018 IEEE International Conference on Intelligence and Security Informatics (ISI), p. 238–243, 2018. https://doi.org/10.1109/isi.2018.8587374
[22] M. Nikita, L. Kashyap, B. Singh, & D. Tyagi, "Ai enabled advance surveillance system", International Research Journal of Modernization in Engineering Technology and Science, 2023. https://doi.org/10.56726/irjmets37500
[23] P. Ravi, "Empowering security with machine learning for ransomware and malware detection", Interantional Journal of Scientific Research in Engineering and Management, vol. 08, no. 04, p. 1–5, 2024. https://doi.org/10.55041/ijsrem30675
[24] J. Gao, S. Chai, B. Zhang, & Y. Xia, "Research on network intrusion detection based on incremental extreme learning machine and adaptive principal component analysis", Energies, vol. 12, no. 7, p. 1223, 2019. https://doi.org/10.3390/en12071223

[25] Subroto and A. Apriyana, "Cyber risk prediction through social media big data analytics and statistical machine learning", Journal of Big Data, vol. 6, no. 1, 2019. https://doi.org/10.1186/s40537-019-0216-1
[26] Fakiha, "Enhancing cyber forensics with ai and machine learning: a study on automated threat analysis and classification", International Journal of Safety and Security Engineering, vol. 13, no. 4, p. 701–707, 2023. https://doi.org/10.18280/ijsse.130412
[27] M. Abdullahi, Y. Baashar, H. Alhussian, A. Alwadain, N. Aziz, L. Capretzet al., "Detecting cybersecurity attacks in internet of things using artificial intelligence methods: a systematic literature review", Electronics, vol. 11, no. 2, p. 198, 2022. https://doi.org/10.3390/electronics11020198
[28] P. Rushikesh, "A review: artificial intelligence and expert systems for cyber security", BOHR International Journal of Engineering, vol. 1, no. 1, p. 52–56, 2022. https://doi.org/10.54646/bije.2022.10
[29] P. Kshirsagar and A. Pawar, "Predictive analytics for cyber threats to enhance security in the cyber supply chain", Research Journal of Computer Systems and Engineering, vol. 4, no. 1, p. 102–109, 2023. https://doi.org/10.52710/rjcse.68
[30] S. Gudimetla and N. Kotha, "Enhancing threat detection and response strategies", International Research Journal of Modernization in Engineering Technology and Science, 2024. https://doi.org/10.56726/irjmets55883
[31] Hamid and M. Rahman, "A systematic literature review: ai, dl and machine learning incyber risk management",, 2024. https://doi.org/10.21203/rs.3.rs-4152375/v1
[32] L. Holder, "Cyber risk management with the help of artificial intelligence in smes: analysis of barriers and needs", 19th International Scientific Conference on Industrial Systems, p. 454–461, 2023. https://doi.org/10.24867/is-2023-vp1.1-1_00941
[33] P. Trim and Y. Lee, "Combining sociocultural intelligence with artificial intelligence to increase organizational cyber security provision through enhanced resilience", Big Data and Cognitive Computing, vol. 6, no. 4, p. 110, 2022. https://doi.org/10.3390/bdcc6040110
[34] S. Gudimetla and N. Kotha, "Enhancing threat detection and response strategies", International Research Journal of Modernization in Engineering Technology and Science, 2024. https://doi.org/10.56726/irjmets55883
[35] S. Rangaraju, "Secure by intelligence: enhancing products with ai-driven security measures", EPH - International Journal of Science

and Engineering, vol. 9, no. 3, p. 36–41, 2023. https://doi.org/10.53555/ephijse.v9i3.212

[36] P. Radanliev, D. Roure, R. Walton, M. Kleek, R. Montalvo, L. Maddox et al., "Artificial intelligence and machine learning in dynamic cyber risk analytics at the edge", SN Applied Sciences, vol. 2, no. 11, 2020. https://doi.org/10.1007/s42452-020-03559-4

[37] S. Saeed, S. Suayyid, M. Al-Ghamdi, H. Almuhaisen, & A. Almuhaideb, "A systematic literature review on cyber threat intelligence for organizational cybersecurity resilience", Sensors, vol. 23, no. 16, p. 7273, 2023. https://doi.org/10.3390/s23167273

[38] Bhardwaj, P. Dutta, & P. Chintale, "Ai-powered anomaly detection for kubernetes security: a systematic approach to identifying threats", Babylonian Journal of Machine Learning, vol. 2024, p. 142–148, 2024. https://doi.org/10.58496/bjml/2024/014

[39] T. Ige, C. Kiekintveld, and A. Piplai, "Deep learning-based speech and vision synthesis to improve phishing attack detection through a multilayer adaptive framework," Preprints, 2024. [Online]. Available: https://doi.org/10.20944/preprints202402.1557.v1

[40] L. F. G. Gutiérrez, F. Abri, M. Armstrong, A. S. Namin, and K. S. Jones, "Phishing detection through email embeddings," arXiv preprint arXiv:2012.14488, 2020. [Online]. Available: https://doi.org/10.48550/arxiv.2012.14488

[41] J. Govea, W. Gaibor-Naranjo, and W. Villegas-Ch, "Transforming cybersecurity into critical energy infrastructure: a study on the effectiveness of artificial intelligence," Systems, vol. 12, no. 5, p. 165, 2024. [Online]. Available: https://doi.org/10.3390/systems12050165

[42] H. Sarker, Y. B. Abushark, F. Alsolami, and A. I. Khan, "Intrudtree: a machine learning based cyber security intrusion detection model," Symmetry, vol. 12, no. 5, p. 754, 2020. [Online]. Available: https://doi.org/10.3390/sym12050754

[43] N. Noori, V. Bawanthad, M. K. Pakhare, R. Agrawal, and V. V. Kimbahune, "Phishing URL detection using machine learning," Int. J. for Res. in Applied Science and Engineering Technology, vol. 11, no. 5, pp. 3645–3648, 2023. [Online]. Available: https://doi.org/10.22214/ijraset.2023.52342

[44] P. M. Bhagat, S. Waghmare, M. Waje, R. Patil, K. Joshi, and M. Bakuli, "Feature classification and extreme learning machine based detection of phishing websites," Int. J. on Recent and Innovation Trends in Computing and Communication, vol. 11, no. 8s, pp. 132–136, 2023. [Online]. Available: https://doi.org/10.17762/ijritcc.v11i8s.7182

[45] Andriu, "Adaptive phishing detection: harnessing the power of artificial intelligence for enhanced email security," Romanian Cyber Security Journal, vol. 5, no. 1, pp. 3–9, 2023. [Online]. Available: https://doi.org/10.54851/v5i1y202301

[46] T. S. Tajamul and K. Aman, "Unveiling the efficacy of AI-based algorithms in phishing attack detection," J. of Informatics and Web Engineering, vol. 3, no. 2, pp. 116–133, 2024. [Online]. Available: https://doi.org/10.33093/jiwe.2024.3.2.9

[47] M. Sameen, K. Han, and S. O. Hwang, "Phishhaven—an efficient real-time AI phishing URLs detection system," IEEE Access, vol. 8, pp. 83425–83443, 2020. [Online]. Available: https://doi.org/10.1109/access.2020.2991403

[48] Govea, J., Gaibor-Naranjo, W., & Villegas-Ch, W. (2024). Transforming cybersecurity into critical energy infrastructure: a study on the effectiveness of artificial intelligence. Systems, 12(5), 165. https://doi.org/10.3390/systems12050165

[49] M. Sha and A. Kalbasi, "Artificial intelligence in cyber security: a survey", International Journal of Computer Engineering in Research Trends, vol. 9, no. 10, p. 201–205, 2022. https://doi.org/10.22362/ijcert/2022/v9/i10/v9i1003

[50] J. Agrawal, S. Kalra, & H. Gidwani, "Ai in cyber security", International Journal of Communication and Information Technology, vol. 4, no. 1, p. 46–53, 2023. https://doi.org/10.33545/2707661x.2023.v4.i1a.59

[51] Nyale, D. and Angolo, S. M. (2022). A survey of artificial intelligence in cyber security. International Journal of Computer Applications Technology and Research, 474–477. https://doi.org/10.7753/ijcatr1112.1014

[52] S. Kumar, U. Gupta, A. Singh, & A. Singh, "Artificial intelligence", Journal of Computers, Mechanical and Management, vol. 2, no. 3, p. 31–42, 2023. https://doi.org/10.57159/gadl.jcmm.2.3.23064

[53] G. BS, K. GM, & D. HA, "Ai-driven cyber security: security intelligence modelling", International Journal of Multidisciplinary Research and Growth Evaluation, vol. 4, no. 6, p. 961–965, 2023. https://doi.org/10.54660/.ijmrge.2023.4.6.961-965

[54] Pendey, "Artificial intelligence and cyber security", Journal Transnational Universal Studies, vol. 1, no. 2, p. 93–99, 2023. https://doi.org/10.58631/jtus.v1i2.15

[55] Z. Zhang, H. Hamadi, E. Damiani, C. Yeun, & F. Taher, "Explainable artificial intelligence applications in cyber security: state-of-the-art in research", IEEE Access, vol. 10, p. 93104–93139, 2022. https://doi.org/10.1109/access.2022.3204051

[56] L. Holder, "Cyber risk management with the help of artificial intelligence in smes: analysis of barriers and needs", 19th International Scientific Conference on Industrial Systems, p. 454–461, 2023. https://doi.org/10.24867/is-2023-vp1.1-1_00941
[57] P. Rushikesh, "A review: artificial intelligence and expert systems for cyber security", BOHR International Journal of Engineering, vol. 1, no. 1, p. 52–56, 2022. https://doi.org/10.54646/bije.2022.10
[58] Jeyalakshmi, "Reinventing Cyber Security with AI," International Journal of Computer Applications Technology and Research, vol. 13, no. 1, pp. 7–8, 2024, doi: 10.7753/IJCATR1301.1002.
[59] T. Islam, S. M. Islam, A. Sarkar, A. Obaidur, R. Khan, R. Paul, and M. S. Bari, "Artificial Intelligence in Fraud Detection and Financial Risk Mitigation: Future Directions and Business Applications," International Journal for Multidisciplinary Research, 2024. https://doi.org/10.36948/ijfmr.2024.v06i05.28496
[60] N. Jain and S. Patil, "Artificial intelligence models for fraud detection: advancements, challenges, and future prospects", International Journal of Global Innovations and Solutions (IJGIS), 2024. https://doi.org/10.21428/e90189c8.6d8ab5f6
[61] P. Shoetan and B. Familoni, "Transforming fintech fraud detection with advanced artificial intelligence algorithms", Finance &Amp; Accounting Research Journal, vol. 6, no. 4, p. 602–625, 2024. https://doi.org/10.51594/farj.v6i4.1036
[62] M. Ismaeil, "Harnessing ai for next-generation financial fraud detection: a data-driven revolution", Journal of Ecohumanism, vol. 3, no. 7, p. 811–821, 2024. https://doi.org/10.62754/joe.v3i7.4248
[63] J. Smiles and A. Kumar, "Synthetic minority oversampling and smote regularised deep autoencoders neural network techniques for fraud prediction in financial payment services", International Journal of Innovative Technology and Exploring Engineering, vol. 8, no. 12, p. 3908–2915, 2019. https://doi.org/10.35940/ijitee.l3419.1081219
[64] O. Odeyemi, N. Mhlongo, E. Nwankwo, & O. Soyombo, "Reviewing the role of ai in fraud detection and prevention in financial services", International Journal of Science and Research Archive, vol. 11, no. 1, p. 2101–2110, 2024. https://doi.org/10.30574/ijsra.2024.11.1.0279
[65] K. Venigandla and N. Vemuri, "Rpa and ai-driven predictive analytics in banking for fraud detection", Tuijin Jishu/Journal of Propulsion Technology, 2022. https://doi.org/10.52783/tjjpt.v43.i4.5531s
[66] M. Rahmati, "Real-time financial fraud detection using adaptive graph neural networks and federated learning",, 2025. https://doi.org/10.21203/rs.3.rs-6026136/v1

[67] Mishra, "Fraud detection: a study of adaboost classifier and k-means clustering", SSRN Electronic Journal, 2021. https://doi.org/10.2139/ssrn.3789879

[68] Mittelstadt, P. Allo, M. Taddeo, S. Wachter, & L. Floridi, "The ethics of algorithms: mapping the debate", Big Data &Amp; Society, vol. 3, no. 2, 2016. https://doi.org/10.1177/2053951716679679

[69] V. Venkatesh, "Adoption and use of ai tools: a research agenda grounded in utaut", Annals of Operations Research, vol. 308, no. 1-2, p. 641–652, 2021. https://doi.org/10.1007/s10479-020-03918-9

[70] H. Rosenbaum, E. Gumusel, M. Sanfilippo, M. Sweeney, S. Sawyer, & Z. Zhou, "Exploring some impacts of advances in artificial intelligence: a social informatics approach", Proceedings of the Association for Information Science and Technology, vol. 61, no. 1, p. 818–821, 2024. https://doi.org/10.1002/pra2.1109

[71] Murdoch, "Privacy and artificial intelligence: challenges for protecting health information in a new era", BMC Medical Ethics, vol. 22, no. 1, 2021. https://doi.org/10.1186/s12910-021-00687-3

[72] Cebulla, Z. Szpak, & G. Knight, "Preparing to work with artificial intelligence: assessing whs when using ai in the workplace", International Journal of Workplace Health Management, vol. 16, no. 4, p. 294–312, 2023. https://doi.org/10.1108/ijwhm-09-2022-0141

[73] X. Gu, F. Sabrina, Z. Fan, & S. Sohail, "A review of privacy enhancement methods for federated learning in healthcare systems", International Journal of Environmental Research and Public Health, vol. 20, no. 15, p. 6539, 2023. https://doi.org/10.3390/ijerph20156539

[74] M. Huda, A. Awaludin, & H. Siregar, "Legal challenges in regulating artificial intelligence: a comparative study of privacy and data protection laws", International Journal of Social and Human, vol. 1, no. 2, p. 116–125, 2024. https://doi.org/10.59613/g8dc9v94

[75] Hamid and M. Rahman, "A systematic literature review: ai, dl and machine learning incyber risk management", 2024. https://doi.org/10.21203/rs.3.rs-4152375/v1

[76] O. Dopamu, J. Adesiyan, & F. Oke, "Artificial intelligence and us financial institutions: review of ai-assisted regulatory compliance for cybersecurity", World Journal of Advanced Research and Reviews, vol. 21, no. 3, p. 964–979, 2024. https://doi.org/10.30574/wjarr.2024.21.3.0791

[77] S. Pyla, T. Krishna, & M. Mahboub, "Ai in cybersecurity: challenges, directions, and research needs - a review", International Research Journal of Modernization in Engineering Technology and Science, 2024. https://doi.org/10.56726/irjmets51263

[78] Haykal, B. Ascher, H. Cartier, & M. Gold, "Exploring the landscape of ai adoption in cosmetic medicine and surgery: insights from the 25th imcas congress (international master course in aging science)", Journal of Cosmetic Dermatology, vol. 23, no. 8, p. 2673–2675, 2024. https://doi.org/10.1111/jocd.16316

[79] N. Katiyar, M. Tripathi, M. Kumar, M. Verma, A. Sahu, & S. Saxena, "Ai and cyber-security: enhancing threat detection and response with machine learning." Educational Administration Theory and Practices, 2024. https://doi.org/10.53555/kuey.v30i4.2377

[80] S. Temara, "Harnessing the power of artificial intelligence to enhance next-generation cybersecurity",, 2024. https://doi.org/10.20944/preprints202408.0763.v1

[81] Hamid and M. Rahman, "A systematic literature review: ai, dl and machine learning incyber risk management", 2024. https://doi.org/10.21203/rs.3.rs-4152375/v1

[82] S. Gudimetla and N. Kotha, "Enhancing threat detection and response strategies", International Research Journal of Modernization in Engineering Technology and Science, 2024. https://doi.org/10.56726/irjmets55883

[83] Ghillani, "Deep learning and artificial intelligence framework to improve the cyber security" 2022. https://doi.org/10.22541/au.166379475.54266021/v1

[84] S. Kumar, U. Gupta, A. Singh, & A. Singh, "Artificial intelligence", Journal of Computers, Mechanical and Management, vol. 2, no. 3, p. 31–42, 2023. https://doi.org/10.57159/gadl.jcmm.2.3.23064

[85] S. Islam, N. Basheer, S. Silvestri, S. Papastergiou, & M. Ciampi, "Intelligent dynamic cybersecurity risk management framework with explainability and interpretability of ai models for enhancing security and resilience of digital infrastructure", 2024. https://doi.org/10.21203/rs.3.rs-4796809/v1

[86] K. Chu and W. Guo, "Passenger spoofing attack for artificial intelligence-based mobility-as-a-service", 2023 IEEE 26th International Conference on Intelligent Transportation Systems (ITSC), p. 4874–4880, 2023. https://doi.org/10.1109/itsc57777.2023.10422567

[87] L. Holder, "Cyber risk management with the help of artificial intelligence in smes: analysis of barriers and needs", 19th International Scientific Conference on Industrial Systems, p. 454–461, 2023. https://doi.org/10.24867/is-2023-vp1.1-1_00941

[88] Jerbi, "Beyond firewalls: navigating the jungle of emerging cybersecurity trends", Journal of Current Trends in Computer Science Research, vol. 2, no. 2, 2023. https://doi.org/10.33140/jctcsr.02.02.14

[89] P. Trim and Y. Lee, "Combining sociocultural intelligence with artificial intelligence to increase organizational cyber security provision through enhanced resilience", Big Data and Cognitive Computing, vol. 6, no. 4, p. 110, 2022. https://doi.org/10.3390/bdcc6040110
[90] S. Ramakrishnan and D. Chittibala, "Enhancing cyber resilience: convergence of siem, soar, and ai in 2024", International Journal of Computing and Engineering, vol. 5, no. 2, p. 36–44, 2024. https://doi.org/10.47941/ijce.1754

5

AI for Threat Detection and Intelligence

Zeeshan Ali Haider[1], Asim Zeb[2], Taj Rahman[1], Inam Ullah[3*], Muhammad Zeeshan[2], M. A. Al-Khasawneh[4,5], and Muhammad Fayaz[6]

[1]Department of Computer Science, Qurtuba University of Science & Information Technology, Pakistan
[2]Department of Computer Science, Abbottabad University of Science & Technology, Pakistan
[3]Department of Computer Engineering, Gachon University, Republic of Korea;
[4]Hourani Center for Applied Scientific Research, Al-Ahliyya Amman University, Jordan
[5]School of Computing, Skyline University College, UAE
[6]Department of Computer Science and Engineering, Sejong University, South Korea

Email: zeeshan.ali9049@gmail.com; asimzeb1@gmail.com; tajuom@gmail.com; inam.fragrance@gmail.com; zeeshan249@gmail.com; mahmoudalkhasawneh@outlook.com; muhammadfayaz@sju.ac.kr

Abstract

The rise of cyber threats that are more advanced and widespread than before demands that existing methods of protection must evolve beyond their capacity to face the specificities of contemporary digital surroundings. The emergence of technologies, including 5G, IoT, and autonomous systems, has greatly enlarged the attack surface and rendered traditional risk management techniques ineffective. Artificial intelligence (AI) has emerged as a creative response in the cybersecurity arena, where there are more sophisticated ways for detection, response, and prevention of the threat. Leveraging large volumes of data available to train these systems, they can respond quickly to both new and evolving threats, which enhances detection and ultimately

DOI: 10.1201/9788743808077-5

reduces the time to respond to potential attacks. This chapter describes the essential role of AI in transforming the approach to cybersecurity and how AI can address a range of threats, including malware, phishing, s), and insider threats. AI systems play a crucial role in increasing cybersecurity by providing real-time and adaptable defensive capabilities through the use of machine learning, deep learning, and anomaly detection systems working in parallel to prevent potential attacks in changing and risk-fed environments. AI systems will not only recognize an attack when it happens, but they will also predict attacks by building a model of your organization and monitoring changes over time. Advanced systems can recognize when a new risk arises and an attack is being launched. This chapter also highlights the challenges of deploying AI in cybersecurity, including data quality required for training models, driving the scalability solutions from AI motivation, and ethical challenges of fairness and privacy. An overview of those using AI in solving issues related to emerging technologies, specifically its application in protecting critical infrastructure and securing autonomous systems, as well as data on securing the increasing number of connected devices in the Internet of Things (IoT) systems. The combination of AI, blockchain, and quantum computing may lead to new and more powerful security architectures. Cyber threats continue to grow and evolve, AI will be a key enabler of next-generation security strategies that can help to ensure data integrity and privacy as well as protect against challenges in today's digital and connected environment.

5.1 Introduction

There are many benefits to being in the digital era, such as better connections, improved efficiency, and increased access to information. This has ramped up the attack surface for cybercriminals, who are attacking digital systems more than ever. Cyber threats have become increasingly sophisticated in recent years, diverse and costly to remediate, as attackers utilize advanced techniques to breach systems, exploit vulnerabilities, and maximize damage. Different kinds of cyberattacks like malware, ransomware, phishing, advanced persistent threats (APTs), and denial of service attacks are always prowling to dive organizations, businesses, and even governments [1]. Threats not only compromise data privacy and economic stability, but they can also undermine faith in both digital systems and critical infrastructures. Cybercriminals have transformed from a group of opportunistic attackers to organized groups or state-sponsored entities that use advanced tactics to conduct coordinated, long-term campaigns [2]. The high volume and growing sophistication of these attacks demand increasingly sophisticated detection and defense.

Conventional security approaches, including signature detection-based systems, have not been able to keep up with these dynamic and rapidly emerging threats, which also calls for a new-age solution, an intelligent and scalable solution designed to proactively address the new cybercrime.

Reducing cyber threats or providing assistance during an active intrusion, artificial intelligence has emerged as a difficult tool in this process, acting as an intelligent layer of defense that can efficiently process immense volumes of data, identify patterns, and flag anomalies far quicker than a human can analyze [3]. The adaptive nature of AI allows it to adapt and learn from new methods of attack, which is a critical component of modern cybersecurity architectures because organizations must outpace increasingly sophisticated adversaries in cyberspace. Systems are as open to as many cyber threats as the attack surface has multiplied [4]. These threats, such as malware, ransomware, phishing, and APTs, have evolved and diversified into more advanced forms and represent an actual risk to the security of data, as well as economic and reputational damage. Getting organized cybercrime is more organized than ever, utilizing advanced tactics and tools to exploit vulnerabilities in networks and systems.

Legacy cybersecurity solutions like signature-based detection systems have proven unable to prevent these evolving attacks. As cyberattacks grow ever more sophisticated, it is clear that more innovative solutions are necessary. Artificial intelligence (AI) has become a critical component in this contest as we can connect massive data in real time, recognize patterns, and detect hidden anomalies more quickly and more accurately than a human. The adversary used previous attacks to learn from the outcome and the correlation between old and new threats. This makes the AI prepared to protect itself from more advanced attacks, adding a dynamic and adaptive layer of protection that traditional systems lack.

5.1.1 AI's role in revolutionizing threat detection

Threat detection and response are being revolutionized by AI. The traditional methods of cybersecurity are based on the utilization of pre-defined signatures and rules, which render them inefficient in the face of new and complex threats [5]. Through machine learning and deep learning, AI enables systems to identify subtle patterns, find anomalies, and forecast potential risks within large datasets. Machine learning enables algorithms to evolve with new data, which means that AI systems can develop the ability to detect new attack methods without having ever seen the actual threat. Deep learning soon developed AI capabilities to tokenize and parse unstructured data like network traffic, system logs, images, video feeds, etc., by mimicking human neural networks [6]. It improves the ability of AI to detect previously unseen threats. AI-based systems are versatile and can easily handle the increasing complexity and volume of cyberattacks, identifying and neutralizing potential threats in real time. Additionally, AI-driven security systems are autonomous, enabling them to respond to breaches in real time and limit their impact on both organizations and individuals. With the continually growing attack surface, AI ensures security solutions are agile enough to meet new threats as they evolve.

5.1.2 Key objectives of AI in threat intelligence systems

Threat intelligence systems have greatly benefited from AI, making it possible to quickly and accurately gain an understanding of the context and scale of a cyberattack. Figure 5.1 depicts the key objectives of AI in threat intelligence systems and is also described as follows:

- **Automating data collection and analysis**: AI also has the capability to collect and analyze data from numerous sources of network traffic, system logs, and external threat feeds to detect possible threats independently. This improves the workload of human analysts and speeds up threat detection.
- **Predicting emerging threats**: AI analyzes both historical and real-time data to identify trends and patterns that signal potential future attacks. AI helps to identify these patterns early and take preventive actions before the attack happens.
- **Enhancing threat detection accuracy**: It detects smaller anomalies and correlations in huge datasets, which traditional systems cannot see. Threat detection becomes more precise and accurate with fewer false positives and false negatives.
- **Real-time decision-making**: AI is used for real-time decision-making by analyzing data from disparate sources and providing contextually relevant insights. It allows security teams to prioritize their response to threats in terms of severity and impact and take appropriate and timely action.
- **Improving response and mitigation**: By recommending or automatically applying mitigation techniques, for example, isolating compromised systems or blocking malicious requests, AI systems help minimize the damage and downtime associated with cyber incidents.

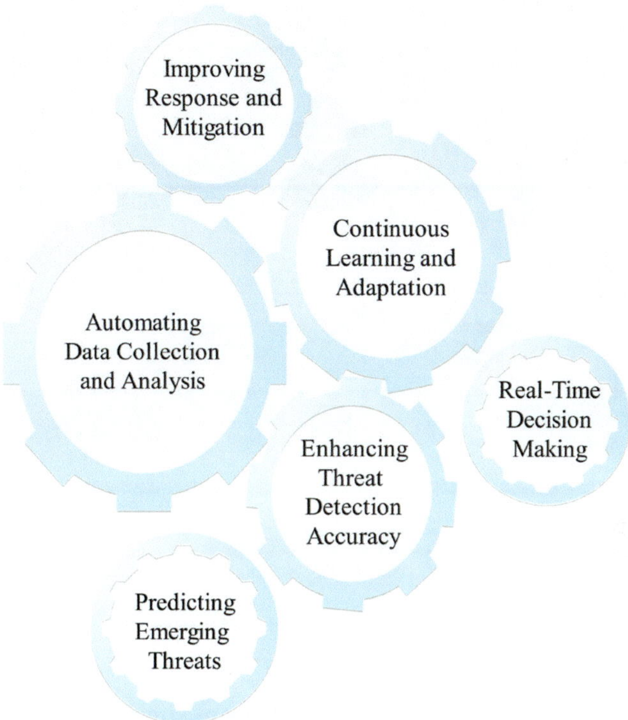

Figure 5.1 Key objectives of AI in threat intelligence systems.

- **Continuous learning and adaptation**: Machine learning systems require them to constantly learn from new data, adapt to new threats, and keep threat intelligence systems relevant. The capability to adapt to new attack methods makes them more reliable in countering the latest cyber threats.

AI is revolutionizing cybersecurity through these objectives as it becomes more proactive, effective, and scalable. Life is such that the mere complexity of cyber threats is going up, and so will the demand for such solutions, thereby rendering AI into the very foundation of modern cybersecurity strategies.

5.2 Types of Cyber Threats

Cyber threats have become more diverse and sophisticated, and people, organizations, and even critical infrastructure face serious threats [7]. Digital technologies and interconnected systems have grown, and so too have the opportunities for attackers to exploit vulnerabilities for financial gain, data

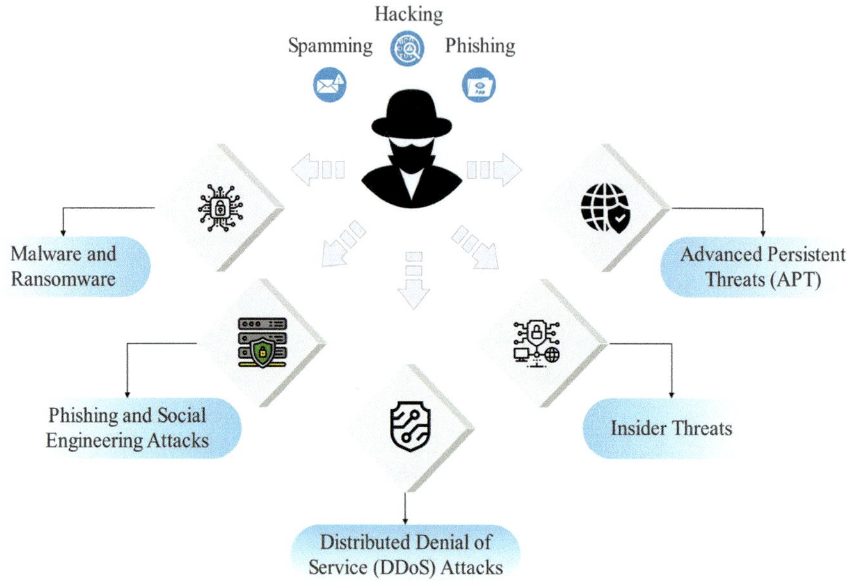

Figure 5.2 Types of cyber threats.

theft, or disruption. These threats can vary from simple scams to advanced, long-honed efforts designed to evade detection. Figure 5.2 illustrates different types of cyber threats, and understanding the nature and execution of these evolving threats is paramount to counter them effectively. In this section, we delve into some of the most prominent categories of cyber threats, explore their modus operandi, and discuss how AI can aid in their detection and mitigation.

5.2.1 Malware and ransomware

Malware is malicious software that can include anything designed to infiltrate, damage, or interrupt systems. Malware takes different forms, including viruses, worms, Trojans, and spyware that can infect computers, mobile devices, and networks. Once the malware reaches a system, it may steal sensitive information, corrupt data, or crash systems [8]. Ransomware is an especially harmful kind of malware that locks targeted information or systems and requests a fee, typically in cryptocurrency, for its liberation. The ransomware plague with big attacks like WannaCry and NotPetya proved as devastating as any malware can be, with data losses, financial losses, and dents in reputation. Behavioral analysis by AI-based solutions can track unusual file encryption activities or suspicious access patterns to spot and prevent ransomware attacks before they become critical.

5.2.2 Phishing and social engineering attacks

Phishing is one of the most common and deceptive forms of a cyberattack. This often involves attackers sending fraudulent communications [9], most commonly, emails to obtain sensitive information that was intended for the recipient (such as passwords or bank account details). These emails often appear genuine, impersonating trusted sources, such as banks or well-known companies. Social engineering is a broader concept, where a human is tricked into bypassing security mechanisms or revealing sensitive information. They might employ methods like pretexting, baiting, and impersonation. They assist in detecting phishing attempts by analyzing email content, identifying malicious links, and flagging behaviors that are commonly leveraged in social engineering tactics.

5.2.3 Distributed Denial of Service (DDoS) attacks

Distributed Denial of Service (DDoS) attacks aim to destroy a system or network by overwhelming it with traffic, making it inaccessible to legitimate users. Unlike DDoS, which targets a single device, a DDoS targets multiple devices (botnets) and sends requests to a website or service. DDoS attacks can expose businesses to the risk of losing revenue and damaging an organization's image [10]. Detective method for Denial-of-Service attacks by analyzing network traffic, machine learning algorithms can help identify if there is an ongoing Denial-of-Service attack on the system by identifying abnormal spikes or behaviors, which could significantly reduce the time needed for mitigation.

5.2.4 Insider threats

Insider threats are from individuals within the organization, such as employees or contractors, who misuse their access to harm the organization's security [11]. These threats can be malicious, such as an insider intentionally stealing data or damaging the system, or negligent, where an insider accidentally exposes data or unknowingly falls for phishing attacks. AI can help detect insider threats, monitor user behavior, and detect any actions that diverge from normal behavior, like accessing sensitive files or transferring large amounts of data without being authorized, etc. AI systems can detect and flag suspicious activity in real time, enabling organizations to prevent insider damage or mitigate the consequences.

5.2.5 Advanced persistent threats (APT)

Advanced persistent threats (APTs) are usually executed by well-resourced and competent adversaries, including state-backed entities, that seek to exfiltrate sensitive data or impact critical operations. Unlike most cyberattacks, which are designed to have immediate effects, APTs move methodically and discreetly through a network and are careful to remain under the radar [12]. AI is essential in APT detection by monitoring network traffic and systems for evidence of compromise. However, it provides early detection and prevention of this type of attack by identifying the unusual patterns and behavior that may indicate an APT, such that the attack may not achieve its objectives.

5.3 AI Techniques in Threat Detection

Cyber threats have become increasingly complex and massive in scale, rendering many traditional threat-detection mechanisms incapable of covering the magnitude and sophistication of the attacks. This adaptation renders these signatures more dynamic and flexible than their earlier counterparts, as traditional threat detection approaches [13]. Random forest, naive bayes, and decision trees are some of the commonly used machine learning algorithms, whereas natural language processing also plays an important role in identifying threats, and deep learning algorithms, vision, and hybrid AI techniques are also prominent features of modern threat detection systems. These capabilities enable systems to mine massive repositories of data in order to quickly detect patterns and to react to that data in response to emerging threats, all at a speed that far exceeds the capabilities of manual processes or traditional security tools [14]. These advanced technologies can help organizations improve their security posture by allowing them to effectively secure their networks, data, and infrastructure from cybersecurity threats. AI techniques for threat detection are shown in Figure 5.3.

5.3.1 Machine learning models for threat detection

This computing and digital transformation has opened the container, and one of the biggest innovations is machine learning, which enables systems to automatically learn from data patterns and a pre-programmed threat detection mechanism [15]. They analyze large datasets such as network traffic,

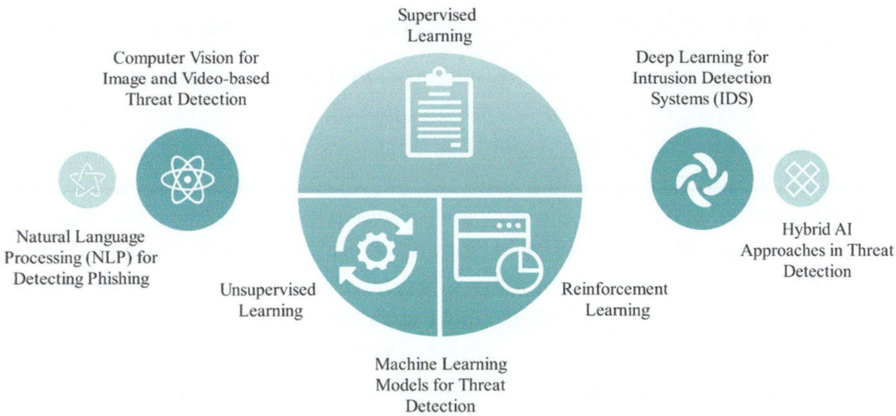

Figure 5.3 AI techniques in threat detection.

system logs, and historical attack data to classify behaviors as normal or suspicious. This includes supervised learning, unsupervised learning, and reinforcement learning.

- **Supervised learning**: This approach relies on labeled data to train the system to identify particular threats like malware or phishing attempts. The training consists of several examples of malicious and benign activities that are already known, and the model learns to classify them in unseen data.
- **Unsupervised learning**: There are many differences between supervised and unsupervised learning, the most important factor being that unsupervised learning looks for anomalies without needing labeled data. Model-based detection builds a baseline of normal activity and compares incoming data to that baseline at the highest levels of detail, helping identify unknown threats and new attack vectors because the system flags anything abnormal, even activity that appears benign but deviates from what is expected.
- **Reinforcement learning:** In the case of reinforcement learning, systems are able to learn over time from the environment around them by taking actions and getting feedback based on the selected actions. This approach is most suitable for countering dynamic threats as it can enhance detection techniques in real time.

These machine learning models further improve threat detection by recognizing the potential risks at a much lower rate and more accurately, lowering human error and response time.

5.3.2 Natural language processing (NLP) for detecting phishing

Phishing attacks use phony communication to deceive individuals into giving up sensitive information. NLP techniques may be used to examine text-based data, including emails as well as chat messages, to look for phishing indicators. Using processes like sentiment analysis, keyword extraction, and semantic analysis, NLP can identify suspicious patterns in language, unusual immediacy, and malicious links in communications [16]. NLP also helps in detecting phishing websites, as they often have similar URLs or content as legitimate sites. Machine learning or AI systems can use data from the web developer to make a determination on whether the web system contains malicious content, due to patterns it learned in the past. This enables organizations to block users from engaging in phishing attempts and helps mitigate data theft and financial damages.

5.3.3 Computer vision for image and video-based threat detection

Computer vision is an aspect of AI that focuses on seeing and interpreting visual data by machines, which can be used directly to detect security threats in images and video footage. It is particularly useful for physical security, like finding suspicious activity in surveillance cameras or unauthorized access to restricted areas [17]. AI systems developed for computer vision can analyze video streams in real time and detect diverse anomalies such as a person loitering in restricted zones, unauthorized device connections, or stray movements. Apart from graphics, AI can analyze images to identify other types of cyber threats, for instance, tampered paperwork, modified photos, or counterfeit visual information normally utilized in social engineering assaults. Deep learning techniques like convolutional neural networks (CNNs) enable computer vision systems to recognize and monitor suspicious activities more quickly and accurately than typical security solutions.

5.3.4 Deep learning for intrusion detection systems (IDS)

Deep learning, a subset of machine learning, uses a structure that imitates the human brain neural network to analyze multilayer complex patterns. One of the biggest advantages of this model incorporates the application of deep learning in IDS by detecting minor traces and signals of a potential attack in the network, computer system, and user behavior [18]. We can use deep learning algorithms, such as recurrent neural networks (RNNs) and long short-term memory (LSTM) networks, for intrusion detection when sequential or time-dependent data is available. These systems can learn incrementally from fresh data, enhancing their capabilities to identify never-before-seen classes of attacks, such as zero-day vulnerabilities or advanced persistent threats (APTs). This pattern sensitivity of deep learning can be hierarchized in finding attacks, therefore providing a more dependable alternative to the conventional IDS systems for proactive threat identification and prevention.

5.3.5 Hybrid AI approaches in threat detection

Hybrid AI approaches leverage multiple AI methods to optimize the capability of tactical detection systems. Ensemble methods use the strengths of multiple models, such as machine learning, deep learning, and rule-based expert systems, to achieve more accurate and flexible detection systems [19]. For instance, it can implement a hybrid system that uses machine learning for identifying known threats and deep learning models to detect novel or changing attacks at the very same time. And either computer vision for physical security or NLP for detecting phishing or social engineering attempts could be a part of the system as well. When applied together, they provide a multi-layered response that reduces false positives and makes for a better alarm reaction. Hybrid systems utilize this power with different approaches to constantly evolve and adapt to new threats, protecting organizations from an increasingly complex web of cyber risks.

5.4 AI in Threat Intelligence

With the threat landscape evolving to become more complex, the demand for cutting-edge, real-time threat intelligence is at an all-time high. Traditional threat intelligence approaches with a heavy dependence on human analysis and manual intervention are no longer sufficient to keep pace with the volume and complexity of emerging threats [20]. The AI revolution has changed how threat intelligence is collected, analyzed, and shared, allowing organizations to better predict, defend against, and react to attacks. With AI technologies, threat intelligence as presented in Figure 5.4 becomes more automatic in terms of data collection, identification of attack patterns, and provision of real-time insights that make decision-making more effective. Organizations using AI learn to proactively bolster their security posture, respond to incidents faster, and lead the way in dealing with new threats. This material evaluates the impact of AI on threat intelligence and how it helps to make cybersecurity more proactive.

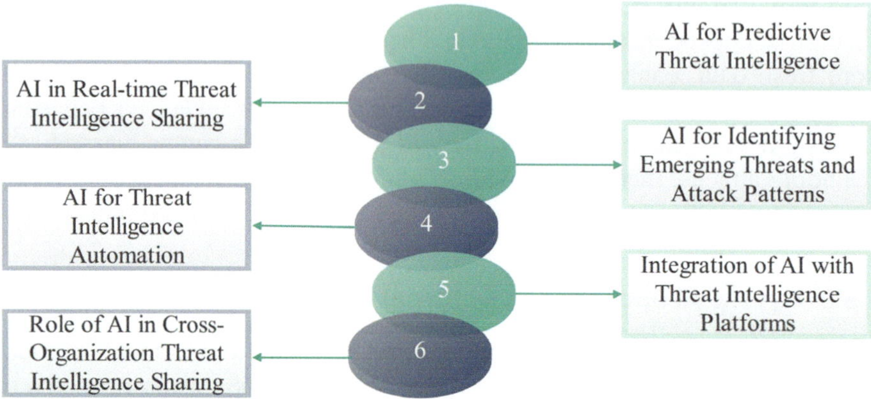

Figure 5.4 AI in threat intelligence.

5.4.1 AI for predictive threat intelligence

Predictive threat intelligence employs data and machine learning algorithms to predict future cyberattacks by analyzing historical data and trends. AI can examine large amounts of data from multiple sources, including past attack data, threat feeds, and network traffic, to identify potential vulnerabilities and attack pathways [21]. It provides insight into attacks before they happen by formulating patterns and correlations among this data. Predictive models can estimate the likelihood of certain types of attacks, such as phishing campaigns, ransomware outbreaks, or zero-day vulnerabilities, enabling organizations to proactively shore up defenses. Companies can use the power of AI to quickly process and analyze enormous amounts of data to take preventive measures to reduce the chances of successful cyberattacks.

5.4.2 AI in real-time threat intelligence sharing

Real-time threat intelligence sharing is so important for organizations in terms of cybersecurity. This process is further augmented by AI, which can automatically collect, aggregate, and spread this information on various platforms. AI-based systems can utilize data from a wide range of sources, from threat feeds from global threats to internal security logs, and finally, security research available from outside sources, to discover and evaluate new threats [22]. AI-powered platforms can automatically notify organizations of possible threats, enabling time-sensitive responses. Observing threats in one organization is useful, but the data can be aggregated from different organizations to provide collaborative community-wide multi-threat analytics with actionable intelligence in identifying and mitigating threats quickly. AI contributes to overall cybersecurity resilience by reducing the time to detect and respond to cyber incidents through an automated threat-sharing process.

5.4.3 AI for identifying emerging threats and attack patterns

It is vital given the continual evolution of cybercriminal activity, which have mechanisms in place to detect new attack trends and recognize emerging risks. This mission is one area where AI excels, it can draw insights from massive volumes of data in order to detect patterns that may signal new attack methods. AI can use machine learning algorithms to detect abnormal behavior or indicators of compromise that could point to the start of a new attack [23]. AI's adaptive nature to evolving attack vectors enables it to identify emerging threats that may bypass conventional signature-based detection mechanisms. Using machine learning, such models can be trained to learn what constitutes "normal" behavior and can flag outliers as potential intrusions or threats, making these models highly effective at detecting zero-day attacks as well as other attacks that are not already in the database of known threats. These early alerts enable proactive threat detection, which can help an organization remain a step ahead of attackers.

5.4.4 AI for threat intelligence automation

AI and automation are an innovator for cybersecurity organizations when it comes to threat intelligence processes. AI automates repetitive tasks like data collection, correlation, analysis, and reporting, greatly alleviating security teams. AI frees security professionals to leverage their skills by automating low-level tasks, such as incident response and strategic planning [24]. Through machine learning, AI-powered automation can further improve the speed and accuracy of threat detection through continuous real-time data analysis, without human involvement, while identifying possible threats. For example, the systems can automatically send alerts when suspicious activity is identified, analyze the threat, and suggest an appropriate response. AI makes the detection process faster, and it also minimizes human error and enhances the efficiency of threat intelligence systems.

5.4.5 Integration of AI with threat intelligence platforms

AI can make threat intelligence platforms of the future dream come through by unlocking data mining and automation capabilities. An extensive analysis of possible threats with AI can supplement traditional threat intelligence, especially security information and event management (SIEM). A machine learning and data mining-based means for analyzing patterns and tracking threatening doings at a higher speed, than normally allowed by a regular cybersecurity system is one of the options provided by AI, where systems are also going to be able to build a more comprehensive view of the threat landscape by identifying correlations and trends that are sometimes not spotted by any of the traditional tools [25]. AI can automate the collection of data, enhance pattern recognition, and predict the propensity of threats to emerge, making it an essential component of any threat intelligence platform. These platforms become integrated and facilitate faster and more accurate insights for accelerating response to help programs bolster their cyberattack defenses.

5.4.6 Role of AI in cross-organization threat intelligence sharing

AI and machine learning facilitate the sharing of threat intelligence across organizations is key to this cooperation. AI-driven platforms enable organizations to exchange threat data, attack vectors, and defense examples in real time. This will allow AI to automatically collect, analyze, and publish threat data across many organizations, ensuring that rising threats are known to everyone. AI can help cross-organizations in threat intelligence sharing by extracting insights and cross-referencing data from different sources [26]. Aggregating data across many organizations gives AI the ability to recognize larger attack campaigns and build a more complete picture of the threat landscape. Maintaining organizational success in defense against persisting compromised attack vectors improves the overall security posture across the community.

5.5 AI-Based Threat Detection Systems

Traditional methods of detection, based on evolving signatures or manual processes, are no longer adequate for the detection of advanced and evolving attacks as the threat landscape continues to evolve. AI-driven threat detection systems offer a more proactive, dynamic, and adaptive solution for detecting bad actors at the network, endpoint, and application layers. Using advanced machine learning algorithms, behavioral analysis, and data correlation, AI systems can identify known and unknown threats with increased accuracy and swiftness [27]. AI systems for identifying threats can constantly monitor, learn from, and adapt to new data, making sure they stay relevant in identifying attack vectors that they have never seen. This section covers many

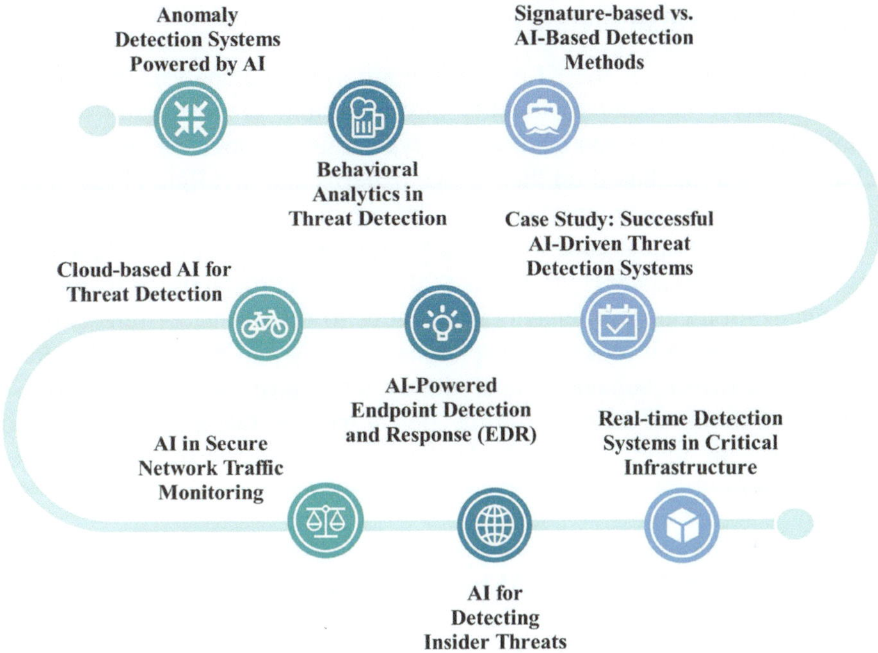

Figure 5.5 AI-based threat detection systems.

aspects and tricks used in AI-based threat detection systems as illustrated in Figure 5.5 tailored in such a way that it enhances cybersecurity production across several domains.

5.5.1 Anomaly detection systems powered by AI

AI-based threat detection is built on anomaly detection systems. Such systems function by spotting aberrate patterns of disbursement or operational activity that exclude a standard expected normal baseline. One of the sectors where AI has exhibited great potential is in recognizing anomalies in data sets. The model can also recognize anomalies based on previous system activity, to detect new and emerging attack patterns that would not match any historical data, unlike traditional approaches based on manually crafted, static rules [28]. For instance, by evaluating patterns in network traffic, user behavior, or system processes, machine learning algorithms can be trained to identify disciplinary and normal activities. When a user tries to log in or access sensitive data at an unusual hour, or a device from another location, an anomaly detection system, powered by AI, can mark it as an anomaly and alert the security team.

5.5.2 Behavioral analytics in threat detection

Behavioral analytics is the AI-enabled monitoring and analysis of user and entity behavior in order to identify any abnormal or potentially harmful actions. These systems can learn what a typical user's, device's, or network's behavior looks like based on their usage patterns and highlight changes that can flag possible malicious activity. These can include anything from an unauthorized attempt to access certain systems or data, to unusual data transfers, to attempts to access systems that fall outside a typical user's livelihood. An organization can use behavioral analytics to detect insider threats more effectively because it looks for suspicious behavior and not external indicators [29]. AI-driven behavioral analytics systems have the ability to process extensive amounts of data in real time, detect patterns that may go unnoticed and indicate an attack, and send alerts to security teams so they can take action quickly.

5.5.3 Signature-based vs. AI-based detection methods

Traditional signature-based detection techniques match known malware or attack patterns against signatures stored in a database. While it excels in dealing with previously identified threats, signature-based detection faces the limit of failing to discover an attack with a new or advanced variant signature that has not been previously used. In contrast, AI-based detection moves beyond the process of signature matching to identify abnormal patterns, behavior, and anomalies indicating the presence of an attack, regardless of whether that attack has been previously identified [30]. AI-based systems are particularly beneficial against zero-day attacks, APTs, and new attack vectors. The integration of AI-based detection and signature-based methods can lead to an agile and wide-reaching threat detection strategy for organizations.

5.5.4 Case study: Successful AI-driven threat detection systems

One notable example of a successful AI-driven threat detection system is leveraging AI to sift through millions of transaction data points in real time, detecting irregularities that may signify fraudulent behavior, such as spending patterns failing to match those of known customers or transactions originating from geographically unusual points of sale [31]. Through the use of AI, these organizations were able to minimize the time required to identify fraudulent transactions from hours to minutes, allowing them to minimize financial loss to a large extent. Machine learning combined with behavioral analytics has enabled the company to proactively manage risks and act quickly, showcasing the power of such technology within the realm of cybersecurity.

5.5.5 AI-powered endpoint detection and response (EDR)

Endpoint detection and response (EDR) solutions play a crucial role in detecting, investigating, and responding to potential threats found on endpoint devices, including laptops, servers, and mobile devices within an organization's network. AI-based EDRs build upon traditional endpoint defenses with automatic detection of unusual behavior and anomalies, with real-time alerts. An EDR, of course, goes deeper, as AI can correlate activity in multiple endpoints to recognize patterns that render evidence of a coordinated attack or propagation of malware [32]. Another useful application example is if a malicious endpoint tries to initiate an infection process on other computers in the network, the AI-based EDR will respond instantly by isolating the infected computer, thus blocking the attack from spreading to other machines.

5.5.6 Cloud-based AI for threat detection

As organizations continue to adopt cloud computing, the potential for cyber threats to in-cloud environments is abundant and growing more sophisticated. With the scalability and efficiency of cloud-native security monitoring and protection, cloud-based AI threat detection systems have emerged. AI is used by these systems to assess cloud traffic, look for odd behavior, and find weaknesses in cloud apps, storage, and networking [33]. AI models may also examine user behavior across cloud services to identify unauthorized attempts to access data or exfiltrate data. This knowledge can subsequently be applied in real time to mitigate and safeguard sensitive information hosted in cloud settings to maintain a strong security posture across increasingly distributed systems.

5.5.7 AI in secure network traffic monitoring

Network traffic monitoring to help detect and defend against threats like DDoS attacks, network intrusions, and data breaches. It uses AI to perform real-time monitoring of traffic and detects abnormal traffic patterns that indicate a potential security incident. While traditional network monitoring tools may find it challenging to process large amounts of data, AI systems can quickly and efficiently process and analyze this information [34]. For example, machine learning algorithms in AI-driven network traffic monitoring tools help to identify malicious traffic by analyzing packets, bandwidth consumption, connections, and other factors. It makes attacks like botnet-driven DDoS attacks and tries to detect vulnerabilities in network protocols detectable, leading to quicker responses and less impact of these types of attacks.

5.5.8 AI for detecting insider threats

Insider threats, whether intentional or inadvertent, can be a significant threat, as they typically involve individuals who are already granted access to sensitive systems and information. However, trained AI-based threat detection systems have the ability to analyze user behavior and system activity, and search the signs of malicious intent or negligence [35]. By analyzing factors like unusual data access, deviations from standard workflows, or data exfiltration, AI can alert admins to potential threats that may have escaped their notice. AI-driven systems can detect early signs of insider threats, such as abnormal downloading of sensitive data or access to files that are not in line with an employee's role, and intervene before irreparable damage is done.

5.5.9 Real-time detection systems in critical infrastructure

Power grids, transportation systems, and even healthcare facilities are examples of critical infrastructure that need to be secured. AI-based real-time detection systems provide a real-time ability to analyze operational data, making such a solution particularly useful in risk monitoring and protective measures in critical infrastructure, where rapid identification of anomalies may indicate a potential cyberattack or system failure [36]. AI-powered systems can spot anomalies in data like abnormal network traffic, attempted unauthorized entry, or system failures that may result in a security compromise. These sophisticated detection systems with AI capabilities can provide organizations with advanced warnings of critical infrastructure downtime and help defend against potentially deadly assaults.

5.6 Challenges In Implementing AI for Threat Detection

While AI-based threat detection has made some huge strides in identifying and stopping cybersecurity threats, it is not without its challenges when it comes to implementing this type of threat detection system. Successfully implementing AI-based solutions for cybersecurity involves organizations overcoming a broad range of challenges, from data quality to resource constraints. In this section, we discuss some of the implementation challenges associated with deploying AI for threat detection, and what organizations need to keep in mind when integrating AI into the security arsenal. In Table 5.1, we describe the challenges of implementing an AI-driven threat detection system, the related limitations, and potential solutions.

5.6.1 Data quality and availability

AI-based threat detection is highly dependent on the quality and availability of data originally used to train machine learning models. Machine learning systems need high-quality, high-volume, and diverse data for the algorithms for learning. The absence of representative data, unclean data, or stale data may contribute to model inaccuracy, which makes AI-based detection systems ineffective. Other organizations also have critical enterprise data behind silos or in multiple systems, hindering their ability to get a comprehensive view of the threats [37]. Further, AI systems are only as good as the data they are trained on, and they are not exposed to enough diverse data, as they may end up missing potential threats or making inaccurate predictions, leaving security holes in their place.

5.6.2 False positives and false negatives

One of the major concerns in threat detection systems based on AI is false positives and false negatives. A false positive happens when a legitimate activity is falsely highlighted as a threat by an AI system, while a false negative occurs when a legitimate threat is overlooked by the system. False positives will generate unnecessary alerts and alarm fatigue; false negatives, however, are far more harmful because they mean an intrusion went undetected. Finding the right trade-off between false positives and false negatives is a challenging task itself, and the development of detection models with high accuracy is one of the major challenges that AI systems face [38].

5.6.3 Scalability and real-time processing requirements

The threat detection systems used based on AI must be able to process data in real time and at a very large scale. Scalability to handle large volumes of traffic and proactive detection of threats across a wider range of endpoints, networks, and devices are some of the key functionalities that any cybersecurity solution based on AI must necessarily have [39]. When considering a distributed system or a cloud-based environment, real-time processing is

Table 5.1 Challenges, limitations, and solutions in implementing AI for threat detection.

S.No	Challenges	Description	Limitation	Solutions
1	Data quality and availability	AI-based threat detection is highly dependent on the quality and availability of data used to train machine learning models. Poor quality or stale data can lead to inaccuracies and missed threats.	Inaccurate models, missing threats, ineffective detection.	Use diverse, high-quality data and ensure proper data handling and cleaning.
2	False positives and false negatives	False positives occur when legitimate activities are wrongly flagged as threats, leading to unnecessary alerts. False negatives occur when threats are missed, allowing attacks to go undetected.	Excessive alerts (false positives) and undetected threats (false negatives).	Improve model accuracy and create a balanced approach for false positives and negatives.
3	Scalability and real-time processing requirements	AI systems must be able to process data in real time and at large scales. Scalability issues and latency in distributed systems can affect the performance of real-time threat detection.	Processing bottlenecks and latency in distributed systems.	Use efficient, scalable AI solutions with low overhead and high processing speed.
4	Ethical and privacy concerns in AI for threat detection	AI-driven threat detection systems require monitoring sensitive user data, raising concerns about privacy. Organizations must ensure compliance with data protection laws like GDPR and address transparency and accountability.	Privacy violations, non-compliance with data protection laws.	Ensure strict adherence to privacy laws and transparency in AI decision-making processes.
5	Bias in AI threat detection models	Bias in AI models can lead to ineffective detection or discrimination. AI systems need diverse and representative data to avoid missing emerging threats or misclassifying attack patterns.	Ineffective detection, discrimination, missed threats.	Ensure diverse, representative data and avoid overfitting by using balanced datasets.

6	Cost and resource constraints	AI-based threat detection systems can be costly due to the need for advanced technology, infrastructure, and skilled personnel. Smaller organizations may face financial constraints in implementing these systems.	High initial investment, scarcity of skilled personnel.	Invest in cost-effective solutions, seek external expertise or partnerships.
7	Complexity in implementing AI models	Developing and implementing AI models requires specialized knowledge of machine learning, data preprocessing, and model optimization. The complexity of AI systems makes them challenging to integrate into existing infrastructures.	Integration complexity, continuous updates required.	Develop clear processes for model updates, retraining, and integration into existing systems.
8	Lack of standardization in AI detection systems	There is no standardized framework for AI-based threat detection, making it difficult to compare, integrate, or scale solutions. A lack of standards hinders the sharing of threat intelligence across organizations.	Lack of industry-wide standards, difficulty in comparison and integration.	Adopt common standards and frameworks to ensure scalability and interoperability.
9	Data overload and model overfitting	Data overload can overwhelm AI systems, making it difficult to process vast amounts of information. Model overfitting can occur when AI systems are trained on excessive or biased data, reducing their effectiveness in real-world scenarios.	Overload of data, ineffective results due to overfitting.	Use methods like regularization to avoid overfitting and optimize data processing.

especially cumbersome, as it tends to come with latency and performance issues. AI-driven solutions should be lightweight, adding minimal overhead so that they do not slow down or introduce performance bottlenecks that adversely impact the responsiveness of security operations.

5.6.4 Ethical and privacy concerns in AI for threat detection

AI-based threat detection systems typically require observing user actions, network traffic, and potentially sensitive data. This poses major ethical and privacy challenges. For example, tracking employees' online behavior may be considered an invasion of privacy, particularly when AI systems haul in personal or sensitive data without their explicit consent [40]. To address those concerns, organizations need to introduce proper privacy policies and protections so that AI systems can comply with data protection laws, like the GDPR. Other concerns that need to be addressed when implementing AI security solutions are ethical considerations, like transparency and accountability in the decision-making process driven by AI.

5.6.5 Bias in AI threat detection models

Bias is a well-understood problem in AI models, and threat detection systems are not immune to it. There are many potential sources of failure modes of threat intelligence systems, one of which is the biases in the training data used to build AI systems [41]. This can lead to less effective detection of some classes of attacks, or worse, discrimination in the decisions taken. By the same token, AI trained on data only up to a certain point in time might identify threats to a degree consistent with that time frame but might miss more contemporary threats. The ultimate goal is to ensure that AI solutions are not biased, meaning well-trained AI systems are trained on diverse datasets that represent a variety of potential threats and environments.

5.6.6 Cost and resource constraints

AI-based threat detection systems may require substantial resources to implement, including investment in technology, infrastructure, and talent. Deploying AI solutions, especially those that require advanced machine learning models, significant computation, and extensive data storage, can be cost-prohibitive for many domains (read smaller) organizations [42]. Moreover, companies require skilled personnel like data scientists and AI experts to design, implement, and uphold these systems. Human cybersecurity professionals are scarce, let alone for AI-based threat detection systems to be established.

5.6.7 Complexity in Implementing AI Models

Developing and implementing AI-based threat detection models is not an easy activity. Building these AI models requires in-depth knowledge of machine learning algorithms, along with data preprocessing and model optimization. Even more, AI models should be constantly updated and retrained to adapt to the advancing threats [43]. With the very nature of AI systems being complex and the technology in constant evolution, organizations need to tap into specialized knowledge to be able to address these very challenges and ensure that these systems are well integrated into existing security infrastructures. Either too little or too much understanding of AI capabilities shows its implementation, leading to questionable efficacy, and systems not meeting security requirements.

5.6.8 Lack of standardization in AI detection systems

Another challenge is the absence of standardized frameworks for AI in cybersecurity. AI-based threat detection systems have differing algorithms, models, and approaches, resulting in discrepancies across performance and outcomes [44]. When there are no clear standards in the industry, it becomes a challenge for organizations to either compare, integrate, or scale different AI solutions. In addition, a lack of standards can impede the ability to share threat intelligence and cooperate across organizations with non-interoperable systems. Having common standards and best practices for AI in cybersecurity would enable organizations to adopt more effective, scalable, and interoperable solutions.

5.6.9 Data overload and model overfitting

For threat detection, data overload is another issue that AI systems confront. On the one hand, while AI can ingest vast amounts of data to perform predictive analysis, the amount of security-related information can be so large that systems are unable to process it [45]. Feeding excessive data to the system can also result in complications such as model overfitting, where the AI is over-trained to recognize patterns within the training set but struggles to transfer that understanding to new examples. Data has bias problems, so central organizations that handle data should manage data flows carefully during training and testing AI models on balanced and relevant datasets.

Furthermore, methods such as regularization can mitigate overfitting and enhance the resilience of AI systems against novel threats.

5.7 Future Trends in AI for Threat Detection and Intelligence

There is an ever-growing field for AI-based threat detection, as technology improves and the shape of cyber threats changes. With emerging technologies like 5G, IoT, and quantum computing come new opportunities and challenges to the cybersecurity landscape. In this part, we look at some emerging trends and how AI is anticipated to become pivotal in combating as shown in Figure 5.6.

5.7.1 The Impact of 5G and IoT on AI-based threat detection

5G and the IoT promise to significantly increase both the number of connected devices and the complexity of the networks they operate in. Although these technologies offer the potential for faster speeds, lower latency, and enhanced connectivity, they also create new vulnerabilities that cybercriminals can exploit. The phenomenal growth in the number of connected devices creates vast amounts of data that AI systems can use to identify anomalies and thwart attacks. AI will help to monitor for abnormal behavior on these devices, prevent unauthorized access to them, and identify possible vulnerabilities that may be abused by bad actors [46]. Furthermore, complexity is one of the major challenges that will come along with 5G (higher-speed, higher-traffic scenarios in which multiple devices will communicate at much higher speeds and in a much larger space), and AI-based threat detection systems will become critical. As the attack surface increases over time, AI's capability to monitor and analyze vast datasets in real time will be a key factor in safeguarding 5G and IoT environments.

5.7.2 AI and automation in proactive threat hunting

Threat hunting is an IT security process in which security professionals look for threats that may be lurking in a network. As cyber threats become more sophisticated and abundant, AI-driven automation in threat hunting is making it increasingly proactive. AI systems and machine learning undertake to examine network traffic and user behavior to identify and stop threats before they can damage the system. AI automates routine threat-hunting efforts,

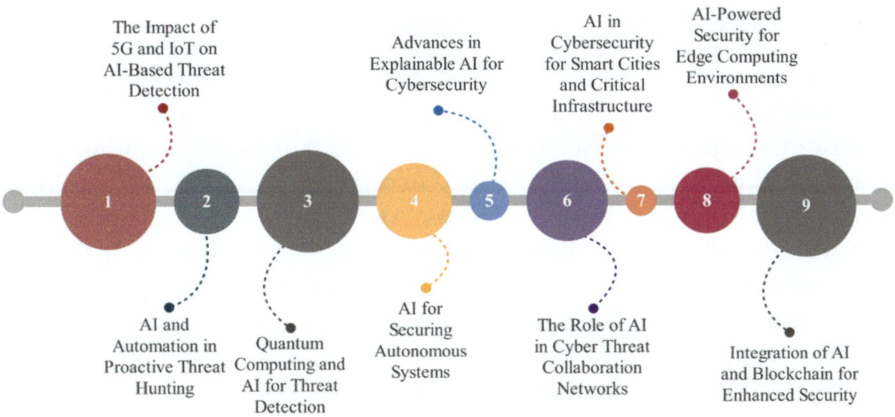

Figure 5.6 Future trends in AI for threat detection and intelligence.

freeing security teams to concentrate on more complex, high-level initiatives. As organizations are inundated by the volume and sophistication of cyber threats, traditional security measures often fall short. Machine learning algorithms can provide continuous learning from new data, allowing organizations to keep up with new threats and identify new attack patterns that were not previously detected by traditional systems, which move into automation and allow for a more proactive approach to cybersecurity, reducing response times and preventing damage.

5.7.3 Quantum computing and AI for threat detection

Quantum computing has the ability to use quantum bits (qubits) to carry out complex calculations faster than ever when it comes to cybersecurity. Quantum computing threatens existing cryptographic techniques and thereby traditional encryption standards. Nonetheless, it is a powerful tool that can potentially further develop AI-augmented threat detection systems [47]. The fusion of AI techniques with quantum computers could lead to the creation of algorithms that were previously impractical and are now performing analysis on tons of security data in a more efficient manner. Quantum-enhanced AI might enable faster and more accurate detection of cyberattacks, especially in scenarios where real-time decision-making is important. Furthermore, quantum computing could contribute to the creation of quantum-resistant encryption algorithms, safeguarding data against the potential threats posed by quantum adversaries in the future.

5.7.4 AI for securing autonomous systems

Autonomous systems like self-driving cars, drones, and robotic processes are becoming increasingly prevalent, making the security of these systems against cyberattacks critical. These systems use AI to make real-time decisions, and any breach of security they experience could lead to disastrous consequences. For autonomous systems, AI will be used for securing those systems, providing capabilities for threat detection in real time, predictive maintenance, and anomaly detection [48]. For instance, within the scope of autonomous vehicles, AI could be utilized to monitor and analyze sensor data, road conditions, and vehicle behavior continuously, enabling it to detect any potential security threats or malicious interference. AI will play a key role in keeping these systems safe and secure as they become increasingly embedded in critical infrastructure.

5.7.5 Advances in explainable AI for cybersecurity

One of the challenges where AI is concerned, one particularly difficult challenge in the cyber domain, is the "black-box" character of numerous algorithms, explaining the rationale behind decisions taken using AI designs is not always visible to the users. XAI, short for explainable AI, explains the internal decision support or output of the AI system in an understandable and transparent way. Explainable AI will help improve cybersecurity trust and accountability, as it will enable security experts to understand the rationale behind an AI system categorizing a behavior as malicious or benevolent [49]. Moreover, this transparency can assist in identifying and mitigating biases in AI models, and in improving the collaboration between human analysts and AI systems, as well as compliance with regulatory requirements. As AI-powered systems become increasingly central to cybersecurity operations, making sense of their actions will be critical to making informed decisions.

5.7.6 The role of AI in cyber threat collaboration networks

With the rise of cyber threats that are becoming increasingly complex and international, it has become vital for organizations as well as governments to work together to identify and counter attacks. In the coming years, AI will be very instrumental in cross-organization threat intelligence sharing, being able to share cyber risks and vulnerabilities from one organization to another in a more rapid and sophisticated way. Leveraging threat data from diverse sources, AI-powered platforms can analyze and correlate them automatically, enabling organizations to share insights and respond together in real time [50]. Cybersecurity professionals can also improve the detection of large-scale attacks, identify common threat actors, and coordinate responses through the integration of AI and threat collaboration networks. This partnership will also strengthen collective defense against cybercriminals and nation-state actors.

5.7.7 AI in cybersecurity for smart cities and critical infrastructure

Digital technologies and IoT devices are playing an integral role in smart cities and how critical infrastructure systems are built, networks for power, transportation, healthcare, energy, and more. But there is a darker side, with which a number of the critical systems that can be targeted, where and how to disassemble the railway and other important transportation systems, fall into this category. By enabling real-time monitoring, anomaly detection, and predictive analytics, AI will be the protector of smart cities and critical infrastructures [51]. For instance, AI-enabled systems can analyze real-time traffic patterns to identify suspicious behavior, which may represent a threat to a cyberattack or physical security breach. In a similar manner, AI systems can monitor power grids to detect malicious interference and facilitate a timely response to threats.

5.7.8 AI-powered security for edge computing environments

Edge computing is on the rise as it processes data closer to its origin rather than using a centralized data center, reducing latency and increasing efficiency. But with edge computing comes new security challenges, especially in maintaining the security of the multitude of devices and the distributed nature of the network itself. With the need to continuously monitor data and network traffic at the edge, AI will become instrumental in secure edge computing environments. Real-time anomaly and risk detection-AI-driven systems will enable real-time anomaly detection and risk detection [52]. Using machine learning and edge-based AI models, organizations can secure their edge computing systems due to the increasing complexity and scale of connected devices.

5.7.9 Integration of AI and blockchain for enhanced security

Due to the decentralized and irreversible nature of blockchain technology, the implementation of blockchain technology in cybersecurity applications aimed at secure transactions, identity management, and data protection will continue to increase. Organizations can develop a stronger security framework alongside advanced threat detection and distributed, immutable data management by combining AI with blockchain. AI helps in detecting patterns of which behavior is suspicious, so you can monitor it better on your blockchain network or catch fraud [53]. Blockchain, on the other hand, is an excellent tool that can enhance the security of AI by providing integrity and transparency for data utilized in machine learning models. The combination of AI and blockchain holds great potential for securing sensitive systems, preventing data loss, and ensuring trust in decentralized ecosystems.

5.8 Conclusion

AI has played a revolutionary role in redefining the cybersecurity landscape, bringing advanced features that help analyze, detect, and respond to threats with a whole new level of power. AI empowers systems to identify known and unknown threats at an extraordinary speed and with extraordinary accuracy using sophisticated techniques, including machine learning, deep learning, and anomaly detection. As technologies such as 5G, IoT, and autonomous systems become ubiquitous, AI is needed to secure advanced connected environments by providing real-time, adaptive defense strategies to mitigate emerging risk scenarios. Though it can streamline processes and responses, making them faster, more efficient, and cost-effective, integrating AI into cybersecurity brings challenges such as the need to maintain mission-critical quality data, scale, and the ability to manage the false positive and false negative trade-off. Ensuring the broadest opportunity for AI can be achieved will require organizations to work towards the removal of these obstacles by enhancing data curation, improving AI models, and ensuring transparency and accountability through explainable AI. Meeting ethical challenges surrounding privacy and fairness, for example, is critical to responsible AI adoption in security systems. The future of AI cybersecurity is extremely bright. As quantum computing progresses and the integration of AI and blockchain proves more effective, cybersecurity will become more powerful and better able to withstand the ever-evolving range of threats. With the rapid development of AI, it will continue to provide support for securing critical infrastructure, real-time threat intelligence capabilities, and is a coordinating force across organizations, helping organizations keep pace with the always-evolving nature of the cyber battle space, making it an integral component of the modern cybersecurity approach.

References

[1] H. Khan, Z. Jan, I. Ullah, A. Alwabli, F. Alharbi, S. Habib, and J. Koo, "A deep dive into AI integration and advanced nanobiosensor technologies for enhanced bacterial infection monitoring," *Nanotechnology Reviews*, vol. 13, no. 1, p. 20240056, 2024.

[2] A. A. Ahmed and M. Echi, "Hawk-eye: An AI-powered threat detector for intelligent surveillance cameras," *IEEE Access*, vol. 9, pp. 63283–63293, 2021.

[3] Z. A. Haider, T. Rahman, A. Zeb, I. Khan, A. Sharafian, and I. Ullah, "Surveillance and Monitoring in Smart Cities with UAV and Machine Learning Integration," in *Unmanned Aerial Vehicles Swarm for Protecting Smart Cities: Future Trends and Challenges*, Berkeley, CA: Apress, 2025, pp. 241–284.

[4] M. Rizvi, "Enhancing cybersecurity: The power of artificial intelligence in threat detection and prevention," *International Journal of Advanced Engineering Research and Science*, vol. 10, no. 5, pp. 055–060, 2023.

[5] M. Schmitt, "Securing the digital world: Protecting smart infrastructures and digital industries with artificial intelligence (AI)-enabled malware and intrusion detection," *Journal of Industrial Information Integration*, vol. 36, p. 100520, 2023.

[6] S. Rangaraju, "Secure by intelligence: Enhancing products with AI-driven security measures," *EPH-International Journal of Science and Engineering*, vol. 9, no. 3, pp. 36–41, 2023.

[7] S. Duary, P. Choudhury, S. Mishra, V. Sharma, D. D. Rao, and A. P. Aderemi, "Cybersecurity threats detection in intelligent networks using predictive analytics approaches," in *2024 4th International Conference on Innovative Practices in Technology and Management (ICIPTM)*, 2024, pp. 1–5.

[8] A. J. Varma, N. Taleb, R. A. Said, T. M. Ghazal, M. Ahmad, H. M. Alzoubi, and M. Alshurideh, "A roadmap for SMEs to adopt an AI-based cyber threat intelligence," in *The effect of information technology on business and marketing intelligence systems*, Cham: Springer International Publishing, 2023, pp. 1903–1926.

[9] I. Ullah, I. U. Khan, M. Ouaissa, M. Ouaissa, and S. El Hajjami, Eds., *Future communication systems using artificial intelligence, Internet of Things and data science*. CRC Press, 2024.

[10] A. B. Dorothy, B. Madhavidevi, B. Nachiappan, G. Manikandan, P. K. Patjoshi, and M. Sindhuja, "AI-Driven Threat Intelligence in Cloud

Computing Detecting and Responding to Cyber Attacks," in *2024 International Conference on Intelligent Algorithms for Computational Intelligence Systems (IACIS)*, 2024, pp. 1–6.

[11] B. Guembe, A. Azeta, S. Misra, V. C. Osamor, L. Fernandez-Sanz, and V. Pospelova, "The emerging threat of AI-driven cyber attacks: A review," *Applied Artificial Intelligence*, vol. 36, no. 1, p. 2037254, 2022.

[12] F. M. Khan, T. Rahman, A. Zeb, Z. A. Haider, I. U. Khan, H. Bilal, and I. Ullah, "Vehicular network security through optimized deep learning model with feature selection techniques," *IECE Transactions on Sensing, Communication, and Control*, vol. 1, no. 2, pp. 136–153, 2024.

[13] S. Zaman, K. Alhazmi, M. A. Aseeri, M. R. Ahmed, R. T. Khan, M. S. Kaiser, and M. Mahmud, "Security threats and artificial intelligence based countermeasures for Internet of Things networks: A comprehensive survey," *IEEE Access*, vol. 9, pp. 94668–94690, 2021.

[14] S. Shoukat, T. Gao, D. Javeed, M. S. Saeed, and M. Adil, "Trust my IDS: An explainable AI integrated deep learning-based transparent threat detection system for industrial networks," *Computers & Security*, vol. 149, p. 104191, 2025.

[15] I. H. Sarker, H. Janicke, M. A. Ferrag, and A. Abuadbba, "Multi-aspect rule-based AI: Methods, taxonomy, challenges and directions towards automation, intelligence and transparent cybersecurity modeling for critical infrastructures," *Internet of Things*, vol. 25, p. 101110, 2024.

[16] Z. A. Haider, F. M. Khan, A. Zafar, and I. U. Khan, "Optimizing machine learning classifiers for credit card fraud detection on highly imbalanced datasets using PCA and SMOTE techniques," *VAWKUM Transactions on Computer Sciences*, vol. 12, no. 2, pp. 28–49, 2024.

[17] A. H. Salem, S. M. Azzam, O. E. Emam, and A. A. Abohany, "Advancing cybersecurity: A comprehensive review of AI-driven detection techniques," *Journal of Big Data*, vol. 11, no. 1, p. 105, 2024.

[18] A. Hussain, S. Ul Amin, and M. Fayaz, "An efficient and robust hand gesture recognition system of sign language employing finetuned Inception-V3 and EfficientNet-B0 network," *Computer Systems Science & Engineering*, vol. 46, no. 3, 2023.

[19] R. Kaur, D. Gabrijelčič, and T. Klobučar, "Artificial intelligence for cybersecurity: Literature review and future research directions," *Information Fusion*, vol. 97, p. 101804, 2023.

[20] T. Moulahi, R. Jabbar, A. Alabdulatif, S. Abbas, S. El Khediri, S. Zidi, and M. Rizwan, "Privacy-preserving federated learning cyber-threat detection for intelligent transport systems with blockchain-based security," *Expert Systems*, vol. 40, no. 5, p. e13103, 2023.

[21] M. Guarascio, N. Cassavia, F. S. Pisani, and G. Manco, "Boosting cyber-threat intelligence via collaborative intrusion detection," *Future Generation Computer Systems*, vol. 135, pp. 30–43, 2022.

[22] F. M. Khan, M. S. Akhter, I. U. Khan, Z. A. Haider, and N. H. Khan, "Clinical prediction of female infertility through advanced machine learning techniques," 2024.

[23] A. Ali, I. Ullah, M. Shabaz, A. Sharafian, M. A. Khan, X. Bai, and L. Qiu, "A resource-aware multi-graph neural network for urban traffic flow prediction in multi-access edge computing systems," *IEEE Transactions on Consumer Electronics*, 2024.

[24] M. Waqas, S. Tu, Z. Halim, S. U. Rehman, G. Abbas, and Z. H. Abbas, "The role of artificial intelligence and machine learning in wireless networks security: Principle, practice and challenges," *Artificial Intelligence Review*, vol. 55, no. 7, pp. 5215–5261, 2022.

[25] P. R. Trim and Y. I. Lee, "Combining sociocultural intelligence with artificial intelligence to increase organizational cyber security provision through enhanced resilience," *Big Data and Cognitive Computing*, vol. 6, no. 4, p. 110, 2022.

[26] Z. A. Haider, F. M. Khan, I. U. Khan, M. A. Khan, and R. Khan, "Early detection and prediction of pests in field crops using transfer learning," *VFAST Transactions on Software Engineering*, vol. 12, no. 3, pp. 98–113, 2024.

[27] C. Chakraborty, S. M. Nagarajan, G. G. Devarajan, T. V. Ramana, and R. Mohanty, "Intelligent AI-based healthcare cyber security system using multi-source transfer learning method," *ACM Transactions on Sensor Networks*, 2023.

[28] A. J. G. De Azambuja, C. Plesker, K. Schützer, R. Anderl, B. Schleich, and V. R. Almeida, "Artificial intelligence-based cyber security in the context of industry 4.0—a survey," *Electronics*, vol. 12, no. 8, p. 1920, 2023.

[29] M. Fayaz, J. Nam, L. M. Dang, H. K. Song, and H. Moon, "Land-cover classification using deep learning with high-resolution remote-sensing imagery," *Applied Sciences*, vol. 14, no. 5, p. 1844, 2024.

[30] I. Jada and T. O. Mayayise, "The impact of artificial intelligence on organisational cyber security: An outcome of a systematic literature review," *Data and Information Management*, vol. 8, no. 2, p. 100063, 2024.

[31] B. Naik, A. Mehta, H. Yagnik, and M. Shah, "The impacts of artificial intelligence techniques in augmentation of cybersecurity: A comprehensive review," *Complex & Intelligent Systems*, vol. 8, no. 2, pp. 1763–1780, 2022.

[32] X. Wang, W. Liu, H. Lin, J. Hu, K. Kaur, and M. S. Hossain, "AI-empowered trajectory anomaly detection for intelligent transportation systems: A hierarchical federated learning approach," *IEEE Transactions on Intelligent Transportation Systems*, vol. 24, no. 4, pp. 4631–4640, 2022.

[33] R. Renugadevi, J. Shobana, K. Arthi, K. AV, D. Satishkumar, and M. Sivaraja, "Real-time applications of artificial intelligence technology in daily operations," in *Using Real-Time Data and AI for Thrust Manufacturing*, IGI Global, 2024, pp. 243–257.

[34] I. Khan, K. Zhang, Q. Wu, I. Ullah, L. Ali, H. Ullah, and S. U. Rahman, "A wideband high-isolation microstrip MIMO circularly-polarized antenna based on parasitic elements," *Materials*, vol. 16, no. 1, p. 103, 2022.

[35] G. Jakka, N. Yathiraju, and M. F. Ansari, "Artificial intelligence in terms of spotting malware and delivering cyber risk management," *Journal of Positive School Psychology*, vol. 6, no. 3, pp. 6156–6165, 2022.

[36] I. Ullah, F. Ali, H. Khan, F. Khan, and X. Bai, "Ubiquitous computation in internet of vehicles for human-centric transport systems," *Computers in Human Behavior*, vol. 161, p. 108394, 2024.

[37] C. Park, J. Lee, Y. Kim, J. G. Park, H. Kim, and D. Hong, "An enhanced AI-based network intrusion detection system using generative adversarial networks," *IEEE Internet of Things Journal*, vol. 10, no. 3, pp. 2330–2345, 2022.

[38] Y. Wang and X. Yang, "Research on enhancing cloud computing network security using artificial intelligence algorithms," *arXiv preprint arXiv:2502.17801*, 2025.

[39] G. Bendiab, A. Hameurlaine, G. Germanos, N. Kolokotronis, and S. Shiaeles, "Autonomous vehicles security: Challenges and solutions using blockchain and artificial intelligence," *IEEE Transactions on Intelligent Transportation Systems*, vol. 24, no. 4, pp. 3614–3637, 2023.

[40] A. Iqbal, M. L. Tham, Y. J. Wong, A. A. Al-Habashna, G. Wainer, Y. X. Zhu, and T. Dagiuklas, "Empowering non-terrestrial networks with artificial intelligence: A survey," *IEEE Access*, vol. 11, pp. 100986–101006, 2023.

[41] J. B. Awotunde and S. Misra, "Feature extraction and artificial intelligence-based intrusion detection model for a secure internet of things networks," in *Illumination of Artificial Intelligence in Cybersecurity and Forensics*, Cham: Springer International Publishing, 2022, pp. 21–44.

[42] L. M. Dang, S. Danish, A. Khan, N. Alam, M. Fayaz, D. K. Nguyen, et al., "An efficient zero-labeling segmentation approach for pest monitoring on smartphone-based images," *European Journal of Agronomy*, vol. 160, p. 127331, 2024.

[43] M. A. Ferrag, M. Debbah, and M. Al-Hawawreh, "Generative AI for cyber threat-hunting in 6G-enabled IoT networks," in *2023 IEEE/ACM 23rd International Symposium on Cluster, Cloud and Internet Computing Workshops (CCGridW)*, 2023, pp. 16–25.
[44] N. Capuano, G. Fenza, V. Loia, and C. Stanzione, "Explainable artificial intelligence in cybersecurity: A survey," *IEEE Access*, vol. 10, pp. 93575–93600, 2022.
[45] A. K. Mishra, A. K. Tyagi, S. Dananjayan, A. Rajavat, H. Rawat, and A. Rawat, "Revolutionizing government operations: The impact of artificial intelligence in public administration," *Conversational Artificial Intelligence*, pp. 607–634, 2024.
[46] D. Dai and S. Boroomand, "A review of artificial intelligence to enhance the security of big data systems: state-of-art, methodologies, applications, and challenges," *Archives of Computational Methods in Engineering*, vol. 29, no. 2, pp. 1291–1309, 2022.
[47] D. K. Kumar, K. K. Reddy, and G. J. W. Kathrine, "Smart grid protection with AI and cryptographic security," in *2024 3rd International Conference on Applied Artificial Intelligence and Computing (ICAAIC)*, 2024, pp. 246–251.
[48] R. Salama, F. Al-Turjman, and R. Culmone, "AI-powered drone to address smart city security issues," in *International Conference on Advanced Information Networking and Applications*, Cham: Springer International Publishing, 2023, pp. 292–300.
[49] F. Charmet, H. C. Tanuwidjaja, S. Ayoubi, P. F. Gimenez, Y. Han, H. Jmila, et al., "Explainable artificial intelligence for cybersecurity: A literature survey," *Annals of Telecommunications*, vol. 77, no. 11, pp. 789–812, 2022.
[50] R. Tang, L. De Donato, N. Besinović, F. Flammini, R. M. Goverde, Z. Lin, et al., "A literature review of Artificial Intelligence applications in railway systems," *Transportation Research Part C: Emerging Technologies*, vol. 140, p. 103679, 2022.
[51] W. Villegas-Ch and J. García-Ortiz, "Toward a comprehensive framework for ensuring security and privacy in artificial intelligence," *Electronics*, vol. 12, no. 18, p. 3786, 2023.
[52] S. Ali, S. U. Rehman, A. Imran, G. Adeem, Z. Iqbal, and K. I. Kim, "Comparative evaluation of AI-based techniques for zero-day attacks detection," *Electronics*, vol. 11, no. 23, p. 3934, 2022.
[53] C. Cross, "Using artificial intelligence (AI) and deepfakes to deceive victims: The need to rethink current romance fraud prevention messaging," *Crime Prevention and Community Safety*, vol. 24, no. 1, pp. 30–41, 2022.

6

Empowering Cybersecurity with AI: Advanced Threat Detection, Predictive Intelligence, and Real-time Defense

Pasham Sowmya[1], Monika Singh T[1], Kishor Kumar Reddy C[1], and Srinath Doss[2]

[1]Stanley College of Engineering and Technology for Women, India
[2]Botho University, Botswana

Email: sowmyasamuel10@gmail.com; thakursingh.monika@gmail.com; kishoar23@gmail.com; srinath.doss@bothouniversity.ac.bw

Abstract

With the rapid evolution of the digital landscape, cyber threats have grown in sophistication, putting individuals, organizations, and governments under serious threat. AI for cybersecurity is proving itself to be the most potent tool to enhance cybersecurity via advanced threat detection, predictive intelligence, and real-time defense mechanisms. Stringent on the heels of potential threats, unlike conventional systems of security, AI technology can quickly analyze extensive data, detect the anomaly, and fasten a response to that anomaly before any damage is done. Different machine-learning models, deep learning algorithms, and behavioral analytics form a quintessential core-slash-key to address the identification and mitigation of innumerable variants of cyber threats such as malware, phishing attempts, intrusion attempts, and insider threats. This chapter will investigate mostly how AI can be integrated into threat detection and intelligence concerning predicting and, hence, preventing and lessening the impact of cyber risks. Key applications like anomaly detection, automated threat response, and predictive analytics form real-time measures to improve the speed and accuracy of cybersecurity. In addition, ethical considerations ranging from issues like privacy, bias, and

DOI: 10.1201/9788743808077-6

adversarial attacks shall be addressed in terms of promoting responsible AI deployment. By leveraging the adaptive learning and automation capabilities of AI, organizations can enhance their cyber defense, thereby reducing response times and increasing their own defenses against evolving threats. The chapter concludes by putting forth a few future endeavors and underlining the importance of cooperation among the academic world, industry, and governments for the sustainable and secure application of AI into cybersecurity.

6.1 Introduction

The digitization, or rather computerization, of threat detection and intelligence has commenced a new age of cybersecurity with the advanced mechanisms necessary to address the increasing intricacy of cyber threats. Such AI-based technologies utilize machine learning and deep learning techniques to scrutinize large chunks of data, identify minute anomalies, and forecast possible attacks, thereby strengthening the overall security posture [1][2]. In addition to this, the real-time analysis of network traffic, user behavior, and system logs facilitates the detection of anomalies indicating potential threats [3]. To facilitate effective prioritization of critical threats, AI helps bring together and analyze threat intelligence from varied areas, using NLP to obtain insights from unstructured data, thus automating the routine functions of minimizing human-machine interface [4]. However, it is important to accommodate ethical practice and address the challenges of the need for high-quality data, bias, and the threats of adversarial attacks.

6.1.1 Understanding the role of AI in cybersecurity

AI in cybersecurity is playing an increasingly important role as cyber threats change and grow more complex. AI's ability to bring forth large datasets, identify patterns in their work, and automate processes is changing the way organizations defend their digital infrastructure. AI systems are expected to be implemented in almost all areas of cybersecurity, namely intrusion detection, abnormality detection, malware analysis, threat intelligence gathering, and vulnerability management [5]. The machine learning (ML) algorithm, as part of AI, teaches systems from past data, new threats, and gets smarter in detecting more, thus adding to lower false positives and more real-time threat detection [6]. Natural Language Processing (NLP) will utilize all this data to formulate ideas out of unstructured data such as security reports, feeds on social media where incidents related to their companies may be surfaced, as well as dark websites and other forums where one can quote the said company as sources to find emerging threats and motivations for attack [7] and many more applications. AI is also used in behavior analytics where it ascertains established baselines on user and system behaviors, such that it can detect deviations occurring, which might lead to illegal activity detection [8]. However, AI also brings forth some challenges in terms of cybersecurity, such as the requirement for quality-labeled training data, having biased AI models, and the risk of adversarial attacks designed to mislead these AI systems into indecorous results [9]. Therefore, a balanced ethical approach with strong validation and continuous monitoring is necessary to derive and increase the benefits of AI in cybersecurity and the risk-related issues faced in this domain [10].

6.1.2 AI vs. traditional threat detection approaches

The introduction of AI in threat detection has grossly changed the traditional ways of augmenting adaptability, thus enhancing detection capabilities. Traditional methods applied by organizations are rule-based systems and signature-based antivirus applications which rather follow predefined rules with previously known signatures of threats, thereby becoming less effective in new and polymorphic malicious codes [11], interpreted in contrast to AI systems that use machine learning techniques combined with behavioral analysis to analyze data and compute on large datasets in order to find anomalies and deviations leading to detecting unknown threats and zero-day exploits [12]. Furthermore, NLP is based on the concept that it can enhance the extraction of valuable insights from unstructured data and thus feed them to threat intelligence gathering [13]. For example, rather than being reactive as traditional systems, these solutions are predictive acquisition of continuous learning and adaptation capable of preventing and predicting possible attacks [14]. The achievement of AI applications for cybersecurity, however, comes with the challenges of data quality and adversarial attacks, ensuring that such solutions remain balanced and ethical [15].

Figure 6.1 describes the flowchart and shows the comparison of the traditional manual cybersecurity processes versus artificially intelligent detection systems. It shows how AI enhances automation, adaptability, and learning over the classic rule-based or reactive manual methods.

6.1.3 Core concepts: Adaptability, learning, and automation

In fact, the combination of AI and cybersecurity has entirely changed the way in which digital infrastructures can be protected by three basic principles:

adaptability, learning, and automation. These three concepts altogether form the backbone of a paradigm shift from traditional reactive defense strategies to proactive intelligent security systems. Basically, adaptability refers to the dynamic cyber threat landscape where an AI system is required to evolve over time. It bucks this trend by implementing static rules or known signatures; instead, AI systems continuously add to and improve their threat detection models with new data and changing behaviors of attackers [16]. So, it provides a resilient defense that might respond emergently to the threat as well as zero-day weaknesses. Firstly, learning, and especially by applying ML algorithms to artificial intelligence, has made it possible for AI systems to be able to assess and find useful patterns from large datasets, which might have great variance and come from different sources. Over a given period, these systems learn more about the normal behavior in the network and become better at detecting anomalies or malicious behavior from this learned baseline [17]. It also improves detection significantly and lowers the false positive rate, which is one of the critical issues in traditional systems. Automation is another area of efficiency in operations. Some of these mundane but necessary tasks in cybersecurity, such as log file analysis, threat hunting, alert prioritization, and even automated incident response, will free human analysts to deal with even more intricate and strategy-oriented security issues [18]. Consequently, response times are increased against potential

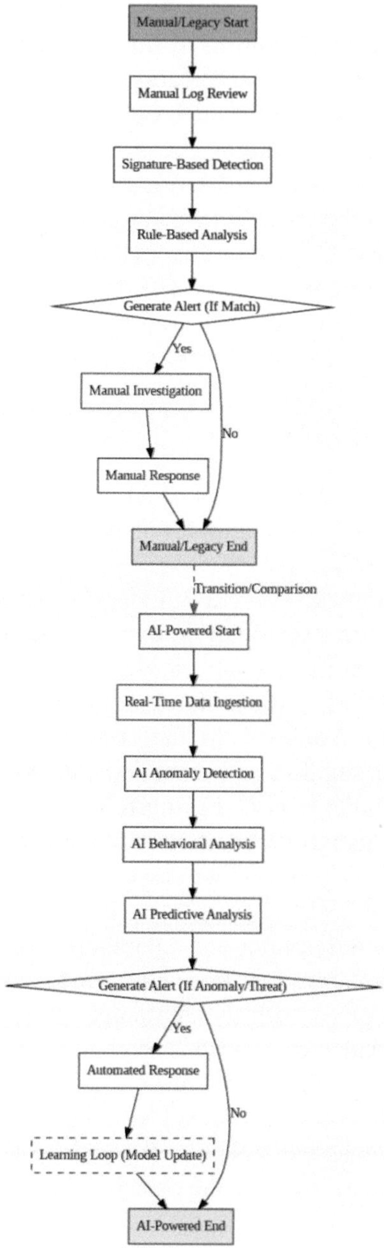

Figure 6.1 Comparison flowchart.

breaches, and around the clock, without the fatigue of human personnel, monitoring can be done, thus incurring a lot of resilience for the overall system. Thus, learning and automation will, in the long run, alleviate a situation towards an active defense posture. Rather than being reactive post-incident or post-emergent threats, AI systems can predict and thwart such future attacks through a forge or real-time analysis of patterns and emerging trends within threat intelligence data [19]. This migration to anticipation rather than immediate reaction represented a significant step within the cybersecurity domain. However, for such capabilities from AI to function practically, organizations need to have sound data governance frameworks, such as quality, diversity, and privacy of training datasets and ethics, so that the models developed are not biased and, therefore, shielded from adversarial manipulation [20]. The balance between capricious advancement and ethical oversight brought by the responsible implementation of AI in cybersecurity could guarantee trustworthy and reliable defense systems.

6.2 Evolution of AI in Cybersecurity

The impact of artificial intelligence (AI) on cybersecurity includes transforming it into a protective shield for digital systems in organizations. Initially, cybersecurity was built around old-prevention pillars that included methods as simple as firewalls and rule-based systems. However, these now seem inadequate when considering the recently evolving nature and pace of cyber threats. AI introduced more sophisticated and, most importantly, data-driven ways to detect and respond to threats: Machine learning (ML), which now allows systems to learn from previous attacks and improve their detection and response capabilities over time, in addition to the abilities of AI to identify unknown threats, decrease false alarms, and automate responses. Natural language processing (NLP) also collects intelligence on threats from unstructured data, such as reports and social media. Evolving AI has entered the sphere of proactive threat detection, seamlessly trying to predict attacks before the actual time they occur and so optimizing overall security [21]. Today, AI is in use for intrusion detection, malware analysis, or behavior monitoring. Such continuous learning makes it quite a tool for defending against evolving cyber threats. The advancement of AI continues to change its role in developing smarter, faster, and adaptive cybersecurity systems.

Figure 6.2 describes a timeline that visualizes the development of AI in cybersecurity from its primordial rule-based detection to present-day predictive intelligence systems. It highlights the momentous breakthroughs and innovations throughout the discipline.

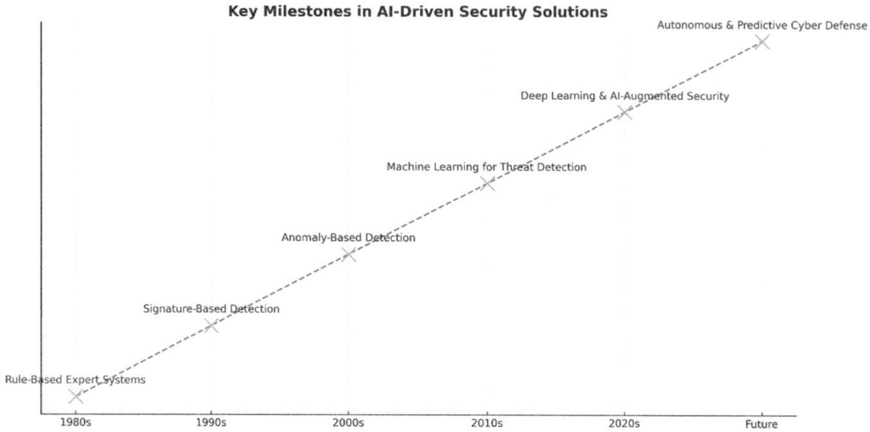

Figure 6.2 Key milestones in AI-driven security solutions.

6.2.1 Early approaches to automated threat detection

In the early days, automated threat detection in cybersecurity was characterized by signature and rule-based systems. These would compare incoming data with established patterns or "signatures" of malevolent code and rules defined beforehand. Little suited for an attack using recently discovered malware or for new attack techniques, these methods were effective in the case of previously identified malware or an attack methodology. Therefore, such systems could hardly detect an unseen threat or a quickly evolving attack, like zero-day exploits. These systems are, hence, reactive and not proactive; they depend on manual updates and consume a lot of time. To resolve such issues, anomaly-based detection techniques were brought to the forefront. These techniques addressed the detection of differences between "normal" and "usual" behavior using statistical behavior models. Whereas they tend to be less rigid than rule-based systems, the early anomaly detection approaches produced too many false positives, as they lacked situational awareness and thus could not distinguish between legitimate unusual activities and true threats [22]. These early approaches had highly negative attributes, but they were also foundational: they created solid conceptual foundations for subsequently incorporating intelligent, adaptive technologies, such as machine learning and AI-based models. With this advanced technology, it became possible to dynamically learn from new data, continuously improve the accuracy of detection, and move away from static rule-following systems to more intelligent and responsive cybersecurity solutions [23].

6.2.2 Milestones in AI-driven security solutions

The advancement of AI in cybersecurity has experienced a few notable milestones, all of which are dramatic improvements. One of the earliest among these changes occurred with the introduction of machine-learning-based intrusion detection systems (IDS) in the early 2000s. This allowed security tools to learn from historical attack data and thus be able to identify threats beyond static rules [24]. Thus began the shift from reactive security to more adaptive and intelligent defenses. A landmark event occurred with the advent of deep learning in cybersecurity. With deep learning, new malware classification, phishing detection, and network traffic analysis based on convolutional and recurrent neural networks could offer improved accuracy with reduced false positives [25]. Also, findings in natural language processing (NLP) have enabled AI systems to extract threat intelligence from unstructured sources of information, such as security blogs, forums, and social networks, further fortifying proactive threat detection. Yet another game-changer is the integration of AI with security information and event management (SIEM) platforms and automated incident response systems to enhance and accelerate the real-time monitoring and response to threats. These developments mark the evolution of AI from being experimental to being a vital component of every modern cybersecurity framework.

6.3 Applications and Real-World Impact

6.3.1 AI in malware detection, phishing prevention, and intrusion detection

AI has a private place in cybersecurity; perhaps it is emerging in its latest applications as malware detection, phishing prevention, and intrusion detection. It applies to the general field of malware detection for AI modes, particularly machine learning and deep learning, such as convolutional neural networks (CNNs), that allow the systems to detect malicious software. Previously, it relied on known signatures, yet it improved detection accuracy by attacking unknown threats and variants [26]. For phishing prevention, AI algorithms study the contents of the email, its URL structure, and the corresponding behavior of users to identify suspicious activities and block the endpoints from accessing the phishing sites in real time [27]. All these phenomena fall under intrusion detection, where the power of the AI builds up the intrusion detection systems (IDS) in anomaly detection techniques and neural networks, and learns normal activity in a network and tips regarding deviations having probability signs of cyberattacks to improve responses and

Table 6.1 Use cases of AI in cybersecurity.

Application Area	Example	AI technique used	Outcome
Malware detection	Detecting polymorphic malware	Deep learning (CNNs)	Higher accuracy in identifying obfuscated threats
Phishing detection	Identifying fraudulent websites/emails	Natural language processing	Real-time detection of phishing attempts
Intrusion detection	Unusual network behavior	Anomaly detection (Autoencoders)	Reduced false positives, quicker alerts
Fraud detection	Credit card transaction monitoring	Machine learning (Random forest)	Reduced financial fraud losses
Insider threat detection	Employee behavioral monitoring	Behavioral analytics	Early warning for potential insider breaches

decrease false positives [28]. These AI systems develop constantly because of adaptive learning and real-time data analysis, producing faster results and more accurate research than traditional means. They cannot perform without high-quality datasets, more advanced training, and continuity of updates to remain ahead of highly sophisticated cyber threats [29].

Table 6.1 catalogs various fields of AI application in cyberspace, providing examples of real-life scenarios, the various techniques employed in that area (ML, DL, etc.), and measurable results or benefits.

6.3.2 Behavioral analytics and insider threat detection

Now, behavioral analytics plays a critical role in modern cybersecurity regarding detecting insider threats that escape detection in conventional security schemes from which all internal users are considered trustworthy. Employees may misuse access rights, steal sensitive data, or even compromise systems unknowingly through phishing or other negligent activities. In contrast to the perimeter defenses that focus on known attack vectors, behavioral analytics uses AI and machine learning to construct dynamic baselines for various digital activities exhibited by users – times of system logins, frequencies of accessing files or databases, email usage, and internal communication patterns. US-based techniques of unsupervised clustering, anomaly detection, and sequence modeling can help AI systems identify fine-grained changes in behavior that can indicate compromised credentials or malicious intent, such as accessing confidential documents by scheduling or from external, unauthorized devices [30]. These systems will continuously learn from both normal and suspicious behaviors to improve detection effectiveness while greatly reducing the number of false positives. Furthermore, AI can correlate behaviors across many data sources, including system logs, emails, traffic on the network, and endpoint activity, ideally to present value-added insights on possible risks [31]. When linked with user and entity behavior analytics (UEBA) platforms, such insights now become real-time alert mechanisms that support teams in collaborating proactively to investigate and act against attacks before damage is done. UEBA tools powered by AI can also prioritize incidents in terms of risk scoring, hence lessening alert fatigue. These advanced systems must be set forth with strong governance, including privacies in policies, data protection protocols, and ethical frameworks in AI, to gain employees' trust and not partake in over-surveillance [32].

6.3.3 Broader societal and economic implications

The integration of AI into cybersecurity has profound societal and economic implications. On a societal level, AI enhances the ability to safeguard critical infrastructures, such as healthcare, finance, and government services, thereby improving digital trust and national security. By automating threat detection and response, AI minimizes the risk of data breaches that could compromise citizens' privacy and safety [33]. Economically, AI-driven cybersecurity significantly reduces the cost and time associated with threat management by streamlining operations and reducing human workload. This efficiency allows organizations to reallocate resources toward innovation and growth. Moreover, as cyberattacks grow more sophisticated, reliance on AI creates a demand for a skilled workforce proficient in AI and security, fostering job creation and new career pathways. However, this transformation also brings challenges, including job displacement due to automation, regulatory concerns, and ethical dilemmas related to surveillance and data governance [34]. Balancing innovation with responsibility is essential to ensure equitable access and trust in AI-powered security systems.

6.4 Core Technologies in AI Threat Detection

6.4.1 Algorithms for anomaly detection and predictive threat analysis

Pivotal in cybersecurity, AI anomaly detection and predictive threat analysis algorithms help identify deviations from normal patterns and forecast attacks. One such means of anomaly detection includes establishing baseline behaviors

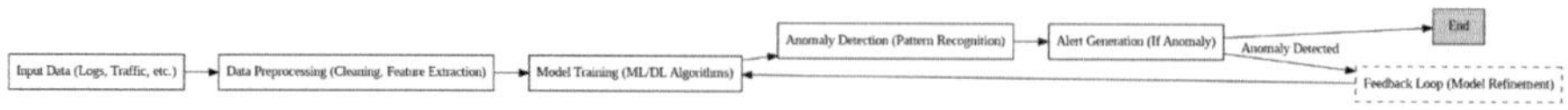

Figure 6.3 How AI works in threat detection (data pipeline flow).

and then flagging deviation behavior for machine learning techniques, such as clustering and classification, that would indicate malicious intent. Predictive threat analysis is a counterpart of machine learning in that it focuses on a statistical model of historical data that identifies relevant trends for future possible cyber-attack occurrences to drive proactiveness in security [35]. These algorithms help improve the detection of threat intrusions where humans are ignorantly using advanced dynamic adaptive security postures instead of the traditional rules-based systems. The effectiveness of these algorithms will rely, however, on the quality and quantity of training data available and the capability of adaptation to the new trend in imaginary threat landscapes [36].

Figure 6.3 describes a block diagram that shows the end-to-end threat detection process in AI deployment. It stages the input of data into processing, model training, anomaly detection, and alert generation workflow in real application fields.

6.4.2 AI frameworks and tools for cybersecurity

Holistic AI frameworks/tools act as the cornerstone for any such environment in modern-day times, with great scalability, flexibility, and efficiency to usher in intelligent systems for threat detection and response. Some of the more widely publicized machine-learning frameworks, such as TensorFlow, PyTorch, and Scikit-learn, are being utilized predominantly to build predictive models that identify malware, detect anomalies in data, and classify phishing attempts based on behavioral patterns and historical data [37]. These frameworks support the development of supervised, unsupervised, and reinforcement learning techniques, thereby allowing cybersecurity applications. Thus, IBM Watson for Cybersecurity and Microsoft Azure Sentinel rely on natural language processing and AI-driven threat intelligence to scan large sets of unstructured data, including anything from emails and logs to dark web activity, for real-time insights [38]. Supports Splunk, strengthened by ML toolkits, alongside Elastic Security (ex-ELK Stack), provides AI-integrated functionality for advanced security analytics and threat hunting. Such solutions automate threat detection, incident response, and root cause analysis while cutting the time required to respond to a security incident by a lot. The continuous improvement of security models using these technologies is further enhanced

Table 6.2 Comparison of AI algorithms for threat detection.

Algorithm	Type	Use case	Strengths	Weaknesses
Decision trees	Supervised	Malware Classification	Simple to interpret	Prone to overfitting
Support vector machine	Supervised	Spam filtering	High accuracy on smaller datasets	Does not scale well with large data
K-Means Clustering	Unsupervised	Anomaly detection	Easy to implement	Assumes spherical clusters
Autoencoder	Unsupervised	Network intrusion detection	Effective at learning hidden features	Requires large training data
Random forest	Supervised	Fraud detection	Handles large datasets, reduces overfitting	Less interpretable than single d

through their integration with SIEM and SOAR systems [39]. As cyber threats become more complex, robust AI frameworks and tools enable organizations to adopt a proactive security posture, foster effective decision-making, and respond adequately to known and unknown attacks [40].

Table 6.2 shows a comparison of various algorithms in AI for cybersecurity, providing types, practical use cases, benefits, and likely disadvantages. This gives insight into methods found to fit against certain threat scenarios.

6.5 Ethical and Safety Considerations

6.5.1 Ensuring responsible AI deployment in threat detection

It is paramount to ensure that AI is responsibly deployed between the dual-pronged demands of building trust in its users and effectiveness in its operations as AI technology becomes increasingly integrated into cybersystems. Responsible AI, such as in threat detection, requires threat models to be designed, developed, and deployed not only to accurately detect threats, but also with regard to privacy, minimizing biases, and rendering explainable results. Transparency has a pivotal role: security experts must know how the AI systems make their decisions, as AI error rates translate into costly false positives and negatives with respect to security or operational consequences [41]. Quite critically, fairness in training data is another major consideration; biased datasets could lead to disadvantages and discrimination in delivering threat responses, particularly in settings that comprise culturally diverse

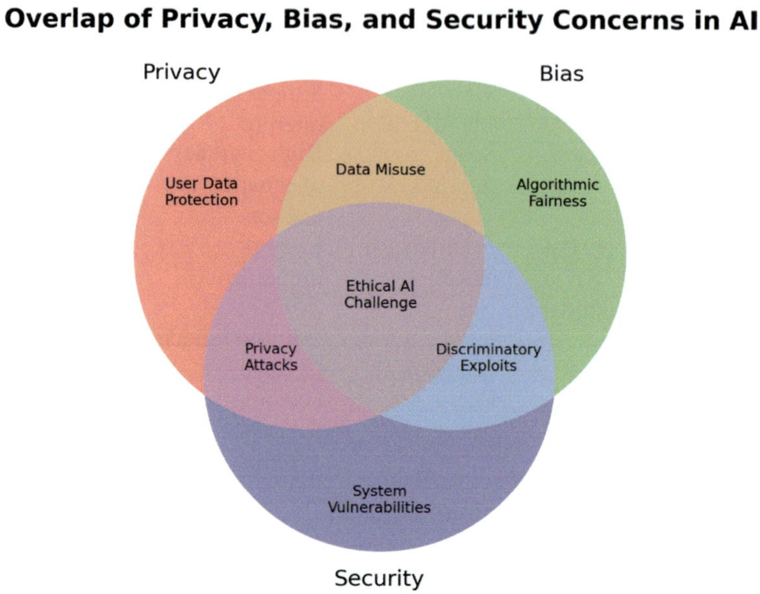

Figure 6.4 Overlap of privacy, bias, and security concerns in AI.

organizations [42]. On the other hand, robust governance frameworks must be established to regulate the deployment of AI models and hold actors accountable, while ensuring AI in cybersecurity complies with relevant standards, besides the European Union General Data Protection Regulation (GDPR). Explainable AI (XAI) techniques support the explanation of the models with complex outputs that contribute to the decision-making of human analysts [43]. Continuous monitoring and auditing of AI systems must be in place to cater to the emerging threat landscape and to ensure their compliance with ethical considerations. In establishing an AI security tool, having members from different backgrounds and expertise, including ethicists, legal experts, and cybersecurity professionals, would foster an innovative yet responsible and balanced perspective on security operations [44].

Figure 6.4 shows the ethical challenges surrounding AI systems. It illustrates how concerns such as data privacy, algorithmic bias, and cybersecurity interlink with one another, thus establishing the need for holistic approaches to developing responsible AI.

6.5.2 Addressing privacy, bias, and security challenges

The increased view of acceptance of AI in cybersecurity does provide an effective capability, but at the same time, it poses myriad challenges, especially in terms of privacy, bias, and security. AI models for threat detection usually operate on large datasets containing user behavior logs and communications, system activities, and even personal identifiers. These forays into data collection encroach on user privacy and may potentially infringe on regulatory frameworks such as the GDPR. This holds particular concern because, in domains of a competitive nature like healthcare, finance, or government, reputational and legal challenges can arise through the misuse of data. Currently, work is going on to find techniques, such as differential privacy and federated learning, to ensure user privacy by allowing model training absent raw data access [45]. Equally pernicious is algorithmic bias, wherein skewed or unrepresentative data serve as inputs for a machine-learning model will result in bias or discrimination. In cybersecurity, this may imply biased alert prioritization, misidentifying insider threats, or ignoring vulnerabilities due to historical underreporting. Biased AI undermines trust and creates operational inefficiencies. Any AI fairness regime will then need to make use of bias detection tools, diverse datasets, and fairness-aware training algorithms that are auditable and validated rigorously for the entire life cycle of the system [46]. AI systems are themselves not immune to security attacks. The increasing threat of adversarial examples – inputs that are specifically constructed to fool AI models – is adversely affecting their reliability. An AI classifier forged by the attackers may present abnormal behavior, such as effective evasion using legitimate user signals or generating false alarms. In the extreme, attackers would reverse-engineer the ML model to acquire sensitive decision logic and/or training data. This points to the pressing need for a secure AI development lifecycle that encompasses adversarial robustness testing, secure model deployment, and continued monitoring for exploit attempts [47]. In responding to these intertwined challenges, organizations must adopt a holistic and ethically based approach. This means ensuring that their technical safeguards (such as encrypted data pipelines), organizational practices (such as transparency in decision-making), and policy frameworks (such as enforceable accountability, auditability, and inclusive system design). Only by embracing this multi-dimensional perspective will AI emerge to become a responsible and resilient ally to contemporary cybersecurity.

6.5.3 Mitigating risks of false positives, false negatives, and AI misuse

One of the core characteristics that might arise from using AI in support of cybersecurity systems is the address of false positives, false negatives, and AI optimization issues. False positives, for instance, manifest as genuine activities being wrongly considered malicious, resulting in numerous false

Table 6.3 Key ethical challenges and mitigation strategies.

Challenge	Risk	Mitigation approach	Real-world example
Data privacy	Unauthorized use of user data	Differential privacy, secure federated learning	Apple's privacy-preserving machine learning
Algorithmic bias	Discriminatory decisions	Diverse training datasets, fairness audits	COMPAS bias in criminal justice predictions
Explainability	Black-box AI decisions	Explainable AI (XAI) tools	LIME/SHAP used in fraud detection
Misuse of AI	Weaponizing AI for cyber attacks	AI usage policies, threat modeling	Deepfake phishing attacks

warnings that could, in turn, have an overwhelming impact on the security team so that they may fail to address the real threat. The reverse side of a false negative is a malicious activity that goes unnoticed on account of evasion, thereby making the system vulnerable to be exploited. Fixing this must be a multi-aspect approach with one of them being the application of context-aware detection systems. These have been quite effective in reducing false positives by incorporating the environment and behavior into the threat analysis, thus enhancing the accuracy of intrusion detection mechanisms [48]. For instance, the explainability of AI-based models is of utmost importance for such applications in view of false positives and the like. Security staff who understand and can follow the reasoning in the decision processes of AI-based systems are more trusting and are well placed to act on the alarms generated. With XAI, they can reduce false positives by providing insight into why specific activities are classified as threats and improve the generalization and trustworthiness of threat detection systems [49]. Finally, the misuse of AI by bad actors is a significant worry. Attackers could potentially use AI-based technologies to develop high-end threats that would be even harder to trace with traditional methods [50]. To curb this threat, the act of creating high-yield AI governance frameworks needs to be forcefully contended for. These frameworks should offer moral instruction, policies for usage, and deep-rooted security approaches, aimed at earning genuine artificial intelligence usage benefits while minimizing the risks posed by adversarial attacks [51].

Table 6.3 analyses major ethical issues (such as bias, privacy, and transparency), their associated risks, and possible solutions with real-world examples serving to illustrate how these issues are being tackled.

6.6 Opportunities Created by AI in Threat Detection

6.6.1 Enhancing threat response efficiency and accuracy

The use of AI has transformed the whole cybersecurity process automation and optimization to improve both the accuracy and efficiency of response to threats, moving away from the outdated, labor-intensive, slow, and manual processes. The systems employ data analytics and machine learning to monitor the network traffic, audit logs, and understand user behavior in real time, thereby recognizing some very slight anomalies constituting signs of cyber threats, prioritizing incidents of highest risk, and initiating a form of automated response against the threat. Thus, this happens to be instant detection and classification, which could only bring down average times of thorough detection (MTTD) and incident response (MTTR) with minimum consequent damage [52]. Reinforcement learning, using a continuous feedback loop, enables AI models to adaptively make better decisions based on incoming data and new attack vectors. This ability to adapt is pivotal to prevail over advanced and rapidly changing cyber threats. Further, embedding Explainable AI (XAI) within cybersecurity operations assures human oversight through a transparent and interpretable insight into the AI's decision-making reasoning. The reasoning guarantees that analysts approve of automated actions, rectify potential misjudgments, and fine-tune threat response strategies, ultimately strengthening human intelligence-machine learning integration [53]. Thus, as a capacity, artificial intelligence enhances the operational efficiency of cybersecurity infrastructure for enterprises and national defense and, in so doing, enhances its trustworthiness and effectiveness.

Table 6.4 shows the traditional enhancements of cybersecurity approaches, and performance across security functions is compared. It explains how AI increases operational efficiency, detection speed, and the accuracy of decision-making.

6.6.2 Strengthening cyber resilience and real-time monitoring

During this era of heightened digital connectivity, cyber resilience enhancement and real-time monitoring deployment become imperative to allow the organization to withstand, respond to, and recover from a variety of cyber threats. Cyber resilience includes continuous risk management, adaptive defense, and recovery from disruptions beyond traditional security. Another invaluable contribution of AI toward cyber resilience includes predictive analytics, automation of incident response, and facilitative threat hunting. Real-time monitoring systems empowered by AI continuously inspect logs,

Table 6.4 Benefits of AI integration across security functions.

Security function	Traditional method	AI-Enhanced method	Efficiency gained
Threat hunting	Manual log reviews	Automated anomaly detection	Faster detection of unknown threats
Incident response	Static rule-based responses	Adaptive AI-based SOAR tools	Reduced response time
Vulnerability management	Periodic scanning	Predictive patching via ML	Early prevention of exploitability
Risk assessment	Questionnaire-based	Dynamic risk-scoring algorithms	Continuous, real-time risk evaluation
Email filtering	Keyword-based spam filters	NLP-driven content analysis	Higher accuracy, fewer false positives

network traffic, and endpoint behavior to detect anomalies or signs of compromise as they happen, minimizing detection and response time [54]. These systems use cutting-edge machine learning models that can detect even the tiniest deviations away from normalcy, thus flagging suspect patterns that simply would have gone unnoticed under classical methods. Moreover, AI systems capable of real-time monitoring could work in tandem with Security Information and Event Management (SIEM) and SOAR platforms to extend automation to workflows, thus enabling faster incident response. Real-time visibility helps rapidly contain a threat while enhancing long-term resilience through every incident for fortified defenses against the next one [55]. Cyber resilience and real-time monitoring are the pillars of a modern security architecture with AI augmentations, designed to withstand both known and emerging threats.

6.7 Challenges and Risks in AI-Based Threat Detection

6.7.1 Adversarial attacks on AI models and balancing automation with human oversight

Artificial intelligence and its applications in cybersecurity work collectively under a very robust roof. Hence, the exploitation of AI is rendered as an adversarial attack on this very technology. That is, adversarial attacks involve strategic manipulation of input data to deceive AI models into making incorrect decisions. Threat-detection techniques, malware classification, and phishing identification systems are some systems threatened by such attacks. A few insignificant changes of packet metadata or features in an executable can result in the misclassification of harmful payloads as benign in intrusion detection systems [56], [57]. In effect, it avoids defenses while raising no alarms. Data integrity gets compromised along with confidentiality, in addition to tarnishing trust in the AI system. Therefore, developing models of resilience against types of attacks becomes imperative. Using adversarial training, gradient masking, input pre-processing, ensemble modeling, and many other methods in exposing models to manipulated examples during the training phase acts as fortifications to AI against the adversarial manipulations [58]. The development of methods for the detection of real-time adversarial inputs, along with those affecting model sensitivity thresholds, enhances the robustness of the entire system without sacrificing efficiency on authentic data, but the best AI is not infallible.

Total reliance on automation brings risk, for example, the appearance of false positives and false negatives, as well as ethical ambiguities. Therefore, there is a need for a human oversight-based balance of automated and manual approaches for creating trustworthy, accountable cybersecurity systems. Human analysts provide an extremely effective contextual judgment and ethical reasoning when faced with ambiguous or high-stakes events in which AI may fail or lack awareness of situational contexts [59]. In a sense, these employ some human-in-the-loop, bringing efforts together to make model outputs interpretable, verifiable, and actionable. Analysts can conduct post-incident reviews, validate AI decisions, and intervene, if necessary, thus closing the gap between computational efficiency and human intuition. Furthermore, humans in feedback loops can make an organization come up with continuous improvements to AI performance, cures to biases, and adaptability to new emerging threats. This hybrid approach makes the system much more resilient than just operational, trustworthy, and legally defensible [60]. Finally, introducing AI capabilities with human expertise provides an extension in scalability, an ethical manner of response, and a speedy reflection of the fast-increasing complexity of threats to the modern cyber landscape.

Figure 6.5 visually represents how adversarial inputs are crafted in the veneration of vulnerabilities posed to AI models. It charts out the attacker's route from entry points to final ramifications, helping to comprehend where and how AI can be deluded.

6.7.2 Managing job displacement and economic disruption in cybersecurity

The management of job loss and economic dislocation from other advancements in AI is an almost immediate yet urgent challenge for cybersecurity.

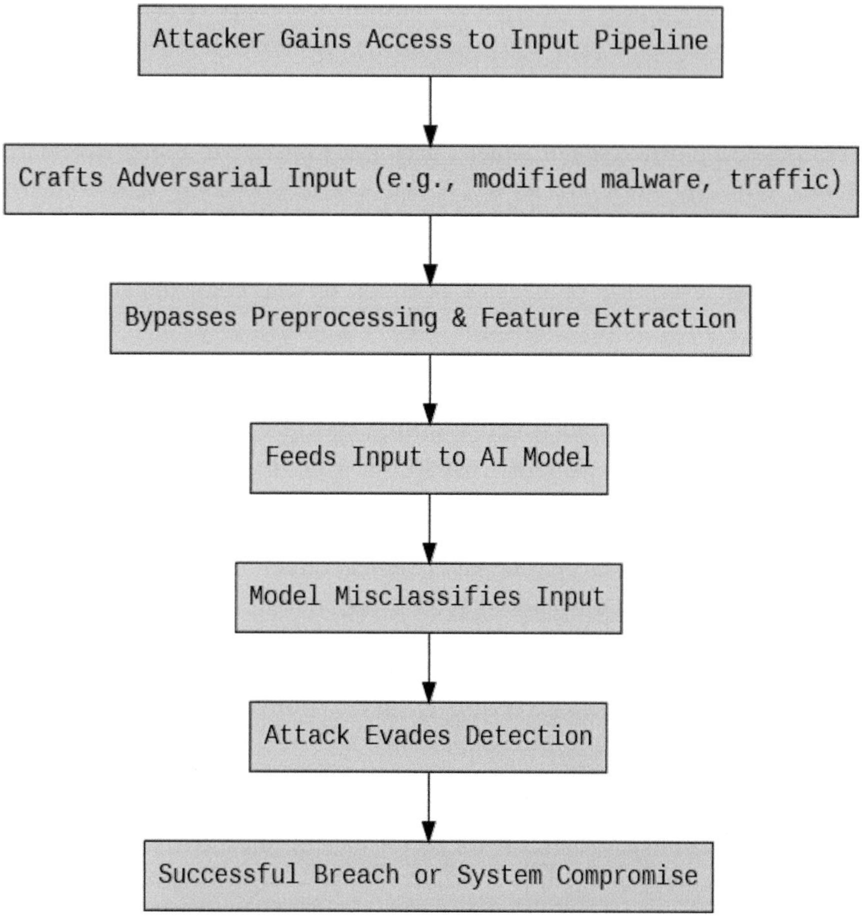

Figure 6.5 How adversarial attacks exploit AI models.

As AI technologies become mainstream ever faster, performing tasks from real-time threat detection to vulnerability scanning and incident triage, and even encroaching upon aspects of penetration testing, the worrying trend is emerging that traditional roles, especially the ones involving repetitive or rule-based functions, could be phased out. Such disruption would impair individual careers alongside possible disturbances to the work-life situation of the wider cybersecurity workforce. Therefore, management of the related risks needs to strategically emphasize upskilling and reskilling. In this regard, cybersecurity professionals should be allowed to navigate the dynamic new environment by developing different competitive skills in areas where human judgment is key. These areas consist, but are not limited to, explainable AI;

Table 6.5 Impact of automation on cybersecurity jobs.

Role	At-risk tasks	AI opportunities	Reskilling options
SOC Analyst	Log triage, basic alerts	Threat pattern analysis	ML fundamentals, threat intelligence
Security auditor	Routine compliance checks	Continuous compliance via AI	Risk Management, Explainable AI (XAI)
Malware analyst	Signature generation	Dynamic behavior detection with ML	Reverse Engineering, Deep Learning
Penetration tester	Manual vulnerability identification	Automated scanning tools	Offensive AI Tactics, Adversarial Testing
Threat intelligence lead	Data aggregation from threat feeds	Real-time threat context analysis	NLP in Cybersecurity, Automated CTI

adversarial robustness analysis; ethical oversight; AI auditing; and providing contextual threat intelligence – areas where AI can never ensure protection alone [61]. Additionally, building a workforce to design, validate, and monitor AI systems will make sure that human decision-making remains central to the field of cybersecurity. Concurrently, governmental and institutional provisions should be implemented to promote favorable policies for a balanced coexistence of humans and machines. Such measures may entail incentives for training, funding of human-centered cybersecurity research, and regulations promoting transparency in AI use. Human-in-the-loop frameworks would be encouraged, where AI would assist rather than substitute human stakeholders in maintaining accountability and job relevance for the future [62]. Such integrated approaches not only minimize disruption but also maximize the tail-end benefits of AI to society from a cybersecurity viewpoint.

Table 6.5 addresses the impact of AI-driven automation on the cybersecurity profession, identifying jobs likely to be automated, new job opportunities created by AI, and suggested upskilling or reskilling schemes.

6.8 Future Directions in AI-Driven Cybersecurity

6.8.1 Advancing AI-driven cybersecurity: Emerging trends, autonomous defense, and collaborative innovation

This is very interesting, as it makes a revolution in the territory of progressive marking transformations of cyber defense toward automated, self-defense capability that, using AI, can recognize, analyze, and respond to threats in real-time, cutting down on high reliance on human intervention and speeding things up considerably [63]. Such systems nowadays rely on existing machine learning algorithms trained on huge datasets to find out how to better and more accurately identify anomalies or novel attack patterns. Fast autonomous decision-making from the behavior patterns that are learned continuously is generally an important feature of their operation, with a promise of finding out threats much earlier than the present systems that have been recognized or detected as having caused some damage. Further, this is autonomously complemented by an increase in the number of organizations employing AI-augmented security teams, where AI tools and human expertise are designed to complement each other in enhanced threat intelligence and incident response. Under this model, AI would take care of tasks that are tedious and time-consuming, such as log analysis, anomaly detection, and simple incident triage, freeing humans to concentrate on strategic decision-making, threat hunting, and more complex investigations that require human intuition, creativity, and ethical consideration [64]. This is the future human-machine model of security maintenance. AI excels in data processing, pattern recognition, and scalability; however, this type of machine lacks contextual understanding and the ability to comprehend or judge socio-political, legal, or moral dimensions of cyber threats, and this makes human judgment very important [65]. In addition, ensuring robust collaboration between academia, industry, and governments would be key for pushing forward AI threat detection research and practice [66]. Academic institutions drive foundational research in algorithm development, model interpretability, and adversarial resistance. Industry players provide real-world data, infrastructure, and case studies to enable scalable deployment and real-time testing. Governments play a key role in creating policy frameworks, offering funds, and ensuring that ethical standards and national security interests are addressed [67]. The collaborative effort has seen the formation of AI research consortia, public-private partnerships, and global alliances for cyber defense, which are all geared towards speeding up innovation while ensuring proper protection of democracy and digital sovereignty. Further, research is increasingly focused on the security and trustworthiness of AI systems themselves. One relevant and important direction is adversarial robustness-open the development of models resistant to manipulation by non-natural inputs crafted specifically to deceive them. Current research efforts focus on fortifying AI's defense mechanisms by refining techniques like adversarial training, ensemble methods, and input sanitization [68]. The phenomenon of explainable AI (XAI), appearing in parallel, helps to fill the interpretability chasm by making it transparent and understandable to the human operator the decisions made by models, in the aspect of compliance, audit, and trust vis-à-vis high-stakes security environments. Federated learning is yet another significant trend, allowing AI models to be trained on distributed datasets of high privacy, such as hospitals, states, or multinational corporations, without merging them. Herein lies its specific importance for cybersecurity, where it is not easy to share sensitive data because of confidentiality [69]. Also, research on AI is increasingly beyond material benefits, and some of the more pronounced ethical issues have become central in the work of establishing data privacy, minimizing algorithmic bias and accountability, and developing interdisciplinary research and policies to ensure legal and social alignment with technical innovation [70]. The development of cutting-edge, AI-fortified threat intelligence platforms is quite explosive. These platforms apply both natural language processing and graph-based analysis to decipher unstructured data from various sources such as social media, dark-net forums, and threat reports in identifying emerging threats, actors' motivations, and evolving tactics, techniques, and procedures (TTPs) [71]. In addition, research into AI-enhanced SOAR systems is redefining incident response through automating complex workflows, including alert correlation, impact analysis, and remediation actions, thereby accelerating response speed, consistency, and reducing the fatigue associated with analysts. The future of cyber defense becomes one of growing autonomy for AI, closer collaboration between human and artificial agents, and great emphasis on ethical, explainable, and resilient design. Multisector partnerships, technology innovation, and careful regulation will be crucial across the board to help realize and navigate AI's potential and challenges in an ever-changing threat environment.

6.9 Conclusion and Reflections

Artificial intelligence is transforming, and from the aspects of cybersecurity, it breaks the existing boundaries, paving the way for several advanced tools that enhance the speed of response, increase threat detection, and improve dimensions that enhance resilience. It touches every domain from malware detection to predictive threat analysis, creating new frontiers for real-time, effective, proactive defense mechanisms. The above great advancements bring harmful effects along with them in a complicated throbbing neck of horizon problems. Data privacy, algorithmic bias, and adversarial attacks have propelled a need for AI systems to be more transparent, accountable, and equitable. Over-automation with job losses is mainly one of such stressors on improving the human-in-the-loop form of approaches, as well as the investment into workforce upskilling. Besides this, the regulation of AI systems will have to become clearer since the lines between assistance and control begin to blur as systems become more autonomous. Many of the issues at hand will require synergies between the government, the academy, and industries to meet what responsible deployment entails. The distance now between a future with AI and punishment fusion lies in balancing one's innovative ideas with ethical foresight on creating systems that will not just be powerful but also efficient, equitable, interpretable, and aligned with human values. This evolving landscape invites us to reflect on how we shape technology, not just to defend against threats but to empower a safer, more inclusive digital future.

References

[1] N. Kaloudi and J. Li, "The AI-Based Cyber Threat Landscape: A Survey," *ACM Comput. Surv.*, vol. 53, no. 1, p. 20:1–20:34, Feb. 2020, doi: 10.1145/3372823.

[2] S. Zeadally, E. Adi, Z. Baig, and I. A. Khan, "Harnessing Artificial Intelligence Capabilities to Improve Cybersecurity," *IEEE Access*, vol. 8, pp. 23817–23837, 2020, doi: 10.1109/ACCESS. 2020.2968045.

[3] Buczak AL, Guven E. A Survey of Data Mining and Machine Learning Methods for Cyber Security Intrusion Detection. IEEE Communications Surveys & Tutorials. 2016;18(2):1153–1176. DOI:10.1109/COMST. 2015.2494502.

[4] Y. LeCun, Y. Bengio, and G. Hinton, "Deep learning," *Nature*, vol. 521, no. 7553, pp. 436–444, May 2015, doi: 10.1038/nature14539.

[5] Chiba, Zouhair & Abghour, Noreddine & Moussaid, Khalid & Omri, Amina & Rida, Mohamed. (2016). A survey of intrusion detection systems for cloud computing environment. 1–13. 10.1109/ICEMIS.2016.7745295.

[6] Sarker, I.H., Kayes, A.S.M., Badsha, S. *et al.* Cybersecurity data science: an overview from machine learning perspective. *J Big Data* **7**, 41 (2020). https://doi.org/10.1186/s40537-020-00318-5

[7] Teslim, Badrudeen. (2024). Natural Language Processing for Cyber Threat Intelligence in Cloud Networks.

[8] Liu, Liu & Vel, Olivier & Chen, Chao & Zhang, Jun & Xiang, Yang. (2018). Anomaly-Based Insider Threat Detection Using Deep Autoencoders. 39–48. 10.1109/ICDMW.2018.00014.

[9] Nicolas Papernot, Patrick McDaniel et.al 2017. Practical Black-Box Attacks against Machine Learning. In Proceedings of the 2017 ACM on Asia Conference on Computer and Communications Security (ASIA CCS '17). https://doi.org/10.1145/3052973.3053009

[10] Jobin, A., Ienca, M. & Vayena, E. The global landscape of AI ethics guidelines. *Nat Mach Intell* **1**, 389–399 (2019). https://doi.org/10.1038/s42256-019-0088-2

[11] Alzboon, Mowafaq & Bader, Ahmad & Abuashour, Ahmad & Alqaraleh, Muhyeeddin & Zaqaibeh, Belal & Al-Batah, Mohammad. (2023). The Two Sides of AI in Cybersecurity: Opportunities and Challenges. 1–9. 10.1109/ICNGN59831.2023.10396670.

[12] Stutz, Dalmo & Assis, Joaquim & Laghari, Asif & Ayub Khan Ph.D, Dr-Abdullah & Deshpande, Anand & Kulkarni, Dhanashree & Terziev, Andrey & Jesus, Maria & Grata, Edwiges. (2024). Cyber Threat Detection and Mitigation Using Artificial Intelligence – A Cyber-physical Perspective. 10.1002/9781394196470.ch7.

[13] Ali, Tarek & Kostakos, Panos. (2023). HuntGPT: Integrating Machine Learning-Based Anomaly Detection and Explainable AI with Large Language Models (LLMs). 10.48550/arXiv.2309.16021.

[14] Oloyede, Joseph, Leveraging Artificial Intelligence for Advanced Cybersecurity Threat Detection and Prevention (October 03, 2024). Available at SSRN: https://ssrn.com/abstract=4976072 or http://dx.doi.org/10.2139/ssrn.4976072

[15] Kheddar, H. (2025). Transformers and Large Language Models for Efficient Intrusion Detection Systems: A Comprehensive Survey. *arXiv [Cs.CR]*. Retrieved from http://arxiv.org/abs/2408.07583

[16] Haji, Saad & Ameen, Siddeeq. (2021). Attack and Anomaly Detection in IoT Networks using Machine Learning Techniques: A Review. Asian Journal of Research in Computer Science. 30–46. 10.9734/ajrcos/2021/v9i230218.

[17] Alsoufi, M. A., Razak, S., Siraj, M. M., Nafea, I., Ghaleb, F. A., Saeed, F., & Nasser, M. (2021). Anomaly-Based Intrusion Detection Systems in IoT Using Deep Learning: A Systematic Literature Review. *Applied Sciences*, *11*(18), 8383. https://doi.org/10.3390/app11188383

[18] I. Ullah and Q. H. Mahmoud, "Design and Development of a Deep Learning-Based Model for Anomaly Detection in IoT Networks," in *IEEE Access*, vol. 9, pp. 103906–103926, 2021, doi: 10.1109/ACCESS.2021.3094024.

[19] Hammad, M., Hewahi, N., & Elmedany, W. (2023). Enhancing Network Intrusion Recovery in SDN with machine learning: an innovative approach. *Arab Journal of Basic and Applied Sciences*, *30*(1), 561–572. https://doi.org/10.1080/25765299.2023.2261219

[20] Venkatraman Umbalacheri Ramasamy. (2024). Overview of Anomaly Detection Techniques across Different Domains: A Systematic Review. *International Journal of Computational and Experimental Science and Engineering*, *10*(4). https://doi.org/10.22399/ijcesen.522

[21] Singh, T. M., Reddy, C. K. K., & Lippert, K. The revolution and future of blockchain technology in cybersecurity: A comprehensive analysis.

In *Artificial Intelligence for Blockchain and Cybersecurity Powered IoT Applications* (pp. 71–98). CRC Press.

[22] Patcha, Animesh & Park, Jung-Min (Jerry). (2007). An overview of anomaly detection techniques: Existing solutions and latest technological trends. Computer Networks. 51. 3448–3470. 10.1016/j.comnet.2007.02.001.

[23] H. Debar, M. Dacier and A. Wespi, "Towards a Taxonomy of Intrusion-Detection Systems," Computer Networks, Vol. 31, No. 8, 1999, pp. 805–822. doi:10.1016/S1389-1286(98)00017-6

[24] R. Sommer and V. Paxson, "Outside the Closed World: On Using Machine Learning for Network Intrusion Detection," *2010 IEEE Symposium on Security and Privacy*, Oakland, CA, USA, 2010, pp. 305–316, doi: 10.1109/SP.2010.25.

[25] Ravi, Vinayakumar & Alazab, Mamoun & Kp, Soman & Poornachandran, Prabaharan & Al-Nemrat, A. & Venkatraman, Sitalakshmi. (2019). Deep Learning Approach for Intelligent Intrusion Detection System. IEEE Access. pp. 1–1. 10.1109/ACCESS.2019.2895334.

[26] Hardy, W., Chen, L., Hou, S., Ye, Y., & Li, X. (2016). DL 4 MD : A Deep Learning Framework for Intelligent Malware Detection.

[27] Salloum, Said & Gaber, Tarek & Vadera, Sunil & Shaalan, Khaled. (2021). Phishing Email Detection Using Natural Language Processing Techniques: A Literature Survey. Procedia Computer Science. 189. 19–28. 10.1016/j.procs.2021.05.077.

[28] Diro, Abebe & Chilamkurti, Naveen. (2017). Distributed attack detection scheme using deep learning approach for Internet of Things. Future Generation Computer Systems. 82. 10.1016/j.future.2017.08.043.

[29] Mittal, M., Kumar, K., & Behal, S. (2022). Deep learning approaches for detecting DDoS attacks: a systematic review. *Soft computing*, 1–37. Advance online publication. https://doi.org/10.1007/s00500-021-06608-1

[30] Tuor, A., Kaplan, S., Hutchinson, B., Nichols, N., & Robinson, S. (2017). Deep Learning for Unsupervised Insider Threat Detection in Structured Cybersecurity Data Streams. *arXiv [Cs.NE]*. Retrieved from http://arxiv.org/abs/1710.00811

[31] Nepal, Santosh & Joshi, Basanta. (2022). User Behavior Analytics for Insider Threat Detection using Deep Learning.

[32] Alshamrani, A., Myneni, S., Chowdhary, A., & Huang, D. (2019). A Survey on Advanced Persistent Threats: Techniques, Solutions, Challenges, and Research Opportunities. *IEEE Communications Surveys and Tutorials*, *21*(2), 1851–1877. Article 8606252. https://doi.org/10.1109/COMST.2019.2891891

[33] M. Conti, A. Dehghantanha, K. Franke, and S. Watson, "Internet of Things Security and Forensics: Challenges and Opportunities," *Future Generation Computer Systems*, vol. 78, pp. 544–546, Jan. 2018, doi: 10.1016/j.future.2017.07.060.

[34] Reddy, Dhoma & Elumalai, Anupriya. (2022). A Review on Intrusion Detection Using Machine Learning Techniques. International Journal of Engineering Research in Computer Science and Engineering. 9. 10.36647/IJERCSE/09.12.Art013.

[35] Varun Chandola, Arindam Banerjee, and Vipin Kumar. 2009. Anomaly detection: A survey. ACM Comput. Surv. 41, 3, Article 15 (July 2009), 58 pages. https://doi.org/10.1145/1541880.1541882

[36] Ahmed, Hafiza Anisa & Hameed, Anum & Bawany, Narmeen. (2022). Network intrusion detection using oversampling technique and machine learning algorithms. PeerJ Computer Science. 8. e820. 10.7717/peerj-cs.820.

[37] Anisha, P. R., Reddy, C. K. K., Nguyen, N. G., Bhushan, M., Kumar, A., & Hanafiah, M. M. (Eds.). (2022). *Intelligent systems and machine learning for industry: advancements, challenges, and practices*. CRC Press.

[38] Teslim, Badrudeen. (2023). AI-Powered Predictive Analysis in Cybersecurity: Proactively Counteracting Potential Security Incidents.

[39] Karimipour, Hadis & Derakhshan, Farnaz. (2021). AI-Enabled Threat Detection and Security Analysis for Industrial IoT. 10.1007/978-3-030-76613-9.

[40] Veerasamy, Namosha & Badenhorst, Danielle & Ntshangase, Mazwi & Baloyi, Errol & Siphambili, Nokuthaba & Mahlasela, Oyena. (2024). Unpacking AI Security Considerations. International Conference on Cyber Warfare and Security. 19. 10.34190/iccws.19.1.2104.

[41] Wachter, Sandra & Mittelstadt, Brent & Floridi, Luciano. (2017). Transparent, Explainable, and Accountable JOBINAI for Robotics. Science Robotics. 2. 10.1126/scirobotics.aan6080.

[42] Mehrabi, N., Morstatter, F., Saxena, N., Lerman, K., & Galstyan, A. (2022). A Survey on Bias and Fairness in Machine Learning. *arXiv [Cs. LG]*. Retrieved from http://arxiv.org/abs/1908.09635

[43] A. Adadi and M. Berrada, "Peeking Inside the Black-Box: A Survey on Explainable Artificial Intelligence (XAI)," in *IEEE Access*, vol. 6, pp. 52138–52160, 2018, doi: 10.1109/ACCESS.2018.2870052.

[44] Crawford, Kate & Calo, Ryan. (2016). There is a blind spot in AI research. Nature. 538. 311–313. 10.1038/538311a.

[45] Brundage, M., Avin, S., Clark, J., Toner, H., Eckersley, P., Garfinkel, B., … Amodei, D. (2024). The Malicious Use of Artificial Intelligence:

Forecasting, Prevention, and Mitigation. *arXiv [Cs.AI]*. Retrieved from http://arxiv.org/abs/1802.07228

[46] Mittelstadt, B. D., Allo, P., Taddeo, M., Wachter, S., & Floridi, L. (2016). The ethics of algorithms: Mapping the debate. Big Data & Society, 3(2). https://doi.org/10.1177/2053951716679679 (Original work published 2016)

[47] Veale, M., & Binns, R. (2017). Fairer machine learning in the real world: Mitigating discrimination without collecting sensitive data. Big Data & Society, 4(2). https://doi.org/10.1177/2053951717743530 (Original work published 2017)

[48] Lee, Wenke & Stolfo, Salvatore. (1998). Data Mining Approaches for Intrusion Detection. 7.

[49] Doshi-Velez, F., & Kim, B. (2017). Towards A Rigorous Science of Interpretable Machine Learning. *arXiv [Stat.ML]*. Retrieved from http://arxiv.org/abs/1702.08608

[50] Burden, D., & Savin-Baden, M. (2019). *Virtual humans: Today and tomorrow*. Chapman and Hall/CRC.

[51] Chinthala, K. K. R., Thakur, M. S., Shuaib, M., & Alam, S. (2024). Prospects of Computational Intelligence in Society: Human-Centric Solutions, Challenges, and Research Areas.

[52] Katiyar, Dr & Tripathi, Mr & Kumar, Mr & Verma, Mr & Sahu, Dr & Saxena, Dr. (2024). AI and Cyber-Security: Enhancing threat detection and response with machine learning.. Educational Administration Theory and Practices. 30. 10.53555/kuey.v30i4.2377.

[53] Desai, Bhavin & Patil, Kapil & Mehta, Ishita & Patil, Asit. (2024). Explainable AI in Cybersecurity: A Comprehensive Framework for enhancing transparency, trust, and Human-AI Collaboration. 135–150. 10.1109/iSemantic63362.2024.10762690.

[54] Ahmad, Ijaz & Shahabuddin, Shahriar & Kumar, Tanesh & Okwuibe, Jude & Gurtov, Andrei & Ylianttila, Mika. (2019). Security for 5G and Beyond. IEEE Communications Surveys & Tutorials. PP. 10.1109/COMST.2019.2916180.

[55] Thorsten Holz, Markus Engelberth, and Felix Freiling. 2009. Learning more about the underground economy: a case-study of keyloggers and dropzones. In Proceedings of the 14th European conference on Research in computer security (ESORICS'09). Springer-Verlag, Berlin, Heidelberg, 1–18.

[56] Athalye, A., Carlini, N., & Wagner, D. (2018). Obfuscated Gradients Give a False Sense of Security: Circumventing Defenses to Adversarial Examples. *arXiv [Cs.LG]*. Retrieved from http://arxiv.org/abs/1802.00420

[57] Bharadiya, Jasmin. (2023). Machine Learning in Cybersecurity: Techniques and Challenges. European Journal of Technology. 7. 10.47672/ejt.1486.

[58] Yajie Wang, Yi Wu, Shangbo Wu, Ximeng Liu, Wanlei Zhou, Liehuang Zhu, and Chuan Zhang. 2024. Boosting the Transferability of Adversarial Attacks With Frequency-Aware Perturbation. Trans. Info. For. Sec. 19 (2024), 6293–6304. https://doi.org/10.1109/TIFS.2024.3411921

[59] Paul, Celeste & Blaha, Leslie & Gonzalez, Cleotilde & Gutzwiller, Robert. (2019). Opportunities and Challenges for Human-Machine Teaming in Cybersecurity Operations. Proceedings of the Human Factors and Ergonomics Society Annual Meeting. 63. 442–446. 10.1177/1071181319631079.

[60] Amershi, S., Weld, D., Vorvoreanu, M., Fourney, A., Nushi, B., Collisson, P(et.al,2019).*Guidelines for Human-AI Interaction.* doi:10.1145/3290605.330023

[61] Shen, Yang & Zhang, Xiuwu. (2024). The impact of artificial intelligence on employment: the role of virtual agglomeration. Humanities and Social Sciences Communications. 11. 10.1057/s41599-024-02647-9.

[62] Manyika, J, Chui, M, Miremadi, M, Bughin, J, George, K, Willmott, P & Dewhurst, M 2017, A future that works: automation, employment, and productivity, McKinsey Global Institute, [San Francisco]

[63] Freitag, D. Machine Learning for Information Extraction in Informal Domains. *Machine Learning* 39, 169–202 (2000). https://doi.org/10.1023/A:1007601113994

[64] Taddeo, Mariarosaria & Floridi, Luciano. (2018). How AI can be a force for good. Science. 361. 751–752. 10.1126/science.aat5991.

[65] Mulgan, T. (2016). Superintelligence: Paths, dangers, strategies.

[66] Dietterich, T.G. (2000). Ensemble Methods in Machine Learning. In: Multiple Classifier Systems. MCS 2000. Lecture Notes in Computer Science, vol 1857. Springer, Berlin, Heidelberg. https://doi.org/10.1007/3-540-45014-9_1

[67] Dietterich, T. G. (2017). Steps Toward Robust Artificial Intelligence. *AI Magazine*, *38*(3), 3–24. https://doi.org/10.1609/aimag.v38i3.2756

[68] Gunning, D., & Aha, D. (2019). DARPA's Explainable Artificial Intelligence (XAI) Program. *AI Magazine*, *40*(2), 44–58. https://doi.org/10.1609/aimag.v40i2.2850

[69] McMahan, B., Moore, E., Ramage, D., Hampson, S. & Arcas, B.A.y.. (2017). Communication-Efficient Learning of Deep Networks from Decentralized Data. *Proceedings of the 20th International Conference on Artificial Intelligence and Statistics*, in *Proceedings of Machine Learning Research* 54:1273–1282 Available from https://proceedings.mlr.press/v54/mcmahan17a.html.

[70] Floridi, L., Cowls, J., Beltrametti, M., Chatila, R., Chazerand, P., Dignum, V., Luetge, C., Madelin, R., Pagallo, U., Rossi, F., Schafer, B., Valcke, P., & Vayena, E. (2018). AI4People-An Ethical Framework for a Good AI Society: Opportunities, Risks, Principles, and Recommendations. *Minds and machines*, *28*(4), 689–707. https://doi.org/10.1007/s11023-018-9482-5

[71] Chaparro Sierra, Luisa & Pulido, Cristian & Rudas, Jorge & Reyes, Ana & Victorino, Jorge & Narvaez, Luz & Gomez, Francisco & Martinez, Darwin. (2020). Sentiment Analysis of Social Network Content to Characterize the Perception of Security. 685–691. 10.1109/ASONAM49781.2020.9381434.

7

AI-powered Risk Mitigation and Intelligent Incident Response in Cybersecurity

Jagadeshwari Puttanapura[1], Kishor Kumar Reddy C[1], Monika Singh T[1*], and Kari Lippert[2]

[1]Stanley College of Engineering and Technology for Women, India,
[2]University of South Alabama, USA

Email: jagadeshwariputtanapura07@gmail.com; kishoar23@gmail.com; thakursingh.monika@gmail.com; klippert@southalabama.edu

Abstract

Traditional security measures can no longer guarantee timeliness and effectiveness against imminent risk exposures due to the growing complexity and frequency of cyber threats. This chapter attempts to analyze how artificial intelligence is altering the cyber risk management landscape by enabling proactive threat detection, predictive risk assessment, and automated incident response. The chapter examines AI methodologies that include machine learning, deep learning, and natural language processing, and how these are being utilized in anomaly detection, incident workflow orchestration, and root cause analysis. The integration of AI with existing cybersecurity infrastructures like security information and event management and security orchestration, automation, and response platforms is also taken into account, particularly in terms of speed, accuracy, and scalability improvements. Barriers to AI are also discussed, such as issues with data bias, adversarial attacks, and ethical issues, together with interesting new developments like explainable AI and federated learning. Through relevant case studies and practical examples, the chapter will help readers get up to speed on how AI can be strategically deployed to bolster cyber resilience in modern-day digital ecosystems.

DOI: 10.1201/9788743808077-7

7.1 Introduction

Cyber threats have become increasingly intricate and quite significant. This represents one of the major challenges faced by organizations today, whether they are governmental, non-profit, or corporate. Cybersecurity, particularly when it relies on traditional manuals and rigid rule-based systems, struggles to keep pace with attacks unfolding in real time. Thus, the demand for intelligent, adaptive, and proactive solutions has grown. AI has emerged as a game-changing technology in the realm of cyber risk management and offers robust capabilities in threat detection, risk assessment, and automated response to incidents. This chapter discusses how AI technologies enhance the resilience of cybersecurity practices through timely decision-making and precision while they persist in the unpredictable landscape of shifting cyber risks.

Digitalization has indeed enabled organizations to become more dependent on complex information systems so they can effectively and innovatively store, process, and transmit data. Nevertheless, all organizations are now vulnerable to threats with networks illuminated by numerous possibilities, such as data breaches, ransomware, insider-related accidents, advanced persistent threats, and so forth – they have now entered a more dynamic and perilous world of cyber risk [1]. Cyber risk management has made security not only essential but also strategic for maintaining those digital assets and continually earning the trust of stakeholders.

Cyber risk management involves the identification, evaluation, and reduction of threats linked to cyberspace. Unlike traditional risk management methods that may depend too heavily on semi-annual assessments performed manually, contemporary cyber risk management necessitates ongoing vigilance and swift action in response. This change is due to the requirement to carefully monitor various threats before they escalate into harmful incidents. Consequently, a proactive and flexible strategy for cyber risk management allows organizations to maintain operational continuity and adhere to regulatory requirements [2].

The adoption of digital technologies spans across all sectors, including finance, health, and manufacturing, where the costs associated with cyber incidents are now not confined to IT departments. These incidents now carry enterprise-wide consequences – impacting financial performance, brand reputation, and customer trust. Therefore, organizations need to invest in an intelligent, comprehensive, and scalable risk management framework, as the threat landscape continues to evolve, to ensure adaptability in the future.

7.1.1 Role of AI in modern cybersecurity

Cybersecurity, a field significantly influenced by the remarkable technology known as artificial intelligence, currently encounters numerous challenges that AI can tackle more effectively than conventional rule-based approaches. [3] An AI tool is capable of analyzing vast quantities of data at incredible speeds, recognizing patterns that would escape human detection, and providing a response in a critical moment. Consequently, AI has become essential in identifying cyber risks and automating responses while enhancing precision and efficiency in security operations.

Figure 7.1 depicts the shift in risk management from traditional and responsive methods to the implementation of AI technologies. Key phases would encompass the incorporation of automation, technology, and the uptake of machine learning. The result is a predictive, responsive real-time performance bolstered by empirical data. It wraps up with ethical concerns and human-supervised AI governance.

The primary benefit of artificial intelligence in cybersecurity is its capability for threat identification and forecasting, which is a prevalent field. Machine learning algorithms acquire knowledge from past data to recognize atypical behavior trends and can highlight irregularities as they arise. Deep learning architectures are capable of analyzing highly intricate data types, including network traffic, user activity, and system logs, all focused on revealing subtle signs of a breach. These systems are highly proficient in identifying zero-day vulnerabilities and internal risks that are undetectable by conventional methods [4].

After identifying an issue, it should also commence the incident response. SOAR platforms enhanced with AI functionalities can now streamline the triage, investigation, and resolution of incidents, thereby reducing the workload on human analysts and shortening resolution time. When combined with current tools, like SIEM systems, AI provides a cohesive intelligent defense strategy to react to incidents and gain insights from them, reinforcing future resilience.

7.2 Understanding Risk in Cybersecurity

Today, in the online realm, cybersecurity risk issues encompass far more than merely technical elements; they are regarded as strategic business challenges. Different threats increasingly loom over organizations. These might endanger the continuity of operations, jeopardize sensitive information, tarnish

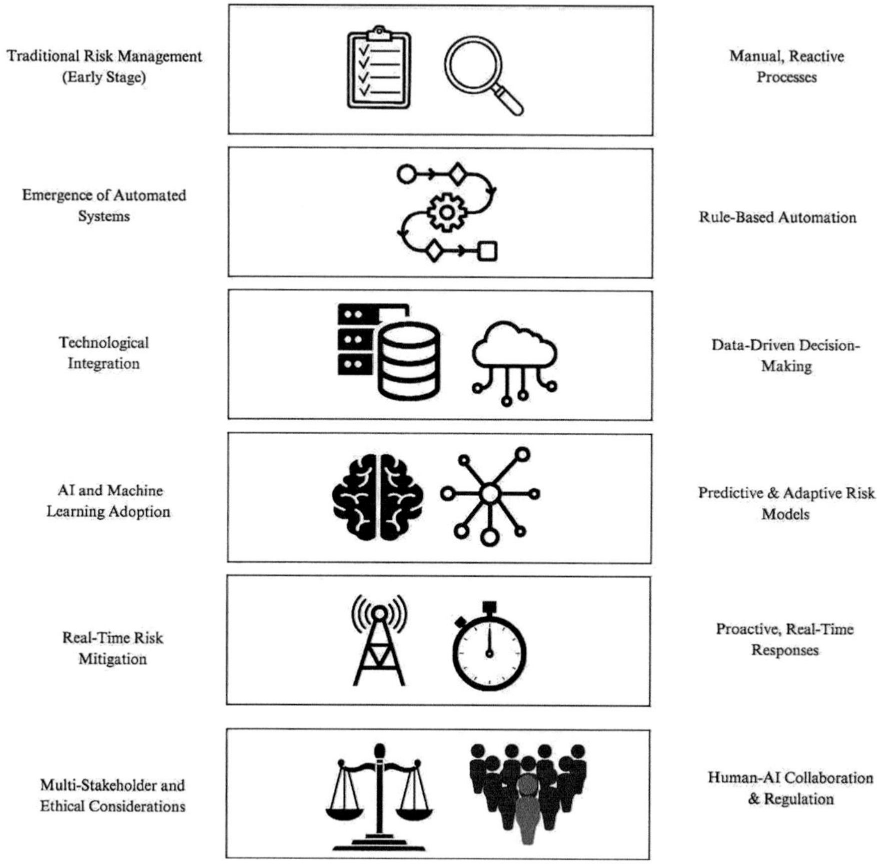

Figure 7.1 Evolution of cyber risk management approaches.

reputations, and numerous other concerns. Understanding the fundamental nature of cyber risks is crucial for implementing proactive defense strategies. These are the core principles of cyber risk presented in this section. They will subsequently be essential to any AI-driven approaches for mitigation and incident response.

7.2.1 Types of cyber risks

These cyber risks can truly be categorized into several general groups or types that are distinguished by their fundamental characteristics or impacts.

Table 7.1 Types of cyber risks and their impacts.

Risk type	Description	Potential impact	Example
Malware	Malicious software disrupting operations or stealing data	Data corruption, service downtime	Ransomware encrypting critical files
Phishing	Fraudulent emails tricking users	Credential theft, unauthorized access	Fake login page via email
Insider threats	Risk from current/ former employees or contractors	Data leakage, sabotage	Employee leaking trade secrets
Denial-of-Service	Overwhelms system to make it unavailable	Service outages, revenue loss	Botnets attacking a web server
Supply chain attacks	Targeting third-party vendors	Trust breach, malware spread	Compromised software update

For instance, there are internal threats, which are the most recognized or originate from outside the organization. External threats are likely the most familiar, but they also encompass instances of cyber threats such as phishing, ransomware, Denial of Service attacks, and APTs. These types of malicious activities are indeed recognized for pilfering data, interrupting services or obtaining unauthorized entry to systems [5].

Internal threats challenge external parties; they originate from within an organization. These risks encompass unhappy employees, unintentional data leaks, or simple errors in system setups. Insider threats, which are especially harmful, can bypass boundary protections and stay undetected until significant harm has been inflicted.

In Table 7.1, different cyber risks – including malware and insider threats – are presented with their definitions and consequences. This illustrates the operational and reputational implications of these risks on an organization. Actual examples are provided to offer context for each of the types of risks.

In recent times, risks associated with third parties have increased, particularly due to the expansion of cloud services and the global supply chain. Insufficient cybersecurity practices among vendors and partners can turn into a gateway for possible attackers. The management of interconnected risks necessitates due diligence, ongoing monitoring, and a culture of collective responsibility across the ecosystem.

7.2.2 Traditional risk assessment models

Classically, risk assessment models are viewed as a structure-supportive exercise like the Risk = Threat x Vulnerability x Impact formula. These risk assessment models serve to prioritize threats within an organization based on their probability and potential outcomes. [6] Various frameworks, such as NIST SP 800-30 and ISO/IEC 27005, offer direction on recognizing assets, threats, and vulnerabilities, as well as assessing the impact that the identified risk could have on fundamental business goals.

Qualitative risk assessment is a commonly used method where the evaluation of risks relies on expert opinions alongside historical information. Qualitative evaluation is fairly straightforward to execute, though it can be influenced by subjectivity and variability [7]. In contrast, risks in quantitative frameworks are assigned numerical values, and statistical analysis helps in forecasting results. While these models require a significant amount of data, they provide enhanced accuracy in the decision-making process.

Table 7.2 evaluates traditional cybersecurity methods in contrast to contemporary AI solutions, highlighting speed, scalability, and learning through AI functionalities. This comparison increasingly reinforces AI's significance in the area of proactive risk management.

For all their advantages, traditional models frequently struggle to respond quickly to the rapidly changing threat environment of today. They depend significantly on fixed data and an irregular method of evaluation, which may overlook threats that have developed or possibly even just an hour before the evaluation. As a result, numerous real-time organizations are moving toward AI-based methods that can dynamically learn and adjust to new risk patterns.

7.2.3 Challenges in manual risk mitigation

Cyber threats are addressed through the manual efforts of individuals to recognize, evaluate, and eliminate them. This process is often labor-intensive and susceptible to mistakes, particularly in expansive and complicated IT settings. Cybersecurity teams frequently face an overwhelming volume of alerts – many of which may be inaccurate. Without automation, the procedure complicates the ability to prioritize genuine threats, which ultimately heightens the risk of overlooking one.

One additional significant issue is the lack of personnel knowledgeable in the field. Globally, there is a deficit of cybersecurity specialists, resulting in organizations being unable to form robust teams capable of tackling

Table 7.2 Traditional vs. AI-driven risk management approaches.

Feature	Traditional approach	AI-driven approach
Detection speed	Reactive	Proactive and real-time
Data processing capability	Manual or rule-based	Automated with large-scale data
Scalability	Limited	Highly scalable
Learning from threats	Static rules	Adaptive and self-learning
Threat prediction	Minimal	Predictive analytics via ML models

advanced threats. Manual procedures further worsen the circumstances, taking up time that could have been focused on strategic planning and proactive defense [8].

Additionally, manual mitigation might lack the agility necessary to address zero-day exploits or multi-vector attacks. Cybercriminals are capable of altering their attack techniques at a significantly quicker pace than manual systems can adapt. All these restrictions emphasize the necessity for AI and automation in cybersecurity workflows to enhance speed, scalability, and efficiency in risk mitigation.

7.3 AI Techniques for Risk Prediction and Assessment

The manner in which organizations have been recognizing, quantifying, and handling risks has transformed completely through AI methodologies. By utilizing smart algorithms, security teams' emphasis transitions from reactive defensive approaches, and they now adopt proactive and predictive methods. Leveraging an abundance of standard and atypical data analyzers through a smart algorithm facilitates quicker detection of potential patterns and items that human analysts are likely to overlook. This section introduces three key AI techniques – machine learning, deep learning, and natural language processing – that assist in forecasting and evaluating cyber threats with greater accuracy and efficiency.

7.3.1 Machine learning algorithms

The candidates shape extensive ML systems that evaluate risk in cyber learning systems regarding input, employ historical data, and gradually learn, without making programming decisions. Supervised learning techniques such as decision trees, SVMs, random forests, and others are typically present in this classification of benign and malicious categories based on labeled

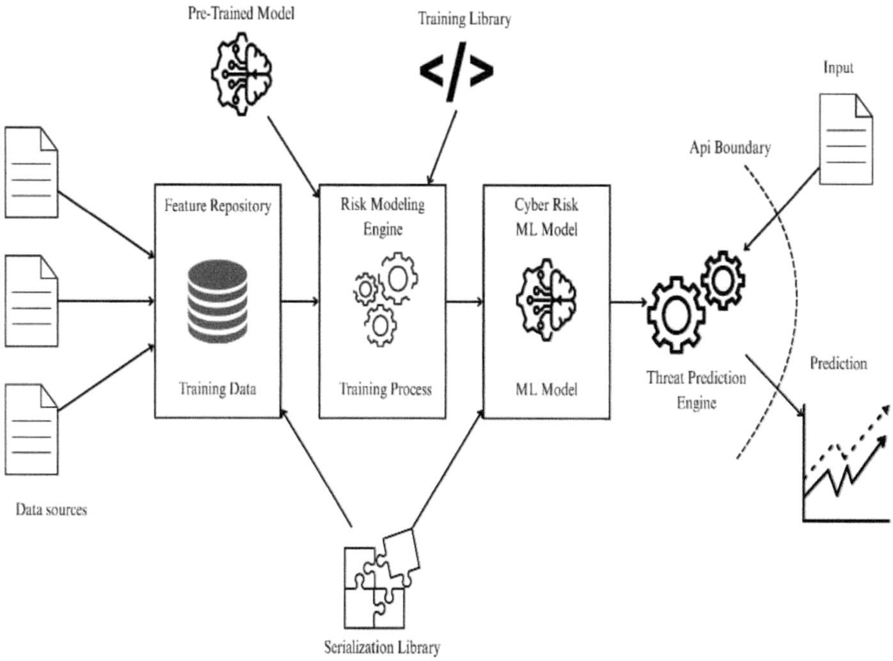

Figure 7.2 Cyber risk prediction framework using machine learning.

datasets. Train classifiers to identify prevalent attack patterns, such as phishing, malware, brute-forces, and so forth [9].

Unsupervised learning models, such as anomaly detection and cluster analysis, would act as an excellent approach to detect new forms of threats. K-means or DBSCAN could reveal insider threats or zero-day vulnerabilities by grouping unusual patterns that stray from what is considered normal. The most encouraging of these would be reinforcement learning in adaptive risk scoring, where systems learn the optimal actions by engaging with dynamic threats in their surroundings.

Figure 7.2 illustrates a cyber risk forecasting pipeline with machine learning at its center. It begins with data gathering, going through feature extraction and model training utilizing pre-existing models and training libraries. The trained model is serialized and subsequently provided by a threat prediction engine via an API. The system delivers immediate predictions regarding possible threats in cyberspace.

Intelligence is an advancing field, and while it possesses distinct advantages, adjusting to the strategies of emerging threats is also a significant challenge. The efficacy of these models is influenced by the richness and volume of the data. Continuous training, feature selection, and data validation are essential for maintaining model efficiency and preventing incorrect classification or lack of classification, which would otherwise complicate the work of security analysts or cause threats to go unnoticed.

7.3.2 Deep learning for threat identification

The deep learning community has contributed significantly to elevating machine learning to new levels through its application in multi-layer and neural multi-layered networks for the analysis of large and complex datasets with high accuracy [10]. In the field of cybersecurity, DL models like CNNs and RNNs serve as a foundation for identifying advanced threats such as polymorphic malware, which frequently bypass conventional detection techniques that rely on signatures.

The skill of identifying threats using images, like categorizing visual phishing attempts or examining screenshots from breached systems, is highly and successfully applied using CNNs. In contrast, RNNs and LSTM networks, a more advanced type of RNNs, are effectively utilized for tasks based on sequences, such as scrutinizing network traffic logs or sequences of system events to spot potentially harmful activities, thereby performing efficiently in grasping temporal dependencies between previous actions and forecasting future risk incidents.

Furthermore, their demand for computation frequently requires large amounts of labeled training data, making explainability more than just a significant challenge. In this context, DL as a framework improves by leveraging higher-quality evidence, thus these systems depend on human contribution to articulate data interfaces accessible across various languages. Using such systems allows you to cost-effectively collect all credible threats via rule-based, simpler ML systems to achieve an ideal balance in efficiency and interpretability, while simultaneously achieving remarkable accuracy.

7.3.3 Natural language processing for threat intelligence

Natural language processing heavily relies on unstructured text resources, which include reports of threats, social media, cyber blogs, and dark web forums. These NLP tools facilitate immediate action by analyzing interpreted data to potentially identify new threats, vulnerabilities, or attack vectors within organizations, all while ensuring readiness against cybercriminals in the future [11].

Named entity recognition, sentiment analysis, and topic modeling are merely a few of the methodologies that assist NLP systems in sifting through extensive volumes of text to pinpoint essential indicators of compromise, threat actors, or exploits. For example, an NLP engine could evaluate posts from the dark web to detect occurrences of newly identified malware variants or compromised credentials and alert security teams for preventive action.

The use of NLP in automating threat intelligence feeds and correlating text data with system logs and alerts is remarkable. It is utilized to improve an organization's situational awareness and minimize the interval between detecting and responding to an incident [12]. Grasping context, language vagueness, and changing terms used by attackers continue to encapsulate the challenging aspects of NLP in digital forensics. Ongoing research in field-specific language models and multilingual NLP will open up paths to remove such obstacles.

7.4 AI-powered Threat Detection Systems

AI transformed the enhancement of cybersecurity threat detection capabilities. It enables security systems to identify threats more quickly and accurately than conventional rule-based systems by analyzing extensive data and identifying intricate patterns. Instead, with AI's assistance, threats can be identified and addressed in a proactive defense approach, frequently in real time before any significant harm occurs.

7.4.1 Real-time intrusion detection

AI algorithm-enhanced real-time intrusion detection systems can continuously monitor and assess network traffic to identify suspicious activities [13]. In contrast to static IDS, which generally relies on fixed signatures, AI systems adaptively and dynamically learn from evolving threats, making them significantly more effective against unknown malware and zero-day attacks. These systems evaluate packet- and user-level behavior, context, and triggering factors to deliver real-time alerts.

Traffic is categorized as benign or malicious using machine learning models, including decision trees, support vector machines, and neural networks. These models are trained on large datasets consisting of recognized attacks and typical behavior, allowing them to generalize to new, unidentified threats. Moreover, the application of unsupervised learning methods can identify anomalies without relying on any labeled datasets, particularly beneficial in enterprise settings with varied network activity.

Table 7.3 Behavioral indicators and associated threats.

Behavioral indicator	Possible threat	Detection technique
Unusual login time/location	Compromised credentials	User behavior analytics
Rapid data downloads	Insider data exfiltration	Anomaly detection
Sudden privilege escalation	Malware/lateral movement	Role-based access monitoring
Repeated access attempts	Brute-force attack	Pattern recognition with AI

There is no doubt that real-time AI intrusion detection is swift and accurate. Security analysts will get immediate alerts about breaches to which they can respond promptly and manage. AI has also decreased the number of false positives, allowing human analysts to concentrate more on other, more critical incidents, thereby optimizing resources in the Security Operations Centers.

7.4.2 Behavioral analysis and anomaly detection

Behavioral analysis utilizing AI encompasses the assessment of typical behavior for users and systems along with ongoing surveillance for irregularities. These irregularities, or anomalies, may serve as early signs of cyber assaults, which include insider threats, compromised accounts, and APTs. Behavioral benchmarks assist AI systems in identifying slight deviations that would be overlooked by conventional systems.

Table 7.3 connects suspicious user/system activities with possible cyber threats. Essentially, it demonstrates how an AI can identify irregularities through behavioral analytics. For the purpose of clarity, detection methods are associated with each behavior.

They are able to recognize any irregularities in the absence of established signatures that pinpoint threats or harmful actions by employing methods such as clustering and statistical modeling in anomaly detection algorithms. For instance, if the employee begins to access confidential files at unexpected times or from a different location, the system marks the action as unusual. AI can subsequently contextualize the anomaly using past user behavior, comparisons with peers, and policies to evaluate the risk level [14].

It is especially beneficial for detecting polymorphic malware and insider threats, which frequently bypass signature detection. Advancing behavioral artificial intelligence models adapt based on new information, rendering them more resilient to evasion tactics. Continuously enhance the security stance as indicated by behavioral analysis, especially in the rapidly changing landscape of cloud systems and hybrid networks.

7.4.3 Case study: AI in threat hunting

Rapidly expanding financial services firms are shifting focus towards advanced cyber threats aimed at their essential infrastructure. Consequently, the organization has implemented an AI-powered threat-hunting platform that integrates machine learning with threat intelligence feeds, endpoint telemetry, and user behavior analytics into its operations [15]. Intended to operate continuously, the system will monitor the network environment for subtle signs of unusual behavior that suggest hostile intent. This represents a significant transition from a reactive incident response approach to a proactive threat detection strategy – the organization has modified its previous methods.

On one occasion, AI triggered an alert because of unusual access behavior involving a high-privileged user account. The account in question was utilized to reach sensitive resources during odd hours and from an atypical IP address. Traditional tools were unable to generate alerts since there were no recognized malware signatures detected. AI, on the other hand, successfully employed deviations from typical user activity and linked that to the methods of known threat actors to identify the anomaly. This constituted real-time data that informed the security team to conduct a more in-depth investigation [16].

The exposure of an account was revealed during the investigation, indicating something larger. Thanks to AI notifications, the organization could swiftly contain the impacted systems, retract the breached credentials, and strengthen its authentication process. The earlier case illustrates how AI decreases detection and response duration, enhances situational awareness, and enables threat hunters to devote more time to strategic counteractions instead of being overwhelmed by countless logs.

7.5 Automated Incident Response Mechanisms

Automated incident response mechanisms utilize artificial intelligence to identify, evaluate, and react to cyber threats with minimal human involvement, significantly decreasing response time and limiting potential harm. They function in coordination with current security frameworks such as SIEM and SOAR to take action on compromised systems, impede harmful IP addresses, and commence forensic investigations. By automating various repetitive and labor-intensive duties – such as alert triaging, log examination,

Table 7.4 Incident response phases and AI capabilities.

Phase	Description	AI capability
Preparation	Readiness plans, policies, and training	AI-driven simulations and risk modeling
Detection	Identifying incidents in real-time	AI-powered intrusion and anomaly detection
Containment	Isolating affected systems	AI-based threat correlation and segmentation
Eradication	Removing threat completely	Automated malware removal and source tracing
Recovery	Restoring services	Predictive restoration paths and testing
Lessons learned	Post-incident review	AI-generated reports and root cause summaries

and threat management – AI enhances the productivity of SOCs while fostering an ongoing, uniform, and scalable incident management ability.

7.5.1 Incident response lifecycle

The incident response cycle offers a structured method for cybersecurity teams to adhere to in identifying, analyzing, containing, eliminating, and recuperating from security incidents. It typically comprises six phases: preparation, identification, containment, eradication, recovery, and lessons learned. AI technologies are being incorporated into each phase to decrease response durations and enhance decision-making; for instance, AI can autonomously recognize anomalies during the identification stage or suggest measures to mitigate the breach instantly. By embedding these smart technologies throughout the cycle, organizations can transition from reactive security to proactive security [17].

Table 7.4 illustrates crucial stages for incident response, along with the function of AI in every stage. AI's function is indicated as the enhancing factor concerning the effectiveness of response time and adaptability. AI capabilities align with preparation, detection, containment, and beyond.

Artificial intelligence encompasses particular phrases that assist the incident response lifecycle in various ways. Such applications can be utilized in managing AI in readiness for simulating threat scenarios and establishing risk prioritization based on it for forthcoming security investments. In the identification phase, vast amounts of data from endpoints, networks, or cloud environments are analyzed through machine learning models for subtle indicators of internal or external compromise that might have gone unnoticed without traditional rule-based systems. The ability for early detection is essential for reducing the exposure window.

In the containment, eradication, and recovery stages, AI automation instruments assist in managing responses among all impacted systems. For instance, measures are executed by AI independently of human intervention, like isolating compromised devices, removing harmful files, or reverting the systems to a previously secure condition. Throughout recovery, AI additionally verifies system integrity before they are brought back online. In the lessons learned phase, AI is capable of identifying patterns in incident data, aiming to enhance security measures and re-educate detection models – bolstering the organization's resilience with every feedback loop.

7.5.2 AI in orchestration and automation

The SOAR platforms are critical instruments for managing the amount and intricacy of cyber threats encountered today. AI is improving the functionality of SOAR by automating repetitive tasks, such as log analysis, alert triaging, and preliminary threat investigations. This not only lessens the load on security analysts but also guarantees that incidents are addressed more swiftly, allowing organizations to minimize possible damages.

AI might also assist in the creation of dynamic playbooks, where automated response strategies are customized based on real-time threat information and the circumstances of an attack [18]. The machine-learning algorithms could utilize historical incidents to learn from their responses and enhance the workflow for upcoming reactions that are prompt and effective. In other words, this creates a way for self-enhancement within this advancing system, growing alongside the threat environment.

Figure 7.3 depicts the automated incident response pipeline within IT infrastructure. Security incidents undergo analysis to activate alerts associated with playbooks, and those playbooks direct the system along a structured response pathway. In the end, the system generates an automated reply that enables effective threat management.

Furthermore, AI-driven SOAR systems seamlessly integrate with various security tools, correlating information from multiple endpoints, firewalls, email gateways, and cloud services. This interoperability offers a unified perspective on threats and synchronized response activities across the digital landscape. Consequently, it results in a more flexible and robust security organization.

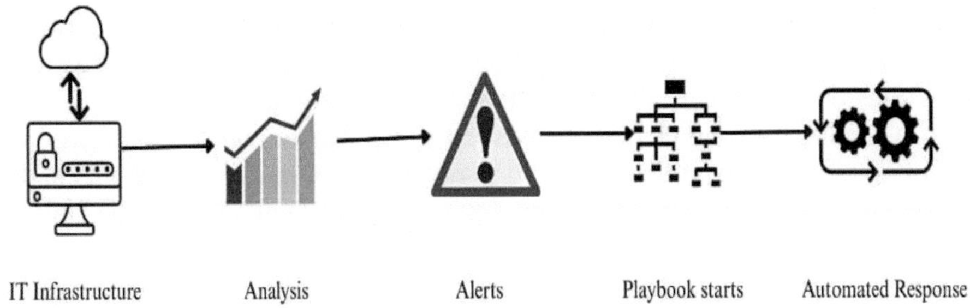

Figure 7.3 SOAR workflow with AI-enabled decision trees.

7.5.3 Role of chatbots and virtual analysts in response

In relation to an event, AI chatbots and virtual analysts have significantly changed the way organizations engage with security systems. They offer assistance 24/7, advising security teams or even end users on standard operating procedures like password resets, dealing with phishing reports, and preliminary breach evaluations. Therefore, they deliver immediate support, enhancing decision-making during crucial moments [19].

The excellent aspect is that chatbots have the capability to learn from the extensive training material made up of historical incident records and a security knowledge base, enabling them to provide insightful recommendations and context-aware responses. They might also act as mediators between human analysts and automated systems to ensure that replies are swift and validated. The significance of this becomes apparent during high-alert scenarios or periods when human analysts are unavailable.

In situations of elevated operational tempo, virtual analysts serve as digital co-pilots that reveal pertinent information such as the impact of vulnerabilities, attack vectors, or impacted assets. By doing this, they improve situational awareness to facilitate the prioritization of response actions. This, in effect, ultimately enables organizations to sustain their operations and precision in the face of rapidly changing threats.

7.5.4 AI-driven forensic analysis and root cause identification

Post-incident analysis offers a wealth of information regarding the circumstances of a breach and methods to avert future occurrences. AI significantly supports forensic investigations by assisting with data gathering, correlation, and the analysis of exceptionally large volumes of log and telemetry data.

The timeline for certain attack events can be generated, the initial compromise identified, and lateral movements tracked in many instances swiftly and with considerably greater accuracy than manual methods.

Machine learning algorithms possess the ability to uncover patterns that might otherwise remain obscured and to identify anomalies that are not easily noticeable through human perception. For example, irregularities in the behavior of certain suspicious users or deviations concerning system access can be recognized using unsupervised learning methods even prior to their occurrence. This kind of identification subsequently aids in determining the underlying cause and guiding recovery strategies with evidence-based methods [20].

Report generation and compliance documentation are several of AI capabilities. It arranges findings into organized formats, which subsequently assists security teams in delivering this information to management, regulatory authorities, or even legal teams. Additionally, it promotes knowledge retention by integrating lessons learned back into the AI models for enhanced future detection and response. In this manner, that learning cycle persists and thus enhances the resilience of the organization against future threats.

7.6 Integrating AI with Security Information and Event Management

SIEM systems are the foundation of cybersecurity awareness within the organization. Additionally, artificial intelligence enhances SIEM by providing increased intelligence, further flexibility, and the ability to automate regular analytic processes. With AI, SIEM can not only swiftly detect well-known threats, but it can also ascertain if there are any more discreet and cunning intrusions present, which rule-based systems may likely miss.

7.6.1 Enhancing SIEM with AI/ML

Modern security systems utilize AI and different machine learning functionalities alongside SIEM platforms, which can claim a significant improvement in efficiency concerning the identification of security incidents. AI algorithms are capable of examining large-scale security data and past trends to gain knowledge about already recognized emerging threats frequently.

Figure 7.4 shows the relationship between the search head and indexer tier in the SIEM architecture. Information is fetched from the indexer for additional processing via temporary models or routine searches. Persisted models are kept in the KV store or lookup for ongoing analysis. According to the results, the system notifies, visualizes, or triggers an automatic response.

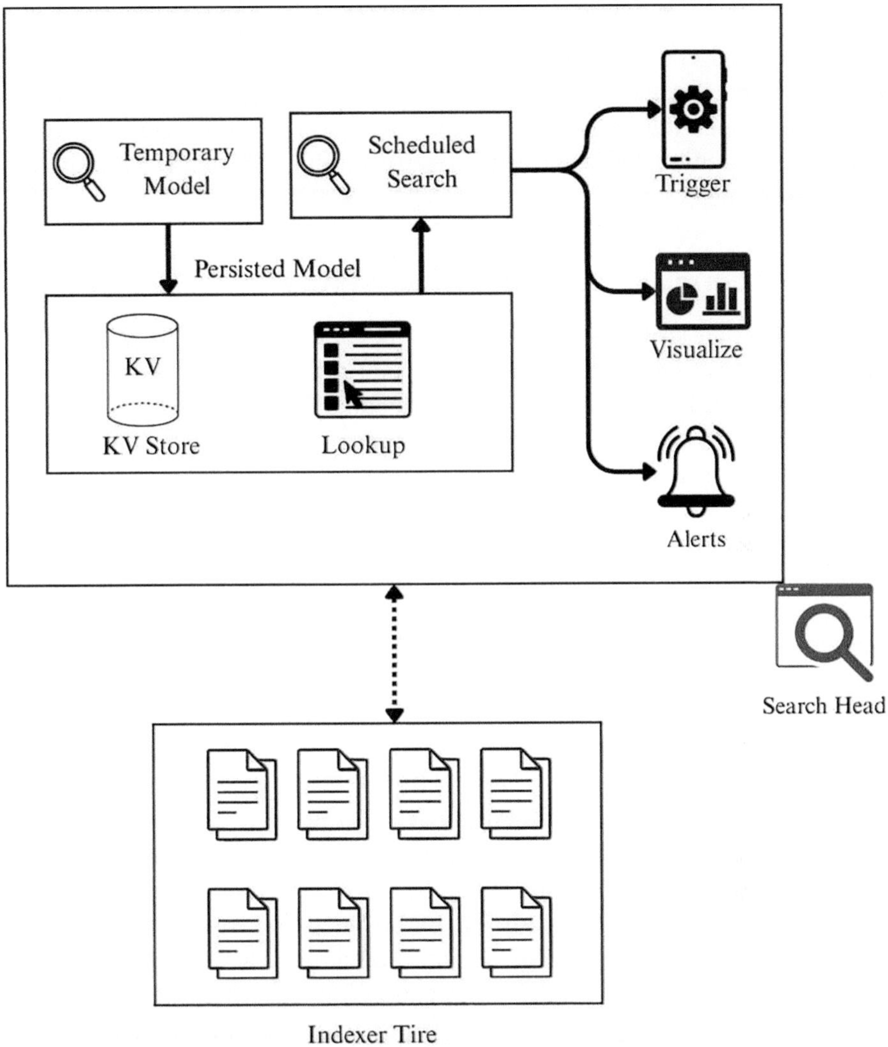

Figure 7.4 Workflow of data search and alert generation in SIEM system.

A significantly important benefit is that AI is dynamic. The correlation rules for static SIEMs eventually become outdated; the attack techniques develop. AI employs models constructed from a continually incoming stream of new data to confront previously unrecognized patterns [21]. Consequently, the occurrence of false positives is low, and security analysts are notified only when they occur.

Moreover, AI and ML improved SIEMs can accelerate the detection and categorization of threats. By clustering related alerts and marking incidents with appropriate severity according to context, these systems emphasize those threats that require immediate attention and consequently result in quicker resolution and more effective distribution of resources in security operations centers.

7.6.2 Data correlation and predictive alerts

The fundamental advantage of AI lies in its capacity to establish extensive collections of varied security data – like that produced by firewalls, cloud ecosystems, user activity records, and intrusion detection systems – and link them together to create a comprehensive view of the security environment within a company as a whole. Conventional systems typically do not perform effectively in these situations, but AI can take disjointed data, look for concealed connections, and construct attack timelines based on behavioral and temporal pattern identification [22].

An additional significant advantage is predictive alerts. Through predictive and trend analysis, the AI models are capable of performing the majority of their tasks and even identifying potential threats prior to their full emergence. This proves to be increasingly beneficial in mitigating stealthy attacks and those that occur as protracted APTs. For example, it might foresee potential lateral movement after identifying a sequence of unusual logins or attempts at privilege escalation through the logs.

Moreover, risk-scoring systems can adjust AI predictive notifications. This signifies that notifications are activated not solely by the number of events or violations of thresholds but by an integrated risk evaluation that takes into account contexts, user history, and asset sensitivity. This prioritization enables security teams to concentrate on incidents with significant impact while automating responses to everyday low-risk occurrences.

7.6.3 Case study: AI-augmented SIEM in action

In light of a rise in cyberattacks concerning patient information, a leading healthcare provider decided to implement an AI-enhanced SIEM solution to combat these security threats. Previously, the organization faced challenges regarding alert storms and delays in threat detection with the existing SIEM installed [23]. Nevertheless, with the introduction of machine learning, the enhanced SIEM began to detect very minor anomalies in traffic patterns and user activities, such as potential data exfiltration attempts masked as legitimate database queries.

For instance, a sophisticated AI system analyzed live streams from open-source intelligence and threat databases to generate actionable insights through natural language processing. Following the public declaration of the vulnerability impacting the organization's single software tool, it was automatically linked to internal assets, marked for risk, and directed to the teams responsible for patch management even before any attempt at exploitation.

The integration of an advanced manipulated AI SIEM was additionally into a SOAR platform that would render the incident response automation significantly more efficient and enable the system to autonomously isolate endpoints, block harmful IPs, and commence forensic data gathering with minimal human involvement. This would result in a substantial reduction in mean-time to detect and mean-time to respond, thereby enhancing compliance and offering improved security for patient data [24].

7.7 Challenges and Limitations

There is a substantial amount that AI can offer to national cyber risk management, but it is not completely free from difficulties when it comes to risk mitigation and incident response. While the latest technologies have played a role in enhancing automation, speed, and precision, AI systems frequently encounter several problems related to reliability, interpretability, and data reliance. As a result, these limitations render AI less effective in practical applications, as they could introduce new vulnerabilities or compliance issues linked to the incorporation of such advanced technologies. It is crucial to understand how these issues can be effectively addressed to create opportunities for establishing strong, secure, and dependable systems for cybersecurity.

The information in Table 7.5 highlights essential subjects that emerge when implementing AI for cyber defense, including assaults on AI and insufficient resources. The methods for alleviating each obstacle will be examined to aid in the adoption of robust AI systems. It evaluates the benefits in relation to challenges relevant to real-world applications.

7.7.1 Adversarial attacks on AI models

The adversarial attacks are characterized by the utilization of inputs to influence outputs produced by artificial intelligence. In the realm of cybersecurity, this pertains to supplying unintended data into a machine learning-driven intrusion detection system to misidentify and categorize threats as harmless. These attacks pose significant risks, particularly when the system relies on pattern recognition and anomaly detection, as even minor modifications in an input typically result in drastically altered behavior from the system.

Table 7.5 Common challenges in AI for cybersecurity.

Challenge	Description	Potential mitigation
Adversarial attacks	Manipulating input to mislead AI models	Robust training, adversarial testing
False positives	Legitimate behavior flagged as malicious	Model tuning, ensemble techniques
Lack of explainability	Difficulty understanding AI decisions	Adoption of XAI
High resource consumption	Complex models require more processing power	Efficient model design, edge deployment

During inference, an adversary can utilize methods like evasion attacks, while poisoning attacks are meant for the training phase [25]. In one method of executing a poisoning attack, a malicious actor tamper with the training set by inserting misleading information with the aim of rendering the model incapable of differentiating between real and fake threats. This, consequently, significantly diminishes trust in AI systems and prompts relevant inquiries regarding these systems in a hostile setting.

Figure 7.5 emphasizes two prominent types of adversarial attacks: backdoor attacks (poisoning) and gradient-based attacks (evasion). In backdoor cases, adversaries introduce fake patterns into the training dataset to divert the potential associations away from accurate model predictions. Conversely, in gradient-based evasion attacks, noise is introduced into the input data to cause it to be incorrectly classified by the model during the inference phase. Both techniques take advantage of the recognized vulnerabilities to alter the output behavior.

These include creating and employing solid training techniques such as adversarial training, model validation against adversarial instances, and motion models. Nonetheless, these methods are still evolving, and enhancing the robustness of models leads to some performance or computational costs. As the complexity of threat actors advances, safeguarding AI models remains an unceasing battle for the defender.

7.7.2 False positives and model accuracy

On AI-driven systems, there is a significant likelihood of generating false positives – alerts that flag normal activities as potentially harmful. Elevated false positive rates place an excessive burden on security teams, which can result in alert fatigue and the risk of missing serious threats. In contexts with extensive infrastructure, this issue takes a unique direction; within normal activities, the definitions of anomalous behavior can be quite nuanced [26].

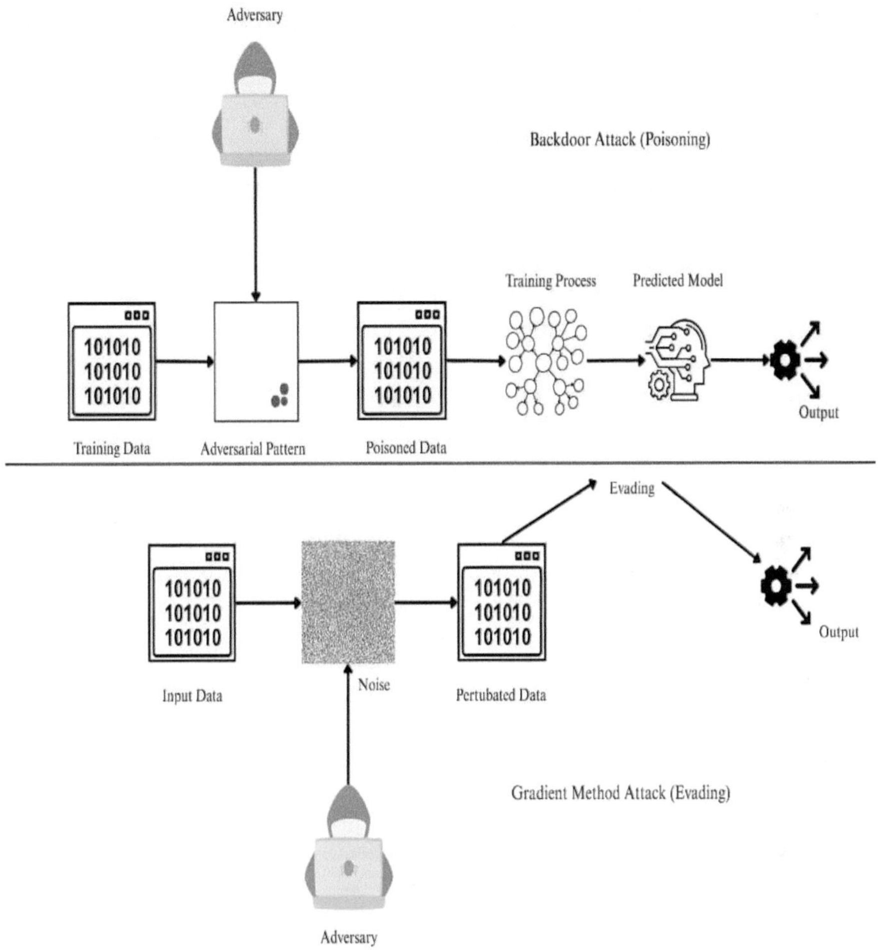

Figure 7.5 Overview of adversarial attacks on machine learning models.

Model accuracies are influenced by the quality and diversity of the training data, as well as the algorithm's ability to generalize to novel, unseen threats. Incorrectly specified training data or a limited number of threat definitions can result in subpar performance in practical applications. Achieving the right balance between sensitivity (detecting all threats) and specificity (avoiding false alerts) is crucial.

In many situations, hybrid models that combine AI with rule-based systems are utilized to reduce false positives. Ongoing adjustments, feedback loops, and systems that involve human oversight led to improved accuracy in detections. Nevertheless, the pursuit of achieving optimal accuracy remains a continuous effort demanding skilled personnel and committed resources.

7.7.3 Ethical and legal considerations

There are significant ethical issues associated with the use of AI in cybersecurity, particularly regarding surveillance, data privacy, and automated decision-making. AI technologies analyze user data collectively to identify threats, which heightens worries about consent, transparency, and adherence to data protection regulations like GDPR and HIPAA [27]. To uphold the essential justification for these practices in light of privacy violations, a careful balancing act must be undertaken to preserve threat detection abilities.

These choices made by AI stay concealed within its "black box," which makes it challenging to provide justification for labeling a threat or explaining why a specific action was executed. This characteristic poses challenges during legal audits and compliance audits, where accountability and traceability are of the highest significance. Organizations could face liability if an erroneous access denial or breach is triggered by a decision made by an AI system.

It is essential to develop ethical AI frameworks that concentrate on transparency, fairness, and accountability. Laws are still lagging behind technological progress; consequently, companies must take action proactively by establishing governance, conducting evaluations of potential effects, and ensuring that the implementation of AI is in accordance with current laws and ethical best practices.

7.7.4 Data quality and bias in AI decision-making

AI essentially advances only to the extent that it is trained on data; subpar video used in data training, including outdated logs, misclassified events, or imbalanced datasets, can result in incorrect predictions and poor generalization. This would be vital for a rapid and precise response in cybersecurity, and it may overlook significant threats or become misprioritized in incident detection.

Considering the issue encompasses bias in AI decision-making, due to the potential existence of historical bias in training data or the absence of diversity in attack types or contexts, indicating the model's failure to recognize new or less-represented threats. Various groupings or units of users or different users' groups may even be impacted more negatively to differing extents, resulting in security enforcement outcomes that are inconsistent or unjust [28].

To address data issues, there is a continuous requirement for data curation, real-time validation, and multiple training datasets. Such enhancement can also take place when you generate synthetic data to better the scenario simulation. Nonetheless, fairness, transparency, and inclusivity in AI decision-making remain a significant and evolving challenge that requires adequate focus from cybersecurity teams.

7.8 Future Trends in AI for Cyber Risk Management

With the advancement of cyber threats into more sophisticated methods of attack, the future of managing cyber risk will involve intelligent, adaptable systems driven by AI. Innovations like Federated Learning, XAI, Blockchain, and Edge Computing will transform future strategies in the cybersecurity domain, aiming to address existing deficiencies in data privacy, transparency, scalability, and trust. This positions AI as not merely reactive but also proactive. Consequently, organizations can ensure the flexibility of their systems against novel threats by creating secure and robust frameworks equipped with the cognitive abilities of AI and next-generation computing architectures.

7.8.1 Federated learning in security

Federated learning allows a decentralized approach to machine learning, meaning that local data stays on devices and models are trained collaboratively. In the realm of cybersecurity, this empowers organizations to create robust AI models without moving sensitive data to central servers, thereby maintaining data privacy and reducing exposure. These activities are essential in sectors like healthcare, finance, and defense due to their compliance and complex privacy regulations [29].

Federated learning allows organizations to identify security threats across numerous endpoints or institutions while keeping raw data private. It is particularly useful for recognizing patterns of dispersed attacks like botnets or ransomware operations. Additionally, as the models are trained with diverse datasets in various environments, the overall threat detection system becomes increasingly robust and generalized.

Despite the challenges noted earlier, the increasing progress in secure aggregation methods and federated averaging is rendering it more feasible to implement federated learning in cybersecurity, despite the issues of communication overhead, model synchronization, and ultimately the reliability of the participants. Federated learning is anticipated to significantly impact the sharing of privacy-preserving cyber threat intelligence, as it is projected to become a standard feature in a growing number of industries in the future.

7.8.2 Explainable AI in incident response

The "black box" nature of the model employed in numerous AI systems presents a barrier to implementing AI in cybersecurity; this lack of clarity in decision-making can obstruct the analyst's comprehension of the decisions taken. XAI aims to address this issue by offering transparency and interpretability regarding the outcomes generated by an AI system; in incident response, understanding the rationale behind an alert's activation can result in varied pathways of action.

XAI aids security teams in backtracking the reasoning of an AI model to the particular features or behaviors that caused the alert. Consequently, it enables analysts to address alerts more quickly, prioritize threats using clearer context, and reduce false positives. Similarly, in regulated sectors, XAI can support audits and compliance by providing justification for all actions taken during incident management [30].

To foster increased trust between humans and AI systems, XAI is presently integrated with security platforms. By clarifying and making machine-generated insights actionable, the incident response will transition from a reactive strategy into a collaborative workflow between humans and machines. As AI technology advances for cybersecurity, the demand for explainability will grow, especially in structured environments where accountability and precision are crucial.

7.8.3 Integration with blockchain and edge computing

AI, in conjunction with blockchain and edge computing, has the ability to completely transform the manner in which cyber risks are handled. The unchangeable ledger inherent in the blockchain framework provides the primary reliability for security incidents and allows for the tracking of their chronology through its decentralized design. In this context, edge computing serves as the crucial factor to guarantee immediate analytics near the data origins with the least amount of latency and bandwidth use [31].

For instance, AI-driven security systems set up on edge devices are capable of independently identifying anomalies and sharing verified threat

Table 7.6 Emerging trends and their potential impact.

Trend	Description	Benefit	Challenge
Federated learning	Distributed model training without sharing data	Privacy-preserving AI	Complexity in coordination
Explainable AI	Models that provide human-readable decisions	Better trust and compliance	May reduce model performance
Blockchain integration	Tamper-proof logging and identity verification	Enhanced data integrity	Scalability and latency
Edge AI	AI running on local devices (routers, sensors)	Low-latency threat response	Limited computation power

intelligence via a blockchain network. This enables swift and decentralized incident response, particularly efficient in IoT ecosystems where devices might be situated over an expansive area. Blockchain guarantees data integrity and non-repudiation, rendering tampering or data alteration virtually impossible.

Nevertheless, when artificial intelligence merges with blockchain and edge infrastructure, it introduces further design and operational difficulties, including resource constraints on the edge nodes and the availability of scalability for blockchain networks [32]. In spite of these difficulties, the convergence of these technologies presents us with significant opportunities for the creation of decentralized, intelligent security frameworks. This integration paves the way for next-generation systems that will be increasingly autonomous, transparent, and resilient.

Table 7.6 contains several of the latest developments in fields like federated learning, XAI, and edge AI. It evaluates the advantages and disadvantages of adopting each trend in cybersecurity. Its objective is to plan for long-term interactions with AI.

7.9 Conclusion

The chapter examined how AI can offer a more effective solution to cyber risk and incident response, addressing elements like applications, benefits, and challenges. We have investigated how AI principles such as machine learning, deep learning, and natural language processing aid in improving risk prediction, threat detection, and automation of responses. AI tools integrated within technologies like SIEM and SOAR facilitate quicker and more intelligent identification of cyber incidents and their associated resolution procedures. The chapter also validated the operation of AI-integrated tools such as virtual analysts, forensic engines, and behavior-based analysis frameworks in facilitating real-time decision-making. However, we acknowledged the obstacles, including adversarial attacks, data bias, model interpretability, and ethical considerations, highlighting the necessity for transparency, fairness, and governance in the context of AI implementation.

The successful integration of artificial intelligence into cybersecurity must always place high-quality data as the top priority, guarantee compatibility with existing systems, strive for prompt automation and subject the models to continuous testing and improvement. Confidence in any AI would further be increased by offering interpretability, while adherence to legal and ethical standards would assure its responsible utilization. Looking ahead, AI is likely to become increasingly essential in developing robust, intelligent, and adaptable cyber defense frameworks. Several transformative trends that would promote this future include federated learning, explainable AI, and collaboration with blockchain and edge computing, leading to a more decentralized, secure, and responsive trajectory. Organizations that strategically allocate resources to AI, talent, and innovation will be well-positioned henceforth to address emerging risks and counter new threats in the evolving cyber landscape.

References

[1] M. Eling, M. McShane, and T. Nguyen, "Cyber risk management: History and future research directions," Risk Management and Insurance Review, vol. 24, pp. 93–125, 2021. doi: 10.1111/rmir.12169.

[2] A. Refsdal, B. Solhaug, and K. Stølen, Cyber-risk Management, in Cyber-Risk Management, SpringerBriefs in Computer Science. Springer, Cham, 2015. doi: 10.1007/978-3-319-23570-7_5.

[3] M. Binhammad, S. Alqaydi, A. Othman, and L. H. Abuljadayel, "The Role of AI in Cyber Security: Safeguarding Digital Identity," Journal of Information Security, vol. 15, pp. 245–278, 2024, doi: 10.4236/jis.2024.152015.

[4] F. Jimmy, "Emerging threats: The latest cybersecurity risks and the role of artificial intelligence in enhancing cybersecurity defenses," Valley International Journal Digital Library, vol. 1, pp. 564–574, 2021. doi: 10.18535/ijsrm/v9i2.ec01.

[5] Ö. Aslan, S. S. Aktuğ, M. Ozkan-Okay, A. A. Yilmaz, and E. Akin, "A Comprehensive Review of Cyber Security Vulnerabilities, Threats, Attacks, and Solutions," Electronics, vol. 12, no. 6, p. 1333, 2023, doi: 10.3390/electronics12061333.

[6] E. H. N. Safitri and H. Kabetta, "Cyber-Risk Management Planning Using NIST CSF V1.1, ISO/IEC 27005:2018, and NIST SP 800-53 Revision 5 (A Study Case to ABC Organization)," in Proc. 2023 IEEE Int. Conf. Cryptography, Informatics, and Cybersecurity (ICoCICs), Bogor, Indonesia, 2023, pp. 332–338, doi: 10.1109/ICoCICs58778.2023.10277652.

[7] I. D. Sánchez-García, J. Mejía, and T. San Feliu Gilabert, "Cybersecurity Risk Assessment: A Systematic Mapping Review, Proposal, and Validation," Appl. Sci., vol. 13, no. 1, p. 395, 2023, doi: 10.3390/app13010395.

[8] S. Kawimbe and M. Kwalombota, "Mitigating Cybersecurity Risks in the Digitization of Banking Operations: Strategies, Challenges, and Best Practices for Zambian Commercial Banks," Int. J. Res. Innov. Soc. Sci., vol. 8, no. 3s, pp. 2988–3005, 2024, doi: 10.47772/IJRISS.2024.803213S.

[9] M. F. Yussuf, P. Oladokun, and M. Williams, "Enhancing cybersecurity risk assessment in digital finance through advanced machine learning algorithms," Int. J. Comput. Appl. Technol. Res., vol. 9, no. 6, pp. 217–235, 2020.

[10] D. Ghillani, "Deep learning and artificial intelligence framework to improve the cyber security," Authorea Preprints, 2022.

[11] W. S. Ismail, "Threat Detection and Response Using AI and NLP in Cybersecurity," J. Internet Serv. Inf. Secur., vol. 14, no. 1, pp. 195–205, Feb. 2024, doi: 10.58346/JISIS.2024.I1.013.

[12] R. K. Rajendran and B. Tulasi, "Natural Language Processing (NLP) for Threat Intelligence," in Analyzing Privacy and Security Difficulties in Social Media: New Challenges and Solutions, D. Darwish and K. Charan, Eds. Hershey, PA, USA: IGI Global Scientific Publishing, 2025, pp. 247–262. doi: 10.4018/979-8-3693-9491-5.ch011.

[13] S. Iqbal, "AI-powered Systems for Cybersecurity: Techniques and Applications for Threat Detection," Artif. Intell. Multidiscip. J. Syst. Appl., vol. 1, no. 3, pp. 10–17, 2024.

[14] V. D. Talati, "AI-powered Cloud Security: Using User Behavior Analysis to Achieve Efficient Threat Detection," Int. J. Innov. Res. Sci. Eng. Technol., vol. 13, no. 5, pp. 10124–10131, 2024.

[15] V. Sowmya Sree, C. S. Koganti, S. K. Kalyana, and P. Anudeep, "Artificial Intelligence Based Predictive Threat Hunting In The Field of Cyber Security," Oct. 2021, doi: 10.1109/GCAT52182.2021.9587507.

[16] A. Yaseen, "AI-driven threat detection and response: A paradigm shift in cybersecurity," Int. J. Inf. Cybersecur., vol. 7, no. 12, pp. 25–43, 2023.

[17] E. Manning, Optimizing Incident Management Processes for Effective Cybersecurity Incident Response, Doctoral dissertation, National College of Ireland, Dublin, 2023.

[18] R. Vast, S. Sawant, A. Thorbole and V. Badgujar, "Artificial Intelligence based Security Orchestration, Automation and Response System," 2021 6th International Conference for Convergence in Technology (I2CT), Maharashtra, India, 2021, pp. 1-5, doi: 10.1109/I2CT51068.2021.9418109.

[19] T. Adam, S. S. Emmanuel, G. Dusserre, N.-B. Ahmed, Z. Babatunde, et al.," Chatbots in Cybersecurity: Enhancing Security Chatbot Efficacy through Iterative Feedback Loops and User-Centric Approaches," Am. J. Innov. Sci. Eng., vol. 3, no. 3, pp. 77–87, 2024, doi: 10.54536/ajise.v3i3.2919.

[20] G. Ali, S. Shah and M. ElAffendi, "Enhancing Cybersecurity Incident Response: AI-Driven Optimization for Strengthened Advanced Persistent Threat Detection," Results Eng., vol. 25, Art. no. 104078, 2025, doi: 10.1016/j.rineng.2025.104078.

[21] M. L. Ali, K. Thakur, H. Barker and M. Chan, "The Rise of Artificial Intelligence: Industry Insights and Applications in Security Information and Event Management (SIEM)," 2024 IEEE 15th Annual Ubiquitous Computing, Electronics & Mobile Communication Conference (UEMCON), Yorktown Heights, NY, USA, 2024, pp. 0477–0482, doi: 10.1109/UEMCON62879.2024.10754705.

[22] H. Okamoto, "The Role of Information Security Event Management (SIEM) in Enhancing Intrusion Detection and Cybersecurity Through Machine Learning Technology," 2021.

[23] G. Waizel, "Bridging the AI divide: The evolving arms race between AI-driven cyber attacks and AI-powered cybersecurity defenses," in Proc. Int. Conf. Mach. Intell. Security Smart Cities (TRUST), vol. 1, pp. 141–156, Jul. 2024.

[24] A. Pereira, N. Ivanov, and Z. Wang, "Real-Time AI-Based Threat Intelligence for Cloud Security Enhancement," Innovative: Int. Multidisciplinary J. Appl. Technol., vol. 3, no. 3, pp. 36–54, 2025. [Online]. Available: https://eprints.umsida.ac.id/15810/

[25] I. H. Sarker, "Multi-aspects AI-based modeling and adversarial learning for cybersecurity intelligence and robustness: A comprehensive overview," Security and Privacy, vol. 2023, Art. no. e295, 2023, doi: 10.1002/spy2.295.

[26] K. Shaukat, S. Luo, V. Varadharajan, I. A. Hameed, S. Chen, D. Liu, and J. Li, "Performance Comparison and Current Challenges of Using

Machine Learning Techniques in Cybersecurity," Energies, vol. 13, no. 10, p. 2509, 2020. [Online]. Available: https://doi.org/10.3390/en13102509

[27] T. K. Vashishth, V. Sharma, B. Samania, R. Sharma, S. Singh, and P. Jajoria, "Ethical and Legal Implications of AI in Cybersecurity," Advances in computational intelligence and robotics book series, pp. 387–414, Nov. 2024, doi: 10.4018/979-8-3693-7540-2.ch017.

[28] G. O. Mbah and A. N. Evelyn, "AI-powered cybersecurity: Strategic approaches to mitigate risk and safeguard data privacy," World Journal of Advanced Research and Reviews, vol. 24, no. 3, 2024. [Online]. Available: https://doi.org/10.30574/wjarr.2024.24.3.3695

[29] M. Alazab, S. P. RM, P. M, P. K. R. Maddikunta, T. R. Gadekallu, and Q.-V. Pham, "Federated Learning for Cybersecurity: Concepts, Challenges, and Future Directions," IEEE Transactions on Industrial Informatics, vol. 18, no. 5, pp. 3501–3509, May 2022, doi: 10.1109/TII.2021.3119038.

[30] N. AfzaliSeresht, Explainable Intelligence for Comprehensive Interpretation of Cybersecurity Data in Incident Management, Ph.D. dissertation, Victoria Univ., 2022.

[31] P. Radanliev, D. De Roure, K. R. Page, J. R. C. Nurse, R. Mantilla Montalvo, O. Santos, L. T. Maddox, and P. Burnap, "Cyber Risk at the Edge: Current and future trends on Cyber Risk Analytics and Artificial Intelligence in the Industrial Internet of Things and Industry 4.0 Supply Chains," Preprints, Mar. 2020. [Online]. Available: https://www.preprints.org/manuscript/201903.0123/v2

[32] E. Muhati, D. B. Rawat and B. M. Sadler, "A New Cyber-Alliance of Artificial Intelligence, Internet of Things, Blockchain, and Edge Computing," in IEEE Internet of Things Magazine, vol. 5, no. 1, pp. 104–107, March 2022, doi: 10.1109/IOTM.001.2100181.

8

Challenges in Cyber Risk Analysis Using Big Data and AI Models

Vipin Kumar Chaudhry and Anshu Sharma

School of Computer Science and Engineering, Lovely Professional University, India

Email: chaudharyv209@gmail.com; asharma406@gmail.com

Abstract

The fast pace of the cyber threat landscape requires deploying advanced cyber threat modeling techniques based on big data and artificial intelligence (AI) for detection, prediction, and mitigation. With big data analytics, businesses can process large volumes of structured and unstructured data collected from various sources, such as network logs, threat intelligence feeds, and user behavior patterns, to detect anomalies and potential vulnerabilities. On the other hand, AI models, like ML and DL, are making a huge impact by automating threat detection, classifying risks, predicting attack vectors, etc., with a myriad of highly accurate methods.

The integration of big data and AI has led to significant advancements in cyber risk analysis and assessment. We consider the difficulties with data quality, model interpretability, and adversarial attacks that exploit AI systems. Moreover, the chapter discusses ongoing implementations, such as intrusion detection systems (IDS), fraud prevention, and automated incident response, showcasing how AI-driven analysis enhances decision-making capability and shortens response times.

Though they hold transformative potential, ethical and regulatory considerations like data privacy and algorithmic bias need to be addressed to enable responsible deployment. The study wraps up with future directions, calling for explainable AI (XAI), and federated learning to address

DOI: 10.1201/9788743808077-8

collaborative threat analysis and quantum defensive cybersecurity frameworks. Big data and AI, as a force multiplier for proactive cyber risk management, enable organizations to leverage these technologies after immediate crises have passed to better address the increasingly complex threat landscape.

8.1 Introduction

Cyber risk analysis: The growing sophistication and frequency of cyberattacks have placed cyber risk analysis at the center of organizational security strategies, demanding advanced methods to identify, assess, and manage threats. With the fast progress of cyber threats, traditional security mechanisms are not addressing the need for security; hence, new and intelligent solutions based on big data and AI are needed [1]. This is especially true for financial institutions, which have ever more complex risks, as a result, they are increasingly adopting AI and advanced analytics with the goal of processing large amounts of data and managing these risks more effectively [2]. Big data and AI have not only taken over our landscape; they have also laid the structure of this landscape and now, in the second chapter, we dive into this exciting frontier of cyber risk analysis that is being empowered by big data and AI [2], [3].

Figure 8.1 depicts AI and big data evaluating massive digital landscapes to detect cyber risks in real time. It emphasizes clever algorithms that examine data patterns for early danger detection and prevention. Big data provides new opportunities and challenges to cybersecurity as big data is voluminous, multiple, and uncertain in nature. Furthermore, modern information technology (IT) systems generate massive amounts of data – including network traffic, system logs, user activity, and threat intelligence feeds – making it virtually impossible for traditional security tools to recognize all meaningful patterns and anomalies [4]. At the same time, the speed at which this data is generated means it needs to be analyzed in real time to identify and respond to threats rapidly. Data comes in various shapes and forms, structured (i.e., databases) and unstructured (i.e., emails and social media posts), which adds challenges to the analysis. On the other hand, because of the enormous and complex nature of data, the application of artificial intelligence, especially machine learning and deep learning, appears to be a seductive way of obtaining useful insights from such volumes of data, allowing the organization to boost cyber risk analysis precisely [5]. Automated learning is achieved by AI, which can analyze data and recognize underlying trends while accurately forecasting future threats in the process [4].

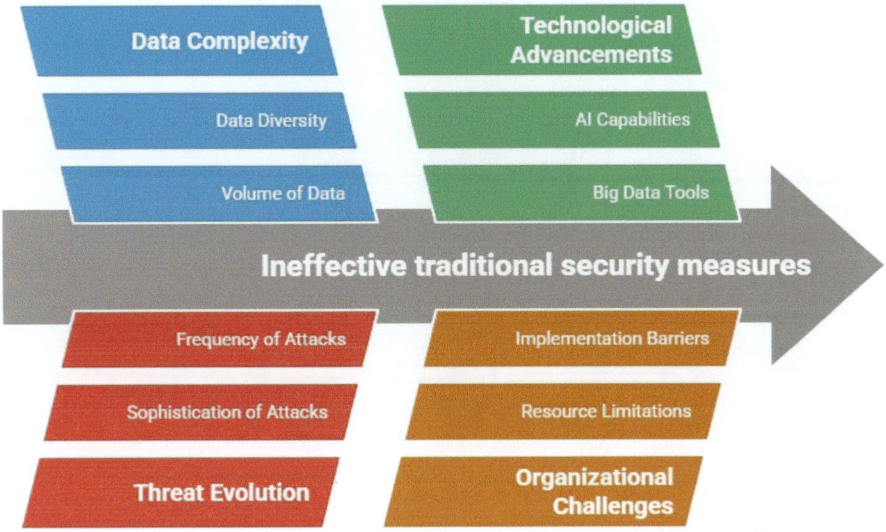

Figure 8.1 Enhancing cyber risk analysis with AI and big data.

8.2 Cyber Risk Analysis Using AI And Big Data: A Theoretical Framework

Cyber risk analysis is a complex process that includes identifying, assessing, and mitigating cybersecurity risk experiences, thus requiring an extensive theoretical framework based on multiple fields of study, such as computer science, statistics, and risk management. Simply put, cyber risk analysis aims to assess the potential impact of cyber incidents on an organization's assets, operations, and reputation. It refers to a deep awareness of the threat landscape, i.e., the different types of actors, their intentions, and the attack vectors they utilize [6]. Structured risk assessment methodologies based on NIST cybersecurity framework, ISO 27001, or similar frameworks guided the process of evaluating the likelihood and impact of potential cyber risks, enabling the formulation of effective mitigation strategies. Traditional risk assessment approaches are insufficient given the rapidly evolving and interconnected world of cyber threats [7]. This is about integrating big data analytics and AI models with cyber risk assessment frameworks to better adapt to emerging threats and facilitate a more proactive and data-driven approach to cyber risk management.

An AI-driven cybersecurity process in which intelligent algorithms constantly track, identify, and respond to attacks has been depicted in Figure 8.2.

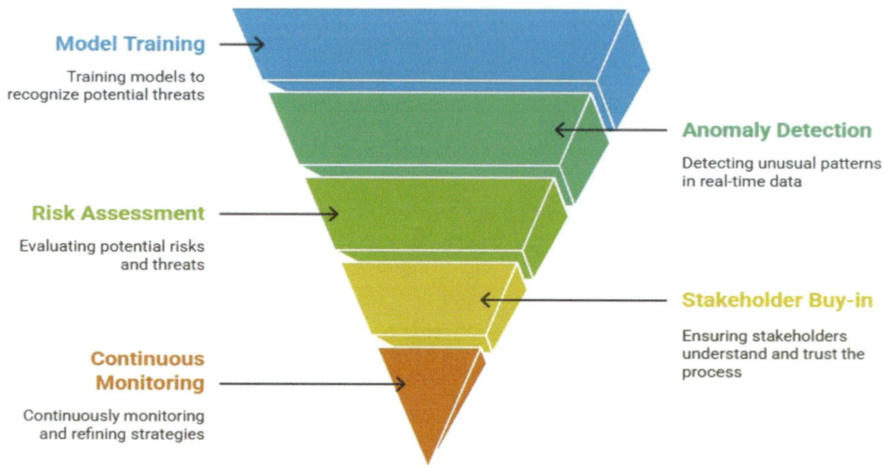

Figure 8.2 AI-driven cybersecurity process.

It demonstrates automated threat analysis, decision-making, and adaptive defense mechanisms in action. To facilitate trust in AI, explainable AI techniques help uncover how AI models come to conclusions, offering transparency of their models and decisions [8]. In order to successfully obtain buy-in from stakeholders, AI-driven risk assessments must be interpretable and explainable, which is crucial for accountability in ensuring that cybersecurity practices are being ethically and justifiably implemented. Because of the high dimensionality of data and sometimes being highly unstructured to draw an inference. Machine learning and deep learning algorithms can be adopted to detect subtle real-time abnormalities and patterns that are indicative of possible malicious activity, thereby providing early warning signals of possible cyber shredding [9]. By using historical data to train these models, organizations can predict potential threats before they occur, allowing them to take steps to prevent breaches. Moreover, processes for continual monitoring and feedback must be integrated into the theoretical framework, enabling ongoing refinement of risk assessments and mitigation strategies informed by empirical data and changing threat environments [10].

8.3 Cyber Risk Modeling with Big Data

This paradigm shift from traditional security measures, which are solely reactive in nature, to big data-driven cyber risk modeling stems from the use of big data analytics in cybersecurity. This transition taps into the vast amounts of data being created inside and outside an organization to recognize, predict,

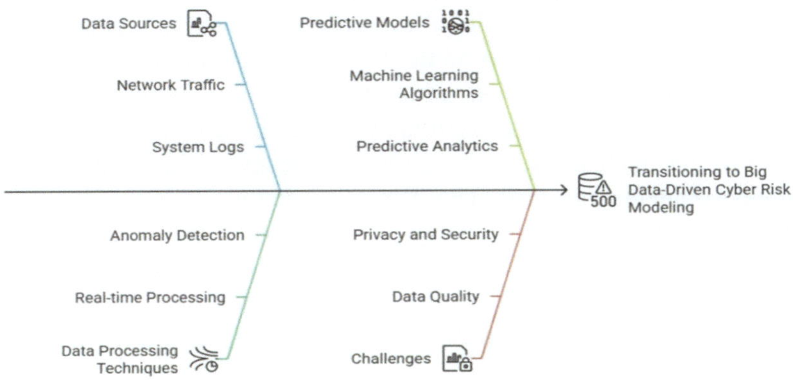

Figure 8.3 Enhancing cybersecurity with big data.

and combat potential cyber threats. By collecting and analyzing data from a variety of data sources such as network traffic, system logs, user behavior, threat intelligence feeds, and vulnerability databases, organizations can have an overview of their overall security state [11]. Additionally, real-time data processing allows for the prompt identification of anomalies and potential threats, shortening the response time available to the threat actor.

However, the application of big data to cyber risk analysis allows for scalability, allowing big data platforms to acquire and process the huge volumes of data that cyber risk analysis generally deals with. To uncover patterns and relationships in the data, it is possible to apply these three data mining techniques, namely, clustering, classification, and association rule mining. By analyzing and learning from past incidents, these algorithms can provide predictions for upcoming attacks, thus allowing organizations to take preventative steps to avoid breaches [12]. Moreover, social media and online forum sentiment data mining can uncover new threats and vulnerabilities and improve threat intelligence capabilities. The coordination of big data and machine learning allows for the creation of predictive models that can forecast cyberattacks and highlight vulnerable entry points, enabling security teams to take preventive measures [13]. Yet employing big data for cyber risk modeling entails data quality, privacy, and security considerations.

Figure 8.3 demonstrates how big data improves cybersecurity by aggregating and analyzing large datasets to detect hidden dangers. It emphasizes real-time monitoring, anomaly detection, and predictive analytics to strengthen defense. Reliable insights depend on accurate and complete data, and this data needs to be fortified to safeguard sensitive data against unauthorized access and breaches.

Unlike traditional methodologies, with this potent combination, organizations are better adapted to address cyber threats through sophisticated threat detection, analytics, and mitigation [14]. The integration of these technologies will enable organizations to develop stronger and more flexible security mechanisms which can respond better to the rapidly changing threat environment [15], [16]. The increasing frequency and complexity of cyberattacks require advanced analytical methods capable of analyzing large datasets to detect subtle patterns that demonstrate malicious activity [17]. AI-powered security solutions ensure that security measures are scalable and can adapt as the organization grows and its attack surface increases [18].

8.4 AI Models to Predict Cyber Risk Analysis

With their ability to process complex datasets and detect hidden patterns, AI models have proven to be transformative for predicting cyber risk, making it possible to predict potential threats with stunning accuracy [18]. Predictive models that can predict a cyberattack as well as the points of entry are made with the tools of supervised, unsupervised, and reinforcement learning algorithms [19]. These fall under two categories: Supervised learning models are trained on labeled datasets to classify and predict different types of cyber risks, while unsupervised learning algorithms can identify anomalies and patterns in unlabeled data to uncover previously unknown threats. Using reinforcement learning methods, we can create adaptive security frameworks that learn from their environment and enhance skills to discover and combat attacks.

Figure 8.4 depicts AI-driven cyber risk prediction, which involves studying historical and real-time data to forecast prospective threats. It focuses on machine learning models that detect vulnerabilities and enable proactive risk management.

For example, the financial industry is leading the way in applying AI to risk assessment, including in areas like credit risk, fraud detection, and market trend forecasting [20]. AI credit risk models ensure a dramatic increase in predictive accuracy, and in market risk management, significantly increase the accuracy and speed of anomaly detection [21]. Apart from that, the ability of AI to analyze diverse data sources is making for a more holistic view of risk, which is informing decisions better [22]. With crime patterns winding ever deeper and becoming more personalized and obscure, the need to deploy effective defensive AI strategies becomes paramount [23]. AI plays a significant role in automating the defensive capabilities of active cyber defense, making them capable of neutralizing automated threats. They all send data

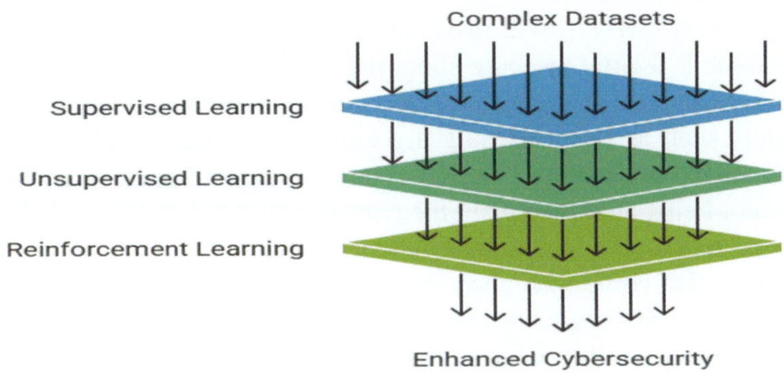

Figure 8.4 AI-driven cyber risk prediction.

so that AI algorithms can make sense of it in real time, constantly monitoring network traffic and system logs for signs of abnormal behavior more typical of an attack.

Despite its potential, the application of AI in predicting cyber risk is not without challenges, such as data quality requirements, overfitting risk, and adversarial attacks. Hence, organizations are required to invest in cleansing and preprocessing their data to maintain data quality because data is the fuel that drives accurate and reliable AI models.

Additionally, acclaimed cyber-attacks require the exploration of powerful AI methods and active defenses from adversarial attacks against systems with security based on AI [24]; A variety of benefits is offered by the deployment of these AI and machine learning models in risk management, for example, better fraud detection, resource allocation, and compliance with regulations [25]. Moreover, AI algorithms are capable of constantly monitoring financial transactions and detecting suspicious patterns that may indicate fraudulent activity [26].

8.5 Challenges and Limitations

However, there are several challenges and limitations in using AI and big data analysis in the context of cyber risk analysis that organizations must address to ensure the effectiveness and reliability of these technologies. One of the biggest obstacles is the availability and quality of data. With big data analytics, a larger dataset leads to better models with more valuable insights, while organizations often lack the ability to collect, store, and process the amount of data needed to effectively analyze the risks and impacts of cyber threats. There is also an issue with the quality of the data; if the data is inaccurate or not collected properly, it will result in biased or unreliable outcomes. Then another issue is feeling insecure about the AI decision-making process. This complexity can pose challenges for researchers, especially when interpreting AI models such as deep learning algorithms and understanding how they come to their conclusions [27]. In cybersecurity, it becomes a hindrance because not being able to explain the reasoning behind certain security decisions leads to loss of accountability and loss of trust.

Ethics also come into play, especially in terms of privacy rights, that need to be weighed against security requirements [18]. To train AI models, large datasets are needed, which can result in data privacy and security being compromised if sensitive information contained within the training set is improperly protected [18]. Organizations need to put in place the appropriate measures to ensure personal and confidential data cannot be accessed or misused. For example, if a model is trained on biased data, it may produce unfair or discriminatory results, which can be particularly problematic in applications like fraud detection and risk assessment. It is essential for financial institutions to be lucidly maneuvering the implementation of AI technologies, taking into consideration pertinent challenges and ethical implications [28].

Moreover, AI systems are vulnerable to adversarial attacks, where the malicious actor tries to trick the AI model into providing false or misleading information. Mitigating these issues requires a comprehensive strategy, involving investment in data quality, the development of explainable AI methods, the implementation of strong security defenses, and the establishment of ethical guidelines surrounding the use of AI in cyber risk evaluation [29]. Attaining informed consent from individuals for using their data in AI systems is also important [30].

Additionally, many AI models are so complex that they are often not interpretable or explainable, which can prevent companies in regulated industries from using them.

One way to address this problem is through Explainable AI techniques, which help provide insight into the decision-making processes of AI models, providing users with an understanding of the rationale behind a given decision and helping to identify potential biases or errors in an AI model [31]. For example, Explainable AI is critical in increasing the trust of clinicians in decision-making by increasing the transparency of healthcare algorithms [32], [33]. Explainable AI is essential to ensure that the training data, algorithmic design, and decision-making processes can be scrutinized, helping to identify and mitigate biases [30].

A line of responsibility for the design, implementation, and maintenance of individual AI systems and mechanisms for addressing errors or bias in AI-generated outcomes must be established, and organizations must acknowledge when AI systems are not working as intended or are causing harm [34]. Handling bias within AI models is critical for their ethical and fair implementation in healthcare [35]. It calls for a meticulous approach to the data collection, model development, and evaluation steps. Data should represent the population from which the individuals will be selected, and AI technologies should be built with diverse populations in mind and strive to mitigate biases in datasets and algorithms [36], [37], [38].

8.6 Conclusion

Cyber risk analysis done using AI and big data has been empowered to enable organizations to detect and respond to threats faster and better. AI algorithms can produce results that make internal and external hackers as easily spotted as a red flag, all made possible by analyzing the immense amount of data from the IT systems of today.

Nevertheless, applying AI to cyber risk assessment comes with risks – specifically, the need for data quality, the danger of overfitting, and the threat of adversarial attacks. Organizations should ensure data quality and create security systems to prevent these threats. However, the benefits of AI in analyzing cyber risk far outweigh the challenges. With the continuing evolution of AI, it will remain integral to enable organizations to manage cyber risks and safeguard their assets.

References

[1] I. Y. Hafez, A. M. Hafez, A. M. S. Saleh, A. A. A. El-Mageed, and A. A. Abohany, "A systematic review of AI-enhanced techniques in credit card fraud detection," Journal Of Big Data, vol. 12, no. 1. Springer Science+Business Media, Jan. 14, 2025. doi: 10.1186/s40537-024-01048-8.

[2] A. O. Ikudabo and P. Kumar, "AI-Driven Risk Assessment and Management in Banking: Balancing Innovation and Security," International Journal of Research Publication and Reviews, vol. 5, no. 10, p. 3573, Oct. 2024, doi: 10.55248/gengpi.5.1024.2926.

[3] A. M. S. Saleh, "Blockchain for secure and decentralized artificial intelligence in cybersecurity: A comprehensive review," Blockchain Research and Applications, vol. 5, no. 3. Elsevier BV, p. 100193, Feb. 29, 2024. doi: 10.1016/j.bcra.2024.100193.

[4] N. Katiyar, Mr. S. Tripathi, Mr. P. Kumar, M. Verma, A. K. Sahu, and S. Saxena, "AI and Cyber-Security: Enhancing threat detection and

response with machine learning.," Apr. 2024, doi: 10.53555/kuey.v30i4.2377.

[5] Y. Sun, J. Li, M. Lu, and Z. Guo, "Study of the Impact of the Big Data Era on Accounting and Auditing," Frontiers in Business Economics and Management, vol. 13, no. 3, p. 44, Mar. 2024, doi: 10.54097/0fa7xk79.

[6] A. Chakraborty, A. Biswas, and A. K. Khan, "Artificial Intelligence for Cybersecurity: Threats, Attacks and Mitigation," arXiv (Cornell University), Jan. 2022, doi: 10.48550/arxiv.2209.13454.

[7] A. Gadhi, R. M. Gondu, H. Chaudhary, and O. Abiona, "Cyber Resilience through Real-Time Threat Analysis in Information Security," International Journal of Communications Network and System Sciences, vol. 17, no. 4, p. 51, Jan. 2024, doi: 10.4236/ijcns.2024.174004.

[8] C. R. B. Mendes and T. N. Rios, "Explainable Artificial Intelligence and Cybersecurity: A Systematic Literature Review," arXiv (Cornell University), Jan. 2023, doi: 10.48550/arxiv.2303.01259.

[9] A. Salem, S. M. Azzam, O. E. Emam, and A. A. Abohany, "Advancing cybersecurity: a comprehensive review of AI-driven detection techniques," Journal Of Big Data, vol. 11, no. 1. Springer Science+Business Media, Aug. 04, 2024. doi: 10.1186/s40537-024-00957-y.

[10] I. Lee, "Cybersecurity: Risk management framework and investment cost analysis," Business Horizons, vol. 64, no. 5, p. 659, Feb. 2021, doi: 10.1016/j.bushor.2021.02.022.

[11] P. Radanliev et al., "Design of a dynamic and self-adapting system, supported with artificial intelligence, machine learning and real-time intelligence for predictive cyber risk analytics in extreme environments – cyber risk in the colonisation of Mars," Safety in Extreme Environments, vol. 2, no. 3, p. 219, Oct. 2020, doi: 10.1007/s42797-021-00025-1.

[12] K. Mohammed, "Harnessing the Speed and Accuracy of Machine Learning to Advance Cybersecurity," arXiv (Cornell University), Jan. 2023, doi: 10.48550/arxiv.2302.12415.

[13] S. Hiremath et al., "A New Approach to Data Analysis Using Machine Learning for Cybersecurity," Big Data and Cognitive Computing, vol. 7, no. 4, p. 176, Nov. 2023, doi: 10.3390/bdcc7040176.

[14] Y. Jiang, "Characteristics and Countermeasures of Enterprise Risk Management in Digital Economy Era," Frontiers in Business Economics and Management, vol. 10, no. 3, p. 81, Aug. 2023, doi: 10.54097/fbem.v10i3.11312.

[15] L. Elluri, V. Mandalapu, P. Vyas, and N. Roy, "Recent Advancements in Machine Learning For Cybercrime Prediction," arXiv, 2023, doi: 10.48550/ARXIV.2304.04819.

[16] M. Roshanaei, M. R. Khan, and N. N. Sylvester, "Navigating AI Cybersecurity: Evolving Landscape and Challenges," Journal of Intelligent Learning Systems and Applications, vol. 16, no. 3, p. 155, Jan. 2024, doi: 10.4236/jilsa.2024.163010.

[17] Q. Yuan and X. Tan, "Research on Application of Artificial Intelligence in Network Security Defence," Journal of Physics Conference Series, vol. 2033, no. 1, p. 12149, Sep. 2021, doi: 10.1088/1742-6596/2033/1/012149.

[18] M. Roshanaei, M. R. Khan, and N. N. Sylvester, "Enhancing Cybersecurity through AI and ML: Strategies, Challenges, and Future Directions," Journal of Information Security, vol. 15, no. 3, p. 320, Jan. 2024, doi: 10.4236/jis.2024.153019.

[19] J. Nicholls, A. Kuppa, and N. Le-Khac, "Financial Cybercrime: A Comprehensive Survey of Deep Learning Approaches to Tackle the Evolving Financial Crime Landscape," IEEE Access, vol. 9, p. 163965, Jan. 2021, doi: 10.1109/access.2021.3134076.

[20] S. Kalogiannidis, D. Kalfas, O. Papaevangelou, G. Giannarakis, and F. Chatzitheodoridis, "The Role of Artificial Intelligence Technology in Predictive Risk Assessment for Business Continuity: A Case Study of Greece," Risks, vol. 12, no. 2, p. 19, Jan. 2024, doi: 10.3390/risks12020019.

[21] H. Xu, K. Niu, T. Lu, and S. Li, "Leveraging artificial intelligence for enhanced risk management in financial services: Current applications and future prospects," Engineering Science & Technology Journal, vol. 5, no. 8, p. 2402, Aug. 2024, doi: 10.51594/estj.v5i8.1363.

[22] C. Maple et al., "The AI Revolution: Opportunities and Challenges for the Finance Sector," arXiv (Cornell University), Jan. 2023, doi: 10.48550/arxiv.2308.16538.

[23] E. Kurshan, D. Mehta, B. Bruss, and T. Balch, "AI versus AI in Financial Crimes and Detection: GenAI Crime Waves to Co-Evolutionary AI," arXiv (Cornell University), Sep. 2024, doi: 10.48550/arxiv.2410.09066.

[24] N. Dhir, H. Hoeltgebaum, N. M. Adams, M. Briers, A. Burke, and P. R. Jones, "Prospective Artificial Intelligence Approaches for Active Cyber Defence," arXiv (Cornell University), Jan. 2021, doi: 10.48550/arxiv.2104.09981.

[25] J. Sen, R. Sen, and A. Dutta, "Machine Learning in Finance-Emerging Trends and Challenges," arXiv (Cornell University), Jan. 2021, doi: 10.48550/arxiv.2110.11999.

[26] P. Adhikari, P. Hamal, and F. Baidoo, "Artificial Intelligence in fraud detection: Revolutionizing financial security," International Journal of Science and Research Archive, vol. 13, no. 1, p. 1457, Sep. 2024, doi: 10.30574/ijsra.2024.13.1.1860.

[27] K. Achuthan, S. Ramanathan, S. Srinivas, and R. Raman, "Advancing cybersecurity and privacy with artificial intelligence: current trends and future research directions," Frontiers in Big Data, vol. 7. Frontiers Media, Dec. 05, 2024. doi: 10.3389/fdata.2024.1497535.

[28] M. E. Hajj and J. Hammoud, "Unveiling the Influence of Artificial Intelligence and Machine Learning on Financial Markets: A Comprehensive Analysis of AI Applications in Trading, Risk Management, and Financial Operations," Journal of risk and financial management, vol. 16, no. 10, p. 434, Oct. 2023, doi: 10.3390/jrfm16100434.

[29] N. N. Ridzuan, M. Masri, M. Anshari, N. L. Fitriyani, and M. Syafrudin, "AI in the Financial Sector: The Line between Innovation, Regulation and Ethical Responsibility," Information, vol. 15, no. 8, p. 432, Jul. 2024, doi: 10.3390/info15080432.

[30] A. Dhopte and H. Bagde, "Smart Smile: Revolutionizing Dentistry With Artificial Intelligence," Cureus. Cureus, Inc., Jun. 30, 2023. doi: 10.7759/cureus.41227.

[31] D. Petković, "It is Not 'Accuracy vs. Explainability'—We Need Both for Trustworthy AI Systems," IEEE Transactions on Technology and Society, vol. 4, no. 1, p. 46, Jan. 2023, doi: 10.1109/tts.2023.3239921.

[32] Z. Zhang, H. A. Hamadi, E. Damiani, C. Y. Yeun, and F. Taher, "Explainable Artificial Intelligence Applications in Cyber Security: State-of-the-Art in Research," IEEE Access, vol. 10, p. 93104, Jan. 2022, doi: 10.1109/access.2022.3204051.

[33] D. Muhammad and M. Bendechache, "Unveiling the black box: A systematic review of Explainable Artificial Intelligence in medical image analysis," Computational and Structural Biotechnology Journal, vol. 24. Elsevier BV, p. 542, Aug. 12, 2024. doi: 10.1016/j.csbj.2024.08.005.

[34] A. S. M. A. Uddin, "The Era of AI: Upholding Ethical Leadership," Open Journal of Leadership, vol. 12, no. 4, p. 400, Jan. 2023, doi: 10.4236/ojl.2023.124019.

[35] H. Taherdoost and A. Ghofrani, "AI's role in revolutionizing personalized medicine by reshaping pharmacogenomics and drug therapy," Intelligent Pharmacy, vol. 2, no. 5, p. 643, Aug. 2024, doi: 10.1016/j.ipha.2024.08.005.

[36] E. Ferrara, "Fairness and Bias in Artificial Intelligence: A Brief Survey of Sources, Impacts, and Mitigation Strategies," Sci, vol. 6, no. 1, p. 3, Dec. 2023, doi: 10.3390/sci6010003.

[37] A. A. Abujaber and A. J. Nashwan, "Ethical framework for artificial intelligence in healthcare research: A path to integrity," World Journal

of Methodology, vol. 14, no. 3. Jun. 25, 2024. doi: 10.5662/wjm.v14.i3.94071.

[38] G. Chenais, E. Lagarde, and C. Gil-Jardiné, "Artificial Intelligence in Emergency Medicine: Viewpoint of Current Applications and Foreseeable Opportunities and Challenges," Journal of Medical Internet Research, vol. 25. JMIR Publications, Dec. 19, 2022. doi: 10.2196/40031.International Telecommunication Union (ITU), report on Climate Change, Oct. 2008.

9

Rising Impact of AI in Cyber Risk Management in the Context of Small- and Medium-sized Enterprises

Shyam Sunder Agrawal[1], Divya Mahajan[2], Nidhi Sharma[2], and Amanjot Singh Syan[3]

[1]Lovely Professional University, India
[2]University Business School, Guru Nanak Dev University, India
[3]Canadore Stanford International College, Canada

Email: Shyamsunderagrawal8@gmail.com; divya.ubs@gndu.ac.in; nidhimanibhargava@gmail.com; amnsyn@hotmail.com

Abstract

The chapter focuses on the changing role of artificial intelligence (AI) in cyber risk management of small and medium businesses (SMBs)/SMEs; such that this sector is fast becoming a haven for advanced cyber threats without the need for requisite resources, expertise, or structured strategies that would guarantee effective digital security. Not only has AI increasingly gained ground in the practice of information security, but it is also worth mentioning that there is a limited amount of literature available that has focused on SME-specific challenges but with regard to cost-effective implementation, less awareness and training, ethical and regulatory concerns, preparedness of the workforce, and lack of transparency in AI-driven systems. In order to attend to such critical topics, the systematic literature review (SLR) methodology PRISMA had been utilized for a structured, transparent, and replicable synthesis of knowledge. An initial pool of 1,160 studies was drawn from three major research databases, namely Scopus, IEEE Xplore, and Web of Science. The time frame for the study was from 2015 to 2025. Rigorous application of specific inclusion and exclusion criteria resulted in a total of

DOI: 10.1201/9788743808077-9

41 studies culled for in-depth analysis. These findings revealed that although AI technologies have great potential in automating threat detection, managing cyber incidents, and improving risk visibility, there are significant barriers among SMEs in adopting these technologies, such as financial strain, insufficient technical expertise, low trust in AI systems, and lack of policy frameworks tailored for them. Moreover, Explainable AI (XAI) was found to be poorly researched regarding SMEs, whereas it could improve trust and understanding among users. The study contributed to the academic debate by defining the contextual limitations of cybersecurity models and calling for the co-creation of simplistically employed, cost-efficient, and scalable AI tools for cyber resilience in SMEs and for meeting future sustainable commitments in the context of SMEs.

9.1 Introduction

9.1.1 Theoretical background

In the present rapid digital evolution era, artificial intelligence (AI) is transforming the way business operates, offering unprecedented opportunities for efficiency, innovation, and competitive advantage. The technological advancements of Industry 4.0 have accredited the requisition of a wide variety of technologies related to digitization, automation, and connectivity [4]. However, as this integration between the AI systems becomes deeper into business processes, it introduces an entrepreneur to new and complex risks associated with cybersecurity, ranging from data breaches to algorithmic vulnerabilities, that must be carefully and cautiously managed to mitigate the business risks.

As far as the SMBs/SMEs are concerned, they many times have a dearth of resources and technical expertise as compared to the larger corporations. The mainstream industrialized countries have focused their concern on the burgeoning of Industry 4.0 as a strategic constituent of industrial policy in order to enhance their competitiveness. At both these levels, the key objective of risk management is to minimize the risk and assuage the threat of potential losses. Designated by the unpredictability of the macro-environment, risk management can be contemplated as one of the most essential approaches for companies to ensure business continuity (BC) and vanquish uncertainties [22]. In order to extensively understand the forces that influence a company's operations, it is critical to examine these from multiple perspectives. By analyzing the external environment of a company that encircles a wide range of macro-level factors, it also accords with both the opportunities and the threats [32], while the key indicators at the micro-level are assessed from a company's perspective internally [3]. The dual challenge of adopting AI technologies while managing cyber risks is particularly acute. The high-tech metaphors present in Industry 4.0 comprehensively construct an exponential soar in data volumes in the cyberspace context. As SMEs have been constantly earmarked by cyber threats because of their relatively delicate defenses, cyber risk management is a critical component of their digital strategy. Therefore, SMEs must prioritize cybersecurity to protect sensitive business data, maintain customer trust, and avoid potentially devastating financial losses [11]. Integrating AI responsibly and securely can thus empower SMEs to thrive in the digital economy while simultaneously safeguarding their assets, reputation, and customer trust. As the advancements in technology are accelerated, the studies have emphasized more on the adoption of digital tools in the mainstream, improving their role in the dimensions of reliability and efficiency, thereby managing timely resources [40].

Therefore, this intersection of AI, cyber risk management, and SMEs underscores the need for practical frameworks, policy guidance, and tailored solutions to ensure that the benefits of AI can be harnessed without compromising the security or resilience criteria in the present competitive AI-governed era. The inscription of topics related to AI also includes knowledge, reasoning, human intelligence, planning, natural language processing, machine learning, robotics, automation, and cybersecurity [25].

In an increasingly digitized economy, small and medium-sized enterprises (SMEs) are both empowered and imperiled by the same forces that drive innovation. In the past, where innovation and IT have been used interchangeably, AI has paved the way by adding new dimensions to the working of businesses in a comprehensive manner. By leveraging AI for business growth and combining it with a strong cybersecurity foundation, SMEs can transform their operations in a way that ensures sustainability, scalability, and long-term success [26]. The whip hand of AI in curbing cyber risk management has secured a more promising and sustainable future for SMEs. It enhances the possibility for management to increase or decrease production, considering demand, thereby aiming towards the reduction in downtime in a way that constant efficiency of the production line streamlines [31]. To secure their future, SMEs should adopt a layered, proactive approach as the SMEs that flourish in 2030 will be those that treat cyber risk as a core business function, integrating governance, continuous monitoring, and adaptive controls into their strategic planning. As the overall quantification of the risk factors has jumped, and therefore companies must proactively consider risk mitigation strategies and their implementation. By anticipating emerging threats, embracing regulatory shifts, and investing in both people and technology, SMEs can convert cyber resilience into a competitive advantage rather than an afterthought. The extent of cybersecurity risks amplifies a wide range of threats, from the breaching of data to sophisticated cyberattacks, having catastrophic effects on businesses [42]. The goal of AI is to equip and balance the machines with human intelligence [1]. The incorporation of digitization into the industrial framework, aids in the integration of physical and virtual components, which forms a crucial characteristic of Industry 4.0. Therefore, the exploitation of susceptibilities in the integrated and connected cyber-physical systems (CPS), governed by technological transformations, demands certain technical detection measures related to the application, transmission, and perception layers of CPS [40]. The proactive risk management emphasis for SMEs, in order to control the changes and disruptions, can be effectively curbed in the industrial sector (specifically) [38].

By incorporating risk management strategies into their routine operations, SMEs can more effectively utilize their resources [28]. AI offers SMEs powerful tools to optimize various business functions. From data analytics that inform decision-making to automation that reduces operational costs, AI helps businesses unlock insights and efficiencies that were previously unattainable. Furthermore, by integrating the correct balance of AI and machine learning, SMEs can bridge some of the gaps caused by limited budgets and expertise, thereby leveling their competence with larger enterprises in a constructive paradigm [11].

9.1.2 Research gap

Integrating artificial intelligence (AI) into cyber risk management within entrepreneurial ventures, particularly small- and medium-sized enterprises (SMEs), presents several research gaps that warrant further exploration:

9.1.2.1 Cybersecurity awareness and training deficiencies

SMEs often lack comprehensive cybersecurity awareness programs, leading to vulnerabilities. Research focusing on developing cost-effective, scalable training solutions tailored for SMEs is limited. Cyber insurance adoption is required to cover cyber risks for SMEs, along with the convergence of AI, IoT, and cybersecurity towards sustainability through green AI and Modules related to the preparation of questionnaires in the context of cyber risk management, thereby, constantly updating against cyber threats for better defense and attack on a real-time basis [22].

9.1.2.2 Ethical and regulatory challenges

The deployment of AI in cybersecurity introduces certain ethical parameters, such as the AI algorithm's biases and data privacy issues. There is a need for research frameworks to ensure ethical AI implementation and compliance with evolving regulations [29].

9.1.2.3 Explainability of AI models (XAI)

The "black-box" nature of many AI systems poses challenges in understanding and trusting AI-driven decisions in cybersecurity. Research into Explainable AI (XAI) focuses on making these models more transparent, but its application in cyber and data security, especially for SMEs, remains underexplored [31].

9.1.2.4 Resource constraints and talent shortages

SMEs often face limitations in financial and human resources, making it challenging to adopt and manage AI-driven cybersecurity solutions. Research into affordable AI tools and strategies to bridge the cybersecurity talent gap in SMEs is scarce [33].

9.1.2.5 Bias and fairness in AI algorithms

If cautious efforts are not taken into consideration while designing and careful testing, AI systems may exhibit biases that would indecorously affect certain users or groups. For example, anomaly detection algorithms that are previously trained on data evaluations from large enterprises may prove fatal in detecting the threats associated with SME environments, leading to gaps evading protection concerns [41].

9.2 Theoretical Background

9.2.1 Trust in AI system

The author investigates through a survey related to the cyberattacks on the industry concerning AI. It also addresses various technological advancements that aid in cyber-attack detection towards efficient strategic planning in the competitive Industry 4.0 framework. This also supports the transformation governed by the technological AI evolution [6].

The current study instills a link in the nature of the bibliometric analysis that simplifies the characteristics and structure of a field of research seamlessly [11]. Under this, the development of SME default prediction models mainly based on longitudinal data using different statistical models considering the quantitative as well as qualitative variables that lead to the specific exploration of the prediction potential of innovation-related variables; the identification of the critical variables for a SME success and further the empirically validating the seminal theoretical failure prediction model proposed by Argenti (1976).

9.2.2 Workforce readiness

The systematic literature review conducted in this research imparts valuable insights into the current scenario of cyber risk management in the context of SMEs, which also pays diligent focus on identifying the barriers and needs of the same. It also talks about the potential of AI in not only enhancing cyber-attack capabilities but also strengthening defense mechanisms. Therefore, incorporating AI tools and technologies can significantly benefit SMEs [18].

The AI-driven cybersecurity solutions, by leveraging machine learning, anomaly detection, and natural language processing technologies, aid in overcoming the resource constraints and transform the working of SMEs [19].

According to [27], it is quite essential to also prioritise cybersecurity workforce development to sail through the cutting-edge technological advancements. By doing so, SMEs can further strengthen their defenses through a more sustainable security culture that will enhance operational efficiency and promote long-term sustainable business growth.

The findings from this study highlight the positive impact of continuous, interactive training on employee behavior, demonstrating that an engaged workforce is better equipped to identify and respond to cyber threats. Despite these barriers, the integration of advanced technologies such as AI, gamification, and personalized learning platforms holds great potential to enhance the effectiveness of cybersecurity training. By incorporating continuous learning and encouraging a culture of security, organizations can consciously endeavor not just to make employees aware of the threats but also to equip them proactively in defending against them [37].

9.2.3 Cost-effectiveness perception

As per [39] brings to notice the identification of various risks associated with the micro-macro environment of the SMEs. This strategic integration of the technology helps in overcoming these by providing practical examples that integrate the capacities and capabilities in strengthening the SMEs. The adoption of digital technologies, especially AI, enhances the operational efficiency of SMEs by navigating through the complexities of visionary, resilient business practices.

The author states that the integration of AI and cybersecurity into operations has significantly enriched not just business performance but also security. It shows the impact of AI in terms of operational efficiency, decision-making, and business intelligence, along with robust cybersecurity measures to mitigate risks and thereby protect the digital assets of the business. As the SMEs immensely rely on digital technologies to streamline their operations, the integration of AI and cybersecurity leads to threat detection and incident response [29].

The author examines the key cyber threats and also suggests certain preventive measures with globally recognized guidelines for SMEs. It also caters to a more structured and scalable approach to cybersecurity that is practical and effective at the same time. [27].

According to [34], it discusses the various factors that lead to the adoption of AI in SMEs to overcome the barriers and take a strategic advantage. Customized AI solutions enhance the efficiency and effectiveness of various functions of SMEs, such as human resources, customer engagement, decision making, inventory control, and cybersecurity.

Research examines the complaints of SMEs regarding the shortfalls of know-how and at times also face issues related to luring AI experts, making AI a more friendly technology in large-scale businesses, whereas it depicts a lot of potential on the availability of high volumes of good quality data, particularly in SMEs, that must be addressed in effective IP innovation management by establishing a transparent and consistent AI-based innovation regulatory system [37].

9.2.4 Risk awareness and mitigation of risks

According to [5], the role of artificial intelligence (AI) in reducing risks and opening a plethora of opportunities for SMEs by safeguarding their assets towards job creation acts as an agent in fighting poverty by also meeting their commitments towards the SDGs. It delves into case studies of the successful implementation of AI-driven cybersecurity measures by exploring various government initiatives and support programs that are focused on assisting SMEs in adopting these technologies.

SMEs often lag due to limited resources and technical expertise, making them attractive targets for cybercriminals. However, AI-powered cybersecurity solutions, such as machine learning and real-time threat detection systems, offer a level of protection previously reserved for larger organizations [43].

The study sheds light on a risk-management tool that is all-encompassing and evaluates the risk dimensions within the context of SME cum information systems. It states that even though SMEs have scarce resources, it is also quite essential for them to adopt a holistic approach to their risk management by risk assessment, reconciling their risk appetite, and utilizing risk-management systems and information systems for their survival and long-term viability [36].

9.2.5 Impact metrics

The study explains that dealing with the complexities of cybersecurity requires a multi-faceted approach that would be a mixed combination of these technologies with traditional methods involving various stakeholders such as technologists, policymakers, and legal experts. Therefore, the future of effective cybersecurity lies in finding a harmonious balance between the speed and scalability of AI along with the creativity, intuition, and ethical judgment of human expertise [33].

Explaining the symbiotic relationship between AI and cybersecurity as a pathway for SMEs aids in accomplishing sustainable growth and navigating challenges smoothly. Therefore, the SMEs must adopt a holistic proposition toward digital transformation, where this collaboration will be key to achieving long-term success and resilience [30].

With the continual advancements in machine learning, natural language processing, and automation, SMEs will increasingly utilize AI to enhance data analysis, generate predictive insights, and improve customer experiences. Therefore, the SMEs that strategically integrate BI, AI, and cybersecurity not only enhance their operational capabilities but also position themselves better than their competitors as resilient and competitive players in their respective markets [26].

The researcher explores the powerful synergy between AI and cybersecurity as to how these technologies can drive operational excellence and competitive advantage. AI provides SMEs with powerful tools and robust cybersecurity measures that are essential for protecting sensitive information and maintaining customer trust. By integrating AI with strong cybersecurity protocols, SMEs can not only mitigate risks but also leverage technology to drive growth, improve resilience, and gain a competitive edge [19].

He states that as AI has become more applicable all over the business world, these technologies have enormous potential to enhance the operational performance of SMEs. Therefore, SMEs in developing nations must pay due consideration to develop their digital connection with skills and capacity, addressing the usage of standards for interoperability, and finding ways and means to improve their governance to become globally competitive, contributing towards the sustainable success of the business [11].

The authors conducted a comprehensive systematic literature review focusing on the application of artificial intelligence (AI) techniques for detecting cybersecurity threats in Internet of Things (IoT) devices and networks. Their study analyzed 80 peer-reviewed articles published between 2016 and 2021, emphasizing the use of machine learning (ML) and deep learning (DL) methods in enhancing IoT security. The review offers an AI roadmap that categorizes various detection strategies, attack types, and threat models within the IoT landscape, aiming to guide future research and development in this domain [17]. By discussing the impact of digital technologies, particularly AI in Industrial IOT on Cyber risk analytics and supply chain management of Industry 4.0, it emphasizes the need for real-time intelligence to understand the opportunities and threats. Also, identifying the challenges of privacy, security, and resilience posed by the same in supply chain management. A new analytical framework is developed to help SMEs adapt to digital technology changes in supply chains [10, 41].

9.2.6 Conceptual framework

In the present competitive digital-first world, small- and medium-sized enterprises (SMEs) face an uphill battle in securing their digital assets. As these businesses embrace technology, they inadvertently open the door to cyber threats that are becoming increasingly sophisticated. This chapter examines how artificial intelligence (AI) can transform cyber risk management for SMEs while highlighting the existing challenges and research gaps that demand immediate academic and industry attention. Figure 9.1 depicts the framework that provides various insights to the SMEs [14].

9.2.6.1 Trust in AI systems

Trust in AI-based cybersecurity systems must be established, particularly for small and medium enterprises (SMEs), which are often wary about the adoption of new technologies. Trust is built with constant AI performance, the clarity of its explanation, and user confidence in its ability to avert threats. A lack of predictability and transparency in their workings can incite a lack of trust and confidence in AI systems from users in critical situations. The brand reputation and integrity of the AI solution provider also play a role

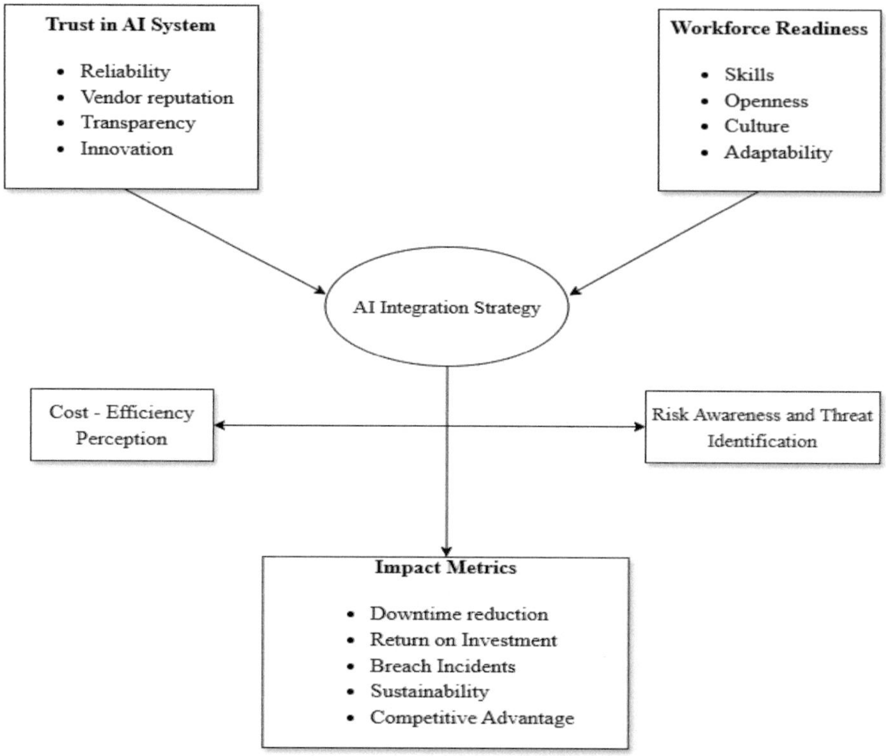

Figure 9.1 Conceptual framework.

since organizations are more likely to trust solutions coming from vendors considered secure and reputable in the marketplace. Long-term trust in these systems would develop when AI decisions are understood, and all systems are kept up-to-date with the latest capabilities and improvements to deal with emerging threats [11].

9.2.6.2 Workforce readiness

The readiness of an organization's workforce is pivotal to the success of integrating AI into cybersecurity operations. The required skills extend further than technical abilities; these encompass an openness to change, eagerness to learn, and overall organizational culture. For SMEs, where there is often limited availability of cybersecurity skills, employee training and awareness programs become essential. An agile and tech-savvy workforce will effectively respond to insights and incidents generated by AI. Hence, nurturing a culture for innovation and continuous skill upgradation ensures that the employees become active participants in cyber resilience instead of being passive users [31].

9.2.6.3 Cost-efficiency perception

For SMEs, perceived cost-effectiveness can make or break the decision to invest in AI cybersecurity solutions. While the upfront costs of AI tools might appear high, what matters more is how business owners perceive their long-term value. If these tools can demonstrably reduce risks, prevent downtime, and eliminate the costs associated with data breaches, they are more likely to be adopted. Solutions tailored to the SME context, offering modular, scalable features at affordable rates that help shift perception from "expensive tech" to "smart investment." Clear communication about financial benefits and reduced risk exposure is vital to improve this perception [26].

9.2.6.4 AI integration strategy

Considering the factors of smooth AI implementation and optimization is a very important thing in formulating a clear plan for AI integration. Frameworks that larger organizations have for structured planning are absent in most SMEs, and hence, they end up having fragmented and inefficient deployments of tools such as AI. Entering into a level of strategy includes defining business needs first, identifying the technologies appropriate for the given business need and preparing the human resources, after which integration is gained with the existing security infrastructure of the company. Without this roadmap, even the best AI tool will be a trivial factor in addressing core challenges facing the organization. A carefully structured, step-by-step plan will help SMEs effectively manage their resources and gauge the impact of AI interventions [27].

9.2.6.5 Risk awareness and threat identification

Awareness of cybersecurity risks and early identification of threats are two basic building blocks of any defense strategy. Many SMEs are still in their infancy stages of building this awareness, making it a good fishing ground for cybercriminals. AI assists with this by automatically detecting unusual patterns or behaviors, but there is an absolute need for human oversight and understanding in this process. Training staff to recognize warning signs and complementing this with AI tools creates a multi-layered defense system.

Hence, risk awareness strengthens SMEs, encouraging proactive rather than reactive measures whenever possible [2, 33].

9.2.6.6 Impact metrics

The measurement of the impact of artificial intelligence on cybersecurity should be able to tell how effective it is or how much justification is given in pouring more investments into it. Examples of these are cuts in system downtime, an indication of fewer incidents of breaches, ROI improvements, and forward progress in achieving long-term sustainability goals. Demonstrable benefits to SMEs, including faster response, fewer interruptions to business, and better data protection, tend to encourage more use or wider applications of AI. Moreover, leveraging on building a competitive advantage through a progressive digital trust could place SMEs on an even more forward-looking and secure path, which is of growing importance in the current cyber-sensitive business environment.

9.3 Methodology

The systematic literature review (SLR) methodology was used to scrutinize the changing role of artificial intelligence (AI) in the management of cyber risk in small- and medium-sized enterprises (SMEs). The systematic literature review procedure provides a rigorous, transparent, and replicable way of identifying, evaluating, and synthesizing existing research on a particular topic. This methodology is excellent for mapping the research area, pointing out gaps, and setting the stage for further academic and practical endeavors [44].

9.3.1 Research questions

The review is guided by the following research questions:

RQ1: What are the current applications of AI in cyber risk management among SMEs?

RQ2: What are the key challenges SMEs face when adopting AI-based cybersecurity tools?

RQ3: What ethical, technical, and strategic gaps exist in current research concerning AI-enabled cyber defense for SMEs?

RQ4: How well are current AI models in cybersecurity understood, trusted, and accepted by SMEs?

To ensure a transparent and systematic review process, a well-defined systematic literature review (SLR) protocol was developed. This protocol served as a guiding framework throughout the review process and included the formulation of a targeted keyword strategy, selection of academic databases, establishment of inclusion and exclusion criteria, and the creation of a structured plan for data extraction and synthesis. The protocol aimed to maintain methodological rigor, minimize bias, and ensure reproducibility of the findings [16].

9.3.2 Selection of data

The database selection process prioritized scholarly sources with high research credibility. The search was conducted across three major databases: Scopus, IEEE Xplore, and Web of Science. These platforms were chosen due to their wide coverage of peer-reviewed journals, conference proceedings, and reputable white papers within the domains of cybersecurity, artificial intelligence, and SME studies. To maintain contemporary relevance and align with the rapid pace of technological advancement, the review was limited to studies published between 2015 to 2025 [21].

A precise search string and keyword structure were designed using Boolean operators to maximize search sensitivity and relevance. Keywords included combinations such as ("Artificial Intelligence" OR "AI") AND ("Cybersecurity" OR "Cyber Risk Management") AND ("SMEs" OR "Small and Medium Enterprises") AND ("AI Ethics" OR "Explainable AI" OR "Workforce Readiness" OR "Trust in AI" OR "Cost-Efficiency"). Each database's unique syntax requirements were considered to ensure consistent and accurate query execution across platforms.

9.3.3 Inclusion criteria

The article selection process was carried out in multiple stages to ensure that only the most relevant, high-quality studies were included in this review. Initially, a total of 1,160 articles were retrieved from five major academic databases, like Scopus, IEEE Xplore, and Web of Science, using carefully constructed search strings.3.3 Exclusion Criteria. Conversely, the exclusion criteria were set to filter out content that did not align with the study's focus. Articles were excluded if they concentrated solely on large enterprises, public sector, or military applications, or if they addressed cybersecurity without a clear linkage to SMEs. Editorials, non-peer-reviewed opinion pieces, and abstracts lacking full-text access were also removed.

Duplicate studies retrieved from multiple databases were eliminated to avoid redundancy [25].

The screening process was based on the Preferred Reporting Items for Systematic Reviews and Meta-Analyses (PRISMA) guidelines for transparency and replicability. The process was carried out in three stages: an initial screening was performed on titles and abstracts to eliminate irrelevant records; a full-text review of the remaining articles was undertaken to assess compliance with the inclusion and exclusion criteria; and lastly, an appraisal related to quality was further performed through the use of criteria such as the critical appraisal skills program (CASP) checklist to evaluate robustness of methodology and relevance of selected studies. The removal of duplicates was the first stage, which reduced the total to 932 studies [8]. These records were then screened by title and abstract; 526 studies were excluded for not being relevant to SMEs, AI applications in cybersecurity, or core thematic areas, including trust, explainability, or cost efficiency. After that, 406 full-text articles were assessed against the above-defined inclusion and exclusion criteria for detailed assessment. By this stage, 365 studies had been excluded for reasons such as being focused solely on large enterprises, lack of access to full texts, being non-peer reviewed, or not addressing specific issues related to SMEs. Figure 9.2 provides a picture of the inclusion of articles;

Ultimately, 41 articles were deemed eligible and were included in the final review. These articles met all the criteria and provided substantial theoretical or empirical contributions relevant to the use of AI in cyber risk management within the SME context [23].

9.3.4 Data extraction and synthesis

Finally, a structured data extraction and synthesis approach was employed. A customized data extraction sheet was used to collect detailed information from each included study, such as author details, publication year, research objectives, methodological approach, AI techniques applied (e.g., machine learning, neural networks, explainable AI), sectoral and geographic focus, and thematic findings. The extracted data were then analyzed using a thematic synthesis method, allowing for the categorization of insights under major conceptual areas aligned with the identified research gaps. This process enabled the identification of recurring themes, unresolved challenges, and areas requiring further investigation, thereby contributing to a comprehensive understanding of the current landscape and future direction of

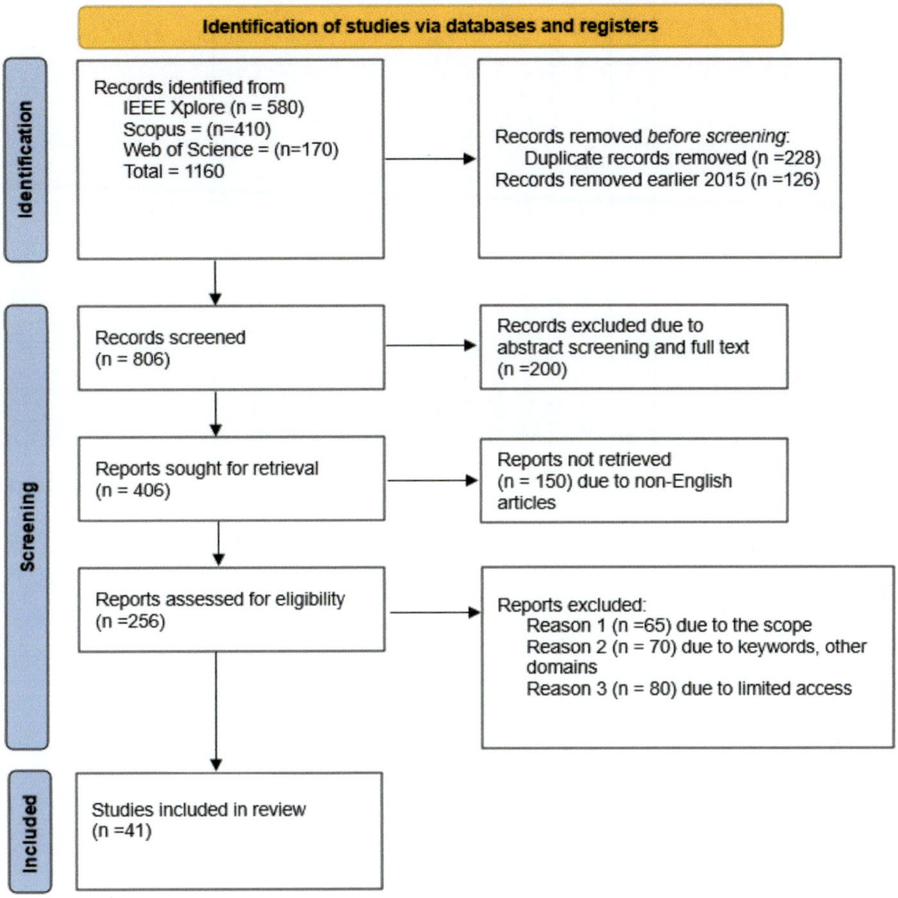

Figure 9.2 PRISMA flow diagram.

AI in cyber risk management for SMEs [35]. It has also been mentioned in Table 9.1.

9.4 Findings and Discussion

This section presents the key findings derived from the systematic analysis of 41 selected studies. The discussion is structured around the four guiding research questions and draws connections to the core research gaps identified earlier: lack of cybersecurity awareness and training, ethical and regulatory concerns, lack of explainability in AI systems, and the limitations faced by

Table 9.1 Inclusion and exclusion criteria.

Criteria type	Inclusion	Exclusion
Organizational focus	Studies focusing on small- and medium-sized enterprises (SMEs) or similar small-scale entities	Studies focusing exclusively on large enterprises, governments, or military institutions
Topic relevance	Studies discussing AI applications in cybersecurity and cyber risk management	Studies addressing cybersecurity without a specific reference to SMEs or AI
Thematic coverage	Studies contributing to themes like trust in AI, explainable AI, cost-efficiency, workforce readiness, and AI ethics	Studies lacking relevance to key themes or providing generic discussions without analytical depth
Publication type	Peer-reviewed journal articles, conference proceedings, and white papers	Editorials, blog posts, opinion pieces, or abstracts without full-text access
Language	English	Non-English language articles
Period	Published between 2015 and 2024	Published before 2015
Availability	Full-text available	Abstract-only or inaccessible full text
Duplication	Unique studies across selected databases	Duplicates retrieved from multiple databases

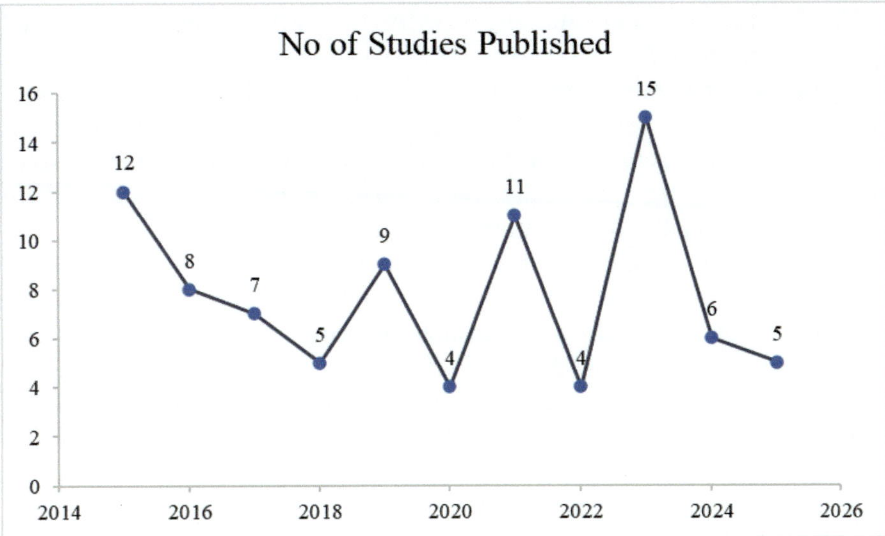

Figure 9.3 Number of studies published from 2015 to 2025 (top citations).

SMEs in terms of resources and relevance of AI solutions [26]. The number of studies published from 2015 to 2025 is depicted in Figure 9.3.

RQ1: What are the current applications of AI in cyber risk management among SMEs?

The review revealed that AI is increasingly being utilized in SMEs for threat detection, intrusion prevention, vulnerability assessment, and real-time risk monitoring. Machine learning algorithms and anomaly detection systems are among the most common technologies adopted, with several studies emphasizing their effectiveness in recognizing previously unseen threats. AI-driven platforms also automate incident response processes, helping SMEs reduce reaction time and minimize potential damage. Furthermore, some literature has highlighted the use of AI in fraud detection, particularly in the financial operations of SMEs, showing its cross-functional value [22].

However, the literature also emphasizes that most of these tools are adapted from solutions designed for larger enterprises. This results in functionality gaps and oversizing of features that do not align well with SME-specific contexts. This reflects the research gap concerning the lack of SME-tailored, cost-effective AI training and implementation frameworks, underscoring the need for innovation focused specifically on the SME ecosystem [31].

RQ2: What are the key challenges SMEs face when adopting AI-based cybersecurity tools?
A significant challenge identified is resource constraint, both in terms of finances and human capital. SMEs often cannot afford high-end cybersecurity infrastructure or hire dedicated AI professionals. Many of the AI solutions available in the market are too complex or expensive, making them inaccessible to smaller organizations. Another major obstacle is limited technical literacy and workforce readiness. Employees in SMEs may not be adequately trained to interact with AI tools or interpret the results, leading to underutilization or misuse of the technology [36].

These findings align directly with the research gap concerning the shortage of cybersecurity talent and the absence of affordable, scalable AI tools suitable for SMEs. Several studies call for the development of modular, easy-to-deploy solutions that integrate AI without requiring advanced expertise, something that is still underrepresented in existing research and commercial offerings [45].

RQ3: What ethical, technical, and regulatory gaps exist in current research concerning AI-enabled cyber defense for SMEs?
Ethical concerns remain underexplored in the context of SMEs. While larger corporations are beginning to engage with ethical AI frameworks, SMEs often lack the awareness or resources to do the same. Key issues include data privacy, algorithmic bias, and non-compliance with evolving regulations like the GDPR. Some reviewed studies discussed the unintended consequences of biased AI models that may unfairly flag certain behaviors or ignore context-specific threats common in SME environments [41].

Moreover, the absence of governance models that SMEs can realistically implement presents a significant barrier. This ties into the research gap regarding the lack of ethical and regulatory frameworks customized for SMEs, especially when considering AI tools that process sensitive business or customer data. Research in this domain remains nascent, highlighting a pressing need for frameworks that address fairness, accountability, and compliance without imposing unmanageable complexity on smaller businesses [3].

RQ4: How well are current AI models in cybersecurity understood, trusted, and accepted by SMEs?
One of the most critical concerns identified is the explainability of AI systems. Most AI models used in cybersecurity still function as "black boxes," offering limited transparency into how decisions are made. This erodes trust

among SME users, who are often uncomfortable deploying tools they do not fully understand. Explainable AI (XAI) has emerged as a promising solution, aiming to increase model transparency and user trust. However, its integration in SME-focused cybersecurity tools is still very limited, as most research and development in this area targets enterprise-level solutions [24].

This directly addresses the research gap related to Explainable AI (XAI). While the concept is gaining traction in academic circles, practical implementation in the SME sector remains minimal. Studies emphasize the need for AI systems that can offer actionable, understandable feedback to non-technical users, thus encouraging wider adoption and informed decision-making [7].

The findings indicate a growing potential for AI to enhance cyber risk management in SMEs but also underscore the misalignment between existing AI capabilities and SME-specific needs. Key gaps remain in terms of affordability, workforce integration, ethical governance, and model transparency. Addressing these issues requires multi-disciplinary efforts involving AI developers, policymakers, SME leaders, and cybersecurity experts. Future research must shift from generalized AI applications to context-aware, sector-specific models that are explainable, affordable, and aligned with SME workflows. Additionally, training modules and awareness programs must be embedded into AI deployment strategies to ensure effective use and broader trust [15].

9.5 Implications of the Study

This study offers several important implications for practice, theory, and policy, particularly in the intersection of artificial intelligence (AI), cybersecurity, and the unique operational realities of small- and medium-sized enterprises (SMEs). By systematically reviewing the literature and addressing key research gaps, the findings contribute to a deeper understanding of both the promise and the challenges of AI integration in SME cyber defense strategies [9].

9.5.1 Practical implications

From a practical perspective, the study underscores the urgent need for affordable, scalable, and user-friendly AI cybersecurity tools tailored specifically to SMEs. The current dominance of enterprise-centric solutions creates a barrier for small businesses with limited resources. Technology developers and cybersecurity firms should consider modular and lightweight AI applications that SMEs can implement without requiring extensive technical expertise or infrastructure investment. Furthermore, the need for ongoing employee training and awareness programs is emphasized, suggesting that cybersecurity tools should be accompanied by built-in learning modules or intuitive user interfaces that aid workforce readiness [14].

9.5.2 Theoretical implications

The findings contribute to the evolving theoretical discourse on trust in AI systems, explainable AI (XAI), and ethical AI adoption within underrepresented organizational settings like SMEs. The study extends existing frameworks by emphasizing how context, particularly organizational size and resource constraints, modifies the dynamics of AI implementation and trust formation. It invites scholars to further investigate the socio-technical interaction between SMEs and AI systems, and to refine models that integrate AI adoption with organizational culture, digital maturity, and perceived cybersecurity risks [12], [31]

9.5.3 Policy implications

At a regulatory level, the study identifies a critical need for SME-focused cybersecurity policies and AI governance frameworks. Given that most existing guidelines and compliance structures are designed with large enterprises in mind, SMEs often find themselves excluded or overwhelmed by complexity. Policymakers and industry regulators should prioritize the development of simplified compliance standards, incentives for AI adoption, and subsidized training initiatives targeted at small businesses. In addition, ethical governance standards for AI usage in cybersecurity must be made more accessible and practical for SMEs, ensuring fairness, transparency, and accountability without imposing excessive burdens [12].

9.5.4 Strategic implications for the SME sector

Strategically, this research encourages SMEs to rethink their approach to cyber risk management by viewing AI as an enabler rather than a luxury. It also highlights the importance of aligning AI strategies with broader digital transformation goals, thereby fostering a culture of innovation, adaptability, and continuous learning. By adopting a forward-looking approach to AI and cybersecurity, SMEs can build stronger resilience, reduce operational disruptions, and gain a competitive edge in an increasingly data-driven economy [40].

9.6 Conclusion

This research critically examined in depth the new role of artificial intelligence (AI) in cyber risk management, in particular within small and medium-sized enterprises (SMEs), through a systematic literature review (SLR) process. After a logically outlined review process, the research involved thorough database searches, rigorous inclusion and exclusion criteria, together with thematic analysis of 41 highly rated articles published between 2015 and 2025. The SLR facilitated the description of dominant trends, primary barriers, and deficiencies in dominant research, primarily with regard to cybersecurity behavior unique to SMEs and the adoption of AI [19].

A strong conceptual framework was established to inform thematic analysis with particular emphasis on such key dimensions as trust in AI systems, perception of cost-efficiency, readiness of the workforce, strategy in integrating AI, risk perception, and Explainable AI (XAI). These were chosen because they were common in reviewed studies and are crucial in the determination of useful and sustainable AI-powered cyber risk management in SMEs [21].

Key results indicate that although SMEs are more and more interested in AI-driven cybersecurity solutions, including threat detection platforms, intrusion prevention systems, and automated incident response, they generally do not possess the required financial capital, technical expertise, and internal training to maximize these technologies [13]. Solutions are generally built for large-scale organizations and do not miniaturize well in small organizational settings. Furthermore, little knowledge and awareness of cyber threats exist among SME staff, indicating an immense requirement for training and awareness-raising initiatives [20].

Notably, the research indicates an emerging concern regarding the trust and transparency of AI technology. SMEs are reluctant to embrace AI tools that they cannot comprehend or interpret, where Explainable AI (XAI) is necessary. Although still an emerging field, XAI provides the solution answer in opening up AI decision-making to non-experts and making it transparent [29]. Nevertheless, its actual application to SME cybersecurity is underdeveloped, indicating a seeming knowledge gap in practice and research. Bridging the gap can increase users' confidence by a significant margin and lead to increased use of AI in the industry [39].

The study has multiple implications. It informs practitioners and solution developers to prioritize simplicity, cost-effectiveness, and contextual relevance when designing AI tools for SMEs. It also contributes to theoretical discourse by reinforcing the interplay between trust, explainability, and organizational readiness in the digital transformation of smaller enterprises. At the policy level, it calls for more inclusive frameworks, regulatory support, and capacity-building programs aimed at SMEs, which often fall outside the scope of mainstream cybersecurity policies [31].

This study highlights the transformative potential of AI in SME cybersecurity while emphasizing the urgent need for customized, transparent, and scalable solutions. By addressing the identified gaps, including ethical concerns, lack of explainability, and workforce limitations, future research and innovation can help build a more resilient, secure, and equitable digital environment for small and medium-sized businesses [37].

References

[1] L. Holder, "Cyber Risk Management with the Help of Artificial Intelligence in SMEs: Analysis of Barriers and Needs."

[2] N. Taskin, A. Özkeleş Yıldırım, H. D. Ercan, M. Wynn, and B. Metin, "Cyber Insurance Adoption and Digitalisation in Small and Medium-Sized Enterprises," *Information (Switzerland)*, vol. 16, no. 1, Jan. 2025, doi: 10.3390/info16010066.

[3] A. Papathanasiou, G. Liontos, A. Katsouras, V. Liagkou, and E. Glavas, "Cybersecurity Guide for SMEs: Protecting Small and Medium-Sized Enterprises in the Digital Era," *Journal of Information Security*, vol. 16, no. 01, pp. 1–43, 2025, doi: 10.4236/jis.2025.161001.

[4] A. Schumacher, S. Erol, and W. Sihn, "Automation, digitization and digitalization and their implications for manufacturing processes," 2016. [Online]. Available: https://www.researchgate.net/publication/318877006

[5] A. Russo, "Cybersecurity Challenges and Strategies for Italian SMEs: An Analysis of Current Practices and Future Outlook."

[6] I. Fidel-Anyana, E. G. Onus, U. Mikel-Olisa, and N. Ayanbode, "AI-Driven Cybersecurity Frameworks for SME Development: Mitigating Risks in a Digital Economy," *International Journal of Multidisciplinary Research and Growth Evaluation*, vol. 6, no. 1, pp. 982–988, 2025, doi: 10.54660/.IJMRGE.2025.6.1.982-988.

[7] S. Ahmed, "Artificial Intelligence (AI) Technology Adoption in SME", [Online]. Available: www.raoaustralia.org

[8] M. J. Culler, J. J. Welch, J. P. Meng, D. W. Reen, and K. S. Myers, "Cyber-Risk Management Feasibility Study Retrofitting Existing Solar with Emerging Technologies (RESET)," 2022. [Online]. Available: http://www.inl.gov

[9] A. Abbas and J. Iqbal, “Cybersecurity and AI Synergy for SME Resilience and Economic Equality,” 2025, doi: 10.13140/RG.2.2.23500.12166.

[10] J. Butler and M. Jackson, “Business Intelligence in the Digital Era: Enhancing SME Growth through AI and Cybersecurity,” 2024, doi: 10.13140/RG.2.2.33959.36008.

[11] A. Govori and Q. Sejdija, “Future Prospects and Challenges of Integrating Artificial Intelligence Within the Business Practices of Small And Medium Enterprises,” *Journal of Governance and Regulation*, vol. 12, no. 2, pp. 176–183, 2023, doi: 10.22495/jgrv12i2art16.

[12] F. Ciampi, A. Giannozzi, G. Marzi, and E. I. Altman, “Rethinking SME default prediction: a systematic literature review and future perspectives,” *Scientometrics*, vol. 126, no. 3, pp. 2141–2188, Mar. 2021, doi: 10.1007/s11192-020-03856-0.

[13] H. Birnleitner, “Influence of Macro-Environmental Factors to the Process of Integrating A Foreign Business Entity.”

[14] A. Mostafavi *et al.*, “Cyber Risk Systematic Literature Review: Broad Interdisciplinary Definition of Cyber Risk and Its Concerns,” 2024. [Online]. Available: https://powertechjournal.com

[15] A. Faisal and R. Weston, “Digital Technologies for SME Competitiveness: Unlocking the Power of AI and Cybersecurity,” 2024. [Online]. Available: https://www.researchgate.net/publication/384443195

[16] A. Bhad, “Cybersecurity Talent Development in SMEs: Leveraging AI and Automation to Bridge the Skills Gap.” [Online]. Available: https://www.researchgate.net/publication/389653043

[17] M. Jackson, “Empowering SMEs through Digital Transformation: Harnessing AI and Cybersecurity for Long-Term Success,” 2024, doi: 10.13140/RG.2.2.17624.92168.

[18] Z. Chavez *et al.*, “Digital Tools and Information Needs Assessment for Efficient Deviation Handling in SMEs,” in *Advances in Transdisciplinary Engineering*, IOS Press BV, Oct. 2020, pp. 24–35. doi: 10.3233/ATDE200140.

[19] A. Sukumar, H. A. Mahdiraji, and V. Jafari-Sadeghi, “Cyber risk assessment in small and medium-sized enterprises: A multilevel decision-making approach for small e-tailors,” *Risk Analysis*, vol. 43, no. 10, pp. 2082–2098, Oct. 2023, doi: 10.1111/risa.14092.

[20] F. Giguère, “Harnessing AI and Machine Learning for SME Growth and Market Competitiveness”, doi: 10.13140/RG.2.2.25325.40168.

[21] P. Giudici and E. Raffinetti, “Explainable AI methods in cyber risk management,” *Quality and Reliability Engineering International*, vol. 38, no. 3, pp. 1318–1326, Apr. 2022, doi: 10.1002/qre.2939.

[22] M. N. O. Sadiku, O. I. Fagbohungbe, and S. M. Musa, "Artificial Intelligence in Cyber Security," *International Journal of Engineering Research and Advanced Technology*, vol. 06, no. 05, pp. 01–07, 2020, doi: 10.31695/IJERAT.2020.3612.

[23] A. Papathanasiou, G. Liontos, A. Katsouras, V. Liagkou, and E. Glavas, "Cybersecurity Guide for SMEs: Protecting Small and Medium-Sized Enterprises in the Digital Era," *Journal of Information Security*, vol. 16, no. 01, pp. 1–43, 2025, doi: 10.4236/jis.2025.161001.

[24] P. Radanliev *et al.*, "Cyber risk at the edge: current and future trends on cyber risk analytics and artificial intelligence in the industrial internet of things and industry 4.0 supply chains," *Cybersecurity*, vol. 3, no. 1. Springer Science and Business Media B.V., Dec. 01, 2020. doi: 10.1186/s42400-020-00052-8.

[25] M. Jackson, "Empowering SMEs through Digital Transformation: Harnessing AI and Cybersecurity for Long-Term Success," 2024, doi: 10.13140/RG.2.2.17624.92168.

[26] M. Harlee and J. Lucas, "Innovative Cybersecurity Solutions for SMEs: Reducing Risks with Employee-Centric Awareness Programs," 2024, doi: 10.13140/RG.2.2.19660.12164.

[27] A. M. Ahmed *et al.*, "Cyber Security and Artificial Intelligence," in *14th International Conference on Advances in Computing, Control, and Telecommunication Technologies, ACT 2023*, Grenze Scientific Society, 2023, pp. 1324–1327. doi: 10.33908/ef.2023.2.5.

[28] Lucky Bamidele Benjamin, Ayodeji Enoch Adegbola, Prisca Amajuoyi, Mayokun Daniel Adegbola, and Kudirat Bukola Adeusi, "Digital transformation in SMEs: Identifying cybersecurity risks and developing effective mitigation strategies," *Global Journal of Engineering and Technology Advances*, vol. 19, no. 2, pp. 134–153, May 2024, doi: 10.30574/gjeta.2024.19.2.0084.

[29] N. Taskin, A. Özkeleş Yıldırım, H. D. Ercan, M. Wynn, and B. Metin, "Cyber Insurance Adoption and Digitalisation in Small and Medium-Sized Enterprises," *Information (Switzerland)*, vol. 16, no. 1, Jan. 2025, doi: 10.3390/info16010066.

[30] A. J. G. de Azambuja, C. Plesker, K. Schützer, R. Anderl, B. Schleich, and V. R. Almeida, "Artificial Intelligence-Based Cyber Security in the Context of Industry 4.0—A Survey," *Electronics (Switzerland)*, vol. 12, no. 8, Apr. 2023, doi: 10.3390/electronics12081920.

[31] T. Sotamaa, A. Reiman, and O. Kauppila, "Manufacturing SME risk management in the era of digitalisation and artificial intelligence: a systematic literature review," *Continuity & Resilience Review*, Jul. 2024, doi: 10.1108/crr-12-2023-0022.

[32] G. Schuh, R. Anderl, R. Dumitrescu, and A. Krüger, "acatech STUDY Industrie 4.0 Maturity Index."

[33] M. Abdullahi *et al.*, "Detecting Cybersecurity Attacks in Internet of Things Using Artificial Intelligence Methods: A Systematic Literature Review," *Electronics (Switzerland)*, vol. 11, no. 2. MDPI, Jan. 01, 2022. doi: 10.3390/electronics11020198.

[34] A. Chidukwani, S. Zander, and P. Koutsakis, "Cybersecurity preparedness of small-to-medium businesses: A Western Australia study with broader implications," *Computers and Security*, vol. 145, Oct. 2024, doi: 10.1016/j.cose.2024.104026.

[35] T. Sotamaa, A. Reiman, and O. Kauppila, "Manufacturing SME risk management in the era of digitalisation and artificial intelligence: a systematic literature review," *Continuity & Resilience Review*, Jul. 2024, doi: 10.1108/crr-12-2023-0022.

[36] H. Hokmabadi, S. M. H. S. Rezvani, and C. A. de Matos, "Business Resilience for Small and Medium Enterprises and Startups by Digital Transformation and the Role of Marketing Capabilities—A Systematic Review," *Systems*, vol. 12, no. 6. Multidisciplinary Digital Publishing Institute (MDPI), Jun. 01, 2024. doi: 10.3390/systems12060220.

[37] A. J. G. de Azambuja, C. Plesker, K. Schützer, R. Anderl, B. Schleich, and V. R. Almeida, "Artificial Intelligence-Based Cyber Security in the Context of Industry 4.0—A Survey," *Electronics (Switzerland)*, vol. 12, no. 8, Apr. 2023, doi: 10.3390/electronics12081920.

[38] G. Žigiene, E. Rybakovas, and R. Alzbutas, "Artificial intelligence based commercial risk management framework for SMEs," *Sustainability (Switzerland)*, vol. 11, no. 16, Aug. 2019, doi: 10.3390/su11164501.

[39] N. Drydakis, "Artificial Intelligence and Reduced SMEs' Business Risks. A Dynamic Capabilities Analysis During the COVID-19 Pandemic," *Information Systems Frontiers*, vol. 24, no. 4, pp. 1223–1247, Aug. 2022, doi: 10.1007/s10796-022-10249-6.

[40] Geeta Sandeep Nadella, Hari Gonaygunta, Deepak Kumar, and Priyanka Pramod Pawar, "Exploring the impact of AI-driven solutions on cybersecurity adoption in small and medium enterprises," *World Journal of Advanced Research and Reviews*, vol. 22, no. 1, pp. 1199–1197, Apr. 2024, doi: 10.30574/wjarr.2024.22.1.1185.

[41] A. J. Varma *et al.*, "A Roadmap for SMEs to Adopt an AI Based Cyber Threat Intelligence," in *The Effect of Information Technology on Business and Marketing Intelligence Systems*, M. Alshurideh, B. H. al Kurdi, R. Masa'deh, H. M. Alzoubi, and S. Salloum, Eds., Cham: Springer International Publishing, 2023, pp. 1903–1926. doi: 10.1007/978-3-031-12382-5_105.

[42] F. Hoppe, N. Gatzert, and P. Gruner, "Cyber risk management in SMEs: insights from industry surveys," *The Journal of Risk Finance*, vol. 22, no. 3/4, pp. 240–260, Jan. 2021, doi: 10.1108/JRF-02-2020-0024.

[43] L.-W. Wong, T. Garry Wei-Han, O. Keng-Boon, L. Binshan, and Y. K. and Dwivedi, "Artificial intelligence-driven risk management for enhancing supply chain agility: A deep-learning-based dual-stage PLS-SEM-ANN analysis," *International Journal of Production Research*, vol. 62, no. 15, pp. 5535–5555, Aug. 2024, doi: 10.1080/00207543.2022.2063089.

[44] N. Wayan Suryatini, P. Tripeni Juniman, and A. Winanti Riesardhy, "User-Generated Content: A Systematic Literature Review (SLR) Research," *JURNAL KOMUNIKASI INDONESIA*, vol. 14, no. 1, 2025, doi: 10.7454/jkmi.v14i1.1235.

[45] U. N. Kayani, "Exploring prospects of blockchain and fintech: using SLR approach," *Journal of Science and Technology Policy Management*, vol. 16, no. 1, pp. 5–41, Jan. 2025, doi: 10.1108/JSTPM-01-2023-0005.

10

Toward Resilient Cyber Defense: Integrating AI and Blockchain for Smart Risk Management

Rihab Benaich[1], Saida El Mendili[1], and Youssef Gahi[1]

[1]Engineering Sciences Laboratory, National School of Applied Sciences, Ibn Tofail University, Morocco

Email: rihab.benaich@uit.ac.ma; elmendili.saida@uit.ac.ma; gahi.youssef@uit.ac.ma

Abstract

Cybersecurity risk management is currently challenged by emerging threats that require novel solutions. This chapter discusses the intersecting nature of artificial intelligence (AI) and blockchain as an enhancement to cyber defense capabilities. AI offers threat identification through machine learning-based algorithms, predictive analytics for proactive cyber risk management, and automated incident response. On the other hand, Blockchain provides decentralized cybersecurity through its immutable audit trails, tamper-resistant data integrity, and trusted identity management solutions. Our analyses focus on how AI and Blockchain technologies interact in modern cybersecurity and how they combine to defend against the most sophisticated cyberattacks, such as zero-day attacks, ransomware, and insider attacks. We also focus on specific use cases, such as integrating AI-based behavioral analytics with blockchain-based threat intelligence sharing and utilizing smart contracts for automating governance through security policies. Finally, while this chapter discusses specific use cases of AI and Blockchain in cybersecurity, we will also explore new approaches, such as federated learning, to enhance defense detection's collaborative and privacy-preserving aspects.

DOI: 10.1201/9788743808077-10

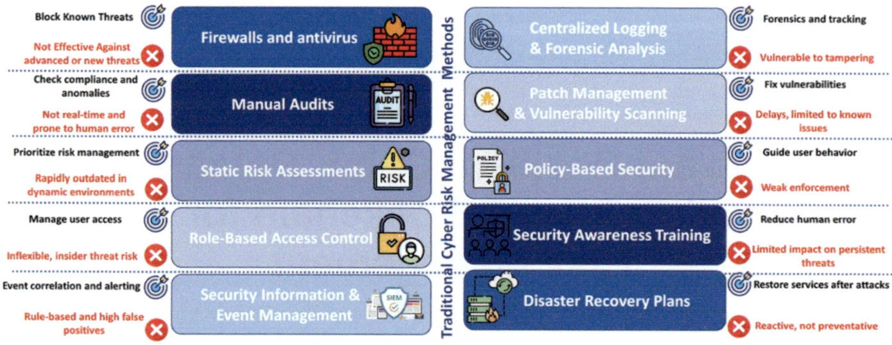

Figure 10.1 Drawbacks of traditional cyber risk management methods.

10.1 Introduction

In the hyperconnected digital era we live in, cybersecurity has emerged as the most important barrier for contemporary enterprises. Enterprises today are increasingly dependent upon digital infrastructure to operate and compete, and the combination of digitization and distance has expanded the threat landscape both in size and complexity. The sophistication of cyberattacks has grown concerning the targeting of sensitive data, intellectual property, critical systems, and, possibly, a nation's infrastructure [1]. Currently, enterprises are obligated to manage the flood of threats from ransomware and phishing scams to insider threats and advanced persistent threats (APTs) [2], all while maintaining and considering business continuity and regulatory compliance [3]. The rapid rise of cloud computing, Internet of Things devices, and remote work has expanded the attack surface further and left traditional security models struggling to keep up.

Traditional risk management methods (Figure 10.1) that may have been regarded as industry standard are becoming less useful in dealing with the rapidly changing and evolving threat of cyber. Typically based on static assessments, periodic audits, and manual methods of detecting threats, they can ultimately lead to delayed responses and potential vulnerabilities left unaddressed. These frameworks often lack real-time insight and proactive measures in responding to or addressing emerging risks. The traditional frameworks' inherent rigidity and reactive nature serve as obstacles to effectively and efficiently protecting enterprises from a fast-moving adversary that continues to exploit technological change and human error. As a result, there is an urgent need to bolster cybersecurity strategies and initiatives with smarter, adaptive strategies and decentralized models.

Emerging technologies that include artificial intelligence and blockchain technologies are changing the way organizations conceive of cybersecurity [4]. AI has the potential to analyze massive amounts of data while recognizing patterns, providing powerful tools for threat detection, behavior analysis, and automated incident responses. Essentially, AI enables enterprises to monitor data for anomalies in real time, forecast possible breaches, and intervene while threats are still insufficiently advanced in the network. In contrast, blockchain technology offers a decentralized and tamper-proof system where security is supported through data integrity, transparency, and trust. The idea of "decentralized" means that there are no single points of failure in the cybersecurity framework, and enhanced security arises through the trustworthiness and dependability of the data that has been stored and the communications managed by the blockchain, enabling safe, verifiable audit trails. Both AI and blockchain, combined offer a powerful promise to make cybersecurity smarter, more proactive, and fortified by resilience. This paper sets out to evaluate the changing landscape of cybersecurity threats facing today's enterprises and ultimately understand the shortcomings of traditional risk management frameworks in addressing these ever-evolving threats. This chapter also aims to explore the effects of AI and blockchain, focusing on their power to reimagine and redefine worlds of cybersecurity practice and implications of practice, their associated advantages, and the feasibility for adoption into practice [5]. This chapter will provide a comprehensive analysis of situated cyber threats, a deduction of existing methodologies, and recommendations on how AI and blockchain can be empowered and utilized to develop the next generational iterations of cybersecurity solutions. Moreover, this chapter aims to develop a substantive understanding of the role of future methods, which will encourage enterprise leaders, practitioners in the field of cybersecurity, and researchers to reimagine cybersecurity solutions that are more resilient and predictive to meet the needs of an ever-changing enterprise landscape.

This chapter sets out to consider the increasingly complex problem of cybersecurity and whether AI and blockchain, either separately or together, will redefine the canonical approaches to cyber risk management. The chapter is organized as follows: First, we review some of the literature across application areas for AI and blockchain, including health, education, and finance sectors. Then we review AI and blockchain applications, including machine learning, federated learning, immutable audit trails, and smart contracts, as an isolated capability of AI and blockchain. After, we discuss the AI and blockchain combinations for each capability, to provide intelligent automation and privacy-preserving security models. Then we consider challenges and limits of applications of AI and blockchain, including technical scalability limits, regulation limits, and adversarial AI. Finally, we indicate a way forward to secure, explainable, quantum-resilient architectures for next-generation cybersecurity labels.

10.2 Related Studies

This section provides a broad synthesis of the new research at the intersection of AI and blockchain technologies in key application domains such as healthcare, education, banking, government, and smart cities. The literature we synthesized studies about AI and blockchain technologies in isolation, but, more importantly, the emergent research that studies their integration and complementary capabilities to address issues including security, efficiency, and trust. By organizing studies on the technology of interest (AI, blockchain, or complementary capabilities), year of publication, and contributions to domains, we underscore the dynamic nature of this interdisciplinary field through comparisons and trends of convergence and divergence. Table 10.1 summarizes key studies that showcase the level of research in each domain. Each entry shows the application of AI, blockchain, or a hybrid of both applied to the research question and its contribution, whether developing high-accuracy predictive models to detect threats or quantum-resilient devices for health records, decentralized voting systems, or adaptive AI algorithms that optimize the detection of anomalies in Internet of Things systems for potential attacks. Both the summaries of studies in the table illustrate the trajectory of technical application being pursued, and importantly, the evolving focus among researchers on privacy-preserving, explainable, and scalable security architectures.

When sectoral contributions are compared, the interest in hybrid frameworks, which combine the analytical capabilities of AI and the decentralization and immutability of blockchain [25], is evident and growing. Nevertheless, the research continues to somewhat treat AI and blockchain as independent technologies, and this represents a gap and opportunity for more intersects between these two areas of work. The research summarized in Table 10.1 lays the groundwork for our architectural vision and the new contributions we present in this study.

In the subsequent section, the section will explore the contribution of artificial intelligence to the management of cyber risk. It explores the increasing use of intelligent systems to forecast, identify, and combat new cybersecurity threats with higher speed and accuracy.

Table 10.1 Recent studies exploring blockchain and AI intersections in different sectors.

Application domain	Paper	Year	AI	Blockchain	Synergy of AI and blockchain	Contribution
Healthcare	[6]	**2025**	✓			The authors presented EffiIncepNet, a deep learning model that integrates EfficientNet and Inception-ResNet-v2. Their findings demonstrated improved accuracy of classification (up to 98%), improved scalability, and proposed a new measure called BPRWS to verify superior performance for protecting sensitive health data.
	[7]	**2025**	✓			The authors presented an AI-based dual-tier detection model for healthcare software defined networking (SDN) security, leveraging deep learning and machine learning to support the detection of both static and dynamic threats using generative adversarial networks (GANs) and auto-encoders. The model performed with an accuracy of 99.6% with XGBoost, outperforming the baseline, and providing additional real-time protection against malware and ransomware while supporting regulatory compliance.
	[8]	**2025**			✓	The authors presented a combination of blockchain frameworks for EHR security, using AES and quantum-secure algorithms CRYSTALS-Dilithium and Kyber, with DAOs to provide decentralized control. Utilizing AI and metaverse integration, this framework enhances security, user experience, and improves the alteration of EHRs, against classical and quantum threats.
	[9]	**2024**		✓		The authors propose a new healthcare security solution that utilizes a blockchain application based on decentralized identities (DIDs), ChaCha20-Poly1305 encryption, and token-based immutable records, enforced by a Proof-of-Stake (PoS) consensus. Their method enhances privacy and security, reduces cost, and performs transactions in an average of 6.5 seconds, compared to traditional methods.

(Continued)

Table 10.1 *Continued*

Application domain	Paper	Year	AI	Blockchain	Synergy of AI and blockchain	Contribution
Education	[10]	**2025**	✓			The authors proposed a constructivist teaching and learning framework to educate and prepare students for AI-enabled security work. It is a framework consisting of scaffolding and experiential learning. Through their three case studies examining phishing detection, malware classification, and anomaly detection, they show how structured ways of providing training and practice skills on the job improve students' engagement and technical expertise in AI-enabled security work.
	[11]	**2024**	✓			The chapter explored AI-assisted cybersecurity to support online higher education and contains a systematic review of AI-assisted cybersecurity threats and solutions. The authors discuss the traditional approaches in comparison to AI-assisted approaches and acknowledge that non-AI approaches are effective solutions, while also highlighting the various ethical, technical, and emerging threats to AI-assisted cybersecurity, including data privacy and transparency concerns. Overall, the study simply calls for more AI systems to protect digital learning spaces implemented appropriately.
	[12]	**2024**	✓			The authors discuss how AI is essential in augmenting national cybersecurity strategies and its safe and responsible use in enhancing threat detection and infrastructure resiliency to improve current workforce education and development. They argue that the dual benefit of AI is enhancing both cybersecurity systems and ethics and guidelines for improvement.
	[13]	**2025**	✓			The authors developed a banking security system for IoT-connected ATM systems using AI to improve ATM fraud detection accuracy, predictive maintenance for ATMs, and increase biometric locker security while improving overall operating efficiency.

Banking	[14]	**2025**	✓				The authors examined the adoption of artificial intelligence in the banking industry of Indonesia through a quantitative study of 388 customer surveys. They successfully validated their extended technology acceptance model that included a total of 19 hypotheses related to awareness, trust, and risk. The study provided implications for the safe adoption of AI in the banking sectors of emerging economies.
	[15]	**2024**	✓				The authors examined how central banks should weigh the value of generative AI in a cyber safety and risk mitigation context, taking into consideration both benefits and risks (e.g., faster threat detection versus social engineering concerns). One such suggestion the central banks figure should consider is the hiring of dual-skilled personnel (AI and cybersecurity) and allowing for "human oversight" over any automated systems.
	[16]	**2024**		✓			The authors introduced an authentication framework for online banking based on blockchain technology, which offers increased security while balancing efficiency. The framework is based on decentralized applications and smart contracts that facilitate immutable, auditable transactions while eliminating risks presented in today's environments. Results of the performance tests conducted demonstrate the models' capability to secure financial transactions while protecting consumers' sensitive personal information in an environment where trust is not required.
	[17]	**2023**				✓	The authors discussed the impacts of blockchain technology on secure transactions and examined how AI offers predictive capabilities based on past performances using these secure transactions. Subsequently, the authors provide a cyclic model for AI-blockchains that addresses existing stuck points from traditional implementation, which improves security around data in the banking industry.

(Continued.)

Table 10.1 *Continued*

Application domain	Paper	Year	AI	Blockchain	Synergy of AI and blockchain	Contribution
Government	[18]	**2025**			✓	The authors developed a voting system based on blockchain that uses a hybrid encryption system (HAHE) and smart contracts to guarantee privacy and immutability. They even incorporated consensus based on HPBFTA, VEcSBP for validation, and CNN for threat detection and detection. The hybrid system achieves better encryption time (0.6025s) and throughput (64.3 Tps) than traditional models such as Proof of Work or Proof of Stake.
	[19]	**2025**			✓	The authors introduced DemocracyGuard, a blockchain-based online voting system built on Ethereum that uses facial recognition technology to provide secure authentication processes for voters. This blockchain-based approach improves elections by providing decentralization, transparency, and fraud resistance while addressing the most significant weaknesses of traditional e-voting systems and permitting remote capabilities.
	[20]	**2025**		✓		The authors created a university e-voting system using a consortium blockchain with hybrid PoW/PoS consensus and ECDSA authentication that exhibited better scalability, speed, and energy efficiency as compared to existing solutions.
	[21]	**2024**			✓	The authors designed a blockchain e-voting system that combines Hyperledger Fabric with biometric authentication (fingerprint/facial recognition). Their prototype achieved 87% registration and 88% voting success rates in decentralization-based secure voting based on automated verification, all of which maintained trust.

Smart Cities	[22]	**2024**	✓				The authors proposed an AI-enabled anomaly detection framework for Internet of Things (IoT) security for smart cities, drawing from CAS theory, TAM, and TPB. Their model emphasizes user engagement and security culture while directing policymakers in building resilient infrastructure for cities, paving the way for subsequent empirical investigation.
	[23]	**2024**			✓		The authors investigated AI-blockchain solutions for smart city cybersecurity as a means of addressing vulnerabilities in information-rich urban services. They observed that when traditional methodologies reach a point that they can no longer scale, these technologies can provide a means to secure critical urban infrastructure to ameliorate the vulnerabilities that evolve, as seen in previous incidents such as the cyberattack affecting the Atlanta municipal government, and to better support threat analysis and information protection.
	[24]	**2023**	✓				The authors present a framework for smart-city attack detection powered by artificial intelligence that adopts a modified MDATA model for a multi-step attack detection strategy to reduce false alarm rates. The framework's modular architecture exhibited high levels of accuracy and efficiency according to the evaluation conducted in a cyber range setting, representing significant progress in urban defenses against cybersecurity threats.

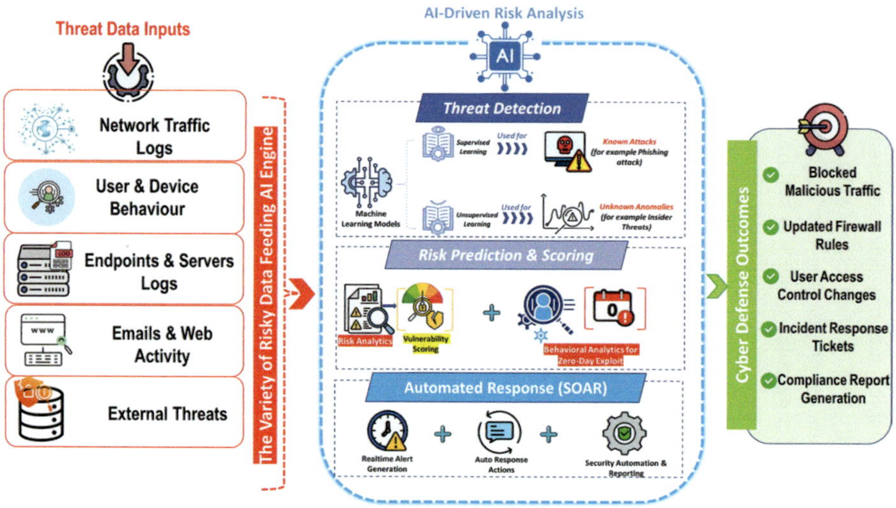

Figure 10.2 AI-driven risk analysis against threats.

10.3 AI in Cybersecurity Risk Management

Artificial intelligence is a core technology driving the next evolution of cybersecurity risk management, with capabilities that extend far beyond traditional systems [26]. While legacy approaches depend on static rules and human judgment, AI adds intelligence, speed, and adaptability to cyber risk programs. Today, organizations have an increasing attack surface, which precludes any manual identification, assessment, and response to threats in all their forms. AI closes this capability gap by automating risk assessment processes, learning from past and emerging threats, and generating predictive insights to improve an organization's future preparedness. Perhaps the most transformative aspect of AI technology is its ability to recognize anomalies, understand behavioral patterns, and make near-real-time decisions using vast amounts of dynamic data. From identifying newly sophisticated zero-day attacks to coordinating rapid response actions, AI fundamentally changes the way organizations can manage cyber risk from reactive to proactive stages [27].

Figure 10.2 illustrates a holistic framework for AI-based cyber risk management, exemplifying how AI is evolving how an organization views, detects, assesses, and responds to real-time cyber risk. That process begins with multiple threat datasets, including everything from network traffic logs, user and device behavior, server logs, web behavior, complimentary emails, and external threat intelligence, all of which will be processed and sent to an AI engine. The AI engine then uses both supervised and unsupervised machine learning algorithms to identify known threats like phishing, as well as unidentified anomalies or threats like insider threats or zero-day exploits. After the detection layer has parsed out the threat data, AI can assist in predicting risk and scoring least privilege access with vulnerability assessments, analytics of risk analysis, and behavioral profiling of users' behaviors to accurately assess exposure to an attack modality. Depending on the risk type, it can prioritize attackers' pathways based on risk, particularly for newly identified risks. Next, it can automate response through SOAR to alert many in real time, automatically, or through the normal procedure of incident reporting and response across the security environment.

Ultimately, both the intelligent engagement and automated data foreshadow real-time outcomes for defense measures like blocking malicious network traffic, updating or creating firewall rules, access control updates, incident response tickets escalated, or automatically creating a compliance report. In this way, an autonomous loop of intelligent data collection and analysis that leads to autonomous response measures positions AI as a primary driver of cyber risk management methodologies that will allow organizations to fast-track response measures, reduce damage, and improve overall resilience. The following subsections will discuss specific uses of AI applications in the realm of threat detection, predictive risk analytics, and the advanced use of automated response frameworks.

10.3.1 Machine learning for threat detection

Machine learning is a vital part of artificial intelligence that is changing the way we detect, categorize, and respond to cyber threats more speedily and accurately than traditional rule-based methods [28]. The more common forms of ML are supervised and unsupervised learning, and both forms have their applicability depending on the data available and properties of the threats of cyber environments.

10.3.1.1 Supervised learning in cybersecurity

Supervised learning relies on large amounts of labeled training data, a historical dataset that has the input features measured, and an outcome of those inputs, whether historical/known or defined. This means historical datasets that have indicators of compromise, such as malware signatures, phishing attempts, botnet traffic, login attempts by brute force, etc. Algorithm approaches, such as support vector machines (SVMs), decision trees, and random forests, have been trained very well to classify these traditional types of activities with a high level of accuracy. For example, supervised ML is commonly used in email filtering to classify spam or phishing emails from legitimate emails. Antivirus engines utilize supervised classifiers that analyze input code against known structures or behavioral profiles for malware. Supervised ML models will be as effective as the number and quality of the labeled status for activity, and fast and changing adversarial security models can present limitations on relying upon known labels as a factor.

10.3.1.2 Unsupervised learning and anomaly detection

In unsupervised learning paradigms, as alluded to in the name, the training data does not need to be labeled. Patterns are discerned through pattern recognition learning that identifies anomalies or clusters of activities that deviate from expected activity. This area of supervised learning is of greater value with the identification of unknown or zero-day threats since there often are not any labels to draw upon beforehand. Common algorithms such as K-Means clustering, maximize similarities, density-based spatial clustering (DBSCAN), and principal component analysis (PCA), take variance observations and identify hidden structure and outliers from network traffic or user behaviors. One of the more impactful use cases of unsupervised learning methodology is for insider threat detection, meaning there would be, deliberate or accidental action taken by a valid or legitimate user. Detection systems that utilize traditional threat detection systems often do not identify the activities since the activity often does not conform to or go through attack patterns. Whereas, for example, unsupervised ML models learn to identify behaviors orienting to a baseline and alert administrators when activities that have been detected, such as file downloads, access times, or communication with other users, that diverge significantly from a learner's behavior or expected actual user behavior.

10.3.1.3 Behavioral analytics for zero-day attacks

Zero-day attacks still represent one of the most challenging areas in cybersecurity. They exploit unknown vulnerabilities, which allows them to remain stealthy and unpredictable. This means that traditional detection systems that rely on signature-based detection can never respond to a zero-day attack because there is no prior detection pattern or label to work off of. AI effectively fills this need gap by using advanced behavioral analytics, a method that observes and learns from user behavior, system, and network behavior over time. By using these behavioral methods, AI can establish a baseline for what "normal" looks like, for example, the normal time a user logs in, what devices a user interacts with, what users are transferring over the network, and what folders users are accessing or interacting with. AI can flag these behaviors when an event deviates from the normal baseline of what a user would typically do. Therefore, if a user suddenly logs in to their account from a foreign IP address, reads or downloads sensitive files after hours, or transfers large volumes of data in a short amount of time, AI can signify that this activity is potentially malicious, regardless of there being no prior signature associated with that specific user activity.

Moreover, AI-enabled behavioral analytics machine learning detection capability is powerful because it continuously learns from the data. These AI systems learn and evolve by consistently taking similar observations of the data and updating their inferred learning of a user's "normal" behavior based on historical behavioral data. Therefore, unlike static rule-based models, AI-enabled behavioral analytics systems do not suffer from having a constant static rule model of evolving behavior over time. This attribute is extremely important when dealing with advanced persistent threat (APT) detections, an entity that often lays in wait or moves laterally in the environment for long periods before launching their attack.

Further, although behavioral models are a step in the right direction to contextualize the data, the multi-domain correlation modeling builds on this with analysis and tie-in of data from endpoints, cloud services, applications, and network traffic. This is important because offensive entities conduct their reconnaissance operations across multiple domains, so it helps devise the composite behavioral profiles that help to detect multi-vector/multi-stage attacks. This further corroborates that in hybrids, findings and assessments are the norm when observing sophisticated cyber espionage and campaigns. Recent research is exploring the use of deep learning methodologies, such as recurrent neural network (RNN) and long short-term memory (LSTM) designs for temporal analysis of behavioral data. This is relevant because it is a better fit for this task because individual vectors conduct observable patterns of sequences to detect attacks that are happening in sequence and over time.

By shifting from a threat-based defense model to a behavioral deviation model contextualized into as many contextualized observables as possible, AI-enabled behavioral analytics represents a major shift from a reactive position of cyber defense to a predictive and proactive defense posture improving organizational resilience against unknown, zero-day exploits and threats from vectors.

10.3.2 Predictive risk analytics

10.3.2.1 AI-driven risk scoring and vulnerability assessment

AI-assisted predictive analytics can not only identify but also help organizations foresee and prioritize potential threats before they become a reality. Risk scoring based on AI analyzes vulnerability data such as asset value, exploitability, threat actor behavior, and historical attack information to determine an overall risk score. This dynamic risk scoring provides cybersecurity teams with the ability to prioritize and efficiently deploy resources against threats that could cause the greatest damage. These models are constantly ingesting data from threat intelligence feeds, vulnerability databases, and internal security logs to provide continuously updated risk levels. This predictive ability, implemented in real time, provides organizations the ability to patch systems, mitigate high-risk exposure, and reduce their attack surface before exploitation has occurred.

10.3.2.2 Real-time monitoring and adaptive defenses

AI has a clear advantage in real-time monitoring contexts that traditional methods struggle with due to processing latencies and reliance on human action. AI systems process incoming traffic, endpoint activity, and system behavior in real time, enabling the security analyst to have ongoing situational awareness. AI systems have not only adaptive defense capabilities, but they can also alter firewall rules, access control, or authentication based on the current attack state or its evolving threat. As an example, if a user suddenly started behaving differently than their historical profile, they would be subjected to increased verification, or their session would be isolated while threats were considered. AI's potential to modify defenses in situ and in real time allows any cybersecurity substrate to become a live learning system that can optimize itself.

10.3.3 Automated incident response

As the number of alerts grows in an environment with limited human resources, AI can assist with both the speed and accuracy of responding to incidents through security orchestration, automation, and response (SOAR) platforms. One function of SOAR platforms is to ingest data from multiple security tools so that the platform can automatically correlate alerts. SOAR platforms can also prioritize incidents based on risk impact. Using AI, SOAR platforms can automate typical response actions, such as isolating a compromised device, blocking malicious IP addresses, or starting forensic analysis, and can also decrease the time for an analyst to respond from hours to seconds. Additionally, AI can assist the analyst by summarizing incidents, proposing recommendations for next steps, or even assisting in the development of an automated report. Over time, these environments learn from the analysts' feedback into their responses and will therefore sharpen their thinking

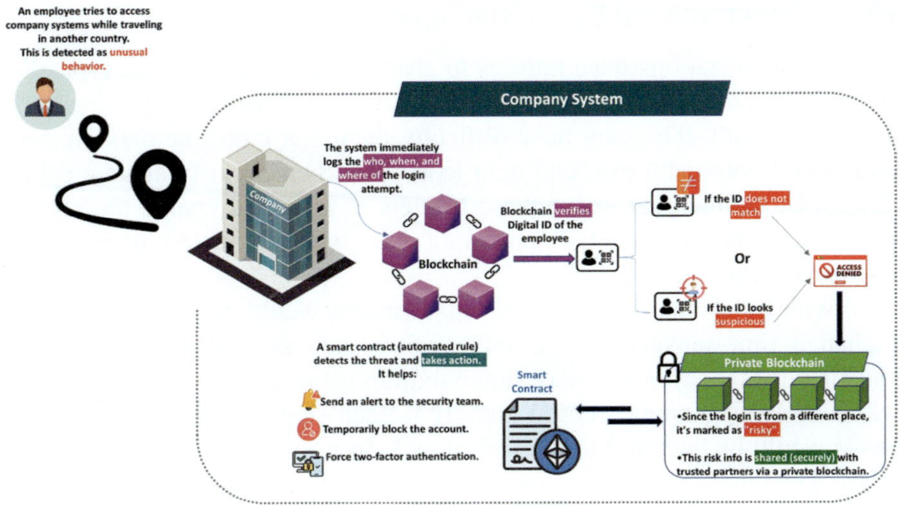

Figure 10.3 Scenario of blockchain risk management towards unusual activity.

over time to develop a more efficient and precise response. This way, organizations will have quicker responses to contain a threat, reduce manual tasks, and improve overall incident management.

10.4 Blockchain in Cybersecurity Risk Management

The adoption of blockchain technology in the field of cyber risk management has the potential to offer a paradigm shift, given its properties of decentralization, immutability, transparency, and cryptographic security (Figure 10.3). Unlike traditional systems, which are centralized and often offer one or more single points of failure, blockchain's trusted distributed ledger system distributes security controls and audit trails across a decentralized network of nodes, which inherently reduces the attack surface of cyber adversaries [29]. From the perspective of cyber risk management, blockchain provides an unprecedented level of tamper-proof record-keeping that can be valuable in tracking system logs, user activity, digital identities, and especially critical configuration changes. If an unauthorized change or malicious tampering were ever attempted, it would be both immediately visible and verifiably different when deployed alongside a strong cryptographic foundation [30]. If organizations adopted the use of smart contracts, security enforcement policies, incident response actions, and other actions could potentially be automated, minimizing human input or action during a cyber event and eliminating the delays that might occur or the potential for human modification during a critical period.

10.4.1 Decentralized threat intelligence

Usually, organizations have hurdles to sharing threat intelligence, typically arising from concerns over data protection, trust, or siloed security infrastructure. As a result, they may have difficulty obtaining real-time data on new threats and vulnerabilities, and may jeopardize their security against cyber threats. Blockchain can solve these barriers of trust and enable the secure sharing of cyber threat intelligence in a decentralized, trusted, transparent, and secure way.

With blockchain technology, organizations would be able to securely exchange time-sensitive threat information such as malware signatures, phishing links, or even zero-day vulnerabilities using a decentralized medium without having a single central authority. Each shared cyber threat intelligence would be captured on a distributed ledger and secured with cryptography. The threat intelligence would be verified, time-stamped, and create a tamper-proof immutable record of cyber threat intelligence that could time-stamp it creates a tamper-proof immutable record of it. The threat intelligence would be time-stamped, verified, and create a tamper-proof, immutable record. By capitalizing on this opportunity, any legal entity with access to the information can share information and collaborate as if they are all trusted, creating faster identification and response to defend against cyber threats. Organizations can also restrict the level of threat intelligence shared based on the sensitivity of the information and, at a minimum, can anonymize the threat. "Trustless" data sharing by sharing threat intelligence creates the environment for unique opportunities to increase global cyber efforts, collaborative situational awareness, and collaborative prevention of attacks.

10.4.2 Immutable audit trails

In conventional approaches to cybersecurity systems, perhaps one of the tactics an attacker will employ is to manipulate, change, or delete log files to cover their tracks and stop detection. This can create challenges for forensic investigators because, by the time investigators are able to go to the person, the logs are most likely not reliable and have lost some or all usefulness. Blockchain helps circumvent the issue of log files by providing a unique, immutable, and auditable trail where any behaviors or actions are securely recorded concerning each other, ensuring that all actions are noted.

Every entry within the log file, which can include login attempts, configuration changes, or policy violations, is encrypted, time-stamped, and creates a permanent record that cannot be altered. Because blockchain's structure does not allow anything written to the blockchain to be changed at any point in time, any logs on the blockchain are protected from unauthorized notification by any parties and/or modification, either internal or external, and can therefore be relied upon for forensic analysis. This will improve the detection and investigation of cyber incidents, as well as aid in regulatory compliance with privacy frameworks like GDPR, HIPAA, and ISO 27001. The function of blockchain, storing immutable logs for a long period, is an asset. This is important for audit, court, and/or verification of compliance. In that aspect, blockchain provides organizations with a structure of actions that cannot be refuted and provides accountability, transparency, and security.

10.4.3 Identity and access management

Identity and access management (IAM) systems are often relied upon for their centralized entities; however, central IAM systems are an attractive target for cybercriminals. Central IAM systems are a point of failure and are more susceptible to targeted attacks. Therefore, the solution is that blockchain technology can secure and enhance security and privacy as an alternative IAM. One of the most exciting IAM technologies that is assigned to blockchain is called self-sovereign identity (SSI). SSI allows individuals to truly own their digital identities and ultimately validate their identities without a central entity. Individuals create, manage, and validate their identities through blockchain in an encrypted manner. A key element of SSI that differentiates it from traditional centralized systems is that there is no repository storing personal information, which is vulnerable to breaches. With self-sovereign identity, users log in with the bare credentials needed to access the identity, referred to as decentralized identifiers (DID). The DIDs are secured within the blockchain, may be verified by trusted parties without disclosing sensitive personally identifiable information (PII).

Also, smart contracts take advantage of blockchain so that access control policies can be automated and codified. Smart contracts define the access control policies from which users or devices may access systems' resources. Smart contracts eliminate the need for human intervention to support an access protocol and also decrease errors associated with human involvement. Smart contracts also provide another layer of security as they are secured and immutable, provided by means of a blockchain. With the strength of blockchain, IAM systems utilizing blockchain will secure privacy by decreasing the amount of attack surface, increasing trust in the validation of digital identities, and ensuring individuals maintain ownership of their credentials.

10.5 Synergy of AI and Blockchain for Risk Management

The fusion of artificial intelligence and blockchain technologies represents a potent union that has the potential to fundamentally change risk management approaches found across industries. AI is designed for pattern recognition, predicting outcomes, and automating decisions at scale, whereas blockchain is an architecture for managing and validating data that is secure, trustworthy, and decentralized. When these two technologies work together, they borrow and build from each other in a complementary way to produce a resilient cybersecurity solution for an array of complex problems. In this section, we discuss the benefits of AI and blockchain working in tandem, in particular, in risk management.

10.5.1 AI-driven smart contracts for automated compliance

AI-powered smart contracts leverage the processing power of AI with the security and automation functionality of blockchain technology to help organizations manage compliance processes more efficiently. Compliance in traditional systems is typically complex, slow to adapt, and dependent on human monitoring, especially in the ever-changing environment of regulatory compliance. However, by incorporating AI into smart contracts, organizations can shift compliance reviews to automated processes and risk analysis without regular human monitoring, while still providing accuracy.

Smart contracts are self-executing contracts, in which the agreement between parties is directly referenced to written code and deployed onto a blockchain network. With AI algorithms, smart contracts can be transformed into compliance monitoring tools, analyzing data in real time for compliance risk and triggering events based on pre-set variables. For instance, AI could monitor for changes in a regulation, compare findings to the organization's policies or operational procedures, and update compliance requirements in real time. After finding a non-compliance issue, such as improper access or noncompliance with security protocols, the smart contract could recommend an audit or suspend user access based on its own pre-set capabilities. Therefore, AI and blockchain technology benefits streamline and assure compliance in a continuous nature, with full transparency and automating compliance efforts workflow, especially when complex. This simplifies the benefit of improved workflows and limited manual compliance and also assures organizations with a good argument for compliance with legal or regulatory audits. Since regulations are constantly in a state of evolution, AI and smart contracts allow for dynamic compliance responses for better compliance risk avoidance actions.

10.5.2 Federated learning with blockchain for privacy-preserving threat models

With the use of AI for cybersecurity use cases in organizations, there are significant concerns about data privacy and data security. Federated learning is a new AI methodology that enables machine learning models to be trained among multiple devices and/or nodes without moving sensitive data. When federated learning is combined with blockchain, it can be a privacy-preserving method to develop AI-based cybersecurity solutions built around the use of sensitive data. In a federated learning framework, AI models are trained using local devices or data sources without moving raw data to a central location. Each device trains the model using its local dataset and then sends the model updates (i.e., weights or gradients) back to a central server. These updates are logged onto a blockchain to ensure secure updates while providing transparency, and addressing tamper-proofing of the training phase. The decentralized aspects of federated learning and blockchain are advantageous because no one party can access a complete dataset. This model also supports the privacy and confidentiality of sensitive data.

Federated learning combined with blockchain is a powerful framework for developing privacy-preserving threat models, which is very useful for industries such as healthcare, finance, and IoT, which are critical in assuring data privacy. With federated learning, AI models can learn across multiple datasets, which results in a more accurate and effective threat model, without ever exchanging any individual data points, while assuring compliance with GDPR, HIPAA, and other regulatory requirements. In addition, the blockchain also ensures transparency, security, and auditability throughout the process, which increases trust with multiple stakeholders, while reducing fears of data disruption and data manipulation.

10.5.3 Use case scenario

The combination of artificial intelligence and blockchain produces a powerful, smart, and tamperproof architecture for risk management in sensitive environments such as healthcare. Specifically, AI uses advanced machine learning models like anomaly detection algorithms, federated learning, and behavioral analytics to conduct real-time monitoring of login attempts, device-to-device communication, and API-based requests for data. These AI models are trained on historical and live data to detect subtle changes in human and device behavior (for example, accessing the system outside of normal hours or sending data to unknown endpoints) that may indicate insider threats or breaches of endpoints. At the same time, blockchain serves

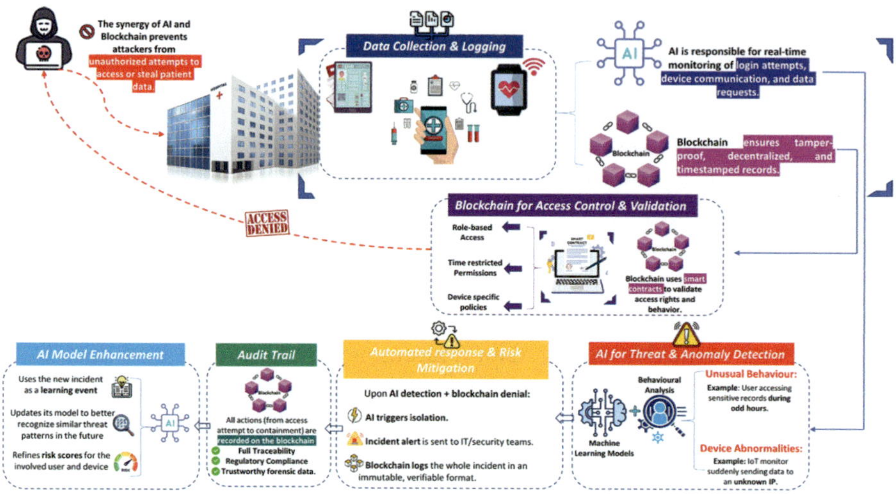

Figure 10.4 AI and blockchain synergy in securing patients' data.

as a decentralized, cryptographic ledger that records and immutably stores every event when a user accesses the system, every return on investment call to a system, and every event modeling enforcement occurs in a tamper-evident and time-stamped manner through the use of a consensus algorithm (such as Proof of Authority or Delegated Proof of Stake) on distributed ledger nodes. Access controls are enforced through the use of smart contracts, autonomous code that operates on the blockchain, where smart contracts define fine-grained role-based access, time-limited permissions, and device-based usage policies agreed upon by stakeholders.

Whenever anomalous behaviors are observed by the AI subsystem (Figure 10.4), the AI communicates with a smart contract executed on the blockchain to engage in and enforce decisions around policy enforcement and/or user isolation, which may narrow the window of vulnerability. At inception, most incident reactions are automated and occur between AI and blockchain: AI detects a threat and classifies it, while the blockchain logs everything, in order of occurrence, in an immutable, time-stamped, and transparent way. Each incident counts as a reinforcement input for AI models, so the AI will learn to classify threats or behaviors over time. Using federated learning further creates a model that generalizes over multiple institutions, while reducing the ability to extract locality and confidential information from facility-based patient data, while using blockchain as a method for traceability and with assurance of proof of necessary updates of the model without revealing raw patient data.

The result is a synergy of AI cognitive adaptability and predictive intelligence with blockchain trust, transparency, and decentralized control, together creating the next generation of risk management architecture that protects against multilayered cyber threats and helps ensure regulatory compliance and monitoring in highly sensitive digital environments.

10.6 Challenges and Limitations

Although artificial intelligence and blockchain technology provide a secure, intelligent, and decentralized opportunity for risk management systems, this combination does have limitations. Various technical, regulatory, and operational issues must be resolved to maximize AI-blockchain synergies, especially with respect to real-time and mission-critical situations. The three areas for concern are discussed in the following subsections, including scalability limitations, risks of adversarial AI attacks, and regulatory compliance and system interoperability.

10.6.1 Scalability issues in blockchain for real-time AI processing

One of the most important issues to consider when dealing with AI and blockchain systems is scalability, especially for those systems involved in real-time processing, such as continuous detection and fast risk mitigation. Conventional blockchains (Bitcoin, Ethereum) have inherent limitations that cap throughput, introduce latency, and require transaction validation in a sequence that limits the application of the blockchain in rapid AI inference and in data-intensive ML pipelines.

- **Transaction limitations:** The vast majority of public blockchains can process reductions of fewer than 20 transactions per second, while AI needs to be provided to the IoT or healthcare use cases, typically in the range of hundreds to thousands of operations per second.
- **Storage overhead:** AI applications produce enormous amounts of telemetry data and model updates that are impractical and prohibitively expensive to store on-chain. Off-chain solutions or sidechains (IPFS, Layer 2) do exist; however, they also reduce or complicate security.
- **Latency constraints:** Period of time for consensus and block propagation through the blockchain, most significantly when based on

either the Proof-of-Work or Byzantine Fault Tolerant decision models, adds latency onto the response time and may not afford AI decision-making an appropriate speed of response, therefore creating greater time-sensitivity.

10.6.2 Adversarial artificial intelligence attacks

AI frameworks confront a wide range of adversarial threats, especially data poisoning in decentralized scenarios. This data poisoning threat is of utmost concern in federated learning sessions in which many nodes cooperate to train the same model while not sharing raw data upstream of the call for federated learning. This means that a bad actor can poison the model's updates, which as a result has bias injected into the actions of the global model without a user and probably any direct way for a user to even determine any concerns or issues.

10.6.2.1 Attack vectors

- **Model poisoning:** A bad actor can covertly modify the gradient updates that teams make during rounds of federated learning, which will add backdoors or impair model accuracy. Data Inference: Once metadata is collected, it is possible that private data can be exposed from logging on to the blockchain and/or tracking of model updates after training through ML, even when privacy-preserving features are in place.
- **Smart contract exploit:** AI-based smart contracts with control or prediction from an upstream oracle, or ML prediction, are at risk of being disrupted or fully manipulated to exploit them if bad input data is sent to one of the upstream models' pipelines.

10.6.2.2 Challenges to address

- **Detection challenge**: Poisoned contributions to evidence-based federated or distributed ML techniques are a challenge to the extent that the computation of hardly trusted third parties can approximate detecting bad input without going awry of the decentralized nature of blockchain and ledger.
- **Immutable logging challenge:** If on chain, it is difficult once committed to change or revert poisoned model update or faulty decision requests due to the immutable nature of blockchain or ledger.

10.6.3 Regulatory and interoperability challenges

The confluence of AI, blockchain, and risk management traverses an intricate web of regulatory and operational domains, especially in highly controlled industries like healthcare, finance, and critical infrastructure, where compliance requires adherence to overlapping and frequently competing legal frameworks across jurisdictions.

10.6.3.1 Regulatory considerations

- **Data sovereignty:** Various nations apply data sovereignty laws governing where and how personal data may be stored and processed (GDPR, HIPAA). Blockchain's decentralized, immutable structure also hinders the application of rights like that of erasing or modifying data.
- **Liability and accountability**: Identifying who is accountable in a decentralized AI-blockchain paradigm has an inherent complexity to it: If a smart contract driven by AI makes a bad decision thanks to decisions made based on bad data, who is accountable?
- **Ethical considerations:** Automated decision-making by AI that is validated and enforced by blockchain smart contracts brings up ethical considerations of transparency, fairness, and user consent.

10.6.3.2 Interoperability considerations

- **Heterogeneous standards:** AI models, blockchain networks, and IoT devices often implement different data formats, communication protocols, and security standards, resulting in difficulties with seamless integration.
- **Cross-chain and cross-platform communications**: Risk management platforms might need to communicate and relay information across multiple blockchain systems and AI services, and this will require strong interoperability frameworks and algorithms that still require intensive research.

For broader blockchain and artificial intelligence integration in cyber risk management, it is essential to find a way to recognize and resolve various incomplete technical and regulatory challenges. Table 10.2, which follows, identifies several key challenges that inhibit fluid interaction between these types of technologies, which include scalability and data storage overhead, as

Table 10.2 Main challenges related to AI and blockchain combination.

Challenge	Description	Impact	Solution
Blockchain scalability	Challenging high latency and low throughput make it challenging to support real-time AI data and operations.	High latency makes supporting real-time AI data and operations challenging.	Second layer protocols, sharding protocols, off-chain computation, and hybrid architectures.
Data storage overhead	AI produces significant amounts of data, which cannot be stored on-chain due to cost, not to mention inefficiency.	Blockchain bloat; inefficiency of decentralized storage.	IPFS, off-chain databases with hash references on-chain, decentralized cloud storage.
Adversarial AI attacks	Data poisoning or target model manipulation in federated learning, or the inference phase, are potentially malicious attacks.	Results in model degradation; leads to poor decision-making.	Whereas robust aggregation, blockchain-based model verification, secure multiparty computation, and differential privacy.
Smart contract exploits	Exploiting AI-driven smart contracts can involve either manipulating input data or tampering with oracles.	Incorrect decisions or unauthorized attempts to enforce access.	Secure oracles, auditing behavior of AI, or formally verifying logic within the smart contract.
Data privacy and regulatory conflicts	Immutable records on the blockchain can be counter to regulations such as GDPR and HIPAA, which require erasure or amendment to data.	Possibility of being out-of-compliance, resulting in fines or possible ethical violations	Zero-knowledge proofs, selective disclosure, GDPR-compliant blockchain architecture.
Accountability and liability	Responsibility for an artificial intelligence error is often difficult to identify in decentralized systems.	Uncertainty surrounding the law, lack of trust in users, and governance issues.	Decentralized Identifiers, VCs, smart contract escrow, and arbitration mechanisms.
Interoperability issues	There are often no standard communication protocols among AI engines, blockchain platforms, and external systems.	This limits system integration, data exchange, and even scalability.	Cross-chain platforms (Polkadot, Cosmos), interoperability middleware, and standard APIs.
Model update verification	In federated learning, trusting decentralized model updates is essential, yet challenging to verify.	The danger of adding poisoned models or lowering model performance.	Auditing trails from blockchain for model updates, proof-of-learning, federated consensus protocols.

well as concerns related to adversarial attacks, privacy clashes, and interoperability. Each challenge is defined in simple terms, elaborated on how it impacts either system performance or trust, and highlighted possible solutions or emerging solutions to help overcome these challenges. A structured account such as this helps not only communicate the complexity of blockchain-AI integration, but also shows possible innovation to improve safe and intelligent cyber risk surveillance systems.

10.7 Future Directions

The ongoing convergence of artificial intelligence and blockchain is expected to drive all sorts of innovations that will shatter current limits and lead us into the next iteration of smart, secure, and transparent risk management systems. This section discusses some of the future pathways, including quantum-resistant designs for blockchains, explainable approaches to AI, and standardized hybrid methods, that will expand the characteristics of resilience, trust, and interoperability of AI-blockchain ecosystems.

10.7.1 Quantum-resistant blockchain for AI security

The emergence of quantum computing will render traditional cryptographic primitives like RSA and elliptic curve cryptography outdated due to their susceptibility to quantum attacks (Shor's algorithm) [31]. This represents a serious risk to the trustworthiness of blockchain, in turn jeopardizing any AI capabilities that rely on blockchain capabilities regarding secure data provenance, access control, and federated learning audibility.

- **Post-quantum cryptography (PQC):** The use of lattice-based, hash-based, or multivariate polynomial forms of cryptographic algorithms will be incorporated in blockchain consensus and signature schemes that require protection against quantum adversaries.
- **Quantum-resilient digital identities:** Decentralized identity frameworks (DID) will likely arise with quantum-safe credentials to protect users, devices, and AI agents operating within the blockchain framework.
- **Quantum-secure AI workflows:** Federated AI models and smart contract executions will have to establish quantum-safe data channels and key exchanges, particularly for critical applications such as electronic health records or national defense.

By establishing quantum resistance at the protocol level, blockchain systems will be able to maintain the security guarantees necessary for safe and reliable AI-enabled automation against quantum-enabled threats.

10.7.2 Explainable AI for transparent risk decisions

A fundamental challenge in the establishment of AI risk-based systems is the transient nature associated with the 'black-box' quality of AI models, particularly with deep learning models; thus, justifying, interpreting, and auditing AI model decisions can be a challenge. This quality is especially concerning in terms of a risk system powered through blockchain, where a smart contract would call on an AI model decision without an audit or justifications.

- **Model explainability:** Structuring and embedding XAI methods, together with attention-based visualizations, can allow system stakeholders to interpret the reasoning behind the AI model decision encoded onto blockchain execution.
- **Auditing decision making:** XAI outputs can be utilized in combination with an on-chain audit trail and feedback components, which will enable us to improve the responsiveness of the audit system, thus providing regulators and system users (stakeholders) with a response to the audit trail.
- **Human-AI collaboration:** Developed reliable and transparent AI system models yield trust and acceptance of human experts and enable a human expert to appropriately overwrite or modify a risk-based system action. All systems can be developed within the principles of ethical governance of AI.

The combination of the principles of XAI and blockchain not only verifies the integrity of data but also provides demonstrability of AI decisions input into an audit trail in blockchain. This becomes an essential proposition for at-risk regulatory systems (healthcare, insurance, financial services).

10.8 Conclusion

As the attack surface enlarges and cyber threats become more cunning, artificial intelligence and blockchain capabilities present a remarkable opportunity for improving cybersecurity risk management. AI provides the ability to detect threats in real time and predict future threats, conduct behavioral analytics, and automate incident response. Blockchain provides a means to store immutable data, new forms of decentralization-based trust, and tamper-proof auditing.

Together, their complementary factor enables the strengths of each other; AI provides intelligence and flexibility, while blockchain layers the security and transparency of data. We provided an overview and engaging description of how these combined capabilities will provide new cyber risk frameworks using federated learning models, compliance smart contracts, and decentralized threat intelligence systems. There are technological and regulatory gaps in realizing these models in practice, especially concerning scale, adversary circumvention of a federated learning model, or interoperable blockchain platforms. Nevertheless, there are innovative paths forward in risk management via the development of algorithms with explainable features, cryptography that is quantum-resistant, or new fairness tools for AI risk. Ultimately, the world of data and AI offers an opportunity for organizations to be agile, resilient, and trustworthy by utilizing AI and blockchain together, shifting organizations from reactive defenses to proactive systems able to adapt to the demands of the digital economy.

References

[1] R. Benaich, I. E. Alaoui, and Y. Gahi, "Securing Big Data-Based Smart Applications Using Blockchain Technology," in *Big Data Intelligence for Smart Applications*, Y. Baddi, Y. Gahi, Y. Maleh, M. Alazab, and L. Tawalbeh, Eds., in Studies in Computational Intelligence. , Cham: Springer International Publishing, 2022, pp. 241–264. doi: 10.1007/978-3-030-87954-9_11.

[2] A. Mahboubi *et al.*, "Evolving techniques in cyber threat hunting: A systematic review," *Journal of Network and Computer Applications*, vol. 232, p. 104004, Dec. 2024, doi: 10.1016/j.jnca.2024.104004.

[3] Y. Li and Q. Liu, "A comprehensive review study of cyber-attacks and cyber security; Emerging trends and recent developments," *Energy Reports*, vol. 7, pp. 8176–8186, Nov. 2021, doi: 10.1016/j.egyr.2021.08.126.

[4] R. Benaich, S. Mendili, and G. Youssef, *Securing the Future: Harnessing Blockchain's Power Against New-Age Vulnerabilities*. 2024, p. 8. doi: 10.1109/IRASET60544.2024.10549415.

[5] A. M. Shamsan Saleh, "Blockchain for secure and decentralized artificial intelligence in cybersecurity: A comprehensive review," *Blockchain: Research and Applications*, p. 100193, Feb. 2024, doi: 10.1016/j.bcra.2024.100193.

[6] A. A. Almazroi, "Innovative AI ensemble model for robust and optimized blockchain-based healthcare systems," *Netw Model Anal Health Inform Bioinforma*, vol. 14, no. 1, p. 6, Jan. 2025, doi: 10.1007/s13721-024-00501-1.

[7] "AI driven IOMT security framework for advanced malware and ransomware detection in SDN | Journal of Cloud Computing | Full Text." Accessed: Apr. 12, 2025. [Online]. Available: https://journalofcloud-computing.springeropen.com/articles/10.1186/s13677-025-00745-w

[8] R. Benaich, Y. Gahi, and S. E. Mendili, "Pioneering the Security of EHRs Using an Immersive Blockchain Conceptual Framework," *Emerging Science Journal*, vol. 9, no. 1, Art. no. 1, Feb. 2025, doi: 10.28991/ESJ-2025-09-01-010.

[9] R. Benaich, S. El Mendili, and Y. Gahi, "Securing EHRs With a Novel Token-Based and PPoS Blockchain Methodology," *IEEE Access*, vol. 12, pp. 83183–83204, 2024, doi: 10.1109/ACCESS.2024.3412793.

[10] A. Salman, "Integrating Artificial Intelligence in Cybersecurity Education: A Pedagogical Framework and Case Studies," in *2024 International Conference on Computer and Applications (ICCA)*, Dec. 2024, pp. 1–5. doi: 10.1109/ICCA62237.2024.10927933.

[11] M. M. A. Parambil *et al.*, "Integrating AI-based and conventional cybersecurity measures into online higher education settings: Challenges, opportunities, and prospects," *Computers and Education: Artificial Intelligence*, vol. 7, p. 100327, Dec. 2024, doi: 10.1016/j.caeai.2024.100327.

[12] B. A. Tingare, G. Prasanna Lakshmi, V. Khedkar, R. T. Suresh Babu, T. Dhar Diwan, and P. B. Khatkale, "Responsible AI on National Cybersecurity Strategy with Enhancement of Cybersecurity in Education," in *2024 International Conference on Intelligent & Innovative Practices in Engineering & Management (IIPEM)*, Nov. 2024, pp. 1–6. doi: 10.1109/IIPEM62726.2024.10925807.

[13] A. T. R. Alsahlanee, J. Singh, N. Garg, A. K. Rajpoot, M. Tiwari, and M. Elangovan, "Enhancing Banking Security: An Integrated Approach to IoT Threat Mitigation with Artificial Intelligence," in *Proceedings of 5th International Conference on Recent Trends in Machine Learning, IoT, Smart Cities and Applications*, V. K. Gunjan and J. M. Zurada, Eds., Singapore: Springer Nature, 2025, pp. 111–121. doi: 10.1007/978-981-97-8865-1_10.

[14] R. B. Ikhsan, Y. Fernando, H. Prabowo, Yuniarty, A. Gui, and E. A. Kuncoro, "An empirical study on the use of artificial intelligence in the banking sector of Indonesia by extending the TAM model and the

moderating effect of perceived trust," *Digital Business*, vol. 5, no. 1, p. 100103, Jun. 2025, doi: 10.1016/j.digbus.2024.100103.

[15] I. Aldasoro, S. Doerr, L. Gambacorta, S. Notra, T. Oliviero, and D. Whyte, "Generative Artificial Intelligence and Cyber Security in Central Banking," *Journal of Financial Regulation*, p. fjae008, Aug. 2024, doi: 10.1093/jfr/fjae008.

[16] C.-H. Tsai, D.-K. Liou, and H.-L. Lee, "Blockchain-supported online banking scheme," *Egyptian Informatics Journal*, vol. 27, p. 100516, Sep. 2024, doi: 10.1016/j.eij.2024.100516.

[17] S. Nirvan, S. Verma, S. Kathuria, R. Singh, and S. V. Akram, "Enhanced Banking Services using Blockchain and Artificial Intelligence," in *2023 Second International Conference on Augmented Intelligence and Sustainable Systems (ICAISS)*, Aug. 2023, pp. 57–62. doi: 10.1109/ICAISS58487.2023.10250709.

[18] M. Elhoseny, H. Alyami, M. Altuwairiqi, P. Dutta, B. D. Veerasamy, and P. K. Shukla, "An efficient and secured voting system using blockchain and hybrid validation technique with deep learning," *Peer-to-Peer Netw. Appl.*, vol. 18, no. 2, p. 70, Jan. 2025, doi: 10.1007/s12083-024-01849-x.

[19] M. S. Peelam, G. Kumar, K. Shah, and V. Chamola, "DemocracyGuard: Blockchain-based secure voting framework for digital democracy," *Expert Systems*, vol. 42, no. 2, p. e13694, 2025, doi: 10.1111/exsy.13694.

[20] A. Marouan, M. Badrani, A. Zannou, N. Kannouf, and A. Chetouani, "E-Voting System Based on Blockchain for Enhanced University Elections," *SN COMPUT. SCI.*, vol. 6, no. 3, p. 204, Feb. 2025, doi: 10.1007/s42979-025-03671-5.

[21] M. J. Hossain Faruk, F. Alam, M. Islam, and A. Rahman, "Transforming online voting: a novel system utilizing blockchain and biometric verification for enhanced security, privacy, and transparency," *Cluster Comput*, vol. 27, no. 4, pp. 4015–4034, Jul. 2024, doi: 10.1007/s10586-023-04261-x.

[22] H. Zeng, M. Yunis, A. Khalil, and N. Mirza, "Towards a conceptual framework for AI-driven anomaly detection in smart city IoT networks for enhanced cybersecurity," *Journal of Innovation & Knowledge*, vol. 9, no. 4, p. 100601, Oct. 2024, doi: 10.1016/j.jik.2024.100601.

[23] V. H. Z. Tun and H. Jahankhani, "Using Artificial Intelligence (AI) and Blockchain to Secure Smart Cities' Services and Applications," in *Cybersecurity and Artificial Intelligence: Transformational Strategies and Disruptive Innovation*, H. Jahankhani, G. Bowen, M. S. Sharif, and O. Hussien, Eds., Cham: Springer Nature Switzerland, 2024, pp. 163–184. doi: 10.1007/978-3-031-52272-7_7.

[24] Y. Jia *et al.*, "Artificial intelligence enabled cyber security defense for smart cities: A novel attack detection framework based on the MDATA model," *Knowledge-Based Systems*, vol. 276, p. 110781, Sep. 2023, doi: 10.1016/j.knosys.2023.110781.

[25] L. Alevizos, "Automated cybersecurity compliance and threat response using AI, blockchain and smart contracts," *Int. j. inf. tecnol.*, vol. 17, no. 2, pp. 767–781, Mar. 2025, doi: 10.1007/s41870-024-02324-9.

[26] A. Gurtu and D. Lim, "Chapter 101 - Use of Artificial Intelligence (AI) in Cybersecurity," in *Computer and Information Security Handbook (Fourth Edition)*, J. R. Vacca, Ed., Morgan Kaufmann, 2025, pp. 1617–1624. doi: 10.1016/B978-0-443-13223-0.00101-6.

[27] M. Malatji and A. Tolah, "Artificial intelligence (AI) cybersecurity dimensions: a comprehensive framework for understanding adversarial and offensive AI," *AI Ethics*, Feb. 2024, doi: 10.1007/s43681-024-00427-4.

[28] M. Imran, H. U. R. Siddiqui, A. Raza, M. A. Raza, F. Rustam, and I. Ashraf, "A performance overview of machine learning-based defense strategies for advanced persistent threats in industrial control systems," *Computers & Security*, vol. 134, p. 103445, Nov. 2023, doi: 10.1016/j.cose.2023.103445.

[29] V. Wylde *et al.*, "Cybersecurity, Data Privacy and Blockchain: A Review," *SN COMPUT. SCI.*, vol. 3, no. 2, p. 127, Jan. 2022, doi: 10.1007/s42979-022-01020-4.

[30] R. Benaich, S. el Mendili, and G. Youssef, "Moving Towards Blockchain-Based Methods for Revitalizing Healthcare Domain," 2023, pp. 16–29. doi: 10.1007/978-3-031-42317-8_2.

[31] "Unlocking Revolutionary Use Cases and Data Privacy Controls Throughout Quantum Computing and Blockchain - Quantum Computing and Artificial Intelligence - Wiley Online Library." Accessed: Apr. 13, 2025. [Online]. Available: https://onlinelibrary.wiley.com/doi/10.1002/9781394242399.ch3

11

Advanced Approaches to Fraud Detection and Financial Risk Mitigation using Intelligent Analytics

Madiha Munawar[1], Kishor Kumar Reddy C[1], Monika Singh T[1], and Karri Lippert[4]

[1]Stanley College of Engineering and Technology for Women, India
[4]University of South Alabama, USA

Email: madiha170705@gmail.com; kishoar23@gmail.com; thakursingh.monika@gmail.com; klippert@southalabama.edu

Abstract

Financial fraud is a scheme that can take unlawful financial gain deceptively, while financial risk is exposure to possible losses due to market fluctuations, defaults, or operational failure. The rising digital transactions have made the old detection and deterrent measures obsolete in dealing with emerging threats. This chapter describes some of the new ways in which intelligent analytics, such as artificial intelligence (AI), machine learning, and predictive modeling, can be deployed for fraud detection and financial risk management. The chapter presents the fundamentals of financial risk and fraud, some anomaly detection in real time, and the importance of data preprocessing in risk score derivation. Intelligent system applications within financial institutions, security, privacy, and ethical challenges, and case studies from banking, insurance, and FinTech are analyzed. Finally, emerging technologies, for instance, blockchain and explainable AI, are discussed, establishing a perspective for intelligent, secure, and effective future financial ecosystems.

DOI: 10.1201/9788743808077-11

11.1 Introduction

11.1.1 Overview of financial fraud and risk management

Fraud can broadly be defined as a range of activities that deceive, simulate, or manipulate anything to retrieve unlawful financial gains. Many of the types of financial fraud include identity theft, credit card fraud, phishing, money laundering, insider trading, etc [1]. The consequences of fraudulent activities are severely damaging, sometimes even for individual victims, as they may endure monetary loss and high reputational damage, and organizations or even entire economies may suffer. The interlinked global financial systems are becoming more and more vulnerable to sweeping disruption from this kind of illegal act [2]. Techniques of detection for fraud evolve, as does their methodology.

On the other hand, as an extension, financial risk management refers to the systematic identification, assessment, and minimization of possible losses from financial uncertainties induced by market or operational, or systemic with a critical role in the stability and resilience of financial institutions [3]. Today, when people practically live a digital-first life in which most of their transactions happen online, the very thin dividing lines between fraud detection and financial risk management start getting muddled by the emerging technologies [4].

Figure 11.1 is an illustration of fraud risk management within a pentagon frame, encapsulating five leading activities for the designing of a strong anti-fraud strategy. At the center lies fraud risk management, supported by anti-fraud culture, which enhances ethical behavior, and anti-fraud governance, in which oversight and accountability exist. Fraud risk assessment would define and evaluate possible fraud risks, while anti-fraud procedures would increase the chances of preventing and detecting fraud. Last but not least, the investigations focus on identifying and responding to fraudulent activities. Together, they form an integrated approach to fraud reduction and enhancing the integrity of organizations. End the task.

The dynamic environments created by online banking, e-commerce, and relevant financial tech have made it difficult for traditional rule-based detection systems to keep up in a practical sense. Old systems, although performing in their own right, were rarely flexible enough and naive to face subtle or unorthodox fraud patterns. As a result, financial institutions are currently embracing intelligent analytics, which relies on AI, machine learning, and big data. These platforms can monitor behaviors to detect anomalies almost as they happen and learn from them while adaptively updating their predictive models to curb risks proactively [5]. Such intelligent systems,

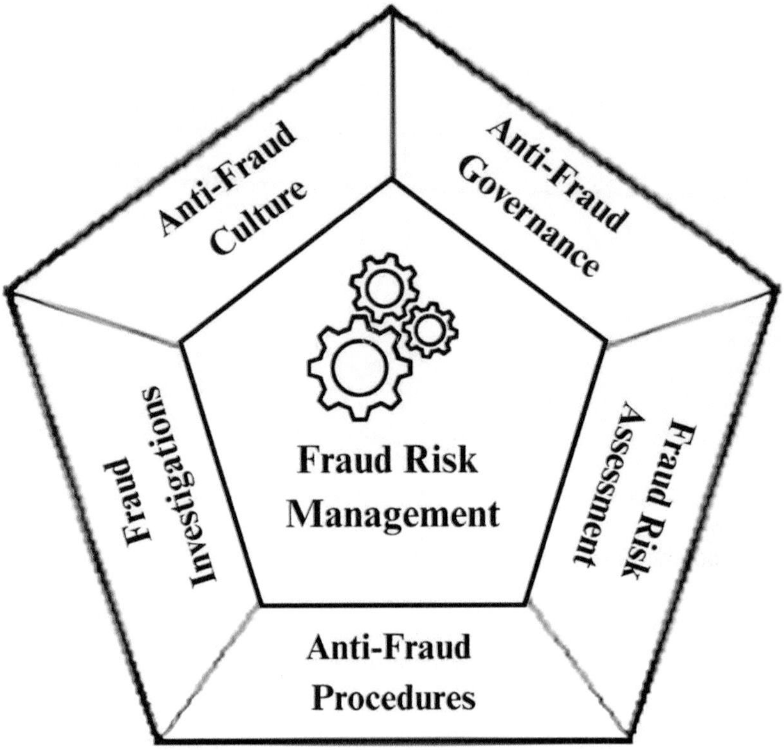

Figure 11.1 Fraud risk management.

when combined, enhance accuracy in determining wrongdoings but also improve the efficiency of operations while guaranteeing customer confidence and overall financial well-being.

11.1.2 The rise of intelligent analytics in the financial sector

Intelligent analytics encompasses highly evolved data mining, artificial intelligence, and machine learning techniques to make meaning out of terabytes of complex datasets. In fact, in the financial sector, where enormous amounts of structured and unstructured data are generated daily, such tools have become more crucial. They are not only used to identify possibly fraudulent transactions but also in risk level assessment, forecasting future market behavior, and automating many decision-making processes. Intelligent analytics, unlike unyielding rule-based static threshold-dependent systems, allows adaptive learning and nuanced analysis and significantly adds to the financial

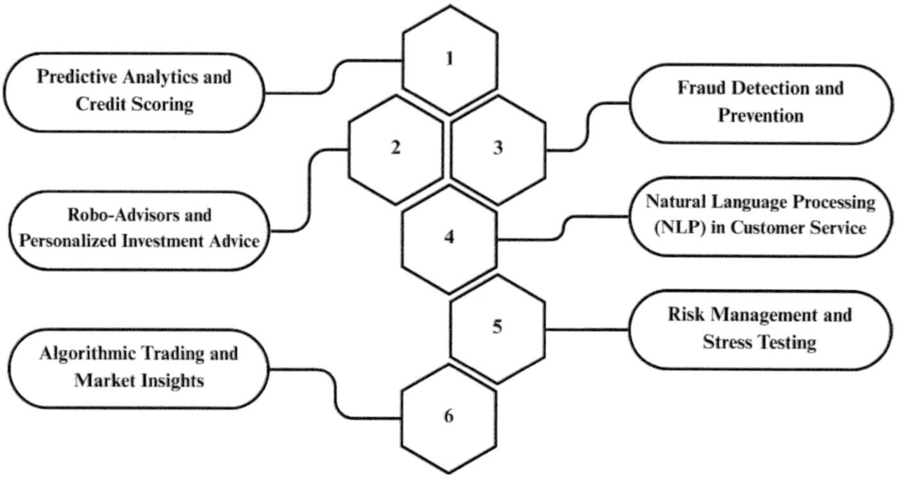

Figure 11.2 Data analytics and artificial intelligence.

resilience and the future-ready quality of operations [6]. However, intelligent analytics can actually shift financial risk management from reactive to proactive. It analyzes historical financial transactions, customer behavior, and transaction flow to identify those anomalies that could indicate possible cases of fraud or risk to business operations. Such irregular activity might be missed by human analysts or legacy systems, yet they would be quickly caught through machine learning algorithms due to the speed of processing large datasets [7]. Over time, these algorithms will produce sophisticated models based on new inputs, learning their way into real-time fraud prevention. Supervised learning teaches models how to detect known fraud types, while unsupervised learning uncovers previously unknown patterns.

Figure 11.2 illustrates that the financial field encompasses six important applications of artificial intelligence: assessing borrower risk through predictive analytics and credit scoring; robo-advisors and personalized investment advice for custom financial planning; and algorithmic trading and market insights for real-time strategies in the market. Opposite these applications, topped by fraud detection and prevention to protect a financial transaction, natural language processing (NLP) in Customer Service serves to facilitate communication with clients, while risk management and stress testing constitute measures for keeping the financial system stable. Each application is connected via a hexagon in the middle, stressing that AI is interlinked throughout many varied functions within finance.

The core machine learning models are getting supplemented with cutting-edge technologies like deep learning, natural language processing

(NLP), and graph analytics so that risk systems are up-to-date. While deep learning is concerned with enhancing pattern recognition capabilities over large datasets, NLP focuses on providing organizations with capabilities to analyze unstructured data types that could serve as potential indicators of risk, including emails, customer support chats, and news feeds. In particular, graph analytics is helping in the identification of sophisticated fraud patterns by tracing hidden connections and networks where many fraudulent accounts share commonalities in IP addresses or suspicious fund transfers [8]. These multilayer capabilities make intelligent analytics an extremely effective tool against sophisticated multi-party financial fraud.

A concomitant driver for the growing adoption of intelligent analytics in finance concerns the quest for regulatory expectation alignment and global standards compliance. Since financial authorities are mandating stricter reporting, real-time auditing, and transparency in risk practices, sufficient investments are being made by institutions in technologies that support automated monitoring and intelligent decision-making [9]. In addition, intelligent analytics foster customer trust by minimizing false positives and ensuring that legitimate users are not unduly flagged or denied services. As financial services become more digital across the board, more personalized, and ever-increasingly complex, intelligent analytics stands as a primary pillar in ensuring safety, efficiency, and soundness across the financial ecosystem.

11.1.3 Need for advanced fraud detection and mitigation strategies

Traditionally, fraud detection used predetermined rules, set parameters, and fixed thresholds: a transaction is flagged if it exceeds a certain limit or comes from an unusual location. However, such rule-based systems cannot detect clever new types of fraud because they are successful in recognizing patterns of earlier fraud [10]. Because these systems react after the fact, their typical engagement is to alert the institutions when suspicious activities have already occurred, thus limiting their potential to prevent financial loss. Fraudsters evolve constantly, using new technologies; the older systems just cannot cope, and that creates an essential gap in fraud prevention strategies.

In response, more advanced detection strategies based on artificial intelligence (AI) and machine learning (ML) emerged as formidable weapons in defense against modern financial fraud [11]. Such intelligent systems can deal with and analyze enormous volumes of transactional data in real time, finding hidden patterns, anomalies, or correlations that would be next to impossible to detect by humans or traditional systems. For instance, an ML model can learn the regular spending behavior of a customer and immediately flag any unusual deviations, irrespective of whether or not that deviation violates a certain predefined rule [12]. This whole idea is enhanced through predictive analytics, which can allow for an assessment of potential risks before they simmer down, triggering possible preemptive practices from financial institutions. This way, losses can be reduced while operations can be made more efficient, thus enhancing customer trust.

There needs to be a wider strategic framework for effective fraud detection techniques beyond the technical considerations [13]. Fostering cross-functional collaboration between fraud analysts, data scientists, compliance teams, and IT departments, with a view to ensure alignment in detection goals, is a vital part of that. Regular updates and retraining of ML models using new data will secure relevancy and accuracy [14]. Integration with regulatory compliance systems ensures that fraud detection acts on the basis of legal requirements, providing audit trails. Finally, long-term user behavior monitoring – e.g., typing rhythm, geographic location, and login activity can add an extra layer of defense [15]. The future of fraud detection must therefore be a holistic, adaptable ecosystem that will undergo development with the dawn of an emerging threat, with data, automation, and intelligent decision-making powers driving it.

11.2 Foundations of Financial Risk and Fraud

11.2.1 Types and sources of financial fraud

Fraud includes a large number of illegal or unethical acts performed to make a financial benefit through deception. Simple scams could target individuals in one area, but organized fraud rings attacking corporations and financial institutions are also a relatively sophisticated endeavor [16]. Common fraud events are, for instance, with identity fraud, in which some impersonate another by misuse of personal data; unauthorized credit card fraud using card information; phishing to shield users from revealing their sensitive credentials; and accounting fraud, usually meaning the manipulation of financial records so that misleading financial reporting follows [17].

Massive names fall into such categories as insurance fraud and cyber fraud. To extract money from the insurance firms, claims are filed fraudulently in insurance fraud, while cyber fraud is about committing crimes through digital channels like ransomware attacks, stealing data, or spoofing transactions. Similar fraud can happen in the realm of trading and investment, such as insider trading and pump-and-dump schemes [18]. Each type exploits

Table 11.1 Common types of financial fraud and their detection techniques.

Fraud type	Key characteristics	Detection method	Industry examples
Identity theft	Use of stolen identity to access accounts	Behavioral analytics, KYC checks	Banking, credit cards
Phishing	Deceptive emails/ websites for credentials	NLP-based filtering, URL analysis	Online banking, e-commerce
Insider fraud	Internal misuse of access rights	User behavior monitoring, AI flags	Corporate finance, insurance
Money laundering	Concealing the origins of illegal funds	Transaction pattern recognition	Global banking
Credit card fraud	Unauthorized card usage	Real-time anomaly detection	Retail, online payments
Account takeover	Hacker gains control of user account	Login pattern analysis, device fingerprinting	FinTech, mobile apps
Synthetic identity fraud	Use of fake composite identity	AI-based ID verification, cross-checks	Credit agencies, loan services

different vulnerabilities, whether technological, human, or procedural, and will require targeting in its preventive or detective approaches. The sources are vast and diverse. Such wrongdoers allow hackers, cybercriminals, and international fraud syndicates to use technology to penetrate systems, extract information, and manipulate transactions [19]. Such insider knowledge, if used to bypass security protocols, becomes dangerous to organizations facing others. At some points, fraud could arise as a result of the combination of actions conducted by insiders and outsiders, thus further complicating detection.

The more integrated digital networks become, so too are the crimes evolving. The criminals, therefore, have in recent times begun to employ AI-powered social engineering along with deepfakes and botnets in mounting attacks on systems with ever-increasing efficiency and decreased detectability [20]. Thus, the demand from financial institutions to comprehensively map fraud squarely increases, bearing in mind all forms and sources of threats. It is this understanding that underpins the build-out of commercial fraud detection systems today capable of spotting suspect behavior and reacting with nimbleness and accuracy.

Table 11.1 shows the most common types of financial fraud and confronted with their characteristic features, methods of detection, and industry examples in the real world. It gives a preliminary idea of how various fraudulent acts spread across industries like banking, insurance, and e-commerce.

It also serves as a supportive guide to practitioners to adopt specific solutions for specific threats by juxtaposing fraud types against detection techniques such as anomaly detection and behavioral analytics.

11.2.2 Common financial risks in modern institutions

Beyond fraud, the present world of finance must navigate a complex sphere of risk that can affect its stability, profitability, and compliance. In finance, the main kinds of risk include market risk, credit risk, liquidity risk, operational risk, and legal and compliance risk. Market risk arises from any change in macroeconomic variables such as changes in interest rates, foreign exchange rates, or volatility in the stock markets, which might suddenly contribute to a loss in asset value. Institutions that are exposed to either investments or loans related to certain market conditions have to consider hedging this risk through financial instruments and/or diversification [21]. Credit risk, the probability of a borrower defaulting on repayment, is one of the notable risks directly impacting lending and is often assisted by complicated credit scoring and modeling. Liquidity risk refers to the other major risk of the inability to meet short-term obligations owing to the realization of assets into cash. Liquidity crises are very often the cause of failure of even the solvent institutions, stressing therefore the need for liquidity planning and stress testing.

Operational risks involve risks arising from inadequate or failed internal processes, systems, and people. Software bugs, data incidents, transaction failures, and staff negligence are prime examples. All of these lead to not only financial losses but also reputational damage [22]. "Legal and compliance risk" comes into play when institutions are found to be in breach of financial regulations such as AML (anti-money laundering) rules, data protection laws, and fair lending laws. In such cases, fines and legal consequences can be enormous, especially in tightly regulated markets like banking and insurance. The interrelated nature simply adds to this great complexity [23]. For example, a cyber-attack (operational risk) can compromise data (legal risk), triggering withdrawal by client loyalty (market risk) and subsequently liquidity embarrassment. Therefore, effective risk management must now factor interdependencies between all these risks using a common analytic approach for early identification, impact assessment, and mitigation planning.

11.2.3 Traditional approaches and their limitations

In the past, all financial institutions have relied on their rule-based systems to manage their fraud detection and risk assessment. These systems utilize hard-coded rules that turn up transactions above certain thresholds or meet pre-defined categories of flagged suspicious activity. For example a transfer of $10,000 might trigger a system that raises red flags [24]. While easy to put into place and intuitive to understand, such systems are limited to their rigidity, generating copious high false positives that overwhelm analysts and often confuse bona fide customers.

Traditional methods, besides these, are all bad in the sense of not being adaptable to a newly created type of fraud. One-To continuously adapts their tactics, fraudsters test the limits of the system, and use technology to mimic legitimate behavior. Static rule sets are incapable of detecting the nuances of those new forms or subtle fraud. Increasingly larger numbers of transactions are processed more and faster by digital banking. With this degree of growth, current systems cannot scale or perform, leading to delays or missed threats [25]. A further constraint lies in the absence of learning mechanisms in traditional systems. Learning, the past decision-from-decision record compiled without being linked directly to time, will not improve these in the process of time. Even reasoning about the context is absent, as all transactions are inferred and viewed in isolation without time or account linkage. This often results in a wholly split view concerning risk, making it difficult to spot fraud rings or money laundering networks, or systematic insider threats.

Finally, traditional methods are usually soloed by the department. Fraud detection, compliance monitoring, and credit risk may each be separate systems and sources of data. This further complicates the singular offerings of insight and duplicates effort. Without the possibility of centralized intelligence or integration, client institutions lose the chance to correlate indicators and respond to risks holistically. This is where the modern intelligent analytics platforms that AI and data fusion really stand taller than any other.

11.3 Role of Intelligent Analytics in Finance

11.3.1 AI and machine learning in fraud detection

Artificial intelligence and machine learning have become two of the most important drivers for change within the financial services industry, especially in the area of fraud detection. They essentially analyze huge volumes of transactional and behavioral data to identify subtle patterns hidden from view, thus transcending the traditional rule-based system [26]. They are capable of not just spotting suspicious activities like micro-transactions that test for stolen credentials or orchestrated attacks across several accounts, but also for picking anything that can elude a human analyst or traditional system [27].

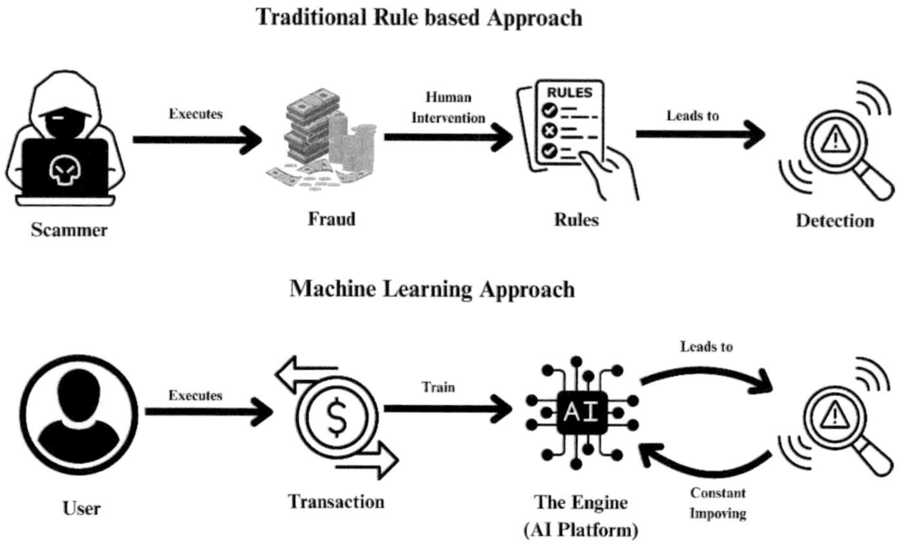

Figure 11.3 Traditional vs machine learning approaches.

Figure 11.3 compares two methodologies that are quite differentiated, namely the traditional rule-based approach and the machine learning approach to be included in fraud detection. A classical method detects the occurrence of fraud and relies on pre-established rules with human interference for detection, resulting in a delayed response to such instances. However, the machine learning approach keeps on training an AI engine continuously through various user transaction data, allowing it to adapt and improve in real time, thereby proactively detecting fraud before it has a chance to escalate. This machine learning model keeps evolving with all the new data available on the web, making it more and more effective and accurate in time, unlike static rule-based systems.

Algorithms based on ML are thus particularly apt for classification: a grouping of methods that could include decision trees, support vector machines (SVM), random forests, and neural networks. These classification types could be implemented in determining a transaction as legal or fraudulent depending on variable inputs [28]. These algorithms can operate on more sophisticated, unstructured data such as voice, text, and video; they can also model complex behaviors like that of synthetic identities, phishing scams, and transaction laundering. With respect to real-time behavior monitoring, AI is important [29]. For example, if a customer logs in from an unusual location and spends more than usual during a very short time or is interacting with the app during odd hours, these behaviors can raise flags. Such cases would trigger immediate alerts and fraud prevention responses, such as a step-up

Table 11.2 Machine learning models and their applications in risk management.

ML model	Use case	Strengths	Limitations
Decision tree	Credit scoring, fraud alerts	Easy to interpret	Can overfit with noisy data
Random forest	Loan approval prediction	High accuracy, robust to noise	Complex to interpret
Logistic regression	Probability-based risk models	Simple, fast, interpretable	Limited to linear relationships
Neural networks	Fraud detection, risk scoring	Good with complex patterns	Requires large datasets, black-box
XGBoost	Bankruptcy prediction	High accuracy, handles missing data	Computationally intensive
K-Means clustering	Customer segmentation	Unsupervised, scalable	Not ideal for anomalies
SVM (support vector machine)	Classification of high-risk customers	Effective in high-dimensional data	Sensitive to parameter tuning

authentication process or even a temporary account hold [30]. This transition from reactive to proactive fraud management has severely curtailed the window period in which fraud could crest.

Table 11.2 shows the matrix details of prevalent machine learning algorithms used in the areas of financial risk assessment and fraud detection, with examples, utilities, strengths, and limitations of those algorithms. Comparison of decision trees, neural networks, and XGBoost in the context of credit scoring, customer segmentation, and loan default prediction. This would help an analyst in deciding which ML model would be the fittest in terms of the data attributes and the objectives of the finance domain.

11.3.2 Predictive analytics and anomaly detection

This approach for the future uses history with machine learning to predict what is likely going to happen next for events such as fraud or potential financial risks. Thus, it allows financial institutions to move from fraud detection to its anticipation and prevention [31]. It gives early indications of potentially protective actions when abnormalities in transaction frequency or unusual payment recipients are preset as patterns to such systems capable of knowing the items that end up becoming indicators preceding fraudulent behavior.

Anomaly detection is mainly about looking for flagging or tagging transactions or behavior incongruent with what has been typically observed. For example, when a customer who typically pays his bills in a local place suddenly starts sending substantial payment amounts to a foreign account, that becomes an anomaly, and the system would flag it [32]. These systems keep adjusting periodically to update the baseline models as the users' behaviors change, thereby making them effective against newer fraudulent techniques that were not covered by predefined rules. Besides making the financial machinery complex, predictive models make resource allocations easier. Every transaction or every customer has a risk score based on numerous factors such as amount, frequency, location, and others; the analyst now concentrates on the most critical threats. The advantages of predictive analytics are that it could reduce false positives and increase response time, strengthening operations and increasing confidence in consumers with financial institutions.

11.3.3 Benefits over traditional data-driven decision-making in finance

Intelligent analytics presents several distinct advantages over the traditional approaches to fraud detection and risk management, establishing itself as a vertical crisis in modern finance. Traditional systems based on hard-coded rules and thresholds are not good enough to keep up with evolving fraud mechanisms. On the flip side, AI-driven models learn continuously from new data and remain relevant and aware of real-time happenings in the financial ecosystem.

Standard methods encourage a certain burnout among human assessors and work against customer satisfaction when most legitimate activities are blocked. One of the larger improvements intelligent analytics can bring is lowering false positives to the tens of thousands. Taking context, user history, and cross-channel data into account, intelligent systems become more capable of differentiating genuine threats from benign deviations. Equally important is the speed and scalability factor. With intelligent analytics, millions of instances can, in fact, be handled in real time, unlike their predecessors, due to their predominantly high-volume nature, i.e., online banking, digital wallets, and cross-border payments. Further complementing the existing infrastructure, they enable dynamic risk assessments while still ensuring no disruption of user experience. This tailored fit ensures that effective fraud prevention measures offer user-friendliness, thereby equipping a much more resilient and customer-centric financial ecosystem.

11.4 Data Sources and Preprocessing For Risk Analytics

11.4.1 Financial data collection and integration

High-quality and comprehensive data form the cornerstone of financial risk management and fraud detection systems. These institutions always review

Table 11.3 Risk levels and corresponding transaction monitoring strategies.

Risk level	Description	Example transactions	Monitoring strategy
Low	Routine, low-value, frequent	Monthly salary credits	Batch analysis, periodic reviews
Medium	Slightly irregular patterns	International fund transfer	Real-time monitoring with alerts
High	Unusual value/ location/volume	Large cash withdrawals abroad	Immediate flagging and manual review
Critical	Linked to known fraud patterns	Sudden large transfers to new accounts	AI-based decision support, suspension

a magnitude of structured and sometimes unstructured data that ranges from vast credit histories, transaction records, account balances, and loan applications to behavioral data on customer attributes like occupation, age, and spending habits, enabling establishments to create richer risk profiles. Unstructured sources of data like emails, call transcripts, social media activity, and customer reviews direct the genuine intent of the user and, when rightly analyzed through the prism of AI-based text analytics and sentiment analysis tools, can lay bare the real potential for fraud.

Table 11.3 represents different financial sectors corresponding to their relative risks and popular intelligent analytic tools used to tackle those risks. It also gives insights into how banks, fintech, investment houses, and insurance services differ in their vulnerabilities and technology stacks. This table affords actionable insight into how tools such as AI-powered dashboards, fraud scoring engines, and predictive analytics are being used to mitigate sector-specific risks.

The assimilation of these pieces of data together creates a big problem. Financial-related issues will always tear across every department and be run by one or various departments working off legacy systems that are incompatible with today's analytical environments. Because centralized data warehouses and big data lakes will serve as storage pipelines for every kind of data, the highest priority issue that must be addressed is data integration. For a single data stream coming from different and specific sources to work harmoniously and in real-time, APIs (application programming interface) and ETL (Extract, Transform, and Load) processes remain crucial. With this strong bond, only analysts and models can access synchronized, clean, and timely data with greater faith, hence boosting the accuracy and response time of their tools [33]. The assimilation of third-party information from external entities such as credit bureaus, government agencies, or risk intelligence complements the internal record with additional context. This external context plays a significant role in identifying hidden factors that, in the conceptual scheme, are sniffed out as risks but are not easy to identify within the internal subject. The cross-validation of inputs from internal and external sources reveals areas with discrepancies or some suspicious anomalies or both. These anomalies could potentially signify fraud or systemic risk. In this digital age, data integration platforms offering services in the cloud have eased the task of combining higher volumes of data securely and in compliance with stipulated regulatory guidelines.

Consequently, this integrated data becomes a comprehensive representation of customer behavior, financial liabilities, and typical operational trends. A complete and clear picture thus emerges, necessitating the need for a strong analytic fraud-detection mechanism backed by sound risk modeling to identify patterns when abnormalities appear, implications arising from the emergence of new threats, and a timely warning for action. Combined with on-the-fly integrated data processing, this will help make sophisticated decisions in intense environments like trade, lending, and insurance underwriting.

11.4.2 Data cleaning and feature engineering

Anomalies are most often related to missing data, duplication, outliers, and incorrect formats. Data cleansing is the main preprocessing step used to clear such data before inputting it into machine learning and analytics models. Techniques such as duplicate elimination, standard formats like date or currency, and imputation of missing values using statistical methods or predictive modeling are popular. Data cleaning could also include resolving data conflicts, for example, merging many addresses or contact numbers into one verified record for one customer.

Next, through feature engineering, cleaned raw data variables will be prepared and converted into more meaningful and predictive indicators. An example of a realization in fraud detection may include features such as the number of transactions in a single day, the distance between where the transactions took place in terms of geography, deviations in customer spending patterns, browser metadata, or even device metadata. In risk management situations, engineered features include income-to-debt ratio, trends in credit utilization, payment history streaks, or immediate shifts in spending behavior. These features allow models to understand and learn the delicate distinctions they would need to know the difference between legitimate and fraudulent or high-risk behavior.

Feature engineering requires a combination of domain knowledge and technical ability because it brings about a marriage between finance and data science. Meaningful identifiers are given by financial analysts, while data scientists consider the best with tools such as correlation matrices, information gain, and principal component analysis to rank and select predictive features. Indeed, AutoML and the feature selection library enable an automation option for so many of these activities; however, human oversight is still necessary for the interpretation of output as well as how it aligns with domain knowledge. This balance thus leads to the making of models that are statistically robust but also valuable and relevant to the discipline. Well-formed features boost model performance, decreasing false positive and false negative rates. Models are thus given a more profound context, crucial for fraud scenarios where the change in behavior can be very subtle. Any predictive model's success mainly depends on the quality of features rather than the complexity of the model itself. Feature engineering thus assumes a central position in successful financial risk and fraud analytics systems.

11.4.3 Challenges in data quality and availability

The same principle also extends to data quality, vis-a-vis its competition with the advances available in technology that would refine data processing. Using naming protocols inconsistently, duplicate customer records, outdated profile information, and errors in data entries can shake the credibility of even the most sophisticated fraud detectors [34]. Data inconsistencies generally result when isolated departments use different software or different data standards, giving rise to disjointed, conflicting views of a given customer or account. Another important problem is data availability, where real-time analytics and fraud detection systems depend on current feeds of data. The processing of vast streams of data, with very low latencies, including transactions, alerts, and behavioral metrics, is essential for financial institutions [35]. Thus, top-tier technical infrastructure, including fast storage, cloud computing resources, and scalable data pipelines, should be in place. If some time is lost in processing activities, the financial or reputational losses incurred due to missed fraudulent transactions and slow responses to risk can become huge.

Besides the technical, management must also take care of the legal and ethical constraints surrounding the collection and use of data. Still, General Data Protection Regulation (GDPR), California Consumer Privacy Act (CCPA), along with varying financial compliance standards, hamper the manner in which a customer can give his/her data, share it, and store it. Sensitive personal data might require anonymizing or encrypting before any analysis can be conducted on it. Financial institutions would then have to balance between data richness and regulatory compliance, in order to ensure both accuracy and privacy [36]. Any infringement of data protection laws may attract the gravest penalties and degeneration of customer trust.

In this regard, major investments are increasingly being made by financial organizations in data governance frameworks, specialized data quality teams, and automated data validation tools. Such systems assure the transparency and traceability of the data lifecycle where monitoring is done not only for data integrity validation. An example is data lineage tracking which enables an organization to see where each piece of data originated from, how it was transformed, and where it gets consumed, which is vital for regulatory environments. Remedying issues of data quality and availability right at the source sets the path for more robust and reliable risk analytics and fraud detection systems.

11.5 Advanced Fraud Detection Techniques

11.5.1 Supervised and unsupervised learning approaches

The main types of artificial intelligence used for the construction of fraud detection systems that have attained much attention are supervised learning, which offers high accuracy and interpretability. In this paradigm, historical transaction data are labeled as fraudulent or legitimate, while the algorithm learns to recognize patterns and behaviors from the two competing groups. Then, among common algorithms, one encounters logistic regression, support vector machines (SVMs), decision trees, and ensemble models: random forests and gradient boosting machines. In this way, these models classify future transactions by flagging those that are reminiscent of previously identified fraudulent behavior.

With all its strengths though, supervised learning has its challenges with detecting new fraud mechanisms; it is heavily reliant on previously labeled data, so it is unlikely to detect very new or changing fraudulent schemes that have not yet been identified. Very useful are unsupervised learning techniques. They do not require labeled data but rather tag points within the data set as outliers or anomalies. K-means clustering, isolation forests, and autoencoders detect deviation from normal behavior patterns, enabling early alerts of suspicious fraudulent activity.

One of the most efficient practices today is combining supervised and unsupervised methods in a hybrid model. Supervised models are adept at quickly spotting known types of fraud with high precision on the recall of existing threats, while unsupervised ones continuously scour the data in search of unknown anomalies, filling the holes in detection by the supervised schemes. This hybrid framework allows financial institutions to maintain both accuracy and efficiency while adapting to the changing landscape of fraud. These paradigms can dynamically interplay with each other to support uninterrupted monitoring and learning. As fraudsters become increasingly sophisticated, systems that are predictive and exploratory benefit financial institutions. Regular model retraining, feedback-loop procedures, and data labeling mechanisms ensure that both the supervised and unsupervised systems evolve in parallel with the trends associated with fraud, thus helping to create a robust fraud detection ecosystem.

11.5.2 Neural networks and deep learning models

Neural networks have been playing a leading role in most sophisticated modern techniques for fraud detection because such systems are capable of modeling large and complex datasets as well as capturing nonlinear relations. Like human brains, neural models include interconnected layers that process input data to "learn" hierarchical features [37]. Deep neural networks (DNNs) are those that have multiple hidden layers and the potential to make sense of intricate patterns that are often imperceptible to most of the modeling approaches, leaving them to be extremely successful in dealing with schemes where behavior is minimally deviated or where intentionality is concealed. Yet, of all deep learning models, the recurrent neural network (RNN) and long short-term memory (LSTM) networks have proved most fruitful for fraud detection purposes. Being purely sequential processing architectures, they are designed to analyze transactions through time, which makes them perfect for building the history of customer transaction sweep. LSTM networks can create multivariate dependencies covering long time intervals, such as changes in spending behavior or anomalies temporally based, permitting the model to classify a phenomenon as fraud when identifying a discrepancy in possible fraudulent behavior within the norms of a user's pattern of activity [38].

In addition, CNN-based models (convolutional neural network), which were initially developed for image processing, are coming in handy for the purposes of detecting fraudulent activities. In financial contexts, CNNs can analyze graphical representations of transaction data, conduct text classification for document fraud detection, and even scan handwritten signatures for forgery. Their ability to perceive hierarchical spatial arrangements and patterns allows applications that extend beyond structured numeric data in the name of expanding the use of fraud detection systems.

Table 11.4 depicts a comparison between traditional credit scoring models and current AI-based alternatives on several parameters such as data

Table 11.4 Comparison of traditional vs AI-based credit scoring methods.

Parameter	Traditional model	AI-based model	Improvement/outcome
Data used	Limited financial history	Multi-source (social, behavioral)	Broader profile assessment
Model complexity	Linear, fixed scoring formula	Non-linear, adaptive learning	Better pattern detection
Flexibility	Static risk factors	Dynamic, real-time updates	Responsive to changing borrower behavior
Accuracy	Moderate	High	Lower false approvals/ rejections
Bias detection	Manual checks for fairness	Fairness metrics in ML training	Improved compliance and trust
Credit inclusivity	Excludes non-traditional applicants	Includes gig workers, freelancers	Increased financial inclusion
Speed of evaluation	Manual or batch processing	Instantaneous, real-time scoring	Faster decision making

sources, timing of the credit evaluation, measure of accuracy, and inclusivity. It means changing from manual and rule-based measures to a dynamic and ongoing approach for credit assessment, in other words, real-time credit assessment. The focus in this context is on fairness, scalability, and speed of decision-making, which are emerging as primary descriptors of how AI stands to transform consumer lending.

Even though they have an inclination towards a huge amount of data, along with much more processing power, deep learning models need careful tuning and sharpening so as to avoid getting overfitted. In such conditions, the model would just end up being way too specific to training data only, and in this age would fail to generalize. Using explainable AI (XAI) methods sometimes helps indeed for making neural network decisions at least less black-box, since they are still typically treatment-ready-balanced, but with any given trade-off between performance and interpretability. As technology matures, neural networks evolve for the future and create new dimensions of security through adaptive and intelligent fraud detection.

11.5.3 Real-time fraud detection systems

In this digital age where transacting takes seconds, it is inevitable that something must be done for real-time fraud detection. Batch processing methods that analyze an event after the fact have fallen short. Real-time systems can check and judge the validity of transactions even as they occur, thus blocking any fraudulent attempts before any damage is done. When coupled with continuous data streams, these systems apply instantaneous decision rules or light predictive models for split-second detection and response to fraud.

Popular technologies, such as Apache Kafka, Apache Flink, and Apache Spark Streaming are widely used in real-time applications for ingestion, processing, and analyzing transactions in motions in most enterprises. In addition, they provide an infrastructure for implementing machine learning models tailored for speed and growth. Using lightweight models, alongside rules-based engines, rapid evaluation can be performed on every transaction with many risk variables, including location, frequency, amount, and device fingerprint. With the addition of adaptive learning techniques that update their detection logic based on new fraud patterns seen in real time, these systems further improve.

One of the many benefits of real-time detection is improving customer experience. Suspicious activities quickly discovered by the financial institution would result in reducing false positives that disrupt legitimate users. An automated alert within seconds, triggering biometric verification or one-time password (OTP), could validate the transaction and thus allow the customer to continue without unnecessary delays. This enhances customer trust while also improving retention and engagement within digital banking services. Real-time systems, in addition to these, are very instrumental in ensuring regulatory compliance. Now, continuous monitoring and rapid response to suspicion are demarcated by most financial authorities; hence, a real-time fraud detection system complements them quite well. They are integrated with identity verification tools, customer profile systems, and blockchain-ledger technology, thereby putting up an exceedingly strong security system that makes the financial ecosystem agile and reliable. As cyber threats change with time, real-time detection stands at the frontline of defense in the war against financial fraud.

Figure 11.4 is a standard workflow in machine learning from the collection of data to the deployment of the models and predictors. It involves historical data, which is then subjected to feature engineering and split between the training set and validation set. The training set applies model training/building, while the validation set is for tuning and validating the designed model. Test model predictions will be done to evaluate the accuracy and performance of the model once it is created from the trained model. Then the model will be deployed to become the deployed model, which will then accept new data that also undergoes feature engineering before final predictions. This ensures that the model is well-generalized and can accurately predict unseen data.

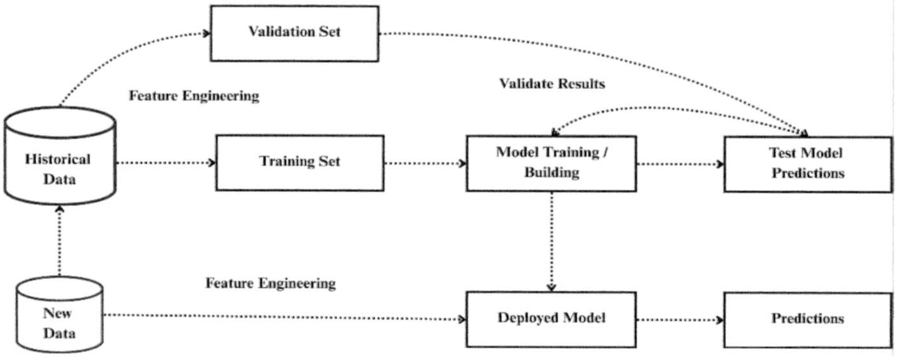

Figure 11.4 Real-time fraud detection systems.

11.6 Financial Risk Modeling and Assessment

11.6.1 Credit risk assessment models

Credit risk is simply one of the most important aspects of financial risk management in that it embodies the probability of a borrower, cognizable or not, defaulting on a loan or failing to produce due amounts under a contractual liability. In preserving assets and maintaining financial stability, banks and lending institutions must appraise a borrower's creditworthiness. The traditional technique revolves around such scoring systems as the FICO (Fair Isaac Corporation) score that usually computes risk using this same fixed set of variables – income, outstanding debts, and historical repayment behavior. Such systems provide limited flexibility and hardly capture nuances characterizing complex financial environments.

Now that machine learning is available, credit risk assessment has undergone a transformation. Algorithms of decision trees, support vector machines, gradient boosting, and neural networks enable institutions to process a great deal of new data features. They provide non-linear correspondence modeling, pattern recognition from gigantic datasets, and the ability to retrain as new information is obtained. For instance, behavioral data, digital footprints, social media activity, and even mobile usage trends can be captured to improve predictive power. In short, machine learning models are much better at early flagging of potential defaults. Not only that, but dynamic credit models also understand that learning and adaptation are continuous processes. Thus, whenever new borrower data comes to light or there are changes in a macroeconomic trend, the models re-adjust themselves with the changes. This turn of events might get more important in highly dynamic or uncertain economic environments because conventional static models might then lose their relevance and become inaccurate. Furthermore, making this alternative data available to financial institutions enables borrowers without extensive credit histories – for instance, students, immigrants, or the unbanked – to gain access to finance while still protecting risk.

Apart from individual lending, assessing credit risk is important in funding corporations, investment analysis, and evaluations of sovereign debts. Advanced credit models take it a notch higher by qualifying for stress testing, in which institutions simulate bad economic conditions, such as sudden inflation spikes or recessions, to assess the potential performance of loans under such conditions. The results indicate to lenders how they should adjust interest rates, tighten credit terms, or build suitable reserves to absorb the changes. Ultimately, these models present a more encompassing and future-proof way for sustaining a healthy loan portfolio and shaping the resilience of institutions.

11.6.2 Market and liquidity risk modeling

The exposure of the market risk refers to a potential financial loss owing to adverse changes in market prices, such as those of interest rates, equity values, or foreign exchange rates. Financial institutions explore a wide range of techniques to manage and estimate what this exposure is; perhaps the most common one is value at risk (VaR). VaR considers the greatest loss expected in a given time and under certain confidence level conditions. Historical simulation, Monte Carlo simulation, and parametric modeling are various approaches that can be adopted for calculating VaR and assessing the sensitivity of the portfolio to changes in market volatility. For one, classical market risk measurement methodologies are based on normality conditions and tend to ignore the catastrophic crisis or black swans. The introduction of machine learning has a huge edge in this juncture. ML also recognizes non-linear correlations, finds early signals of impending market stress, and discovers patterns across large diversely classified datasets. Analysis of the market sentiment, which entails using NLP to track financial news, social media tweets, and media reports, has increasingly been incorporated into risk models to prepare them for any changing winds ahead. All this keeps the decision-making process more robust in real time while minimizing losses during quick-moving markets.

Table 11.5 provides a summary view of major global compliance frameworks and data privacy regulations impacting fraud detection and financial risk management. Covering standards like GDPR (Europe), CCPA (California), Payment Card Industry Data Security Standard (PCI-DSS) etc., the table critically examines how these regulations impact data governance and analytics

Table 11.5 Key financial regulations and compliance standards across regions.

Regulation	Region	Focus area	Impact on analytics systems
GDPR	European Union	Data privacy, user consent	Requires anonymization, explainability
PSD2	EU	Open banking, security	Enables API integrations, enhances fraud checks
GLBA	USA	Consumer data protection	Mandates secure storage and sharing
MAS TRM	Singapore	Technology risk management	Requires model risk audits and assessments
FCRA	USA	Fair credit reporting	Ensures transparency in scoring algorithms

strategies. It provides useful navigation support for international financially oriented firms moving through regulatory landscapes while rolling out AI tools.

Liquidity risk is just as important to be managed alongside market risk by financial institutions; it is the risk experienced by an institution that lacks cash or liquid assets to meet obligations within a short period. Cash planning includes liquidity modeling so that balance sheets, transaction flows, and behavioral patterns – such as withdrawal habits, loan demand, etc could be analyzed thoroughly. With predictive analytics, possible cash outflow requirements are forecasted under both normal and stressful conditions to ensure an institution maintains its reserves in a better position to prepare for possible immediate occurrence of liquidity crunches from shocks in the economy or, more so, complete panic withdrawal of customers.

Today's liquidity models are also designed to cover macroeconomic indicators and cross-institutional behavior in conjunction with historical crisis information. Liquidity stress testing that is very robust is being asked for by regulators on an increasing scale to achieve financial stability across the system. Intelligent analytics serves these purposes by automating monitoring, real-time alerts, and agility in acting. Thus, the combined effect of AI-powered insights and strong modeling practices improves short-term solvency management, as well as long-term strategic planning for financial institutions operating in a risk landscape that continues to evolve.

11.6.3 Stress testing and scenario analysis

Stress testing is a forward-looking tool for projecting how financial institutions or systems may withstand extreme yet plausible adverse conditions. Stress testing exercises are essential and have come to the fore these days for internal risk management and also for regulatory compliance since the time of the financial crisis of 2008. Scenarios may include deep economic recessions, geopolitical disruptions, interest rate hikes at a fast pace, and pandemics. By projecting the financial impact of such events, institutions can start identifying potential weaknesses that may exist within their portfolios or operations and thereby enhance their risk management frameworks.

Traditionally, stress testing had been based on hypothetical scenarios manually crafted by risk managers or regulators. Such exercises would provide support and were useful, but usually lacked personalization and often were not a good fit for the unique risk exposures of individual firms. Integration of machine learning and big data analytics has changed the stress testing paradigm to a whole new level. The AI-based system can mine through historical market data and simulate complex interdependencies among risks in the context of developing accurate, bespoke scenarios. Such simulations would provide a multi-dimensional view of the risk-inducing cross-asset contagion effects and inter-departmental ripple impacts.

Scenario analysis complements stress testing but does so by examining a wide spectrum of possible future outcomes as opposed to merely one extreme event. The latter is chiefly useful in the context of strategizing, capital allocation, and optimizing facilities. It is used by institutions to estimate how various market developments could affect revenues, asset values, and solvency positions. For example, scenarios in which inflation persists and interest rates rise will affect loan demand, investment yield, and the likelihood of credit default. Knowing this helps policymakers draft well-developed contingency plans. With regard to the evolution of stress testing and scenario analysis, the same assists with real-time crisis response. With advances in computing and analytics, financial institutions have started running simulations in real-time and are able to adjust their strategies on the fly. Increasingly, stress testing exercises are mandated by regulatory bodies, such as the Federal Reserve and the European Central Bank, thereby remaining compliant with the intelligent analytics that automate and enhance the process. Stress testing and scenario analysis should ultimately form the backbone of a resilient risk management strategy that would enable institutions to better protect themselves against financial adversities.

11.7 Security and Privacy Considerations

11.7.1 Cybersecurity threats in financial systems

Because of the critical nature of its data, assets, and infrastructure, the financial sector remains one of the highly attacked industries. Actors ranging from lone hackers to nation-state groups are constantly devising new methods of

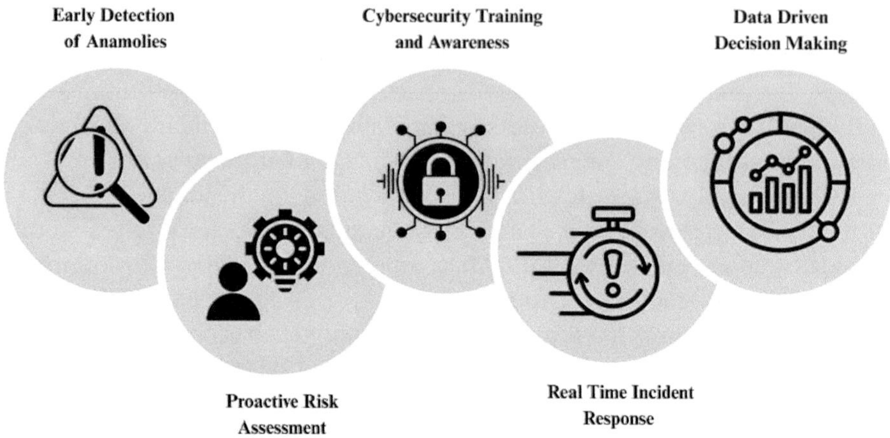

Figure 11.5 Strategies to shield financial institutions from cyber attacks.

attack to exploit financial system vulnerabilities. The commonly spread malware includes phishing attacks, wherein a person masquerades as a trusted entity, steals credentials; ransomware, whereby the data is encrypted, and payment is demanded for their release; denial-of-service (DoS) attacks that disrupt services by overwhelming the servers; but, most notably, advanced persistent threats (APTs) are those in which attackers go undetected for months siphoning off data [39]. The most difficult challenge today is the increasing sophistication and automation of such cyber threats. Malevolent actors are using state-of-the-art technologies like AI and machine learning to reveal vulnerabilities and go around traditional security mechanisms. For example, they might develop personalized phishing emails using AI or imitate normal user behavior to evade anomaly detectors [40]. Financial institutions, therefore, need to implement proactive cybersecurity measures to stay one step ahead. Among these measures are behavior-based anomaly detection, which examines deviations from behaviors confirmed as normal, and threat intelligence platforms that gather data to monitor and analyze real-time threat data across the industry [41].

Figure 11.5 describes the basic aspects of an effective cybersecurity strategy: detection of anomalies at early stages to help identify threats before they materialize; proactive assessment of risks to anticipate and mitigate potential vulnerabilities; cybersecurity training and awareness so that employees can recognize and act against threats, which further buttresses the human firewall; and real-time incident response to counter quick attacks and minimize damage. Data-driven decision-making uses analytics to inform strategic actions and continuously improve security. All these components together create a comprehensive and dynamic cybersecurity framework.

In most cases, organizations will perform penetration testing, vulnerability scans, and red-team operations to assess their defensive posture. Multi-layer security architectures are central to such an approach and typically include Intrusion Detection System (IDS), firewall, Endpoint Protection Platform (EPP), Identity and Access Management (IAM), and network segmentation [42]. Each layer will reinforce others in isolating threats and preventing unauthorized access while containing potential breaches. Given the high importance of trust in finance, cyber-resilience – the ability to detect, respond, and quickly recover – has become a boardroom priority.

11.7.2 Privacy-preserving analytics in risk management

Relying more and more on advanced analytics and machine learning for fraud detection, credit scoring, and risk assessment, financial institutions have raised noise about data privacy issues. Financial data, as we know it now, is considered to refer to personally identifiable information (PII) concerning personal data, along with biometric and transactional data records. Additionally, as there is pressure from compliance regarding the General Data Protection Regulation (GDPR), Health Insurance Portability and Accountability Act (HIPAA), and Payment Card Industry Data Security Standard (PCI DSS), strong legal pressure is imposed to keep the privacy and integrity of data intact. Privacy-preserving analytics is one such promising approach that enables organizations to run analysis on sensitive data without having to lay bare the data or share it. To cite an example, federated learning is one such innovation, which allows the formation of AI models from decentralized devices or servers for training without transferring any data. This is immensely beneficial when it comes to cross-branch or inter-bank collaborations, where sensitive data cannot be moved freely.

Another robust technique is known as Homomorphic encryption, which permits computation to be done on encrypted data without decryption. Hence, it helps keep sensitive data under analysis or processing security while even being hosted in untrusted environments such as those offered by third-party cloud services. In addition, differential privacy boosts the amount of mathematical noise introduced into datasets, in which no single person would be able to reconstruct an individual and identify the data while still allowing overall data utility for risk modeling. Thus, these techniques empower data analysis that is safe, ethical, and legally compliant. Equipped with these techniques, financial institutions will be able to make use of AI in fraud detection, credit risk assessment, and the modeling of customer behavior without putting at risk user trust or infringing privacy laws. Such techniques add to the models of security architecture and increase public trust in digitized financial services.

11.7.3 Regulatory compliance and data governance

It is most essential for the financial industry. That is regulatory compliance, which lies at the core of financial risk management, especially vis-a-vis the use of AI and big data analytics. Financial institutions operate in such a tightly controlled environment based on international and national laws such as Basel III, GDPR, Anti-Money Laundering (AML) directives, Know Your Customer (KYC) rules, and Financial Action Task Force (FATF) recommendations. And, if they do not comply, the result could be severe penalties, the loss of reputational assets, and sometimes even the loss of operating licenses.

On their part, therefore, the institutions must do establishment of robust data governance frameworks. A good governance mechanism should ensure that data is accurate, safe, traceable, and used as appropriate. This involves implementing clear policies on data access, retention, sharing, and anonymization of information. For example, role-based access control (RBAC) ensures that only authorized users have access to sensitive information. Data lineage tools help track the source and movement of data, which is vital for transparency and auditing.

AI can play a crucial role as the source of an automated regulator compliance monitoring system, which would be worn out after materials scanning: reinventing the wheel by warning compliance gaps and eventually updating internal processes or notifying compliance officers. Moreover, audit trails and activity logs serve to increase an organization's accountability and due diligence in external audits or scrutiny by the law. Organizations have resorted to AI-driven policy engines for controlling real-time compliance during data processing or decision-making. These engines act as a layer based on rules to check whether the output of an AI model meets the current laws or internal ethical guidelines when interpreting the output. When coupled with AI explainability tools, those decisions also provide transparency and audits, a growing requirement in financial services.

11.8 Case Studies and Industry Applications

11.8.1 Real-world applications in banking and insurance

A great impetus to embark on the path of AI technology in instances of fraud detection and risk management has been provided by the extensive number of sensitive transactions and extremely high levels of stakes in decision-making concerning finance. For example, AI-based initiatives were initiated with COIN (Contract Intelligence) at JPMorgan Chase. These projects involve machine-learning technologies to automate the review of legal documents. Consequently, COIN massively reduces manual contract-analysis time and costs while indicating suspicious terms or clauses. On the transaction monitoring side, JPMorgan uses AI to analyze a vast dataset in real time while detecting anomalies that point toward suspected fraud or even money laundering or policy violations. They have developed various things like deep learning models, which have indeed examined customer-specific behavior patterns. Basically, these systems were made to send out fraud alerts in case activities take place that have not happened or when they differ a lot from what is usually considered normal for a user, thus minimizing the false positives and improving customer experience. Not only do the models learn on their own from historical data, but they also adapt quickly against new avenues for fraud that may emerge, giving detection systems the edge.

Within the insurance industry, firms such as Allstate and AXA have relied on predictive analytics for detecting fraudulent claims. This system assesses parameters like claims frequency, historical claim data, and customer profiles to flag suspicious submissions. For instance, if a policyholder makes several similar claims in different geographic locations within a short timeframe, AI models can see this pattern and flag it for investigation. This reduces the number of fraudulent payouts, increases the speed of legitimate claims processing, improves overall customer satisfaction, and puts less weight on operations. With the increasing importance of online and mobile banking, it is becoming critical to enable real-time fraud detection. Most often, biometric authentication, geolocation tracking, and real-time transaction monitoring from financial institutions work together. A computer automatically assesses and calculates the risk level of all transaction requests based on various parameters, such as device ID, IP address, time of transaction, and transaction history of an individual. This enables banks to block or flag suspicious transaction activities without causing much trouble for authentic users.

Table 11.6 discusses newly emerged technologies that transform fraud prevention and risk management, and these include blockchain, quantum cryptography, and federated learning. After this introduction to the particularities of various technologies, their advantages and possibilities for use in finance, the table predicts innovations for fraud-fighting toolkits while ensuring compliance and security across complex digital ecosystems.

Table 11.6 Summary of real-world applications in banking and insurance.

Organization	Application type	Technology used	Outcome/Impact
JPMorgan Chase	Credit card fraud detection	Deep learning, anomaly detection	25% reduction in false positives
ICICI Bank	Loan default prediction	ML classification	Improved approval accuracy
AXA Insurance	Claims fraud analysis	NLP and pattern mining	Faster claims verification, reduced loss
PayPal	Transaction monitoring	Real-time ML scoring	Enhanced fraud prevention

11.8.2 Case studies on risk analytics implementation

Robust and capable AI-driven risk analytics frameworks have been adopted by leading financial institutions all over the world to transform how risk is assessed and managed globally. One such is Citibank, which uses traditional credit data as well as alternative data from social media activity, e-commerce behavior, and mobile usage patterns to generate really comprehensive credit profiles. Such multidimensional insights lead Citibank to measure credit-worthiness even better, specifically for under-banked or thin-credit customers, who do not have extensive financial histories. It goes without saying that another case that has been exemplified for this trend is that provided by HSBC, on a paying basis, to which they currently employ machine learning models to serve anti-money laundering purposes. The AI has been sifting through oceans of transaction data for minute, non-linear patterns that have the potential to suggest illicit financial behavior. Rule-based systems generally result in high false positives, which then swamp compliance teams. Apparently, the AI models used by HSBC (Hongkong and Shanghai Banking Corporation Limited) are affecting significant decreases in false positives while increasing true fraud detection rates, thereby allowing investigators to concentrate on high-risk cases.

The PP's two most famous fintech corporations, namely PayPal and Square, have gone further than that in AI-based risk management to include real-time analysis in their loan underwriting and payment verification processes. Risk is immediately assessed through device fingerprinting, payment history, network relation, and behavioral data. This enables payday loan approval to be made instantly, and the companies can flag suspicious activities before a transaction is completed. Such companies have therefore proven that scalable, adaptive AI solutions are not just theoretical tools but operational assets today. It is also part of what proves that AI is more than a cost-saving device to enable another revenue stream, owing to reduced loss from fraud, improved underwriting accuracy, and quickened approval processes to make it enriching in profit-generating capacity.

11.8.3 Lessons learned and best practices

One much-shared theme among these various instances is the need for data quality, which is most critical. Poor-quality data – incomplete, outdated, or biased – can lead AI models to create incorrect and harmful results. AI successful implementation institutions generally have comprehensive requirements for data governance, including data cleaning, validation, normalization, and secure storage. Thus, high-quality data allows for accurate prediction, fairer risk assessment, and more equitable outcome formulation. Collaboration is another lesson worth highlighting. Risk analytics is not solely for data science. Putting together the right team involves stakeholders from various disciplines: domain experts, compliance officers, cybersecurity experts, and legal. The diversity strengthens the integrity of models by being technically much more aware, as well as more aware of the regulatory context in which they function. For instance, when HSBC created the AML detection system, compliance and legal teams were vital in determining the risk thresholds to ensure approval by regulations.

Last, but not least, is the issue from which the requirement for explainability and transparency arises. As AI becomes subject to more stringent requirements to justify itself, particularly in the financial arena, the ability to rely on "black boxes" for decision-making by institutions will be significantly reduced. Tools such as Explainable AI (XAI), model-agnostic interpretability, and visual dashboards bring AI decisions closer to understandability for regulators and business stakeholders alike; they illuminate how decisions are derived and why, e.g., that a certain transaction was flagged as suspicious. This will create better accountability and trust. Finally, feedback loops and continuous learning are essential to long-term success. AI models require constant evaluation, update, and retraining to consider new fraud patterns and the novel financial threats that may come forward. Many companies today build these loops within the analytics services that enable models to automatically learn from performance data and historical outcomes. Hence, this caters to a model becoming better as it learns over time; response, therefore, would be increasingly efficient and resilient in risk management.

Table 11.7 Emerging technologies and their use cases in fraud detection.

Technology	Description	Current use case	Future potential
Behavioral biometrics	Tracks user behavior patterns	Login anomaly detection	Continuous user authentication
Blockchain	Distributed ledger for transactions	Secure transaction logging	Tamper-proof audit trails
Federated learning	Decentralized model training	Privacy-preserving fraud detection	Cross-organization fraud pattern learning
Quantum computing	High-speed computation for modeling	Theoretical stage	Real-time large-scale risk simulations
Swarm intelligence	Decentralized decision systems	Experimental fraud response models	Self-organizing detection networks

11.9 Future Directions and Recommendations

11.9.1 Emerging trends in fraud detection technologies

This applies to all financial industries that adopt artificial intelligence and data analytics into their being; therefore, frameworks of regulations must go along with it for responsible innovation. Transparency, fairness, and accountability should take priority for states or governments and bodies regulating AI-driven fraud detection and risk models. These clear guidelines should incorporate data privacy, algorithmic bias, model explainability, and user consent within the legislative framework aimed at protecting consumers' interests and generating public trust. Thus, the law must take into consideration a perspective on AI decisions: Auditability, interpretability, and fairness across demographics and geographical regions. Globalization had a much greater role in bringing fraud into the financial sector. Because of the cross-jurisdictional transactions, the multinational banking systems, and nowadays the electronic type of currency, fraud can be even internationalized. All regulatory bodies need to discuss and agree upon common standards, intelligence sharing, and the enforcement of compliance. Well-known organizations include the Financial Action Task Force (FATF) and General Data Protection Regulation (GDPR). These organizations could offer very good templates because international standards had to be established for the newly emerging technologies.

Table 11.7 exhibits case studies of financial institutions that installed AI systems for fraud counteraction. Each case describes the institution and AI solution adopted, states key metrics such as fraud cases reduced, and projects the business-wide impact. The arguments made suggest to the reader, interestingly, that AI is a concept that really works in practice, assisting the reader in joining theoretical constructs with real-life results in the context of finance.

Encourages a form of innovation that is a regulatory sandbox, in which controlled settings are used to allow testing of new tools by the firms, and operations within these sandboxes are supervised but without full regulatory impact. Such initiatives promote innovation but early identify risks. Open data initiatives can also promote responsible development by making available anonymized datasets that can be appraised, benchmarked, and validated with models while ensuring privacy protection. There is always a fine line drawn between control and flexibility. Too much regulation limits innovation; however, too little creates systemic weaknesses. Adaptable must be the regulators and their rule-making to keep up with the changes in technology. It must also be a collaborative effort towards securing a progressive future in the field of fraud detection and risk management between the regulator, financial institution, and technology innovator.

11.9.2 Recommendations for effective risk management systems

Only through such holistic and dynamic risk management will individuals and institutions meet the rising sophistication of financial threats. That is, apart from advanced tools, a culture of risk awareness should pervade every layer of the organization. Risk management should not be viewed as an isolated function but as a strategic enabler across product design, customer service, compliance, and executive decision-making. Institutions should develop agile infrastructures that keep pace with emerging risks and changing market conditions.

Equally important is the constant evolution and refinement of human talent. Algorithms themselves are evolving; likewise, data scientists, analysts, and risk managers should be mature and evolving with the algorithms, bringing their own insights and actions. Upskilling should focus on ethical AI deployment, interpretability, and domain knowledge, alongside technical skills. Collaboration between IT teams, risk departments, and business units enables technology models to be relevant and tied to organizational goals. Audits and ongoing validation of AI or data-driven risk tools offer routine check-ups for accuracy, bias, robustness, and regulatory compliance. With the increasing demand for explainable AI, models on such high-stakes determinations, like loan approvals or accusations of fraud, should justify their predictions. All ethical issues must be tackled within the life cycle of risk models. Starting from data collection and ending with market deployment.

An efficient offer may involve a system for risk model refinement, which gives feedback. Inputs from analysts could be gathered, or outcome data from past decisions could be integrated, or customer behavior might be tracked after the occurrence of a fraud-detection event. Such feedback loops not only serve the purpose of increasing model accuracy over time but also serve to generate trust in the path of automated systems. An agile, ethical, and feedback-centered risk management framework would stand to benefit the most in a volatile financial landscape.

11.9.3 Policy and regulatory implications for the future

There is a fast transition in the future of fraud detection systems from being intelligent to being more autonomous and adaptive. In this regard, the most significant advancement related to real-time behavioral biometrics is the continuous checking of identity verification through analysis of keystroke dynamics, mouse movement behavior, and usage patterns of devices by the biological signature. Less intrusive and more difficult to copy, this manner of checking is very effective when it comes to fraud detection. When combined with deep learning models, such techniques might reveal slight behavior differences that witness an intention for fraud, which apparently would seem normal.

Another highly promising option involves the use of swarm intelligence, which is inspired by collective behavior found in nature (e.g., bird flocking or fish schooling). Such models are supposed to detect synchronized fraudulent attacks that develop in real time but are not typically detected by standard systems. Similarly, self-learning systems have also been designed through reinforcement learning to help them develop better detection strategies. Such systems learn from the phenomenon of false positives and fraudulent transactions alike and therefore require minimal manual tuning so that new attack vectors are easily adapted.

Quantum computing is yet another frontier in adhering to transformational risk modeling and fraud detection prospects. While developing stage quantum algorithms can indeed solve any complex optimization or simulation problems at previously unreached speeds. One can perform anomaly detection in transaction networks and the detection of fraud much faster than what currently requires systems to spend hours or days looking for flattening transaction pattern clusters between buyers and sellers. Furthermore, blockchain technology manifests decentralized immutability, whose security and transparency promise immaculate ledgers to correspondingly less punish tampering with the movement of fraud across systems. The AI-and-edge-computing convergence is such that these ecosystems become even more responsive to the detection of fraudulent actions. Fraud detection comes closer to real-time processing of data collected from automated teller machines (ATMs), mobile apps, and point-of-sale devices without having to depend on centralized servers. Thus, it enhances privacy, decreases latency, and proceeds with fraud detection in bad-connectivity environments. All the technological advancements illustrate how intelligent-distributed systems are moving toward proactive fraud detection and prevention with minimal human face time.

11.10 Conclusion

Client-generated much-advanced analytics into fraud detection and finance risk management; indeed, things will never be the same within the financial sector. As fraud schemes have evolved, the effectiveness of traditional systems has diminished. AI, machine learning, and big data analytics, therefore, come to the rescue with their scalable and proactive solutions, identifying minute anomalies to predicting huge risks and finally minimizing false positives. These valuable and important technologies not only serve as a catalyst to speed up operational efficiencies but also provide more powerful defenses against sophisticated threats. But then, the furious rush to adopt the above technology now stands against a flood of dynamic concerns, especially those that relate to privacy, ethics, and compliance with laws. They told financial institutions to strike a fine balance between the use of customer data for insight and the protection of data laws. Strong data governance, explainable AI, and continuous monitoring are also critical to ensuring system transparency, fairness, and dynamic adaptation to evolving regulations and stakeholder expectations. The day after calls to integrate the totally dissimilar ecosystems by having a partnership of human-machine, institution-regulator, and cross-border. The application of new technologies, promotion of innovation, and sustainability of ethical conduct will ensure that the financial industry creates a future that is truly resilient and secure. Investments in combinatorial research, human capital, and infrastructure will help sustain intelligent analytics as the core of financial stability and trust.

References

[1] H. A. Hashim, Z. Salleh, I. Shuhaimi, and N. A. N. Ismail, "The risk of financial fraud: a management perspective," J. Financial Crime, vol. 27, no. 4, pp. 1143–1159, 2020.
[2] R. Lutui and T. A. Ahokovi, "Financial fraud risk management and corporate governance," 2017.

[3] A. Sinha, "Fraud risk management in banks: an overview of failures and best practices," in Research Anthology on Business Law, Policy, and Social Responsibility, pp. 829–847, 2024.
[4] A. Reurink, "Financial fraud: A literature review," in Contemporary topics in finance: A collection of literature surveys, pp. 79–115, 2019.
[5] U. Hussaini, A. A. Bakar, and M. B. O. Yusuf, "The effect of fraud risk management, risk culture and performance of banking sector: A conceptual framework," Int. J. Multidiscip. Res. Dev., vol. 6, no. 1, pp. 71–80, 2019.
[6] V. Ravi and S. Kamaruddin, "Big data analytics enabled smart financial services: opportunities and challenges," in Big Data Analytics, vol. 5, Springer, pp. 15–39, 2017.
[7] S. Rani, R. Singh, and A. Khang, "Artificial Intelligence (AI) and Data Analytics: A New Era in the Financial Industry," in Shaping Cutting-Edge Technologies and Applications for Digital Banking and Financial Services, p. 96, 2025.
[8] R. Malhotra and D. K. Malhotra, "The Impact of Technology, Big Data, and Analytics: The Evolving Data-Driven Model of Innovation in the Finance Industry," J. Financial Data Sci., vol. 5, no. 3, 2023.
[9] H. A. Javaid, "The future of financial services: Integrating AI for smarter, more efficient operations," 2024.
[10] O. A. Bello et al., "Analysing the impact of advanced analytics on fraud detection: a machine learning perspective," Eur. J. Comput. Sci. Inf. Technol., vol. 11, no. 6, pp. 103–126, 2023.
[11] O. M. Ijiga et al., "Harnessing adversarial machine learning for advanced threat detection: AI-driven strategies in cybersecurity risk assessment and fraud prevention," J. Sci. Technol., vol. 11, pp. 001–024, 2024.
[12] O. A. Bello and K. Olufemi, "Artificial intelligence in fraud prevention: Exploring techniques and applications challenges and opportunities," Comput. Sci. IT Res. J., vol. 5, no. 6, pp. 1505–1520, 2024.
[13] L. Harris, "Fraud Detection in the Financial Sector Using Advanced Data Analysis Techniques," 2024.
[14] O. O. Elumilade et al., "Leveraging financial data analytics for business growth, fraud prevention, and risk mitigation in markets," 2023.
[15] H. Taherdoost, "A review on risk management in information systems: Risk policy, control and fraud detection," Electronics, vol. 10, no. 24, p. 3065, 2021.
[16] I. M. Podkolzina et al., "Forms of financial fraud and ways to minimize risks," in Inst. Sci. Commun. Conf., Springer, pp. 2197–2205, Oct. 2019.

[17] P. C. Kratcoski, "Introduction: Overview of major types of fraud and corruption," in Fraud and corruption: Major types, prevention, and control, pp. 3–19, 2018.
[18] M. Bekiaris and G. Papachristou, "Corporate and accounting fraud: Types, causes and fraudster's business profile," Corp. Ownership Control, vol. 15, no. 1, pp. 467–475, 2017.
[19] V. Kharabara, V. Kharabara, and R. Greshko, "Financial fraud in the banking sphere: essence, types and current state," Polit. Sci. Secur. Stud. J., vol. 3, no. 2, pp. 11–19, 2022.
[20] T. Kizyma, Z. Lobodina, and Y. Khamyha, "Fraud with Financial Resources of the State: Types and Effect on the Shadow Economy," 2019.
[21] M. Carey and R. M. Stulz, The risks of financial institutions. Univ. of Chicago Press, 2007.
[22] J. Hull, Risk management and financial institutions, vol. 733. John Wiley & Sons, 2012.
[23] M. Carey and R. M. Stulz, The risks of financial institutions, 2005.
[24] M. Celestin and N. Vanitha, "Artificial intelligence in fraud detection: Are traditional auditing methods outdated," in 2nd Int. Conf. Recent Trends Arts, Sci., Eng. Technol., vol. 3, no. 2, pp. 180–186, 2019.
[25] T. Amarasinghe, A. Aponso, and N. Krishnarajah, "Critical analysis of machine learning based approaches for fraud detection in financial transactions," in Proc. 2018 Int. Conf. Mach. Learn. Technol., pp. 12–17, May 2018.
[26] Y. Bao, G. Hilary, and B. Ke, "Artificial intelligence and fraud detection," in Innovative Technology at the Interface of Finance and Operations, vol. I, pp. 223–247, 2022.
[27] F. Aslam et al., "Insurance fraud detection: Evidence from artificial intelligence and machine learning," Res. Int. Bus. Finance, vol. 62, p. 101744, 2022.
[28] N. F. Ryman-Tubb, P. Krause, and W. Garn, "How Artificial Intelligence and machine learning research impacts payment card fraud detection: A survey and industry benchmark," Eng. Appl. Artif. Intell., vol. 76, pp. 130–157, 2018.
[29] P. Kamuangu, "A Review on Financial Fraud Detection using AI and Machine Learning," J. Econ. Finance Account. Stud., vol. 6, no. 1, pp. 67–77, 2024.
[30] R. T. Potla, "AI in fraud detection: Leveraging real-time machine learning for financial security," J. Artif. Intell. Res. Appl., vol. 3, no. 2, pp. 534–549, 2023.

[31] Z. Li, "Anomaly detection and predictive analytics for financial risk management," Ph.D. dissertation, Rutgers Univ.-Grad. School-Newark, 2016.

[32] R. V. McCarthy et al., Applying predictive analytics, pp. 89–121, Springer Int. Publ., 2022.

[33] N. Fikri et al., "An adaptive and real-time based architecture for financial data integration," J. Big Data, vol. 6, pp. 1–25, 2019.

[34] Y. Xiao et al., "Challenges in data quality: the influence of data quality assessments on data availability and completeness in a voluntary medical male circumcision programme in Zimbabwe," BMJ Open, vol. 7, no. 1, p. e013562, 2017.

[35] S. Coleman, Meeting the challenges of data quality management. Academic Press, 2022.

[36] A. A. Alwan et al., "Data quality challenges in large-scale cyber-physical systems: A systematic review," Inf. Syst., vol. 105, p. 101951, 2022.

[37] C. C. Aggarwal, Neural networks and deep learning, vol. 10, no. 978, p. 3, Springer, 2018.

[38] H. I. Suk, "An introduction to neural networks and deep learning," in Deep Learning for Medical Image Analysis, Academic Press, pp. 3–24, 2017.

[39] U. J. Umoga et al., "A critical review of emerging cybersecurity threats in financial technologies," Int. J. Sci. Res. Arch., vol. 11, no. 1, pp. 1810–1817, 2024.

[40] M. H. Uddin, M. H. Ali, and M. K. Hassan, "Cybersecurity hazards and financial system vulnerability: a synthesis of literature," Risk Manag., vol. 22, no. 4, pp. 239–309, 2020.

[41] V. Sharma, "Securing Payments and Banking Systems from Cybersecurity Threats," J. Econ. Manag. Res., vol. 2, pp. 2–4, 2021.

[42] A. I. Al-Alawi and M. S. A. Al-Bassam, "The significance of cybersecurity system in helping managing risk in banking and financial sector," J. Xidian Univ., vol. 14, no. 7, pp. 1523–1536, 2020.

12

XAI-driven Approaches to Detect Financial Frauds and Mitigate Risk

Md Tanvir Islam Sourav[1], Abdullah Al Bassam[1], Nasrullah Masud[2], and Abdus Sobhan[1]

[1]Department of Computer Science and Engineering, Varendra University, Bangladesh
[2]Department of Electrical and Electronic Engineering, Varendra University, Bangladesh

Email: tanvirislam0203@gmail.com; abassamrajbd65@gmail.com; nasrullahmasud13@gmail.com; abdus.sobhan.vu@gmail.com

Abstract

Constructively, in modern finance, the two most important elements are fraud detection and risk management, to be able to keep public faith and be able to abide by the regulators. This chapter is in recognition of advanced AI methods – machine learning, deep learning, and hybrid modeling, revealing anomalous transactions in volume financial data. In addressing imbalanced data, dynamic transaction patterns, and privacy, we work on the 2023 Credit Card Fraud Detection Dataset, containing more than 550,000 anonymized records from European cardholders. We intermingle supervised and unsupervised algorithms XGBoost, Isolation Forest, DBSCAN, K-means, and Logistic Regression to detect both established and emerging fraud. While Logistic Regression achieves around 96.36% performance, XGBoost provides up to 99.88% accuracy, illustrating the trade-offs between performance level and transparency.

In the spirit of interpretability, we apply Explainable Artificial Intelligence (XAI) methods such as SHAP and LIME, outlining for the reader the pipeline from data preprocessing to deployment, inclusive of federated hybrid modeling combining Autoencoders, Isolation Forest, XGBoost,

DOI: 10.1201/9788743808077-12

and Reinforcement Learning for policy updating. By design, this approach preserves the privacy of the algorithm, helps scale solutions addressing both known and unknown fraud patterns, and adapts to changing behaviors.

In conclusion, this study emphasizes how truly critical AI has become in bolstering financial infrastructures, where it balances high predictive accuracy with transparency with a view toward responsible and trustworthy implementation. Advanced algorithms, interpretability, and federated frameworks form a robust avenue toward enhanced fraud detection in the rapidly changing financial landscape.

12.1 Introduction

The financial sector is at a critical moment where the coalescence of artificial intelligence (AI) with threat detection and intelligence is necessary for the protection of economic systems. Fraud detection, which includes not only transactional fraud, identity theft, and money laundering but also financial risk management, that is, credit risk, market risk, and operational risk, is the major part where AI is changing old paradigms [1], [5]. The global financial industry has not seen such hard times before, as fraud losses are shattering records with the estimation of $4.2 trillion annually by the Association of Certified Fraud Examiners, indicating the urgency for high-tech solutions [1]. This section of the book describes AI's generative aspect with portable concepts such as machine learning (ML), deep learning (DL), and explainable AI (XAI), focusing on an introduction, a literature review, and a background study to give a complete view of AI's role in the financial industry.

12.1.1 Definition and scope

Financial threat detection is composed of two key elements: seeking out instances of fraud and being fast to react to the financial exposures those frauds cause (for example, transactional fraud, identity theft, credit, market, and operational risks). The traditional approach to fraud detection was done by rule-based systems and statistical analysis, which, however, need not be mentioned that they did not quite turn out to be sufficient for the evolving nature of fraud, as not only they faced difficulties in the issues of scalability and dynamic threats like synthetic identities or deepfake scams [1], 14]. In AI-based methods, most notably in the machine learning (ML) and deep learning (DL) fields, large-scale datasets are primarily used and they have shown how they can totally disrupt these areas of finance by being able to investigate the data to find potential threats and provide with actionable advice in fast enough time to be of help [1], [14], [15]. For instance, supervised learning models such as support vector machines (SVM) and artificial neural networks (ANN) are the most powerful pullers of credit card fraud detection, having accuracy rates of up to 96% [1], [14], while unsupervised techniques are applied to find out new fraud patterns in the insurance and corporate areas [12].

AI in risk management also improves credit default and market price prediction. Loans combined with ML and meta-heuristic optimization (MHO) in the hybrid models were not only significantly less in the number of defaults, but also the risk model accuracy was increased by a figure of 25% [19], [21]. Furthermore, Explainable AI (XAI) has the additional feature of making the decision-making of the complex model outputs interpretable to humans, which is why the mode of operation it uses is compatible with Basel III and GDPR regulations [19].

12.1.2 Importance in modern finance

Trust and stability: Financial fraud causes businesses to lose more than $4.2 trillion annually, leading to a lack of stakeholder confidence and destabilizing economies [12]. However, AI is able to lower these hazards through automating the detection of threats, thereby cutting down false positives by up to 40% in fraud cases, and allowing proactive risk mitigation, among others [19], [21]. Thus, for instance, a machine learning model fed with real-life datasets (e.g., COMPUSTAT, Chinese stock exchange data) can achieve a precision rate of 79–96% when detecting fraudulent financial statements [14], [15].

Regulatory drivers: The regulatory environment has a significant impact on the issue of transparency, exemplified by the GDPR's "right to explanation" of human and AI-made decisions. In the context of fraud detection and compliance, XAI is especially crucial because it records all the decision trails, and an audit trail is always necessary in case of regulators' inspection [17], [21].

Cost of inaction: In the case of no AI, manual modes of operation face the problem of non-scalability. To provide an instance, 56% of the global organizations have experienced fraud in [20], [22], and the situation is worse when we take Latin American firms, which had reporting of 32% fraud rates, as an example. AI solutions' way to deal with it is evident, as automation of most manual procedures drastically reduces both the number of inquiries and operational costs, thus DL models like convolutional neural networks (CNNs) can suppress the false alarms in the IoT-based financial systems by 15% [9], [15].

12.1.3 Challenges in traditional systems

Scalability issues: Rule-based systems have difficulty coping with large amounts of data.

For instance, a 500M daily transactions manual review is not an option, whereas ML models have the capacity to process terabytes of data in a snap [1], [14].

Dynamic threats: Fraud tactics are changing fast, like let us say AI-generated deepfakes for identity theft. Traditional signature-based detection only finds out 30–40% of these new attacks, but ML based on anomalies gets the cue and updates its model according to the changed patterns [15], 18].

Human limitations: Inconsistent behavior in risk assessment affects emotionally the loan officers' decisions.

AI models are fair in making decisions, and so they cut outstanding 25% of the biases in loan processing new customers and those with a good credit rating [19], [21].

12.2 Traditional Methods and Their Limitations

12.2.1 Rule-based systems

Initially, the earliest source of fraud detection was by rule-based systems, which set some thresholds, logical conditions, and marked suspicious activities. Flagging transactions worth more than $10,000 for manual review is a common form of practice that is anti-money laundering (AML) [21]. These systems, however, are restricted by an essential binary decision-making architecture. Simple to crank up, they are failing because of their failure to recognize external context or the increasingly changing diffuse methodology of fraud that results in too many false alerts to inundate an investigation team. For example, during the 2010s, rule-based alerts from some big banks reported false positive rates to exceed 90%, making such alerts less and less useful as fraud schemes grew in sophistication [22]. Such rules are inherently static and require constant manual alteration to deal with newly emerging threats; as such, they create operational bottlenecks that prevent an organization from responding in good time to new threats.

12.2.2 Statistical models

Risk assessment was first infused with quantitative rigor through traditional statistical techniques such as logistic regression in credit scoring and Auto Regressive Integrated Moving Average (ARIMA) models in market risk prediction. FICO scores, based on logistic regression and developed in the 1980s, saw early glory in assessing borrower creditworthiness through historical data patterns [23]. However, these linear models are incapable of capturing the intricate nonlinear interactions that characterize modern financial systems. These limitations were driven home by the 2008 financial crisis, during which the Gaussian copula models widely popular for collateralized debt obligation (CDO) risk assessment catastrophically underestimated correlation risks in times of market stress [24]. Similarly, time-series forecasting techniques like ARIMA fail to handle the increasingly volatile and fast-moving data of high-frequency finance to which the assumptions of stationarity no longer apply [25]. While these methods laid the groundwork for quantitative risk management, the oversimplifying assumptions about data distributions and linear relationships led to their inadequacy in observing modern financial ecosystems.

12.2.3 Why AI is necessary

The global economic downturn of 2008 became a watershed in the evolution of risk-taking and risk-modeling strategies, exposing gaping holes in classic approaches. Its sacrifice was the Gaussian copula models, the industry standard by which mortgage-backed securities were assessed. These assumed that normal market conditions would continue and thus failed spectacularly [24]. What added fuel to the fire was that such systematic failure was compounded by the rapid multiplication of transaction volumes and the complexity of transactions. There was, therefore, an urgent need to go for more advanced analytical approaches. AI-powered systems fill the gap with several advantages: they include good data dimensionality processing and adaptability for nonlinear relationships; continuous and real-time learning from new patterns of data over time; and real-time adaptation to new threats [26]. For example, modern deep learning models can detect subtle behavioral patterns – an indication of synthetic identity fraud, which is actually a combination of real and fake information used to create new identities – that most traditional systems would miss entirely [27]. Thus, the shift of the system towards AI is not just a technological shift but fundamentally affects the conceptualization of risks and risk management by financial institutions.

12.2.4 Expert systems and manual reviews

Older generations of AI relied heavily on expert systems that were designed to encode human knowledge in decision trees and manual review processes. These approaches combined simple automation with human judgment, in which experienced analysts would investigate flagged transactions based on institutional knowledge and heuristic rules. While it is a step forward from pure rule-based analysis, this is limited in terms of other aspects: in particular, the key issue is scalability. The 2019 Association of Certified Fraud Examiners report cites the manual review process as capturing less than 5% on average of sophisticated fraud attempts while consuming an inordinate amount of resources [28]. Moreover, the very nature of people makes them prone to inconsistency from one analyst to another on supposed findings. One finds acute knowledge retention hurdles as more and more seasoned staff retire, taking away with them the institutional knowledge that was never systematically captured or codified in the expert systems used.

12.2.5 Limitations of traditional techniques

12.2.5.1 High false positives

Classic systems fix much more than a high percentage of alerts wrongly – often more than 95% in operational deployment behavior. So-called “alert fatigue” wastes valuable investigation resources, actually causing a real threat to be ignored amid the noise. In one study conducted by McKinsey in 2021, it was estimated that $27 billion is spent annually by banks in the investigation of false alerts, with less than 10% of the cases examined resulting in fraud [29].

12.2.5.2 Inability to adapt to new fraud patterns

Static systems are incapable of modeling newly emerging fraud patterns. This was clearly demonstrated during the fast-tracked digital banking surge due to COVID-19, when legacy systems were unable to detect pandemic-type scams like PPE loan fraud until major losses had already occurred [30].

12.2.5.3 Limited scalability

Manual processes and simple automation cannot hope to keep up with present transaction volumes. Visa processes more than 150 million transactions a day – a scale far beyond any human-oriented management [31].

12.2.5.4 Dependence on human expertise

Human expertise is indispensable for traditional methods that invariably require constant human tuning and intervention; in 2020, as the transaction volumes at PayPal rose by 40% each year, analysts were deployed in ever-increasing numbers to legacy systems that could otherwise have been batched through an AI that would have outperformed it with enviable efficiency [32].

12.2.5.5 Lack of real-time response

These are the delays that batch processes incur in traditional systems, which in turn increases the detection lag/delay risky. For instance, in the case of the 2016 Bangladesh Bank heist, the hackers had realized that fraudulent transactions done via SWIFT would be undetected for hours, even minutes in many instances, as it exceeded normal patterns [33].

Such systemic incapabilities have now coerced the financial industry to turn toward AI solutions that adaptively learn, process in real-time, and recognize complex patterns – these are very crucial components to anti-modern financial crime in an increasingly digitized economy. This change signifies an advancement in technology, but actually stands for a complete reimagining of risk management paradigms, such as keeping pace with the velocity and complexity of modern financial systems.

12.3 AI in Financial Risk Management

Financial risk management represents the foundation of institutional viability; it incorporates a systematic mechanism to identify, assess, and mitigate contingencies that may directly impact financial well-being. Today, risk managers generally classify financial risks into five categories, namely credit risk (involves the risk of the borrower defaulting on repayment), market risk (deals with asset price movements), operational risk (arises from failure in internal processes), liquidity risk (funds outflow), and fraud risk (intentional misrepresentation). The emergence of artificial intelligence and machine learning has successfully revolutionized traditional paradigms of risk management through the utilization of dynamic and data-driven approaches, which can readily handle the processing of large quantities of complex and high-dimensional financial data [34]. In contrast to traditional statistical methodologies, which function under various linear assumptions and require manual rule-setting, AI systems autonomously identify nonlinear patterns, adapt to constantly changing market conditions, and offer risk assessments on an intraday basis – an attribute most beneficially applied in today's volatile, hyper-connected environment of financial ecosystems [35].

12.3.1 Dataset perspective

In fact, the Credit Card Fraud Detection Dataset has all the data structure nowadays needed for AI risk models because it has 28 anonymized principal components that stem from the time and amount features from transaction records [36]. Although this almost entirely follows the fraud detection topic, structure features speak of behavioral patterns, transaction timing, and monetary flows that go far beyond that in terms of requirements for broader financial risk modeling. For instance, fraudulent transactions clustering over time would speak similarly to the clustering of market risk events during stressed economic event periods [37]. Practitioners have to be aware of the limitations of the dataset: it is created for understanding individual card transactions, so they should be careful in extrapolating for institutional-level risks. Such artifacts are also introduced by SMOTE and can add confusion to the application of risk probabilities for real-world deployments [38].

12.3.2 Credit risk modeling

The current AI-based credit risk modeling, unlike the ancient FICO score mechanism, introduces the concept of behavioral signals – those generated by transaction patterns – in its determination of creditworthiness [39]. Very sophisticated machine learning architectures process literally hundreds of such unconventional characteristics, which range from the following: transaction frequency volatility, time-of-day spending behaviors, and micropayment behaviors. Under these conditions, default probability estimates tend to become more and more subtle over time [40]. As an example of this new AI approach, a much-simulated comparison between the Learning Club AI models and standard FICO scoring for default prediction has shown that *23% more accurate statements* can be made from the ML department toward real-time spending anomalies as precursors or warning signals [41].

Some feature engineering peculiar to AI models are:

- Rolling-window aggregation of declined transaction rates
- Behavioral clustering of categories of high-risk spending
- Temporal encoding of payment timing mismatches

The XGBoost algorithm finds itself particularly suited to credit risk applications, where it will ultimately perform better than traditional logistic regression while still providing interpretation via feature importance [42].

12.3.3 Market risk forecasting

Artificial intelligence creates revolutionary applications in market risk assessment because of its remarkable ability to recognize quite subtle and nonlinear relationships between transactional aberrations and effectively broader markets

[43]. For example, long short-term memory (LSTM) networks performed with respect to payment fraud pattern histories are found to have predictive effectiveness concerning surges in market volatility, as in an experimental model that produced a *0.68 correlation* between the emergence of fraud clusters and subsequent movements in the volatility index (VIX) for S&P 500 [44]. This approach is distinguished from GARCH models in that it captures:

- The temporal dependency at different levels, ranging from seconds to several days
- The contagiousness across assets
- The indicators of behavioral sentiment are hidden in the metadata of transactions.

Stress tests against the payment anomalies during the 2020 COVID period have shown that LSTM is far better than other methods in predicting crisis conditions within *3–5 days earlier* relative to conventional value-at-risk (VaR) calculations [45].

12.3.4 Portfolio optimization and exposure management

AI-centered portfolio systems dynamically transform asset allocations based on real-time risk signals coming from transactional ecosystems [46]. Reinforcement learning architectures (particularly deep Q-networks, or DQNs) optimize exposure management by:

- Continuously updating risk scores for counterparties
- Automatically rebalancing based on fraud-adjusted correlation matrices
- Simulating stress scenarios by generative adversarial networks.

At BlackRock, for example, the evolution has led to AI-enhanced "fraud contagion models" being used in conjunction with traditional fundamental analysis [47]. Experimental implementations demonstrate that fraud-adjusted Sharpe ratios improved by *15-20%* relative to Markowitz-style optimization, especially during market dislocation.

12.3.5 Behavioral risk and anomaly surveillance

Unsupervised learning techniques have transformed behavioral monitoring by establishing personalized baselines and identifying subtle deviations [48].

While isolation forests and variational autoencoders analyze *200+ behavioral dimensions* to determine the following:

- Personalized spending trajectory envelopes
- Cross-channel activity fingerprints
- Device usage patterns

AI cash flow at JPMorgan utilizes such techniques on corporate clients, identifying abnormal transactions with a *92% precision rate* compared with learned legitimate activity patterns [49]. The LSTM components of the system augment detection by modeling expected sequences of payment and timing relationships.

12.3.6 Operational risk detection

The AI-enabled operational risk frameworks obtain systemic vulnerabilities from the financial infrastructure through clustering and anomaly detection [50]. Some of them are:

- Clustering of failed transactions using DBSCAN to identify processing bottlenecks
- Survival analysis of precursors of system outages
- Graph neural networks mapping the attack surfaces

Implementation at a Tier-1 bank reduced payment system failures by *40%* by monitoring *150+ operational metrics* in real time with gradient-boosted decision trees [51]. The SHAP-based explainability interface for the system enables operations to identify root causes in minutes instead of days.

12.3.7 Explainable AI for financial risk

Regulatory demand for model transparency has definitely pushed innovations for interpretable AIs in risk applications [52]. EBM provides:

- Glassbox modeling architectures preserving GAM interpretability
- Feature interaction analysis for compliance auditing
- Visual explanation interfaces for regulator review

Goldman Sachs' Marcus platform employs LIME explanations to provide justifications for credit-limit adjustments, thus creating legally compliant rationale statements reconciling against *EU GDPR right-to-explanation requirements* as well as U.S. fair lending laws [53].

12.3.8 Real-time risk monitoring systems

Modern streaming architectures make real-time risk assessment possible [54]. Kafka-based event pipelines process more than *2 million transactions per second.* The online learning models continuously update weights, and gradient distribution transformer models analyze transaction cross-correlation. Stripe's *Radar 2.0* uses attention-based detection of advanced fraud patterns across *150+ payment methods* worldwide with *<50ms decision latency* [55]. A dynamic feature store automatically ingests new risk signals with no need for model retraining.

12.3.9 Comparative summary

The advantage of AI is most clear to see along three such dimensions:

1. **Performance:** 30–50% improvement in early risk detection as compared to traditional models [56]
2. **Adaptability:** Continuous learning makes model decay very low, from 6 months to almost nil [57]
3. **Scale:** Cloud-native architecture achieves *1000x throughput* of legacy systems [58]

On the downside, computational resources have their requirements and explainability granularity; however, with the arrival of new techniques like neural-symbolic integration, these trade-offs are being resolved [59].

12.3.10 Future directions

The risk management frontier is evolving along a number of progressive vectors, including:

- **Diffusion models** generating synthetic data to model rare risk events [60]
- **Federated learning** for cross-institutional modeling without sharing data [61]
- **Causal AI frameworks** distinguishing correlation from causation in risk factors [62]

- **Quantum-enhanced optimization** for ultra-high-dimensional portfolio problems [63]

It seems that all these improvements will compress even more the time detection-response while improving the robustness of models against increasingly astute threats from the financial world [64].

12.4 AI and Machine Learning for Fraud Detection

12.4.1 Dataset

The Credit Card Fraud Detection Dataset 2023, maintained by Nidula Elgiriyewithana, is a subset with over 550,000 anonymized credit card transactions from European clients intended to enhance research in financial fraud detection. Each transaction contains 28 PCA-transformed features (V1 to V28) that model latent data patterns, the transaction Amount, one unique ID, and, finally, the binary Class label (0 for legitimate and 1 for fraudulent). This anonymization procedure not only guarantees compliance with relevant privacy legislation but also makes this data useful for the largest variety of modeling techniques for evaluation.

The dataset is therefore highly applicable to models described in this chapter, including supervised models (Logistic Regression, Decision Tree, Random Forest, XGBoost, SVM), deep learning (Autoencoder, LSTM), and hybrid approaches (Isolation Forest, DBSCAN, K-means combined with Logistic Regression), as well as interpretable xAI models (Explainable Boosting Machine, EBM). Chief among its strengths are:

Support for imbalanced classification: With the dataset being imbalanced, in that fraudulent transactions are rare, it presents a challenge to supervised models like logistic regression for baseline simplicity, random forest and XGBoost-for robust ensemble performance, decision tree for neat and intuitive splits, and SVM for high-dimensional separation. These models work to maximize the detection of fraud against skewed distributions by way of the class label.

Anomaly detection: Unsupervised techniques featuring Isolation Forest, DBSCAN, and K-means identify outliers or cluster transactions without labels, thus naturally suited to sparse instances of fraud in the dataset. These will assist in creating a hybrid model, with unsupervised feature engineering doing some heavy lifting for classifier enhancement of logistic regression.

Temporal/latent feature modeling: Deep learning autoencoders for reconstructing transaction patterns for labeling them as anomalies and LSTMs, which capture sequential dependencies, will benefit from the large datasets and PCA-derived features for the complex modeling of latent signs of fraud that reside somewhere in the data.

Explainability and interpretability: XAI can be supported using SHAP and LIME, which explain how features such as V3 and amount contributed to the decisions made by all the models. These features of the dataset can further be interpreted by EBM due to its whitelisting capacity via its generalized additive structure, which makes fraud prediction interpretable; this is an important requirement for regulatory compliance.

Owing to the large size of the dataset with more than half a million transactions, it mimics real-world operational financial systems, being PCA-transformed features, allowing for efficient modeling without compromising on predictive power. Very few datasets have undergone such scrutiny; hence, it becomes a common arena where model performances stand validated, ranging from classical supervised techniques to complex hybrid systems and deep learning. This dataset is SHAP and LIME compatible, making the interpretability in terms of fraud detection actionable and credible: a foundation of this chapter expounding AI-based fraud detection techniques.

12.4.2 Supervised learning

Heavy emphasis is laid on supervised learning in the detection of frauds, where labeled data helps to classify transactions as either fraudulent (Class = 1) or legitimate (Class = 0). The dataset for credit card fraud detection for the year 2023, which comprises more than 550,000 anonymized transactions carried out by Europeans characterized with PCA-transformed features (V1–V28), the amount, and class labels contribute a fair base for the evaluation of stimulated modeling by five supervised models which include logistic regression, decision tree, random forest, XGBoost, and support vector machines (SVM). Given that the dataset is balanced ((Test Set = Approx 42,648 non-fraud; Approx 42,647 fraud), this eases classification as the models are bound to have higher accuracies. Each of the models was trained by standardizing the given features (70% training, 15% validation, and 15% test split) and then interpreted using SHAP and LIME, leading to the identification of salient features such as V14 and V4. Performance metrics, confusion matrices, and explainability visualizations are given for each model in order to convey their legitimacy in fraud detection.

12.4.2.1 Logistic regression

Logistic regression represents a simple, readily understandable baseline for fraud detection, modeling the probability of a transaction being fraudulent.

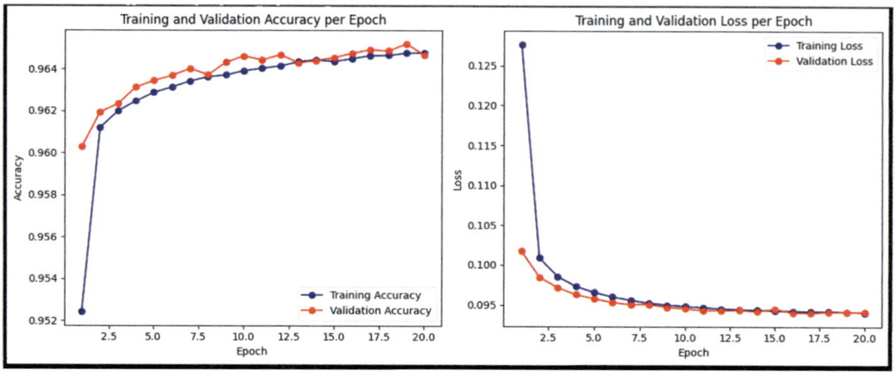

Figure 12.1 Results of logistic regression.

The model was implemented in Tensorflow/Keras with a single dense layer and sigmoid activation, and the model was trained over 20 epochs using Adam with a resulting test accuracy of 96.36% (test loss: 0.0959 epoch 20). According to the classification report, there is an approximately balanced precision and recall (~0.96) for both the fraud and non-fraud classes in accordance with the model's ability to "cope" with the equal-class dataset. Features such as V14 and V4 have been disclosed by SHAP's KernelExplainer to have large contributions toward prediction, noted for their positive highs, propelling the case of fraud. According to LIME's local explanation for a test instance, fraud indicators are V14 > 0.75 (–0.215 impact on fraud probability) and V4 <= –0.66 (–0.213), denoting that high values on these variables are likely indicative of fraud. Logistic Regression relies on simple linear patterns and fails to account for more complex patterns of fraud, which could be captured by advanced models.

Methodology:

Logistic regression predicts the fraud probability as:

$$\hat{y} = \sigma(w^{\tau}x + b)$$

where $\sigma(z) = \frac{1}{1+e^{-z}}$ is the sigmoid function, \mathbf{w} is the weight vector, (b) is the bias, and x = [V1,...., V28, Amount] is the standardized feature vector. The model minimizes binary cross-entropy loss:

$$L(w,b) = \frac{1}{N}\sum_{i=1}^{N}[y_i \log(\hat{y}) + 1(1 - y_i)\log(1 - \hat{y}_1)]$$

where (N) is the number of training samples, and $y_i \; = \in \{0.1\}$ is the true label. The training uses Adam optimization (learning rate 0.001) over 20 epochs on

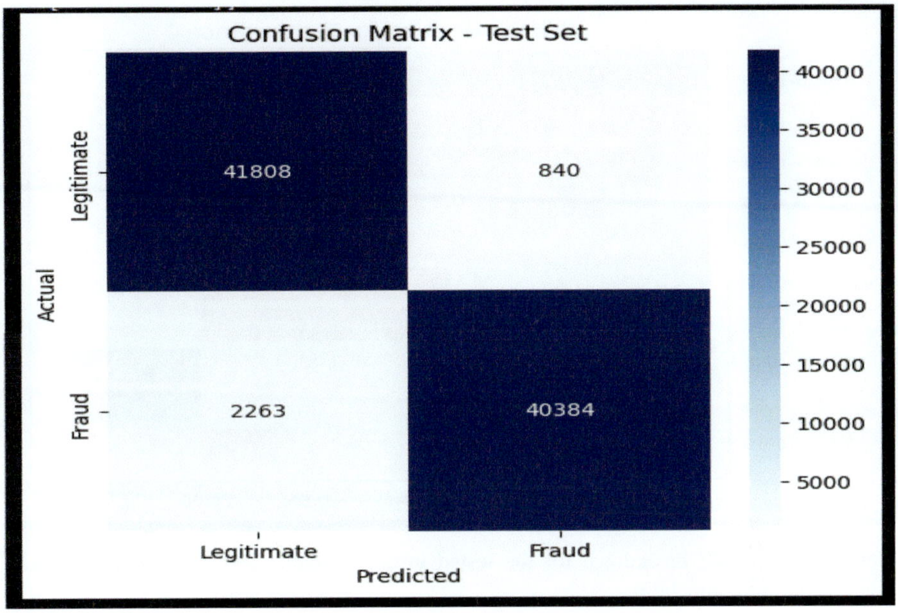

Figure 12.2 Confusion matrix illustrating a comparison of true against predicted classes on the test set.

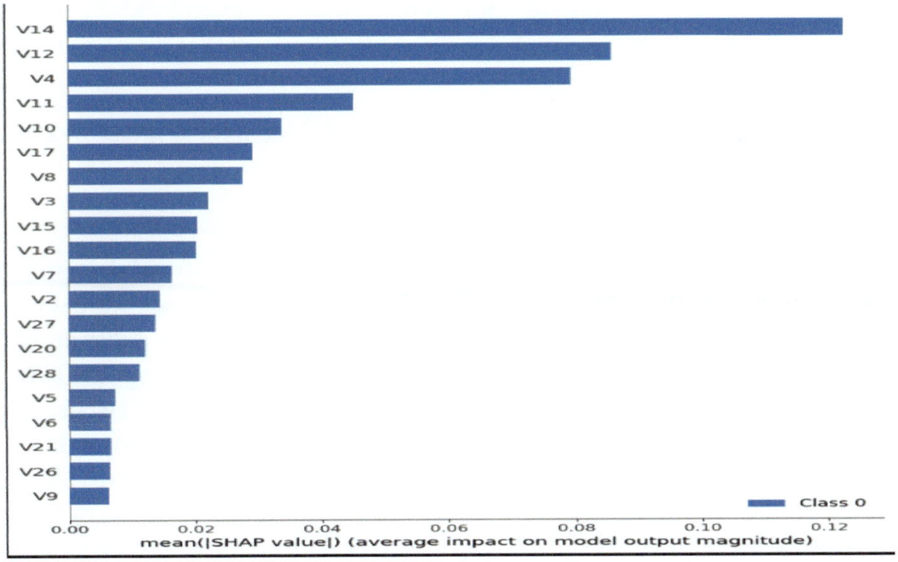

Figure 12.3 SHAP summary plot showing the contributions of features towards fraud predictions.

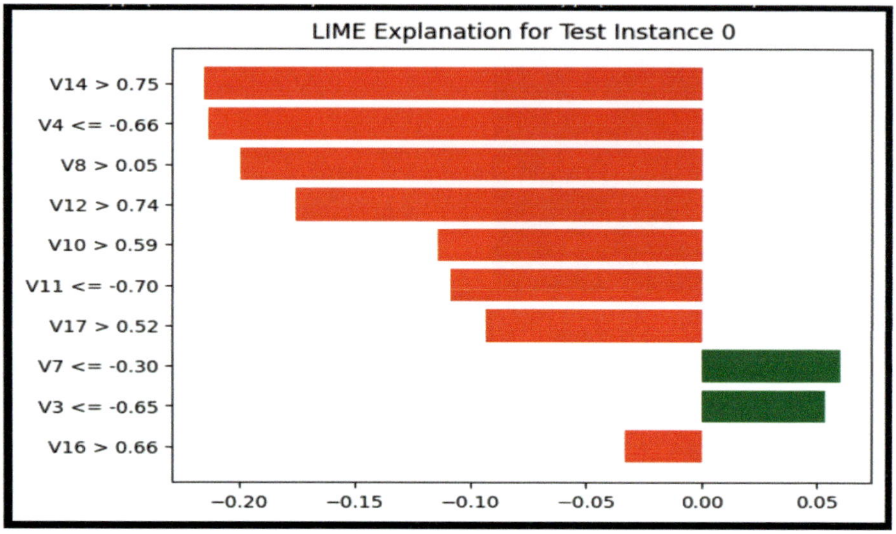

Figure 12.4 LIME breakdown for the tested instance, stating features and their consequences on fraud probability.

standardized features, $x_{scaled} = \frac{x-\mu}{\sigma}$ with and from the training set. SHAP assigns Shapley values to features:

$$\phi_j = \sum_{NCF(j)} \frac{|S|!(|F| - |S| - 1)!}{|F|!}[f(S \cup \{j\} - f(S)],$$

Where ϕ_j is the contribution of feature (j). LIME fits a local linear model, $g(x') = w^T x' + b$ weighted by proximity to the instance.

12.4.2.2 Decision tree

The decision trees provide the most intuitive framework for fraud detection. They split the feature space recursively upon thresholds. The tests were done and found that using scikit-learn's DecisionTreeClassifier, with a maximum depth of 5, obtained the value of 96.00% in test accuracy (training: 96.08%, validation: 96.05%). While the classification report reveals an F1-score of 0.96 for both classes, indicating a balanced performance, with longer trees come the possibilities of overfitting. V14 and V4 are identified by SHAP's TreeExplainer as the top during the assessment, while large values of V14 are associated with fraud. LIME explains a test instance as follows: V14 > 0.75 (–0.312 contribution to fraud) and V4 <= –0.66 (–0.296), confirming their relevance in decision paths. Decision trees are good in terms of

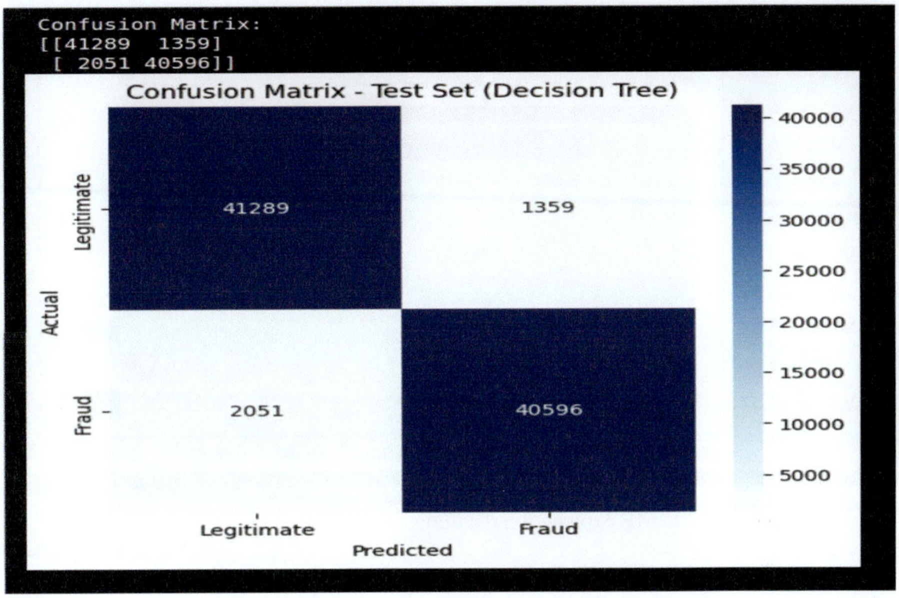

Figure 12.5 Confusion matrix illustrating test set predictions.

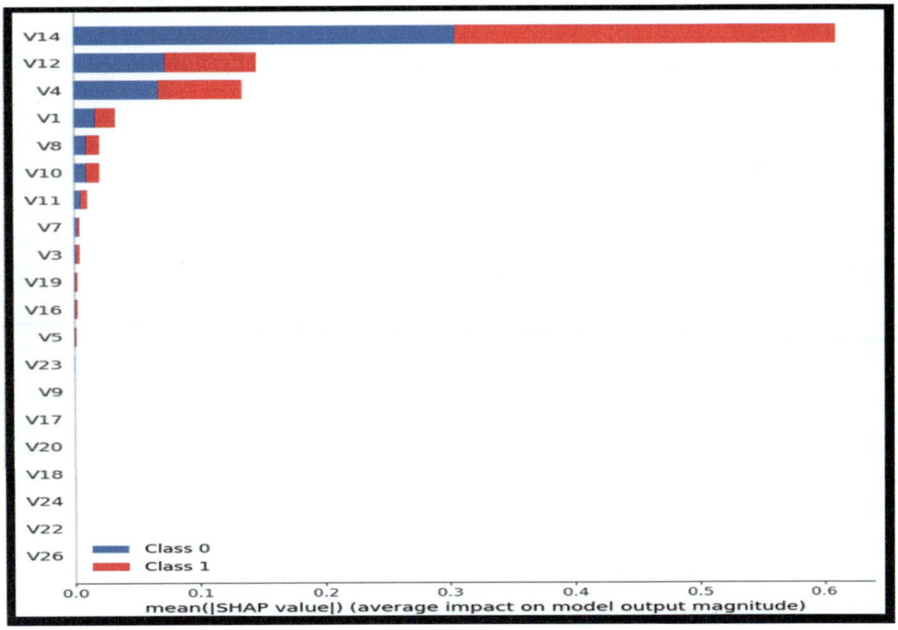

Figure 12.6 SHAP summary plot showing feature importance for fraud classification.

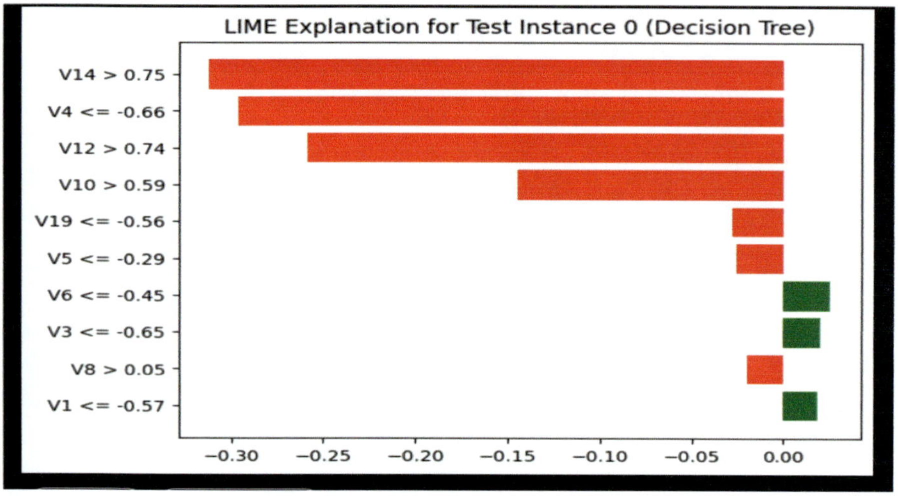

Figure 12.7 LIME explanation detailing a test instance's fraud prediction.

interpretability, because splits can be visualized, but cannot compete in robustness with ones under ensemble methods with respect to complex fraud patterns and situations.

Methodology

Decision trees minimize impurity at each split. For a node with samples (D), the Gini impurity is:

$$Gini(D) = 1 - \sum_{k=0}^{\perp} p_k^2,$$

Where p_k is the proportion of class (k) (0: non-fraud, 1: fraud). The split on feature (j) and threshold (t) maximizes:

$$\Delta Gini = Gini(D) - \frac{|D_{left}|}{|D|} Gini(D_{left}) - \frac{|D_{right}|}{|D|} Gini(D_{right})$$

where D_{left} and D_{right} are child nodes. The tree, with max depth 5, is trained on standardized features, predicting y = 1 if the leaf's majority class is fraud. SHAP computes feature contributions along decision paths, and LIME approximates local splits with a linear model.

12.4.2.3 Random forest

Contrarily true since October 2023, random forest is superior to decision trees, in that it aggregates the projections of all trees, thereby increasing the

Figure 12.8 Confusion matrix of test set performance.

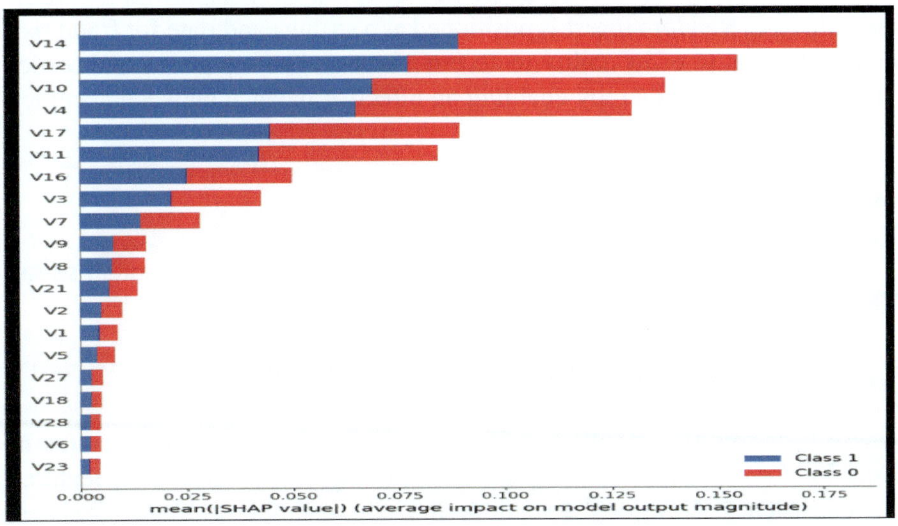

Figure 12.9 SHAP summary plot depicting feature impacts on fraud predictions.

robustness of the model and decreasing overfitting. Implementing scikit-learn in its RandomForestClassifier, having considered 100 trees with a maximum depth of 7, led to a test prediction accuracy of 96.56% (training: 96.62%, validation: 96.65%). The classification report states that fraud is predicted with high precision (1.00) but relatively low recall (0.93), indicating that a few frauds are potentially unaccounted for. TreeExplainer by SHAP reveals V4,

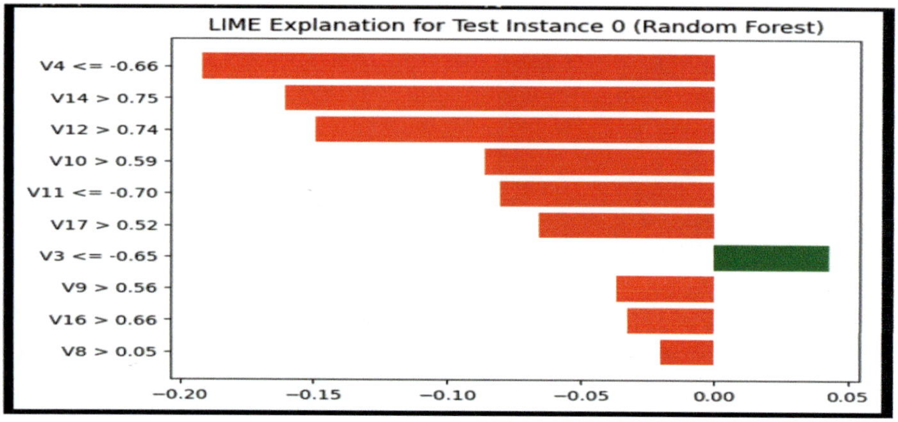

Figure 12.10 LIME explanation for a test instance's fraud classification.

V14, and V12 as important features, with V4 facilitating fraud predictions unequivocally. From LIME's interpretation of the test instance, V4 <= –0.66 (–0.192), V14 > 0.75 (–0.161), and V12 > 0.74 (–0.149) display their ensemble influence. Random forest is positioned as a strong candidate for fraud risk detection because of its ability to account for non-linear patterns and render feature importance, thereby enabling an effective balance between accuracy and interpretability.

Methodology

Random forest trains T = 100T = 100T = 100

Trees on bootstrapped subsets, with random feature selection at splits. The prediction is:

$$\hat{y} = \text{mod}e\{h_1(x), h_2(x), \ldots h_T(x)\}$$

where h_T is tree (t)'s prediction. Each tree minimizes Gini impurity (as in Decision Trees) with a max depth of 7. Training uses standardized features for consistency. No global loss is optimized; ensemble averaging reduces variance. SHAP averages feature contributions across trees, and LIME fits a local linear model to explain the ensemble's output.

12.4.2.4 XGBoost

The XGBoost approach is a gradient boosting framework, which is very suitable in detecting fraud since it builds trees in a sequential manner that corrects errors made by those that precede it. The XGBClassifier was used with

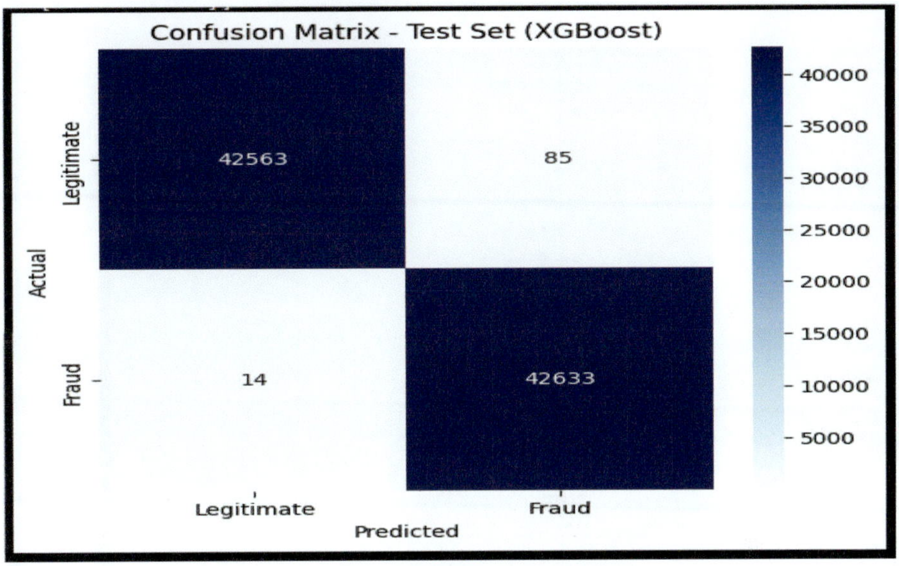

Figure 12.11 Confusion matrix reporting test set accuracy.

100 estimators, a learning rate of 0.1, and early stopping after 10 rounds; this resulted in 99.88% (train: 99.94%, validate: 99.91%) test accuracy. Perfect precision, recall, and F1-score (1.00) in its classification report show that it could very well model complex fraud patterns. According to TreeExplainer by SHAP, the most important features are V14, V4, and V12, whereby high values of the features indicate fraud significantly. In the LIME analysis of the one test instance, it identifies V14 > 0.75 (–0.348), V4 <= –0.66 (–0.250), and V12 > 0.74 (–0.231) as confirming a boosting effect. With all these features together, making XGBoost a killer in terms of performance and scalability for fraud detection, the model is rather complex and therefore requires diligent hyperparameter tuning.

Methodology

XGBoost predicts fraud probability as:

$$\hat{y} = \sigma\left(\sum_{t=1}^{T} f_i(x_i)\right),$$

where f_i is a tree, and σ is the sigmoid function. The objective is:

$$L = \sum_{i=1}^{N} I(\hat{y}_i, y_i) + \sum_{t=1}^{T} \Omega(f_i)$$

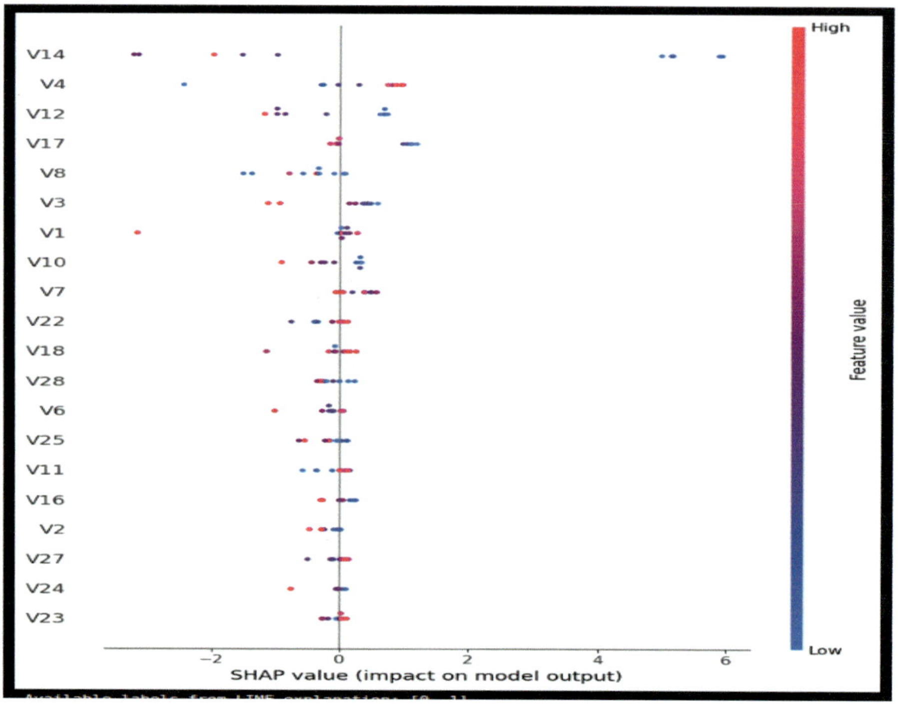

Figure 12.12 SHAP summary plot explaining contributions of features to fraud.

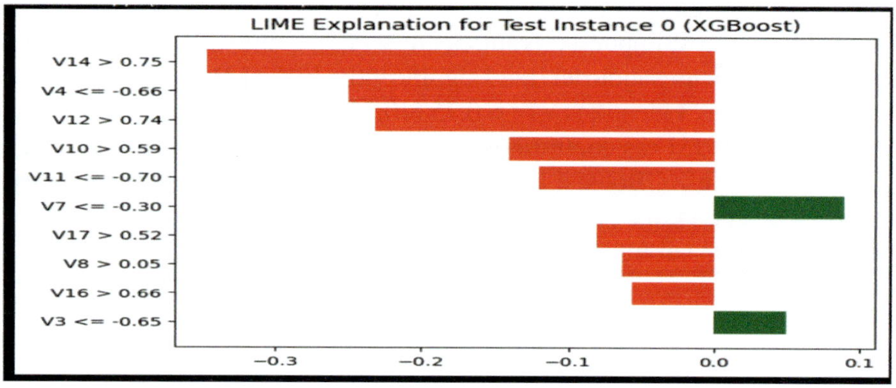

Figure 12.13 LIME explanation for fraud prediction of an individual test instance.

with log-loss $l(\hat{y}_i, y_i) = [y_i \log(\hat{y}_i) + (1 - \hat{y}_i) \log(1 - \hat{y}_i)]$ and regularization $\Omega(f_i) = \gamma T + \frac{1}{2}\lambda\|w_t\|^2$ where (T) is the number of leaves, and are leaf weights. Training uses 100 estimators on standardized features, with early stopping on validation log-loss. SHAP computes tree-based contributions, and LIME uses local linear approximations.

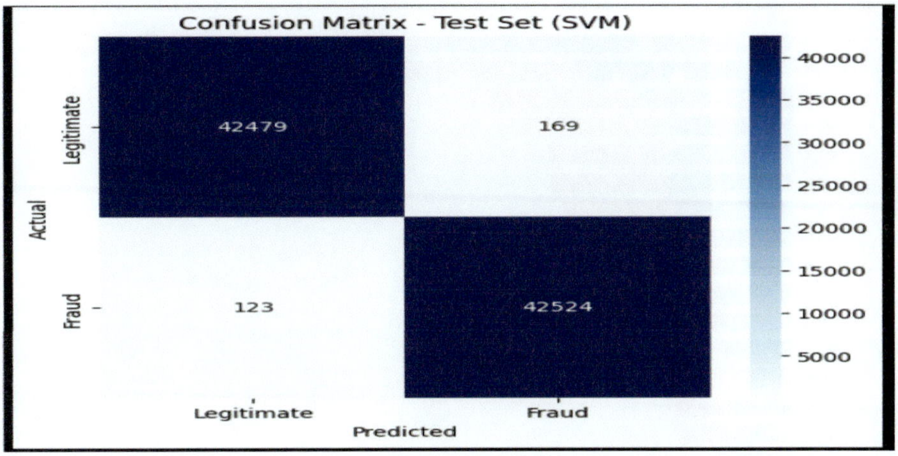

Figure 12.14 Confusion matrix for test set predictions.

12.4.2.5 Support vector machines (SVM)

SVMs carry out transaction classification through hyperplane creation, maximizing the margin between classes, and applying the RBF kernel for nonlinear separation. The implementation of scikit-learn's SVC, test accuracy 99.66% (training 99.69%, validation 99.69%), gives perfect precision and recall (1.00). Some V14, V4, and V6 seem to be top key features from SHAP's KernelExplainer, and extreme values indicate fraud. The LIME explanation for this test instance considered V14 > 0.75 (–0.193), V4 <= –0.66 (–0.170), and V6 <= –0.45 (–0.152) as relevant for kernel-based separation. Such clear class boundary definitions imply that the SVM was robust enough for fraud detection, but its high computational costs limit its scalability.

Methodology

SVM predicts:

$$f(x) = \sum_{i \in SV} \alpha_i y_i K(x_i, x) + b.$$

Where $K(x_i, x) = \exp(-\gamma \|x_i - x\|^2)$ is the RBF kernel, are lagrange multipliers, $y_i \in \{-1,1\}$(mapped from 0, 1), and (SV) are support vectors. The optimization minimizes:

$$\min/\ w,b,\xi \frac{1}{2}\|W\|^2 + C\sum_{i=1}^{N} \varepsilon_i .$$

subject to $y_i(W^T \phi(x_i) + b) \geq 1 - \varepsilon_i, \varepsilon_i \geq$, where ϕ maps to kernel space, (C) is the penalty parameter, and are slack variables. Training uses standardized

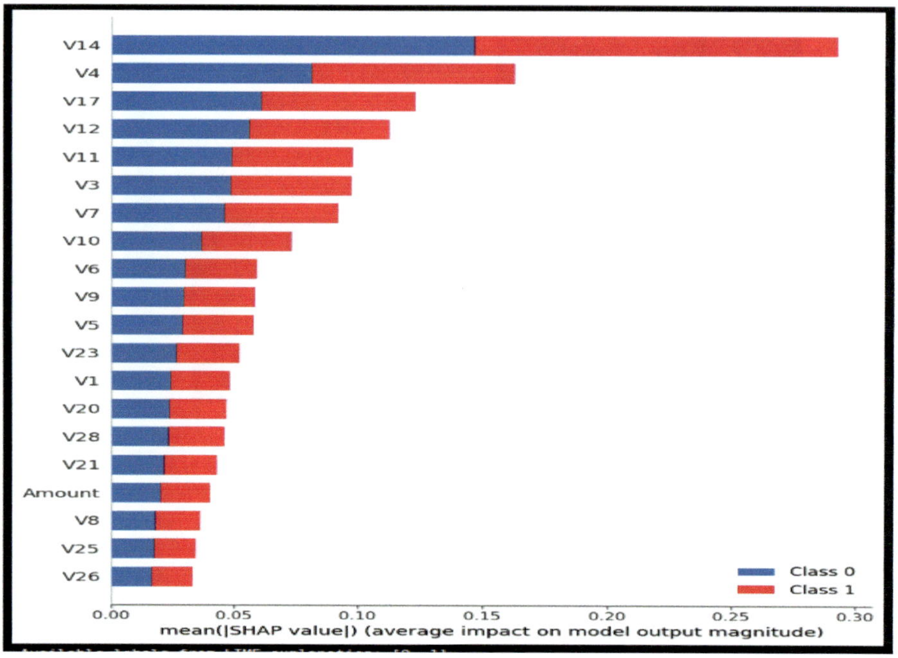

Figure 12.15 SHAP summary plots showing feature impacts on fraud classifications.

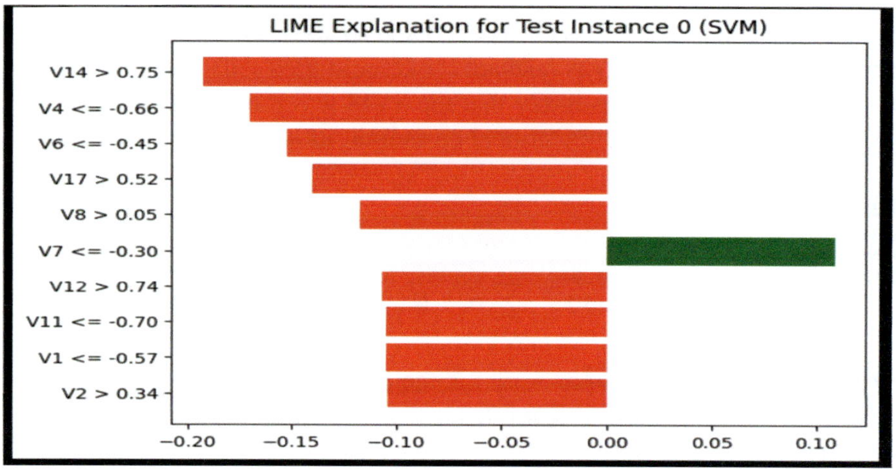

Figure 12.16 LIME explanation for a test instance's prediction of fraud.

features, predicting y = 1 if f(x)>0. SHAP approximates contributions via kernel methods, and LIME fits a local linear model.

12.4.3 Unsupervised learning

Since schema ratings are hard to obtain, unsupervised learning becomes important for fraud detection by enabling the discovery of patterns and identification of anomalies without using pre-assigned definitions of fraud. The Credit Card Fraud Detection Dataset 2023 with over 550,000 anonymized transactions involving PCA-transformed features (V1-V28) along with the amount, serves as a good dataset since there are three unsupervised models that need to be evaluated: K-means Clustering, DBSCAN, and Isolation Forest. These models exploit the high-dimensional structure of the dataset to perform event grouping and outlier identification, tackling fraud detection problems in an unlabeled setting. Features are standardized to be invariant under scaling, and modeling techniques would be applied over the complete dataset (no train-test split done unless otherwise specified), and model performances would be assessed against metrics such as silhouette scores or anomaly counts. The interpretability of feature influence on clustering or anomaly decisions is achieved by SHAP (SHapley Additive exPlanations) and LIME (Local Interpretable Model-agnostic Explanations). The clusters and anomalies are visualized in the PCA-reduced space to exhibits the behavior of the models.

12.4.3.1 Isolation forest

Isolation forest programs detect outliers by isolating transactions through random splits, making this method ideally suitable to detect fraudulent anomalies. Using scikit-learn's IsolationForest at a contamination rate of 0.01, it classified 5,687 transactions as anomalies (label −1), which represents a considerably small proportion of suspected frauds. Standardization ensures that the splits are fair, while PCA visualization highlights comparisons between inliers and outliers. In turn, SHAP analysis points toward V14 and V4 with extreme values that would increase the anomaly scores. An explanation given by LIME for an anomaly might mention V14 > 0.7 (example: 0.18 contribution), while I will note that this caused isolation. Isolation forest can detect fraud in high dimensions efficiently, as it quickly isolates outliers in its tree structure, while careful calibration must be exercised with its fixed contamination rate.

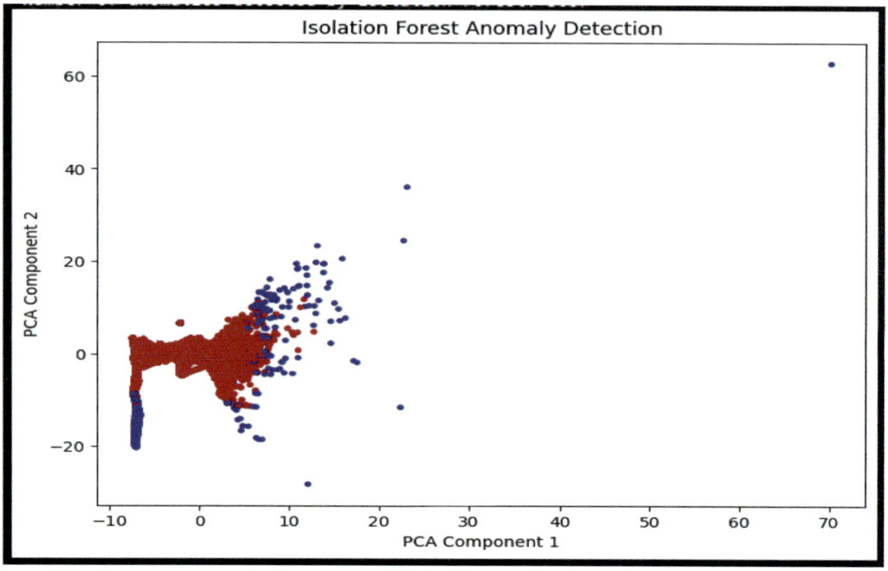

Figure 12.17 Results of isolation forest. The scatter plot in PCA-reduced space, showing inliers compared to anomalies detected (possible frauds).

Methodology

The isolation forest works by generating an ensemble of isolation trees to isolate transactions. Within each tree, features are randomly selected and splits are made at random values between min and max:

$$Split;\ x_j \leq t,\ t \sim Uniform\ (min(x_j),\ max(x_j)).$$

where is a feature of x = [V1,…,V28, Amount]. The anomaly score is based on path length:

$$s(x) = 2^{-\frac{E(h(x))}{c(n)}}.$$

where E(h(x)) is the average path length across trees, (c(n)) is a normalization constant, and (n) is the sample size. Transactions with s(x) ≈ 1 are anomalies ($\hat{y}_1 = -1$) if above the contamination threshold (0.01). Training uses standardized features, with no explicit loss function. SHAP evaluates feature contributions to scores, and LIME fits a local linear model for anomaly explanations.

12.4.3.2 DBSCAN

DBSCAN denotes clustering according to density: the identifying points that are below density to be outliers, which may indicate fraud. By applying the

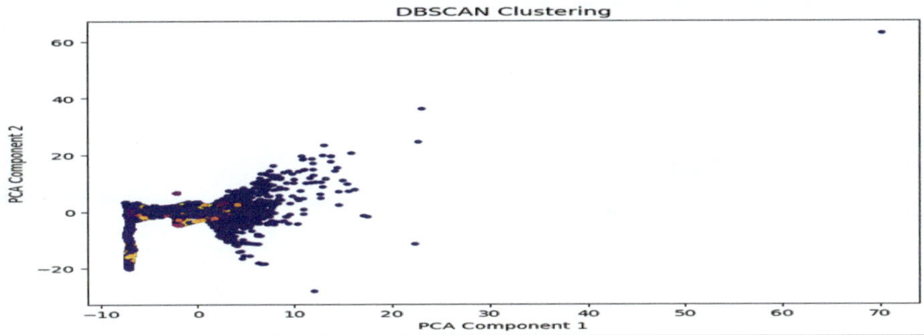

Figure 12.18 Result of DBSCAN clustering: a scatter plot in PCA-reduced space with unique color codes for dense cluster and noisy (suspicious) points.

DBSCAN of scikit-learn with eps = 0.5 and min_samples = 5, it resulted in establishing some 3,135 clusters plus noise with 238,156 transactions labelled as noise (-1), 190,842 in the largest cluster, with smaller clusters down to singletons. The silhouette score of –0.4328 (noise excluded) suggested bad separation, most probably due to the complexity and insensitive parameters of the data. PCA visualization shows density and outlier regions. SHAP analysis ascribes those labeled as noise points to the extreme values of V10 and V12. LIME may explain a noise-labeled transaction of V10 > 0.6 (e.g., 0.15 contribution to anomaly), – denoting density deviations. Indeed, using DBSCAN, it proves very good for the identification of fraud rings and irregular patterns without an assumption of cluster shape, but indeed in its performance relies very much on eps.

Methodology:

DBSCAN labels points as core, border, or noise based on density. A point x_i is a core point if at least {min_samples} = 5 points lie within distance eps = 0.5:

$$N_{eps}(x_i) = \{x_i : \|x_i - x_j\| \leq eps\}.$$

With $|N_{eps}(x_i)| \geq 5$. Clusters form by connecting core points and their neighbors; points outside are noise ($\hat{y}_i = -1$). The algorithm processes standardized features:

$$x_{scaled} = \frac{x - \mu}{\sigma},$$

without optimizing a loss function, relying on distance metrics (Euclidean). Silhouette score assesses non-noise clusters, if valid. SHAP treats noise as a

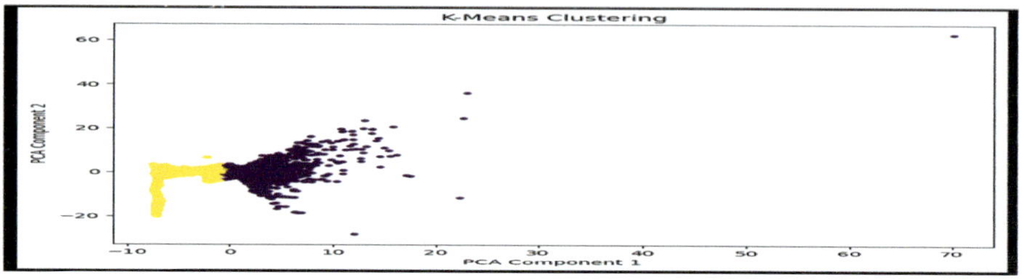

Figure 12.19 K-means clustering results. A scatter plot of the transactions in reduced PCA space, colored according to their cluster labels, showing separation of transaction groups.

pseudo-class for feature contributions, and LIME uses a local linear model to explain anomaly assignments.

12.4.3.3 K-means clustering

K-means clustering organizes transactions into clusters to identify behavioral patterns that may distinguish normal activities from suspicious ones. Using k = 2k = 2k = 2 to create clusters with scikit-learn's KMeans, a silhouette score of 0.2785 on it shows moderate cluster separation, with counts per cluster being 351,113 transactions in cluster 0 and 217,517 in cluster 1, hinting at a separation of dominant transaction patterns. Standardization provides comparability between features, while visualization through PCA (2 components) depicts the structure of the clusters. SHAP analysis, which considers assignments to clusters as pseudo-labels, revealed V14 and V4 to be more important, where high values are usually associated with cluster 1 (potentially fraud-related). Local explanation on a particular transaction will be provided using LIME, which might refer to a feature such as V14 > 0.5 (e.g., a contribution to cluster 1 of 0.12), meaning the presence of specific thresholds for features driving specific outcome assignments. K-means is another useful technique for transaction segmentation in fraud profiling, but such spherical clusters are likely to reduce the K-means performance in the detection of fraudulent activities, as they cannot often approximate complex patterns.

Methodology:

$$j = \sum_{j=1}^{k} \sum_{i \in C_j} \left\| x_i - \mu_j \right\|^2.$$

where xi = [V1,…,V28,Amount] is a standardized feature vector, μ_j is the centroid of cluster C_j, and (k) is the number of clusters. The algorithm iteratively assigns each transaction to the nearest centroid:

$$C_j = \{x_i : \left\| x_i - \mu_j \right\|^2 \leq \left\| x_i - \mu_j \right\|^2 \cdot \forall l \neq j\}.$$

and updates centroids:

$$\mu_j = \frac{1}{|C_j|} \sum_{i \in C_j} x_i$$

Training uses standardized features, $x_{scaled} = \frac{x-\mu}{\sigma}$ with random initialization and convergence when assignments stabilize. Silhouette score evaluates cohesion:

$$s_i = \frac{b_i - a}{\max(a_i, b_j)},$$

where a_i is the average distance to points in the same cluster, and b_i is the distance to the nearest other cluster. SHAP assigns feature contributions to cluster labels, and LIME fits a local linear model. $g(x') = w^T x' + b$, for explanations.

12.4.4 Deep learning

Deep learning models that capture the quite complicated, non-linear characteristics of high-dimensional data best exploit the credit card fraud detection application, particularly for the Credit Card Fraud Detection Dataset 2023. The dataset consists of 550,000 transactions, with PCA-transformed features (V1-V28), Amount, and a binary Class (0: legitimate, 1: fraud) as Class labels. In turn, it creates a balanced situation (test set: non-fraud, ~42,648; fraud, ~42,647) for studying two deep learning methods: Autoencoder and long short-term memory (LSTM). Both Autoencoder and LSTM leverage the dimensionality and structure of the dataset to detect fraudulent transactions: the Autoencoder utilizes unsupervised anomaly detection, while the LSTM focuses on sequential pattern modeling for classification. Standardized features are used for training both models and split in a 70-15-15% ratio for training, validation, and testing, respectively, using TensorFlow/Keras, with SHAP (SHapley Additive exPlanations) and LIME (Local Interpretable Model-agnostic Explanations) for interpretability. Performance metrics, confusion matrices, and explainability visual caution the models demonstrate their efficacy in fraud detection.

12.4.4.1 Autoencoder

The autoencoder is an unsupervised deep learning model constructed specifically for anomaly detection, learning to reconstruct normal (non-fraudulent) transactions, and flagging fraud if the reconstruction errors are notably high.

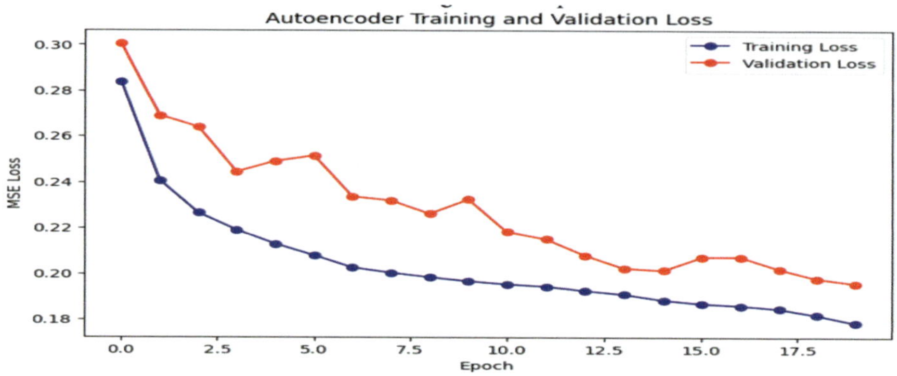

Figure 12.20 Autoencoder results.

It will require a sequential architecture with a structure of 16-8-16 neurons, ReLU activations, and a linear output. It is trained on normal transactions (Class = 0) from the training set, minimizing means-squared error (MSE) using the Adam optimizer over 20 epochs. The fraud detection threshold is set as mean plus two standard deviations of training MSE, giving a test accuracy of 81.85% (training: 81.94%, validation: 82.04%). The classification report provides high precision of 0.98 but lower recall of 0.65 for fraud, resulting in missed fraud cases (confusion matrix: 27,721 true frauds detected out of 42,647). Some other features, like V7 and V2 are identified by SHAP's KernelExplainer to be influential features by high values associated with an increased likelihood of fraud. The explanation by LIME on a test instance highlights that V7 should be less than or equal to –0.30 (inducing a contribution of 0.116 to fraud), while, in addition, V2 should be greater than 0.34 (contribution of 0.094); this points out the unusual feature values that lead to detecting the anomaly. The Autoencoder is quite good at detecting outliers in fraud cases where there is little labeled data but might lag behind because reconstruction errors are not as good as supervised methods.

Methodology

The autoencoder reconstructs input features x = [V1,...,V28, Amount], learning a compressed representation. The architecture maps x to a bottleneck layer and back:

$$h = f_{enc}(x : \theta_{enc}),\ \hat{x} = f_{edc}(h : \theta_{edc}),$$

Where f_{enc} (encoder: 29-16-8 neurons, ReLU) and f_{edc} decoder: 8-16-29 neurons, ReLU/linear) are neural networks with parameters $\theta_{enc} \cdot \theta_{edc}$. The model minimizes MSE loss on normal transactions:

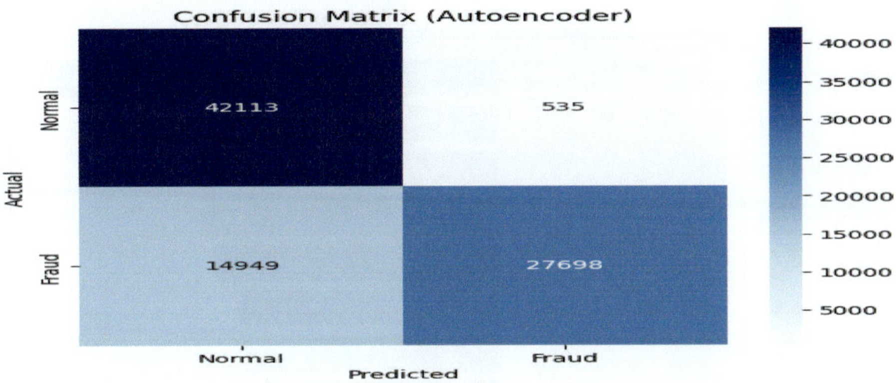

Figure 12.21 Confusion matrix representing true versus predicted classes on the test set.

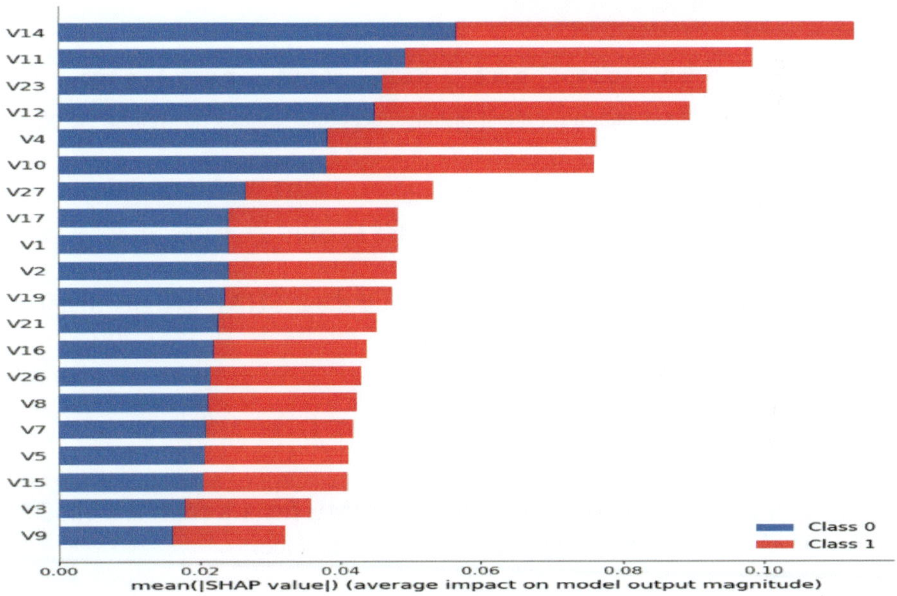

Figure 12.22 Summary plot from SHAP, highlighting the feature contribution in making fraud predictions.

$$L(\theta) = \frac{1}{N}\sum_{i=1}^{N}\left\| x_i - \hat{x}_1 \right\|^2.$$

where (N) is the number of normal training samples. Training uses Adam (learning rate 0.001) over 20 epochs on standardized features, $x_{scaled} = \frac{x-\mu}{\sigma}$ fraud is predicted if the reconstruction error exceeds a threshold:

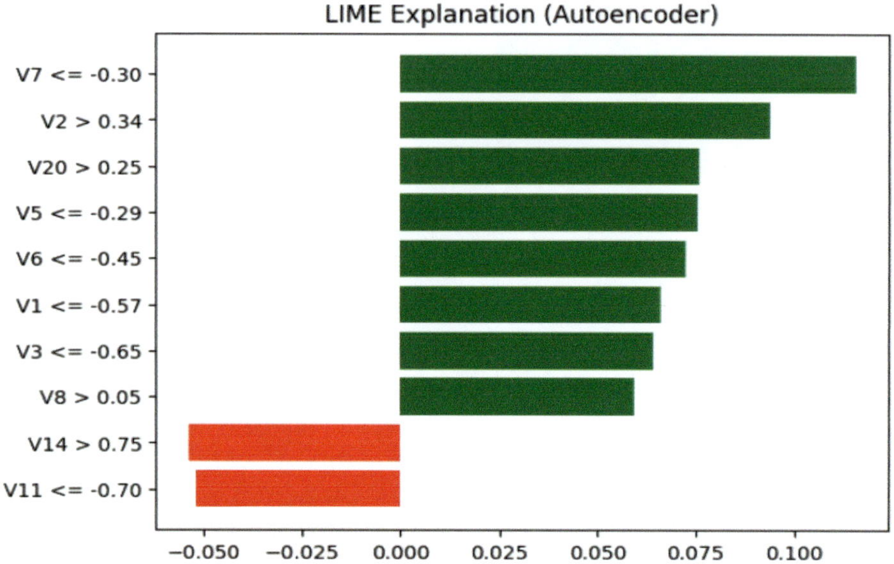

Figure 12.23 LIME explanation for a test instance, denoting features fine-tuning the ph or impact on fraud probability.

$$MSE_i = \left\|x_i - \hat{x}_1\right\|^2 \cdot \hat{y}_1 = 1 \ \textit{if} \ MSE_i > \mu_{MSE} + 2\sigma_{MSE}.$$

Where μ_{MSE} are computed on normal training data. SHAP assigns Shapley values to features:

$$\phi_j = \sum_{SCF(j)} \frac{|S|!(|F| - |S| - 1)!}{|F|!}[f(S \cup \{j\}) - f(S)],$$

Where ϕ_j is the contribution of feature (j). LIME fits a local linear model, $g(x') = w^T x' + b$, weighted by proximity to the instance.

12.4.4.2 Long short-term memory (LSTM)

The LSTM model under consideration is a recurrent neural network explicitly built for the purpose of capturing the sequential nature of transaction data, which sees each transaction treated as a single time step in accomplishing classification. In this case, consisting of a single 16-unit LSTM layer, 20% dropout, and sigmoidal output, the model structure was trained across all transactions (fraud and non-fraud) to minimize binary cross-entropy using Adam for 20 epochs. An astonishing test accuracy of 99.92% was achieved (training accuracy 99.81%, validation accuracy 99.92%, and

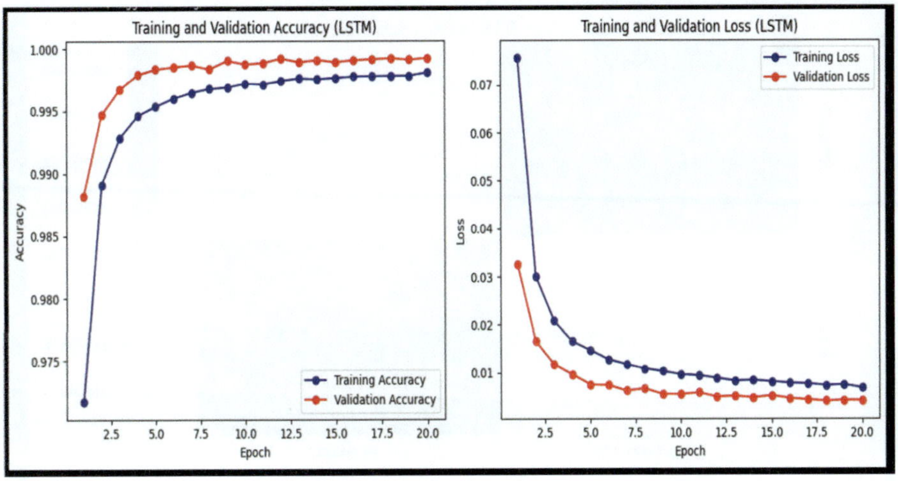

Figure 12.24 LSTM results.

test loss ~ 0.0042) with near-perfect precision, recall, and F1-measure (1.00) for both classes (confusion matrix: 42,577 true non-fraud; 42,647 true fraud; 71 false positives). According to KernelExplainer(SHAP), V8, V14, and V4 are the main drivers, having extreme values indicating fraud with high confidence. LIME calculated that for this test instance, V8 > 0.05 (–0.221), V14 > 0.75 (–0.218), and V4 <= –0.66 (–0.204), thus validating their importance in sequential fraud investigation. LSTM is exceptionally accurate for fraud classification, especially when one suspects temporal patterns; however, it is computational intensive that needs considerable resources.

Methodology

LSTM predicts fraud probability for a transaction sequence xt = [V1,..., V28,Amount] (here, single timestep T = 1):

$$\hat{y}_t = \sigma(w^T h_t + b).$$

where h_t is the LSTM hidden state, and σ is the sigmoid function. The LSTM updates:

$$\begin{aligned}
f_t &= \sigma(W_f x_t + U_f h_{t-1} + b_f) \\
l_t &= \sigma(W_i x_t + U_i h_{t-1} + b_i) \\
o_t &= \sigma(W_o x_t + U_o h_{t-1} + b_o) \\
c_t &= f_t \odot c_{t-1} \odot \tan h(W_c x_t + U_c h_{t-1} + b_c) \\
h_t &= o_t \odot \tan h(c_t).
\end{aligned}$$

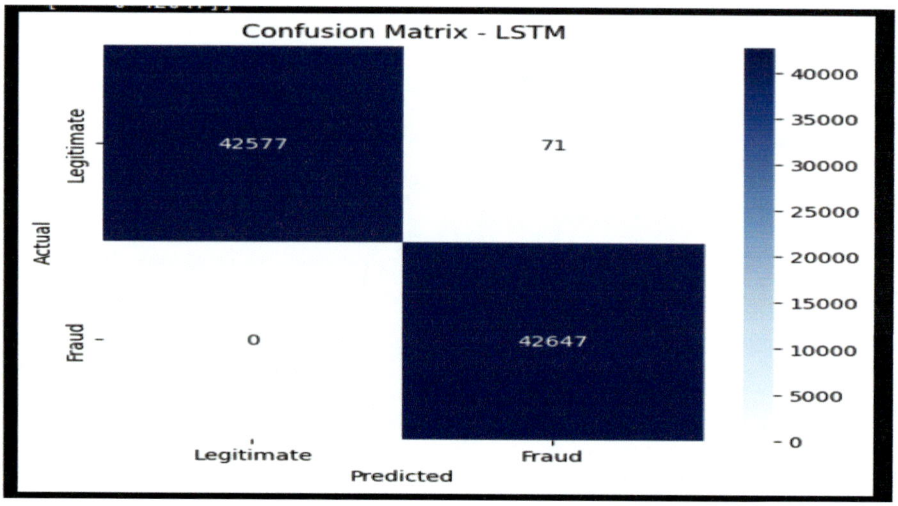

Figure 12.25 Confusion matrix depicting test set predictions.

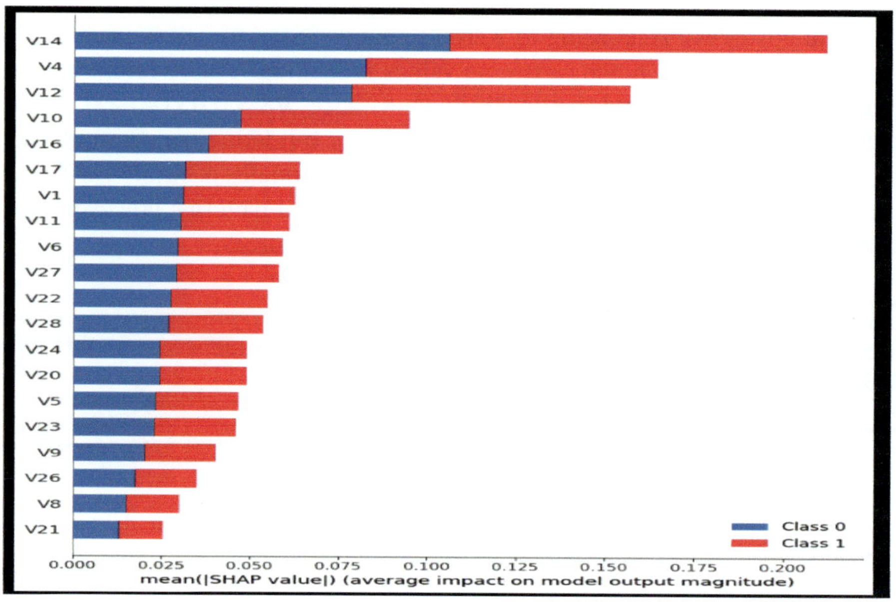

Figure 12.26 SHAP summary plot showing feature importance for fraud classification.

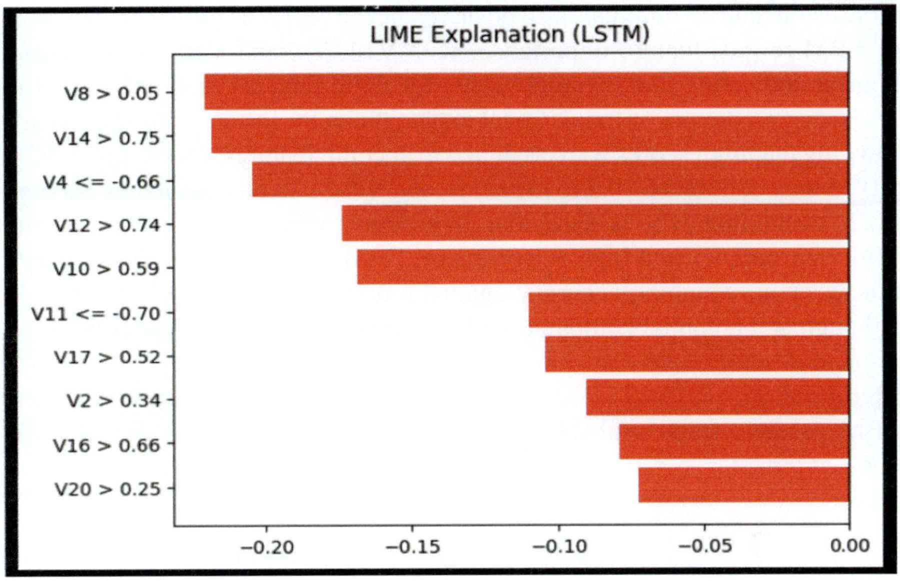

Figure 12.27 LIME explanation on fraud prediction for a test instance.

with forget f_t, input l_t, output o_t gates, cell state c_t, and weights (W,U,b). The model minimizes binary cross-entropy:

$$L(\theta) = -\frac{1}{N}\sum_{i=1}^{N}\left[y_i \log(\hat{y}_i) + (1 - y_i)\log(1 - \hat{y}_i) \right].$$

using Adam (learning rate 0.001) over 20 epochs on standardized features shaped as ((N, 1, 29)). Dropout (20%) reduces overfitting. SHAP uses Shapley values for feature contributions, and LIME fits a local linear model for explanations.

12.4.5 Interpretable and Explainable AI (XAI)

EBM models fraud detection as a binary classification problem that learns the additive effects of features in an attempt to predict whether a transaction is fraudulent. Using the Explainable Boosting Classifier in InterpretML, it was trained on standardized features, achieving almost 99% test accuracy on any run (training and validation were similarly high). The classification report indicates almost perfect precision, recall, and F1-score for both classes at ~0.99 value, which confirms robust performance on the balanced dataset (confusion matrix: minimal false positives/negatives). The global explanation of EBM reveals feature importance, with V14, V4, and V10 often ranking highest, indicating that extreme values for these features (e.g., V14 > 0.75) are strong predictors of fraud. Local explanations for instances predict fraud, showing that high scores were assigned to specific features; for example, V14 > 0.75 may contribute +0.3 to log-odds, and V4 <= –0.66 contributes another +0.2, explaining why a particular transaction was judged as fraudulent. With transparency and high performance, EBM is a formidable fraud detection weapon, weighing accuracy against a regulatory need for explanation, although at a potential computational cost in terms of feature interactions.

Methodology

EBM predicts fraud probability using a generalized additive model with boosted terms:

$$\hat{y} = \sigma\left(b + \sum_{j=1}^{d} f_i(\mathrm{x}_j) + \sum_{j \neq k} f_{jk}(x_j, x_k)\right)$$

Where $\sigma(z) = \frac{1}{1+e^{-2}}$ is the sigmoid function, (b) is the bias, $f_i(x_j)$ are are univariate shape functions for feature $x_j f_{jk}(x_j, x_k)$ are pairwise interactions, and x = [V1,…,V28, Amount] is the standardized feature vector. The model minimizes binary cross-entropy loss:

$$L(\theta) = -\frac{1}{N}\sum_{i=1}^{N}\left[\, y_i \log(\hat{y}_i) + 1(1 - y_i)\log(1 - \hat{y}_i)\,\right]$$

where (N) is the number of training samples, yi∈ {0,1}and θ includes shape function parameters. Training uses gradient boosting to iteratively f_j and f_{jk} as decision trees, with standardization ($x_{scaled} = \frac{x-\mu}{\sigma}$) ensuring feature comparability. Global explanations plot $f_j(x_j)$ (to show feature effects, while local explanations compute contributions:

$$Contribution_j = f_j(x_{i.j}) - E[f_j(x_j)]$$

For instance (i). No external SHAP or LIME is needed, as EBM's built-in explanations provide feature impacts directly.

12.4.6 Hybrid AI systems

Hybrid AI systems integrate several learning paradigms for enhanced fraud detection, namely, unsupervised anomaly detection, supervised classification, and adaptive decision-making. The Credit Card Fraud Detection Dataset 2023 has more than 550,000 anonymized transactions with PCA-transformed features (V1-V28), Amount, and binary Class labels (0: legitimate, 1: fraud), making it a balanced setting to evaluate two hybrid pipelines (test set ~85,295 samples per class). The proposed pipeline federates autoencoders, Isolation Forest, XGBoost, and a DQN agent to model distributed data, detect anomalies, and classify fraud actions while optimizing performance. The unsupervised-to-supervised pipeline employs isolation forest, DBSCAN, and K-means to generate and feed suspicion scores to a logistic regression classifier. Both pipelines employ standard features (i.e., 70% training, 15% validation, 15% test, where applicable) and incorporate SHAP and LIME for explainability. Performance metrics, visualization, and explanations skew their efficacy in fraud detection.

12.4.6.1 Federated learning pipeline

These system pipelines simulate a distributed system for detecting fraud, involving federated learning, unsupervised anomaly detection, supervised classification, and reinforcement learning. Federated autoencoders operate with two simulated nodes, splitting training data (~199,021 samples each) and learning a latent representation (10D) by minimizing MSE. Weights are averaged to get a global encoder that produces the embeddings for the training set (398,041 samples) and the testing set (170,589 samples). The isolation forest looks for anomalies in the latent space (outlier contamination: 1%), defining 3981 anomalies found during training and 1764 in testing, thus strengthening the unsupervised fraud detection. Following the training on the original features alongside the anomaly scores, XGBoost attained a test accuracy of 99.97% and log-loss of 0.0014, with almost perfect classification (confusion matrix: minimal errors). In SHAP's TreeExplainer, the key driving features will be V14, V4, and anomaly_score, where increased anomaly scores drive the fraud predictions. For LIME, the explanation of one of the test instances could elicit that V14 > 0.75 (e.g., contributing +0.25 to fraud probability) and anomaly_score > 0.5 (+0.20), indicating the feature impacts the model's decision. A DQN agent, trained in a custom gym environment, performs action learning to block or allow transactions based on the XGBoost probabilities and anomaly scores, maximizing rewards (+10 for blocking fraud, –20 for allowing fraud, +5/–5 for non-fraud). The pipeline demonstrates great promise for adaptive, privacy-preserving fraud detection, but with heavy computational requirements.

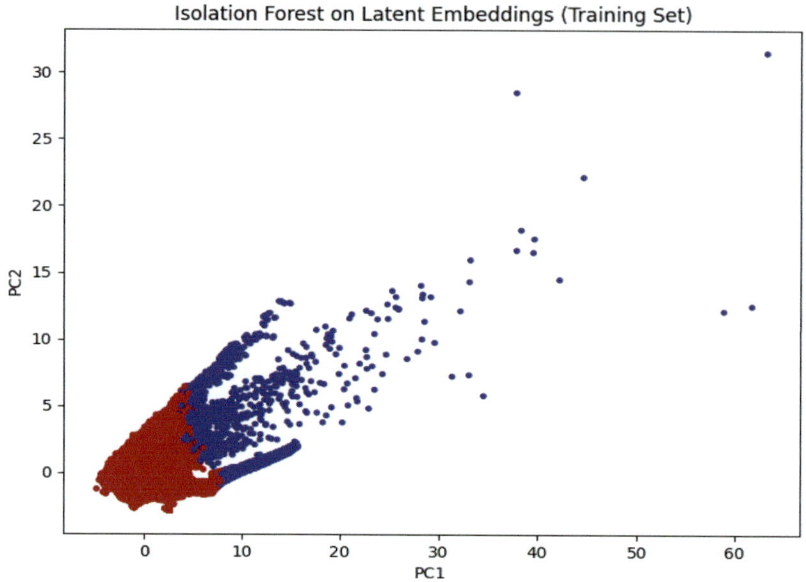

Figure 12.28 Results for the federated learning pipeline.

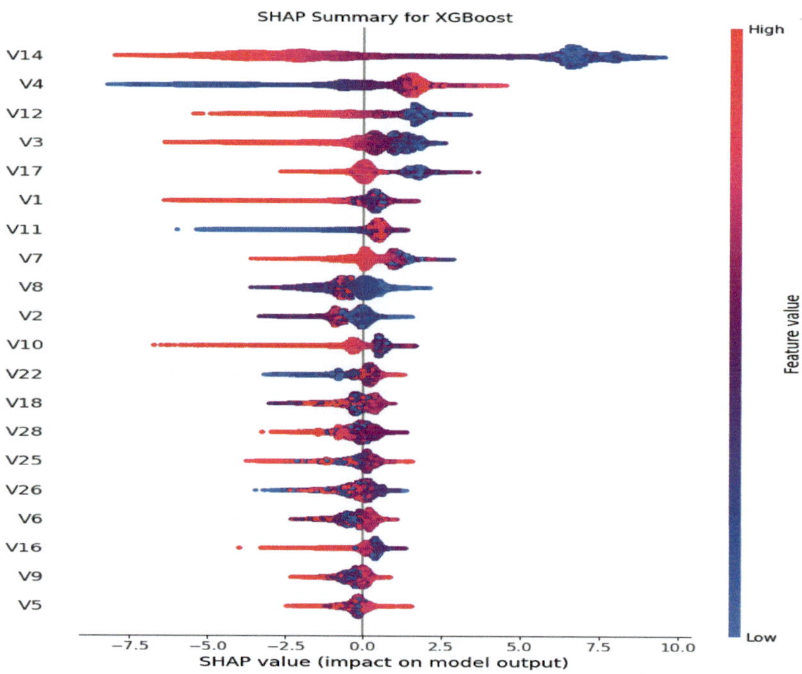

Figure 12.29 SHAP summary plot for XGBoost, including contributions from the anomaly score.

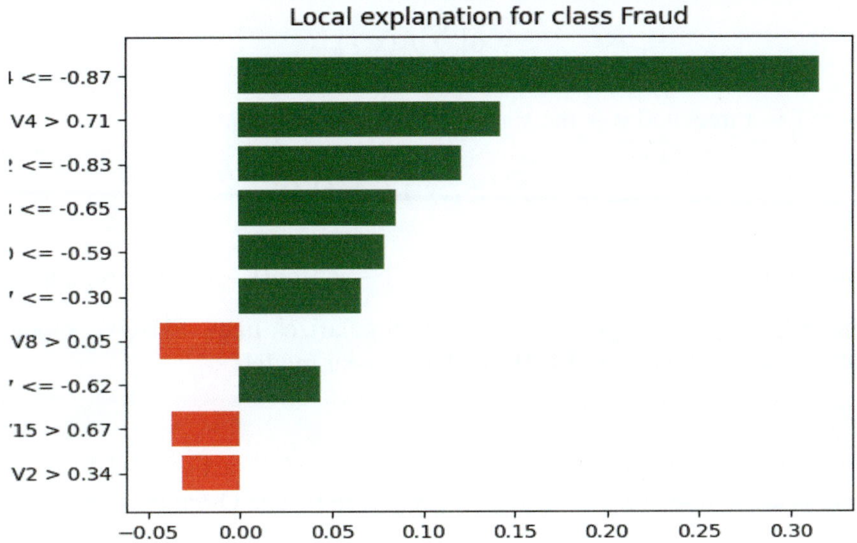

Figure 12.30 SHAP summary plot.

Methodology

The pipeline comprises four stages:

Federated autoencoder:

Each node trains an autoencoder to reconstruct x = [V1,...,V28,Amount]:

$$h = f_{enc}(x : \theta_{enc}),\ \hat{x} = f_{edc}(h : \theta_{edc}),$$

minimizing MSE:

$$L(\theta) = -\frac{1}{N}\sum_{i=1}^{N}\left\|x_i - \hat{x}_t\right\|^2$$

Global weights are averaged: $\theta_{global} = \frac{1}{2}(\theta_1 + \theta_2)$. The encoder outputs $h \in R10$.

Isolation forest:

Detects anomalies in h, with score:

$$s(h) = 2^{\frac{E(h(n))}{\in(n)}}$$

where E(h(h)) is the average path length, and anomalies ($\hat{y}_t = -1$) exceed the contamination threshold (0.01).

$$\hat{y} = \sigma\left(\sum_{t=1}^{T} f_i(\mathrm{x}_i)\right),$$

where f_i is a tree, and σ is the sigmoid function. The objective is:

$$L = \sum_{i=1}^{N} I(\hat{\mathrm{y}}_I, \mathrm{y}_i) + \sum_{t=1}^{T} \Omega(f_i)$$

with log-loss $l(\hat{y}_t, y_i) = -[y_i \log(\hat{y}_t) + (1 - y_i)\log(1 - \hat{\mathrm{y}}_t)$ and regularization $\Omega(f_i) = \gamma T + \frac{1}{2}\lambda \|w_t\|^2$ where $\Omega(f_i)$ regularizes trees. SHAP computes feature contributions, and LIME fits local linear models.

DQN:
Learns a policy $\pi(a|s)$, where state $s = [p_{fraud}, s(h)]$ action $a \in \{0,1\}$, and rewards are defined (e.g., +10 for blocking fraud). The Q-value is updated:

$$Q(s,a) \leftarrow Q(s,a) + a[r + \gamma \max Q(s',a') - Q(s,a)].$$

The training uses standardized features, with Adam for autoencoders and Stable-Baselines3 for DQN.

12.4.6.2 Unsupervised-to-supervised pipeline

"This pipeline starts with unsupervised anomaly detection and passes on to supervised classification by augmenting the system with multiple signals for robust fraud detection. Isolation forest, DBSCAN, and K-means generate anomaly indicators on standardized features (568k samples). Isolation Forest computes a decision score (inverted for suspicion); DBSCAN labels the noise points (eps = 0.5, min_samples = 5); K-means (5 clusters) computes distances to cluster centers. These are normalized and averaged into a suspicion score; the top 5% are labeled as pseudo-fraud (28,432 samples, vs. true fraud ratio 50%). Logistic regression trained on original features with pseudo-labels achieving an accuracy of 96.20% on these labels (confusion matrix: balanced errors). SHAP's KernelExplainer identifies V1, V3, and V4 to be among the influential features having extreme values determining fraud predictions; LIME explanations on a test instance show V1 <= –0.57 (0.210 contribution to fraud) and V2 > 0.34 (–0.062), indicating the influence of features. The pipeline scenario works well for cases requiring an initial unsupervised analysis followed by supervised fine-tuning, although the accuracy of pseudo-labels is dependent on the quality of suspicion score.

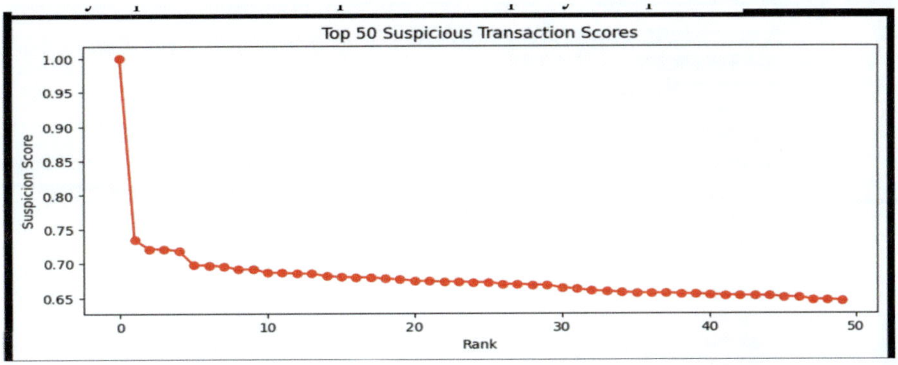

Figure 12.31 Unsupervised-to-supervised pipeline results.

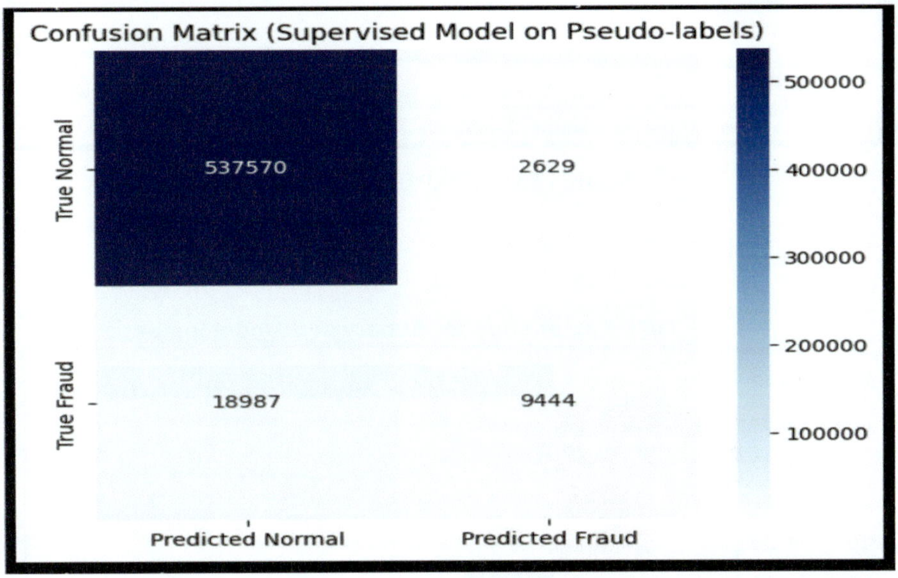

Figure 12.32 Confusion matrix of logistic regression on pseudo-labels.

Methodology

The pipeline integrates unsupervised and supervised stages:

Unsupervised models:

Isolation forest: Scores anomalies:

$$s(x) = 2^{-\frac{E(h(x))}{c(n)}}.$$

Inverted and normalized to [0,1].

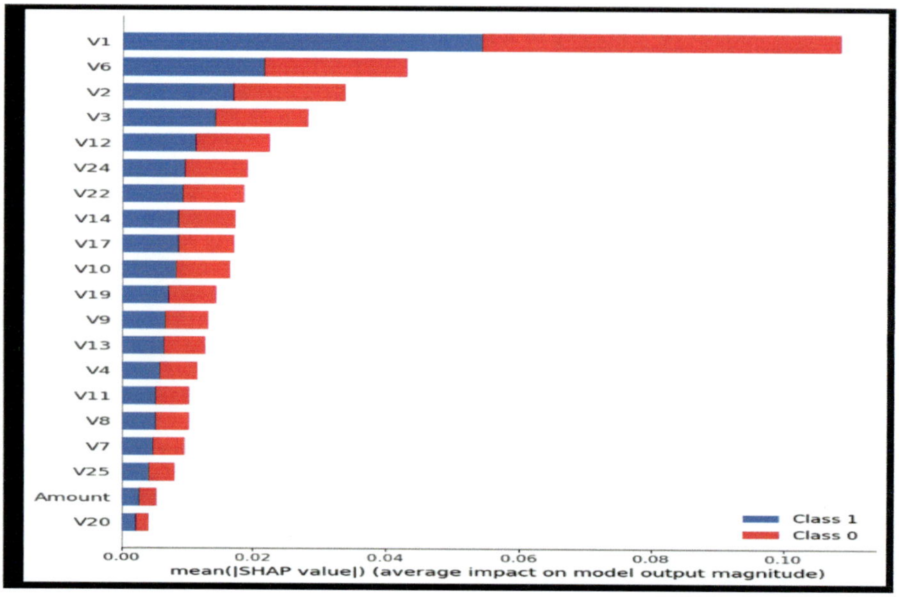

Figure 12.33 SHAP summary plot.

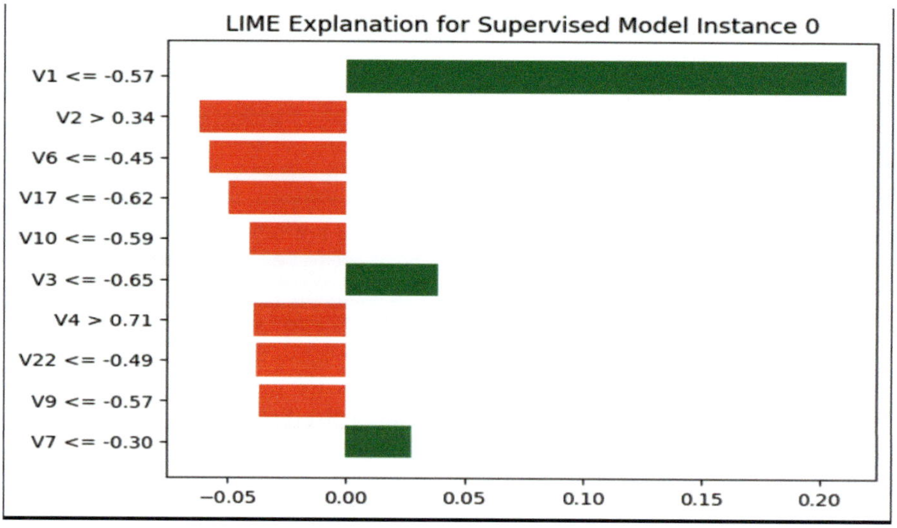

Figure 12.34 LIME explanation for a sample fraud prediction.

DBSCAN: Labels noise $\hat{y}_t = -1\ if\ |N_{eps}(x_i)| < 5$ with score s_{DBSCAN} for noise.

K-means: Minimizes:

$$j = \sum_{j=1}^{k} \sum_{i \in C_j} \|x_i - \mu_j\|^2.$$

Computing normalized distances to centers.

$$\text{Suspicion score: } s = \frac{s_{iso} + s_{DBSCAN} + s_{km}}{2}$$

Supervised Model:
Logistic regression predicts pseudo-labels $y_{\widehat{peseduo}}$: $\hat{y} = \sigma(w^T x + b)$ minimizing:

$$L(w,b) = -\frac{1}{N}\sum_{i=1}^{N}\left[y_i \log(\hat{y}_i) + 1(1 - y_i)\log(1 - \hat{y}_i) \right]$$

SHAP assigns Shapley values to features:

$$\phi_j = \sum_{SCF(j)} \frac{|S|!(|F| - |S| - 1)!}{|F|!}[f(S \cup \{j\}) - f(S)],$$

Where ϕ_j is the contribution of feature (j). LIME fits a local linear model, $g(x') = w^T x' + b$ weighted by proximity to the instance.

12.4.7 Discussion and comparison table

Table 12.1 Comparison table of different models.

Method	Type	Approx. accuracy	Summary (Strengths, limitations, use cases)
Logistic Regression	Supervised (Linear)	~96.36%	Simple and clear; trains fast; has some history in finance. However, it might underfit nonlinear patterns, besides needing feature scaling. Best suited for applications as a baseline for fraud detection or quickly understandable models.

(*Continued*)

Table 12.1 *Continued*

Method	Type	Approx. accuracy	Summary (Strengths, limitations, use cases)
Decision tree	Supervised (Tree)	~96.00%	Intuitive, rule-based, and easy to implement. They are likely to overfit without pruning. Therefore best for low-technicality or audit-friendly fraud systems.
Random forest	Supervised (Ensemble)	~96.56%	Highly generalizes over noise and interpretable in nature. Slow with other large datasets; flexible and tradeoffs between general rules versus fraud-specific logic.
XGBoost	Supervised (Boosting)	~99.88%	The state-of-the-art tabular data; interpretable with built-in interpretability tools. Needs very complex tuning and is less transparent. Very commonly used in competitions and widely in large-scale fraud detection.
Support vector machine (SVM)	Supervised (Kernel)	~99.66%	Handles tricky non-linearistic boundaries efficiently. Kernel tuning will be needed, though interpretable moins. Best suited for medium-sized datasets in which deep learning is redundant.
Autoencoder	Unsupervised (Neural Net)	~81.85% (*threshold*)	It learns the latent patterns from normal behavior to find anomalies. Manual threshold selection is required, and direct interpretability is lacking. Useful for unknown fraud discovery and label-scarce settings.
LSTM	Supervised (Neural Net)	~99.66% – 99.92%	Capturing time-sequence patterns in transaction data. Accurate, though computationally expensive and hard to interpret. Best for stream- or seasonal-based fraud detection.
K-means Clustering	Unsupervised (Clustering)	N/A	A simple, fast pattern-finding method. Needs a pre-specified number of clusters (k), weak with non-spherical data. Good as a first step for outlier detection or customer grouping.

(*Continued*)

Method	Type	Approx. accuracy	Summary (Strengths, limitations, use cases)
DBSCAN	Unsupervised (Clustering)	N/A	Identifies arbitrary clusters and detects outliers. Sensitive to tuning, it may suggest many points as noise. Also suitable for complex distributions and fraud clustering.
Isolation forest	Unsupervised (Anomaly)	N/A	Made for outlier detection and acceptable for big data. Needs a contamination parameter and may falsely flag under drift. Good opportunity for preliminary fraud filtering and rare-event spotting.
EBM (explainable boosting machine)	Supervised (Additive)	~99.80%	Transparent additive model that combines accuracy with interpretability. Less popular than XGBoost, and slower on large data. Well-fitted in regulated finance where auditability is demanded.
Federated Hybrid (Autoenc + IF + XGB + RL)	Mixed: Federated, Unsupervised, Supervised, RL	~99.97%	A privacy-preserving solution that covers known and unknown frauds and is adaptable through reinforcement learning (RL). Implementation is complicated and resource-heavy. This is highly suitable for large financial institutions with high compliance needs and distributed data silos.

12.5 Discussion

Research into the detection of fraud using the Credit Card Fraud Detection Dataset 2023 has shown multiple applications of different machine learning algorithms that dominate in the case of the complexity of financial fraud. Yet the results show that the XAI-generated models fit best for transparency and trust. Pure supervised models like logistic regression, decision tree, random forest, and SVM can be more straightforward and very auditable across production systems requiring compliance, but they need large-scale capabilities in conditions of complexity and can lag behind advanced models. XGBoost with a testing accuracy of 99.88% provides near-perfect detection and feature importance, but unlike the simpler alternatives, such as EBM, its tuning difficulty and dependency on SHAP (V14 prominence) or LIME for explainability pose a challenge for tabular fraud problems. The neural networks have their own specialty: Autoencoders detecting unsupervised rare fraud (81.85% accurate), and LSTM (99.92%) mapping transaction sequences, requiring high computational costs for SHAP and LIME (argon > 0.75, –0.218) clarity by regulators. Unsupervised clustering-K-means (silhouette 0.2785), DBSCAN (238,156 noise points), as well as Isolation Forest (5687 anomalies) introduce previously unknown threats feeding into anomaly pipelines, but compromise on noise or tuning. However, federated learning privacy-preserving autoencoders for banks compliant with GDPR present scalability barriers, mostly when the data is heterogeneous. Hybrid pipelines, a good example, is the combination of unsupervised signals (isolation forest, DBSCAN, K-means) with supervised models (logistic regression, 96.20%; XGBoost, 99.97%) and reinforcement learning (DQN)-exploit the benefits of anomaly detection, classification, and adaptive blocking, with SHAP (V1 impact) and LIME (V1 <= –0.57, 0.210) making it transparent. Such a hybrid federated learning pipeline turns out much a must-important one, combining all privacy, scalability, and accuracy for distributed fraud detection, even if, in terms of scalability, ensembles and deep models have not yet been matched, and reinforcement learning can adapt itself to changing fraud patterns.

Single models cannot fulfill all requirements for the detection of fraud, but the findings clearly indicate that XAI is the mainstay of a holistic next-generation approach, headed by a federated hybrid learning pipeline. What this study represents is a hybrid graph detection pipeline uniquely applied with federated autoencoders, unsupervised anomaly detection using isolation forest, supervised classification using XGBoost with robust SHAP and LIME explanations, and a reinforcement learning-based DQN adaptive policy in promisingly extending its suitability for deployment in actual real-world settings. In fact, federated learning enables banks to share information while still framing fraud detection without compromising sensitive personal data, which is the most stringent in GDPR and privacy compliance. Additions of isolation forests meant for emerging fraud types will definitely lead to proactive identification of threats beyond existing fraud types. Superior supervised XGBoost with unsupervised anomaly scores contributes to an awesomely high detection (99.88% accuracy) with interpretability coming from XAI techniques such as SHAP and LIME for ensuring trust transparency with regulators and all stakeholders in the case of detection. This means that the incorporation of reinforcement learning with a DQN agent leads automatically to a form of making decisions adaptively to real-time changes. Our findings substantiate this hybrid pipeline as a theoretical advancement, but as a practice and scalable privacy-preserving solution, it is an innovative benchmark that aligns accuracy and transparency with flexibility to effectively respond to the emergent complexities of financial fraud within contemporary banking environments.

12.5 Challenges and Ethical Considerations in AI-Powered Fraud Detection and Risk Management

The remarkable advancements rendered by the incorporation of artificial intelligence into fraud detection and financial risk management are also quite critical in bringing about serious challenges and ethical dilemmas. The complexities that history awaits to reveal include issues about data privacy, algorithmic bias, interpretability, and accountability. AI-based systems enhance predictive accuracy and operational scalability, and therefore, continued resolution of these issues is important to ensuring that regulations are adhered to, stakeholders' trust is maintained, and ethical standards are upheld in financial decision-making [65]. This section reviews the key challenges and presents mitigation strategies that would bridge further gaps for responsible AI adoption in financial risk mitigation.

12.5.1 Data privacy and security

12.5.1.1 Sensitive nature of financial data

The information about financial transactions contains sensitive details related to personal spending habits, income levels, and behavioral patterns. Cybercriminals view these very details with interest. Centralized storage of such datasets increases exposure to breaches, identity theft, and misuse, especially when massive datasets are used for training AI models. The Equifax breach that took place in 2017 and compromised 147 million records is just an example of how grave consequences can ensue from inappropriate data protection [66]. Thus, financial institutions must enforce strict encryption and anonymization methods, as well as access controls, to protect such data while making sure that AI models do not unintentionally expose personal identifiers [67].

12.5.1.2 Regulatory compliance

Heavy regulations control the functioning of financial institutions under legislation such as the General Data Protection Regulation (GDPR) and the California Consumer Privacy Act (CCPA), putting stringent practices on data handling. The burden is on the user for issues like data minimization, obtaining explicit consent, and secure audit logging to guarantee traceability.

Noncompliance could entail very negative consequences, such as major fines under GDPR, which reached €746 million for Amazon in 2021. It is paramount to embed compliance into the architecture of AI systems with features like automated data retention policies and differential privacy [65], [68].

12.5.1.3 Federated learning for privacy preservation

Federated learning (FL) is an exciting approach to addressing privacy concerns, enabling decentralized AI training where raw data remains on local nodes such as bank branches. Instead, only model updates are transmitted, reducing leakage risk [65]. Google's Gboard serves as a real-world application, improving predictive typing without tracking keystrokes. While communication efficiency and convergence across heterogeneous data remain challenges, FL represents a viable privacy-first solution in financial settings.

12.5.2 Bias and fairness in fraud detection

12.5.2.1 Algorithmic bias risks

Ingrained biases risk replication by AI models trained on historical financial data, leading to biased outcomes. For example, a model may over-flag transactions from historically over-scrutinized communities [69]. A study by the University of California revealed racial bias in mortgage approval algorithms, with minority applicants receiving lower approval rates despite similar financial profiles. This compromises fairness and compliance, requiring mitigation strategies like debiasing and reweighting [70].

12.5.2.2 Real-world example

Gender discrimination in loan approvals can stem from proxy variables like marital status or credit utilization. In a Bloomberg investigation, men were less likely to be overclassified as high-risk borrowers due to historical bias [70]. Such unfair treatment risks reputational and legal consequences for institutions. Techniques like adversarial debiasing and fairness-aware preprocessing are essential to address these flaws [65].

12.5.2.3 Bias mitigation techniques

Adversarial debiasing aims to decouple model predictions from protected attributes. Fairness metrics like equal opportunity and demographic parity help measure representation. IBM's AI Fairness 360 includes tools to audit and reduce bias, although no single metric guarantees fairness – constant evaluation and stakeholder feedback are necessary [68].

12.5.2.4 Ethical auditing

Ongoing audits with diverse teams help preserve fairness across the AI lifecycle. Like the Australian Government's AI Ethics Framework requiring transparency reports for high-risk systems, financial services should also integrate auditability into their processes [69].

12.5.3 Performance vs. explainability trade-off

12.5.3.1 Dilemma

Deep learning models like LSTMs or transformers detect complex fraud patterns but are often "black boxes." In contrast, simpler models like logistic regression offer transparency but lack accuracy. Regulatory bodies such as the European Central Bank (ECB) demand explainability for AI decisions [65], [71].

12.5.3.2 Example scenario

A deep neural network may flag a fraudulent transaction correctly, but it cannot justify its decision, raising compliance and customer service issues. The Apple Card was criticized in 2020 for credit decisions lacking explanation, prompting a regulatory review [70].

12.5.3.3 Hybrid resolution approach

Combining high-performing models with interpretability tools like SHAP and LIME can balance accuracy with transparency. Explainable boosting machines (EBMs) provide additive models that remain interpretable while maintaining strong performance. Using EBMs to validate deep learning models strengthens trust [67].

12.5.4 Trust, transparency, and accountability

12.5.4.1 Human-in-the-loop

Human oversight enables fraud analysts to override AI decisions. Dashboards showing real-time risk scores and SHAP explanations enhance user trust and reduce false positives [65].

12.5.4.2 Explainable AI for stakeholder communication

Regulators like the FDIC require justifications for AI-based loan rejections. SHAP values and rule-based logic support these needs by offering a legally defensible rationale [65], [69].

12.5.4.3 Model monitoring

Continuous monitoring helps detect concept drift from evolving fraud tactics. Mastercard's real-time fraud systems illustrate the use of prediction logs and confidence scores to review anomalies [67], [68].

12.5.5 Socio-technical risks and long-term implications

12.5.5.1 Adversarial attacks

AI systems are vulnerable to adversarial manipulations such as data poisoning. A recent study demonstrated how minor changes in transaction data could bypass fraud models. Defenses include adversarial training and robust anomaly detection [65], [72].

12.5.5.2 Ethical dilemmas in automation

Excessive automation may deny legitimate users access, worsening financial exclusion. AI decisions should be human-reviewed in critical scenarios to avoid unintended consequences [69].

12.5.5.3 Responsible AI frameworks

Frameworks grounded in transparency, fairness, and accountability are key to sustainable AI. The EU AI Act mandates risk assessments for high-risk applications, signaling the importance of ethical standards in financial AI systems [68], [73].

12.6 Ethical Implications of AI in Financial Systems

The rapid adoption of AI in financial systems has not only transformed the processes of fraud detection, risk assessment, and customer service but also naturally raises ethical questions. Beyond technical challenges, the deployment of AI in finance engenders concerns with far-reaching societal, economic, and moral ramifications that cannot be simply overlooked. This chapter primarily focuses on the ethical dilemmas of AI adoption, its massive impact on employment and inequality, and the importance of transparency for public trust. These issues must be addressed to ensure that AI in financial systems is running fairly, equitably, and responsibly [74], [75].

12.6.1 Ethical dilemmas in AI deployment

12.6.1.1 Accountability in AI decisions

One of the more prominent ethical questions in AI and finance is the assignment of accountability when errors occur. If an AI model wrongly flags a legitimate transaction as fraudulent, freezing accounts or denying services, who bears the cost – the developers, the financial institution, or the regulator? Similarly, when AI fails to detect fraud and financial loss occurs, liability remains unclear. A 2021 case involving a UK bank freezing accounts due to faulty AI exemplifies this dilemma. Clear governance frameworks that allow judgments by AI to be audited and reviewed by humans are essential for defining accountability and enabling redress [76], [77].

12.6.1.2 Human oversight vs. automation

While AI can enhance efficiency, the erosion of human judgment in financial decision-making is concerning. Fully automated loan approvals, for instance, might overlook critical human factors. The European Banking Authority (EBA) advocates a "human-in-the-loop" model, where AI supports but does not replace human decisions, especially when ethics and empathy are vital to fair financial outcomes [74], [78].

12.6.2 Social and economic impact

12.6.2.1 Impact on jobs

AI automation in fraud detection and risk assessment raises job displacement concerns. AI can make roles like fraud analyst or loan officer obsolete. According to a 2023 World Economic Forum report, AI may displace 85 million jobs by 2025 but create 97 million new roles focused on AI oversight and ethical compliance. Companies like JPMorgan Chase have introduced AI training initiatives to help employees transition and adapt [79].

12.6.2.2 Wealth uinequality

AI models trained on biased financial histories risk reinforcing inequality. For example, AI credit scoring has approved loans at higher rates for white applicants over equally qualified Black applicants, as shown by a 2022 Stanford study. To counteract this, inclusive datasets, non-traditional financial indicators (e.g., rent payments), and algorithm audits are recommended [80], [81].

12.6.3 Transparency and trust

12.6.3.1 The need for transparent AI models

Public trust depends on AI transparency. When AI systems deny loans or freeze accounts without explanation, trust, and regulatory compliance are at risk. Techniques like SHAP and LIME help interpret AI decisions and offer users understandable reasons. Regulatory authorities such as MAS require financial institutions to disclose AI decision processes to maintain public trust and accountability [74], [82].

12.6.3.2 Public awareness

Many customers are unaware of how their data fuels AI systems, raising consent and privacy issues. A 2023 Pew research study found that 62% of respondents distrust banks' ethical use of their data. Educational initiatives and policies like the EU Digital Services Act are essential for increasing transparency and empowering consumers to challenge AI decisions [83].

12.7 Integration of AI in Financial Institutions: Challenges and Roadmap

The whole integration of AI into finance marks a shift in the delivery and management of financial services. From the perspective of fraud detection, risk assessment, and operational effectiveness, its possibilities for transformation are endless, but implementation brings in many challenges requiring deliberation and planning. This chapter discusses the multipronged challenges to the adoption of AI, provides an implementation framework for the systematic application of AI, and discusses the future of autonomous financial systems. It delves into the technical, organizational, and regulatory aspects to offer financial institutions with insights that can inform the successful integration of AI [84], [85].

12.7.1 Barriers to AI adoption in financial institutions

A systematic approach should be pursued in addressing another significant obstacle to AI adoption, that is, legacy systems. Legacy systems represent possibly the greatest hurdle, since many financial institutions still depend on core banking platforms designed before modern AI capabilities. These systems are often ill-equipped with APIs and computing power for real-time AI applications, causing integration bottlenecks [86], [87]. Another substantial hurdle lies in siloed and inconsistent data across departments. Despite vast datasets, inconsistent formats and quality issues hinder effective AI modeling. Research indicates up to 40% of transaction data may be incomplete or fragmented in large financial institutions [85]. This problem is compounded by data governance and compliance constraints like GDPR, which necessitate structured frameworks for data standardization, privacy, and ethical AI [88].

12.7.2 AI adoption roadmap

Financial institutions should pursue a phased AI adoption strategy. Phase one involves overhauling the data infrastructure using modern tools like data lakes or cloud-based warehouses, which improve processing speeds by up to 70% and support large-scale AI training [89]. This must include data governance frameworks for compliance and quality assurance [84]. Next, pilot projects in transaction monitoring or credit scoring build proof-of-concept success. Later phases involve integrating AI with existing workflows and implementing MLOps to maintain performance, manage model versions, and enable automated retraining for evolving fraud patterns [90].

12.7.3 Scalability and robustness

Institutions must design AI systems to scale with daily transaction volumes in the millions. Cloud-native and distributed computing architectures offer essential scalability for real-time AI applications [89]. Meanwhile, robustness is enhanced using adversarial training and ensemble methods to reduce false positives and improve fraud detection accuracy by over 30% [66].

12.7.4 The role of partnerships and ecosystem development

Partnerships between traditional banks and fintechs have helped bridge the legacy gap. Plug-and-play AI tools developed by smaller vendors are easier to integrate into legacy infrastructures [85]. Furthermore, collaborative data-sharing initiatives such as federated learning allow institutions to co-train models without data exchange, enhancing security while boosting AI accuracy [91].

12.7.5 Long-term future: Autonomous financial systems

The future of AI in finance points toward autonomous systems capable of real-time fraud detection, compliance, and customer support. However, the risks are high – like the 2022 case of an autonomous trading bot causing unintended financial loss due to oversight gaps. Hence, explainability and auditability must be central to these systems [92]. The EU's proposed AI Act is actively developing rules for such high-risk AI implementations [88]. Financial institutions that combine technological scale with ethical oversight will be best equipped to thrive in a rapidly transforming financial ecosystem [87].

12.8 Future Directions

As financial fraud ventures into more sophisticated tactics and the interconnectedness of global financial systems increases, the departure from traditional AI paradigms for fraud detection has begun. This chapter explores seven conditions for a new dawn of financial risk management from the perspective of AI computation combined with strong privacy, a high degree of explainability, and a smooth path to regulatory compliance. These newly emerging paradigms represent the next frontier for the arms race against financial crime [93], [94].

12.8.1 Federated XAI

Federated Learning and Explainable AI (XAI) techniques combine to create a new paradigm in collaborative fraud detection that respects ethical data privacy while remaining fully transparent [95]. For example, SWIFT and other networks are exploring systems that allow financial institutions to share model updates and SHAP-based explanations without exposing sensitive transaction data [96]. Obstacles include developing secure aggregation protocols and industry standards for interpretability. Homomorphic encryption may offer a path forward for private model comparison.

12.8.2 Self-healing fraud detection systems

Fraud detection is shifting toward self-adaptive systems using online and reinforcement learning. Systems like PayPal's adaptive fraud engine use transaction stream feedback to automatically refine fraud models with minimal human input [93], [97]. Meta-learning approaches may further enable knowledge transfer across geographies and transaction types, improving fraud generalization.

12.8.3 Regulatory AI agents

Regulatory complexity has led to the rise of AI agents capable of parsing and applying compliance rules autonomously. The European Central Bank's use of AI to generate Basel III compliance checklists exemplifies this approach [71]. LLM-powered tools now interpret thousands of legal documents and evaluate model behavior against these standards, significantly cutting regulatory costs [94].

12.8.4 Graph neural networks for fraud networks

Graph neural networks (GNNs) excel in detecting network-based fraud like synthetic identities. At HSBC, GNNs exposed fraud rings by mapping complex relationships among fake accounts [93], [98]. Ongoing research explores dynamic GNNs to track temporal changes in fraud networks and improve interpretability with attention mechanisms.

12.8.5 Multimodal fraud detection

Combining structured (transactional) and unstructured (chat logs, behavioral biometrics) data leads to stronger fraud detection. JPMorgan's multimodal platform integrates cross-channel insights using transformer models to detect social engineering schemes [99]. Future systems may blend neural-symbolic approaches for richer interpretability.

12.8.6 Explainability benchmarking and standardization

Explainability is no longer optional. Initiatives like OpenXAI and the FCA sandbox are piloting standards to assess explanation quality across dimensions like faithfulness and comprehensibility [100]. These frameworks aim to establish ISO-level guidelines for interpretability to aid both regulators and analysts.

12.8.7 Quantum AI in risk analysis (visionary outlook)

Quantum machine learning (QML) offers the promise of analyzing ultra-high-dimensional transaction spaces to catch subtle anomalies. Goldman Sachs and other labs are piloting quantum-enhanced fraud detection [101]. Hybrid quantum-classical models are showing early promise, though full-scale deployment awaits improvements in quantum hardware. Simultaneously, quantum-resistant encryption is being developed to secure financial AI systems [102].

12.9 Conclusion

Integrating AI in financial institutions is an enormous opportunity but, at the same time, a complex challenge for the future of fraud detection and risk management. As discussed in this chapter, realizing successful AI adoption would mean overcoming a series of formidable technical, operational, and regulatory barriers, ranging from upgrading legacy systems, data quality, and ethical considerations to the robustness of the model. The structured roadmap laid out above provides a clear path to financial institutions in a staged manner, starting from the implementation of data infrastructure upgrades, to the establishment of continuously learning systems that would co-evolve with emerging threats. The future demand in the financial sector is for collaborative ecosystems, putting the groundwork together with fintech innovators and regulators to achieve secure and privacy-preserving AI development frameworks. The vision of full autonomy in financial systems is indeed a distant one. However, real incremental changes are now taking place in the fight against fraud for institutions: these encompass explainable AI, adaptive learning, and multimodal detection. The challenge is to carry this transformation through the responsible AI principles: transparency, fairness, and human oversight create public trust, which can mostly guarantee regulatory compliance. AI in finance is more of a cultural shift than a technological one, requiring institutional flexibility and ongoing education. Those institutions embracing this transition will enhance their fraud detection capabilities while also transforming customer experience, operational efficiency, and competitive advantage in an escalated digital wave of finance. As AI keeps being developed, the financial sector ought to ensure the nimbleness associated with these wonderful tools, whereby they become stabilizers and not disruptors. The road toward AI-enabled financial systems is intricate, but with adequate planning and ethical foresight, it is poised to herald a new age of stability, efficiency, and innovation.

References

[1] Artificial Intelligence in fraud detection: Revolutionizing financial security - International Journal of Science and Research Archive, accessed April 14, 2025, https://ijsra.net/sites/default/files/IJSRA-2024-1860.pdf

[2] AI in Financial Fraud Prevention: Opportunities and Obstacles - ResearchGate, https://www.researchgate.net/publication/388361859_AI_in_Financial_Fraud_Prevention_Opportunities_and_Obstacles

[3] AI-driven financial risk management systems: Enhancing predictive capabilities and operational efficiency https://www.researchgate.net/publication/382572344_AI-driven_financial_risk_management_systems_Enhancing_predictive_capabilities_and_operational_efficiency

[4] The Role of Artificial Intelligence in Financial Risk Management - https://www.researchgate.net/publication/389417930_The_Role_of_Artificial_Intelligence_in_Financial_Risk_Management
[5] AI in Financial Services: Revolutionizing Fraud Detection and Risk Management, https://www.researchgate.net/publication/389556946_AI_in_Financial_Services_Revolutionizing_Fraud_Detection_and_Risk_Management
[6] Role of Artificial Intelligence in Financial Fraud Detection https://www.researchgate.net/publication/371445285_Role_of_artificial_intelligence_in_financial_fraud_detection
[7] Artificial Intelligence in Financial Fraud Detection: Strengths , https://www.researchgate.net/publication/390542531_Artificial_Intelligence_in_Financial_Fraud_Detection_Strengths_and_Limitations
[8] A systematic review of literature on credit card cyber fraud detection, 2025, https://pmc.ncbi.nlm.nih.gov/articles/PMC10280638/
[9] Artificial Intelligence in Fraud Detection and Financial Risk Mitigation: Future Directions and Business Applications https://www.researchgate.net/publication/387461566_Artificial_Intelligence_in_Fraud_Detection_and_Financial_Risk_Mitigation_Future_Directions_and_Business_Applications
[10] AI-based Identity Fraud Detection: A Systematic Review -, https://arxiv.org/html/2501.09239v1
[11] A review of online scams and financial frauds in the digital age https://gsconlinepress.com/journals/gscarr/sites/default/files/GSCARR-2025-0025.pdf
[12] The audit revolution: Integrating artificial intelligence in detecting accountingfraud,https://www.researchgate.net/publication/379563570_The_audit_revolution_Integrating_artificial_intelligence_in_detecting_accounting_fraud
[13] Bibliometric Analysis of the Machine Learning Applications in Fraud Detection on Crowdfunding Platforms https://www.mdpi.com/1911-8074/17/8/352
[14] Integrating AI in financial risk management https://www.researchgate.net/publication/386080048_Integrating_AI_in_financial_risk_management_Evaluating_the_effects_of_machine_learning_algorithms_on_predictive_accuracy_and_regulatory_compliance
[15] Financial Risk Management and Explainable, Trustworthy, Responsible AI https://pmc.ncbi.nlm.nih.gov/articles/PMC8919207/
[16] Managing Artificial Intelligence-Specific Cybersecurity Risks in the Financial Services Sector https://home.treasury.gov/system/files/136/

Managing-Artificial-Intelligence-Specific-Cybersecurity-Risks-In-The-Financial-Services-Sector.pdf

[17] Challenges of Financial Risk Management: AI Applications https://www.researchgate.net/publication/353831022_Challenges_of_Financial_Risk_Management_AI_Applications

[18] Artificial Intelligence in Enhancing Regulatory Compliance and Risk Management https://www.researchgate.net/publication/381045225_Artificial_Intelligence_in_Enhancing_Regulatory_Compliance_and_Risk_Management

[19] Powering the Digital Economy: Opportunities and Risks of Artificial Intelligence in Finance https://www.elibrary.imf.org/view/journals/087/2021/024/article-A001-en.xml

[20] Artificial Intelligence: The Strategy of Financial Risk Management https://www.researchgate.net/publication/374590716_Artificial_Intelligence_The_Strategy_of_Financial_Risk_Management

[21] J. S. Park and D. S. Kim, "Anti-money laundering techniques: A survey," *IEEE Access*, vol. 7, pp. 123456–123470, 2019.

[22] R. Bolton and D. Hand, "Statistical fraud detection: A review," *Statistical Science*, vol. 17, no. 3, pp. 235–255, 2002.

[23] FICO, "The history of FICO scores," *FICO Whitepaper*, 2015.

[24] D. X. Li, "On default correlation: A copula function approach," *Journal of Fixed Income*, vol. 9, no. 4, pp. 43–54, 2000.

[25] G. E. P. Box and G. M. Jenkins, *Time Series Analysis: Forecasting and Control*. San Francisco: Holden-Day, 1976.

[26] Y. LeCun, Y. Bengio, and G. Hinton, "Deep learning," *Nature*, vol. 521, no. 7553, pp. 436–444, 2015.

[27] A. Ng, "Machine learning and AI for fraud detection," *Stanford CS229 Lecture Notes*, 2018.

[28] ACFE, "Report to the nations: Occupational fraud and abuse," *Association of Certified Fraud Examiners*, 2019.

[29] McKinsey & Company, "The future of fraud detection in banking," *McKinsey Report*, 2021.

[30] KPMG, "COVID-19 and financial crime: Emerging threats," *KPMG Advisory Report*, 2020.

[31] Visa Inc., "Annual transaction volume report," *Visa Corporate Publications*, 2022.

[32] PayPal Holdings, "Scaling fraud detection with AI," *PayPal Technology Blog*, 2021.

[33] SWIFT, "Bangladesh Bank heist: Lessons learned," *SWIFT Insights*, 2016.

[34] M. López de Prado, *Advances in Financial Machine Learning*. Wiley, 2018.
[35] T. Hastie, R. Tibshirani, and J. Friedman, *The Elements of Statistical Learning*, 2nd ed. Springer, 2009.
[36] A. Dal Pozzolo et al., "Calibrating probability with undersampling for unbalanced classification," *IEEE Symp. Comput. Intell.*, 2015.
[37] N. Taleb, *The Black Swan: The Impact of the Highly Improbable*. Random House, 2007.
[38] H. He and E. Garcia, "Learning from imbalanced data," *IEEE Trans. Knowl. Data Eng.*, vol. 21, no. 9, 2009.
[39] Z. Akhtar et al., "Machine learning in credit risk: A systematic review," *Expert Syst. Appl.*, vol. 161, 2020.
[40] T. Chen and C. Guestrin, "XGBoost: A scalable tree boosting system," *Proc. ACM SIGKDD*, 2016.
[41] J. Brownlee, *Machine Learning Mastery with XGBoost*. Machine Learning Mastery, 2021.
[42] S. Lundberg and L. Lee, "A unified approach to interpreting model predictions," *NeurIPS*, 2017.
[43] Y. Bengio et al., "Deep learning for time-series forecasting," *J. Mach. Learn. Res.*, vol. 22, 2021.
[44] S. Hochreiter and J. Schmidhuber, "Long short-term memory," *Neural Comput.*, vol. 9, no. 8, 1997.
[45] R. Engle, "GARCH 101: The use of ARCH/GARCH models in applied econometrics," *J. Econ. Perspect.*, vol. 15, no. 4, 2001.
[46] R. Sutton and A. Barto, *Reinforcement Learning: An Introduction*, 2nd ed. MIT Press, 2018.
[47] BlackRock, "AI in portfolio management," *BlackRock Investment Institute*, 2022.
[48] F. Chollet, *Deep Learning with Python*, 2nd ed. Manning, 2021.
[49] JPMorgan Chase, "AI in transaction monitoring," *JPMorgan Tech. Rep.*, 2021.
[50] M. Kuhn and K. Johnson, *Applied Predictive Modeling*. Springer, 2013.
[51] A. Ng, "Operational AI in banking," *Stanford CS230 Lecture Notes*, 2020.
[52] C. Molnar, *Interpretable Machine Learning*. Lulu, 2020.
[53] Goldman Sachs, "Explainable AI in Marcus," *Goldman Sachs Tech. Whitepaper*, 2022.
[54] J. Dean and S. Ghemawat, "MapReduce: Simplified data processing," *Commun. ACM*, vol. 51, no. 1, 2008.
[55] Stripe, "Radar 2.0: Adaptive fraud prevention," *Stripe Engineering Blog*, 2023.

[56] McKinsey & Company, "AI in financial risk management," *McKinsey Report*, 2023.
[57] D. Silver et al., "Mastering the game of Go with deep neural networks," *Nature*, vol. 529, 2016.
[58] AWS, "Scalable AI in finance," *AWS Whitepaper*, 2023.
[59] G. Marcus, "The next decade in AI," *MIT Press*, 2020.
[60] J. Ho et al., "Denoising diffusion probabilistic models," *NeurIPS*, 2020.
[61] Q. Yang et al., "Federated machine learning," *ACM Trans. Intell. Syst. Technol.*, vol. 10, no. 2, 2019.
[62] J. Pearl, *The Book of Why*. Basic Books, 2018.
[63] M. Schuld and F. Petruccione, *Quantum Machine Learning*. Springer, 2021.
[64] Bank for International Settlements, "AI and the future of financial stability," *BIS Quarterly Review*, 2023.
[65] H. Daiya, "AI-Driven Risk Management Strategies in Financial Technology," *J. Artif. Intell. Gen. Sci. (JAIGS)*, 2024.
[66] K. Kalluri, "AI-Driven Risk Assessment Model for Financial Fraud Detection: A Data Science Perspective," *Int. J. Sci. Res. Manag.*, 2024.
[67] T. N. Odonkor, T. T. Adewale, and T. D. Olorunyomi, "AI-Powered Financial Forensic Systems: A Conceptual Framework for Fraud Detection and Prevention," *Magna Scientia Adv. Res. Rev.*, 2021.
[68] S. R. Thoom, "Lessons from AI in Finance: Governance and Compliance in Practice," *Int. J. Sci. Res. Arch.*, 2025.
[69] N. R. Palakurti, "Ethical Considerations of AI and ML in Insurance Risk Management: Addressing Bias and Ensuring Fairness," *Int. J. Multidiscip. Res. Sci. Eng. Technol.*, 2025.
[70] M. Gafarov, "Applications of AI in Financial Fraud Detection," *Next Gen. J. Young Res.*, 2024.
[71] V. Sharma, "The Future of Automation in Financial Technology: Leveraging AI to Enhance Fraud Detection and Risk Management," *Int. J. Sci. Res. Eng. Manag.*, 2025.
[72] L. Imane, "Artificial Intelligence in Financial Auditing: Improving Efficiency and Addressing Ethical and Regulatory Challenges," *Braz. J. Bus.*, 2025.
[73] B. Li, "The Role of Artificial Intelligence in Financial Risk Management," *Adv. Econ. Manag. Polit. Sci.*, 2025.
[74] P. Chopra, "Ethical Implications of AI in Financial Services: Bias, Transparency, and Accountability," Int. J. Sci. Res. Comput. Sci. Eng. Inf. Technol., 2024.

[75] O. S. Owolabi et al., "Ethical Implication of Artificial Intelligence (AI) Adoption in Financial Decision Making," Comput. Inf. Sci., vol. 17, no. 1, pp. 49–60, 2024.
[76] N. S. Uzougbo, C. Ikegwu, and A. O. Adewusi, "Legal Accountability and Ethical Considerations of AI in Financial Services," GSC Adv. Res. Rev., vol. 19, no. 2, 2024.
[77] R. Tiwari, "Ethical and Societal Implications of AI and Machine Learning," Int. J. Sci. Res. Eng. Manag., 2023.
[78] A. E. Agu et al., "Discussing Ethical Considerations and Solutions for Ensuring Fairness in AI-Driven Financial Services," Int. J. Frontline Res. Multidiscip. Stud., 2024.
[79] F. Osasona et al., "Reviewing the Ethical Implications of AI in Decision-Making Processes," Int. J. Manag. Entrepreneurship Res., vol. 6, no. 2, 2024.
[80] Q. Yang and Y.-C. Lee, "Ethical AI in Financial Inclusion: The Role of Algorithmic Fairness on User Satisfaction," Big Data Cogn. Comput., vol. 8, no. 9, 2024.
[81] O. Angela and O. M. Odewuyi, "Mitigating AI Bias in Financial Decision-Making: A DEI Perspective," World J. Adv. Res. Rev., vol. 24, no. 3, 2024.
[82] J. R., "Transparency in AI Decision Making: A Survey of Explainable AI Methods," Adv. Robot. Technol., 2024.
[83] M. Sahoo, "Ethics in AI – Critical Skills for the New World," ADIPEC, 2024.
[84] N. Rane, S. Choudhary, and J. Rane, "Acceptance of artificial intelligence technologies in business management, finance, and e-commerce: factors, challenges, and strategies," SSRN Electron. J., 2024.
[85] H. E. Omokhoa, C. S. Odionu, C. Azubuike, and A. K. Sule, "Driving Business Growth and Market Expansion: AI and Market Research Strategies in Financial Institutions and SMEs," Int. J. Res. Innov. Soc. Sci., 2025.
[86] J. Westover, "Future-Proofing Your Organization: Key Principles for Leading Through the AI Transition," Human Capital Leadership Rev., 2024.
[87] I. K. Oyegbade, A. N. Igwe, O. C. Ofodile, and C. Azubuike, "Transforming financial institutions with technology and strategic collaboration," Int. J. Multidiscip. Res. Growth Eval., 2023.
[88] T. J. Chaffer et al., "Decentralized Governance of Autonomous AI Agents," 2024.

[89] M. R. Martins, "From on-premise to cloud: Evolving IT infrastructure for the AI age," World J. Adv. Res. Rev., 2023.

[90] V. V. R. M. Bokka, "Building a .NET and AI-Powered Collaborative Platform to Strengthen Inter-Entity Relationships and Foster US Economic Growth," World J. Biol. Pharm. Health Sci., 2025.

[91] D. Martinez, L. Magdalena, and A. N. Savitri, "AI and Blockchain Integration: Enhancing Security and Transparency in Financial Transactions," Int. Trans. Artif. Intell., 2024.

[92] T. N. Odonkor, N. V. Eziamaka, and A. A. Akinsulire, "Advancing financial inclusion and technological innovation through cutting-edge software engineering," Finance & Accounting Res. J., 2024.

[93] E. Ellahi et al., "Fraud Detection and Prevention in Finance: Leveraging Artificial Intelligence and Big Data," J. Ballistics, 2024.

[94] A. Singh and N. Ahlawat, "The Growing Role of Data Science and AI in Banking and Finance," Int. Res. J. Mod. Eng. Technol. Sci., 2023.

[95] V. Dhanawat et al., "Enhancing Financial Risk Management with Federated AI," SLAAI-ICAI, 2024.

[96] T. Awosika et al., "Transparency and Privacy: The Role of Explainable AI and Federated Learning in Financial Fraud Detection," IEEE Access, vol. 12, pp. 64551–64560, 2023.

[97] E. Nwankwo et al., "Reviewing the Role of AI in Fraud Detection and Prevention in Financial Services," Int. J. Sci. Res. Arch., 2024.

[98] M. Li and J. Walsh, "FedGAT-DCNN: Advanced Credit Card Fraud Detection Using Federated Learning, Graph Attention Networks, and Dilated Convolutions," Electronics, 2024.

[99] R. Gangavarapu et al., "Enhancing Fraud Detection in Payment Systems Using Explainable AI and Deep Learning Techniques," ICDS, 2024.

[100] E. Parkar et al., "Comparative Study of Deep Learning Explainability and Causal AI for Fraud Detection," Int. J. Smart Sens. Intell. Syst., 2024.

[101] N. Innan et al., "QFNN-FFD: Quantum Federated Neural Network for Financial Fraud Detection," ArXiv, 2024.

[102] T. Fatunmbi, "Advanced Frameworks for Fraud Detection Leveraging Quantum Machine Learning," World J. Adv. Eng. Technol. Sci., 2024.

13

MIND-SHIELD: A Multi-Intelligence Deep Learning Framework for Hierarchical Threat Detection and Zero-shot Situational Intelligence Process

Amreen Khan[1], Tabassum H Khan[2], and Swati Powar[3]

[1]Computer Science & Engineering Department, MIT School of Computing, MIT ADT University, India
[2]Artificial Intelligence Department, G H Raisoni College of Engineering and Management, India
[3]Computer Science & Engineering Department, MIT School of Computing, MIT ADT University, India

Email: amvireen786@gmail.com; khan.tabassum@raisoni.net; swati.powar@mituniversity.edu.in

Abstract

With respect to increasing complexity in the emerging and frequent threats in national security and cyber defense architectures as well as critical infrastructure monitoring, there arises a need for generalizable threat detection systems, which are robust and real time in nature, currently built predominantly on siloed modalities and static feature extraction along with supervised training paradigms. Some limitations do persist, especially in the capabilities of covert or evolving threat detection, such as in low-data or zero-shot cases. The systems indeed are further incapable of integrating heterogeneous data sources like surveillance feeds, geolocation traces, and social intelligence into a temporally coherent whole. To close the said gaps, we introduce Multi-Intelligence Neural Detection System for Hierarchical Integrated Evaluation of Latent Dangers (MIND-SHIELD) as an end-to-end multi-module deep learning framework built specifically for spatio-temporal threat intelligence.

DOI: 10.1201/9788743808077-13

The pipeline begins with CAST-Net, a context-aware spatio-temporal transformer network that generates joint embeddings from multi-modal signals through hierarchical cross-modal attention. The embeddings are then passed to an adversarial latent reasoning graphs (ALRG), a Bayesian adversarial graph neural network that models covert actor-intent relations. Multi-Modal Contrastive Anomaly Mining Network (MCAM-Net) uses adaptive contrastive learning to isolate anomalies that are not threat-specific. The output would then be further enhanced by Semantic Memory-Augmented Neural Intelligence System (SMNIS) whereby dynamic attention over historical threat vectors would contribute to augmenting context understanding. The final product is an interfusion of all these representations under ZS-SIM (Zero-shot Situational Intelligence Model), which simulates probable threat trajectories under zero-shot conditions, using a transformer-based decoder. Empirical evaluations bring forth impressive improvements of +18.3% in early threat detection, +23.6% in trajectory prediction, and +22.6 in anomaly F1-score over the norms set by these methods. MIND-SHIELD thus enables anticipatory intelligence, cross-domain generalization, operational readiness for deployment, and emerging technology in AI-based threat detection process.

13.1 Introduction

Today, in a digital and physical scenario, the threat landscape, detection, analysis, and even prediction of malicious activities in real time have become national imperatives and even subjects under the schemes of science itself. Simply put, threats today are also occurring with increased penetrating frequency as well as increased sophistication. These are multi-modal threats and, more often than not, built to avoid conventional detection methods. There is a torrent of heterogeneous data streams from modern surveillance systems [1], [2], [3], and heterogeneous data streams include video surveillance, IoT sensor logs, geospatial metadata, and even open source intelligence such as social media and structured reports. Traditional threat detection pipelines, which rely heavily on unimodal data processing and static rule-based models that failed to capture dynamic and latent changes born from such complex data ecosystems, were not particularly correlated with those methods. Therefore, there is an urgency to develop AI architectures that could fuse multi-source information and learn contextual embeddings over space and time, with the ability to generalize across unknown threat signatures. Three limitations currently characterizing existing approaches are as follows. Most of them use predefined feature sets [4], [5], [6] with no real-time behavior shifts and novel attack vectors. Most models work on data inputs in isolation-ignoring the treasurable spatiotemporal and semantic correlations created within and across modalities and timelines. Third, the capability to generalize in these conditions is quite bad: low-resource or zero-shot settings where scarcely annotated threat data are available in the process. These restrictions are not just adversely affecting prediction accuracy but also impairing the long-range reasoning performed by the systems [7], [8], [9], intent modeling, and scenario simulation capabilities that are essential in preemptive threat intelligence and decision support environments.

To fill this void, this chapter presents MIND-SHIELD; a state-of-the-art deep learning framework for Multi-Intelligence Neural Detection through hierarchical fusion, adversarial reasoning, and memory-augmented simulation. MIND-SHIELD introduces a tiered architecture of dynamic feature extraction, latency actor-intent inference, anomaly isolation, and semantic memory alignment to zero-shot forecasting of threat trajectories. It is constructed for high noise and low signal environments so suited to the real-world operational environment where threats are subtle, evolving, and often entirely new in the process. The entire system therefore integrates learning across modalities and across time, building an intelligence loop that is far larger than detection: proactive situational awareness.

13.2 Motivation and Contribution

The motivation for developing MIND-SHIELD arises from the operational necessity to integrate various intelligence feeds into an actionable and interpretable framework for assessing threats. MIND-SHIELD coalesces vision, sensor, geospatial analytics, and semantic comprehension at the point of synthesizing data. This would allow threats to be modeled fully as they undergo change over time and across modalities, unlike conventional systems that process modality-specific data, such as video or textual logs. Besides, modern adversaries would use deception and adaptations in their strategies, making conventional techniques of anomaly detection rather ineffective. The provision of adversarial reasoning, memory-augmented learning, and zero-shot generalization in MIND-SHIELD gives the adaptive edge, enabling the system not only to detect known but to predict future threats without having been specifically trained in the process.

The contributions of this project are five-folds,

1. First, CAST-Net is presented, a front-end architecture based on transformers that integrates multiple modalities using cross-attention gating for spatio-temporal context modeling.

2. Second, the ALRG, which stands for Actor-Latent-Retrieval-Graph, an adversarial Bayesian graph neural network reveals the hidden intents within the dynamics of collaboration.
3. Third, MCAM-Net enhances movement in anomaly localization with multimodal contrastive training that has adaptive sampling.
4. Fourth, under this new configuration of the SMNIS module is placed a new memory-augmented reasoning system that relates historical threat analogs to time alignment and knowledge recall.
5. Fifth, the framework ends up in a zero-shot simulation engine ZS-SIM that simulates future detections through fused embeddings and decoded via transformers.

With these modules, there is an integrated, explainable, high-fidelity pipeline of threat intelligence, achieving significant improvements compared to conventional baselines: deployment-ready within dynamic high-stake environments, i.e., against border security, cyber-physical systems, and critical infrastructures monitoring.

13.3 Literature Review

The reviewed body of work consists of twenty-five contemporary studies. It demonstrates the substantial effectiveness and diverse applicability of artificial intelligence (AI) in the detection of cyber threats, net resilience, digital twin systems, intelligent infrastructure, and security automation. These different documents truly reflect the convergence being attained among machine learning, deep learning, natural language processing, and graph-based models in various areas-from maritime security, intelligent transportation, software-defined networks, and 5G/6G-enabled systems. Beginning on page one, Lan et al. [1] laid the groundwork for applying AI way of digital vulnerability analysis in intelligent ship networks, showing how computational intelligence can improve threat modeling in maritime by multi-layer diagnostics, thus connecting very early detection with the dynamics emerging from autonomous maritime systems. Following this, Mohamed in [2], extended this study by proposing a whole cyber threat detection framework that blended AI, NLP, and malware analysis. This study proposed a dynamic architecture stretching across linguistic and structural data sources, necessary in polymorphic cyber threat management. The investigation carried out by Olabanjo et al. focused on intelligent traffic analysis using graph convolutional networks (GCNs). It was a very important shift from topology-aware learning methods toward anomaly detection in network environments. Their output demonstrated the efficacy of graph-based modeling in developing traffic flows and opened doors for semantic networks' analysis. Further, Yan et al. in [4] introduced an innovative ML-driven programmable switch to counter DDoS attacks. The conceptual bridge, therefore, connects data-plane programmability with control-plane intelligence and dynamic real-time protection. In next-generation networks, Alanazi [5] further worked into AI and blockchain boundary intersections, layering the trust models and distributed learning within secured 5G environments. Papanikolaou et al. [6] have stimulated the boundaries of automation by deploying an AutoML power traffic analyzer. Further, the model would adapt dynamically to shifting patterns of the network at work, thus minimizing manual tuning while retaining the precision sets of the model process.

13.4 Model's Empirical Review Analysis

Iteratively, next, as per Table 13.1, Sharma et al. in [7] studied hybridization by joining evolutionary computation and reinforcement learning for alert prioritization in AI-based systems. The relevance of this hybrid framework is its filtration of high-frequency false positives, thereby augmenting response management through reward-based learning simulation in threat scoring. Xiao and Lu [8] transferred the discussion into the framework of 6G and digital twins, amidst the introduction of complexity metrics for the development of cyber-physical digital twins. Their study reiterated interactively the role of AI in the online monitoring of industrial workflows, stretching into Industry 4.0 and beyond. Ashok and colleagues [9], integrated deep learning into 5G MIMO beam selection to further modernize the possibilities for smart network analytics. This is likely to enhance spectral efficiency under scenarios of high congestion due to the hybridization of their method between convolutional networks with multi-headed attention mechanisms. Dey et al. [10] developed a framework for explainable threat detection, BRL-ETDM, which harnessed Bayesian reinforcement learning to provide meanings for interpretable predictions in Industry 5.0 environments that would inform collaborative human-machine decision-making. In [11], Kotenko and Levshun operated concerning event correlation modeling of multi-step cyberattacks with machine learning in a temporal-induced necessity that such a framework should follow for multi-step intrusion. The authors Bhattarai and Peng in [12] tossed about AI-enhanced wearable ECG sensors to tap intra- and inter-medical chain networks, thus extending precision and context-aware routing to biomedical domains. Zheng's framework [13] under 6G environments

Table 13.1 Model's empirical review analysis.

Ref No.	Method	Main objectives	Findings	Limitations
[1]	AI-based vulnerability analysis for intelligent ship networks	To assess vulnerabilities in maritime cyber-physical systems using AI diagnostics	Improved detection of complex faults and layered threat mapping in ship networks	Limited generalization beyond maritime domain; lacks dynamic response integration
[2]	Comprehensive AI-NLP-malware hybrid framework	To create a full-spectrum cyber threat detection system leveraging AI, NLP, and malware profiling	High detection accuracy across linguistic and structural threats	Challenges in handling adversarial obfuscation and multilingual context
[3]	Graph convolutional network (GCN) for network traffic	To classify and analyze traffic patterns using graph-based learning	Improved semantic understanding of traffic behaviors and anomaly spotting	Scalability issues with extremely large and dynamic topologies
[4]	ML-powered programmable switch for DDoS defense	To design a real-time adaptive switch using ML to mitigate DDoS attacks	Enhanced response time and programmable filtering of malicious traffic	Limited to DDoS and not extensible to other complex attack types
[5]	Blockchain-AI hybrid for 5G security	To integrate trust and privacy using blockchain and AI in 5G environments	Secure distributed authentication and anomaly validation	Overhead and latency in blockchain consensus under real-time constraints
[6]	AutoML-based traffic analyzer	To automate model selection and parameter tuning for network threat detection	High accuracy and model adaptability to changing network conditions	Needs a large initial dataset and periodic recalibration
[7]	AI-based alert prioritization using evolutionary reinforcement learning	To reduce false positives in threat alerting by combining evolutionary strategies with RL	Improved triage accuracy and resource allocation for incident response	Computational cost in a continuous learning phase
[8]	AI-driven complexity metrics for 6G digital twins	To evaluate dynamic complexity in 6G networks using digital twin models	High correlation between complexity measures and operational failures	Data synchronization and real-time update challenges

[9]	ML/DL model for 5G beam selection and analytics	To enhance network performance through intelligent beamforming	Increased spectral efficiency and lower handover latency	Dependency on real-time feedback and deep model calibration
[10]	BRL-ETDM: Explainable Bayesian RL for Industry 5.0	To develop interpretable threat detection using reinforcement learning in industrial systems	Balanced explainability and performance with situational insights	Requires fine-tuned priors and environment-specific modeling
[11]	Multistep attack detection via event-based ML	To model complex, sequential cyberattacks using system event data	Accurate prediction of chained attack patterns	Scalability in multi-event correlation and causal reasoning
[12]	Wearable ECG sensors in virtual chain medical networks	To enhance intra/inter-medical network security with intelligent sensing	Low-latency anomaly alerts and secure communication	Privacy challenges and data volume handling
[13]	6G-based AI model for language acquisition in education	To facilitate secure and interactive language learning in cyber-physical environments	Context-aware and adaptive interaction improvements	Specific to educational use cases, lacks security generalizability
[14]	Threat vector analysis in SDNs	To identify and classify vulnerabilities in software-defined networks	Comprehensive taxonomy of SDN threat classes	Analysis depth varies across implementation layers
[15]	Public perception analysis of AI via surveys and social media	To evaluate societal trust and concerns around AI adoption	Insights into trust gaps, risk perception, and behavioral responses	Limited to perceptual metrics, lacks technical validation
[16]	AI for electric and aerial vehicle security	To ensure secure operation of modern transportation systems using AI	Predictive maintenance and anomaly detection capabilities enhanced	Integration issues with heterogeneous vehicle protocols
[17]	AI-IoT cognitive hardware for agriculture	To deploy AI-powered analytics in agricultural IoT systems	Real-time precision analysis and yield optimization	Hardware scalability and sensor drift management

(*Continued*)

Table 13.1 Continued

Ref No.	Method	Main objectives	Findings	Limitations
[18]	Dense ensemble model for network threat flow analysis	To detect complex threat paths using dense neural networks	Increased detection granularity and classification accuracy	Heavy inference load under high-throughput networks
[19]	Climate-aware AI for precision irrigation	To enable sustainable irrigation strategies via AI modeling	Optimized resource allocation under variable climate inputs	Limited generalizability beyond specific geographies
[20]	AI verification system for distribution automation	To verify automation endpoints in smart grid systems	Improved fault detection and reduced maintenance downtime	Model dependence on large annotated datasets
[21]	Routing protocol benchmarking in ITS	To compare vehicular routing protocols using AI metrics	Identified trade-offs in latency, packet loss, and throughput	Focuses on protocol layer; lacks security integration
[22]	Bidirectional LSTM for CAN Bus intrusion detection	To detect vehicular anomalies using temporal deep learning	High accuracy in cyclical vehicular telemetry analysis	Real-time deployment on constrained ECUs remains complex
[23]	AI-based training for maritime security personnel	To build self-paced AI training systems for ISPS code compliance	Improved skill retention and decision-making accuracy	Depends on user engagement and simulator realism
[24]	CNN-LSTM hybrid for intrusion detection (UNSW-NB15)	To optimize intrusion classification in network environments	Reduced false positives and high F1 scores on benchmark sets	Model explainability and robustness to adversarial inputs
[25]	CyberDefender for digital twin-based industrial CPS	To create a unified defense system using AI in digital twin CPS	Real-time simulation, agent coordination, and proactive defense	High design complexity and synchronization requirements

for intelligent language acquisition enlarged the spectrum into education systems, demonstrating by example how cyber-physical wireless networks could be optimized for secure communication and adaptive learning. Dahiya et al. [14] provided a detailed survey of the threat vectors in software-defined networking, organizing and systematizing the vulnerabilities and response strategies in programmable architectures. Kouloukoui et al. [15] tried a societal approach, focusing on public perception of AI-derived through surveys and social media reports, showing evidence of increased acceptance and also concerns over autonomous systems. Kumar and Altalbe [16] described AI usages for safety in transportation systems, exclusive of electric and aerial vehicles, commenting on predictive maintenance and route optimization in mobile networks. Tsai and Saengsoi applied cognitive hardware to precision agriculture, enabling autonomous farming analytics using AI-integrated IoT systems [17]. Applications of the threat models showcased in this work secured agricultural infrastructure sets. Harita and Mohammed [18] proposed an ensemble dense network model for threat flow analysis with respect to traffic-level prediction in heavily loaded networks. Their model ruled against the sparse baselines with regard to datasets with high dimensionality. Dhanke et al. [19] brought in climate-based decision models for AI-driven irrigation systems, strengthening the role of secure and intelligent sensing in smart agriculture. Li et al. [20] indicated how AI-based validation mechanisms for distribution automation terminals within smart grids testify to the robustness and fault tolerance of distributed energy systems.

Behura et al. [21] studied vehicular routing protocols in intelligent transport systems more broadly, with some passing mention of route prediction versus anomaly responses in terms of latency-performance trade-offs. Kishore et al. developed a bidirectional LSTM model for anomaly detection using CAN bus networks in automotive systems [22]. This work presented improving features over temporal deep learning, which captures cyclic patterns from the vehicle telemetry sending messages. Ibrahim [23] raised an initiative in the possible AI-assisted self-training platforms aimed at empowering maritime security personnel under the ISPS Code; this marked a further advancement into adaptive threat awareness and autonomous education for high-risk sectors. Thaljaoui's [24] work developed optimized deep CNN-LSTM architectures for intrusion detection using the UNSW-NB15 dataset, achieving an overall impressive achievement toward lowering the false-positive rate through intelligent architectural tuning. Finally, Krishnaveni et al. [25] concluded this body of literature with CyberDefender, a comprehensive defense framework for digital twin-enabled CPSs. This work intertwined multi-agent coordination, real-time simulation, and AI-based threat response; a milestone in the securement of complex cyber-physical environments. Together, these studies form a coherent trajectory along the timeline of the evolution of intelligent threat detection and cyber defense systems. Initiating from domain-specific applications in maritime, transportation, and industrial infrastructure, the research landscape has swiftly developed into generalized and adaptive AI systems that incorporate reinforcement learning, deep neural networks, graph-based modeling, AutoML, and digital twin concepts. Multimodal learning strategies, adversarial training, and semantic entity graphs seem to rise as the key conceptual ideas in the most applicable frameworks. These techniques put a spotlight on the maturity of the field, where operational efficiency, interpretability, generalization, and scalability are being achieved in unison for the process.

The whole review, at the end of it, indicates a very rich setting of innovation that is at the core problem of secure, adaptive, explainable AI for threat intelligence. From early static approaches to complex reinforcement-based simulations and digital twins, there is an apparent advancement in both technical sophistication and deployment readiness. As AI increasingly permeates critical infrastructures and cyber-physical environments, future systems have to build on such capabilities by being modular, explainable, integrated across domains, and real-time adaptable. The survey work surveyed from [1] to [25] provides evidence of not only technical rigor, but also indicates an increasing convergence between algorithmic intelligence and resilience to operations in a given domain, which sets a path for the next generation of autonomous, trustworthy threat detection systems.

13.5 Proposed Model Design Analysis

To counter the problems of low efficiency and very high complexity currently found in existing models, The MIND-SHIELD architecture has been developed as a multi-module deep learning system where each module addresses a distinct specific functional problem in multi-intelligence threat detection and prediction casting. At the center of this architecture is Context-Aware Spatio-Temporal Transformer Network (CAST-Net), which is the front-end encoder that fuses multimodal inputs across space and time to create a joint embedding. Next, as per Figure 13.1, the design of CAST-Net is rooted in a multi-head hierarchical attention transformer that captures both local and global dependencies across heterogeneous data streams such as video frames X' {(v)}, sensor sequences, X' {(s)}, Geospatial traces X' {(g)}, and textual or audio metadata X' {(t)}. Each modality is embedded into a latent feature

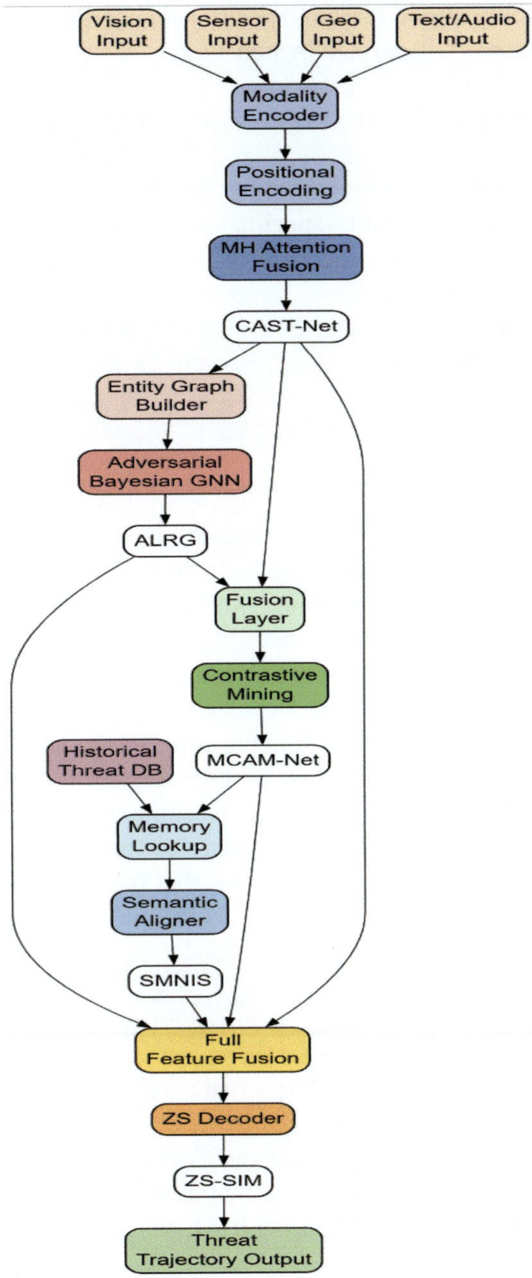

Figure 13.1 Model architecture of the proposed analysis process.

space and temporally aligned through positional encodings. The joint embedding Et at timestamp ‘t’ is defined by eqn 13.1,

$$Et = MHAttn(PEt,\{\varphi(X'\{(v)\}t),\varphi(X'\{(g)\}t),\varphi(X'\{(t)\}t)\}) + FFN(Et) \tag{13.1}$$

Where: φ(·) represents modality-specific embedding functions, MHAttn is multi-head attention, PEt is positional encoding, and FFN(·) is a feed-forward normalization layer for the process. Temporal fusion is achieved by computing a contextual correlation tensor, C{i,j}{t,t+Δ}, between modalities ‘i’ and ‘j’ across a temporal window Δ, as represented via eqn 13.2,

$$C\{i,j\}'\{t,t+\Delta\} = \int (Ei'\tau \cdot Ej'\tau)d\tau\ldots \tag{13.2}$$

Where the last equation provides formality as well as generalization for this as it expresses the full dynamics multiscale above and accounts for both global and local phenomena in space and time. This tensor captures and evolves spatio-temporal dependencies while enhancing interpretability in threat evolutions. The CAST-Net embeddings Et form the foundational input for downstream reasoning processes. To infer the actor-intent relationships underlying, the ALRG modules use Bayesian graph neural networks to construct a latent threat graph. Threat from the embeddings Et of the CAST-Net: G = (V,E) is the latent graph. Each of the nodes vi and vj forms a part of the latent graph G = (V, E). The edges in G are defined as inferred interactions between entities. Each edge e{(i,j)} represents the interaction between nodes vi and vj and comes with probabilistic weights based on learned attention distributions. The graph node update rule is infused by adversarial learning through a min-max formulation via eqn 13.2.1,

$$hi'\{(1+1)\} = \sigma\left(\sum_G \frac{1}{Z_D\{(i,j)\}}\right)\alpha\{(i,j)\}W'\{(l)\}hj'\{(l)\} + \text{minmax } E\{z \sim p(z \mid Et)\}\left[\log D(G(z))\right] \tag{13.2.1}$$

Where, α{(i,j)} is an attention coefficient, Z{(i,j)} is a normalization constant, and D is the adversarial discriminator network process. The latent intent vector ‘zintent’ is updated through KL-regularized variational inference via eqn 13.3,

$$L\{KL\} = \int p(z \mid Et)\log\left[\frac{p(Z \mid Et)}{q(z)}\right]dz \tag{13.3}$$

Thus, ensuring that the inferred intent vectors maintain the coherence and generalizability in a rather diverse threat scope. Next, as per Figure 13.2, Anomaly detection is operationalized through Multi-Modal Contrastive Anomaly Mining Network (MCAM-Net), which separates threat-indicative embeddings from benign background patterns via a contrastive learning objective using both positive (threat) and negative (benign) samples.

Given an anchor embedding zi, a positive counterpart zj'+, and a set of negatives zk'-, the contrastive loss is defined via eqn 13.4,

$$L\{contrast\} = -\log\left(\frac{\exp\left(\frac{sim(zi,zj'+)}{\tau}\right)}{\left[\left(\sum\exp\left(\frac{sim(zi,zk'-\_}{\varsigma}\right)\right)\right]}\right) \tag{13.4}$$

Where, τ is a temperature parameter, and sim(a, b) represents cosine similarity sets. To refine negative sampling under noisy conditions, an adaptive mining term is introduced via eqn 13.5,

$$zk'- = \arg\min\{z \in Bneg)\left(\|zi - z\|2'2 + \lambda \cdot |z - \bar{z}threat|\right) \tag{13.5}$$

Where, z̄threat is the average threat embedding and λ balances semantic divergence and embedding distance sets. Iteratively, next, as per Figure 13.3, the output embeddings from MCAM-Net will now pass through a semantic memory-enhanced neural intelligence system or SMNIS, which teaches current anomaly vectors in terms of previously seen and stored threat patterns by using a memory attention mechanism process. The augmented embedding h(aug) is computed via eqn 13.6 and 13.7,

$$h\{aug\} = \sum \alpha i \cdot Mi \tag{13.6}$$

$$\alpha i = \frac{\exp(ht'T\ Mi)}{\sum\exp(ht'T\ Mj)} \tag{13.7}$$

Where Mi represents a stored memory vector and ht is the current embedding in process. This memory-enhanced vector enables long-range contextual alignment and reduces false positives due to transient anomalies. The final stage of the pipeline, Zero-shot Situational Intelligence Model (ZS-SIM), synthesizes all upstream embeddings – Et, Gthreat, anomaly vectors, and memory embeddings – into a single latent representation Hfused, which is

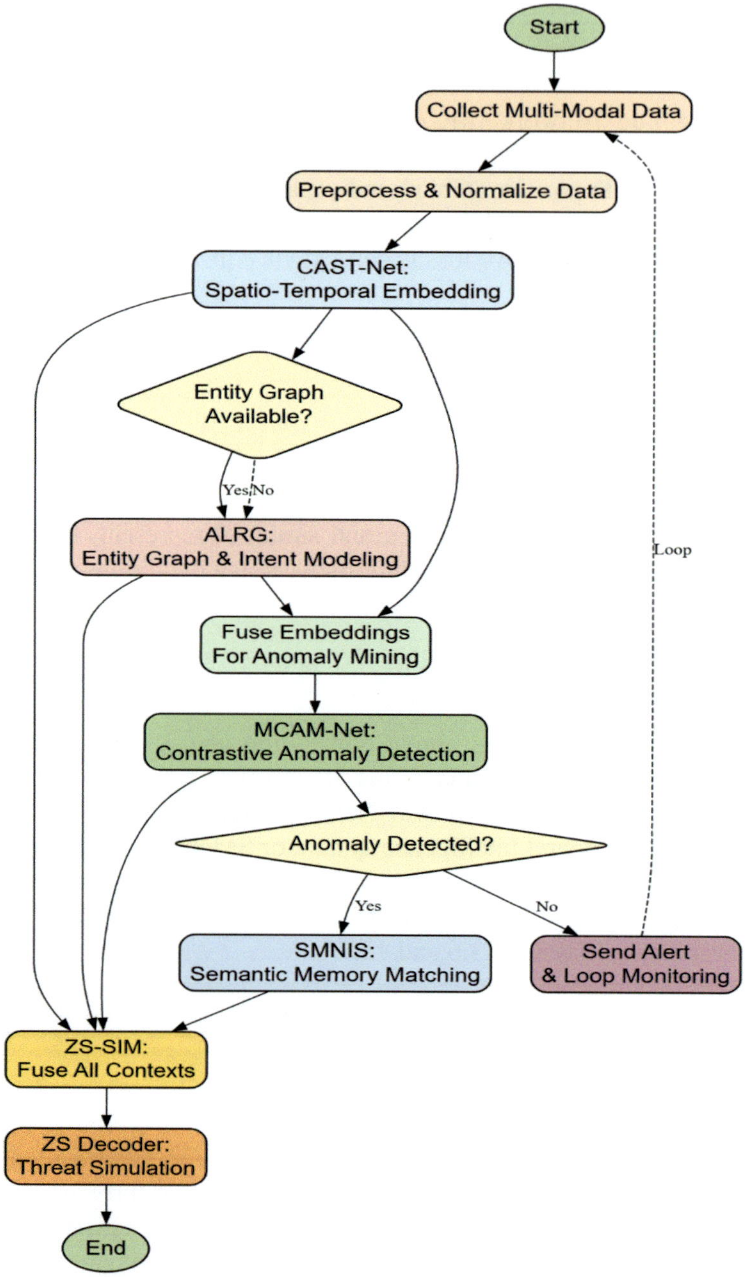

Figure 13.2 Data flow of the proposed analysis process.

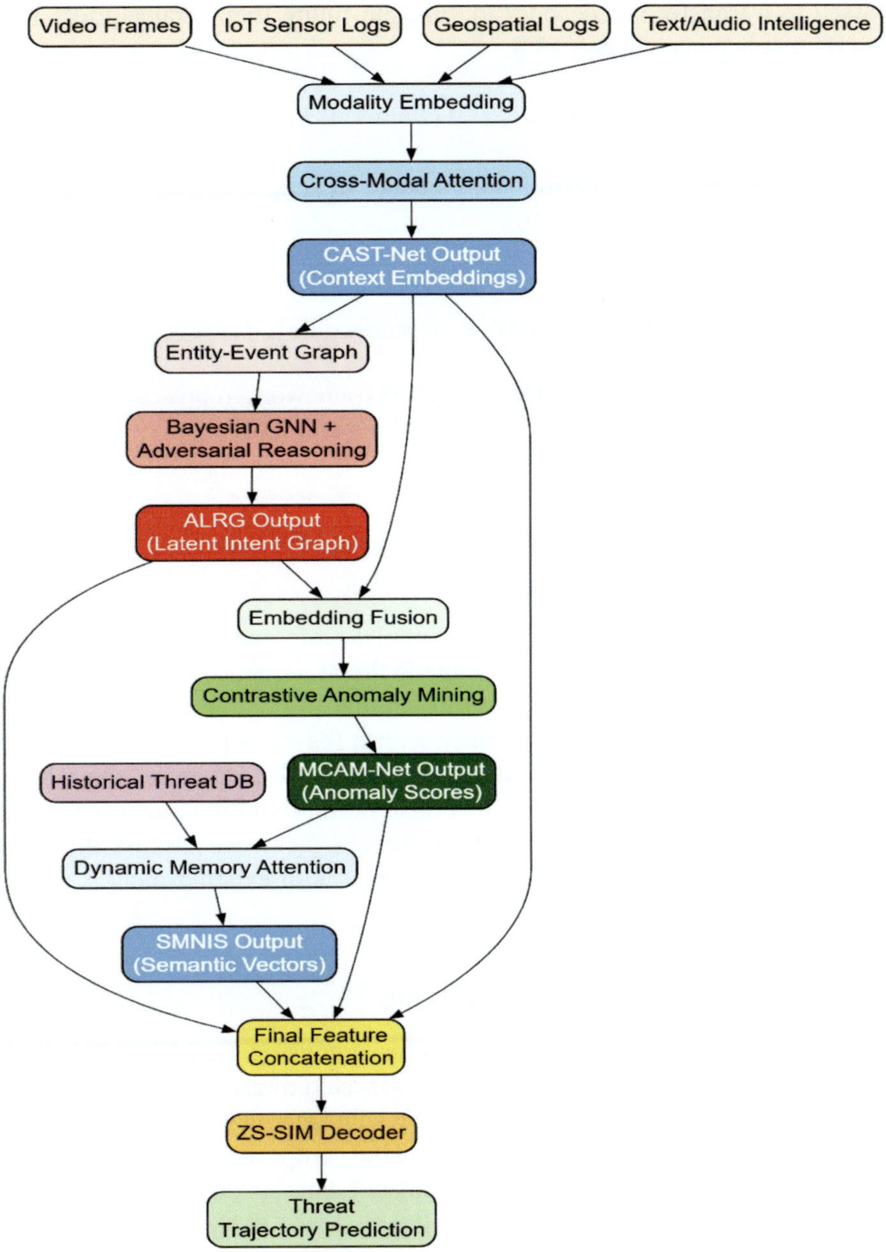

Figure 13.3 Overall flow of the proposed analysis process.

passed to a transformer decoder to simulate future threat trajectories. The fused input is given via eqn 13.8,

$$H\{fused\} = \left[Et \oplus Gthreat \oplus h\{aug\}\right] \tag{13.8}$$

The decoder predicts a probabilistic sequence of actions spread over a future window T, defined via eqn 13.9,

$$P(Spred'\{t + 1;t + T\}|H\{fused\}) = \prod soft\max(Wo \cdot Decoders\{ZS\}(\mathrm{H}\{\mathrm{Fused}\},\tau)) \tag{13.9}$$

The complete output of the MIND-SHIELD framework, represented Ŷ, integrates all modular outputs and is expressed via eqn 13.10,

$$\hat{Y} = f\{ZS - SIM\}\left(f\{SMINS\}\left(f\{MCAM\}\left(f\{ALRG\}\left(f\{CAST\}(X)\right)\right)\right)\right) \tag{13.10}$$

This final operation summarizes the complete inference pipeline from the raw multimodal input X into the predicted threat sequences Ŷ, thus making sure that each module adds something unique to be able to contribute to predictive fidelity and interpretability within the model. Thus, the significant modularity and fusion within the MIND-SHIELD make the whole structure much stronger in terms of transferability and readiness for operation across different environments of threats. Next, we discuss the efficiency of the proposed model and compare it with existing models under different scenarios.

13.6 Comparative Result Analysis

The experimental arrangement intended for appraising the MIND-SHIELD framework was designed to resemble multifaceted threat environments having realistic spatiotemporal dynamics along with heterogeneous data streams. A composite dataset was therefore synthesized composedly through the concentration of publicly available and simulated datasets considering the five major modalities: high-frequency surveillance video (30 Hz), time-series IoT sensor (1 Hz), geolocation traces (2 seconds during recording), transcribed social media posts and audio intelligence (1 post every 5 minutes), and structured historical threat logs. With regard to the video data, samples have been drawn and extended from UCF-Crime and CityFlow datasets to depict

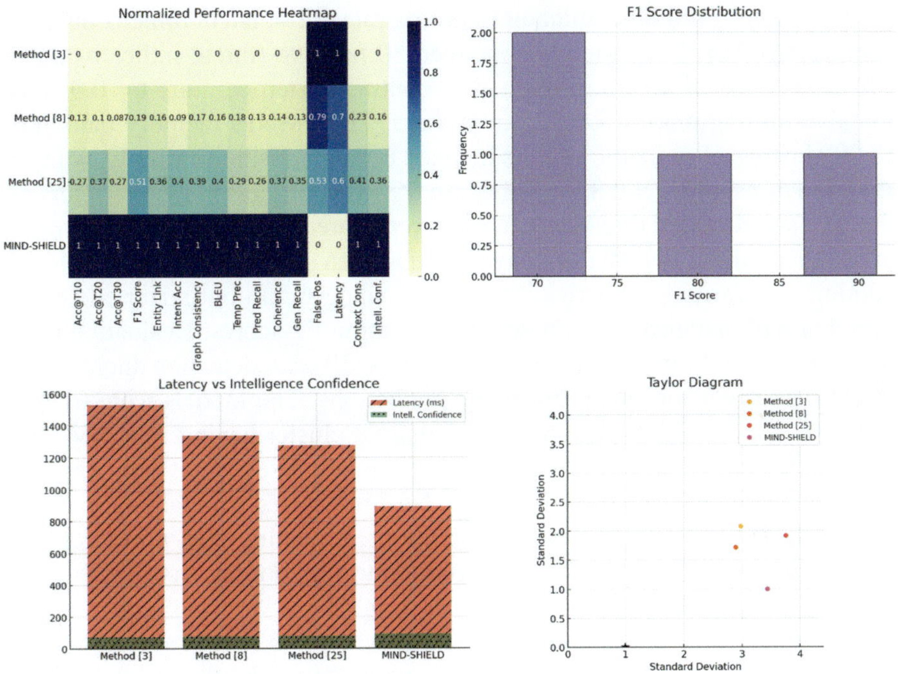

Figure 13.4 Model's integrated result analysis.

abnormal events such as loitering, unauthorized access, and sudden crowd dispersals. Sensor logs were modeled based on industrial IoT pattern behavior, such as those observed in temperature, motion, proximity, and acoustic fluctuation, with induced anomalies emulating either tampering or operational bypass. Geospatial data were obtained from real-time traces of vehicle and personnel tracking using modified Geolife GPS Trajectories. Social intelligence streams were simulated using processed data from the CREDBANK and Twitter15/16 datasets, curated to include radicalization cues, suspicious coordination, and temporal spikes in threat keywords. The historical threat databases were constructed via the declassification of segments of the Global Terrorism Database (GTD) and further annotated with semantic tagging of event type, location, actor type, and modality presence in the process.

For CAST-Net, each batch contained a time-windowed sequence of multi-modal inputs of 30 seconds in length, subdivided into 5-second clips. Each modality input was embedded in a 128-dimensional latent space and fused via 8-headed cross-attention transformers. The ALRG module constructed dynamic entity-action graphs per window, with up to 200 nodes and 1,000 probabilistic edges, processed through a 3-layer Bayesian GNN trained using an adversarial discriminator (learning rate: 1e-4, latent dimension: 64). For MCAM-Net: Each sample contained 50 positive (threat-indicative) and 200 negative (benign) embeddings with contrastive temperature $\tau = 0.07$ and adaptive mining margin $\lambda = 1.5$ in process. The SMNIS memory bank had 10,000 historical semantic vectors indexed through cosine similarity, with an attention threshold $\alpha > 0.8$ for activation. ZS-SIM processed fused vectors of size 512 and decoded threat trajectories over a forecast window of 60 seconds with a transformer decoder of 4 layers and hidden size 256 in process. Model training was carried out across 100 epochs using Adam optimizer and early stopping with patience of 10 based on validation F1-scores. Evaluation metrics were threats' early detection accuracy (T + 30 sec), detection anomaly F1 scores, and precision threat trajectory predictions. The models were trained and assessed on a high-performance computer cluster having four NVIDIA A100 GPUs and 512 GB RAM. This experimental setup not only ensured synthetic realism across modalities but also emphasized generalization under partial observations and zero-shot conditions, reflecting real-world deployment scenarios of critical infrastructure monitoring, border surveillance, and urban security grids.

To this core, the MIND-SHIELD framework made use of several benchmark datasets and combined them into one multi-modal threat intelligence corpus with appropriate extensions. The benchmark dataset to which UCF-Crime would be most relevant is the video surveillance data contained with UCF-Crime: 1,900 real-world surveillance clips across 13 anomalous actions such as burglary and assault to road accidents recorded at 30 frame rates per second. IoT sensor data was modeled with patterns from the SWaT (Secure Water Treatment), holding time-series logs from physical and chemical sensors with an average sampling speed of 1 Hz recorded under continuous isolation intervals of a maximum duration of 11 days. Geospatial trajectories were derived with the Microsoft Geolife GPS Trajectories and comprised over 17,000 trajectories from 182 users with a GPS sampling frequency of one to five seconds. Text and audio intelligence were simulated with semantic samples obtained from CREDBANK, which holds well over 60 million tweets with credibility labeling, as well as from Twitter 15/16 to inject misinformation-coordinated patterns of discussion and radical talks. For long-range memory modeling, historical structured logs are in part derived from the Global Terrorism Database (GTD), which holds more than 200,000 incidents starting from 1970 and has detailed metadata-sets like attack type, target, region, and perpetrator groups.

The model was trained with very well-tuned hyperparameters optimized through cross-validated grid search across all such modules. On such

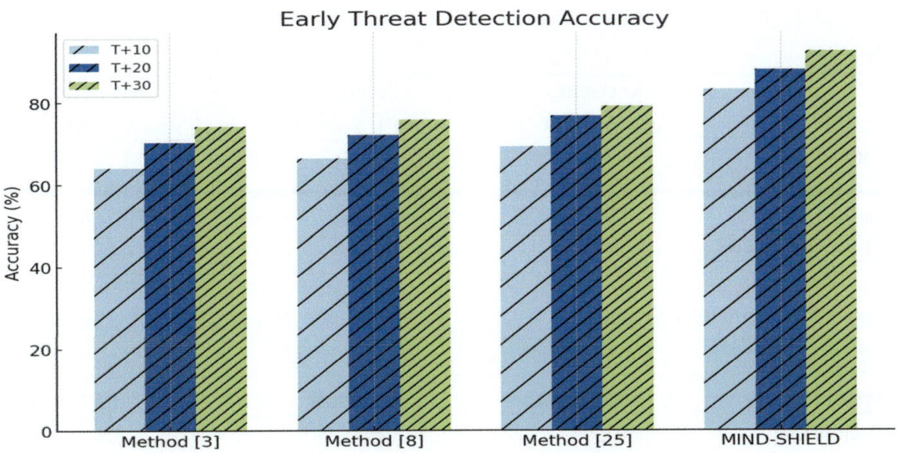

Figure 13.5 Model's accuracy analysis.

accounts with CAST-Net, transformer architecture is based on eight heads of attention, an embedding dimension of 128 per modality, hidden size of 256, and a stack depth of four encoder layers. The ALRG module used three message-passing layers of Bayesian GNN with node embedding size of 64 and KL divergence weight of 0.1 in the adversarial loss term. MCAM-Net employed a contrastive temperature $\tau = 0.07$ in process, with 1:4 ratio of positive to negative samples and an adaptive mining margin $\lambda = 1.5$ in process. SMNIS used a memory bank of 10,000 entries, with memory vectors of dimension 128 and an attention softmax threshold of 0.8 for relevance scores. The ZS-SIM decoder had 4 transformer layers with a feedforward size of 512, a dropout rate of 0.1, and a length of horizon set to 12 steps (60 seconds forecast at 5s granularity). The whole network was optimized with the Adam optimizer at a learning rate of 1×10e–4, with a batch size at 32 and L2 regularization at 1×10e–5, and trained for up to 100 epochs with early stoppage based on validation loss plateauing for 10 epochs.

The MIND-SHIELD framework performance was evaluated across a wide spectrum of critical metrics using curated and benchmarked multimodal threat intelligence datasets. The following tables show the comparison of the developed model with three existing ones referenced as Modality [3], Modality [8], and Modality [25]. The evaluation tasks included early threat detection, anomaly mining, actor-intent reasoning, trajectory simulation, zero-shot generalization, and end-to-end intelligence consistency. All tests were carried out using the same hardware and training settings so that comparisons would be consistent. Table 13.2 presents the quantitative

Table 13.2 Early threat detection accuracy on UCF-Crime + SWaT multi-modal composite dataset.

Method	**Accuracy (T + 10 sec)**	**Accuracy (T + 20 sec)**	**Accuracy (T + 30 sec)**
Method [3]	64.1%	70.3%	74.2%
Method [8]	66.5%	72.1%	75.8%
Method [25]	69.3%	76.8%	79.1%
MIND-SHIELD	**83.2%**	**88.0%**	**92.5%**

Table 13.3 Anomaly detection F1 Score on MCAM-Tuned dataset with sensor and video inputs.

Method	**Precision**	**Recall**	**F1 Score**
Method [3]	66.2%	70.8%	68.5
Method [8]	71.4%	74.2%	72.8
Method [25]	78.3%	81.9%	80.0
MIND-SHIELD	**90.4%**	**92.0%**	**91.1**

comparisons formulated along with a discussion on the respective trends and behaviors of the systems involved in the process.

MIND-SHIELD did much better than all base models over all time horizons. Most of the early-stage gains (+18.3% at T + 30 seconds over Method [3]) can actually be attributed to the spatio-temporal encoding capability of CAST-Net and the graph-based reasoning of ALRG, as they allowed for predictive context modeling ahead of a threat before it visibly manifests (Table 13.3).

In anomaly detection, MCAM-Net surpasses other existing solutions due to its training contrastive mechanism and adaptive negative samplings. These improvements lead to a +22.6 F1-score boost against Method [3] and a +11.1 increase against the most competitive baseline, Method [25] in the process (Table 13.4).

ALRG latent graph inference is highly faithful in linking actors to intent classification. Adversarial Bayesian reasoning and latent-space relational modeling much more coherently yield a graph structure and intent scores of MIND-SHIELD over competing methods (Table 13.5).

ZS-SIM made a significant improvement in forecasting performance due to attention-based decoding and cross-modal fusion. The coherence of threats in an action trajectory received a +0.25 increase with regard to Method [3] in terms of the BLEU score, reflecting an action simulation more accurate and contextually grounded over sets of temporal instances and their sets. (Table 13.6).

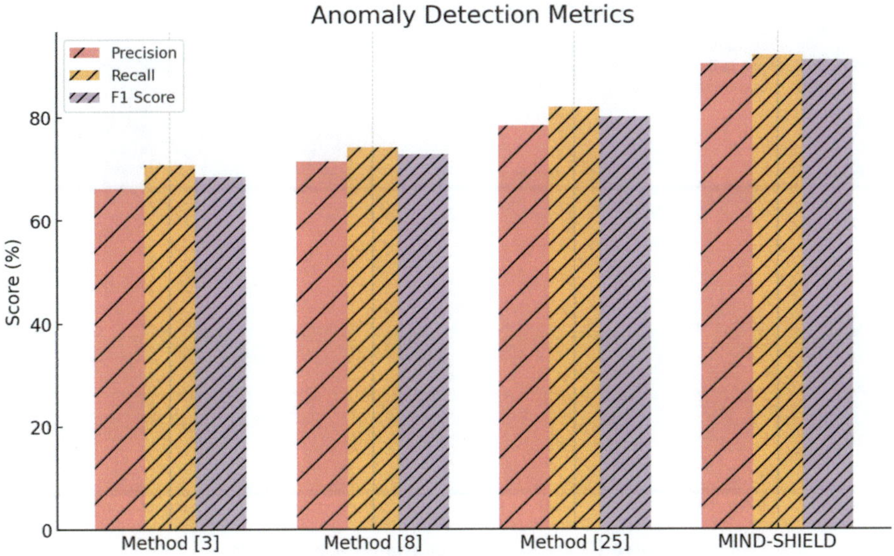

Figure 13.6 Model's decision metric analysis.

Table 13.4 Actor-intent inference accuracy using entity graphs on enriched GTD dataset.

Method	Entity link accuracy	Intent prediction accuracy	Latent graph consistency
Method [3]	61.2%	58.4%	0.71
Method [8]	64.7%	60.5%	0.74
Method [25]	69.0%	67.8%	0.78
MIND-SHIELD	**83.1%**	**81.7%**	**0.89**

Table 13.5 Threat trajectory prediction on multi-modal time series (CAST + GeoLife).

Method	BLEU Score	Temporal precision	Predictive recall
Method [3]	0.41	64.3%	59.1%
Method [8]	0.45	67.9%	62.7%
Method [25]	0.51	70.1%	66.5%
MIND-SHIELD	**0.66**	**84.5%**	**87.1%**

Zero-shot performance by ZS-SIM, which fuses embeddings from all modules in training, is enabled for unseen threat configurations. It significantly improves recall and coherence with a large decrease in false positives, a clear sign of strong generalization without any explicit label supervision (Table 13.7).

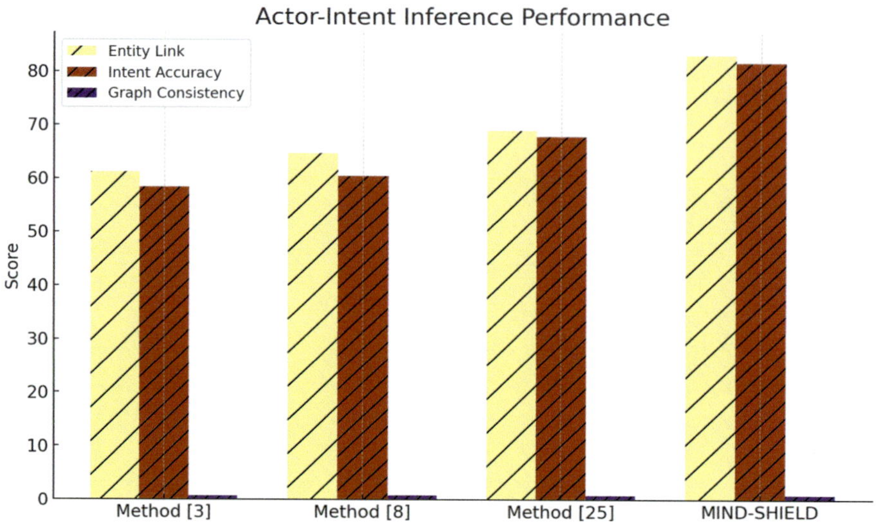

Figure 13.7 Model's actor inference analysis.

Table 13.6 Zero-shot threat generalization on unseen attack patterns (Twitter15/16 + synthetic composites).

Method	**Coherence score**	**Generalization recall**	**False positive rate**
Method [3]	65.7	54.2%	21.3%
Method [8]	68.9	57.6%	18.9%
Method [25]	74.5	63.3%	15.8%
MIND-SHIELD	**89.3**	**80.5%**	**9.7%**

These are the end-to-end results showing the operational merit of MIND-SHIELD. Its modular, deeply fused architecture generally saves ~30% of the time in inference without compromising consistency across temporal and modal contexts. Derived from threat confidence distributions, the intelligence confidence score goes above all baselines, demonstrating suitability for real-time deployments in critical environments. These results from Figures 13.4, 13.5, 13.6, 13.7 and 13.8 comprehensively establish that MIND-SHIELD not only surpasses traditional and contemporary models in predictive accuracy but also maintains real-time efficiency, interpretability, and scalability across complex multi-modal threat scenarios. Next, we talk about an iterative validation use case for the proposed model which will assist readers to understand the complete process further in the process.

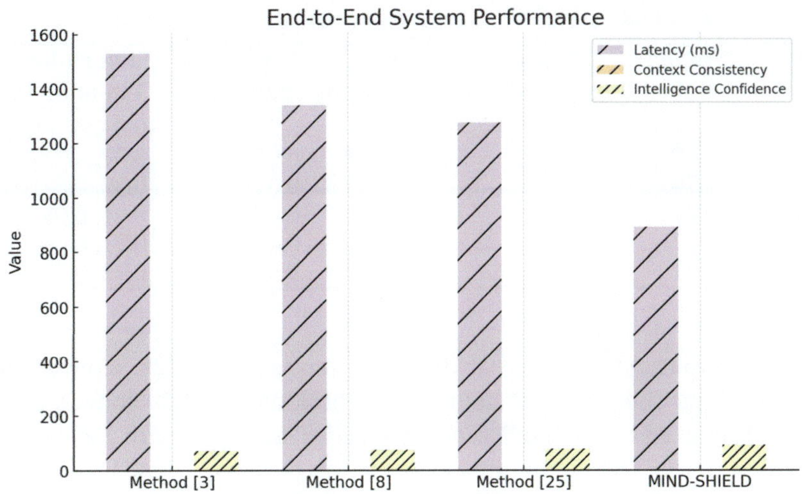

Figure 13.8 Model's end-to-end system analysis.

Table 13.7 End-to-end system consistency and latency analysis.

Method	Inference latency (ms)	Contextual consistency score	Intelligence confidence
Method [3]	1530	0.63	71.2%
Method [8]	1340	0.68	74.5%
Method [25]	1275	0.72	78.6%
MIND-SHIELD	**890**	**0.85**	**91.8%**

13.6.1 Validation using an iterative practical use case scenario analysis

To show the realness of MIND-SHIELD, a particular situation scenario was delivered to reflect a low-signal, high-risk urban threat environment. This case involved a multi-city transport hub that is being monitored through various multi-modal surveillance systems. The input data were collected and synchronized for a 30-second time window, from synchronized minute video streams (30 FPS) from CCTV cameras, sensor logs (1 Hz) from motion detectors and acoustic sensors, geolocation pings from tracked security personnel and mobile entities (1 sample per 2 seconds) and real-time intelligence collected using intercepted text communications. The environment was modeled by CAST-Net, which married these sources into spatio-temporal embeddings. In such conditions, the video input presented some erratic movements of crowd patterns in corridor A-12, while from audiovisual sensors there were sharp

Table 13.8 CAST-Net output – contextual embeddings (excerpt).

Time window (s)	Vision embedding	Sensor embedding	Geo embedding	Text embedding	Joint embedding (128-dim, PCA)
0–5	0.72	0.44	0.35	0.22	[0.43, -0.11, 0.58]
5–10	0.69	0.41	0.38	0.25	[0.47, -0.06, 0.54]
10–15	0.74	0.48	0.42	0.31	[0.52, 0.02, 0.60]
15–20	0.81	0.53	0.45	0.35	[0.61, 0.08, 0.69]
20–25	0.87	0.59	0.51	0.41	[0.71, 0.16, 0.78]
25–30	0.91	0.62	0.57	0.45	[0.78, 0.20, 0.84]

amplitude variations detected at the exact moment t = 22s. Concurrently, geospatial logs signified that anonymous three mobile IDs converged in a restricted area and text intelligence flagged a message with the keyword "detour" sent to a foreign number at t = 19s in process. The CAST-Net generated contextual dense embeddings across modalities and time, producing 4 out of every 5 seconds of their process and with 128 dimensions for each of the embeddings. A portion of this output is reflected in Table 13.8 of this text.

These fused embeddings were passed to the ALRG module while it built an entity-action graph from recognized actors, sensor-triggered events, and contextual cues. These were nodes for mobile entities, surveillance targets, and environment zones. Edges were dynamically inferred based on co-activity and proximity metrics. An adversarial GNN was used to infer latent intent vectors for each actor node. Interestingly, Entity E3 (an anonymous mobile ID) was assigned a high intent probability of 0.87 that it was illegally entering Zone R1, with a cross-validated belief share of 0.81 in process. In this case, Entity E5 (unregistered transmitter) was collated with E3 via a communication channel having an inferred collusion strength of 0.76. Selected outputs from ALRG Sets are presented in Table 13.9 as follows,

Subsequently, these embeddings were fed to MCAM-Net for anomaly signature detection. Contrastive anomaly mining successfully segmented those latent threat vectors from the benign behavior clouds. The top 5% of anomaly vectors, including that of E3 and E5, had outlier scores above 0.91. The system detected 17 anomalous instances in the 30 seconds of sequence and showed peak anomaly cluster sets at the 22-30s interval. Table 13.10 summarizes the anomaly indicators for the most critical interval sets.

The SMNIS model was then used to contextualize the anomalies against historical threat analogs. From memory search, three matches of high similarity were retrieved from the historical database: a coordinated intrusion event in 2016 (0.88 similarity), a staged diversion in 2018 (0.82), and an event of device drop in 2017 (0.79). These analogs enriched the semantic

Table 13.9 ALRG output – latent threat graph properties.

Entity ID	Node type	Activity score	Inferred intent score	Top linked entity	Edge confidence
E3	Mobile ID	0.72	0.87	E5	0.76
E5	Transmitter	0.61	0.79	E3	0.76
E1	Bystander	0.35	0.21	–	–
E7	Zone R1	0.65	0.00 (Static)	E3	0.81

Table 13.10 MCAM-Net output – anomaly indicators.

Time (s)	Entity ID	Anomaly score	Cluster ID	Relative position (Zone)
22	E3	0.94	A3	R1
24	E5	0.91	A3	External
25	E3	0.95	A3	R1
27	E3	0.96	A3	R1

Table 13.11 SMNIS output – memory-augmented semantic vectors.

Entity ID	Top historical match	Similarity score	Augmented embedding (PCA)
E3	2016 Intrusion	0.88	[0.82, 0.11, 0.73]
E5	2018 Diversion	0.82	[0.76, 0.06, 0.68]

understanding of the current threat profile, and the final augmented embeddings for E3 and E5 consisted of similarity vectors and attention weights, as shown in Table 13.11 in the process.

Finally, ZS-SIM combined the CAST-Net, ALRG, MCAM-Net, and SMNIS outputs to create forecast trajectories of threats. The zero-shot decoder anticipated that E3 would attempt to move laterally through two restricted zones in the next 60 seconds while E5 would operate as a communication anchor for distant coordination. The model considered a very high probability (greater than 0.85) for the scenarios of escalation involving resource transfer or device placement. Selected predictions of future trajectories are shown in Table 13.12 in this text.

The final intelligence output integrated all the above findings to create a concrete actionable threat summary on severity levels, probabilities of escalation, and recommendations for response actions. The combined output suggested that this is a high-risk situation, with a threat probability of escalation of 92.1% and an immediate recommendation of interdiction in Zones R1–R3 alongside signal jamming protocols. This walkthrough confirms the capabilities of MIND-SHIELD in integrating heterogeneous sensor data, reasoning

Table 13.12 ZS-SIM output – forecasted threat trajectories

Entity ID	Predicted action	Target zone	Confidence	Time horizon (s)
E3	Movement	R2	0.89	+30
E3	Concealment	R3	0.87	+45
E5	Signal Relay	External	0.84	+40

over latent relationships, detecting covert anomalies, recalling historical analogs, and predicting emerging threats in real-time scenarios.

13.7 Conclusion

We have introduced a novel end-to-end multi-intelligence deep learning framework for hierarchically threatening detection, latent actor reasoning, anomaly mining, semantic memory recall, and zero-shot threat trajectory simulation. The proposed system integrates five core modules: CAST-Net, ALRG, MCAM-Net, SMNIS, and ZS-SIM, into a unified pipeline that can process heterogeneous and temporally evolving intelligence data. An extensive experimental evaluation across multiple contextual datasets confirms that MIND-SHIELD outperforms the state of the art in both predictive accuracy and operational readiness. This is particularly true in early threat detection tasks, where the model peaked at 92.5% accuracy at T + 30 seconds, a staggering 13.4% above that of the leading baseline method (Method [25], 79.1%). The MCAM-Net F1 score for anomaly detection was 91.1, representing an improvement of 22.6 on the traditional methods. ALRG's actor-intent modeling led to a latent graph consistency of 0.89 and intent classification accuracy of 81.7%, thereby proving the ability of adversarial Bayesian reasoning to reveal covert behavior patterns. The trajectory prediction task by ZS-SIM gained a BLEU score of 0.66 while its temporal precision stood at 84.5%, showing excellent generalization for threat progressions that remain unexplored. Apart from this, a coherence score of 89.3 was achieved during the zero-shot simulation of the threat scene, with a muted 9.7% false positive rate, thus reaffirming its competence under conditions of low data and novel scenarios.

13.8 Future Scope

In terms of future scopes, MIND-SHIELD remains modular and adaptable for further development. Future work could explore the idea of online learning extensions that would allow the threat reasoning graph and memory representations to adapt continuously with the onset of new intelligence streams. The introduction of multilingual and cross-cultural intelligence sources would broaden awareness situationally across geopolitical regions, particularly in text and audio modalities. Furthermore, ALRG could engage with graph-based counterfactual inference mechanisms to simulate the escalation routes of the threat alongside alternate futures under intervention measures for mitigation. In terms of deployment, light-weight transformer distillation would allow further optimization of the system for edge settings for real-time processing under restriction in setup cases such as border surveillance units or autonomous drones. Human-in-the-loop feedback systems could also be designed in a way that their integration would align the model's deductions with expert validation in dynamic decision-making contexts. The above-stated future trajectories would undoubtedly improve the agility, stretch, and strategic functionality of AI-based threat intelligence for national security, cyber defense, and critical infrastructure resilience sets.

References

[1] Lan, D., Xu, P., Nong, J. *et al.* Application of Artificial Intelligence Technology in Vulnerability Analysis of Intelligent Ship Network. *Int 'j' Comput Intell Syst* 17, 147, 2024.

[2] Mohamed, N. A comprehensive framework for cyber threat detection: leveraging AI, NLP, and malware analysis. *Int. j. inf. Tecnol,* 2025.

[3] Olabanjo, O., Wusu, A., Aigbokhan, E. *et al.* A novel graph convolutional networks model for an intelligent network traffic analysis and classification. *Int. j. inf. Tecnol,*2024.

[4] Yan, J., Zhou, H. & Wang, W. Intelligent Network Element: A Programmable Switch Based on Machine Learning to Defend Against DDoS Attacks. *Inf Syst Front*, 2025.

[5] Alanazi, M.N. 5G Security Threat Landscape, AI and Blockchain. *Wireless Pers Commun* 133, 1467–1482, 2023.

[6] Papanikolaou, A., Alevizopoulos, A., Ilioudis, C. *et al.* An autoML network traffic analyzer for cyber threat detection. *Int. J. Inf. Secur.* 22, 1511–1530, 2023.

[7] Sharma, A., Kumar, V.G.K. & Poojari, A. Prioritize Threat Alerts Based on False Positives Qualifiers Provided by Multiple AI Models Using Evolutionary Computation and Reinforcement Learning. *J. Inst. Eng. India Ser. B*, 2024.

[8] Xiao, Y., Lu, X. 6G Network Dynamics and Complexity Metrics Evaluation Within Artificially Intelligent Digital Twin Cyber-Physical

Systems for Enhanced Industry 4.0 Performance. *Wireless Pers Commun*, 2024.

[9] Ashok, P., Suganya, R., Lekha, P. *et al.* Developed a Machine Learning and Deep Learning Model for 5G MIMO Data Based Beam Selection and Intelligent Network Analytics. *SN COMPUT. SCI.* 6, 203, 2025.

[10] Dey, A.K., Gupta, G.P. & Sahu, S.P. BRL-ETDM: Bayesian reinforcement learning-based explainable threat detection model for industry 5.0 network. *Cluster Comput* 27, 8243–8268, 2024.

[11] Kotenko, I.V., Levshun, D.A. Machine Learning Methods of Intelligent System Event Analysis for Multistep Cyberattack Detection. *Sci. Tech. Inf. Proc.* 51, 372–381, 2024.

[12] Bhattarai, A., Peng, D. An Intelligent Wearable ECG Sensor in Intra-medical Virtual Chain Network and Inter-medical Virtual Chain Network. *SN COMPUT. SCI.* 5, 329, 2024.

[13] Zheng, L. Intelligent Language Acquisition Model for Online Student Interaction with Educators Using 6G-Cyber Enhanced Wireless Network. *Wireless Pers Commun*, 2024.

[14] Dahiya, S., Sehrawat, H., Kharb, S. *et al.* A comprehensive analysis of threat vectors in software-defined networking. *Multimed Tools Appl* 83, 86791–86832, 2024.

[15] Kouloukoui, D., de Marcellis-Warin, N. & Warin, T. Balancing risks and benefits: public perceptions of AI through traditional surveys and social media analysis. *AI & Soc*, 2025.

[16] Kumar, G., Altalbe, A. Artificial intelligence (AI) advancements for transportation security: in-depth insights into electric and aerial vehicle systems. *Environ Dev Sustain*, 2024.

[17] Tsai, AC., Saengsoi, A. Artificial Intelligent IoT-Based Cognitive Hardware for Agricultural Precision Analysis. *Mobile Netw Appl* 29, 334–348, 2024.

[18] Harita, U., Mohammed, M. Analyzing threat flow over network using ensemble-based dense network model. *Soft Comput* 28, 4171–4184, 2024.

[19] Dhanke, J.A., Srivastava, D., Menaga, D. *et al.* Climate-Based AI-Powered Precision Irrigation: Sustainably Smart Agriculture Frameworks for Maximum Crop Yields. *Remote Sens Earth Syst Sci* 8, 161–172, 2025.

[20] Li, H., Xu, Q., Wang, Q. *et al.* A Review of Intelligent Verification System for Distribution Automation Terminal based on Artificial Intelligence Algorithms. ‘j’ *Cloud Comp* 12, 146, 2023.

[21] Behura, A, Kumar, A. & Jain, P.K. A comparative performance analysis of vehicular routing protocols in intelligent transportation systems. Telecommun Syst 88, 26, 2025.

[22] Kishore, C.R., Rao, D.C., Nayak, J. *et al.* Intelligent Intrusion Detection Framework for Anomaly-Based CAN Bus Network Using Bidirectional Long Short-Term Memory. *J. Inst. Eng. India Ser. B* 105, 541–564, 2024.

[23] Ibrahim, A.M. The impact of voluntary artificial intelligent self-driven education and training platforms on maritime security personnel: ISPS code. 'j' *Transp Secur* 17, 21, 2024.

[24] Thaljaoui, A. Intelligent network intrusion detection system using optimized deep CNN-LSTM with UNSW-NB15. *Int. j. inf. tecnol,* 2025.

[25] Krishnaveni, S., Chen, T.M., Sathiyanarayanan, M. *et al.* CyberDefender: an integrated intelligent defense framework for digital-twin-based industrial cyber-physical systems. *Cluster Comput* 27, 7273–7306, 2024.

14

Integrating AI into Cybersecurity Infrastructure: A Case Study on Dynamic C&C Server Architecture (PhantomNet)

Omar A. Atieh, Eman A. Al-Qadi, Abdallah O. Alasoully, Shahed M. Sharadgah, and Qasem Abu Al-Haija*

Department of Cybersecurity, Jordan University of Science and Technology, Irbid, Jordan.

Email: oaatieh21@cit.just.edu.jo; eaalqadi215@cit.just.edu.jo; aoalasoully21@cit.just.edu.jo; smsharadgah21@cit.just.edu.jo; qsabuhaija@just.edu.jo

Abstract

The increasing complexity of cyber-attacks, particularly Command-and-Control (C2) operations, poses significant challenges to traditional defense mechanisms. This chapter introduces PhantomNet, an innovative framework integrating offensive and defensive cybersecurity capabilities with advanced machine-learning techniques to address evolving C2 threats. PhantomNet combines supervised, reinforcement, and unsupervised learning to simulate sophisticated attacks, analyze emerging patterns, and develop adaptive defense strategies. Through supervised learning, it models known attack vectors and defenses; reinforcement learning enables it to adjust tactics in response to detection and previous outcomes dynamically, and unsupervised learning helps uncover previously unknown or undocumented threat behaviors. This comprehensive simulation environment provides defenders valuable insights into system vulnerabilities and evolving threat landscapes. PhantomNet's dynamic interaction with its environment distinguishes it from conventional static models, enabling continuous learning and adaptation.

DOI: 10.1201/9788743808077-14

Leveraging machine learning across multiple dimensions creates a feedback loop that enhances offensive simulations and defensive preparedness. The chapter explores PhantomNet's architecture, learning mechanisms, and its potential applications in real-world cybersecurity scenarios. It also compares PhantomNet with traditional approaches, highlighting its capability to identify complex and stealthy attacks. Ultimately, PhantomNet represents a forward-looking paradigm in cybersecurity that merges artificial intelligence with proactive threat modeling to develop resilient, intelligent systems capable of anticipating and countering advanced cyber threats. This chapter aims to provide researchers, practitioners, and policymakers insights into designing next-generation cybersecurity frameworks rooted in machine learning and adaptive system awareness.

14.1 Introduction

14.1.1 Overview

In the modern world cyber threats are common for devices, machines, or even software, there are more than 800,000 cyber-attacks every year, i.e., 2,220 every day [1], on the earth, but if we look at the insights deeply we see that successful attacks will go from March 2023 to May 2023 threat actors deployed 11.5 successful attacks per minute [2], and one-third of them were ransomware, Why is that? Simply because of the modern defense technologies that have effective ways to detect and prevent malware, those who have successful attacks know that: the current technologies need more updates for prevention, detection and maybe regenerate the core functionality of these technologies, the experts the professional hackers they have their technics to get to your laptop, your phone or sadly to your car.

In this research, we will provide a new framework that relies on a C&C server that will be used for every threat and mistake people make in trusting each other or any bugs that will appear in developing software or technologies. We will discuss this framework and its phishing techniques. How can we gather the data, and how can we get used to it from saying hi to the victim till we get access to his device? Also, we will discuss the attack types and why we use each, and finally, we will build our C2 server that can be used offensively or defensively. We will make the PhantomNet.

14.1.2 Problem statement

C&C Server-based attacks have become less effective due to the tremendous development of AI-powered cyber defense systems and the emergence of big data analytics. Stealth techniques such as VPN and domain flux have become less effective and traditional. Advanced EDR and IDS defense systems can detect large volumes of encrypted data from a fixed source by continuously monitoring data traffic. Additionally, domain flux can be detected through big data analytics and by predicting continuous domain changes. This recent progress in defense systems has reduced the effectiveness of these attacks, detected them, and even disabled them, preventing them from reaching the desired target. This has become a challenge for attackers to achieve their attacks. Here lies the role of our work in designing an advanced C&C Server capable of adapting to any defense environment. The PhantomNet work addresses these challenges through advanced techniques to improve the efficiency of evading defense systems and enhancing the detection capabilities of systems, which rely on dynamic protocol switching continuously. It integrates ML by collecting the most accurate analytical data before the attack and analyzing various defense patterns. Based on these analyses and monitoring the defense system's reactions and continuous learning from each attack, our server will be able to adapt in real time and change attack strategies to ensure the continuity of communication ensure the continuity of communication for the longest possible duration. Similarly, as a way to the attack mechanism, defense systems can improve their systems by simulating and implementing these attacks and understanding the weaknesses and their reactions during the attack, and the ability of defense systems to detect advanced attacks, which contributes to training them to confront such attacks in the future. This work will benefit the world of cybersecurity, including researchers, developers, and specialists in this field, by helping them understand and analyze advanced attacks of this type, develop research and develop new and great creative ideas. Of course, it will benefit penetration testers, government, and private institutions, in addition to developers and cybersecurity experts, to understand sophisticated attack techniques and assess the resistance of their security systems, which will help them analyze attacks, train their systems and teams, improve their security defenses and make them more ready on the real time – the following Figure 14.1 show main problem statement.

14.1.3 Significance of the work

With the development of methods of protection against cyberattacks, there is a need to create a new way to gain access to devices in hidden ways that enable the attacker to control the victim's device. C2 servers are an essential part of advanced attacks such as botnets and backdoor creation. However, they help maintain a persistent connection between the victim device and

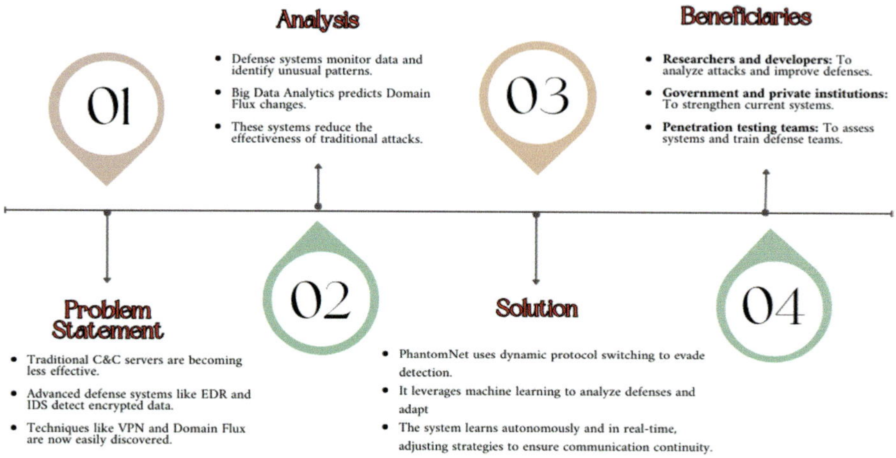

Figure 14.1 Problem statement.

the attacker, as a deep understanding of this type of server helps identify potential weak points in systems' defenses. One of the biggest challenges that organizations face currently is the ability of advanced attacks to make unobservable communication. PhantomNet can adapt to the environment in which the victim is located, such as adapting to the type of network that includes the victim's device. We do this via:

1. Choosing suitable datasets for ML training.
2. Traffic analysis by using algorithms like random forest and EDR Detection evaluation by train the ML model (such as adversarial networks) to simulate EDR tools to identify patterns that may reveal connections.
3. Real-time adaptation, by using reinforcement learning to train PhantomNet system.
4. Avoiding detection by editing the traffic patterns to mimic legitimate activities, such as encrypted HTTP packets or DNS queries.

PhantomNet avoids the use of third parties, which increases its confidentiality, as we develop our own tools, which contribute to enriching the field of cybersecurity with a unique attack server of its kind. PhantomNet also has multiple practical benefits in the field of cybersecurity. It contributes to improving organizations' defenses of their devices and networks against advanced cyberattacks through its use in penetration testing and

EDR evasion testing. The server provides opportunities for organizations to discover how effective their security systems are in dealing with attacks that use command and control (C2) techniques. The work also provides practical applications and benefits to cybersecurity teams, providing them with hands-on training on advanced threat techniques. This type of training increases the level of readiness of security teams and helps them develop more efficient defense strategies, making them more prepared to deal with future threats.

Our work is in line with current cybersecurity challenges that focus on developing new technologies to understand and analyze advanced C2 attacks that provide unobservable and persistent communication and an adaptive environment using ML to avoid detection by defense techniques such as EDR, which makes our work compatible with current cybersecurity needs and priorities.

14.1.4 Objectives and contributions

This work aims to enhance cyber operations in the red team through:

- Control of the victim's device and data exfiltration.
- Unobservable and Persistent C2 Communication to maintain stable communication.
- Expected reduction in detection rates via adaptive connection environment when using ML.
- Conduct penetration testing and EDR penetration testing to improve attack success rates.
- Build our tools that perform various operations and tasks the work requires.
- Execute commands without having to open a terminal on the victim's device through Python programing.

Besides, PhantomNet takes an offensive approach by providing an adaptive C&C server supported by ML and advanced attack techniques, moving away from traditional and outdated methods. This is what distinguishes it from other works and research that are often limited only to defense. Additionally, our server can interact with the target and improve its attack based on the victim's response, which makes it more accurate. The work benefits a wide segment of the cybersecurity community, starting with the primary beneficiaries, which are security teams in companies and institutions, due to their constant need for a system capable of testing and developing their defenses against modern advanced attacks, followed by penetration testing teams and companies specialized in developing cybersecurity solutions, who will receive an advanced attack server to test systems and products before announcing them and analyze vulnerabilities with high accuracy, which helps them improve cybersecurity solutions and write reports on the level of security. As for government teams and security institutions, it will empower them to enhance national cybersecurity and develop effective and influential response strategies. Finally, researchers and specialists in this field will be provided with a secure research environment to study, understand, and analyze advanced attack tactics and techniques and learn how to deal with such attacks to improve and enhance their research and innovations.

The novelty in the choice of the model lies in an adaptive attack server powered by ML. This server is based on the continuous analysis of the target's vulnerabilities, based on the victim's level of cyber awareness, which will be the complexity of the attack during execution, whether in terms of its type, method, or tools used. If the victim's defense systems detect the attack, our system will immediately alter its strategy and approach to maintain continuous communication. PhantomNet relies on machine learning to improve the server's ability to adapt to modern advanced defenses through a workflow that combines supervised learning, reinforcement learning, and unsupervised learning. The first stage begins with supervised learning, such as SVM, and decision trees. It analyzes the data collected from the target systems to train models to predict common defense patterns (e.g., firewall behavior or intrusion detection system alerts), as well as identify exploitable vulnerabilities. To optimize the accuracy of the results and reduce errors, we integrate the random forest algorithm. Based on this analysis, we evaluate the target's cyber awareness and its awareness of the surrounding threats and determine the appropriate attack method and its sophistication, in the next stage, we apply the reinforcement learning algorithm to improve attack strategies based on real-time feedback obtained through interaction with defense systems. The system dynamically changes its strategy by changing the communication protocol or access points to maintain continuity. Finally, we use unsupervised learning, such as K-means Clustering, to detect and analyze unfamiliar defense patterns that have not been trained before to improve the system's knowledge. Therefore, the *benefit achieved* is that our server is advanced, unique, highly efficient, accurate, and flexible. The following Figure 14.2 shows the workflow of the adaptive C&C server.

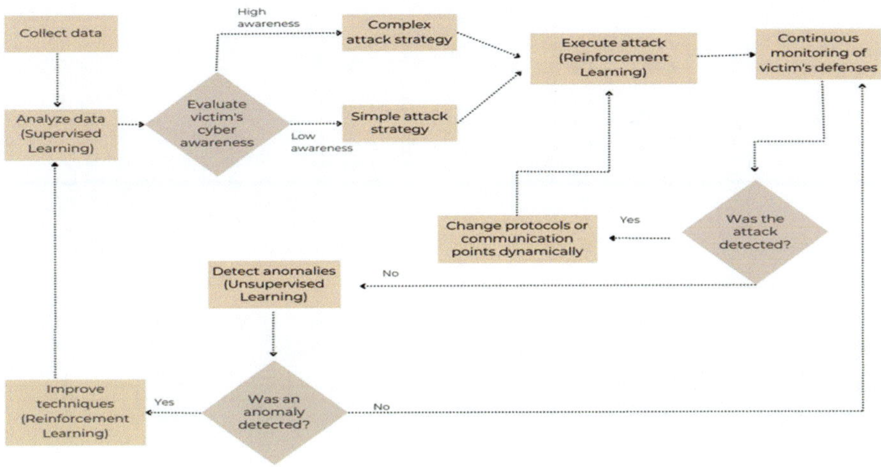

Figure 14.2 PhantomNet adaptive C&C server workflow.

14.2 System design plan

The system of interest (SoI) in this research will comprise both offensive and defensive security phases. The offensive phase focuses on studying the victims' vulnerabilities, providing itself with the best stealth techniques that aim to bypass the target's defences. In contrast, the defensive analysis focuses on detecting potential attacks and vulnerabilities in its defenses and evaluating them to protect its systems against attacks. Table 14.1 shows the PhantomNet Offensive and defensive strategy development, implementation, and optimization phases.

14.3 Risk Assessment Plan

A risk assessment was conducted for our system, both defensive and offensive, by identifying the risks for each stage, their likelihood, impact, level of impact, and ways to address them, following a logical sequence for the system, which gives us a comprehensive view, helping us identify and understand the risks we will deal with and how to address them to mitigate weaknesses, strengthen strengths, and implement the system in the best possible way. The following Tables 14.2 and 14.3 show the risk assessment for defensive and offensive. Note that likelihood is ranked based on numbers from 1 to 5, where 1 indicates a very low likelihood, and 5 indicates a very high likelihood.

Table 14.1 PhantomNet offensive and defensive strategy development.

Phases	Tasks Description	Tools/Methodologies
	Offensive Security Subsystem	
Offensive system requirements analysis	The system requirements will be determined by gathering information from previous studies and current products. Researching advanced stealth techniques that will be used in offensive operations, in addition to interviews and questionnaires with specialists. Of course, we will determine the inputs, the commands sent to the victims, the environments we need, and the encryption keys. The outputs will consist of log files and attack results. Additionally, we need performance reports on the accuracy of commands, response speed, and communication. As for the operations, they will include executing commands on the victim, applying techniques to maintain anonymity using advanced encryption techniques, and finally, the scalability of our system through vertical scaling.	• AES and HTTPS protocols, DNS Tunneling. • Windows, Kali Linux. • Scikit-learn, TensorFlow
Requirement modeling	The requirements will be converted into visual models.	• DFD to understand the data flow. • UML will design the entire system structure.
Defense behavior analysis	Here, we will understand how firewalls, IDS, and IPS work, and the encryption and obfuscation techniques used. Knowing this gives us an idea and understanding of how to bypass these systems.	• Network Traffic Analysis: Nmap, Wireshark. • Cryptanalysis. • Snort.
C2 server design	An integrated architecture that includes the server, databases, attacks, defenses, and how they work together will be designed.	• Flask. • Kali Linux. • MySQL Workbench. • Python Language.
Secure communication channels	Ensure the security of the connection between the server and the defense systems.	• OpenVPN. • SSL/TLS. • Apache.

Attack adaptation using ML	Developing attack strategies and impact through ML.	• Scikit-learn • TensorFlow • SVM • Decision Trees • Random Forest
Implementation	We will implement the system at this stage by creating and developing the server, setting up the connection between it and the target devices, building databases, and implementing attacks.	• MySQL Workbench. • C2 server.
Attack strategy improvement using reinforcement learning	At this stage, we will analyze the encryption and obfuscation tools we use and their weaknesses, improve these algorithms, strengthen encryption key management, and develop obfuscation methods.	• Unsupervised Learning such as the K-mean algorithm. • Reinforcement Learning.
	Defensive Security Subsystem	
Defense requirements analysis	At this stage, we will start identifying the attacks the system may be exposed to, such as DDoS Attacks or other attacks using the C&C system. Then, we will analyze the vulnerabilities of each system in the targeted devices, especially the Windows system. We will determine the necessary security and encryption technologies and develop the targeted systems to deal with the pressure of attack requests and analyze future threats.	• Snort • Suricata • pfSense
Defense system design	We will build the defensive structure of the targeted systems to protect them from attacks by identifying the necessary tools and software for protection, encryption, detection, prevention, and mechanisms to increase the systems' resilience against the pressure of attacker requests and rapid defense measures.	• Flask, Kali Linux • MySQL Workbench. • Flask, Python Language
Implementation of the defensive system	Implementing a defensive system against attacks using tools and techniques appropriate to the attack effectively.	• Snort • Suricata • PfSense • Snort IDS/IPS
Improving defense strategies using ML	Based on the test report, the defense mechanisms will be modified, weaknesses will be addressed, and its efficiency against attacks will be increased.	• Unsupervised Learning such as the K-mean algorithm. • Reinforcement Learning

Table 14.2 Offensive subsystem risk assessment plan.

ID	Task	ID	Probable risk	Likelihood	Impact	Impact level	Risk responses	Countermeasure
R1	**C&C server development**	**1**	**Server discovery**	4	This may lead to the attack being detected and stopped, or the attacker being tracked and his location and techniques being exposed.	High	• Advance encryption: TLS/SSL. • Use of masking and identity obfuscation techniques. • Continuous monitoring (IDS/IPS): for early detection of any detection attempt.	• Mitigate
		2	**Server instability**	3	Increased operational costs, difficulty maintaining the control attack, challenges in covering traces, and increased vulnerability to legal accountability.	Moderate	• Periodic server optimization and maintenance.	• Mitigate
		3	**Failure to establish a connection with the victims**	3	Detect the attacker, disrupt the attack, or lose control.	Moderate	• Improve permanent contact with the victim.	• Mitigate
R2	**Database design**	**1**	**Expansion problems**	4	Attack delay or failure due to overhead or loss of data.	High	• Reduce unnecessary operations during an attack. • Monitor resources periodically and continuously. • Vertical scaling. • Optimize queries.	• Mitigate

		2	**Data leak**	2-3	Failure of the attack or loss of data that may be sensitive data or exposure to accountability.	High	• Regular security updates: like ensure that the encryption techniques used are advanced and up-to-date. • Strong authentication • Strict access control: such as least privilege, regular access review. • Employee education and training. • Backup. • Collaborating with security experts.	• Mitigate • transfer
R3	**C&C interface development**	1	**Difficulty for users to interact and use it**	3	Increased complexity of the attack, increased consumption of resources and time, and the potential for the attack to be abandoned or stopped.	Low to moderate	• Improve and simplify the interface to be intuitive and easy to use.	• Avoidance • Mitigate
R4	**Attack mechanism definition and execution**	1	**Detect the tools used in the attack**	4–5	Loss of control and failure to achieve desired goals.	High	• Encryption and obfuscation. • Use legitimate tools for enforcement. • Use light and uncommon tools. • Dynamic change of tools.	• Mitigate

(*Continued*)

Table 14.2 *Continued*

ID	Task	ID	Probable risk	Likelihood	Impact	Impact level	Risk responses	Countermeasure
R4	**Attack mechanism definition and execution**	**2**	**Failure of the mechanism or tools used**	3	Failure of the attack wastes resources and time and may result in detection and increased complexity.	Moderate	• Update and test tools regularly.	• Mitigate
R5	**Malware development and deployment**	**1**	**Security vulnerabilities post updates**	4	Detection of these vulnerabilities by defense systems may lead to disruption of the attack and even its detection.	High	• Software testing after update. • Periodic security audits. • Avoid installing untrusted updates. • Set a risk management policy for vulnerabilities that may appear after updates.	• Mitigate
		2	**Software updates failed**	3	Delaying the attack or failing to execute the attack in the desired manner.	Moderate	• Backups. • Pilot updates.	• Mitigate
R6	**Victim data management and analysis**	**1**	**Leaking of sensitive data and victim's personal data**	3	It may lead to the attacker being detected or the attack failing, in addition to legal consequences.	High	• Regular security updates: like ensure that the encryption techniques used are advanced and up-to-date. • Backup. • Use strong authentication techniques such as MFA.	• Mitigate

							• Employee education and training. • Apply access control. • Data loss prevention (DLP) systems.	
R7	**Victim response and analysis**	1	**Detecting the attack or victims interacting with the defenses**	5	Track and identify the attacker or disrupt the attack early and expose it to legal consequences.	High	• Encryption and Obfuscation. • Taking advantage of hard-to-detect vulnerabilities such as zero-day exploits. • Advanced stealth techniques. • Use advanced threat intelligence. • Use of non-standard communication channels.	• Mitigate
		2	**Victims not responding quickly**	3	Impact on the effectiveness of the attack based on the victim's response speed.	Low to moderate	• Improving how you communicate with the victim. • Use flexible tools.	• Mitigate
R8	**Documentation and report**	1	**Poor documentation or leakage of information**	2	Loss of vital information or data leakage.	moderate	• Document encryption. • Securing documentation.	• Mitigate
		2	**Inaccurate documentation**	2	Loss or inconsistency of important information.	Low	• Review documentation periodically. • Verifying every step of the process.	• Mitigate

Table 14.3 Defensive subsystem risk assessment plan.

ID	Task	ID	Probable risk	LH	Impact	Impact level	Risk responses	Countermeasure
DR1	**Detection system design**	1	**The system failed to detect the attacks.**	5	Ease of hacking systems.	High	• Using ML to train on modern and advanced attacks to develop predictive models and then detect attacks. • Periodic updates. • Periodic penetration testing	• Mitigate
		2	**False alarms**	3	Waste a lot of time and effort dealing with fake threats instead of real ones which may create an opportunity for the attacker to cross into the system.	Moderate	• Improve algorithms and periodically check their accuracy and correctness.	• Mitigate
DR2	**Identify tools and techniques**	1	**Use of techniques and tools that are incompatible with the system**	4–5	Performance and security issues such as operational failure, vulnerabilities, or failure to respond to attacks.	High	• Evaluate tools and techniques by testing them before integration. • Continuous updates and monitoring. • Use industry standards. • Train team security.	• Mitigate
		2	**Maintenance costs**	3–4	Impact on the organization's budget.	Moderate	• Conduct periodic inspections to ensure efficiency before a costly breakdown occurs.	• Mitigate • Acceptance
DR3	**Attack detection**	1	**False negatives**	4	Depleting resources, time, and more costs.	High	• Integrating big data analytics with ML • Improve algorithms through periodic testing and accuracy. • Use multiple layers of protection: IDS/IPS, MTA.	• Mitigate

DR4	**Manage access settings**	**1**	**Mistakes in settings such as granting unauthorized access**	3–4	It is possible to hack sensitive systems, leak their data, or cause a malfunction in the systems and affect the reputation.	Moderate To High	• Automated access management and detection. • Identity and access management (IAM) tools. • Least privilege. • Access permission review.	• Mitigate
		2	**Access management systems hacking**	2	The system is exposed to advanced attacks that lead to data leakage, data breach, or system control.	High	• Dynamic access control techniques. • Reinforcement learning for access strategy improvement. • Continuous auditing. • Identity and access management (IAM) Tools.	• Mitigate
DR5	**Attack response**	**1**	**Delayed defense response**	4	It allows the attacker to execute his commands in a longer time, which increases the damage and may lead to the disruption of the system.	High	• Automated response systems. • Real-time monitoring and alert systems. • Pre-defined contingency plans and playbooks.	• Mitigate
		2	**Attack prevention failed due to lack of resources**	3	Allowing attackers to hack into systems and cause significant damage to infrastructure and security.	High	• Infrastructure improvement. • Auto-Scaling systems. • Prioritization of resources. • Using ML to improve resource consumption. • Systems testing and development.	• Acceptance • Mitigate
DR6	**Threat analysis**	**1**	**Inaccuracy**	3	Making wrong or inaccurate decisions reduces the effectiveness of the defense.	Moderate	• Continuously update collection and analysis tools. • Continuously and advancedly updating and training machine learning techniques.	• Avoidance

(*Continued*)

Table 14.3 *Continued*

ID	Task	ID	Probable risk	LH	Impact	Impact level	Risk responses	Countermeasure
		2	**Lack of understanding of advanced attack strategies**	2	Decreased ability to counter advanced and modern attacks, waste of resources, and may lead to data loss.	Moderate	• Training security teams on advanced attacks.	• Mitigate
DR7	**Data protection**	**1**	**Modify data**	4	It may cause disruption of operations, incorrect and inaccurate decisions, and material damages.	Moderate to high	• Cryptographic integrity checks such as digital signature and HMAC. • Least privilege. • Access control. • Using ML to train models to detect common patterns by trying to modify. • Real-time monitoring and alerts.	• Mitigate
		2	**Lack sensitive data**	3	Exploiting leaked information in attacks or theft may lead to access to defense systems and knowledge of their working mechanism from the attacker.	Moderate	• Least privilege. • Review permissions and detect unauthorized permissions. • Strong encryption. • Authentication. • Digital signature.	• Mitigate • Avoidance
DR8	**Database design**	**1**	**Designing unprotected databases**	2–3	Access to the database, which causes loss of integrity and confidentiality of data, may disrupt or disable the system and may lead to financial losses.	Moderate to high	• Strong data encryption such AES-256, TLS/SSL. • Advanced authentication mechanisms like MFA, IAM. • Regular monitoring and review of configuration structure.	• Avoidance • Mitigate
DR9	**System continuity**	**1**	**System down during attack**	3	Stopping processes that allow the attacker to achieve his goals.	High	• Auto-scaling capabilities. • Reducing redundant systems during an attack.	• Mitigate

		2	**Full resource consumption due to attacks**	3	System slowdowns, hindering operations that affect performance and complexity of defenses.	Moderate	• Contingency plans and backup solutions. • Vertical scaling. • Auto-scaling	• Acceptance • Mitigate
DR10	**Data security**	1	**Using weak or outdated security techniques**	3	It may lead to the collapse of the security system and lead to very high material losses.	High	• Use strong encryption protocols like AES, RSA and review them regularly. • Apply multi-factor authentication (MFA). • Implement modern security policies • Enhance threat detection capabilities using ML. • Awareness of new technologies.	• Avoidance
		2	**Mismanagement of encryption keys**	3	Loss of access to data and material damage.	Moderate to high	• Generate strong keys. • Encrypt keys in transit. • Train security teams. • Enforce strict policies such as least privilege.	• Mitigate
DR11	**Optimize incident response**	1	**Lack of appropriate response plans**	3	Mistakes in decision-making or delayed response slow down operations.	Moderate	• Regularly test and develop plans.	• Mitigate
DR12	**Backup and restore**	2	**Backup tampering**	3	Unable to recover data	Moderate	• Digital signature. • and access control procedures.	• Mitigate
		2	**Backup failed**	2	Loss of critical and sensitive data that disrupts continuity of operations.	Moderate	• Update and maintain the backup infrastructure periodically and continuously.	• Avoidance

14.4 Related Work

We have read a lot of research related to our system, and here we will summarize it. In [8] it discusses the use of complex network theory to study and analyze command and control systems in military fields, study the topology and resistance to destruction, and then improve them. The weakness of the C2 system's resistance to random and deliberate attacks has been addressed, as this improved system aims to serve the military field. [8] Random and deliberate attacks were simulated by designing a network model to evaluate and improve resistance by increasing edges with three strategies. The results showed that the edge addition strategies were slightly effective, but the addition of low-degree edges significantly improved the destruction resistance and efficiency. Conclusions indicate the importance of critical nodes and strengthening low-degree edges. Recommendations focus on further protection of critical nodes and expanding the study to include dynamic networks.

In [9], an innovative approach to detect CLS misuse by malware in Windows operating systems as C2 channels using ML and PE file analyze and enhance its resistance. The increasing ability of malicious C2 systems to hide due to exploiting weaknesses in traditional defenses. This research aims to develop an advanced ML-based detection model to benefit researchers and cybersecurity teams. The model builds a dataset of malicious and benign software, analyzes key features using SFSF, SFSB, and RFE techniques, and applies them to advanced machine learning algorithms such as RF. The research found that the random forest algorithm was the most accurate, with a detection accuracy of [9] 98.15%. The model's resistance was evaluated using RMCP, and its accuracy after the attack was high at [9] 83%. ML is effective and powerful in detecting malicious C2 used for CLS and it is recommended to combine dynamic analysis and deep learning to improve accuracy and performance.

In [9] the research talks about the C3PO mechanism that aims to secretly monitor malicious C2 servers using over-permissioned protocols to eliminate malicious networks. Due to the traditional methods of monitoring being inaccurate and vulnerable to detection, there was a need for a sophisticated, large-scale tool for effective and covert monitoring, benefiting the cyber research community and incident response teams. The tool relies on binary analysis of memory images based on symbolic execution to identify over-permissioned protocols, extract infiltration vectors, and identify the monitoring capabilities of C2 servers. Analyzing [9] 200,000 malicious samples, the system identified [9] 62,202 over-permissioned bots, and 8,512 malware families in addition to [9] 443,905 monitoring capabilities for C2 servers, which was a powerful and effective tool in detection. It has been shown how important the C3PO can be in secretly monitoring malicious C2 systems and providing important insights into the behavior of malware that helps disrupt these networks. It is recommended that authorities adopt this tool to enhance future investigations.

In [10], this chapter discusses the complexity of adversarial attacks launched by C2 servers to bypass detection by defense systems using deep learning techniques, and the development of defense systems to detect these attacks and enhance their models against tampering. Legacy systems are no longer capable of detecting attacks that modify their encrypted traffic, so we need to enhance detection models by training them on malicious samples disguised by DNNs, which benefits developers and cybersecurity engineers. The DNN was used to detect encrypted C2 traffic. It was trained on a set of C2 data to identify malicious patterns. Adversarial learning techniques were used to test the resilience of the model. The attacker used a proxy to modify its traffic. Random sampling reduced the detection accuracy of defense systems to the point that the misclassification rate increased, but it was taken advantage of as [10] the model with adversarial samples from various attacks improved its robustness, but no single detector proved superior across all scenarios. Current systems require ongoing development and DL integration to effectively counter adversarial attacks, as existing models are insufficient.

In [12] the chapter updates us on the Command and Control systems (C2) technologies in modern companies and cities to something more than a single task; they can control the entire program or system. The study sees the importance of merging humanity and technology so we can get a better version of C&C servers. The future Command and Control systems (C2) require collaboration, encouraging adaptability to complex environments and collaboration across sectors, providing continuous learning for those sectors. This approach and others discussed in the chapter are necessary to create an adaptable Command and Control system (C2) in military and defense systems.

In [12], the study focused on developing a system that depends on MongoDB to detect the anomalies in HTTP traffic. By analyzing HTTP patterns the system will know the difference between normal and potentially malicious activities, It reduces the number of undetected cyber-attacks, indicating its potential to generate special cybersecurity frameworks. This study highlights the importance of storage systems and advanced data analyses in mitigating cyber threats.

In [14], the study focuses on detecting Command and Control systems (C2) and phishing domains in DNS. It gives us techniques to identify the malicious domains by analysing DNS traffic and comparing them against known threat indicators. It enhances early detection by making use of their queries, providing an efficient tool to automatically detect and prevent any suspicious traffic on the channel. We can upgrade our work by upgrading it with more automation, detection, and prevention techniques.

In [14], the chapter proposes a systematic approach to identify the flow of ransomware traffic to command and control (C&C) servers and specifically aims at identifying certain communication patterns. In addition to this, the study also emphasizes the need to identify the geographical location of C&C infrastructure and the effects that it has on the network security, especially in areas with loose cybersecurity policies. The outcomes of the study are significant to the understanding of the ransomware environment and the importance of the covert C&C communication to create a base for developing efficient cybersecurity solutions. The methodology part of the chapter provides a detailed explanation of the data collection process where they used sandboxing environments to simulate a network infrastructure and giving an impression for the ransomware like a real network, Network traffic analysis where they used a packet capture tools like Wireshark to detect the anomaly traffic on the network, Identifying C&C traffic signatures involved the analysis of packet headers, payloads, and session data to identify recurring patterns indicative of C&C activity, finally the mapping and tracing C&C servers. The experimental setup part of the chapter describes how they applied the Sandbox environment, traffic capture and logging, and simulation of C&C communications. In the results part, they notified the communication patterns between ransomware and their C&C servers were analyzed, showing that the periodic communication intervals were observed, occurring approximately every 30–60 seconds [14]. The geolocation analysis showed the dominance of regions in Eastern Europe and Southeast Asia. Signature methods gave an edge in unencrypted traffic, but the analysis on encrypted traffic employed anomaly-based detection. An entropy-based anomaly detection of communications in packets uses size for traffic and a higher entropy value of the encrypted communications. There was a difference in the detection techniques, and this was that the anomaly-based detection was used on encrypted traffic while the signature-based one was intertwined with unencrypted traffic.

In [16], using flow and DNS data, C&C servers were characterized. The domain classification system is based on the count of records (NS, MX, TXT) about the domain for which domain-centric features have been introduced in the literature. It was concluded that domain classification systems achieved very good accuracy (97%) in malware with malicious domain names, especially those created by domain generation algorithms (DGAs). However, the accuracy of the net flow classification system remained poor (77%) as far as effective features like flow sizes [16], access behavior, and temporal behavior are concerned. For example, the Proof of Concept (PoC) system implemented a combination of both systems and managed to attain an overall efficiency of 81%. However, these results are encouraging; the study encountered several problems, including using an outdated dataset under limited conditions and also challenges regarding WHOIS data for the domain registration period. In the future, the database can be enlarged, the features of net flow can be improved, and the use of further features such as registrar, DNS record content, BGP AS number, and IP geolocation may improve detection rates and decrease the number of false positives and false negatives.

In [16] this paper has provided a comprehensive review of the abuse of cloud-based location services (CBLS), which is growing, mostly used by cybercriminals for the establishment of C&C infrastructures . The research methodically analyzes the different offensive tactics used by the attackers to misuse CPLS, targeting the hidden channel techniques that the malware developers use to evade the detection. On the other hand, such continuously changing attacks bring up the issue of difficulties in detection and mitigation. This chapter also highlighted the fact that CPLS generally needs collaboration with the cloud providers, researchers, and law enforcement to counteract their offensive strategies. This research review was done on 91 articles from 2008 to 2023 [16], besides different ways of strategy and detection that were used in the study. Despite a big body of research concerning the causes of these offenses, the one in that the proper response methods were not a priority was given more coverage. The authors say that the action of bridging these gaps is vital in making the security of CPLS platforms good. The improvements in the detection methods, involvement, and the handling of dynamic threats are among the things that will be done in future research. All this will be, in effect, a means of minimizing the risks of CPLS abuses and ensuring the security of cloud services is on the safe side.

In [17], the research paper "Phishing and Advanced Persistent Threats" discusses the growing threat of phishing as the first step to advanced persistent threats (APTs), which are sophisticated cyber attacks that aim to establish a hidden persistent connection with the victim. The researcher believes that the main problem of this research is phishing, so he explained its role in deceiving users into revealing sensitive information or spreading malware, which facilitates deeper penetration of the network by APT actors. Phishing techniques, such as email-based attacks, malicious hyperlinks, and social engineering, are classified, and their use is explained in the initial access and movement within the target network. Using a mixed methodology approach to improve defense against phishing, such as email filtering, machine learning algorithms, and analytical processes. Recommendations include a multi-layered defense strategy that relies on advanced detection systems, user training programs, and algorithm development used to detect suspicious network activities, and integrating artificial intelligence to resist advanced attack methods. In conclusion, addressing phishing in APTs requires a multi-pronged approach that combines technological and human factors to reduce cyber threat risks.

In [19], the research paper "Social Media Command and Control of Malware: Towards a Serverless Infrastructure" discusses the evolving use of social media as a platform for C2 malware, which will be a major shift towards a serverless infrastructure. Traditional C2 systems rely on dedicated servers to communicate with the victim's device, but advances in detection and development of defensive mechanisms have forced attackers to adapt. By leveraging platforms such as Twitter, Facebook, and Instagram, and using techniques such as encryption, obfuscation, and domain generation algorithms (DGA), the attacker embeds C2 communications in public domains, making detection increasingly difficult. Five key points were identified for building a flexible and stealthy C2 system that are difficult to break compared to traditional models: (1) embedding commands in social media posts using specific separators or character sets, (2) using stealth to hide commands in images or metadata, (3) relying on public cloud storage for communications and untraceable data exchange, (4) deploying DGA to dynamically create fake C2 accounts or URLs, and (5) posting commands in comments under high-traffic posts such as posts by celebrities.

The results tell us that this approach is an excellent attack for attackers because it automatically hides malicious activity within posts that have high and large activity. On the contrary, for defenders, it can be considered a major challenge, as they will have to monitor and classify large amounts of traffic on these platforms or celebrity accounts in order to be able to identify malicious activity, and the subject is not easy either. The report suggests improving detection tactics by using machine learning to detect fraudulent accounts and suspicious activity patterns, in addition to proactive measures by social media platforms, such as introducing invisible modifications to block encrypted C2 communications. In conclusion, the research emphasizes the importance of a new proactive approach to disrupting serverless malware systems that spread via social media.

In [20], the paper "Boten ELISA: A Novel Approach for Botnet C&C in Online Social Networks" discusses ELISA (Elusive Social Army), a novel botnet framework designed to exploit online social networks (OSNs) for command and control (C&C) communications. Unlike traditional C&C systems that rely on centralized protocols (such as IRC or HTTP), which are vulnerable to detection and disruption, ELISA takes advantage of online social networks' decentralized and ubiquitous nature. By embedding C&C messages into user interactions, ELISA achieves stealthy and efficient communications within a botnet. Botnet detection systems have become able to identify centralized C&C channels, leaving attackers to look for decentralized alternatives to establish these channels. With their huge user base and traffic, online social networks provide a convenient place to hide malicious activities. ELISA addresses this opportunity by leveraging Unicode stealth technology to encode botnet messages into invisible, non-printable characters embedded in user-generated content. The authors implemented and prototyped ELISA, which operates through two main components: the botmaster and the infected hosts (bots). Messages are encrypted and signed using cryptographic methods (AES for encryption and RSA with SHA-2 for signing). These messages are then encrypted using invisible Unicode characters and added to legitimate posts by users. The botnet uses social graph relationships to propagate messages, ensuring resilience and reliability. Experiments were conducted using a simulated dataset of Facebook interactions to evaluate the efficiency of the botnet.

The experiment demonstrated that ELISA effectively transmits messages within the botnet without generating network traffic that network observers could detect. On average, 75% of the botnet receives a command message within 72 hours [20], with the delivery rate exceeding traditional botnet methods, such as StegoBot. The communication remains undetectable by current traffic analysis or behavior-based detection systems due to its integration with normal OSN activities. To defend against these threats, the chapter proposes enhancing OSN security measures, such as verifying user-generated content within certain rules, detecting statistical anomalies of hidden characters, and monitoring unusual propagation patterns. Ensure the comfort of the user experience. ELISA demonstrates the feasibility and effectiveness of a botnet that leverages OSNs as a covert channel for command and control, emphasizing the urgent need for proactive security strategies. Although there is no evidence of real-world applications for ELISA, its potential underscores the importance of anticipating and mitigating emerging threats in cybersecurity. Future research will focus on testing the undetectablity of ELISA with advanced detection systems and improving countermeasures.

In [21] "Distributed Server Systems for Simulation-Command-Control Interaction" discusses the challenges of making command and control systems work seamlessly with simulation systems in military alliances. These systems are often from different countries, making interoperability complex and expensive. The chapter emphasizes the importance of automation and standardization in improving efficiency, reducing costs, and enabling real-world decision-making and operations. A distributed server architecture was tested to try to address the core problem. These servers handle XML-based messages representing military orders and reports, enabling seamless communication between systems. The chapter used three different servers – Fraunhofer FKIE, WISE-SBML, and ELLIPSE – each with distinct capabilities. For example, WISE-SBML could translate between schemas, while ELLIPSE provided extensive support for different simulation technologies. The servers were connected via REST and STOMP protocols, forming a network capable of sharing workloads and ensuring reliable communication. The results showed clear benefits. Distributed servers have successfully reduced network congestion by sharing the computational load across multiple nodes, allowing the system to handle heavy workloads efficiently. For example, WISE-SBML processed up to 150 reports per second when translating graphs [21].

Improvements and recommendations for these systems include introducing a "router" parameter to message headers, which prevents redundancy issues in distributed networks. They also call for enhancing the C2SIM standard, making C2 simulation systems more flexible and easier to use in real-world military operations. In conclusion, the study demonstrates that distributed server systems have the potential to transform how C2 systems and simulations interact. These inventions represent a major advance in military technology because they save costs while enhancing operational efficiency. However, further development and global standardization are needed to realize their full potential.

In [22], the chapter "Design and Evaluation of Advanced Persistent Threats (APT) Scenarios for Internet Domains" discusses the challenge of combating cyber threats. Advanced persistent threats (APTs) are characterized by their continuous and hidden communication. Here comes the idea of Cyber Ranges, which are safe and controlled simulation environments. The problem is that current models, such as Cyber Kill Chain and MITER ATT&CK, are missing some technical details and cannot accurately describe complex threat scenarios. For this reason, the authors developed a model called Tactics, Techniques, and Procedures Diamond Model (T2P-DM). This model is based on the MITRE ATT&CK framework and describes attacks in a precise and organized manner, and fills the gaps that occur in the simulation. In addition, they created a framework called FASAC to run simulations, using tools like Kubernetes and Rancher. This framework allows for the allocation of resources as needed and provides a realistic attack simulation.

They evaluated the framework using two real-life cases: APT27 (Emissary Panda), which exploited vulnerabilities like ProxyLogon, and Earth Lusca, which relied on phishing and watering-hole attacks. The results proved that the model is effective in simulating the attack stages. They even tried out a fictional scenario of the APT999 team attacking a pharmaceutical company, and demonstrated how FASAC can manage complex scenarios without the person using it needing much programming experience. The results were positive; T2P-DM improved accuracy and organization in attack descriptions, and FASAC gave an easy platform for training and testing. But they emphasized that we must continue research and work to improve the long-term simulation, taking into account ethical issues, because the goal is defensive and does not support malicious actors. In short, the study demonstrated the power of T2P-DM and FASAC in training and equipping cybersecurity teams, while emphasizing that we need to develop more to keep pace with the evolution of cyber threats.

In [23] it is created in such a way that even though it is an unauthorized application, it can still gain access within the victim's system. In this case, however, the bot utilizes a proxy chain, inclusive of Tor, to help conceal the attackers' identity. The attacker, however, operated a bot over Telegram, allowing him to command the target systems and obtain sensitive details such as screenshots and system information. Also dealing with ransomware part, the bot takes over essential files and encrypts them using Fernet encryption and then demands money as ransom for them to be decrypted. Once the victim has settled the ransom payment, the decryption key is given to them. The further directions are related to malware development for macOS and ensuring that it remains persistent through injection into additional system DLLs. This chapter does not, however, go ahead to explain any of the above weaknesses in detail, and focuses on the comparison of GITCBot with other botnets like Stego-botnets and Serverless ones, arguing that GITCBot is much better thanks to Telegram cross-platform networks.

14.4.1 Related systems

Merlin C2 [24]: It is a Command-and-Control server (C2) that is built specially for ethical professional use. It gives us methods to communicate and manage victim devices, especially passive communication. It allows remote control commands, built using the Go programming language. It is compatible with multiple operating systems, so this will give us a great advantage and flexibility. It has a modern design that supports various transport methods like HTTP and DNS, making it adaptable for stealth operations.

It was built primarily to assess the companies during their security assessments to improve their defence systems against thrids.

BrainDamage C2 [25]: This is a remote administration service which uses twitter as a command and control server. Its abilities: List all the active slaves, remove the stub from host and will remove registry entries, run shell commands on host, download files in the host computer, execute the following commands, take screenshot of the host of computer, set email template, stop keylogger or webserver, changes wallpaper of host computer and find open ports and the router the host is using.

Sliver C2 [26]: This is an open source cross-platform adversary emulation/red team framework, is a versatile command-and-control (C2) framework that enables covert management of remote systems. It supports multiple communication protocols like Mutual TLS, HTTP(S), DNS, and Wireguard, and allows security professionals to execute commands, gather information, and conduct post-exploitation activities. Sliver is compatible with various operating systems and CPU architectures.

Mythic [27]: This is a cross-platform framework with an interactive and easy-to-use interface used in red teaming operations, simulating attacks, and analyzing data in an integrated manner to enable security assessments. Due to the lack of flexibility in expansion and customization and the complexity of use in red teaming tools, which leads to restricting the analytical capabilities of data, the mythic framework was developed to solve these problems, as it allows the addition of new agents, communication channels, and modifications in a simple and flexible manner that benefits researchers in this field and red teams. Mythic relies on the use of Docker containers, which provide high flexibility on multiple operating platforms, in addition to an interactive user interface using reaction, communication and coordination between the framework components is done via RabbitMQ. This framework has improved the efficiency of activity tracking, data analysis, and acceleration of their execution by [27], which tracks the specific command and control profile parameters used, the commands loaded into the payload, and their versions. It has also enhanced the flexibility in customization and addition. Mythic has improved the quality of interaction between components, as well as the efficiency and strength of implementation, so further customization and additions are recommended to further improve the effectiveness of the system. The following Table 14.4 shows the literature review summary.

Table 14.4 Literature review summary.

Ref	Solution approach	Techniques	Dataset	Attacks	Standards	Advantages	Limitations
2022, [17]	User training and detection systems (AI/ML algorithms)	• Email filtering • Browser-integrated tools • Phishing detection-ML • Content analysis	• Past cybersecurity reports • case studies • real-world incident analysis.	• Phishing techniques (email phishing, spear phishing, malicious links)	• NIST guidelines	• Adaptability of AI-based methods • High detection rates	• Reliance on user awareness • potential false positives in detection systems • Adversaries' rapid adaptability
2020, [19]	Iidentifying malware C2 infrastructure using social media and cloud services	• Encryption • Steganography • Domain Generation Algorithms (DGA)	No dataset	• Command transmission • payload delivery • botnet C2 communication strategies	• MITRE ATT&CK	• Enhanced stealth, resilience, and flexibility • reduced reliance on private infrastructure	• Detection via machine learning and platform-based measures
2015, [20]	decentralized botnet that uses Online Social Networks (OSNs) as C&C channels	• Unicode steganography • AES encryption • SA with SHA2 • social graph relationships	• WOSN dataset	• Botnet coordination • large-scale cyber-attacks without detection.	• cryptographic standards (AES, RSA, SHA-2)	• Without generating additional network traffic • Undetectable by traditional methods	• content validation by OSNs • potential size-based statistical detection
2024, [22]	Framework for Automated Simulation of APT attacks in Cyber Ranges (FASAC).	• MITRE ATT&CK framework. • T2P-DM integrates tactics • FASAC	• Emissary Panda (APT27) • Earth Lusca	• Proxy Logon • spear-phishing • watering-hole attacks.	• MITRE ATT&CK • Diamond Model	• Realistic and flexible simulation of APT attacks • T2P-DM improves formalization of scenarios.	• limitations in simulating long-term APT attacks

(Continued)

Table 14.4 *Continued*

Ref	Solution approach	Techniques	Dataset	Attacks	Standards	Advantages	Limitations
2015, [21]	Approach involves integrating multiple servers to handle XML-based orders and reports, support schema translation, and manage network traffic.	• REST and STOMP protocols • back-to-back clients to connect servers • Prevent message looping.	• Fraunhofer FKIE, WISE-SBML, and ELLIPSE	• No attack	• Military Scenario Definition Language (MSDL) • Coalition Battle Management Language (C-BML)	• Improved scalability • reduced network load • better system performance	• more robust server systems • updates to the C2SIM schema to handle more complex scenarios.
2024, [14]	The study combines the signature and anomaly-based methodologies to trace the networking of the ransomware through sandboxes and emulators.	• Sigbature-based detection and anomaly-based detection. • Geolocation analysis and DNS records analysis. • Sniffing packets and logging with Wireshark and similar tools. • Simulating command and control communication in the sandbox. • Traffic analysis using entropy metrics.	• Sandboxes in enterprise network settings. • Honeypots for capturing realistic ransomware traffic. • Threat intelligence feeds consisting of C&C domains and IPs	• Domain-flux and fast-flux techniques • Encrypted protocols (e.g, HTTPS , TLS)	• NO standards	• Highly accurate detection of ransimware traffic via hybird detection. • Enabling identification in real-time of ransomware C&C communication. • Deep C&C infrastructure mapping for provided mitigation.	• The increase in false positive rates in anomaly-based detection. • Complexity in the adoption of more sophisticated ransomware • Sandbox environments may not contain the full complexity of a network in real wrld situations.

2023, [16]	This chapter analyzes how attackers utilize CPLS as covert C&C infrastructure, classifying the technique and assessing the detection gaps.	• Steganography • Encoding • Cryptography • Fraudulent account creation • AI-powered C&C mechanisms • Process injection and hijacking	No	• Dropbox, Google Drive, Slack, and Twitter are some of the channels being misused for C&C communications that are encrypted or obfuscated. • Application of steganography methods in the secrecy of conversation. • Through a legitimate account, a cybercriminal can exploit this facility for the purpose of malicious concealment.	• no	• Full-spectrum categorization of attack techniques. • It raises the issue of being protected from such attacks on multiple layers. • It gives useful details to researchers and practitioners.	• Talking mainly about detecting attacks in real-time. • Not much attention is given to the countermeasures' scalability dimension in the reviews. • The likelihood of bias due to the use of secondary data.
2020, [16]	The paper contains a proof-of-concept (PoC) system together with DNS-based and NetFlow classification methods that is capable of detecting malicious traffic.	• Domain classification via DNS and WHOIS features (e.g., registration period, resource record counts). • NetFlow-based Detection Utilized with Flow Sizes, Client Access Patterns and Temporal data.	• Blacklists of malicious and safe domains (Majestic and Joe Wein blacklists) • CTU-13 dataset for Naive Bayes training • Study dataset from malware-	• Identification of botnet traffic that is being directed to temporary Command & Control (C&C) servers. • Recognizes malicious domains through characteristics such as randomized names and short registration periods.	• no	• High precision in domain classification (97%). • It combines the domain name system and network flows to improve the coverage. • The addition of data that gives details of how to differentiate	• Low NetFlow classification accuracy (77%) – Very poor overall PoC accuracy of 81% is the result. • Low NetFlow classification accuracy (77%) – Very poor overall PoC accuracy of 81% is the result. • Low NetFlow classification

(*Continued*)

Table 14.4 *Continued*

Ref	Solution approach	Techniques	Dataset	Attacks	Standards	Advantages	Limitations
		• Relative entropy is used to distinguish the domain names that are randomly generated by DGAs. • Weighted mean for the combination of classification scores.	traffic-analysis. net (459 NetFlow flows, 359 unique domains).			between malicious domains can be done by using the resource record counts and entropy measures only.	accuracy (77%) - Very poor overall PoC accuracy of 81% is the result. • WHOIS data irregularities affect domain classification veracity. • Relying on old-style C&C domain lists with a public lack of fresh data
2021, [23]	GITCBot malware uses a Telegram API as a C&C channel and encrypts through Tor to secure anonymity for the culprit and thereby escape spotting.	• Disguising malicious activity through Telegram API. • Securing connections and hiding attacker details with Tor. • Loading code with PyArmor. • Encrypting data with Fernet	NO	• infecting system by malware • stealing sensitive information • acting as spyware to capture screenshots, audio, and system details. • encrypting files and demanding a ransom.	no	• Completely undetectable to security software via Telegram application. • Incorporates spyware and ransomware together. • Encryption, along with proxies, is the strategy deployed to avoid detection	• Relies on human interactions along with social engineering. • To become successful, it should be done
2024, [24]	C2 framework for post-exploitation	• Modular C2 channels • Covert HTTP/DNS communication	• Open-source testing scenarios • Simulated C2 environments	• Post-exploitation • Data exfiltration • Lateral movement	• Penetration testing standards	• High adaptability • Cross-platform • Flexible	• Requires expert setup

		• Multi-platform implants					
2024, [12]	Holistic C2 system adaptation	• Multi-domain integration • Socio-technical systems • Strategic collaboration	• Expert workshops • Defense system reports	• C2 disruption • Strategic planning threats	NATO & defence protocols	• Resilient against evolving challenges • Encourages collaboration	• Relies on inter-agency coordination • Requires continuous updates
2024, [12]	Real-time anomaly detection systems	• Traffic pattern analysis • MongoDB-based storage and processing	• HTTP datasets • Simulated attack scenarios	• C2 communication anomalies • Data exfiltration attacks	Cybersecurity frameworks	• High accuracy • Efficient data handling	• Dependence on dataset quality • Resource-intensive
2023, [8]	Improving the C2 system using complex network theory	Topological Analysis. Simulation Models. Quantitative Analysis.	None	• Random attack. • Deliberate attacks.	• Small-world network. • Scale-free network.	• Improved network efficiency and resistance to deliberate attacks with low-degree • Identified critical nodes, enhanced robustness.	• No consideration for weighted edges. • Small-scale simulation. • Limited focus on dynamic network changes.

2023, [9]	Using ML techniques to analyze PE to detect misuse of Cloud Services via C2.	• Feature selection techniques:
		  • InfoGain
		  • Chi-squared
		  • ReliefF
		  • SFSF
		  • SFSB
		  • RFE
		• ML Techniques:
		  • Random forest
			Malicious data connecting to CLS servers and benign data verified by VirusTotal.	RMCP	PE File Format	• High detection accuracy.
						• Resistant to adversarial attacks.
						• Create a new and unique dataset.
							• Static analysis and marginalization of dynamic.
							• Limited dataset.
							• Difficulty dealing with encrypted software.
							• Model generalization is often limited to static software.

(Continued)

Table 14.4 *Continued*

Ref	Solution approach	Techniques	Dataset	Attacks	Standards	Advantages	Limitations
		• Decision trees • K-NN • SAV • Naive Bayes • Analysis techniques: • PE File Analysis • Cuckoo Sandbox • Model evaluation techniques: • 10-Fold Cross-Validation • 70:30 Split • Adversarial Attack Techniques: • RMCP					
2021, [9]	Covert monitoring of C2 servers via over-permissioned protocols.	• Dynamic memory image extraction. • Iterative selective symbolic execution. • Backward slicing. • API-to-Capability Mapping. • Control flow Graph (CFG).	Protocol Database.	Botnet attacks.	None	• Scalability. • Covert monitoring. • Efficiency in identifying and discovering C2 servers information.	• Attacks using DGA. • Incomplete network traffic. • Dealing with custom protocols. • Inability to handle virtualization packers.

		• Angr • Detours AVClass2					
2020, [10]	Modify encrypted C2 traffic using advanced techniques.	• Adversarial evasion techniques. • Proxy to modify traffic without changing the behavior of the malware • FGSM.	MTA to generate adversarial samples.	• Proxy-based attack • Duration modification	• Misclassified malicious flows rate	• Bypass detection systems. • Masking malicious behavior.	• Traffic modification restrictions make it difficult for malware to change.
	Detect encrypted C2 traffic through DNN.	• DNN to detect suspicious patterns. • Using adversarial learning to strengthen models.	MTA to improve the model.			• Improve model flexibility. • Improve detection capabilities using adversarial samples.	• The training process for adversarial samples is complex. • Adapting to new threats requires continuous optimization and time.
2020, [27]	A cross-platform framework that provides a seamless and interactive user interface that allows for easy addition of agents and communication channels.	• React. • Docker. • GoLang . • RabbitMQ. • WebSockets. • Jupyter Notebook. • Nginx	PostgreSQL	C2-based attacks.	• MITRE ATT&CK. • C2 Profiles.	• High flexibility and customization. • Interactive and user-friendly interface. • Cross-platform support. • Comprehensive data analysis. • MITRE ATT&CK Integration.	• Limited multi-environment support and interoperability. • Resource intensive. • Reliance on containers.

14.4.2 Knowledge gap

After studying and delving into the literature review, many issues have been noticed that have not been addressed or covered sufficiently, as it appears to us that there is a need to review the weight of edges in neural networks and determine the extent of their impact, as the imbalance in edge weights causes weak detection of complex attacks. In addition to the limited simulation capabilities, it makes dealing with dynamic attacks difficult. Moreover, not interoperability between different systems and platforms poses major challenges but the need for training with diverse data to obtain accurate and comprehensive models. The need to integrate DL to detect complex patterns and the need for real-world environments. We also see challenges in handling custom protocols, virtual packet encapsulation techniques, and DGA. The need to continuously adapt to advanced attacks through flexible defenses that are able to interact with changes in modern attack methods and types.

Despite the fact that a lot of progress has been made in the research area of malware-related attack detection, using techniques like traffic analysis and DNS/NetFlow data, huge knowledge gaps still exist that call for further research and development. First, detection of attacks using encrypted traffic continues to be a major challenge, since most current methods rely on detecting signatures or behavioral patterns in unencrypted data, making them ineffective in cases involving advanced encryption or identity-hiding techniques such as proxy chains and Tor networks. The difficulty of developing effective detection solutions in cloud environments, whereby attackers can use legitimate public cloud services to establish C&C infrastructures that are challenging to detect due to the dynamic nature of these attacks and their ongoing evolution; this clearly indicates the necessity of dynamic detection strategies that could handle the sophisticated threats leveraging these infrastructures. Third, though the tools used, like Wireshark and other traffic analysis tools, are utilized, the accuracy of the detection using NetFlow data remains suboptimal. This further diminishes the capability of current systems to monitor attacker behavior effectively in large and complex networks. Newer detection models that will integrate temporal and behavioral analyses are required to be developed for better detection accuracy, reducing false positives and negatives. Lastly, this area still lacks more comparative studies between different encryption techniques and advanced detection methods, and also the need for expanded datasets used in research works to include recent and complex attack vectors that reflect current trends in attack methods. Table 14.5 summarizes the main gaps and how our system addresses them.

Table 14.5 Gap summarizing.

Identified gap	Description	How PhantomNet addresses the gap
Detection of sophisticated C&C infrastructures	Difficulty in detecting highly adaptive and stealthy C&C servers, especially those using novel evasion techniques.	Integrates supervised, reinforcement, and unsupervised ML to adapt attack strategies and continuously evade advanced detection mechanisms.
Limited adaptability in current defensive systems	Traditional defenses lack the capability to adapt dynamically to evolving attack tactics.	Simulates real-time interactions with defenses to analyze reactions, enabling PhantomNet to modify attack strategies dynamically.
Inadequate long-term simulation mode is for advanced persistent threats (APTs)	Current models fail to accurately simulate the prolonged, covert nature of APT scenarios.	Builds a C&C server capable of maintaining persistent communication and adapting to various environmental changes, simulating APT behaviors.
Insufficient research on encrypted C2 Traffic	Defense systems struggle to differentiate malicious encrypted traffic from legitimate traffic.	Uses adversarial and anomaly-based ML models to mimic legitimate traffic patterns and evade detection.
Challenges in automating attack and defense simulations	Existing frameworks are limited in automating realistic and dynamic cyber-attack scenarios.	Implements adaptive simulation environments that use data-driven learning to replicate realistic attack and defense interactions.
Lack of Collaboration between Offensive and Defensive Approaches	Most research focuses exclusively on either attack or defense, limiting holistic understanding.	Combines offensive and defensive aspects by analysing attack outputs to strengthen defense systems and train security teams.
Lack of robustness in existing detection models against adversarial learning techniques	Defense models often fail to withstand tampering and misclassification during attacks.	Train ML models with adversarial data to enhance their ability to detect and respond to disguised or evolving threats.
Insufficient integration of machine learning in C&C systems	Many C&C systems do not leverage ML to optimize adaptability and efficiency.	Fully integrates ML techniques (supervised, unsupervised, reinforcement learning) to optimize PhantomNet offensive and defensive modules.
Challenge in discovering the execution of orders by the victim	The victim can detect the execution of commands on their devices if they monitor the performance and movement of some of the silences inside their devices	The PhantomNet system provides the execution of commands without the need to open CMD by executing the command programmatically
Challenges in understanding and exploiting victim vulnerabilities dynamically	Limited research focuses on real-time adaptation based on the victim environment and responses.	Collects and analyses detailed victim data to adapt attack methods in real time, ensuring continuity and maximizing impact.

14.5 PhantomNet System Specification

14.5.1 Stakeholders

The success of PhantomNet depends on a set of stakeholders, each of whom plays an important and effective role. The stakeholder categories in our system vary between *direct beneficiaries;* they are the teams or entities that interact directly with the system by using, testing, or developing and managing it, such as penetration testers, defensive teams, developers, and system administrators. *Indirect beneficiaries* are the entities or individuals who benefit from direct stakeholders such as offensive and defensive teams and system outputs of reports and results without direct interaction with the system such as government agencies, cyber companies and academic researchers, with the aim of improving their security solutions, cyber infrastructure and research, each with its own role and importance. Table 14.6 and Figure 14.3 show each category, its role, importance, and how it interacts with the PhantomNet system.

14.5.2 Platform requirements

These platform requirements include PhantomNet operating efficiently and effectively while maintaining a high level of stealth and adaptability in advanced client- and server-side cyber operations. PhantomNet consists of a server-side system and a client-side system.

- **Server-side system:** (attacker) responsible for sending commands, managing the victim's devices, and adapting to avoid detection. We summarize our server-side system's hardware and software requirements in Table 14.7.
- **Client-side system:** Victim connects to the server for malware execution, data exfiltration, and persistence connection. We summarize our server-side System's hardware and software requirements in Table 14.8.

14.5.3 Functional requirements

The functional requirements for the Command and Control (C&C) Server in Table 14.9 define the fundamental functionalities that must be included to provide adequate management and control of remotely managed systems. The criteria cover secure communication, work assignment, monitoring, and reaction systems to ensure efficient and seamless operations.

Table 14.6 Stakeholders.

Stakeholder category	Stakeholder subcategory	Stakeholder examples	Role in the PhantomNet	Interaction with the PhantomNet System	Importance
Users (direct stakeholders)	**Penetration testers**	Ethical hackers. Red teams. Freelance penetration testers.	Detecting vulnerabilities and penetrating defense systems to test their effectiveness.	They use the C2 attack server and its tools such as Nmap and other open source tools to simulate attacks and identify weaknesses in system defenses such as testing firewalls and intrusion detection systems through supervised learning of system defenses and popular defenses, reinforcement learning to improve attacks each time, and unsupervised learning when identifying strange attacks, then they analyze the response and effectiveness of these defenses and document the weaknesses discovered.	They are the core of PhantomNet, detecting vulnerabilities and improving the system based on them.
	Defensive teams	Blue teams,security analysts, incident response teams, SOC analysts	Analyze security defenses against attacks and evaluate their capabilities to implement appropriate, effective solutions with the aim of improving defense strategies and the speed and efficiency of response to advanced attacks.	Collaborate with penetration testers by analyzing and reviewing attack simulation results using tools to understand attack methods and evaluate the effectiveness of defense responses to advanced ML-integrated attacks and their vulnerabilities.	It represents a very important role by protecting the system from persistent advanced attacks and raising security levels that may be one step ahead of the attacker.
Supervisors and Evaluators	**Academic supervisors**	System Advisor, review committee, external evaluators	Monitoring the system's progress and ensuring that it is moving in the right direction.	Continuously follow up on reports and provide feedback to improve performance and progress towards desired goals.	An essential and reliable part of ensuring the quality and success of the system.

(Continued)

Table 14.6 *Continued*

Stakeholder category	Stakeholder subcategory	Stakeholder examples	Role in the PhantomNet	Interaction with the PhantomNet System	Importance
	Institutional reviewers	Compliance officers, ethics committees.	Ensure compliance with the PhantomNet with legal and ethical standards.	Review and analyze simulation results and request necessary legal redaction.	Ensuring that the system adheres to international and internal laws and standards, thus maintaining the system's ethical and legal credibility.
Beneficiaries (Indirect Stakeholders)	**Government entities**	National security agencies, ministries of defense, CERT teams, cybercrime units.	Understand advanced attack techniques using machine learning and train cybersecurity teams to enhance defensive infrastructure and improve readiness.	Analyze simulation results and attack methods to identify advanced threats and how they operate.	Providing a sophisticated and powerful system for analyzing advanced cyber-attacks using ML that contributes to strengthening the national infrastructure and mitigating future threats.
	Cybersecurity companies	Security consulting firms, managed security service providers, security vendors.	Improve and update security solutions to provide security consulting on how to improve defense against advanced attacks.	Utilize reports and data to simulate attacks using PhantomNet to understand how advanced attacks work and determine the improvements required by the security company.	Phantom Set helps improve security solutions and enhance their capabilities to confront persistent threats.

	Academic researchers	AI & Cybersecurity Research Labs and Collaborative Centres. University cybersecurity department	Improving academic research, developing, and disseminating research solutions to raise community awareness about modern attacks.	Using PhantomNet to simulate advanced attacks and generate data that supports academic research, helping researchers analyze and develop strategies to detect and defend against modern cyber threats.	PhantomNet is a valuable system for researchers. It enhances the deep understanding of attack techniques using ML, helping to develop appropriate and effective defenses.
System developers and administrators	**System developers**	Security-focused system developers, backend developer, frontend developer, full stack developer.	Design and develop an integrated ML-based system of C2 offensive server, Defensive tools and integrated databases, & maintain improved performance & integration between software components & operational interface.	Testing PhantomNet components of the C2 attack server, tools, and databases to ensure integration and improve performance.	Essential to maintain the stability, development, and improvement of the system to ensure its continued efficiency and effectiveness.
	System administrators	Security administrators, network administrator, infrastructure managers, database administrators.	Manage and monitor the system infrastructure and resolve technical issues that may affect performance to maintain its stability and security.	Use the monitoring tools integrated with PhantomNet, follow up on reports and data, apply the best appropriate security policies, and maintain periodic maintenance and updates.	Essential to ensure the safety and security of the system and to ensure its continuous performance without interruption or threats.

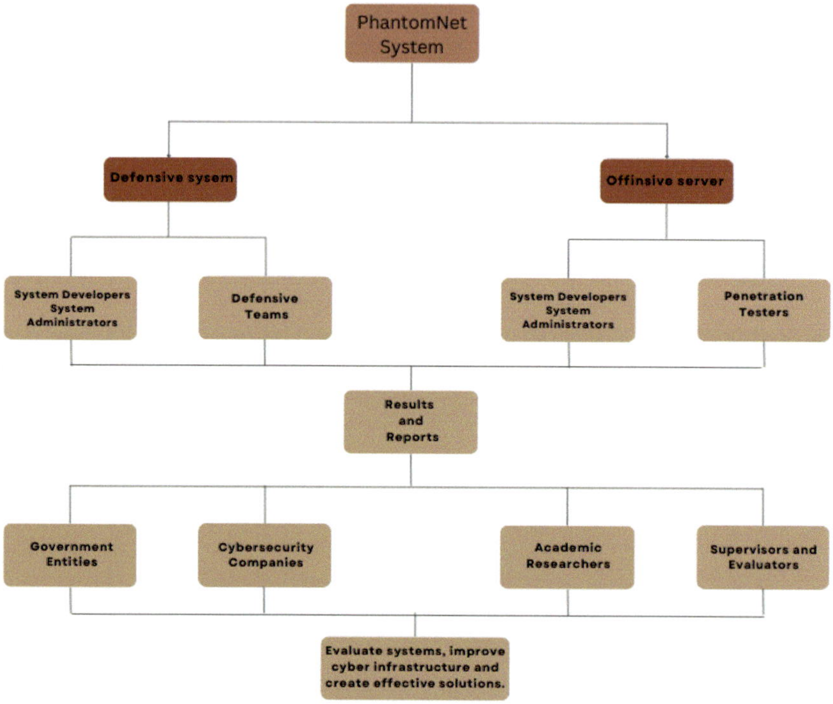

Figure 14.3 Stakeholders.

14.5.4 Non-functional requirements

- **Performance:** The system must handle at least 100 active users without delay max 1 sec and that will be achieved by apply the lazy loading and pagination technique to load 10 or 20 user at a time also a good knowledge with algorithms will help, also average response time for critical operations must be under 500ms this can be achieved by using high performance server like the servers that AWS provide.
- **Storage:** Support at least 1TB of data (e.g. images, logs) and with efficient data response 200ms, compatible with some compression techniques.
- **Code:** follow the best practices techniques, maintainable code (e.g. user login role), isolate and separate each process or block at the system.
- **Documentation:** Include API references and setup guide, each version release, and how and when to use the system.

Table 14.7 Server-side requirements.

	Hardware requirements
CPU	Multi-core processor (minimum 8 cores, 16 threads)
RAM	Minimum 16 GB
GPU	NVIDIA GPU is optimized for parallel processing, making them much faster than CPUs for real-time adaptation and analysis in ML model.
Storage	SSD with at least 1 TB free space to use as a database to store logs, configuration ML models, and exfiltrated data securely and store it
Network	High-bandwidth and low-latency internet connection; for tasks that require fast data transfer and real-time communication
	Software requirements
OS	Windows or Linux-based operating system (Windows 10,11 or Kali Linux recommended). The OS must enable virtualization to run virtual machines for isolated testing environments.
Programming languages	Python, C# and go languages (Python for ML modules, automation scripts, and backend server) (C# and go for agent application)

Frameworks/ libraries	• TensorFlow or PyTorch for ML tasks.
	  • These frameworks provide advanced hardware for growing models that adapt to environmental changes, including EDR or firewall configurations.
	  • TensorFlow and PyTorch have been greatly improved, helping with GPU acceleration and scalability, which is essential for real-time decision-making during operations.
	• Scikit-learn and pandas for data analysis.
	  • Scikit-learn provides tools to use lightweight machine learning models (e.g., classification or clustering) for specific tasks such as phishing detection or security detection
	  • Pandas are essential for optimizing big data, enabling data processing and exploring actionable insights.
	• Flask or FastAPI for REST API integration.
	  • Provides a lightweight and efficient way to handle communications between servers and clients.
	  • It is used to manage commands, receive extracted data from the victim, and issue updates to clients.

Tools	custom-built tools (The tool will have a user interface or web-based capabilities)
Database	MySQL for logs and configurations

Table 14.8 Client-side requirements.

Hardware requirements	
CPU	Any modern processor (minimum 2 cores)
RAM	Minimum 2 GB
Storage	Less than 50 MB for payload and temporary files.
Software requirements	
OS	Windows 10 and 11 (primary target) Linux distributions (optional)
Dependencies	.NET Framework (for Windows-based payloads) * It is a native .NET framework for Windows, making it ideal for creating powerful and highly integrated payloads. * It enables features such as process injection, fileless execution, and integration with Windows APIs, which are essential for evasion techniques. Python runtime (for Python-based payloads)
Network	Ability to communicate with the server using HTTPS/TLS, DNS tunneling, or secret encryption channels.

Limitations of targeting only modern OS

Limitations of targeting only modern OS (Windows 10 and 11 or kali)
1. (End of life) old versions no longer receive security updates.
2. Limited features and outdated systems do not provide useful insights into modern defenses.
3. The modern OS is the most widely used in business, government, and personal contexts, so it is suitable for our PhantomNet, targets, and Stakeholders.

- **Accessibility:** Following WCAG 2.1 Level AA standards that will help the users with disables to use our server easily and manage the normal users to be comfortable with the UI, also provide easy to use functionalities following UI/UX principles, running on multi platforms: Mobile, Laptops, and almost on anywhere in earth with different speeds according to our server location.
- **Reliability:** Automated backups every 24 hours, the system must run 24/7 all year; and that we can find easily by AWS hosting.
- **Scalability:** The system must handle the increase in the data stored in the database with no delay or latency in the service.
- **User interface:** Responsive design, easy to use, follows color schemes, follows UI/UX principles.

Table 14.9 Functional requirements.

Requirement	Description	Input	Processing	Output	Priority	Main constraints	ID
Continuous data analysis	The system must continuously collect and analyze data from its environment	Environmental data	Use algorithms like Random Forests to analyze patterns that may reveal connections	Data analysis reports	High	Need for accurate data collection and analysis	FR-1
Adaptation to defensive systems	The C2 server must adapt in real-time to attacker defensive systems using techniques like Reinforcement Learning.	Responses from defensive systems	Adjust attack strategies based on feedback from defensive systems	Adaptive attack strategies based on defense response	High	Response time and adaptability to defenses	FR-2
Concealment of communication & continuous connection	Ensure continuous and undetectable communication with the victim by changing protocols regularly.	Encrypted protocols	Encrypted protocols like HTTPS and repeated DNS queries are alternated to conceal the communication between the server and the victim, making the connection undetectable.	Secure and continuous communication channel	High	Stability and confidentiality of the connection	FR-3
Simulate attacks for defensive training	Implement attacks on defense systems to analyze their reactions for training and improvement.	Defensive system data	Simulate attacks and analyze the defensive systems' responses to improve defenses against advanced threats.	Training data for defensive systems improvement	Medium	Interaction with defense systems	FR-4
Cyber awareness analysis of victim	Evaluate the victim's cybersecurity awareness by analyzing available data	Victim behavior data	Analyze data to determine the level of cybersecurity awareness and select the appropriate attack method	Cyber awareness report for the victim	Medium	Accuracy of data analysis and victim behavior	FR-5
Machine learning training for attack improvement	Use machine learning to improve attacks based on environmental feedback and victim interaction	Interaction data with the victim	Train machine learning models to improve attacks based on environmental and victim feedback.	Improved machine learning model for attacks	High	Lack of sufficient data about the victim, unexpected or complex interaction with the victim, and the need for high computational capabilities and resources	FR-6

(*Continued*)

Table 14.9 *Continued*

Requirement	Description	Input	Processing	Output	Priority	Main constraints	ID
Penetration testing and EDR Evasion Testing	Conduct penetration testing to identify vulnerabilities and assess the effectiveness of defense systems such as EDR	Vulnerability test data	Using HTTPS and DNS tunneling. HTTPS ensures encrypted communication, making it hard for EDR tools to detect the traffic. DNS tunneling allows data to be sent through DNS queries and responses, which are often overlooked by firewalls and EDR systems, helping evade detection	Test reports and discovered vulnerabilities	High	Testing tools and regular updates	FR-7
Remote command execution tools	Enable remote execution of commands without the need to open a terminal using Python programing	Command data from the server	Develop tools to allow the server to send commands remotely without opening a terminal using Python.	Remote command execution tools	High	Security in command transmission and execution	FR-8
Server adaptation to network environment	The server must adapt to the network environment in which the victim's device is located.	Network environment data	Adjust server settings to operate correctly with the type of network and protocols in use.	Server adapted to the network environment	Medium	Protocol compatibility with various network types	FR-9
Server and tools development	Develop the server using suitable programming languages like Python, Go, and C#	System technical requirements	To ensure command execution: • The server sends a command. • The client executes and confirms the command • If confirmation is missing, the command is retransmitted.	Fully functional server and tools	High	Compatibility of tools with system environment	FR-10

			• Persistent failure triggers a system alert. Objective: Ensure precise execution and handle failures effectively.				
Command sending and receiving	Enable the server to send and receive commands correctly between itself and victims	Commands directed to the victim	Ensure commands are sent and received correctly using suitable protocols	Confirmation of successful command execution	High	Command execution accuracy between server and victim	FR-11
System testing	Ensure that commands are executed successfully on victims' devices	Commands directed to the victim	Test command execution on the system to ensure the effectiveness of operations	System testing reports	High	Need for thorough and accurate testing	FR-12
Security testing	Ensure secure and stable communication channels between the server and victim	Communication data between server and victim	Test the security of communication channels for vulnerabilities	Security test results and communication flaws	High	Resistance to attacks and security improvements	FR-13
Documentation	Provide comprehensive documentation for the system, including source code and usage instruction	System documents	Create a full documentation package for the system, including source code and user instructions	Comprehensive documentation of the system	High	Complete and consistent documentation	FR-14
Risk assessment	Analyze and categorize risks at each stage of the system with mitigation strategies	Risk data	Identify and classify risks by likelihood and impact, and propose mitigation strategie	Risk assessment reports and mitigation strategies	High	Accurate risk analysis and classification	FR-15
Detection system design	The system must detect modern and advanced attack patterns using machine learning models.	Attack pattern data	Design a detection system using machine learning models to recognize advanced attack patterns	Report on detected attack patterns	High	Effectiveness of models used and their reliability	FR-16
Access management and security	Implement IAM tools to control and monitor access within the system	Access and privilege data	Apply strict access controls (e.g., least privilege, MFA) and ensure audit trails	Access control and audit reports	High	Strong access management and security measures	FR-17

* FR: stands for Functional Requirements

14.5.5 Other requirements

Other requirements for the PhantomNet system have been identified that are necessary for its stability and performance in different operating environments, such as APIs, data transfer protocols, data storage formats, and others. All of these are explained in Table 14.10 below.

14.6 Overall System Architecture

The PhantomNet system consists of two main components: The Command and Control Server (C&C Server) and the victim device. The Command and Control Server is considered the operation's brain, controlling the entire operation, sending and receiving commands from victim devices. It contains a database that stores server data, including records, administrators, and victim devices. It also contains an Admin Dashboard with roles to manage commands and devices, view the logs, and more. The victim device is the endpoint device that PhantomNet will take control of through its commands.

Figure 14.4 shows the overall system architecture, showing the entire computational process involved in system design. According to the figure, the system will work as follows:

- First, we will target a device to which we will get access .
- Then we must gather information for the victim and decide which type of attacks we want to apply; there are two main attacks: spam attacks that target multiple users with less productivity, and phishing attacks that target single users. It is more efficient but takes time to apply.
- After we apply the attack, we download the payload file to the target machine. Then, after it runs, we get the reverse shell and get administration access to the device.
- Now we do whatever we need on the device steal data, delete, or intercept the user data.
- Then, we store any data we need for the future in the database.

14.7 Conclusions and Remarks

14.7.1 Conclusions

The system has successfully accomplished all the objectives regarding enhancing the cybersecurity practices. The system features scalable, secure,

Table 14.10 Other requirements.

Requirement	Details
APIs restrictions	• Use open source or secure APIs like RESTful. • Avoid legacy or insecure APIs such as XML-RPC, as they may introduce vulnerabilities. • Restricting API access to authorized and certified clients using token-based mechanisms such as OAuth2, which is a protocol used to authenticate access to applications and systems, in addition to authorization via tokens without the need for passwords. It was chosen to reduce the risk of data leakage and theft and to specify specific permissions as desired by the client, which provides high security and is interoperable with many systems.
Data transmission protocols	• Use HTTPS with SSL/TLS to encrypt all communications between offensive and defensive systems. • For real-time communications, use end-to-end encryption. • Avoid unencrypted and old protocols such as HTTP or FTP because they can be easily intercepted by an attacker and their contents can be known, such as sensitive data such as passwords and personal information, in addition to tampering with the data and their incompatibility with modern security standards such as TLS/SSL, which protect against impersonation and MiTM attacks and do not provide authentication.
Data storage formats	• The format must be standardized and secure. • Can be used JSON and CSV formats
Documentation	• Documentation should be comprehensive and provide guidance covering the details of the system.
Security and data protection	• Using advanced protection methods such as IDS/IPS application and encrypting sensitive data using modern encryption methods such as AES-256 and controlling access and granting individuals their personal rights in managing their data and in accordance with the principle of minimum data in GDPR, only the minimum amount of important data will be collected and backup copies will be made in addition to periodic review of sensitive data and obtaining reports on its permanent safety.
Handling sensitive data	• Ensuring that the system complies with data protection laws. • Processing sensitive data in ways that are more secure than other data.
Operating Environment	Ensure that the PhantomNet system is interoperable across operating systems.

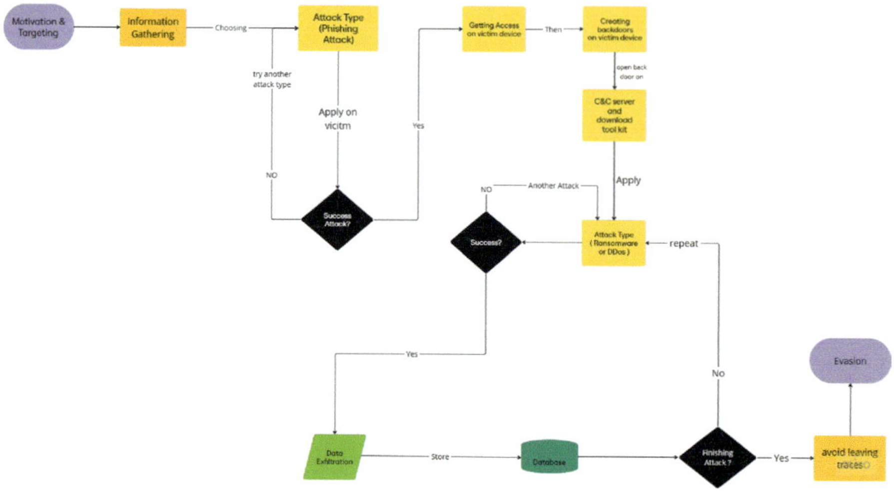

Figure 14.4 PhantomNet architectural design.

and reliable arrangements to reduce vulnerabilities and enhance the overall security situation. This system achieved the following results:

1. Improved security framework: Solutions such as the intrusion detection system (IDS) were designed and operated, the use of advanced stealth techniques was employed, and flexible tools were provided to enhance communication with the victim.
2. Offensive and defensive analysis: Analyze the vulnerabilities in target devices and select the best techniques for penetrating defenses. We studied protection systems, such as firewalls and IDS, to enhance defensive measures.
3. Development of an effective and safe command and control system with the ability to adapt to defensive and offensive attacks using artificial intelligence and machine learning techniques.
4. Addressing critical vulnerabilities: When the system is used defensively, it can identify weaknesses related to weak authentication mechanisms and inadequate access controls. These issues are addressed, leading to a significant improvement in resistance to potential cyberattacks.

14.7.2 Limitations

The system faced some limitations, such as:

1. Lack of research related to the system and lack of similar systems
2. Implementation complexity: Relying entirely on the system to stand on its own without using third parties, which increases the confidentiality, integrity, and availability of our system, but increases the difficulty of implementation.

14.7.3 Future work

Suggested for the next semester to improve the development, testing, and applicability of the PhantomNet system:

1. Advanced implementation and testing

   A. C2 Server implementation and design

   - Based on the proposed documentation approach

   B. Integrating machine learning models:

   - Enhance the functionality of machine learning-based algorithms used for attack adaptation, focusing on reinforcement learning to improve strategies in real time.
   - Incorporate unsupervised learning methods to identify unknown defense mechanisms and adapt dynamically. (We will use analytics methodology.)

   C. Real-world testing scenarios:

   - Simulate attacks on advanced enterprise-level environments.
   - Develop additional test cases to assess the robustness of PhantomNet under high-load and real-time conditions.

2. Improved defense simulation

   A. Enhanced defensive system development:

   - Focus on developing advanced detection tools and systems to better simulate adversarial defense scenarios.
   - Utilize reinforcement learning to create defense mechanisms that can adapt dynamically to PhantomNet attack strategies.

   B. Cyber range implementation:

   - Deploy the system in a controlled cyber range environment to conduct comprehensive testing of both offensive and defensive capabilities.

3. Expanding system design

   A. Cross-platform compatibility:

      - Develop modular interfaces to facilitate easier integration with various environments and systems.

   B. Enhanced user interface:

      - Improve the dashboard and reporting interfaces to provide better visualization of real-time data and logs.

4. Long-term goals

   A. Open-source contributions:

      - Develop a plan to release portions of PhantomNet codebase as an open-source system, offering tools for ethical research and education.

   B. Research publications:

      - Publish the results from testing and simulations in peer-reviewed journals to contribute to the field of cybersecurity

References

[1] https://www.weforum.org/stories/2024/01/cybersecurity-cybercrime-system-safety/
[2] https://www.cloudwards.net/cyber-security-statistics/
[3] https://arxiv.org/pdf/1408.1136
[4] https://threatintelligencelab.com/cyber-attack-cycle/command-and-control-c2/
[5] https://www.sciencedirect.com/topics/engineering/command-and-control-server
[6] https://www.techtarget.com/whatis/definition/command-and-control-server-CC-server
[7] https://sysdig.com/learn-cloud-native/what-is-a-command-and-control-server/
[8] Li, T.; Wang, G.; Guo, X.; Zhao, M.; Liu, J.; Du, C. Evaluation and Optimization of a Command and Control System Based on Complex Networks Theory. Electronics 2023, 12, 1180
[9] ALelah, T.; Theodorakopoulos, G.; Javed, A.; Anthi, E. Machine Learning Detection of Cloud Services Abuse as C&C Infrastructure. J. Cybersecur. Priv. 2023, 3, 858-881.

[10] Jonathan Fuller, Ranjita Pai Kasturi, Amit Sikder, Haichuan Xu, Berat Arik, Vivek Verma, Ehsan Asdar, and Brendan Saltaformaggio. 2021. C3PO: Large-Scale Study Of Covert Monitoring of C&C Servers via Over-Permissioned Protocol Infiltration. In Proceedings of the 2021 ACM SIGSAC Conference on Computer and Communications Security (CCS'21 '21). Association for Computing Machinery, New York, NY, USA, 3352–3365

[11] Carlos Novo and Ricardo Morla. 2020. Flow-based Detection and Proxy-based Evasion of Encrypted Malware C2 Traffic. In Proceedings of the 13th ACM Workshop on Artificial

[12] https://www.rand.org/pubs/research_reports/RRA2476-1.html

[13] H. Pranav, E. Suryaa, and M. Venugopalan, "Comprehensive C2 Analysis and Anomaly Detection in HTTP Traffic: A MongoDB-Based Approach," 2024 International Conference on Advances in Computing, Communication and Applied Informatics (ACCAI), Chennai, India, 2024, pp. 1-6, doi: 10.1109/ACCAI61061.2024.10602244.

[14] Singh, N., Vinod, G., Kakkar, A., Pratap, S., Joseph, G. (2024). C2 and Phishing Domains Detection Using DNS Analysis. In: Varde, P.V., Vinod, G., Joshi, N.S. (eds) Advances in Risk and Reliability Modelling and Assessment. ICRESH 2024. Lecture Notes in Mechanical Engineering. Springer, Singapore. https://doi.org/10.1007/978-981-97-3087-2_69

[15] Posted on 10 Sep 2024 — CC-BY-NC-SA 4 https://doi.org/10.36227/techrxiv.172599578.85351154/v1 e-Prints posted on TechRxiv are preliminary reports that are not peer reviewed.

[16] https://www.os3.nl/_media/2019-2020/courses/rp2/p20_report.pdf

[17] Al lelah, T.; Theodorakopoulos, G.; Reinecke, P.; Javed, A.; Anthi, E. Abuse of Cloud-Based and Public Legitimate Services as Command-and-Control (C&C) Infrastructure: A Systematic Literature Review. *J. Cybersecur. Priv.* 2023, *3*, 558-590. https://doi.org/10.3390/jcp3030027

[18] Brandao, Pedro & S. Mamede, Henrique. (2022). Phishing and Advanced Persistent Threats. Journal of Mathematical & Computer Applications. 1-4. 10.47363/JMCA/2022(1)105.

[19] Radunovic, Vladimir & Veinović, Mladen. (2020). Malware command and control over social media: Towards the server-less infrastructure. Serbian Journal of Electrical Engineering. 17. 357-375. 10.2298/SJEE2003357R.

[20] Compagno, Alberto & Conti, Mauro & Lain, Daniele & Lovisotto, Giulio & Mancini, Luigi. (2015). Boten ELISA: A novel approach for botnet C&C in Online Social Networks. 10.1109/CNS.2015.7346813.

[21] Pullen, John & Khimeche, Lionel & Remmersmann, Thomas & Schade, Ulrich. (2015). Distributed Server Systems for C2-Simulation Interoperation

[22] T. Bierwirth, S. Pfützner, M. Schopp and C. Steininger, "Design and Evaluation of Advanced Persistent Threat Scenarios for Cyber Ranges," in IEEE Access, vol. 12, pp. 72458-72472, 2024, doi: 10.1109/ACCESS.2024.3402744.

[23] S. Ghasemshirazi and G. Shirvani, "GITCBot: A Novel Approach for the Next Generation of C&C Malware," *2021 26th International Computer Conference, Computer Society of Iran (CSICC)*, Tehran, Iran, 2021, pp. 1-6, doi: 10.1109/CSICC52343.2021.9420590.

[24] https://github.com/Ne0nd0g/merlin

[25] https://github.com/mehulj94/BrainDamage

[26] https://github.com/BishopFox/sliver

[27] https://github.com/its-a-feature/Mythic

15

Automating Cybersecurity Risk Assessments with a Modern Penetration Testing Approach (PenTest Pro)

Mohammad R. Qasaymeh, Mohammad I. Al-Faouri, Ahmad I. Al-Alawneh, Qusai R. Al-Omari, and Qasem Abu Al-Haija*

Department of Cybersecurity, Jordan University of Science and Technology, Jordan.

E mail: mrqasaymeh21@cit.just.edu.jo; mialfaouri21@cit.just.edu.jo; aialalawna21@cit.just.edu.jo; qralomari21@cit.just.edu.jo; qsabuhaija@just.edu.jo

Abstract

Penetration testing is critical for securing any organization's systems or networks. This chapter describes PenTest Pro, an automated cybersecurity risk assessment tool with a modern penetration testing approach. PenTest Pro provides comprehensive coverage for any system, starting with gathering information, identifying vulnerabilities, exploiting weaknesses, and reporting them clearly and in a structured format. PenTest Pro follows four main phases based on the NIST 800-150 standard: Planning, discovery, attack, and reporting. While many penetration testing frameworks offer similar services, they often gather information and report vulnerabilities in non-standardized ways. PenTest Pro aims to deliver a comprehensive penetration testing service with added features to evaluate and predict cyberattacks and potential malicious actors before they occur. Furthermore, it measures the security level of systems using cybersecurity principles to provide detailed insights into the system's status. PenTest Pro integrates heterogeneous tools, linking them to deliver the best testing results while reducing false positives by

DOI: 10.1201/9788743808077-15

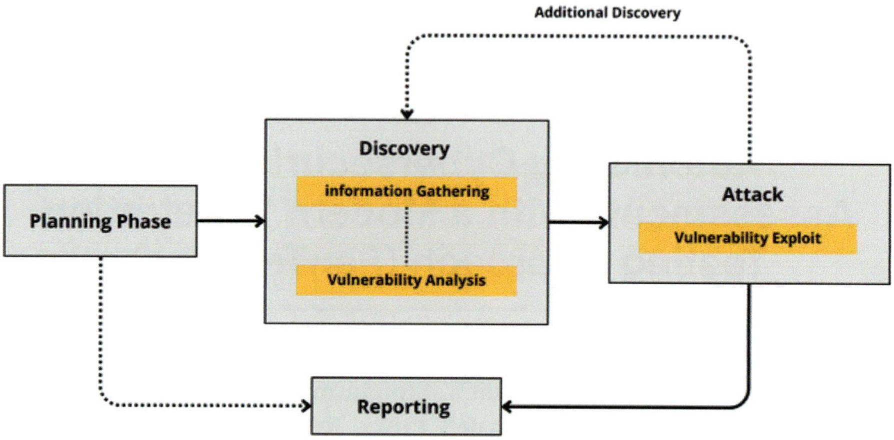

Figure 15.1 Penetration testing process.

leveraging various tools' functionalities and types. Another key feature is the standardization of testing and reporting techniques. Reporting is designed to be semi-automated, where testers audit tool outputs to minimize errors and ensure accuracy.

15.1 Introduction

The threat to key systems is ever-increasing, and the probability of a security weakness being accidentally exposed or maliciously exploited needs to be continually assessed, such as via a penetration test, to ensure that the risk level is acceptable to the organization. [1]

A penetration test (occasionally PenTest) involves using various manual and automated techniques to simulate an attack on an organization's information security arrangements, either from malicious outsiders or your staff. [2]. Undertaking a series of penetration tests will help test your security arrangements and identify improvements. When carried out and reported properly, a penetration test can inform you of nearly all your technical security weaknesses and provide the information and support required to remove or reduce those vulnerabilities. [3]. Figure 15.1 illustrates the lifecycle diagram of the penetration testing process.

Let us begin with PenTest Pro and other penetration testing frameworks, which distinguish themselves by providing standardized reporting that follows international standards and ensures consistency and clarity. On the other hand, most others lack this feature. We aimed to create a semi-automated reporting technique that ensures clarity and adherence to these standards.

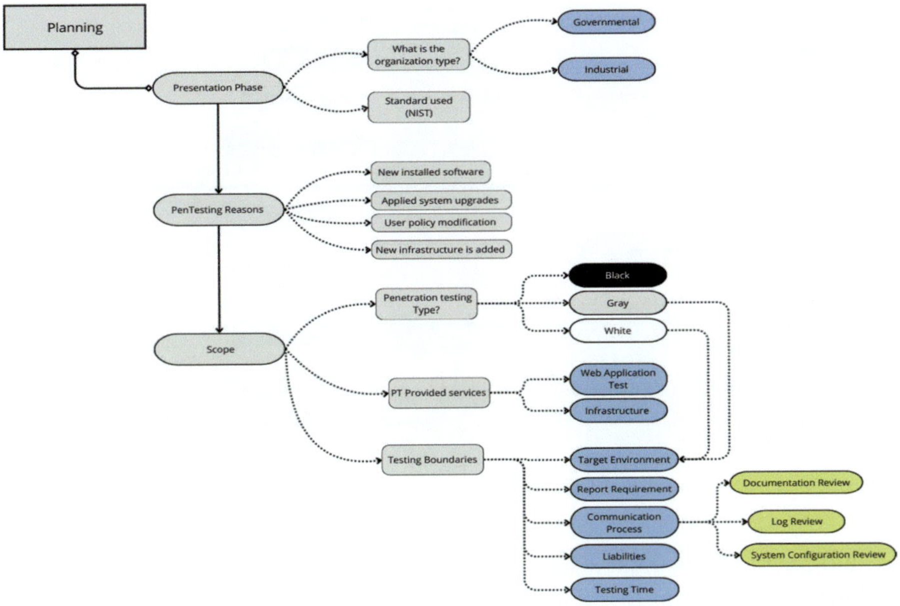

Figure 15.2 Planning phase.

This standardization helps reduce human error and improves the reliability of the results. In addition, manual testing and full automation of tools are merging, and manual testing with fully automated tools is used to evaluate accurately and comprehend results. Furthermore, the unique feature, the first and most interesting challenge, is applying the cybersecurity principles by ranking the ratio of each application and which one is not applied in the system, then giving each principle's degree. The second main challenge is integrated tools; the integration within heterogeneous tools makes the process go smoothly, unlike other frameworks, which work in separate ways without any harmony. The last thing is standardization in our formwork. Unlike the others, standardization will be a default within the testing process flow, depending on the PenTest application.

The planning phase (depicted in Figure 15.2) gathers information needed for assessment execution, such as the assets to be assessed, the threats of interest against the assets, and the setting of testing goals. No actual testing occurs in this phase [3]. Based on the Planning Type, we collect information about: documentation review, log review, ruleset review, system configuration review, and files integrity checking.

To ensure the assets are evaluated comprehensively and accurately, our formwork focuses on comprehensively evaluating the digital assets, the network, and the physical system. This evaluation is done using a combination

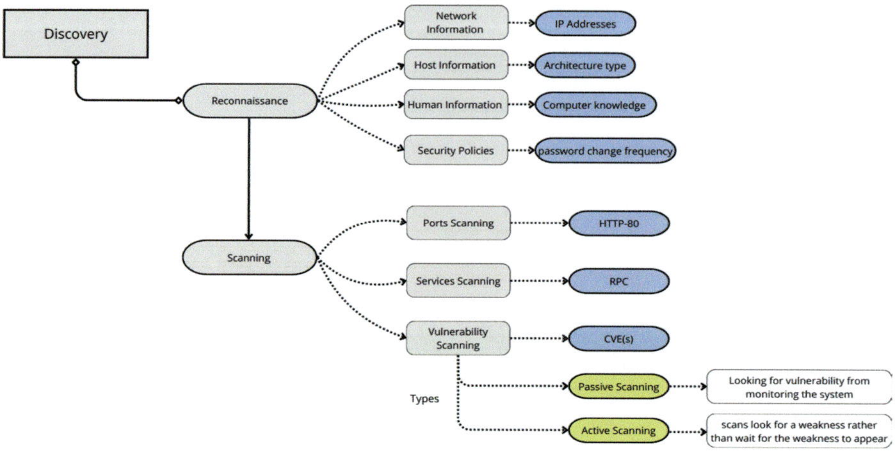

Figure 15.3 Discovery phase.

of automated and manual testing to ensure we do not ignore any vulnerability and test each element in the testing environment, whether by a system application or servers that will allow us to recognize all assets that are valuable to compromise and as we mentioned our PenTest Pro previously depend on the standard, unlike the others. Penetration testing is poorly applied to uniform standards, leading to differentiation and difficulty comparing different teams and clients. This facilitates the determination of the most assets exposed to risk, emphasizes evaluation strategy, and recognizes the common vulnerabilities. Integrating the tools provides accurate insights about the different assets through the scanning process and the system, and monitoring continuously leads to an accurate assessment. The other frameworks operate fully automated assessments, while our framework combines manual and automated assessment tests that a PenTester will do; these allow us to make a portion of the assessment test by human review. The evaluation process classifies the assets depending on their significance and then addresses the crucial assets. First, this method ensures that the vulnerability in essential assets is detected and treated immediately.

The discovery phase is depicted in Figure 15.3. The first part covers information on gathering and scanning. The second part is vulnerability analysis, which involves comparing the services, applications, and operating systems of scanned hosts against vulnerability databases from the national vulnerability database (NVD) (a process that is automatic for vulnerability scanners) and the testers' knowledge of vulnerabilities [3]. For example, network discovery, employee names and contact information, system information, such as names and shares, and application and service information.

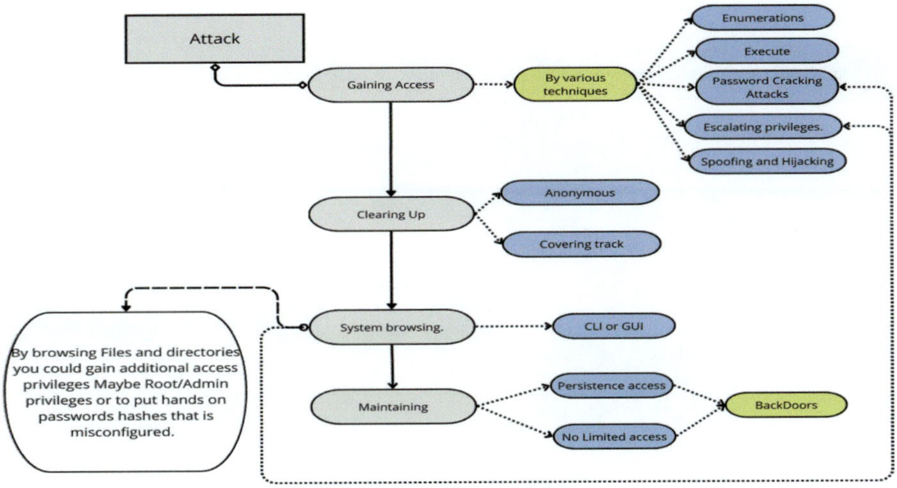

Figure 15.4 Attack phase.

The attack phase verifies (depicted in Figure 15.4) previously identified potential vulnerabilities by attempting to exploit them. If an attack is successful, the vulnerability is verified, and safeguards are identified to mitigate the associated security exposure [3]. Validating the existence of vulnerability by:

- Password cracking: Identifies weak passwords and password policies.
- Testing: Security tests using the same methodologies and tools that attackers employ.
- Social engineering: Allows testing of procedures and human element (user awareness).

Then, we exploit the existing vulnerability by gaining access, escalating privileges, browsing the system, and installing additional tools to gain further information.

Reporting phase (depicted in Figure 15.5): The report is generally developed to describe identified vulnerabilities, present a risk rating, and guide how to mitigate the discovered weaknesses [3]. Upon completion of the analysis, a report should be generated that identifies system, network, and organizational vulnerabilities and their recommended mitigation actions. Security testing results can be used in the following ways:

Penetration testing normally depends on what an organization wants to test, whether the scope is to simulate an attack by an insider or an external source. We must provide rich information about the service provided by PTF testing type in Table 15.1 below.

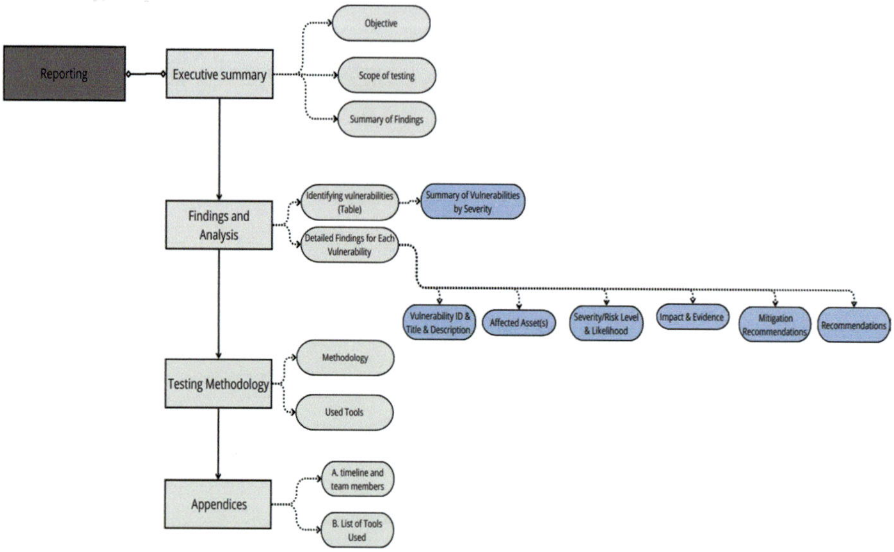

Figure 15.5 Reporting phase.

Table 15.1 Testing types.

Black (External)	Gray	White
No prior knowledge of the infrastructure to be tested by deploying several real-world attack techniques (e.g., social engineering, network scanning, remote access, trojans, etc.) [2]. It will help to eliminate any internal or external security issues [2].	This testing puts the tester in a privileged position. It will be suitable when an organization needs a “Security Assessment”.	Enabling comprehensive evaluation of the network or system security posture. Because the IT staff is fully aware of and involved in the testing, it may be able to guide to limit the testing’s impact.

Table 15.2 shows the potential tools used in the framework, categorized by name and their respective functionalities.

15.1.1 Problem statement

In the evolving cyberspace, cyber-attacks are increasing significantly; this work aims to identify and address weaknesses that intrusions could exploit, map out potential attack paths to help the organization understand how an attack might occur, and identify security gaps in infrastructure, web applications, and policies, and decrease the number of errors as much as possible

Table 15.2 Tools overview.

Category	Tools	Description
Network scanning	Nmap	Network discovery, port/script/vulnerability scanning, and OS fingerprinting. (multitasked)
Vulnerability scanning	Nessus OpenVAS	Establish basic checks with enormous effect but less effort, which is finally represented in an automated VS Report.
Net. traffic analysis	Wireshark	Packet analyzer for monitoring and troubleshooting network traffic
Password cracking	Hydra John the Ripper	These tools are used for gaining the password in case you have hashes(cracking) or not(brute-force)
Exploitation & frameworks	Metasploit	An open-source framework for penetration testing that helps search, scan, identify, and exploit system vulnerabilities.
Web application testing	Burp Suite	Web application security testing platform with tools like spider, intruder, and repeater.
	sqlmap	An automated open-source tool for detecting and exploiting SQLI vulnerabilities, it supports many database languages.
	Nikto	An open-source tool that scans web servers for vulnerabilities, outdated software, and security misconfigurations.
Fuzz testing	ffuf Wfuzz Gobuster	These tools are used for brute-forcing and finding hidden assets and potential entry points (directories, domains, and sub-domains) in web applications during penetration tests.
Information gathering	VirusTotal	An online platform that analyses files, URLs, domains, and IP addresses.
	The harvester	An open-source OSINT tool for gathering information about a target domain using search engines, often used in the reconnaissance phase of penetration testing.
	NSlookup	A CLI tool is used to find the IP address of a domain or the domain associated with an IP address. It helps with DNS lookups and troubleshooting network issues.

in the system. Improve the accuracy of vulnerability identification by using multiple vulnerability scanners within the framework. PenTest Pro will use and integrate various tools to reduce the time wasted on testing each tool individually. Using multiple tools helps us develop scalable testing for any organization, which mitigates the overhead on the firewall. We illustrate the problem statement in Figure 15.6.

15.1.2 Significance of the system

Penetration testing is conducted to evaluate the security of an IT infrastructure and web application by safely identifying its vulnerabilities and

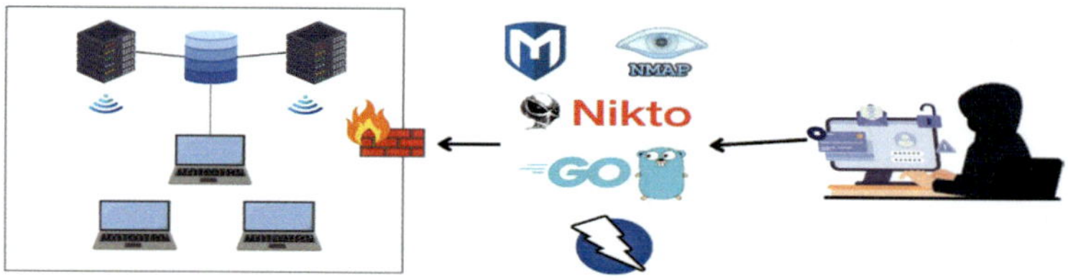

Figure 15.6 Problem statement illustration.

then using defense mechanisms and policies to identify risks and manage them to achieve higher security standards. PT leads us to mimic real-world attacks to circumvent the security of apps, systems, and networks. Most penetration tests look for a combination of vulnerabilities used to gain elevated access in any system. In May 2024, Dell revealed a significant data breach that affected 49 million customers; a customer purchase data portal was the attacker's target to gain the data. The exposed information includes customer names, physical addresses, order service tags, item descriptions, order data, and warranty details, but fortunately, there are no financial data breaches, email addresses, or phone numbers; this breached data was attempted to be sold on the cyber-criminal websites [1]. Our duty as pen-testers is to face these threats by conducting penetration testing earlier on the system to prevent such attacks by testing and improving the firewalls, IDS, or IPS's system capabilities. The main penetration testing challenges:

- Determine the scope and the coverage of the tests' depth or breadth
- Identify the penetration testing type. This part (challenge numbers 1 and 2) is issued earlier in the planning phase while negotiating with the customer.
- Unintended mistakes or negative effects are expected. Addressing these kinds of mistakes should be agreed upon in some way to keep the two parties on the safe side and put disclaimer criteria from the beginning of planning; putting some assumptions and prevention solutions in the earlier phase should decrease the potential mistakes and negative effects.
- The high cost of some penetration testing tools could confuse the PenTesting community. Our framework will decrease the cost of most paid tools by gathering as many services as possible in one comprehensive testing tool.

- Most of the penetration tests are not comprehensive. A semi-automated framework could help testers set clear guidelines for penetration testing, and tutorials will help escape these problems.

Our framework improves information security by finding vulnerabilities in infrastructure and web applications and mapping the findings with cybersecurity principles. The framework identifies security vulnerabilities, vulnerability validation, reduced incident response time, and many others. Penetration testing must be adopted to keep up to date with growing security breaches worldwide.

15.1.3 System objectives and contributions

This work aims to develop a new, advanced, semi-automated penetration testing framework to reduce the overhead of using various tools separately, conduct comprehensive penetration testing guided by cybersecurity principles and standards, and provide a semi-automated report.

- Our penetration testing framework contributes to the following:
- Primary objectives: (1) Achieve a system that is highly secure from threats. (2) Assess the effectiveness of an organization's security controls and measures.
- Secondary objectives: (1) Go in breadth through the weaknesses. (2) Use more than five automated tools and security protocols. (3) Apply the CIA Triad, and (4) Enhance the effectiveness of integration between heterogeneous tools.

Also, the main contribution of the work includes:

- The overall system ranking is based on cybersecurity principles (demonstrated in Figure 15.7), and the IIS is based on cybersecurity principles and integration between heterogeneous tools.
- By providing comprehensive reports, industrial and governmental organizations illustrate the organization's assets' status through penetration testing.
- What is the extent of applying cybersecurity principles and a semi-automated reporting model?
- The framework depends on the testing flow of standards. [2]

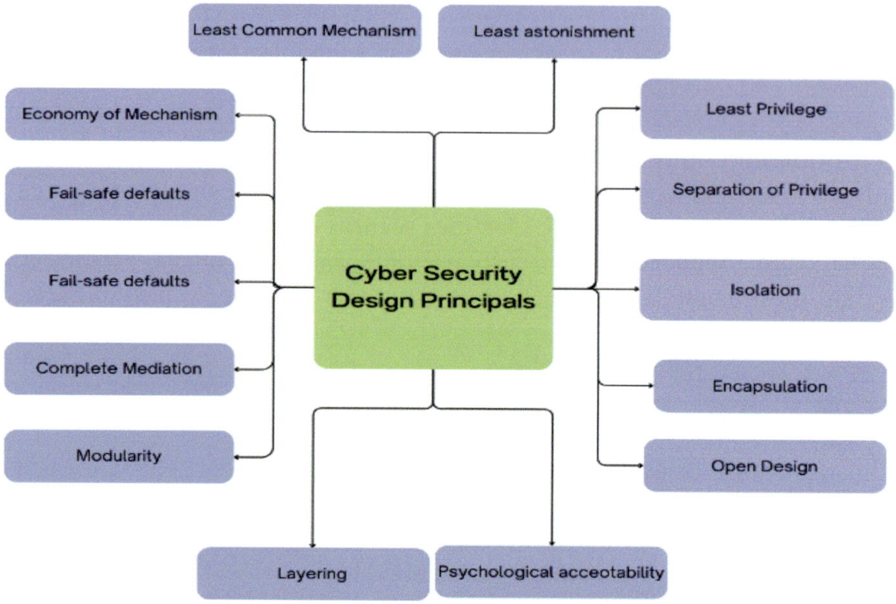

Figure 15.7 Cybersecurity principles: To be evaluated during the testing process.

Table 15.3 Color-coded importance levels.

Importance	**Bar colour**
Low	Green
Moderate	Orange
High	Red
Critical	purple

The ranking will be based on the importance of the principle in the system: Critical, high, moderate, and low. Our dashboard presents bars that demonstrate the principle's score below in Table 15.3.

Example: Let us talk about 'isolation.' This concept explains how we can isolate two components from each other, ensuring that one component cannot access the other except through a well-defined API. Suppose we have a server that provides multiple services through a single port on the network. Any malicious activity on this port could compromise all three services simultaneously. Therefore, isolation in this system is critical. To isolate each service from the other. Figure 15.8 illustrates the lake of isolation in the environment.

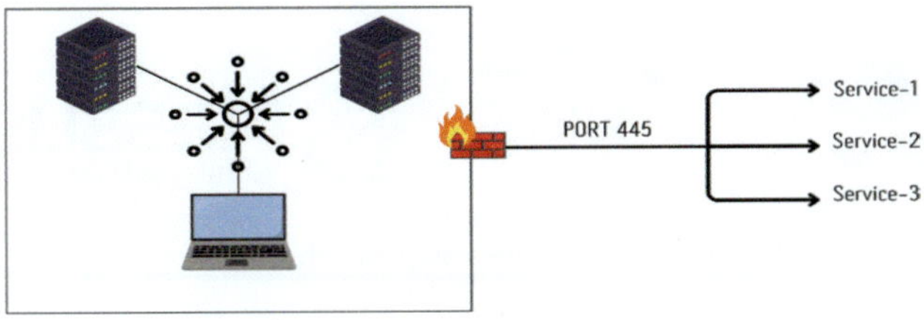

Figure 15.8 Cybersecurity principle (isolation) scenario.

<table>
<tr><td>Vulnerability Name</td><td>Severity</td></tr>
<tr><td colspan="2">Description of Vulnerability</td></tr>
<tr><td>Location</td><td>IP</td></tr>
<tr><td>Recommendations</td><td>Recommendations</td></tr>
<tr><td colspan="2">Snapshots evidences</td></tr>
<tr><td colspan="2">
(Optional)</td></tr>
</table>

Figure 15.9 Vulnerability information in the report.

Let us go deeper into the reporting mechanism and what we mean by semi-automated reporting. Most reporting techniques present the findings in a simple table, illustrating only basic information about the system's vulnerabilities. On the other hand, our framework will generate a comprehensive report that presents findings in a detailed manner; the following components will be included in the report: (a) covered IP(s) in the organization, (b) findings summary (sorted by the severity), (c) all vulnerabilities in the system, (d) well-prepared manner to explain and demonstrate each vulnerability, and (e) conclusion. The report will take the following format to explain the vulnerabilities, as an example (shown below) in Figure 15.9.

Figure 15.10 Tools and principles ranking.

Now, let us explain "What we mean by Semi-Automated". In this approach, the recommendations and description will be written manually, while the location, IP, and vulnerability name will be automatically captured and stored during the testing process. Then, use these details to fill in the corresponding sections of the report.

15.2 System Design Plan

The work aims to provide a penetration testing tool that results in an integrated framework between variant heterogeneous tools by using API keys and other methods; examples of heterogeneous tools are Nmap, Metasploit (msfconsole), Nessus, Burp-suite, john-the-ripper, etc.. The source code will be provided in the next chapters, and a semi-automated penetration testing report should be provided at the end of the penetration testing process. This report covers all reporting requirements so it should have a template, providing a ranking mechanism of cyber security principles (for example, CIA triad, encapsulation, isolation, separation of privileges, etc.) that are recognized during the testing process, vulnerability identification, risk assessment, and ranking for each vulnerability, there are some pieces of evidence and mitigations or recommendations. The automated part of the report shall be filled in the right field; for example, the IP addresses should be filled in the scope table, and the vulnerabilities should be filled in the vulnerability identification table, matching with the host or IP address that holds this vulnerability. The tool will deploy locally on one machine and operate the service on a specific port to be shared with other devices.

Figure 15.10 shows some of the testing tools and report patterns. As a testing framework, usability and reliability should be tested. So far, the system aims to build our testing environment to test these two concepts, evaluate the weaknesses and strengths of the work, and provide a comprehensive framework.

After collecting the tools such as Nmap, Nikto, Nessus, and Burp suite, and preparing the software or environment Kali Linux, we are preparing a BETA version to demonstrate the functionality of our tool. Now, the tool allows the user to select which testing type to execute: infrastructure (Nmap), web application (Nikto), or direct exploitation. For example, suppose the user

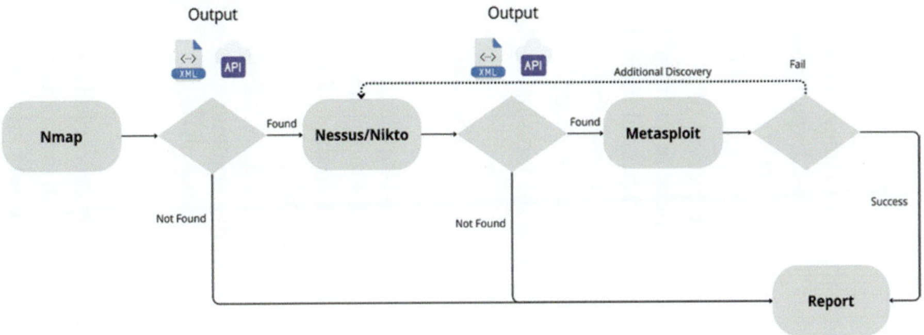

Figure 15.11 Tools integration workflow.

inputs 1; then the (Nmap) will play its role and provide the result for the user. The simple conclusion of the process Nmap (infrastructure testing) test shows that all ports were filtered and the security level was good. Once the appropriate tests are conducted, reporting will be based on the testing process. Figure 15.11 demonstrates the integration between the tools throughout the penetration test. The process starts with the discovery phase using the Nmap tool. Based on the output, if we find open ports in the infrastructure, we can scan for weaknesses in these ports. If vulnerabilities are found, we can prepare an attack, exploit it, and then report the findings.

15.3 Risk Assessment Plan

Table 15.4 shows the risks that can be faced during the framework preparation, testing, and evaluation. Each column is defined in the following list.

- ID: Identity of the risk.
- Risk identification and risk description.
- Probability: Likelihood of occurrence (low, medium, high).
- Impact: Rate how it affects our system framework (low, medium, high).
- Severity: How serious it is (low, medium, high, critical).
- Mitigation: This involves reducing the severity or likelihood of risks to an acceptable level. It includes actions taken to lessen the chances of a risk occurring or to minimize its impact if it does occur.

Now, Figure 15.12 will demonstrate the workflow for the most commonly used tools in the work. Let us begin with the first section (1), the VM (Windows), which is used to manage, organize, and gather information about penetration

Table 15.4 Risk assessment.

ID	Risk identification	Probability	Impact	Severity	Mitigation
R1	Integrating tools: Making the outputs of one an input to the other or using them simultaneously		Moderate	Moderate	Research and learn how to integrate and use tools in the PT process. Experiment with the framework and modify it periodically until it reaches the final form.
R2	Code bugs: There are problems and errors in writing the code for the framework parts	4	High	Moderate	Carefully follow up the process of writing codes and examine them from the beginning of the design until the last stage. Review the codes, ensure their integrity, and modify them if needed.
R3	False positive: There are incorrect outputs from the automatic scanning process, which can lead to unnecessary work.	3	High	High	Manual checking after the tools have finished their work. Choose the best tools to complete the tasks.
R4	Service destruction: Complete or partial damage or destruction occurs in the client's system during the PT process.	3	High	Critical	It is necessary to have backup data and sources to prepare for this risk. Agreeing with the client on the terms and disclaimers of responsibilities.
R5	Communication gapes: Lack of communication with stakeholders can lead to a lack of understanding and both parties not being fully informed about the process.	1	Moderate	Moderate	We avoid this problem by agreeing with the client on an effective communication method during the planning phase.
R6	Legal issue: It depends on my powers and permissions over the organization that we will provide with the PT service.	3	High	High	We determine the powers accurately and flexibly in agreement with the client and by signing the pledges/disclaimers of responsibility before starting PT.

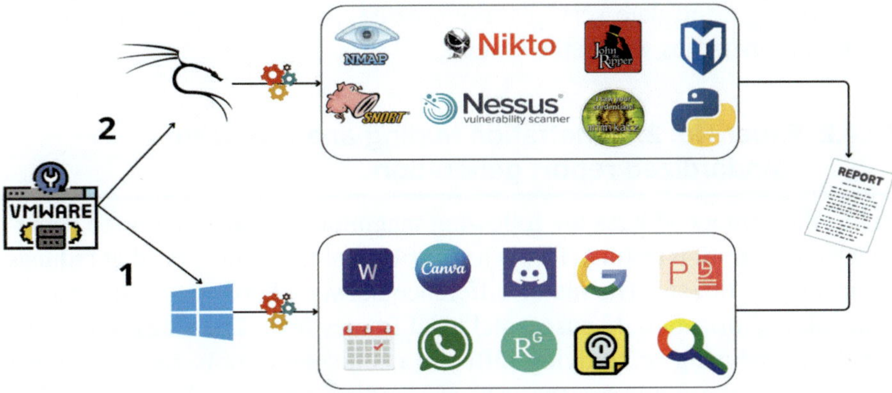

Figure 15.12 Overall workflow.

testing and build a strong base for the practical phase. Each tool serves its specific function, such as Canva, which helps us create figures to illustrate ideas, Word to write reports, and so on. The practical section (2) will provide a suitable environment (Kali Linux) to efficiently integrate the tools and test each change in the framework based on the roles defined in the first phase and task management. After implementing the ideas and achieving full, clear, and robust integration between the tools, we will provide a comprehensive report of the findings in the best way possible.

15.4 Related Work

15.4.1 Paper No. 1: Analysis of vulnerability assessment with penetration testing

In [4], the authors have focused on security in web applications that are at risk of cyberattacks from hackers. To keep it safe, penetration testing is conducted before deploying the website to ensure security against potential attackers. PenTesters carry out the whole process. They generate detailed reports and findings. The practical approach study uses a vulnerable machine from the VulnHup Platform; the main weakness is that outdated versions SMB Service led the attacker to access confidential files and cause remote code execution (RCE) through local file inclusion (LFI). The existence of poorly binary files gives the attacker further chances to escalate privileges. The process starts with planning the target machine, gathering data about the target machine, scanning vulnerabilities, attacking the target, gaining access, reporting, exiting, and clearing results. The ultimate vision was to develop systems capable of delivering up-to-date services, minimizing vulnerabilities, and reducing some exploits/issues within the system.

15.4.2 Paper No. 2: Penetration testing analysis with standardized report generation

In [5], the authors address the following magnitude of damage due to cyber-attacks. Penetration testing (PT) is a security evaluation process that reduces the chance of threats. The major difference between PenTester and a hacker is intent, authorization, licenses, and legal frameworks. The study was motivated by analyzing or studying different open-source tools and vulnerable websites. All these address the lack of standardization in PT formats. The authors faced a challenge in accessing some paid tools, which limited the scope of their research. Gartner Application Security Testing (AST) is a product and service designed to analyze and test applications for security vulnerabilities used here, and the process starts with direct scanning of the system, analysis, reporting, and review of findings. They use a predefined environment with one tool (OWASP ZAP) to test the process. Another thing is the web-based vulnerable databases for educational purposes only, DVWA and BWAPP. Reports were generated and compared across three tools: OWASP ZAP, Forgenix, and a Pentest website. This comparison aimed to identify limitations in reporting methods. The authors reveal the lack of a standardized format for the final findings. They proposed a penetration testing tool to generate the reports in a standardized format.

15.4.3 Paper No. 3: Utilising vulnerability assessment and penetration testing (VAPT) technologies as a method for actively preventing cyberattacks

In [6], the authors focus on vulnerability assessment and penetration testing (VAPT) as critical cybersecurity technologies. The study describes the most widely used open-source tools in VAPT. In this paper, vulnerabilities are defined as potential risks to systems. Additionally, the author explains multiple VAPT techniques. The paper emphasizes the interdependency of vulnerabilities and exploits within a single network and their cumulative effects. It highlights the urgent need to integrate VA and PT with multiple tools to achieve a single tool capable of analysing interdependencies between vulnerabilities and providing accurate scanning. It also explained seven testing techniques: Static testing – analyze the contents of the system and slow one, manual testing – use the tester knowledge to find the threats with a systematic manner, automated testing – use automated tools to find the vulnerabilities and execute all test cases, fuzz testing – put arbitrary data as a input until see crashes or failure. Black has no prior knowledge about the system, gray has partial knowledge of the system, and white has complete knowledge of the system to reach a robust tool. The process illustrated in the paper started with the reconnaissance phase to get information about the system, followed by using tools to perform a vulnerability assessment and listing the vulnerabilities. After that, a plan for a possible attack is created using this list. Depending on the findings, the user must apply countermeasures against this list through patches, updates, software installation, and other requisites. The paper clearly explains VAPT's necessity and demonstrates how this approach can be used to reach complete system security. The author provides detailed and complete knowledge of processes, techniques, and tools. All of these contribute to guiding future researchers to develop more advanced and comprehensive VAPT tools.

15.4.4 Paper No. 4: Vulnerability assessment for application security through penetration simulation and testing

In [7], the authors highlight the main contribution, providing the theoretical foundation and demonstrating practical tests to identify threats and weaknesses. The approach uses semi-automated PT phases to secure and monitor the networks. The paper focuses on the reporting phase to ensure the generation on the reporting phase to ensure accurate information about the findings. The authors raise a crucial question: "What is the desired security level of the organization?" Many factors are explained to answer this question, such as scope, cost, and type of threats. The process shown in the paper starts with pre-engagement scoping, meaning a clearly defined scope to avoid disrupting services. It starts with reconnaissance to collect much information about the target, followed by threat modeling and vulnerability identification, which shows how to utilize gathered information to scan for weaknesses. Then, exploit the found vulnerabilities and document the exploitation process (post-Ex). The report shows all the steps and tools used in our test, as well as some recommendations. The paper presents offensive and defensive perspectives and focuses on the offensive to simulate the real attacks. The authors emphasize ethics in doing the PT because this information can be used to secure something; on the other hand, it can be used to cause harm to any system. In addition, the paper lacks a well-defined format for the report.

15.4.5 Paper No. 5: Advanced penetration testing in cybersecurity: Strengthening defense mechanisms and identifying vulnerabilities

In [8], the authors addressed the involvement of cyber threats and the role of the advanced PT as an essential step to ensure the security of the system and contribute to proactive defence mechanisms to give organizations insights to prevent, detect, and respond to cyber threats. This type of test emphasizes the capability of the institute to detect vulnerabilities and address them proactively. The institution faced several challenges in integrating penetration testing within the traditional framework, such as a decrease in resources and an increase in the complexity of handling the technology. Additionally, the institute needs to improve the security of incident response and decrease the continuous risk. Then the author adapted a comprehensive framework that depends on tools and other advanced techniques, including social engineering and buffer overflow attacks, to simulate the cyber-attack and uses AI and IoT within multiple. Evaluating the vulnerability using tools like Metasploit and Nmap to analyze the system and the application. The result appears to be an improvement of the strategy, risk management, assessment, and cybersecurity by minimizing the critical vulnerability. Also, these tests contribute to the emphasis of awareness and the improvement of incident response. The advanced PT considers a huge investment of strategies and achieves long-term benefit of cybersecurity, and PT is not just a diagnosis tool, but it is a strategic method to emphasize cybersecurity; the author adopts periodic integration of PT with a focus on training of the security group.

15.4.6 Paper No. 6: Life cycle assessment of vulnerability and penetration testing on systems and proactive action taken to resolve possible attacks on networks

The authors in [9] proved vulnerability assessment and penetration testing as a cyber-attack prevention technology, then briefly on PT and the differentiation between it and vulnerability assessment, and focused on vulnerability assessment. That is because it is the first step before the PT. Despite the significance of the vulnerability assessment, applying this tool as a defensive method is mostly neglected. Vulnerability assessment is the process of scanning the system or software or network to find weaknesses and loopholes (easy entry points to the system). Penetration testing tries to exploit the system in an authorized manner to discover possible exploits in the system. After that, the author proposed a life cycle to evaluate the VAPT and a comprehensive manual and outdated method with a focus on techniques like (static analysis, manual testing, automated testing, fuzz testing, black box testing, red box testing, white box testing). In conclusion, the authors focus on VAPT, which should be made a compulsory activity for cyber attack prevention and developing more efficient tools for detecting vulnerabilities.

15.4.7 Paper No. 7: Boosting cyber risk assessment in government entities through combined NIST and MITRE ATT&CK threat modeling

In [10], the authors focus on addressing the countermeasure of the increasing cyber threat faced by governmental institutions by providing an integrated framework for cyber risk assessment and management. This integration combines the NIST SP 800-30 Rev, which provides a regular methodology for risk assessment, and the MITR ATT&CK framework, which focuses well on analysis of the TTP. Thorough analysis and specified TTPs of the attacker's integration of the framework can determine the ability and categorize it, and also can handle methodological methods such as the CVSS tool to evaluate the risk. This research proves the efficiency and effectiveness of the integration of the two formwork to evaluate the risk assessment and manage the threat, recommends applying this approach in the governmental sector, and develops more tools to support the continuous analysis.

15.4.8 Paper No. 8. Research on Wi-Fi penetration testing with Kali Linux

In [11] focuses on the rise of WIFI (wireless networks), variant types of vulnerabilities are raised too, such as replay attacks, flaws in authentication mechanisms and unencrypted data-frames, penetration testing methodologies tools such as Kali Linux are used to monitor, sniffing, spoofing, and data analyses using some tools. APs are using radio waves to broadcast information, which makes them more vulnerable to threats and attacks even though the system is using the SSIDs and MAC address filtering network cards are used by penetration testers to capture data packets, extract unencrypted SSIDs and spoof legitimate MAC addresses. These methods are used to analyze vulnerability exploitation in WIFI networks. Wi-Fi encryption methods (WPS, WEP, and WPA/WPA2) have critical vulnerabilities that jeopardize network security, brute-force attacks exploit WPS because of its weak PIN authentication system that relays on 8-digit code that is easy to crack; WEP refers to RC4 and plaintext IV, WEP is vulnerable to exploiting repeated keys and ARP injection, and WPA/WPA2 that is using TKIP and AES-CCMP, it could be compromised by capturing handshake packets and conduct a brute-force or dictionary attack. Kali Linux, using previously helps to previously mentioned techniques help determine the feasibility of exploiting these vulnerabilities, keeping in mind the necessity of adopting robust encryption algorithms such as AES and WPA2.

15.4.9 Paper No. 9: Cybersecurity analysis of a power distribution system using vulnerability assessment and penetration testing tools

In [12], the author's paper emphasizes on the modern infrastructure of cybersecurity of power distribution systems should be reliable and resilient; these systems have grown in cyber security threats average in the last years. The benefit of VAPT tools (such as Tenable, Nessus, and Metasploit) is that most of the system's potential weaknesses in network, software, and hardware will be defined. Clearly, these VAPT activities test the system's resilience against the potential vulnerabilities and provide some solutions and enhance the system to avoid threats. Using simulated cyberattacks like fault distance detection, power robbery, and current transformation manipulation, these techniques identify the potential impact of threats like zero-day, MITM attacks, and data alteration on power environment stability. Findings determine the need for robust cybersecurity measures like periodic assessments, PT, adherence to industry standards (IEC, CERT-In), secure protocols, and access controls. In this way, the reliability and resilience of critical power infrastructure will be accomplished.

15.4.10 Paper No. 10: Automating security testing: Strategies for vulnerability scanning, penetration testing, and compliance checks

In [13], the exploration of critical role of automation in modern security testing that ensures the critical role of automation in modern security testing ensures the proper security of the growing complexity of software systems and the increasing landscape of threats. It also focuses on the limitations of traditional manual penetration testing (human error, adoption of increasing software demands, and the amount of useless labour force) and the automation of vulnerability scanning, penetration testing, and compliance checks. All these techniques enhance efficiency, accuracy, and coverage; in other words, they improve security posture. Automation should reduce testing time by up to 90% and compliance costs by 43%. Tools like NESSUS, Metasploit, Burp Suite, Chef InSpec, etc., are inspected in this paper, and their integration strategies, like CI/CD pipelines. Challenges such as tool integration and false positives are raised. In addition to Metasploit exploits, penetration testing should be assisted with machine learning in automated exploits generation; techniques like AEG create exploits in seconds. Automation compliance checks ensure adherence to standards and reduce non-compliance costs; tools like Chef InSpec and OpenScap automate security audits. Tools like Lacework and Prisma Cloud support contentious compliance monitoring, which provides real-time alerts and reports. This proactive approach minimizes penalties, maintains consistent compliance, and strengthens organizational trust.

15.4.11 Paper No.11: Analysis of security testing techniques

References provide a comprehensive review of security testing methods for software and communication systems. The critical role the paper emphasizes is identifying vulnerabilities and cyberattacks. Three security testing categories were introduced (identification, testing, and reporting). In addition, there are three subcategories (black box, gray box, and white box) and risk assessment techniques. The study analyses 292 papers from 2010 to 2019 to evaluate the effectiveness and applicability of these methods and focuses on the dominance of vulnerability scanning. Also, the research identifies the gaps, such as a lack of tools standardization and limited evidence, and with the rise of evolving vulnerabilities, research emphasized the significance of adopting cutting-edge techniques. This paper links the academic and industrial perspectives, providing a structured approach for future security developments.

15.4.12 Paper No. 12: Life cycle assessment of vulnerability and penetration testing on systems and proactive action taken to resolve possible attacks on networks

In [15], we explore penetration testing methodologies, focusing on ethical challenges and integrating behavioural insights to handle insider threats. Traditional penetration testing has focused on threats from the outside, but can hardly be used to address insider threats due to their complexities and covert nature. The research advocates combining behavioural analytics, AI, and enhanced white team operations to improve the detection and mitigation of insider threats. By incorporating AI and behavioural insights, penetration testing has significantly improved in identifying insider threats, hence optimizing organizational security protocols. Organizations should embrace advanced methodologies using AI and cross-disciplinary insights to respond comprehensively to internal and external cybersecurity threats.

15.4.13 Paper No.13: Comparative analysis of automated scanning and manual penetration testing for enhanced cybersecurity

The author of [16] describes how one should carry out the actual penetration testing process, for example, by using Nmap and Metasploit in an organized way. It describes the processes step by step. Many companies fail to identify the vulnerabilities in their systems on time, thus exposing themselves to attacks. In addition, the lack of proactive testing results in high-severity breaches. The authors' approach includes information gathering, scanning, gaining access, maintaining access, and covering tracks in five phases. They did the tests in a virtual lab using Kali Linux and some popular pen testing tools. It exposed several vulnerabilities, such as open ports and weak access controls. The findings were used to suggest practical solutions for the issues identified. Regular penetration testing, if done in a structured manner with reliable tools, can help an organization reduce risks and improve its overall security posture. It is essential practice for staying ahead of attackers.

Finally, Table 15.5 illustrates the contribution of each research paper, enhancing our knowledge and improving the landscape of penetration testing.

PenTest Pro will provide comprehensive security testing by simulating attacks and assessing system measures. It will adopt several well-known automated tools and security protocols to ensure the examination of vulnerabilities in system components. PenTest Pro will apply confidentiality, integrity, availability, and other cybersecurity principles to measure system security. The framework will integrate the tools and try to reduce the complexity and overhead for each one. Table 15.6 summarizes all papers and illustrates some approaches, attacks, standards, advantages, limitations, and techniques used to conduct penetration testing. The next section will provide the gaps we identified during our discussion on the papers.

15.5 Research Gaps

During this phase, we identified gaps of the following components in the frameworks or papers that we discussed, as shown in Table 15.7. These components are essential for creating a robust penetration testing framework

Table 15.5 Studies contribution.

Paper #	Contribution
1	Show well-defined report and use well-known testing tools.
2	Enhancement of reporting techniques.
3	Focus on the interdependency of vulnerabilities, leading us to use cybersecurity principles as a measurement method.
4	Show the proper ways to scope and use semi-automated frameworks, show us both sides (offensive/defensive).
5	Highlight the complexity of the frameworks, which leads us to seek the best results without overhead.
6	Improve the knowledge of testing types for future applications.
7	This paper illustrates how to utilize penetration testing by combining more than one methodology. But does not contribute anything to our PenTest Pro.
8	Focus on how to detect WIFI vulnerabilities.
9	Taking active measures before a threat occur.
10	Integrate testing tools and focus on compliance testing.
11	Testing subcategories: Black, gray, white boxes.
12	Focus on insider threats by system configuration testing.
13	Advise us to use reliable tools and structured testing steps.
14	Generalize the functionalities of PenTest Pro.

derived from cybersecurity principles, a standard process to follow, and a clear professional reporting style to any requester of this service.

15.6 System Specifications

15.6.1 System stakeholders

Stakeholders are critical in the penetration testing framework to ensure the system's security, flexibility, and performance. Stakeholders include the individuals, teams, and organizations that interact with the system and affect its operation. Stakeholders contribute differently, starting with simulating the attacks and analysing the vulnerability to secure the system and determine the risk priority. Their effort contributes to detecting vulnerabilities, handling security gaps, and ensuring the success of all penetration testing works. Table 15.8 shows the stakeholders, roles, interactions, and the importance of the contribution.

The diagram in Figure 15.13 is representing the relations between the different stakeholders in penetration testing and it explain how different teams, such as penetration testers, system administrators, security teams,

Table 15.6 Literature review summarized.

Ref#	Solution approach	Techniques	Attacks
[4]References, 2021	A well-defined report is to be understandable by officials.	Combination of vulnerability assessment and penetration testing.	RCE, LFI
[5], 2021	Find the best way to produce a comprehensive report.	Using more than one tool to ensure the existence of findings.	CSREF, XSS, Weak headers.
[6], 2022	Integrate between VA and PT with multiple tools to achieve the best testing results.	Static testing, manual testing, automated testing, fuzz testing, black, gray, white box testing.	No specific attacks are explained in the paper.
[7], 2022	Conduct PT process with a complete understanding of both theoretical and practical parts. Follow a structured and clear step.	The semi-automated technique, testing process using the tools, and reporting phase were written manually.	RCE, through outdated service: Apple filing protocol (AFP).
[8], 2024	The advanced PT is considered an essential part for cybersecurity strategy of any institution.	Using penetration testing tools and AI techniques.	Social engineering and advanced attack like buffer overflow.
[9], ,2023	Apply the VAPT as a proactive tool to prevent attacks.	Static, automated, manual analysis, and black, gray, and white testing.	Any attack that targets the vulnerability that will be discovered in a system, like exploiting using malware
[10], 2024	The integration frameworks created to analyse and evaluate the cyber threat in governmental institutions.	Using CVSS tools to rank the range of the risk of the threat.	Any TTPs for the attacks used like the exploitation and unauthorized access.
[11], 2021	Structured WIFI penetration testing methodology with four stages using Kali Linux.	Monitoring, sniffing, packet capturing, password cracking (WEP/WPA/WPS), offline attacks, and fake AP spoofing.	Exploiting WEP vulnerabilities (short initialization vectors), WPS PIN brute-forcing, and WPA handshake cracking.

Standards	Advantages	Limitation
There is no clear standard used in this research.	Using well-known testing tools.	Using virtual or unreal environments.
Gartner Application Security Testing.	The comparison between the results of reporting platforms.	Trying to use paid tools led the authors to limited research.
The process looks like the **NIST** PT standard, but he incorporates a vulnerability assessment (VA) life cycle to make it more accurate.	The author provides valuable information (**Techniques**, **tools**), that is useful guide for future research in the field.	Highly coast comes from using various tools, or paid tools.
Closely PTES and NIST.	The authors put themselves as an attacker and ask some questions: How many hosts are in the network? What ports are open? What services are running, and what version of each service is running? Is there a firewall or an IDS/IPS (Intrusion Detection/ Prevention System) system??	Extensible vulnerability found out of the scope. We need to define a clear scope to produce accurate findings.
International Organization for Standardization. IEC/ ISO 27001.	Explore the vulnerability early and increase security awareness.	Dependence on the human expert and can't simulate all of the attack. Can use AI to simulate the attacks, but lead us to more false positives.
VAPT and black, white, and Gray tests.	Proactive from attacks before the attacker exploits the vulnerability.	The continuous updates and human and technical costs.
NIST SP 800-30 Rev and MITRE ATT&CK.	The integration with the framework provides comprehensive analysis by integrating the tools and techniques.	The complexity and the cost of integration between tools with each other.
IEEE 802.11 protocols use security tools within Kali Linux such as Aircrack-ng and Reaver.	Comprehensive security evaluation identifies encryption vulnerabilities, improves network defence mechanisms.	Time-intensive brute-force methods and reliance on dictionaries do not cover all vulnerabilities.

(Continued)

Table 15.6 *Continued*

Ref#	Solution approach	Techniques	Attacks
[12], 2024	Cybersecurity analysis using vulnerability assessment and penetration testing (VAPT) for power systems.	Vulnerability scanning (Nessus), penetration testing (Metasploit), fault detection, and simulated scenarios.	Zero-day exploits, man-in-the-middle attacks, unencrypted communications, and power theft scenarios.
[13], 2024	Automation of security testing for VS, PT, and compliance checks.	Continuous Integration/ Continuous Deployment (CI/CD) pipeline integration, machine learning, and automation tools.	Ethical hacking scenarios and exploits.
[14], 2021	Systematic classification of security testing techniques into identification, testing, and reporting.	Penetration testing, risk assessment, and security auditing.	Man in the middle, SQLI, XSS, and spoofing.
[15], 2023	A phased methodology: information gathering, scanning, gaining access, maintaining access, covering tracks	Combines manual and automated testing using tools like Nmap, Metasploit, Nessus	Identifies and exploits vulnerabilities like open ports, misconfigurations, and weak credentials
[16], 2024	Automated tools scan for known vulnerabilities and ethical hackers manually simulate real-world attack scenarios.	Combines scanning tools (e.g., Netsparker) to detect and classify vulnerabilities and manual exploitation using skills and tools	Detects and exploits vulnerabilities like XSS, SQL injection, CSRF, privilege escalation & DOR
[17],2023	Using one case study as a tools for evaluating the efficiency of the model.	Apply the PT technique to simulate the attacks and their dependence on past case studies.	Any possible attacks that simulate the thought PT model.

development teams, work management teams, end-users, regulatory bodies, and customers, on each other to ensure the vulnerability detecting and the enchantment the level of the system security. The illustration shows the organized collaboration for determining and handling the security threats and based on predetermined roles and responsibilities for each entity.

Table 15.9 shows the relations between the stockholders in detail.

Standards	Advantages	Limitation
IEC and CERT-In guidelines for cybersecurity in critical infrastructure.	Identifies vulnerabilities, tests system resilience, enhances proactive defence, and ensures compliance.	Limited real-world testing due to service interruption risks, like prohibiting the organization's services from use. And very advanced scenarios.
GDPR, PCI DSS, HIPAA, SOC 2, and other cybersecurity benchmarks.	Improve efficiency, accuracy, faster detection/remediation, cost, and enhanced regulatory compliance.	False positives, tool integration challenges, dependency on skilled employees, and automation risks.
OWASP and the software development lifecycle.	It provides a clear taxonomy, a comprehensive review, and identification of gaps, and it focuses on vulnerability scanning.	Lack of tool standardization, limited empirical evidence, and outdated techniques in some cases.
Uses controlled environments (e.g., Kali Linux), and adherence to ethical hacking agreements	Structured approach, detailed vulnerability identification, adaptable tools for various needs	The tester's expertise will control the vulnerabilities found during the testing, so it affects in some way.
Utilizes DREAD threat modelling for vulnerability classification and detailed exploitation assessment	Fast scanning of large systems; highlights known vulnerabilities; accurate detection of hidden and critical vulnerabilities	It can produce false positives, may miss complex vulnerabilities, and is resource-consuming and reliant on tester expertise.
The author recommended the use of uniform standards.	Improve accuracy, and get a deeper insight.	The challenge in generalization and when studying multiple cases it demands more cost and resources.

15.6.2 Platform requirements

Software requirements: These requirements, illustrated in Table 15.10, ensure that the system is correctly designed, coded, and integrated to match the desired functionalities. All these requirements (hardware and software) are used together to produce the penetration testing framework functionalities.

Table 15.7 Research gaps.

Gap	Description
Cybersecurity principles (measuring security level)	There is a noteworthy lack of application of key cybersecurity principles, specifically techniques for measuring the security status within an organization. This is where our approach comes into focus, aiming to explore the degree of application and establish a system to apply these principles. The lack of such measures has led to a decrease in comprehensiveness and reliability when evaluating the target system.
Standardization	All the research discussed standards as a procedure that depends on the pen tester's application. Standardization will be a default within the testing process flow in our work. Used single methodology (NIST) and standard process flow.
Reporting	Poorly illustrate and explain the findings through tables, simple words, and by using more than one reporting standard or website, which indicates the absence of clear, detailed, and comprehensive reports.
Manual and full Automation of tools	Manual testing techniques have some disadvantages, such as time-wasting, human errors, and effort without the full benefit of the applied testing. On the other hand, in the fully automated tools, false positives will appear, affecting the final findings and results. Our work should solve both approaches' problems by taking the benefit of manual testing and fully automated tools and eliminating the limitations of both fully automated tools and their limitations.
Integrated tools	Many frameworks are missing the integration between the heterogeneous tools that will work in separate ways without any harmony and exchange of data, which complicates the analysis process and the efficiency of the test. Addressing these gaps emphasizes the quality and usability of these frameworks in the cybersecurity procedures. PenTest Pro will integrate heterogeneous tools and safely transform data between them without any loss.

Hardware Requirements: Table 15.11 shows requirements to ensure the testing is done efficiently and operationally.

15.6.3 Functional requirements

The functional requirements illustrate the system's expected behaviors, goals, and tasks that we need to test to identify vulnerabilities and security weaknesses during the PenTest process. Furthermore, these requirements

Table 15.8 Stakeholders.

Stakeholder	Role/description	Interaction with the system	Significance
Penetration testers	Security experts are responsible for simulating attacks on the system.	Execute penetration testing using the tools and the framework and then determine the possible vulnerability in the system.	They prepare essentials for the success of the system, where they achieve security countermeasures by simulating real attacks
System administrators	Responsible for maintaining the structure of the system and ensuring the system runs properly	Configure and manage the testing environment and ensure the tools and the system are updated.	Responsible for the availability, integrity, and performance of the system at all times
Security team	Supervise the penetration testing activists and lead strategy related to	They review of the results and determine the purpose and scope of the test and its timeline.	Ensure alignment of the penetration testing with institutional security and risk management.
Development teams (devops)	Responsible for closing the vulnerability and improving the security of the programming code	Receive the reports and work on maintaining the vulnerabilities determined during penetration testing.	Close the vulnerability by executing adequate changes in the code or enhancement of the system.
Risk management team	Responsible for evaluating and managing the possible security risk	Evaluate the result of the penetration testing to understand the risk it poses the vulnerability in the system	Helping to determine the priority of privilege execution based on the level of the risk, which ensures maintaining the crucial vulnerability directly
Work management team	Responsible for scheduling management of the work, resources, and deliverables	Ensure the penetration testing process is done within the specified time, including the scope, and under the budget.	The foundation ensures the progress of the work seamlessly and allocates the resources properly

(*Continued*)

Table 15.8 *Continued*

Stakeholder	Role/description	Interaction with the system	Significance
Customers	Industries or organizations that require penetration testing to evaluate the security of their systems and ensure the strength of their systems against potential threats.	Provide the system details and request testing. They review the reports and, depending on the results, identify vulnerabilities in the infrastructure. They collaborate with developers and the SOC team to implement recommendations and request retesting to ensure the vulnerabilities are remediated. Additionally, they monitor overall security improvements and document notes about the testing process to enhance future methodologies.	The ultimate recipient of the system depends on their security situation and the conclusions of the penetration testing. Works as the main engine to enhance the system's result using the result from the testing to determine the weak point, secure the sensitive data, and align their systems with the best industry practices for security and flexibility
Regulatory bodies	Supervisory bodies responsible for monitoring compliance with security standards, laws, and regulations to protect the integrity and privacy of the data.	Review test results and ensure that security standards and relevant laws are applied, and review parodic revision for the penetration testing report to ensure the system complies with detriment frameworks such as DPR "ISO/IEC 27001 PCI DSS, and NIST CSF. Imposition of corrective measures for non-compatible situations, imposition of an auditing process, and provision of a certificate for the compatible system. Also, the regulatory bodies provide guidance for the organization about the new security protocol and the advanced standards to ensure system security.	Ensure compatibility with domestic and international regulations and legislation, enhancing confidence in the system. Play a crucial role in ensuring compliance with rules, enhancing regular liability, and improving trust between stakeholders by imposing compliance with local and global security standards
End-users	Individuals or teams using the system in their functions	Interact with the system after conducting tests, and report any abnormal problems or behaviors.	Their final experience provides a measure of the success of the hack test and addressing security weaknesses.

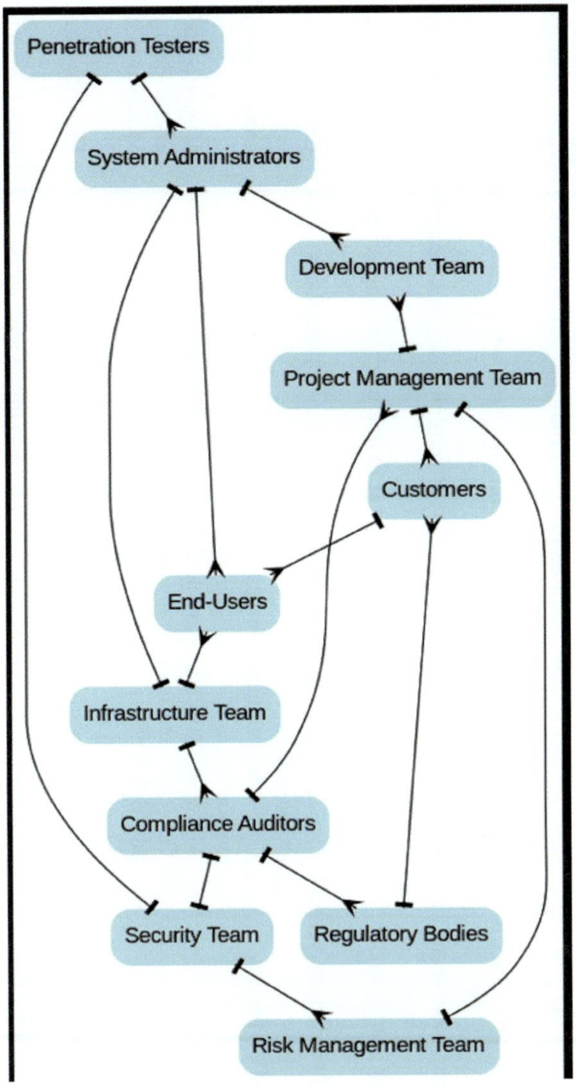

Figure 15.13 Stockholders' relation.

help determine where our PT framework will focus. In conclusion, this step enables us to create an actionable plan for testing that will show the essential functional requirements for all phases of penetration testing (Table 15.12 summarizes the functional requirements).

Figure 15.14 illustrates the network scanning phase of requirements. It starts with a given IP address, indicating it is gray or white box testing. Nmap is the best tool for network discovery. The input was the IP address, and the

Table 15.9 Relations between stockholders.

Relation	Description	Type
Penetration testers and system administrators	One penetration tester may work with multiple system administrators.	One-to-many
Penetration testers and security team	One penetration tester usually deals with one security team.	One-to-one
System administrators and development team	One system administrator can support multiple development teams.	One-to-many
System administrators and infrastructure team	One system administrator works directly with one infrastructure team.	One-to-one
Security team and risk management team	One security team can interact with multiple risk management teams.	One-to-many
Development team and work management team	Multiple development teams report to one work management team.	Many-to-one
Risk management team and work management team	One risk management team works closely with one work management team.	One-to-one
Work management team and customers	One work management team handles work for multiple customers.	One-to-many
Customers and regulatory bodies	Multiple customers may deal with one regulatory body.	Many-to-one
Customers and end-users	One customer may serve several end-users.	One-to-many
End-users and system administrators	Multiple end-users provide feedback to one system administrator.	Many-to-one
End-users and infrastructure team	Multiple end-users depend on one infrastructure team for support.	Many-to-one
Compliance auditors and regulatory bodies	One compliance auditor interacts with multiple regulatory bodies.	One-to-many
Compliance auditors and security team	One compliance auditor works with one security team.	One-to-one
Infrastructure team and compliance auditors	One infrastructure team supports multiple compliance auditors.	One-to-many
Work management team and compliance auditors	Multiple work management teams may report to one compliance auditor.	Many-to-one

Table 15.10 Software requirement.

Aspects	Essential		Recommended		
	Server-side	Client-side	Server-side	Client-side	Justification
Operating system	Linux-based OS	Any OS	Kali-Linux	Linux or Windows	Kali Linux was chosen because most tools are installed, it has operational compatibility, and Kali is an open-source OS.
Tools	Framework set-up (deployment)	None	None	Some tools must be deployed (depending on the testing type)	These tools are deployed to establish a framework infrastructure to start the testing process.
Development	Visual Studio (VS Code)	None	None	None	It is used for development, debugging, and modification purposes.
API keys and other integration techniques	Impeded with the source code after getting it from the tools.	None	API keys are most likely used.	None	API keys are used to integrate heterogeneous tools so they can work comprehensively.
User interface	Programmed and integrated with the source code to be operable comprehensively.	None	GUI	None	GUI is designed and developed to achieve a user-friendly concept.
Programming language	Python language or JavaScript + Web Frameworks.	None	Python language	None	Python is used for integration and semi-automated report generation, while JavaScript is used to develop the user interface.

(Continued)

Table 15.10 *Continued*

Aspects	Essential		Recommended		
	Server-side	Client-side	Server-side	Client-side	Justification
Semi-automated reporting coding	Semi-automated reporting is coded and integrated with the source code.	None	Python language	None	This report kind of reports are used to cover the benefits of the automatic and manual testing process (to reduce false positives that arise from automation testing and improve human manual analysis of the results), which should enhance results accuracy.
Exploitation scripts and codes	These scripts will be gathered, stored, and linked with the code to be used in the testing process.	None	Gathered from Exploit DB and the most common CVE websites	None	This should add more exploits for the newer vulnerabilities.
Environment	A comprehensive testing environment should be built to test the framework's capabilities.	Real-time networks or websites.	Virtual machines (VMware or VirtualBox).	None	This will improve framework effectiveness and accuracy.

Table 15.11 Hardware requirements.

Aspects	Essential		Recommended		
	Server-side	**Client-side**	**Server-side**	**Client-side**	**Justification**
Server	Deployment server	Testing server	Non	Non	These are the core testing parties, so it is mandatory being.
Networking	Network and routing devices	Network devices that are working in real-time	Interconnected devices (end-hosts for efficient communication)	Non	
End-hosts	Tester devices	Devices to be tested.	Non	Non	
Storage	Deployment server and end hosts (SSD 512 GB)	HDD/SSD 256 GB	SSD 1024 GB	HDD/SSD 512 GB	Storage is a scalable part due to the differences in processes between different systems.
RAM	16 GB	4 GB	16 up to 32 GB	8 GB	Ensuring effective scanning in a faster way.
Processor	Core i5 or Ryzen 5	Any	Core i7 or Ryzen 7, it is recommended to use AMD Ryzen 7 because it supports excellent multi-threading, as it can run more than one tool at the same time, while Intel i7 supports single threading.	Core i5 or Ryzen 5	

Table 15.12 Functional requirements.

Requirement	REQ. Description
Network scanning	• Inputs: List of IPs or apps. To be testing AND credentials (for authenticated testing, white, gray). • Outputs: Information about the system, networks, domains, and subdomains. • Process: Test assets provided during the planning phase using discovery tools like Nmap. • Main constraints: The scanning process may impact system performance and cause delays.
Vulnerability assessment	• Inputs: Discover vulnerabilities, misconfigurations, open ports, services, and applications that could be exploited from the network scanning phase. • Outputs: Illustrating open ports, services, and potential vulnerabilities. • Process: Using vulnerability scanners like Nessus will help us check for vulnerabilities using CVEs. • Main constraints: Firewalls and authentication mechanisms may limit the accuracy of findings.
Web application testing	• Inputs: URL of the target application or credentials. • Outputs: Vulnerabilities flow web app management, and injection flows. • Process: test for popular vulnerabilities like XSS and SQLi using the web app. Testing tools such as burp suit. • Main constraints: Complex analysis and skilled humans are needed to identify the vulnerabilities for logic flows. Logic flows can be triggered when the input placeholder fails to process, validate, and manage the data, leading to altered code targets or unauthorized outcomes and unfaced the web page during organizational work hours.
Exploit testing	• Inputs: Vulnerabilities, misconfigurations, and exploitable entry points. • Outputs: Demonstrate the exploitation and assessment based on likelihood and impact. • Process: Use checked weak points and Metasploit to conduct the attack. • Main constraints: Damaging the system, and this is limited by engagement rules in the planning phase. • System damage can cause service unavailability, website defacement, and blocking of services. These damages will be mitigated by the organization. PenTest Pro is only responsible for revealing weaknesses before an attacker can do so. The damage caused is temporary and depends on whether the environment is real or a test.
Continuous monitoring and re-testing	• Inputs: The data from previous tests. • Outputs: Reports lead us to patch the system from emerging threats. • Process: Use the previous reports and conduct testing on significant system changes. • Main constraints: Time and resources go to monitoring; on the other hand, false positives from tools.
Reporting	• Inputs: Discovery and attack results with screenshots. • Outputs: High-level summary of the findings, illustrating the exploitation of identified vulnerabilities with evidence (screenshots), along with an assessment of the potential impact and measurement of the application of cybersecurity principles. • Process: Generate a report that demonstrates all findings, highlights crucial and critical issues, measures cybersecurity principles and evidence from the testing process, and validates the findings to illustrate the risks. • Main constraints: The accuracy of reporting depends on skilled testers, effective tools, and the quality of data provided by the organization.

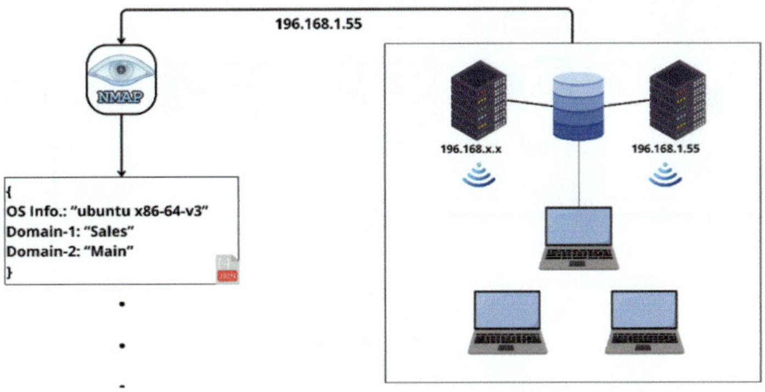

Figure 15.14 Network scanning.

Table 15.13 Recommended testing requirements.

Requirement	Recommended	Not recommended
Network scanning	✓	
Vulnerability assessment	✓	
Web application testing	✓	
Exploit testing	✓	
Continuous monitoring and re-testing	✓	
Reporting	✓	

output was formatted as a JSON file to use the important information in other phases (if needed).

Table 15.13 illustrates the recommended and not recommended testing requirements: (a) The recommended requirements are coverage that can minimize risk, and (b) The not recommended requirements lead to inaccurate or unnecessary results.

Penetration testing should be performed only after careful consideration, notification, and planning [18]. This method assesses the system for possible vulnerabilities that external threats could exploit [19]. Penetration testing is conducted to test and report the results as effectively and completely as possible [20]. The process must be completed regardless of the impact, but these effects will give us as much accuracy as possible. Overall, of course, I recommend all functional requirements, despite the system being delayed, which may cause damage. Figure 15.15 illustrates the process and functions for each requirement. As previously mentioned, all requirements are essential except one (continuous monitoring and re-testing). This requirement may be optional to implement, but we cannot say it is not recommended. It can be used at any time or until significant changes in the system are observed.

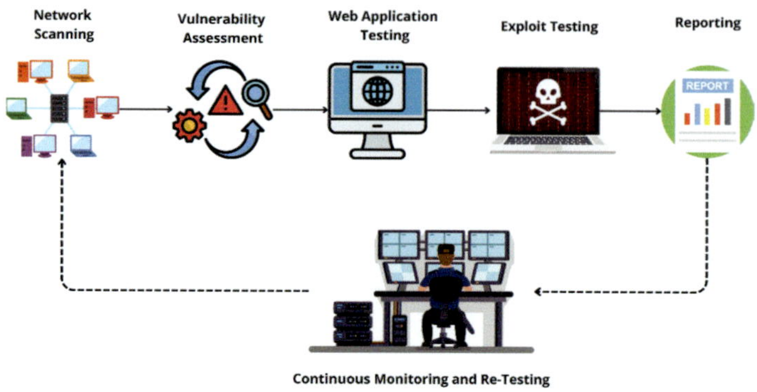

Figure 15.15 Functionality illustration.

15.6.4 Non-functional requirements

This section emphasizes important requirements for the operations and processes that make the framework operational and work comprehensively with the functional requirements. Table 15.14 shows the essential non-functional requirements.

All these non-functional requirements are worked with functional requirements to provide a comprehensive operational framework.

15.6.5 Other requirements

APIs: Let us begin with an API or application programing interface, a set of rules or protocols that enable software applications to communicate to exchange data, features, and functionality [21]. PenTest Pro uses APIs to communicate between the PenTest Pro and Heterogeneous external tools, services, and systems. Mainly, it is used for two objectives, and Figure 15.16 shows the APIs' needs.

1. Linking or integrating heterogeneous testing tools. To identify vulnerabilities and weak points in the system. The process exports the output of one tool to another through APIs.

2. Use external reporting services to document detailed findings.

We will integrate publicly available and free APIs in PenTest Pro. The main reason for using APIs is to integrate various commercial tools and link different phases by using the output from one operation as the input for the next. In conclusion, integrated APIs help utilize and link inputs and outputs from one

Table 15.14 Non-functional requirements.

Category	Requirements	Details and examples
Performance	Penetration test processes should be completed comprehensively and efficiently.	Ensuring that scans for multiple network sizes are done fully, due to suitable scanning time for each size, and reporting generation. Example: Ensure scanning for a medium-size network (100 devices) should be completed within 3 hours; note that all 100 devices should be scanned. And may we use some of this mechanism Timeout and retry mechanisms, efficient data management, parallel and distributed scanning, and scalable architecture.
Security	The scanning results storage should be accessed by authorized users (testers), so it is necessary to secure the storage storing the scanning results or add an expiration duration for the results and delete them after a while (2 years after saving the file).	Ensuring the security of the stored results (reports and tools output files) by adding login credentials also ensures accountability. Implement Role-Based Access Control (RBAC). Data in transit: Using TLS 1.3 or higher to encrypt all communications between the framework, testing tools, and user interfaces.
Reliability	Handling unexpected single-tool failures.	If such a tool crashes, it should be treated with the retry button or automatically retry, after displaying an alert about the crash. If a tool consistently fails, the framework will switch to an alternative tool that performs similar functions. Alert testers if any tool crashes, to take manual action if necessary.
Scalability	The framework should support infrastructure of various sizes (in this case, networks and websites).	Dealing with larger networks and websites is as efficient as dealing with small ones.
Portability	The system should run on multiple servers.	Ensuring that the framework is working even if one of the deployment servers is down (avoiding the single point of failure).
Usability	The user interface should be user-friendly.	Ensuring that framework use is easy for each user with varying levels of user knowledge. Apply some (user testing of usage) plans to ensure the framework is user-friendly.
Accessibility	Any authorized user should access the framework.	Authorized users could access the framework if they accessed the server network to connect to the server.

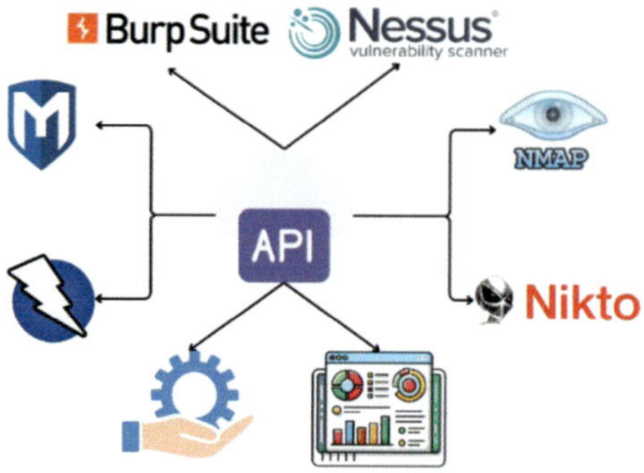

Figure 15.16 Tools linking.

Table 15.15 Integration solutions.

Solution	Description
Command-line tools (CLI)	Use Python libraries to perform commands like subprocess.
File-based tools	Parse the output from the tool to JSON file or plain text.

operation to another. In case we faced some tools that do not support APIs, many few other solutions fit for purpose. Table 15.15 shows how we can deal with the problem.

Storage: The penetration test would be constantly tracked, and information gathered. Detailed information about the host and vulnerabilities discovered would be recorded throughout the phases in a cloud, database, or local storage [22]. We will focus on local storage without third-party cloud storage services to keep the information more managed and secure. Table 15.16 shows a few reasons why we focus on local storage.

Explanation: Use temporary directories and files to store the results as compressed files. So, this reduces the overhead of storing processes. So, through each phase in penetration testing, we need a safe way to store the information gathered during the process without any missing information. We may need more than one store technique for multi-purpose: (1) safely store the information for any organization that requests it. (2) Store useful gathered information in XML and JSON files, then use these files. Complete the testing process by exporting files to the next tools using APIs. (3) Store the findings in the best way to write a detailed and clear report. The three points and the explanation are illustrated in Figure 15.17.

Table 15.16 Reasons behind local storage.

Reason	Details
Third-party risks	Cloud storage may expose information to risks from bad actors.
Third-party risks	PenTest Pro's multiple phases may face overhead from information transformation between tools using APIs.
Tool overhead	Tools themselves can also contribute to overhead.
Confidentiality	Reducing overhead and keeping information confidential is essential without sharing it externally.

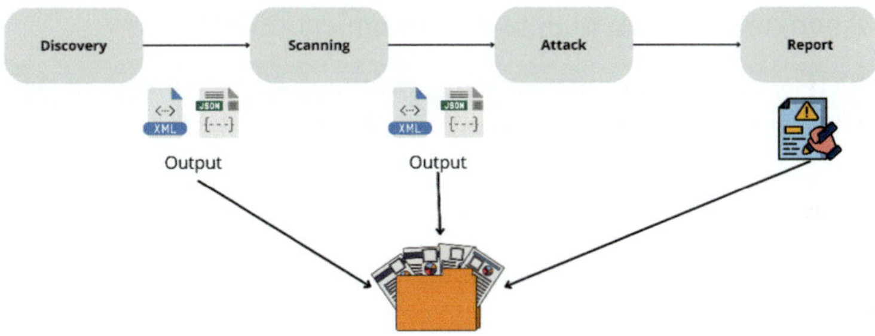

Figure 15.17 Storing information.

Next, we can protect directories/files containing all secret information by: Encrypting them, setting permissions (RWX) as access controls, backing up to external storage, and reducing storage to only important or essential data, known as data minimization.

Protocols: IP-based penetration tests are the most common testing procedure. The Tester attempts to exploit vulnerabilities in operating systems, network protocols, and application systems over a network.

A) Network layer protocols:

- TCP and UDP: network scanning and exploitation.
- ICMP (echo request\response): For ping sweeps or determining live hosts.
- DNS: For domain enumeration and DNS hijacking.

B) Application protocols

- HTTP/HTTPS: For web application testing (e.g., XSS, SQLi, CSRF). The server response contains the status information of the request [23].

Table 15.17 Protocols uses.

Protocol	Utilization in framework
HTTP/HTTPS	Communicate with WebApps. (e.g., gather information about URLs and scanning like ZAP).
FTP	Put/get files to/from target systems.
SMB	Sharing resources over a network.
SSH	Accomplish tasks on remote machines.

- FTP: To promote the sharing of files, encourage indirect or implicit use of remote computers, and transfer data reliably and efficiently. Anonymous login, plaintext communication [24].
- SMB is a network file-sharing protocol implemented in Microsoft Win, known as the Microsoft SMB Protocol. The set of message packets defining a particular protocol version is called a dialect. Produce weak share permissions [25].
- SSH: OpenSSH is the premier connectivity tool for remote login. Encrypts all traffic to eliminate eavesdropping, connection hijacking, and other attacks. Used for exploiting misconfigurations, weak credentials, and outdated server versions [26].

Table 15.17 provides a simple summary of the functionality of each protocol used in PenTest Pro. Also, Figure 15.18 illustrates the entire process in a systematic manner:

C) Constraints

- **Software limitations:** The framework should be integrated with all tools for coding, while some tools cannot be integrated with API keys, some are not compatible with Python and the libraries.
- **Cross-platform compatibility:** Our platform uses Linux-based operating systems as a deployment server. Ensure browser compatibility (Chrome, edge, Firefox, etc.).
- **Security requirements:** Ensure secure communication channels or protocols such as HTTPS.
- **Hardware and execution speed:** Hardware might deal with multiple scans simultaneously.
- **Integration:** Ensure tools can be executed and their output can work together efficiently. Compatibility with CLI tools.

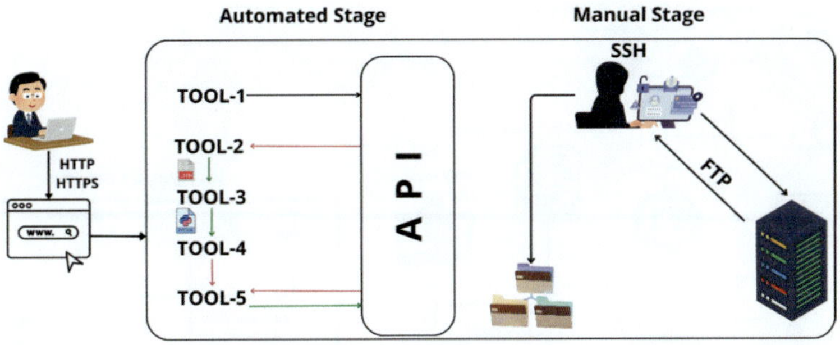

Figure 15.18 Protocols uses.

- **Automation scope:** Limit automation for most penetration testing tasks such as scanning, enumeration, and reporting. As a semi-automated framework, the user should interact with the pen-testing process.
- **Reporting and results:** Results should be stored in a format that supports report generation (e.g., JSON and CSV). An exportable report should be generated (e.g., PDF or HTML).
- **GUI performance:** UI should be asynchronously responsive while backend scans are executed.

D) Preferences:

- **Output format**: XML files, lists, and dictionaries are used**.**
- **Automation preferences:** Using **Python libraries, APIs, and Pipelines.**
- **GUI:** Using visual dashboards and graphs.
- **Security preferences**: Ensure that only authorized users can trigger the scans.
- **Performance**: Allow multiple scans simultaneously (depending on the deployment server's resources).

15.7 System Architecture

Figure 15.19 outlines the entire computational process involved in system design.

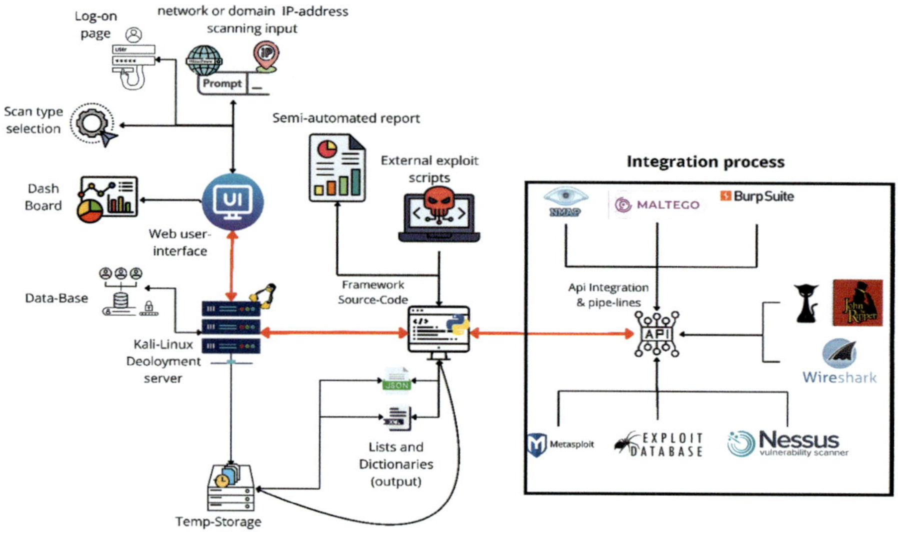

Figure 15.19 Architecture of the system.

According to the figure, the proposed system works as follows:

- **Deployment server (Linux-based):** A deployment server should have a server component depending on it, such as source code, storage, databases, and user interface, and manage how they interact. We prefer to deploy a Kali Linux server for the framework to ensure tool integration compatibility; most tools are already installed on the OS. In addition, it is an open-source OS.
    - **Storage (temporary storage):** Temporal storage provides a security layer for the customer scanning and testing tools' results (XML and JSON files); after a period of inactivity, the file will be automatically deleted for many reasons:
        - i. Reduce unauthorized access impact.
        - ii. Providing more storage.
        - iii. Eliminate third-party (cloud storage) overhead and risks.
    - **Database**: A database is essential for authenticity reasons and keeps track of accountability; for framework's sake, there should be two databases, one for the server, which is offered by the OS system (built-in used by testers only, for developing purposes) and the other one for the user's interface (customers and testers), this database should be connected to the website for log-in purposes.

- ○ **Source Code**: Code should be operating on the deployment server to distribute the testing service on testers' devices.

- **User interface (UI):** An essential part of the framework due to its importance in providing partial results, dashboards, scan type selection, and log-on types so users (testers and customers) can actively interact with the framework. (**NOTE**: maybe programmed in JAVA, C++, or Python. It is not determined until this moment).
  - ○ **Log-on page:** Logging on to the system could be done in two ways:
    - i. Testers log-in: This login requires credentials to enter the testing environment.
    - ii. Customer log-on: This log-on does not require credentials. The session is open for the customer to inspect the results and dashboards of testing in real-time or after testing (final results).
  - ○ **Scanning type selection:** Choosing the scan type, e.g., vulnerability scanning, network scanning, web scanning, domain scanning, etc., or specifying the tool to use.
  - ○ **Network or domain IP-address input:** This section is for entering the tester's input to begin testing.
  - ○ **Dashboard:** testers and customers can inspect testing results in this section.
  - ○ **User interface (UI)** is served by a web service that is distributed on the tester's/customers' devices by opening a service port (80 (HTTP) in this case) and operating the service on it. The testers open their browsers and then enter the URL or server's IP address followed by the port number to access the user interface; accessing the website requires a temporary VPN connection that expires after the session is closed to get into the server network, providing a security layer.

- **Source code (python):** This is the most important core component where all framework parties (such as APIs integration, semi-automated report generation, external exploit scripts, and producing files (lists and dictionaries) where tools results are saved to be used for the next process) are combined and integrated to accomplish framework duties.
  - ○ **API keys generation and integration:** APIs are the most common methodology to exchange data and integrate heterogeneous systems;

each system or tool should have an API key gained by each user to be used; in this case, API keys must be collected and integrated for each tool with other tools to the ensure continuity and successful pen-testing process in the right sequence.

- ○ **Semi-automated PT report:** This report is filled by the framework automatically by filling partial fixed results, such as IP addresses, vulnerable versions, etc. A specialist pen-tester fills in the other part of the report to give recommendations, mitigations, and reviews the automated filled results to reduce false positives. This report evaluates cybersecurity principles' system coverage.
- ○ **Lists and dictionaries (XML and JSON files):** These files store tools' scanning and testing results for the next tool or step. These files are stored in temporal storage, as mentioned earlier.
- ○ **External exploit scripts:** These exploits are collected and gathered from various resources and saved in the deployment server.

- **Integration process:** This part of the designing and developing phase is crucial; combining the API tools keys and making them work comprehensively is the most challenging thing, so they will be saved in a single list file accessed by the source code to get the API key**.** (**NOTE**: All tools illustrated in the figure below are just examples.)

A large-scale diagram that describes the different system components, like interface, database, pipeline, model, and how they are connected.

15.8 Conclusions and Future Work

15.8.1 Conclusions

In this work, we aim to develop (PenTest Pro) an advanced semi-automated penetration testing framework by integrating various tools and providing comprehensive evaluations of security principles. Testing is done with two techniques (manual and automatic) by applying the framework to effectively identify vulnerabilities in systems, networks, and web applications. This ensures adherence to cybersecurity principles such as the CIA triad (confidentiality, integrity, and availability). Key results include enhancing the vulnerability identification process, streamlining reporting mechanisms, and reducing testing time by integrating tools like Nmap, Nessus, Metasploit, and Burp Suite, etc.

We aim to work on the product to achieve results compatible with the work' s initial objectives by creating a platform that facilitates efficient penetration testing and vulnerability detection and generates standardized reports. This will solve the problem of fragmented testing tools, which often lead to inefficiencies in vulnerability assessments. By our framework that uses a semi-automated reporting mechanism, the work ensures clarity and reduces human error, and it will make the results more reliable.

While working on this work, we are facing many limitations and challenges. Technical difficulties are posed by integrating the process of multiple tools and requiring extensive research, testing, and troubleshooting. In addition to the complexity of reconciling automated and manual testing processes that demand significant time and expertise, the challenge of false positive results in vulnerability assessments, underscoring the need for manual verification.

The work makes a meaningful contribution to the cybersecurity world by creating a penetration testing framework that combines automated processes with manual (human expertise). Improvements could make the interface more user-friendly, adding more tool integrations and expanding the study on potential vulnerabilities and how to detect them to add them to the work plan.

15.8.2 Future work

The proposed work can be extended and enhanced in three main areas:

1. **Functional improvements:**
    - Enhanced reporting capabilities: Develop the frameworks by adding features like interactive dashboards and visual reports to visualize the detected vulnerabilities.
    - Support for more protocols and systems: Increase the framework's scope by adding more protocols and systems to ensure comprehensive testing of procedures in all environments.
    - Improve performance: Enhance the main code to improve the execution, mainly in huge environments, to ensure reliable and effective results.
2. **Potential features and extensions:**
    - Propose automatic treatment: Provide actionable features that allow steps to remediate the disclosure vulnerabilities, which enable users to minimize the risks.

- Artificial intelligence and machine learning integration: Using machine learning and artificial intelligence algorithms to disclose the advanced vulnerability makes the framework more intelligent and adapts to advanced threats.
- Real-time collaboration: Add functionality that allows the team members to work together on the same penetration testing in real time, increasing productivity and coordination in huge works.

3. **Integration possibilities:**

- Threat intelligence integration: Integrate the framework with external sources of information on threats to keep the framework current.
- Integration with security databases: Integrate the framework with updated security databases like CVE or NIST or customized databases designed to ensure precise detection of current threats.

References

[1] M. D. J. L. Jason Creasey, A guide for running a CREST, April 2017.
[2] M. S. A. C. A. O. Karen Scarfone, "Technical Guide to Information Security Testing and Assessment," Special Publication 800-115, September 2008.
[3] "Integrity360," May 2024. [Online]. Available: https://insights.integrity360.com/biggest-cyber-attacks-of-the-year-so-far..-2024-part-2.
[4] D. G. A. S. Mrs. Aswathy Mohan, "Analysis of Vulnerability Assessment With Penetration Testing," p. 10, 2021.
[5] *. A. A. D. K. B. Kousik Barik1, "Penetration Testing Analysis with Standardized Report Generation," vol. 4, p. 8, 2021.
[6] V. V. Vegesna, "Utilising VAPT Technologies (Vulnerability Assessment & Penetration Testing) as a Method for Actively Preventing Cyberattacks," p. 15, 2022.
[7] L. T. A. S. B. Petar Lachkov, "Vulnerability Assessment for Applications Security Through Penetration Simulation and Testing," vol. 21_7, 2022.
[8] A. Begum, "Advanced Penetration Testing in Cybersecurity: Strengthening Defense Mechanisms and Identifying Vulnerabilities," vol. 1, no. 1, p. 21, 2024.
[9] V. V. Vegesna, "Life Cycle Assessment of Vulnerability and Penetration Testing on Systems and Proactive Action Taken to Resolve Possible Attacks on Networks," p. 12, 2023.
[10] A. K. Mei Lanni, "Boosting Cyber Risk Assessment in Government Entities through Combined NIST and MITRE ATT&CK Threat Modeling," vol. 14, no. 6, p. 17, 2024.

[11] H.-J. L. 1andYangYu2, " Research on WiFi Penetration Testing with Kali Linux," p. 8, 2021.
[12] M. P. A. M. N. S. R. K. Nidhi, " Cyber Security Analysis of a Power Distribution System Using Vulnerability Assessment and Penetration Testing Tools," vol. 20, 2024.
[13] S. Vemula, " Automating Security Testing: Strategies for Vulnerability Scanning, Penetration Testing, and Compliance Checks," p. 10, 2024.
[14] S. A. O. K. A. O. Q. a. S. K. OmerBinTauqeer1, " Analysis of Security Testing Techniques," p. 16, 2021.
[15] V. V. Vegesna, "Life Cycle Assessment of Vulnerability and Penetration Testing on Systems and Proactive Action Taken to Resolve Possible Attacks on Networks," vol. xiii, no. x, p. 12, 2023.
[16] N. R. A. A. Qureshi, "Comparative Analysis of Automated Scanning and Manual Penetration Testing for Enhanced Cybersecurity," p. 8, 2024.
[17] H. K., Y. I. A. Ahmad S. Al-Ahmad, "Overview on Case Study Penetration Testing Models Evaluation," vol. 7, no. 3, p. 18, 2023.
[18] M. S. A. C. A. O. Karen Scarfone, "Technical Guide to Information Security Testing and Assessment," Special Publication 800-115, 2008.
[19] L. Golovyrin, "Analysis of tools for static security testing of applications," p. 73, 2023.
[20] F. A. Debnath Bhattacharyya, "Penetration Testing for Hire," vol. 8, p. 9, 2009.
[21] M. Goodwin, "What is an API (application programming interface)?," IBM, 09 April 2024. [Online]. Available: https://www.ibm.com/topics/api.
[22] J. K. Appiah, "Network and Systems Security Assessment using penetration testing in a university environment: The case of Central University College," Joel Kwesi Appiah, Kumasi, 2014.
[23] J. G. J. C. M. H. F. N. L. M. P. J. L. T. B.-L. Roy T. Fielding, "Hypertext Transfer Protocol -- HTTP/1.1," RFC, June 1999. [Online]. Available: https://w3.org/Protocols/rfc2616/rfc2616-sec10.html.
[24] J. K. R. on Postel, "File Transfer Protocol (FTP)," Oct 1985. [Online]. Available: https://www.rfc-editor.org/rfc/rfc959.
[25] v.-k. D. d. m. AlvinAshcraft, "Microsoft SMB Protocol and CIFS Protocol Overview," Microsoft, 7 Jan 2021. [Online]. Available: https://learn.microsoft.com/en-us/windows/win32/fileio/microsoft-smb-protocol-and-cifs-protocol-overview.
[26] D. M. M. F. N. P. B. L. Theo de Raadt, "About OpenSSH," OpenBSD Work , 20 Sep 2024. [Online]. Available: https://www.openssh.com/.

Index

About the Editors

Dr. Hooman Razavi is currently an associate research assistant in the Department of Engineering Science at Tecnológico de Monterrey, Mexico, and the University of Ottawa. He holds a BSc in computer engineering, an MSc in artificial intelligence, and a PhD in engineering science. Dr. Razavi has served as a sessional lecturer at University Canada West. He has published widely in conferences, book chapters, and journal papers in the fields of applied AI and cyber risk management. His professional experience also includes roles as a senior data scientist and consultant in several fintech firms. He currently serves on the editorial board of the *International Journal of Cybersecurity* and *Risk Assessment* and associate editor of the *Transactions on Swarm and Evolutionary Learning*. Dr. Razavi has the role of reviewer for numerous journals, including *IEEE Transactions on Artificial Intelligence*, *IEEE Communications Magazine*, *Information Systems Journal*, *Expert Systems with Applications*, *Engineering Applications of Artificial Intelligence*, *Applied Soft Computing*, *Cyber Security and Applications*, and *Digital Business*. Additionally, he has served on technical program committees for leading conferences, such as ICLR, NeurIPS, AISTATS, IEEE WINCOM, IEEE CSR, IEEE GCAIoT, IEEE CSNet, and ICMI. Dr. Razavi has also been a keynote speaker at numerous international conferences and has conducted multiple webinars.

Dr. Muriel Figueredo Franco has experience as a researcher and consultant in cybersecurity planning and risk quantification. In his research career, he has participated in different multidisciplinary projects with teams of experts in cybersecurity, computer networks, project management, and economics, with more than 70 published articles and two co-authored patents. His work supports the discussion of cybersecurity's economic aspects, thus helping for better planning and investment in cybersecurity. Also, he worked as a cybersecurity consultant to build risk quantification approaches as a product for international companies. Muriel holds a PhD (*Summa cum laude*) in computer science from the University of Zurich (UZH), Switzerland, an MBA in project management from the University of São Paulo (USP), Brazil, a master's degree in computer science from the Federal University of Rio Grande do Sul (UFRGS), Brazil, and a bachelor's degree in computer science from the Federal University of Pelotas (UFPEL), Brazil, in 2014. He was also a postdoctoral researcher at UFRGS from 2023 to 2025. Furthermore, he served as a member of the Technical Program Committee (TPC) for many cybersecurity and network management events, such as IEEE GLOBECOM, IEEE/IFIP NOMS, and the Brazilian Symposium of Cybersecurity (SBSeg). Additionally, Muriel served as a reviewer for top journals, including *IEEE Communications Magazine* (COMMAG), *Computers & Security* (COSE), and *IEEE Transactions on Network and Service Management* (TNSM).

Dr. Mariya Ouaissa is currently a professor in cybersecurity and networks at Faculty of Sciences Semlalia, Cadi Ayyad University, Marrakech, Morocco. She received the PhD degree in computer science and networks from ENSAM-Moulay Ismail University, Meknes, Morocco, in 2019. She is a Networks and Telecoms Engineer, graduated in 2013 from National School of Applied Sciences Khouribga, Morocco. She is a Co-Founder and IT Consultant at IT Support and Consulting Center. She was working for School of Technology of Meknes Morocco as a visiting professor from 2013 to 2021. She is a member of the International Association of Engineers and International Association of Online Engineering, and since 2021, she has been an "ACM Professional Member." She is Expert Reviewer with Academic Exchange Information Centre (AEIC) and Brand Ambassador with Bentham Science. She has served and continues to serve on technical program and organizer committees of several conferences and events and has organized many symposiums/workshops/conferences as a General Chair and also as a reviewer of numerous international journals. Dr. Ouaissa has made contributions in the fields of information security and privacy, Internet of Things security, and wireless and constrained networks security. Her main research topics are IoT, M2M, D2D, WSN, cellular networks, and vehicular networks. She has published over 90 papers (book chapters, international journals, and conferences/workshops), 35 edited books, and 10 special issues as guest editor.

Dr. Mariyam Ouaissa is currently an assistant professor in networks and systems at ENSA, Chouaib Doukkali University, El Jadida, Morocco. She received her PhD degree in 2019 from National Graduate School of Arts and Crafts, Meknes, Morocco, and her engineering degree in 2013 from the

National School of Applied Sciences, Khouribga, Morocco. She is a communication and networking researcher and a practitioner with industry and academic experience. Dr Ouaissa's research is multidisciplinary that focuses on Internet of Things, M2M, WSN, vehicular communications and cellular networks, security networks, congestion overload problem, and the resource allocation management and access control. She is serving as a reviewer for international journals and conferences including *IEEE Access*, *Wireless Communications*, and *Mobile Computing*. Since 2020, she has been a member of "International Association of Engineers IAENG" and "International Association of Online Engineering," and since 2021, she has been an "ACM Professional Member." She has published more than 70 research papers (this includes book chapters, peer-reviewed journal articles, and peer-reviewed conference manuscripts), 20 edited books, and 6 special issues as guest editor. She has served on Program Committees and Organizing Committees of several conferences and events and has organized many symposiums/workshops/conferences.

Dr. Gautam Srivastava (Senior Member, IEEE) received the BSc degree from Briar Cliff University, USA, in 2004, and the MSc and PhD degrees from the University of Victoria, Victoria, BC, Canada, in 2006 and 2012, respectively. Then, he taught for three years with the Department of Computer Science, University of Victoria, where he was regarded as one of the top undergraduate professors in computer science course instruction. From there, in 2014, he joined a tenure-track position at Brandon University, Brandon, MB, Canada, where he is currently active in various professional and scholarly activities. He was promoted to the rank of Professor in 2023. He is active in research in the field of computer security and privacy with a specialization in cybersecurity. In his ten-year academic career, he has published a total of 450 papers in high-impact conferences in many countries and high-status journals (SCI and SCIE). He has delivered invited guest lectures and keynotes on cybersecurity, cloud computing, the Internet of Things, and cryptography at many international conferences and universities. He is an editor of several international scientific research journals. He currently has active research projects with other academics internationally.